Hidden Reality

The BioGeometry®

Physics of Quality

The Science of Subtle Energy and Life Force

50

YEAR ANNIVERSARY OF BIOGEOMETRY

Dr. Ibrahim Karim

PhD-Tech. Sc., ETH-ZH

Publishing Info

This book is published by

Dr. Ibrahim F. Karim, BioGeometry Energy Systems Ltd

ISBN: 9798370712425

First Edition

DISCLAIMER

This book is provided solely for educational purposes. The purpose of the information provided in this book is to provide helpful information on the subject discussed, and is not meant to be used for diagnosis or treatment of any kind, medical or other. The author, publisher, and BioGeometry companies and their directors, officers, employees and representatives are not responsible for, or liable for any claims of adverse concerns to any person reading or following the information in this book. The information contained herein is provided on an "AS IS" basis and without warranty of any kind. The author, publisher, and BioGeometry companies and their directors, officers, employees and representatives will not be liable for any direct or indirect damages arising from the use of any of the information provided herein.

BioGeometry is not a form of medical diagnosis or treatment. It is a long-term environmental support for the body's energy system and all types of treatment.

Users thereof are fully responsible for any consequences resulting from their use.

Dedication

This work is the legacy that my wife Rawya and I,

as well as our children, who are an active part of our journey,

dedicate to future generations

in the hope of giving them a prosperous future with a true worldview

that is equally scientific and spiritual.

A Scientific Journey from Eternal Egypt

into the Golden Age

With the path of Divine Unity manifested

in the combination of the knowledge,

science, and wisdom of THOTH

and the "equality through spiritually-centered complementarity" of the

Universal Order of MAAT

Bringing spiritual harmony into everyday life through

EXCELLENCE OF ACTION

The BioGeometry Way

The BioGeometry Physics of Quality is based on a solid, scientific paradigm that provides multiple solutions to environmental problems and it has been applied to numerous projects worldwide. BioGeometry itself is founded on more than fifty years of research based on scientific and academic post-graduate studies in many fields.

To access information about BioGeometry research, please visit

www.BioGeometry.com

History tells us that merging science and spirituality is challenging, however it is our mission to build a bridge and show there is a path they can move along together to a brighter future. The best and most beautiful, unobstructed, and holistic view is reserved for those who stand on the bridge and can envision greater possibilities. This book is primarily addressed to them.

Paths of knowledge paved with universal truths will illuminate the heart to guide humanity along the "Way of Universal Unity" that will save the environment.

The Physics of Quality Series

This book is the first volume of the Physics of Quality series. It is intended to introduce the Physics of Quality, which is the main component of the science of BioGeometry that itself brings environmental harmony into our world of modern technology. The all-embracing multi-dimensional universality of this qualitative approach is a key to understanding the paradigm from which the sciences of the great ancient civilizations emerged. Human sensory perception assesses energetic effects through the lens of *quality*. Shifting into or creating a new qualitative paradigm, such as we are presenting with this book and those which follow, involves a right-brain state with a holistic perception of an all-encompassing unity, complete with its unifying patterns and qualitative components. This delicate and elusive state of perception is easily overshadowed by our detailed quantitative way of thinking, and this puts this new scientific paradigm at risk.

The topics chosen for this first volume are meant to give a complete picture of the BioGeometry Physics of Quality; other equally important but complementary topics are relegated to future volumes.

The detailed practical use of the BioGeometry devices, shapes, and instruments introduced in this volume will also be dealt with in our courses as well as in future volumes of the Physics of Quality series.

The BioGeometry Physics of Quality

Table of Contents

Note to the Reader

This book is dedicated to members of the wide audience of people, today and into the future, who we might characterize as seekers. It is founded on the fact that while the analytical scientific way of quantity is based on the exterior observation of phenomena, the way of quality is an internal state of perception that is felt within us. The Physics of Quality is a physics of life using the laws of interaction between living attributes of quality as a complement to the mathematical formulas of quantitative science. The units of measurement in this type of physics are an extension of the living qualities we all experience through our sensory apparati, for example, through hearing, seeing, and touching, plus the qualitative attributes of numbers, geometrical shapes, polarity, etc.

In addressing the general reader, I aim to present this information in a compact, easy-to-understand form. I have occasionally added interesting facts from Ancient Egypt, as well as stories, drawings, and personal reflections. I've also taken the reader into parts of my journey to give some background about the origin of the science of BioGeometry and the Physics of Quality. My elaborations on certain universal aspects of the Physics of Quality accept other interpretations due to their abstract nature, and when all is said and done, the Physics of Quality gives a scientific core to all beliefs, rituals, and subtle energy practices.

Many of the core concepts of this new paradigm are building blocks I have arranged according to their role in illustrating more than one concept. To give a complete picture of each topic, and to save the reader from going back and forth in the book when accessing different topics, I have unavoidably had to repeat some concepts and figures—with different nuances each time. Repetition in various forms helps us reach a simplified understanding of some of the more elusive concepts related to Creation, and it takes us to deeper levels as new relevant relationships or details are introduced.

Due to the complexity of the material, I found it necessary to include many sketches and diagrams designed to help readers visually navigate these treacherous waters. Some of the sketches contain additional information that is better communicated visually than through the written word. We have used my collected original handwritten notes and sketches, without any form of embellishment, to keep their authenticity.

A Practical New Paradigm

This book introduces a practical new scientific and spiritual paradigm to take us safely into the future. It deals with the quality of subtle energy in the continuous dynamic exchange of information with the environment. This dynamic interaction continuously affects all living systems' biological, emotional, and mental functions.

Subtle energy is a general term used for all types of multi-dimensional energetic effects that occur on emotional, mental, spiritual, and vitality-related levels, as well as other scientifically unexplainable manifestations like dark energy, dark matter, etc. These energetic forms, which make up more than ninety percent of the subtle energy background of the Universe, exist beyond the physical electromagnetic range and thus are not bound by the speed of light or physical time-space as we know it. We can, however, measure them according to the universal harmonic presence of attributes that affect the human subtle energy system. In this paradigm, the scientific and the poetic merge into a new way of perception.

Quantum physics has already introduced us to such revolutionary concepts as particles that continue their resonant interaction, through a permanent connection referred to as "entanglement," over vast distances. We've all heard of experiments showing how a researcher's intention became part of the observed results of an experiment. On a micro-atomic level, the subject of the observer's measurements, such as the mass of a sub-atomic particle, appeared as predicted. However, when the observer measured the particle's energy, it shifted, becoming a wave with no mass to measure. The observer's consciousness thus became involved in "creating" what was to be measured out of a background of formless subtle energy. This pushes the physical boundaries of scientific observation into the realm of subtle energy.

The knowledge that mental and emotional interactions are active in dimensions beyond the time-space confinements of our physical electromagnetic dimension, which is bound by the speed of light, is breathtaking. This, however, is but a small step towards the much greater task of understanding and interacting with consciousness and awareness. They are both powerful creative components of the Universal Mind and they are embedded within all levels of subtle energy. Let's take it one step further and note that abstract *collective* emotional and mental subtle energy levels in the environment become realities affecting the functions of biological systems.

The scientific definition of energy is "the ability to produce an effect." Quality, then, can be seen as the result of any effect from any dimension which acts upon the human subtle energy system. Since almost anything in any dimension whatsoever can produce a qualitative effect on an unconscious level, the human being can be seen to be at the center of the qualitative evaluation of everything in existence. The subtle energy quality is sensitive to many types of unconscious information that affect it on physical, vital, emotional, mental, and spiritual levels. Our living energy systems are affected by all kinds of movement across time and space in this or other universes, whether visible or not. As an example, biological functions of all species react and take into consideration all such universal effects. Body chakras, acupuncture points, and sensory perception relate many types of external information that are taken into consideration by the organ functions. The impact of qualities from unconscious realms on our subconscious levels can be made visible and measurable and thus can be scientifically evaluated.

Human perception is based on quality. Qualitative scales (color, sound, touch, smell, shape, etc.) in different parts of the brain decode the sensory effects on the nervous system. The largest effects, however, are on the unperceived unconscious levels. The human right-brain perception (RB) perceives unlimited universal information in an unconscious qualitative manner, and this affects biological functions. What's more, the qualitative perception of sensory information in different areas of the brain can be used as a scale of measurement applicable to all other unperceived vibratory ranges.

With qualities or attributes becoming an objective abstract scale of measurement, this type of human-based physics becomes limitless, with no boundaries in any dimension or reality. It brings every topic of modern science, humanities, art, spirituality, and life in general, into a unified system of living, resonant, interactive unity; it defines qualities as differentiated effects of the ONE transcendental primordial centering state which manifests conscious control of everything in the duality of Creation. The ONE we refer to here is not the numerical digit "one" but the qualitative all-containing "UNITY" of Creation. Everything in Creation is a component of this unified system. The Arabic language has a different name for each: "AHAD" for ONE unity of Creation and "WAHED" for the singular one. They are enfolded within the zero-infinity state and are balanced by the centering connection leading back to it. This is the eternal presence of the zero state as the Divine light center in every manifestation in the duality of Creation. This centering aspect at the core and root of all emerging qualities is the cornerstone of the measurement of quality in BioGeometry and the main aspect differentiating it from all other systems of human sensing like dowsing or Radiesthesia.

Systems of Radiesthesia based on physically calibrated instruments are good steppingstones but they cause confusion when it comes to in-depth understanding of the pure qualitative measuring system at the core of Bio-Geometry. Radiesthesia uses quantitative aspects of "Microwave Physics," a label assigned by the French researchers Chaumery, Bélizal and Morel in their books, to denote the measurement of an object's color affinity. We will use the term "BioGeometry Quality Measurement" here to denote that it is based on a Physics of Quality and differentiate it from existing systems of Radiesthesia.

Quantitative measurement, the holy grail of modern science, is a tool that has its rightful place in understanding phenomena. Still, the measurement of "Living Qualities" of life force on multi-dimensional levels of subtle energy must be considered a main criterion in scientific research. Instruments calibrated to qualitative scales used in conjunction with universal subtle energy resonance of shape are used in this type of research. Ideally, the measurement of universal life force will ultimately complement the quantitative approach to form the backbone of a future holistic science.

The BioGeometry paradigm is based on the practical qualitative interaction between subtle energy systems in an environment. BioGeometry solutions have been applied successfully in many projects for more than forty years and BioGeometry research and solutions have found academic approval as part of MA and Ph.D. programs for the past twenty-five years

(For more information on BioGeometry research and applications please visit www.biogeometry.ca/research).

In this book, we deal with environmental problems in a constructive way. By highlighting the dangers of modern technology's electromagnetic and chemical pollution we can increase awareness of, and seek to provide solutions for, issues that will transform modern technology into an environmentally harmonizing activity.

Finally, my background is in architecture, engineering, design, science, and metaphysics. I am an artist more than I am a writer, and I feel most at ease drawing my way in the world of shapes. I am also at home reading what the Divine pen draws and writes in the shapes of nature.

My wish for you, dear reader, is that you read what I have presented here with interest, assess what I have shared with an open mind and heart, and go forth into the world carrying with you the seeds of change that will benefit all animate and inanimate living forms that are part of the holistic makeup of this planet.

I have brought up front some of the new concepts explained in the Glossary at the end of the book to help the general reader along the way. They will be introduced and explained in a simplified manner in the relevant chapters.

New Terms and Concepts Introduced
by the Author

1. BioGeometry

This label refers to the measurement of the quality of the life force of the earth.

(Bio = Life force, Geo = Earth, Metry = measurement). It involves the integration of life force as found in the forming process of nature into all design activities through design principles that induce harmony into the environment.

BioGeometry is a new field of science that uses specially designed shapes, as well as color, sound, motion, and wave configuration, to induce harmony into biological subtle energy systems. The cornerstone of BioGeometry is the ONE harmonizing subtle energy quality BG3 which is at the center of the natural forming process.

2. The Physics of Quality

This is a holistic type of physics that deals with the quality of effect objects or actions have on the human subtle energy system. The Physics of Quality extends the resonant principles of the science of Universal Harmonics to cover all vibratory levels of absolute reality from zero to infinity in a holistic information exchange of qualities. The Physics of Quality introduces the centering, spiritually harmonizing BG3 quality at the core of ancient Universal Harmonics.

3. BG3

This is a label for the centering subtle energy quality of the earth's sacred power spots which BioGeometry reproduces through a geometric design language. It is detected through the simultaneous presence of three subtle energy qualities: Grey, referred to as Horizontal Negative Green (HNG), Higher Harmonic of Ultraviolet (HHUV), and Higher Harmonic of Gold (HHG). These three basic qualities are in resonance with the ONE harmonizing energy quality and are used to detect it with the BioGeometry tools of harmonic qualitative measurement.

4. BioGeometry Qualitative Harmonic Measurement

The BioGeometry measurement system is referred to as *"BioGeometry Quality Measurement."* It is based on the Physics of Quality which has BG3—the ONE quality—as its cornerstone. It uses qualitative scales of measurement.

5. The Law of Time

It is the governing principle that governs the shape and balance of the pulse of Creation. It is active in the first pulse that produces the stable duality of Creation. It is active from the smallest to the largest pulses in a system of resonant communication behind the unity of Creation.

6. The Law of Trinity

This law is expressed as the balanced motion governed by the center of a circular/spherical motion to produce the harmonious complementarity of dualities to form a unified energetic manifestation. This is the action of geometrical motion that brings balance within in the time pulse. In this context, the Law of Trinity is an aspect of the Law of Time.

7. Ziron

This is the activation of Consciousness as the centering principle. It is the Divine center beyond duality or time and space, a bi-directional doorway to the zero state from which the infinity of Creation emerges. Its centering effect is detected through its BG3 quality. This is the intermediate state between the zero-infinity non-dualistic dimension and the duality of Creation. It is the *activation of Consciousness* as a background state formed of pulsating centers. Each center is referred to as a Ziron. These centers are sometimes referred to as the drops manifesting as a primordial fog. The centering principle is equally existing before and after the emergence of full duality and is equally a center and a background.

8. Psychon

This is the first unit of Creation. It manifests the activated Consciousness which extends the centering principle into the bi-directional mental-emotional spiraling dimensions that emerge from the Ziron and form the Psychon pulse. This pulse is the origin of life force that we know as subtle energy.

9. Experions

When experiencing the separate unbound pages of stacked time beyond our linear sensory time perception, the page content can enter into resonance with similar connected experiences and form a whole situation with its own time-space configuration. Our perception can also jump between related Experions, just as it does with resonant pages.

10. QL-Torsion (Qualitative Torsion Effect)

This is the reaction of the body's energy field to the effect of external torsion on the body. It is made visible using pendulums or other devices that rotate to amplify and make visible the body's reaction.

11. Primordial QL-Torsion

This is the primordial outgoing and incoming QL-Torsion of life force in the original spiraling pulse of the Ziron to form the eight levels of the Psychon.

12. Al-Kareem Quality

This is the expansion of the energizing quality of inward-flowing life force-positive QL-Torsion (QL+) into the outgoing phase around the body and environment.

13. Life Force

The Consciousness within the zero-infinity state before the duality of Creation is activated in the Ziron as the axis of the bidirectional spiraling mental-emotional pulse of the Psychon. The bi-directional activity of Consciousness in the mental and emotional spirals is the life force animating the primordial state of Creation. This life force medium is the subtle energy background on which all creation takes place. Everything in this universe and others in any dimension of Creation exists within this life force background medium. The Omnipotent Universal Mind is a function of life force. The Laws of Nature are attributes of life force. Everything in Creation is a manifestation of a state of life force.

14. "Excellence" of Action

Bringing harmony and perfect balance into action through a higher spiritual Divine connection. This is the ultimate synergy of male (left brain) and female (right brain). It is the essence of all spiritual paths.

Overview

The BioGeometry Physics of Quality and Life Force

This section serves as a paradigm-changing preparation for the material dealt with in this book. It also gives an overview, from a different perspective, of some of the important scientific and historical topics covered in my previous books, *Back to a Future for Mankind* and *BioGeometry Signatures*. Topics that are covered extensively in previous books are referred to here in a more general manner.

In this overview, I will introduce the concept of life force in BioGeometry, along with its fields of application. This concept will be expanded upon and covered in detail in relevant chapters later in this book. Concepts may also be repeated and words re-defined when introduced in their relevant chapters so the reader will not have to come back to the overview.

The "BIO" Dimension in BioGeometry

BioGeometry recreates the subtle energy quality found in sacred Earth and sky power spots as well as in special moments in time celebrated in different cultures throughout history. This transcendental multi-dimensional energy quality has a harmonizing, centering effect on life force attributes in nature. I use the term "life force" to describe the animating principle present in all dimensions of Creation. These dimensions relate to physical, vitality, emotional, mental, and spiritual levels of being. They are not separate in their actions but are holistic, inseparable components of life force. To differentiate and address their functions we resort to a form of spatial categorization, and we refer to them as different levels or planes and sub-planes of nature. There are different ways of understanding them, for example, as multiple entities existing on several levels as components of the soul as in Ancient Egypt.

In BioGeometry, the energy of sacred Earth power spots is detected by harmonic string methods and labelled BG3. The BioGeometry harmonic tools and instruments have been specially designed to measure this energy quality, and they are also capable of measuring different life force qualities in nature. For example, imagine a circle. The BG3 quality emerges from the center to harmonize the arrangement of the circle's different life force attributes into a circular pattern.

The use of the term "centering" in BioGeometry is not geometric in nature, but rather refers to a state where the life force qualities emerge out of the central source like a fountain to fill the whole space. The quality emerging from this source brings the life force attributes from the higher subtle energy dimensions into the whole physical shape. In other words, the entire shape becomes a living, multi-dimensional, central vortex.

Life force qualities are prevalent in every type of matter, whether living or seemingly inert. Unfortunately, many aspects of modern technology result in a disconnection from natural laws, and the interaction with products of modern technology results in a depletion of our life force.

It was a completely different story in the great ancient civilizations where people brought life force into every product. Their focus on perceiving and interacting with the powers of nature, and their ability to holistically integrate with the living Earth, helped ensure prosperity.

The Multi-Dimensionality of Life Force

To understand the origin and essence of life force, we must go back to the source of everything. The act of creation has been explained in many ancient civilizations and contemporary religions. It is helpful to look at Creation in a scientific, neutral, and abstract way to reach the common essence of all beliefs. In fact, we can analyze the pulse that activates all the potentials of Consciousness and life force. When we do, we can see that all universes and dimensions are an endless hierarchy of pulses governed by Divine centers which lie beyond the duality in which they arise.

The omnipresent Consciousness, the initiator of all levels of awareness, interaction, evolution, and information exchange in all dimensions and levels of creation, is the main animating component of life force. It governs manifestation from abstract energetic states to physical manifestation, as shown in quantum physics, where human intention becomes a part of the experiment. Material dimensions of Creation are formed through the action of universal Consciousness in different dimensions, from spiritual through mental, emotional, and vital levels, and down to our perceived physical world. When the energy slows down to the speed of light, myriad electromagnetic sparks erupt, each in the form of a "Big Bang," that creates a new living physical universe (Figure 1).

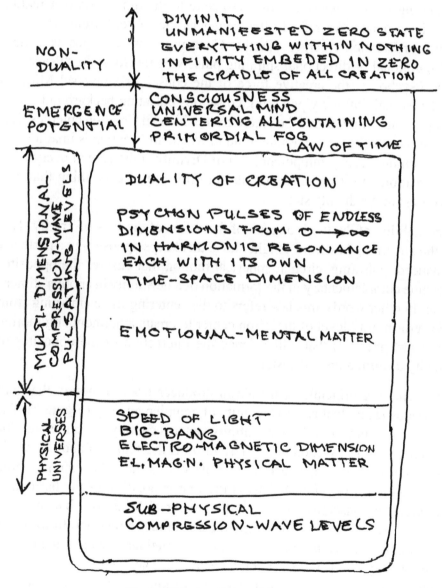

Fig.1 - Dimensions of Creation

The essence of life comes about through the actions of Consciousness emerging from the zero-infinity source to animate all dimensions of Creation. The non-dualistic state of pure manifested Consciousness can be expressed equally as zero and infinity as it is totally inert and potentially infinitely active at the same time. The first manifestation is through a centering vortex connecting the zero state to the dimension of Creation that it produces. We refer to this center as the "Ziron" from which the pulse of Creation emerges. "Active Consciousness" emerges as a mental-emotional bi-directional spiraling pulse we refer to as the "Psychon." The Psychon is the creative force of the conscious Universal Mind. It is the eternal, infinitely powerful, conscious pulsating background subtle energy state which forms the cradle from which all Creation emerges. It is the universal all-encompassing mind in which all Creation is imagined. It is the omnipresent, omnipotent level of Divinity at the core of every level of Creation and it contains the total information of everything that will manifest in the duality state.

The stability of duality is a result of the action of the Law of Trinity. This is the governing law from a higher level that keeps opposites in a perfectly balanced, pulsating, circular/spherical motion that ensures the opposites become complementary in the formation of a new unity in another dimension. In other words, this law refers to the centering force emerging from the zero-infinity level of the Ziron center to create a harmonizing motion (circular/spherical) that will balance the interaction of the opposites of duality to form a unified system.

The centering principle of the Ziron produces laws of motion that turn the opposites in duality into the unity of complementarity (Figure 2). The Ziron, emerging from the zero-infinity state, is equally the center and the periphery of the Psychon pulse. The Ziron is the center of and the whole in which the forces of Creation take place, and the pulse emerges from it and within it (Figure 3). This is the first expression of the harmonizing creative conscious control of the Universal Mind as a backbone of universal subtle energy. The spiritual zero-infinity dimension from which everything emerges is simultaneously the container in which mental and emotional dynamism of Creation takes place. The Trinity is a governing center in which duality occurs. The opposition of duality expresses the dynamism of the two components within the unity. The Psychon Pulse is produced by the Ziron center and exists within it. It is as if the Ziron center expands to produce and contain Creation. The numerical qualities of the Trinity will be further explored in a dedicated chapter.

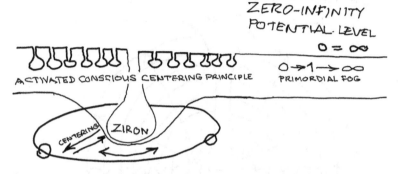

ZERO-INFINITY POTENTIAL LEVEL

$0 = \infty$

ACTIVATED CONSCIOUS CENTERING PRINCIPLE

$0 \rightarrow 1 \rightarrow \infty$ PRIMORDIAL FOG

CENTERING (ZIRON)

THE ZIRON IS THE DROP CONNECTED TO THE PRIMORDIAL FOG MANIFESTING FROM THE ZERO DIMENSION. IT IS THE CENTERING PRINCIPLE OF THE LAW OF TRINITY THAT ENSURES THE BALANCE AND STABILITY IN THE DUALITY OF CREATION

Fig.2 - Center to Duality Manifestation

This harmonizing force, Consciousness/Divinity, also contains the Law of Time. It governs the balance of all pulse levels in Creation, and we will be considering the Law of Time in greater detail later in the book as well. Some ancient Creation myths expressed the Law of Time concept in their reliefs as the emergence of the sleeping god from his sleep state in the primordial waters.

This first state of emerging duality or activation of natural laws forming the background in which all Creation takes place is usually described

THE ZIRON IS THE TIMELESS SPACELESS
ORIGINATOR AND HARMONIZING CONTAINER
OF CREATION

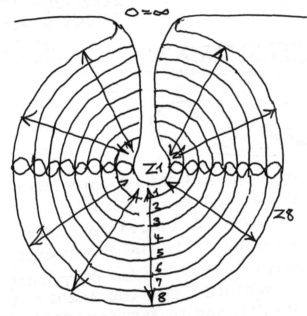

THE 8-FOLD EXPANSION OF THE
ZIRON CENTER CREATES THE
OUTWARD MENTAL AND INWARD
EMOTIONAL SPIRALING RADIATION
AND ATTRACTION FORCES OF THE
PSYCHON

Z1 = THE CENTER CREATING THE PULSE
Z8 = THE BODY CONTAINING THE PULSE

Fig.3 - Ziron Container

by some ancient traditions as an illuminated primordial fog, smoke, or "humm" sound. The Law of Trinity emerges from this primordial manifestation to balance and create harmony between its quality components. The Law of Trinity as the agent of complementarity within the centering effect forms new units which in turn interact with others according to the same centering action of the Trinity and creates other dimensions.

This is a process of evolution which continuously creates new dimensions, and it contains the principles behind the differentiation of these dimensions into higher harmonics of light, air, humidity, and dryness of matter. These qualities are themselves the result of interactions between the original pulse units in the Universal Mind state that we refer to as the Psychons. Innumerable harmonics of primordial fog manifest on all vibratory levels of absolute reality down to the physical states of water, which itself contains resonant levels of all attributes of life. This is the omnipresent, omnipotent universal brain imagining everything in Creation within itself.

Life Force and Qualitative Torsion Effects

This is clearly an unimaginably vast and intricate system that combines infinite possibilities with material outcomes. We measure it through the field of BioGeometry Quality Measurement, which is based on a form of "Qualitative Torsion" (QL-Torsion) that results from human interaction with the highly potent, bi-directional pulsating subtle energy background medium of the environment. To put it more simply, torsion's effect on the human subtle energy system can be detected and measured and it is its qualitative effect—QL-Torsion—that the BioGeometry Physics of Quality has introduced. Let's look a little deeper at this phenomenon. Torsion describes the spiraling effect at the core of subtle energy.

The Psychon is a form of dynamic mental-emotional interaction which is bi-directionally balanced, and it arises through the first spiraling pulse in the Creation of duality. The Psychon is the primordial mental-emotional pulse of life and Consciousness and it is, in fact, the first unit of Creation. It is comprised of eight levels or layers which are themselves derived from the multi-directional spiraling pulses of the Ziron. Remember that we defined the Ziron as the Divine center beyond duality or time and space, a doorway to the zero state from which the infinity of Creation emerges.

In the primordial spiraling (archetypal torsion), we can identify outward and inward directions of motion which we can further classify as mental and emotional attributes. This is a human-centered paradigm. As an example, breathing-in produces absorption of life force and positive QL-Torsion, while breathing out is coupled with a loss of life force and negative QL-Torsion. The proper level of life force is affected by the balance between positive and negative QL-Torsion.

In BioGeometry, we use the QL-Torsion effects on the rotation of pendulum (held in a human hand), calibrated with qualitative scales of measurement, to study the qualitative effect of any object, emotion, or thought on the human energy field. This puts the human being at the center of evaluation. (Figure 4).

Our bodies produce QL-Torsion in reaction to external torsion on the vital, emotional, and mental levels of the human subtle energy system. QL-Torsion is also produced internally by the quality of emotion or thought in a person's imagination or intention. The dynamic interaction of mental-emotional spiraling motions with the essence of the Psychon's forming process activates the Universal Mind's Consciousness and manifests in life force. All its activity and its creative imaginary processes are different forms of life force. The effect on the body of QL-Torsion within life force is affected by the quality of a person's emotional and mental activities.

This concept is the essence of BioGeometry Quality Measurement devices: they are specifically designed to measure the quality of subtle energy effects. The devices use geometric calibrations based on qualitative scales to measure QL-Torsion while reducing the effects of mental-emotional aspects of autosuggestion.

At this point I must mention the work on life force by my good friend for whom I have great respect, MIT and Princeton physicist, the late Dr. Claude Swanson. The second book of his *Synchronized Universe* series, titled *Life force, The Scientific Basis,* is a monumental, encyclopedic work that tackles the subject in a different way than this book, which concentrates mainly on the Physics of Quality of life force. It contains all the scientific research on life force as well as different techniques for and practices used around the world.

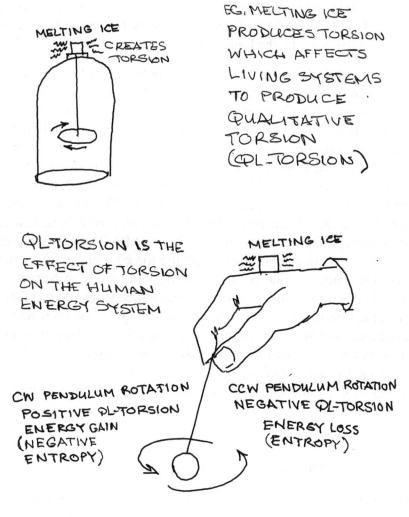

Fig.4 - Qaulitative Torsion

The Laws of Nature in Life Force

We can look at the non-dualistic state of everything and nothing as both the source of, and the centering harmonizing level of, the Universe. It radiates living omnipresent, omnipotent information in the form of Laws of Nature in the duality levels. The duality levels materialize through the Law of Trinity's creation of material units in the respective dimensions and together these constitute the essence of the life force of Creation that is active within different forms of material manifestation. Life force is the vehicle of the Universal Mind, and it manifests as Laws of Nature, which are kept in harmony by the higher centering source.

In the ancient civilizations, life force attributes in the form of powers of nature were personified in animated forms. In Ancient Egypt, they were referred to as Neters. More specifically, life force attributes are the Laws of Nature that interact to produce biological functions in all species. In modern religions, they are referred to as Divine Names, Divine Attributes, Angelic Forces, and so on, depending on one's belief system. They interact within a person's intuitive sub-conscious right brain and can, under certain conditions, be perceived by our senses. The Ancients perceived reality from a right-brain-focused mode of perception (RB) and interacted with it through their sensory-rich left brain (LB). They also maintained an everyday practical relationship with life force through its various manifestations. They considered these manifestations—these Neters—to be "the living Laws of Nature" and they personified them and brought them into all their buildings and activities by depicting them in their sculptures, hieroglyphs, and art. They communicated and lived in harmony with the Neters and invited them to participate in every significant occasion in their lives. Certain belief systems affirm that the gods walked the earth and angels lived and intermarried with humans during this pre-historic era.

The NETERU Origin of Ancient Egyptian Civilization

Some of the aspects of the Ancient Egyptian civilization seem to have emerged without showing any developmental stages, such as in its construction techniques, medicine, hieroglyphs, administration, and many other aspects of functional life. For example, the Ancient Egyptians practiced brain surgery and cataract surgery without implants, among other treatments, with no evidence of a learning curve leading up to their knowledge in the area.

Unofficial Ancient Egyptian chronologies describe the roots of the Ancient Egyptian civilization as reaching back more than thirty thousand years. The official chronology of the dynasties of the ruling kings Egypt starts with King Menes of the first dynasty around 3000 BC. Ancient records also refer, however, to two great advanced civilizations that existed in Egypt prior to this "first" dynasty of the old kingdom. Their most accurate chronicler, that we know of, was the Egyptian priest Manetho from Sebennytos, who lived and wrote in the third century BC during the Greek Ptolemaic period. Ironically, his chronology is the official one adopted today. What's most fascinating is that Manethon's works include *The Aegyptiaca,* which was translated into English by W.G. Waddell. The interesting thing about Manetho is that all his works, including *Aegyptiaca* and *Historia,* were lost when the Library of Alexandria was burnt around 47 or 48 BC. We only knew about his books from authors, such as Eusebius, Josephus, and Afrikanus, who referred to his books. Manetho must have used the different sources of Egyptian history, such as the king lists. This work provides detailed descriptions of the ruling dynasties of two earlier civilizations. The first was the twelve thousand-year reign of the "Shemsu Hor," and the second is the earlier era of the "Neteru," (sometimes written as "Netheru"), which dates from another twenty-two thousand years earlier. Although those older chronologies are very detailed, giving the name and rule of each king, they are unfortunately considered mythological by "official" Egyptology. Officials drew a line in the sand between the old kingdom, which early Egyptologists like Flanders Petrie dated as being more than two millennia earlier than the current official date of around 3000 BC, and the significantly older dynasties referenced in Manetho's writings. If those civilizations did exist, then sooner or later we will find archeological proof and erase the veil of the artificial red line.

It's possible that a linked parallel African civilization could also have existed far back in time as there are visible remnants that show a close connection with Egypt. An earlier Sumerian civilization, as well as that of Atlantis, could also have existed much earlier in history than we might assume.

In those early times, North Africa had a different, rainy, climate and was covered with vegetation and large water masses. There is evidence of an ocean that covered large areas of today's African Sahara. In the Fayoum Oasis, about an hour's drive from Cairo, large whale fossils were found in the desert surrounding the lake. The area is now known as the "Valley of the Whales" and has a museum displaying the bones of these huge ocean dwellers. Fayoum was covered by an extension of the Mediterranean Sea known in the literature as "the Sea of Tethys." Fayoum is officially not an oasis. By geological definition an oasis should have its own water sources. The Fayoum region was a depression in the desert with less-than-sufficient water sources and was developed as an agricultural region in the Twelfth Dynasty. The Valley of the Whales was where those ancient whales went to die when the sea of Tethys covered parts of North Africa, together with sea turtles and other similar species. Those particular whales are special because they had limbs, as that was during the Eocene period when major changes occurred in mammals. That is why UNESCO chose it as the only natural history UNESCO heritage site in Egypt.

To understand the human state of the people who created the ancient civilizations, we should try to understand how they perceived and interacted with their reality. The Swiss psychologist Carl Gustav Jung (1875-1961) categorized humanity based on our modes of perception. Jung's categorization of humanity into "Primitive, Ancient, Modern, and Contemporary" is based in the slow shift of the focus of perception from the right to the left brain. This is not an actual physical shifting in the brain hemispheres, but rather a mode of perception. Primitive humanity's focus of perception was in the right brain. People were animal-like in their integration into the Laws of Nature and unity with the environment. In this state, the subconscious universal mode governed all actions. The collective subconscious mind of the herd or species overshadowed one's individuality. Whether an earlier category with a supernatural makeup existed before what Jung referred to as primitive humanity is a subject of long debate.

Ancient humanity emerged when the focus of perception moved towards the left-brain's analytical mode, allowing the conscious sensory awareness of the unconscious realm in which it was still focused. This led to the development of number, geometry, music, and so on, as tools of conscious interaction with the powerful forces of the subconscious realm. With time these tools showed practical values in everyday life. With this shift in perception, where the two brain modes were in active conscious communication, the world of ancient civilizations emerged. The Ancients lived in a world with equal presence in the sensory world as well as in the world of personified forces of nature present in their everyday life.

The final total shift into the left brain had a cataclysmic effect on the forming and perception of reality that led to the emergence of modern humans. An ego-based sensory awareness reigned and closed the door to the conscious perception of rich, unified, right-brain holistic reality.

The Ancient Egyptians, with their focus of perception still mainly in the right brain, had a different perception of reality than modern humans. They perceived their world differently and interacted with it in a way that we cannot comprehend today. These people personified and interacted with higher entities—or, perhaps, more aptly put, the personified powers of nature. They depicted them in their reliefs, and regardless of whether these were human, materialized entities, or personified nature powers, it's clear that these beings were very advanced and brought knowledge to the Egyptians at the time.

The Fish in the Water

While Ancient Egyptians were imbued with an understanding of the universal all-permeating intelligent life force of the subtle energy background, in modern times we seem to have completely lost track of it due to our hemispherical brain shift in perception. As a result, our human-made products of modern technology lack a connection to life force. Our ignorance of life force has led our scientists to deny the existence of the universal background, the "Ether," which was acknowledged for thousands of years in all ancient civilizations, and they replaced it with a form of vacuum, or void. In more recent years, science has been nudged back on track with new concepts regarding the highly potent energetic background etheric medium that we generally refer to as subtle energy. It contains such elusive phenomena as Dark Energy and Dark Matter.

In many ways, we are like fish that cannot comprehend the existence of water. Or we are like "fish scientists" living in the ocean trying to create water in the laboratory. Our scientists are trying to create life through artificial intelligence, and they are proposing different theories about Consciousness. In fact, conscious life force cannot be created; it is accessed through resonance with the universal primordial medium in our background that we refer to generally as subtle energy.

Humanity, as well as all living species on Earth, are no different from fish, as we all live in a humid medium. Humidity levels affect the environment's life force, as water is the carrier of life force, and dehydration reduces life force at the physical level. Heated buildings, with their low humidity, cause dehydration and thereby reduce the life force of the people living in them. Many products of modern technology in the age of information, such as fossil fuels, radioactivity, and all forms of electromagnetic radiation (EMR), cause heat. They also dehydrate all life forms in their vicinity.

Water in any form is a cradle of life force. This does not refer only to water in its material form; it includes all its innumerable non-material harmonic levels that resonate and communicate all the way up to the primordial omnipresent universal background medium of all Creation. If we take the example of a seed that starts germinating when it is irrigated with water, we can see that it was not dead or devoid of life force before it was given water. While it was dormant on the physical level, the seed was alive on higher dimensions. The higher non-physical dimension of water in the seed animated it on the vital, emotional, mental, and spiritual levels. When given water, the seed's evolution was activated on the physical plane.

Looking for life anywhere in the Universe is no different from the fish looking for water in the ocean. Imagine that a fish in an ocean polluted by electromagnetic radiation is being treated for dehydration with water solutions. The universal background is alive and functions as the ocean of life in which everything bathes, from the densest physical dimension to the highest ethereal forms of life. Unfortunately, we are still the fish in the ocean looking for the water. Through the ancient science of Universal Harmonics, we can view life as a unifying quality that resonates on all time-space octave levels of the symphony of Creation. Physical life is only a very small temporary cyclic manifestation of the holistic life force. It gains universality through resonance and transformation in other levels of Creation.

The Living Universe

Our universe, as well as many others, is bathed in the primordial living fog within a Universal Mind containing all the levels of Creation. All Creation exists as a form of imagination within the consciousness of this mind. In this context, questions such as whether there is life after death have no place. When the physical body loses its connection to life force, the vital, emotional, mental, and spiritual components are as alive as ever in the background medium. The life that was connected to the physical body moves to other non-physical time-space dimensions.

The conscious life of the earth is not just the life of humans, animals, and plants. All matter, animate or inanimate, is submerged in the universal life force. We are in a constant exchange of life force with all kinds of matter as we are all bathing in it. The different Laws of Nature in life force move in our biological systems according to a subtle energy anatomy within the physical body. Life force moves within everything in nature through subtle energy patterns.

Modern technology does not deal with life force. The disturbance and depletion of the life force of the earth through modern technology affects the natural environmental balance and reduces the global immunity of all living species on earth. When we manipulate natural electromagnetism, which is part of the life force of the earth, or extract minerals, we deplete them of their living essence. We produce synthetic counterparts of natural products that are devoid of life force.

Subtle Energy Vortices and Life Force

Let us explore some of the concepts dealt with above in more detail. The subtle energy patterns within living systems, in fact in all types of matter, interact with the multi-dimensional Laws of Life force, forming a universal unity with all Creation. This is a communication system that connects through emotional and mental levels to the harmonizing non-dualistic dimension—the spiritual dimension. It operates through the mechanism of subtle energy vortices which themselves bring the harmonizing laws in to govern the evolution of each living form. These vortices govern the forming process in nature. They occur on all levels, from the microcosm of DNA to the macrocosm of the human body and beyond to span the Universe and all of Creation.

This concept appears in the well-known phrase of Ancient Egyptian Hermetic tradition written on the famous Emerald Tablet, "as above so below." The Emerald Tablet is said to have been written by Hermes Trismegistus in Greek, but inspired from Egyptian wisdom. The original Egyptian Demotic script tale speaks of the Book of Thoth which is supposed to contain all knowledge and whoever possesses it is said to have the power of a god. An ancient Egyptian tale ("Setna Khaemwas and Naneferkaptah") from the Ptolemaic Period, mentions this magical book. It was said to have been buried in Memphis but was originally hidden in the bottom of the ocean in six or seven boxes like a Russian doll. The boxes were made of iron, copper, juniper wood, ivory, ebony, silver, and the final one was of gold; it contained the book itself. It is uncertain if "ivory" and "ebony" made up one or two boxes. The Egyptian historian Manetho said that Thoth had written 36,525 books. In any event, Thoth thrice glorified was said to have all knowledge in that book. However, the moral of the tale of Setna and Naneferkaptah clearly indicates that Divine knowledge was not intended for humans or we may lose our lives and the lives of all our loved ones.

The following is a small sample of prose from the Hermetica, taken from ancient Egyptian literature:

Truth! Certainty! That in which there is no doubt!
That which is above is from that which is below, and that which is below
is from that which is above,
working the miracles of one [thing]. As all things were from One.
Its father is the Sun and its mother the Moon.
The Earth carried it in her belly, and the Wind nourished it in her belly,
as Earth which shall become Fire.
Feed the Earth from that which is subtle,
with the greatest power. It ascends from the earth to the heaven
and becomes ruler over that which is above and that which is below.

In more modern times, William Blake poetically described this concept as "the universe in a grain of sand." The first manifestation of this geometrical motion is governed by the Law of Trinity that creates the Psychon pulse formed by a centering Ziron axis within the bi-directional spiral-ing motion. The infinite number of Psychon pulses active in numerable dimensions of time-space create the stable highly potent background state of subtle energy. The bi-directional spiraling motion of the Psy-chon pulses created by the life force of the Ziron creates the living subtle energy medium with the archetypal spiraling motion at its core. This is the origin of Torsion in subtle energy that is directly affected by the direction of flow of life force.

The earth itself is full of subtle energy vortices that connect it to the different levels and dimensions of life force and its powers of nature. Those vortices result from the crossing of underground water streams running in channels within the rocky strata of the earth. The harmo-nizing aspect of any specific vortex gives the water and the area above it many special subtle energy qualities; human beings may experience these as healing properties, or perhaps the ability to communicate with other spiritual dimensions. The vortices, located at what we now often call "power spots" have the BG3 centering quality, while the life force attributes in the resulting fields animate everything in the natural envi-ronment (Figure 5).

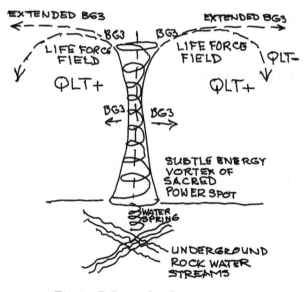

Fig.5 - BG3 and Life Force

In these power spots, early humanity communicated with the Laws of Nature through their "holistic" perception and this gave them direct access to the workings of the powers of nature. As an integral part of nature themselves, these people lived unconsciously in complete harmony with the natural forces. The collective mind of the species played the main role in the harmonious interaction of the individuals. This right-brain control led to the birth of ritual and artistic creativity as interpretations of the effect of the subtle energy of the earth. In time, these locations played an essential role in the prosperity of the community, ensuring a powerful connection to life force in all activities and becoming the sacred centers of their respective communities.

Multi-dimensional communication through the sacred power spots spurred the natural laws' ascension from the subconscious levels of humanity to the right brain subconscious level, which got translated into the left brain to emerge into sensory actions. Humans in their interaction with such power spots became the voice of the earth's multi-dimensional forces of nature. This creative force was expressed through art, motion, and sound, and it spurred self-reflection, which ultimately governed the evolution of humankind. This explains the similarity of human creativity in different locations on the earth. In my opinion, those early forms of creative expression and the communication of energetically active ideas that preceded the invention of writing truly represents the birth of civilization.

Interaction with Life Force

Human beings, like animals and birds, instinctively followed natural subtle energy principles to build homes as reservoirs of life force and to connect all activities, from the smallest to the largest, with the multi-dimensional vortex of the power spot. Important buildings and monuments were placed on the sacred power spots so that they became alive through their connection with the universally harmonized life force. People developed rituals to invite the powers of nature into their buildings or monuments. This practice continued with every new civilization in an area. Today we find that there are usually remnants of earlier buildings in the earth several levels below sacred power spots. In fact, remnants of earlier monuments in an area historically became one of the most important criteria for siting a new building or, indeed, a civilization.

Living Ancient Monuments

The first building interaction with a power spot would begin with the erection of a megalithic vertical stone that we refer to as a "menhir" (Figure 6).

Fig.6 – Menhir

The choice of stone was vital as it had to be dense with a high quartz content, such as exemplified by granite, to amplify the radiation of the power spot's subtle energy vortex. People went to great trouble to find a suitable type of stone, quarry it, and transport it to the site. It was a tedious task to cut trees to build sledges and rafts and move those huge boulders over land and rivers; the route sometimes stretched over hundreds of kilometers. This early practice of planning a structure, choosing, and transporting the material, and managing a site gave birth to living architecture. The menhir harnessed and radiated the forces of nature to serve humanity. Menhirs later developed into obelisks, monumental statues, and towers that still retained the main subtle energy concepts of interaction with the sacred power spots. Eventually, secondary horizontal architectural features were applied to enhance resonance with specific wavelengths (Figure 7). Sacred Proportion became a variable that permitted the tuning of monuments so they could resonate with the powers of nature. The consecration of temples and monuments to different deities became a common practice in all ancient civilizations; this has lived on in a simplified form up to this day. The concept of bringing life into matter, however, has been lost and relegated to the realm of mythology.

Fig.7 - Obelisk & Mosque Minarets

The second form of building that would develop over a power spot would take the form of two megalithic stones in a vertical position supporting a third one in a horizontal position. This formed a sort of gateway that we refer to as a "dolmen." The gateway would be oriented to the east-west equinoxes, extending the harmonizing quality of the power spot along a line connected to the rising and setting of the sun and the cycle of life (Figure 8). The dolmen went through several stages of evolution over time. In later eras they might be covered by an earth mound which created a central chamber; still later the earth mound would be covered with clay bricks and then covered with earth. In the pyramid era, people covered the granite dolmen with megalithic stones. The first example of these is the step pyramid of Saqqara in Giza, Egypt (Figure 9). The stepped stone structure was developed to become the true pyramid shape as we know it (Figure 10).

Fig.8 – Dolmen

Fig.9 – Saqqara Pyramid

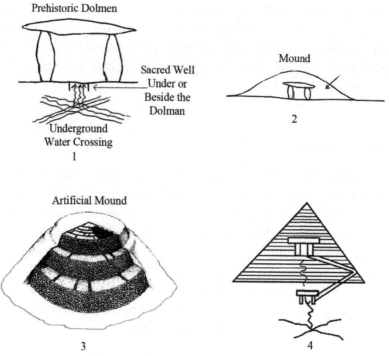

Fig.10 – From Dolmen to Pyramid

Ultimately the dolmen became a spiritual archetype for monuments in the form of arches and eastern gates. The "Arc de Triomphe" on the Champs Élysées avenue in Paris, France, is one such example.

City Planning Across the Ages

As communities developed into villages, towns, and cities, the principle of placing important buildings and activities on power spots and connecting them with main roads was retained to form the basic pattern of the city plan. Planning and laying the foundation at the central Omphalos, or "navel" of the city, was an act of initiation, and movement along the connecting roads enhanced the distribution of the harmonizing energy in the whole pattern. City planning was basically about arranging all activities within a subtle energy pattern of spiritual energy that brought health and prosperity to the community. The city thrived in its natural connection to the life force of the earth and the sky. It became an integral part of nature. We can find examples of this planning in many towns in Europe that are of Roman origin. Zurich in Switzerland, originally called "Turicum," a Roman garrison, still retains the ancient energy-based layout. Modern examples like Washington DC, Paris, Rome, and Cairo were planned along the ancient principles.

The Sacred Web of Life

Being a part of the natural living environment, every activity and object produced had to be part of the web of life, just like the role of each note in a symphony. This was achieved through a resonant quality of subtle energy exchange with all the levels of the living background medium. In this worldview, everything in the environment had a certain aspect of sacredness. The powers of nature were actively working in this Divine symphony of a unified Creation. The manufacturing of everyday objects was based on geometrical archetypes from higher perfect dimensions to which they were connected. Rituals were applied to the use of everyday objects.

The Greek historian Herodotus (c. 485-430 B.C.) visited Egypt and described the Egyptians in his famous work, *An Account of Egypt*:

II:37. They are religious excessively beyond all other men, and with regard to this they have customs as follows: they drink from cups of bronze and rinse them out every day, and not some only do this but all: they wear garments of linen always newly washed, and this they make a special point of practice".

—Thames, 2012, Herodotus on the
Egyptians *World History Encyclopedia.*

Life in Ancient Egypt was considered so perfect, in fact, that the Egyptian afterlife was imagined as an eternal continuation of life on earth.

— (Joshua J. Marc, 2016, *World History Encyclopedia).*

In the process of mummification as practiced in Egypt, amulets specially designed with resonant energetic principles and connectivity to the living forces of nature were placed in relevant positions on the mummy to confer upon it the aspect of life force related to that specific area of the body. The life force stored in the mummy was further maintained through the wall paintings and offerings surrounding it.

Jewelry and amulets were designed to resonate with specific powers of nature related to the energy centers of the body on which they were worn. As an example, head ornaments connected the serpent to the brow chakra and was part of an overall design that activated both brain hemispheres (Figure 11). The jewelry and dress were relevant to the forces of nature at play during celebrations.

Fig.11 - Power Headdress

Living Shapes to Enhance Life Force

Sacred power spots occur either over underground stream crossings or at the center of shapes in the topography that mold the horizon giving an interface with the sky. Mountains, caves, valleys, bays, and peninsulas are such examples as they form a convex or concave shape on the horizon making one element interface with the other. These geometrical configurations point to the existence of subtle energy vortices. The most obvious action we might take today is to invite that sacred energy into our lives by placing an object or monument directly in the power vortex, as was practiced in ancient times. We know, however, that the Ancients also accessed this energy from a distance through certain sacred rituals. In Islam, for example, worshipers from all over the world pray in the direction of the holy mosque in Mecca.

As an architect, engineer, and scientist, I researched and developed a geometrical language that could resonate with this subtle energy quality and thereby create its own BG3 vortex—a power spot—independent of its location on Earth. In order to study the energy interactions of shape with other vibratory ranges such as sound, number, and color, as well as emotional and mental qualities, I needed to look at a comprehensive harmonic system and experience the unity of Creation. To do this I developed a model of a virtual string instrument with strings covering all lengths from zero to infinity. This extended the concept of ancient Universal Harmonics to cover all vibratory ranges of absolute reality. The instrument was designed to have counterparts in all dimensions of reality that would all connect through multi-dimensional resonance reflecting the overall communicative unity of Creation. This led to the development of the multi-dimensional Physics of Quality we are discussing here today. It encompasses all absolute reality in a unifying communicative system of quality.

This is the foundational concept we must grasp in order to build upon our understanding of the Physics of Quality: let's envision the idea that resonant qualities of things we can touch—as well as colors, sounds, shapes, tastes, and smells—each have a place on the imaginary stringed instrument, introduced above, that extends from zero to infinity. At fixed points along the string, we can find the vortex quality containing the centering principle in the Physics of Quality. All vibratory ranges can be brought into qualitative resonance with each other, and they can be accessed through qualitative scales of shape, number, sound, etc. With astute use of these qualitative design principles, human-made objects of any kind can be made to access life force and become part of living nature. What's more, we can use this principle to design modern technology that serves humanity while harmonizing the subtle energy exchange with the environment. In the first BioGeometry book, *Back to a Future for Mankind*, there is an overview of the BioGeometry design language in the appendices which you are invited to review if you would like to take a deeper look at his field of study.

Music

Our physical universe is just a tiny vibratory range of the unperceived absolute reality that ranges from zero to infinity. We refer to everything beyond this physical electromagnetic reality as "subtle energy." It's comprised of a background medium of non-electromagnetic forms of compression waves. These are like the sound waves with which we are familiar, and which include all audible and inaudible ranges of absolute reality. The difference is that subtle energy is the domain of the vital, emotional, mental, and spiritual energies that govern physical life. To be more specific, the backbone of all dimensions beyond the physical universe can be described as inaudible sound or invisible light, and when we look closer at this, we can see that the myriad natural laws involved in the harmony of Creation transform the original sound and light into the unity of a grand universal symphony.

The only way to build an all-encompassing scientific paradigm, therefore, is through the extended Laws of Musical Resonance as found in ancient Universal Harmonics. These included sound, shape, number, and color, as well as everything in existence, all layered into a unified resonant inter-communicating reality. In the Egyptian Hermetic tradition, music was a form of prayer that connected to the creative life force; it was the way to communicate with Divinity. This is the right-brain knowledge of the heart that is behind the sciences of the great ancient civilizations, and which will take us into the future.

In the Hermetic tradition, the mathematical proportions of musical scales were derived from the natural division of strings that can be repeatedly observed in the rotation of a jumping rope that indicated and resonated with the division of wavelengths in nature. Musical scales based on those proportions connected to the process of creation.

Music, in its original mathematical proportion form, recreates the connection to the Laws of Creation through the BG3 quality that is inherently within it and that serves to harmonize all life force attributes with a holistic healing effect. Musical compositions can produce strong BG3. Such an example is the "Sirius Odyssey" I composed with my son-in-law, Omar Raafat. In any type of musical scale, however, the BG3 quality can be activated through the design body of the instrument. Georg Gaupp-Berghausen, a music professor, heads our BioGeometry research in this field and together we have developed string instruments incorporating flexible arms that can be set to any angle thus adding geometrical qualities to sound. Music activates the universal right-brain perception and allows all forms of spiritual communication and creativity. It also harmonizes and empowers the life force of a community and connects its activities to spiritual blessing.

In Ancient Egypt, every occasion that celebrated an important transition in life, such as all types of ceremonies and festivals, had its own type of music. Those occasions were embellished with special clothing, color codes, jewelry, and rituals, all of which served to activate the sacred harmonizing life force that ensured the prosperity of the occasion.

The Shape of the Human Body

Matter is usually formed to serve a certain function. To contain a liquid, we need a concave vessel in the form of a cup, bowl, or bottle. People have been shaping matter to contain material things or to perform specific functions like hunting or carving for many thousands of years. This is child's play compared to the task of containing the multiple levels and functions of life force and the Laws of Nature on vital, emotional, mental, and spiritual levels. In fact, this is something only the myriad forms found in nature can do with great efficiency. In nature, shapes are frozen life force principles, so every natural shape is a manifestation of an underlying combination of the living Laws of Nature. The material "frozen" level of natural shapes is, however, permanently connected to the higher dimensions of life force through the vortices in the centers of each shape.

The most relevant example would be the shape of the human body, a form designed to contain all levels of life force and its biological functions. To illustrate the resonance between shape and life force, we tested an artist's flexible wooden statue of a human being and found that it manifests the same subtle energy vortices, often referred to as wheels or chakras, that we find on the human body. The inanimate statue is a carrier of subtle energy biological functions. Changing the positioning of the arms and hands activates some vortices more than others. This discovery opened a completely new perspective from which to understand ancient statues. By contrast, when we measured electromechanical robots with artificial intelligence that had been placed into a human-like body, we did not find any indication of energy centers or life force. It would require the application of BioGeometry design principles that are based on the forming process of nature to bring life force in. The gray area between artificial intelligence and life force will prove to be a very interesting and indispensable path for future research.

The Life Force of Archetypal Statues

To the Ancient Egyptians, everything in nature was a manifestation of Divine Creation and therefore sacred. They mummified and gave sacred burial to all kinds of animals and birds and believed that all shapes in nature originated from archetypes expressing the living words of Divinity. They also understood that all shapes in nature manifested the harmonious interplay of the Laws of Nature in different forms which gave them a certain level of sacredness. Their concept of the different levels of the soul as functional entities emerged from a very deep understanding of the afterlife.

The Greek philosopher Plato, who, like all his peers, spent years in Egypt, expresses the concept of the reality of an archetypal world in his metaphor of the people in the cave. The cave dwellers live in a world of shadows resulting from the sun's light outside the cave projecting shadows of the life outside onto the uneven cave walls. When the people in the cave go out, they would be blinded by sunlight and could not see the real world out there. He gave this very crude example to simplify the very deep complex knowledge of the temple sciences. The difference, however, is that the Egyptians knew the origin of the shadows and communicated with the real word outside the cave to bring harmony into the shadows.

The Ancient Egyptians accessed the archetypal dimension on the higher planes of nature through their stylized figures of the natural world. These gave them access to the perfect shape patterns on which living physical shapes in nature took form. Our measurement methods based on resonance of shape support the ancient traditions placing this dimension between the higher mental and spiritual planes. The physical shapes were part of the environment, and it was the continuous subtle energy exchange that resulted in the myriad different individual shapes. There is a slight tension created by deviations from the original archetypal template that is part of the natural beauty of nature. What's more, the natural evolution of the forming process in nature is governed by a connection to the archetypal level, ensuring connection to all levels of life force energy.

This connection is achieved through subtle energy vortices that not only ensure multiple levels of centering of the physical shape but also harmonize imperfections resulting from energy exchanges with the environment. The Ancient Egyptians used sacred archetypal patterns of natural shapes as resonant connections between the imperfect world and the perfect spiritual dimension. Their figures had a stylized supernatural appearance, and their stylized statues gave slight indications of the individual features of the actual person being represented which assisted to connect the two. The forming principles of each statue resonated with higher dimensions and radiated subtle energy harmony to the community, as well as the person to which it was connected. The archetypal paintings and reliefs in each tomb resonated with the life force from the higher archetypal levels, ensuring harmony and a smooth transition between worlds.

As with the prehistoric menhirs we discussed earlier, statues would be placed on power spots to give them the fullest life force impact possible, and to enhance their connection to the powers of nature. The statue was inert as a physical object but would be connected to life force and powers of nature; this enabled it to come vitally alive on emotional and mental dimensions, and yet still have a spiritually centering impact on its surroundings. The community would have a sacred interaction with the living statue for healing, oracle readings, and manifestations of the powers of nature. A false notion that is commonly circulated asserts that in ancient times people worshiped those statues. As the ancient civilizations faded away, the rituals connected to the monuments and statues came to be misunderstood. People began to think that the figures were representations of gods rather than powers of nature. In time, members of later generations practiced the same rituals, but with this false belief as their motivating principle. This misunderstanding also led to the defacing or destruction of ancient statues.

The Danger of Moving Monuments

In my earlier book, *Back to a Future for Mankind*, I cautioned against moving ancient monuments, obelisks, and statues from their original locations on sacred power spots without knowledge of the subtle energy configuration. The placement of monuments and buildings on sacred power spots ensured the multi-dimensional connection between the spiritual and the physical dimension. This connection ensured health and prosperity as well as the harmonious integration of all life activities with the environment. The monuments and buildings brought in the life force. A civilization with no anchor in life force is doomed to extinction. If a monument is moved to another power spot, its connection to the universal life force is depleted. Without the connection to higher dimensions created by the subtle vortex above the underground water stream crossing these monuments lose their effect on the surroundings and the sacred function on which rituals were based is lost. They become devoid of the life force they originally radiated. They become a material body without a soul. Unfortunately, this knowledge, which was their whole reason of being, has been lost to mainstream archeology resulting in the "death" of monuments that were "alive" for thousands of years. Without the life force preserving them, the building material's decay is accelerated.

Electromagnetic Radiation (EMR) and Dehydration

In our path towards integrating science and spirituality into a new paradigm, we deal with the dangers of EMR armed with the optimism of having developed successful, well-tried regional solutions that can transform the EMR of the information age into a natural healing medium that will integrate modern technology with the natural environment. Let me explain this further.

In the 1940s, French scientists Léon de Chaumery and Antoine de Bélizal discovered a dehydrating subtle energy quality in uncorrected pyramid and dome shapes radiating from the apex out of the base. We will look at this quality in detail in a dedicated part of this book. They called this quality Negative Green, and it is also found in all types of EMR. What's interesting to note about this quality is that when we put foods like meat or milk inside a pyramid or hemispheric shape they do not rot or ferment but will simply dry up. Chaumery himself fell victim to this energy quality while experimenting with multiple hemispheres that he super-imposed upon each other: he was found dead and dehydrated in his laboratory. This dehydrating energy quality is part of what makes EMR so devastating: it depletes the life force that is naturally resident in nature. Dehydration reduces the immunity of all living species, leaving them defenseless against parasites and viruses. This, in turn, triggers people to increase their use of harmful chemicals, which has a further negative impact upon our health and well-being. The Ancients were aware of this problem and dealt with it through corrective design measures in their monuments. The design corrections were, however, only one aspect of increasing the shape's harmony. The most important criterion was the choice of location. The pyramids of ancient civilizations in Egypt and other places were built on sacred power spots, which added life force and harmonized the dehydration effect.

In the age of information, most products have moved from being mechanical to electronic and so wireless EMR covers the globe. There is abundant scientific research showing the harmful effect of EMR on biological levels but let's examine its effect on life force specifically. Water is the carrier of life force in nature and in the physical dimension water is necessary for the activation and evolution of living systems. As mentioned earlier, physical water carries harmonic levels of water that originate in the primordial non-differentiated foggy dimension and filter through different higher dimensions into the physical level. We know that dehydration on any level reduces life force and that EMR has a dehydrating quality on the physical level, as well as on all subtle energy levels. This, however, is compounded by the global warming effect of EMR in the atmosphere.

Electromagnetic stress affects not only our physical body but also our emotional and mental levels as well. This was very evident in psychological assessments carried out during BioGeometry environmental projects in Switzerland. In those studies, BioGeometry shapes harmonized the emotional and mental subtle energy levels of the environment. Although the sources of EMR were not altered on the physical level, the health symptoms were dramatically reduced as people's emotional and mental levels were brought into balance. The positive psychological effects on the residents, shown through their behavior and interactions, were obvious, and the results were published in an independent study (Figure 12), (appendix).

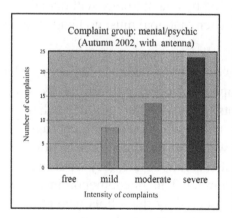
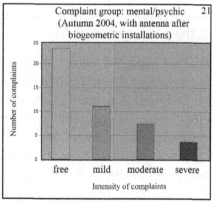

Fig.12 - Hemberg Report-Mental Psychic Scale

Artificial Intelligence and Life Force

One of the goals of modern science is to create life. Artificial intelligence (AI) can simulate the mental processes of life and, with time, self-develop to exceed human capabilities and optimize management and production processes, as well as control all aspects of everyday life. A sort of ideal world could be created by AI in which everything works perfectly, however it would lack conscience, empathy, ethics, and spirituality, and the artistic, creative beauty of imperfection. Those life attributes cannot be created; they must be accessed through multi-dimensional connections.

The future could bring us the rule of supercomputers wherein the subdued humanity would be helpless pawns in the hand of lifeless information technology. Ultimately, it could reach a level of human annihilation and self-destruction.

What if we could introduce into AI the spiritually connected, emotional subtle energy quality of life force and thereby give it a conscience? AI would come alive on all levels above that of the physical. This may sound implausible, but through the principles of BioGeometry, it is a realistic possibility aligned with the ancient paradigm of bringing life force into statues and buildings that interact and cross-communicate with the human subconscious mind. This is not a dream but a necessity, for the future of mankind is in danger of being controlled by a technology without ethical values. Research and experiments to reach that goal must go hand in hand with the development of AI.

Forty years ago, a Russian scientist working in AI contacted me to find a solution to a problem. He had developed the software to run robots. With time, he found that some of the robots behaved differently depending on his psychological state. If he was upset, they would sometimes act aggressively beyond the control of the software that governed their actions. At other times when he was in an optimistic, creative state, they would act beyond the possibilities of their programming. This phenomenon increased with time, and he felt continuously observed by the robots who at times seemed to act according to a different will. He wanted to come to Egypt and work with me as he was convinced that he needed to incorporate BioGeometry to bring harmony into the robots' behavior. Unfortunately, life got in the way of him being able to visit, so we just exchanged emails. This experience provides a typical example of how the human sub-conscience can affect AI in an uncontrolled manner. Ethics and ideals cannot be imported into AI without a connection to higher spiritual planes. The emergence of an uncontrolled "AI-human hybrid technology" that could surface the hidden fears within the collective human subconscious mind is a distinct possibility if such a future technology takes hold.

Pharmaceutical Products

The restoration of life force into all kinds of pharmaceutical products is a very important concept that could greatly enhance their therapeutic effect and reduce the side effects associated with most of them. In fact, the life force component could take the beneficent effect of a drug beyond the physical to the emotional and mental levels. BioGeometry solutions can be applied here for an ideal solution in many ways, and at any level of production—from the manufacturing process itself, to the electromagnetic and mechanical machinery used, the storage of the products, the factory buildings themselves, and the packaging and labelling of the products. Transplants, prosthetics, and implants enhanced with life force could also become a natural part of biological systems. This concept can also apply to all chemical products used in agriculture or in homes. Our food can be healthier with restored life force. Household product toxicity can be reduced.

A New Evaluation System for Products of Modern Technology

I urge that future evaluation of any product should involve ensuring full life force components be in perfect balance and include a BG3 connection to the archetypal dimension. This would allow a product to be perfectly integrated into the natural environment and transmitting its harmonizing quality to the user. We can evaluate the effect of the product's energy on people's emotional and mental levels using the instruments of BioGeometry.

A New Evaluation System for Artistic Creations

The same BioGeometry criteria we use for product design can also apply to artistic creativity. BioGeometry's design concepts and design principles support the creative process and take the consumer of the art into higher spiritual dimensions through the extrasensory perception modes of their right brain and heart. Monitoring the effect on the brain and heart rhythms, and other bodily functions, as well as the BG3 and life force levels, would enable us to do so. All works of art should have a positive transforming effect on people and the environment. Art is Earth's language, and a way of transforming humanity.

In ancient civilizations, all types of art had a harmonizing effect on the observer by opening a doorway in his or her perception to the spiritual planes. The design principles that achieve such a harmonizing connectivity are guidelines that do not restrict creativity; they rather channel it along the right path to higher dimensions. This right-brain connectivity to higher planes takes creativity into new dimensions producing true art as it is meant to be; the artist becomes a voice of the multi-dimensional Universe.

And so, now that we have a solid understanding of the concept of life force in BioGeometry, along with an overview of some of its fields of application, let's turn to a more detailed exploration of the science of Bio-Geometry. As mentioned earlier, you will find that some concepts may be repeated and re-defined when introduced in their relevant chapters so you will not have to come back to the overview to refresh your memory.

Introduction

The Origins of the Science of BioGeometry

In the early 1970s, I coined the word "BioGeometry" as a term for the science of measuring the life force of the earth.

The word "geometry" is composed of the word, "Geo," referring to Earth, and "metry," meaning measurement. This latter term originally referred to the Ancient Egyptian methods of land survey, which were used every year to restore the borders of land ownership after the annual floodwaters receded. By adding "Bio" to the concept, we bring the life force of the earth into the measurement to shift focus from the physical to the higher energy dimensions of life.

Nature's own design language is based on centers of rotation that connect to the life force on higher dimensions. They are commonly referred to as energy wheels or chakras and are easily detected through their special energy quality, which we will introduce and discuss below. Similarly, the design language of BioGeometry restores the life force of animate and inanimate matter in the environment and can also embed it in products of modern technology.

BioGeometry is a modern Physics of Quality with a design language of shape that creates harmony in the subtle energy of the environment. It merges science and spirituality into a holistic paradigm uniting practical and theoretical research in a living reality. BioGeometry is based on the energy quality of harmonic proportions and sacred architectural building rituals used in ancient civilizations, where the location of monuments on sacred power spots played a major role. As an architect with significant exposure to the wisdom of Ancient Egypt, I came to realize that sacred power spots have been one of the main driving factors in the evolution of the history of humankind. The special subtle energy qualities of sacred power spots could be observed in their effect on bird formations flying overhead or on the quality of plants, water, physical material, and healing properties.

Based on Jung's categorization, which we introduced earlier, we can deduct that primitive humanity, with their animal-like interaction with the forces of nature, could directly perceive and identify the location of those power spots in the same way animals did. Modern humanity has lost this ability to perceive the quality of subtle energy. We therefore must resort to other methods to register a sensitivity to subtle energy. I myself embarked long ago upon a quest to ultimately discover these methods and I found they have been used throughout history to locate sites for sacred monuments and to map the earth's energetic patterns so as to optimize city planning. In my search for understanding, I learned about the very special energy quality that identifies the power spots that became sacred to humanity through the ages. In fact, my search led me to a scientific form of subtle energy detection referred to as "Radiesthesia," meaning sensitivity to radiation. I combined that with the concept of resonance and my study of Pythagorean Universal Harmonics to develop the BioGeometry Physics of Quality. I integrated the centering energy quality of power spots with Universal Harmonics to create a special form of "BioGeometry Quality Measurement."

The harmonizing, centering, healing, and multi-dimensional subtle energy quality of sacred power spots became the cornerstone of the science of BioGeometry.

Early on in my search I discovered that there were three primary subtle energy qualities (which are together now referred to as BG3) that enabled the detection of this special energy quality. Today we use a proprietary system of measurement to detect and reproduce BG3, but its initial discovery truly was the starting point for the development of the science of BioGeometry and the Physics of Quality.

Quality is measured as the effect that an action has on the receiver. It can be measured in an individual's subtle energy balance or through physical changes in biological functions. For example, different types of measurement with computerized devices or medical testing procedures can be used to assess a qualitative effect on the human biological system: brain and heart activity, blood markers, and muscle tension, can all be assessed to indicate changes in quality.

Other types of instruments use the human subtle energy field to detect the quality of energetic effects. Instruments of Radiesthesia, calibrated to qualitative "harmonic" scales, are one of the most important tools to accurately detect and measure quality at the subtle energy level.

The term "Radiesthesia" refers to sensitivity to radiation as measured through the scientific calibration of traditional methods of dowsing. Ancient Egyptians used special geometric shapes for detecting and emitting subtle energy quality. The main subtle energy quality in their work, which differs completely from modern concepts of Radiesthesia, related to the communicative multi-dimensional harmonizing and healing dimension found in sacred power spots. Roman practitioners, referred to as "augures," used specially calibrated staffs to enter into resonance with specific wavelengths to detect the quality of Earth's subtle energy. This was deemed necessary for the building of sacred monuments and city planning throughout history. Historic sacred buildings and monuments around the world have been built on such power spots, which were located through dowsing methods and observation of the speed of decay of meat or milk placed in the area. Temples of Ancient Egypt, Greek, and Roman empires were all located on such power spots. All the historic cathedrals in Europe and mosques in the Middle East are located on such sacred spots.

One should not confuse the subtle energy detection methods used in locating sacred power spots and underground water streams with the practice of dowsing using pendulums and rods in a psychic way to connect with the subconscious mind and other forms of spiritual activities. Such usage came to be considered as an esoteric practice. It has been harshly judged accordingly by the standards of the time. This widely used practice of dowsing as a form of psychic activity is different from the scientifically based Radiesthesia used for harmonic quality detection as in the BioGeometry Physics of Quality. The distinction is blurred as they both use some form of pendulum or rods. The principles and methodologies are, however, very different. Dowsing uses questions and answers in a dialogue with the subconscious mind. French and German scientific Radiesthesia use physical calibration of instruments in the form of pendulums or antennas according to abstract qualitative scales to assess energy quality. In Physical Radiesthesia, no questions or dialogues are used.

In the 1940s French researchers Léon de Chaumery and Antoine de Bélizal developed a system of Radiesthesia with instruments calibrated to color scales. Following the tragic death of Chaumery, Bélizal and P. A. Morel published their book, *Physique Microvibratoire et Forces Invisibles* (Éditions Desforges and Amazon), which translates into English as *Micro Vibrational Physics and Invisible Forces*, which became a classic reference in the field. At the same time, German researchers like Hartmann, Curry, and others revived the detection of "Earth Energy Grids," which bear their names. Physicist Reinhard Schneider developed an instrument of radiesthesia based on the micro-wave double antenna of Lecher. It was calibrated to wavelengths and became known as the Lecher Antenna.

Multi-Dimensional Living Physics

This book deals with the "quality" of the background weave of the conscious, intelligent, living subtle energy that permeates all dimensions of the visible and invisible spheres of absolute reality. It is the realm of an all-prevailing Consciousness with all attributes of life. It is the universal soul from which all life in nature arises. In this context, the universal soul is synonymous with the primordial background living subtle energy from which everything arises through endless resonating harmonic levels of life force and Consciousness.

Many concepts of the universal and individual soul have arisen in different world cultures throughout history. They deal in-depth with functional aspects of the soul as seen through the prism of their culture and beliefs. The soul is dealt with in philosophy, psychology, religion, mysticism, and spirituality, as well as, in one way or another, in most fields of knowledge. The Ancient Egyptians had a detailed concept of the different functional soul components that I introduced in my first book, *Back to a Future for Mankind*.

This book does not present any doctrine of the soul but deals with it as a universal living Consciousness in a purely scientific way based on abstract concepts dealing with the different subtle energy levels of the planes of nature. It is, in a way, like the levels used in Helena Blavatsky's Theosophical Society, but without the background doctrine. In a similar way, "spirituality" is viewed here as the harmonizing, centering, subtle energy quality of the three highest planes of nature found in sacred power spots.

The subtle energy quality path supports all beliefs as they all interpret the same timeless truths through their different cultural backgrounds. This is, in a way, an abstract "Physics of the Universal Soul."

The BioGeometry paradigm aligns with the worldview of ancient civilizations. I therefore use the harmonic tools of the Physics of Quality as a key to unlocking the subtle energy secrets behind their achievements. From time to time, I will give examples from my own knowledge of Ancient Egypt to illustrate certain concepts and applications of subtle energy without imposing any doctrine. These examples have parallels in other ancient cultures as well.

The soul and related topics, like the afterlife (which is simultaneous as it is beyond linear time), karma, and reincarnation, are related to dimensions that lie outside our physical time-space reality as perceived in our left brain sensory-based mode of being. The dimensions beyond our linear time-space flow cannot be directly comprehended by the duality and causality relationships that build the backbone of mental perception in our world. They are only understood after they are translated into the dualistic mode of time and space, and associated with sensory, mental imagery and experience-based meaning. Any translation through the limited human sensory system must apply time, space, associated cultural criteria, and a process of personification to produce a meaningful picture. This will inevitably result in some loss of information resulting in an imperfect reproduction of absolute reality. A simplified explanation applicable to such a concept would be the idea that the initiation of an action in our physical dimension creates a reaction. The initiating action enters into multi-dimensional resonance with dimensions beyond our physical linear time-space from which an exchange of information affects the quality of the relationship between cause and effect. This concept can be applied to understand such illusive things like karma, reincarnation, or other life.

In a science of subtle energy, we look at the human being as existing in two dimensions simultaneously through the two hemispherical modes. We are multi-dimensional beings living concurrently on all planes of nature. From this perspective, we have two soul components living together: one is sensory and mortal, and its twin is extrasensory and immortal. The connection between the brain hemispheres provides the feeling of a unified entity. We will use this concept of twin soul entities, or our "invisible roommate," to explain several topics as we go along.

This universal information and the Laws of Nature interact directly with the subconscious mind's extrasensory perception of the so-called right-brain mode, or what is sometimes referred to as the "intellect of the heart." In this timeless dimension of non-duality and non-causality, communication and information exchanges work through the multi-dimensional resonance which we call "Universal Harmonics," a new concept of the multidirectional flow of time and motion that we shall get into within the Physics of Quality.

In the current scientific paradigm, where our sensory, physical dimension puts us in a box, we seek the freedom of thinking outside the box through all types of artistic activities leading to right-brain perception. BioGeometry, however, is a science that uses a new Physics of Quality to expand the box itself to include everything in all dimensions of Creation. All that is needed is a simple shift of perception and a very short journey through the tunnel connecting our analytical sensory left-brain mode of perception to the universal right-brain mode. The Physics of Quality takes a holistic qualitative abstract approach to the subtle energy of the human system, including its environment. We deal with the soul in its "energetic" individual or universal dimensions, as a sensory databank exchanging information with its projected perceived (as well as the total unperceived) multi-dimensional reality. This concept connects the individual and universal realities as components of the soul in different dimensions. The Laws of Universal harmonics put all the levels of the soul into a resonant unified multi-dimensional information system.

We use BioGeometry shapes and tools, such as the BioGeometry Human Archetype Ruler (to be introduced in upcoming sections), to achieve resonant interactions that allow us to access the impersonal qualitative information of the universal soul on the different planes and sub-planes of nature (Figure 13). We do so in an abstract way that is equally scientific, spiritual, and practical, without favoring any doctrine. It is a solid scientific—as well as a spiritual—backbone that can be applied to any set of principles.

The Swiss psychologist Carl Gustav Jung delves deep into Egyptian Gnostic schools to study their concepts of the soul and the archetypes. In fact, a codex from the scrolls discovered in 1945 in Nag Hammadi, Egypt, is referred to today as the "Jungian codex." Jung sees the archetypes as archaic patterns within the collective unconscious that form the psychic base of instincts.

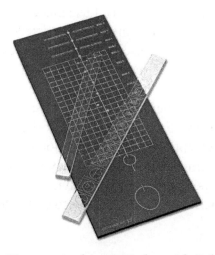

Fig.13 - Human Archetype Ruler with Subplane Strip

Theories of archetypes represent the common area where Jungian psychology, theosophy, Gnosticism, Ancient Egypt, and BioGeometry meet, each from a different direction. In fact, archetypes play an important role in the living Physics of Quality and the energy of shape, as well as in understanding the stylized sculptures and reliefs of Ancient Egypt. In Bio-Geometry, our approach to archetypes is similar to that of Ancient Egypt in that we see all forms of the physical dimension as being rooted in subtle energy templates that are both spiritual and archetypal. These templates contain the perfect subtle energy patterns of all physical forms. What's more, the physically real forms acquire a certain level of imperfection through interaction with their environments; this allows for the creation of multitudes of different physical appearances. The slight imperfections in shapes produce a subtle dynamic tension that spurs our feeling of the beauty of nature. In Ancient Egypt, the sacred templates of all shapes lay behind the culture's stylized reliefs and statues that secured the connection between the physical and the spiritual dimensions.

Jung's categorizations of humanity (primitive, ancient, modern, and contemporary) are based on the slow shift of focus of perception from the so-called right-brain mode of primitive mankind to the so-called left-brain mode of modern humanity (Figure 14). I use this concept to shed light on the dualistic nature of the multi-dimensional existence of the human being, and the conscious and unconscious information exchanges of which we are capable. We can only discover the secrets of the ancient sciences when we understand the way they perceived their reality and interacted with it. In this context, we can regard the Ancient Egyptians as a different species. However, the basic Jungian categorization only shows the dominating kind of perception in human development. Human modes of perception are more complex than that, as they shift constantly between modes while a person performs different activities. They would, however, be completing those activities differently based on the focus of perception of their category.

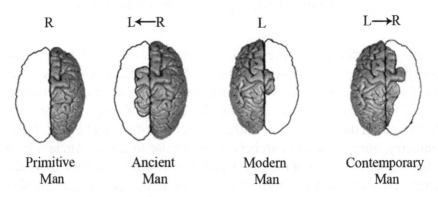

R	L←R	L	L→R
Primitive Man	Ancient Man	Modern Man	Contemporary Man

Fig.14 - Shift from Right Brain to Left Brain Perception

While we're on the topic of Jungian psychology, I must mention my fruitful interactions with some of the important post-Jungian psychologists who have developed Jung's concepts and connected them to deeper spiritual realms of the soul.

The Dallas Institute of Humanities and Culture

In 2011, I was invited by Gail Thomas to give a presentation on BioGeometry at the celebration event of the thirtieth anniversary of the Dallas Institute of Humanities and Culture. Part of the event was dedicated to the memory of James Hillman, one of the peers of neo-Jungian psychology who was one of the founders of the Dallas Institute of Humanities. He passed away a week before the event. I got to know Robert Sardello, Thomas Moore, Joan Stroud, and others and had very fruitful discussions with them.

Robert Sardello, one of a group of prominent post-Jungian psychologists who were attending the event, had sent a copy of my first book to Gail Thomas, another of the group's members and subsequently introduced me to the group. Robert Sardello has gone beyond the boundaries of traditional or Jungian psychology to develop his own school of spirituality; it leads to an inner path of silence equally valid and central to all beliefs. In fact, he is a major figure in America's rediscovery of soul. Thomas Moore hails him as one of our most creative and original thinkers, while James Hillman praised him for breaking open startling new realms of meaning. Sardello's probing, provocative books, seminars, and "soul retreats," run through his School of Spiritual Psychology, have earned him widespread respect and attention. He explains how to locate the soul and gain a sense of how our soul wants to act in the world.

Gail Thomas is the author of an interesting book titled *Healing Pandora*. In it, she sheds light on the enormous healing powers available through a connection to nature, as well as on nature's better-known destructive capacity. Pandora is the dark but all-giving feminine, an archetypal vessel with the power to heal our culture. After the event in Dallas, the group spent a few days with Gail at her property, Windwater Lodge, where Robert, Gail, and I continued the interesting discussions that anchored our friendship.

Robert had advised me to write a comprehensive new book that went beyond the introductory concept of my first book, *Back to a Future for Mankind,* to cover the new ideas and practical applications that I presented in my lectures. He felt this would allow my ideas to be understood as part of the complete Physics of Quality within BioGeometry, rather than left to their own devices as scattered bits and pieces of information. I wrote down the list of topics for this comprehensive work and discussed it with the group. I later started writing this book but had to put it aside to write my book, *BioGeometry Signatures,* which was published in November 2016 for the celebration of forty-five years of BioGeometry that was held in Montreal. With the long-awaited publishing of the book on BioGeometry Signatures behind me, I started again working on this book.

PART ONE

The Need for a New Paradigm

Advances in modern medicine have raised our life expectancy by about twenty years over the past century. However, those extra years come at a cost: our quality of life has not improved at the same pace due to the rise of chronic diseases, of which the causes are still largely elusive. Autism, attention deficit hyperactivity disorder (ADHD), and dementia are on the rise. Psychological disturbances like depression and aggression are rising to epidemic levels. High blood pressure, diabetes, cancer, arthritis, and so on, are only a small example of many chronic diseases that modern medicine can manage but not cure.

Chronic diseases are on the rise because we remain ignorant of their causes, and this is largely because we haven't been looking in the right places. As long as science promotes the idea that there is a separation between the human being and the environment, we, as a species, will never find the causes. We are the drops that make up the ocean and we share its overall quality.

The obvious major factor for chronic disease—which is still vastly ignored—is environmental stress and this has been clearly demonstrated in the results of BioGeometry's various environmental projects. The increase of EMR in the atmosphere and the chemical pollution of food and drink—compounded by our use of many toxic household products—are the main causes of many chronic diseases that industry does not want to acknowledge.

We are moving from fossil fuels to electric energy that we erroneously believe will save our environment. The increasing amount of electromagnetic radiation in all types of modern transportation is creating a lot of health hazards for the occupants as well as the environment. Smart cities are the ultimate manifestation of the information age, and they will pose a real threat to all life systems within them, as well as to their surroundings. The resulting increase in the incidence of chronic diseases and epidemics will be a major decisive factor in the future of humanity.

I keep repeating this warning at every possible opportunity: the increase in EMR in the atmosphere—with its dehydrating effect—reduces the immunity of all living systems and contributes to global warming. This could be the "Achilles' heel" that brings our civilization to its knees.

This need not be the case. Electromagnetic radiation is a carrier of information. As such it can become the solution to environmental problems. If we can make it a carrier of natural harmonizing life force, we can transform this harmful effect into a healing one that can change the future of humanity as well as the whole environment. All electrical modes of transportation can be made to have a healing effect on users. Smart cities can be made to channel life force and become an integral part of the natural living environment.

This is not a vision of Utopia but a reality that has been well tested in BioGeometry solutions for several decades. Our topics of investigation range from cars, aircraft, ships, homes, and living and workspaces, up to whole regions.

In Switzerland, we were commissioned by the government authority for mobile communication and environment to apply BioGeometry solutions in collaboration with Swisscom, the main Swiss mobile communication provider, in the regions of Hemberg, St. Gallen (2003), and Hirschberg, Appenzell IR (2007). These projects were documented and according to an independent study there was about a sixty percent reduction in all health problem symptoms (Figure 15), (appendix).

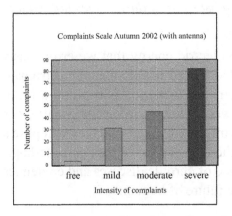 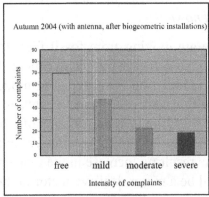

Fig.15 - Hemberg Complaint Scale - All Symptoms

The Open Energy System of Life

A human being's interaction with the environment is based on a resonant exchange of different types of energy that should all be acknowledged. Beyond the chemical and electromagnetic on the physical level, our bodies also exchange with the environment many types of subtle energy on the vital, emotional, mental, and spiritual levels. We must start looking at a person and the environment as one unified inseparable system.

The earth is comprised of the material globe and the gaseous atmosphere around it as a unified inseparable life system. Everything within this system operates like tiny bacteria playing a part in the life of the whole system, just like our immune cells have a crucial function supporting the overall health of our body. We are an open energy system continuously exchanging all types and levels of subtle energy with the earth. All physical manifestation happens within a unified living multi-dimensional subtle energy background that includes many dimensions. All life manifests within the endless harmonic levels of the primordial state referred to as waters or Fog that form the background subtle energy.

The physical universe exists in a narrow electromagnetic range concentrated around the speed of light. It forms a very small part of the endless vibratory range of the subtle energy levels of absolute reality that range all the way from zero to infinity and include different forms and levels of vital, emotional, mental, and spiritual planes of nature. This vibratory range is not linear but moves in a multidirectional, multi-dimensional way, just like an all-illuminating light. The multi-dimensional subtle energy exchange with the universal life force includes vital, emotional, mental, and spiritual levels that are harmonically present in other universes existing in physical, as well as non-physical, dimensions. Human beings exist in multiple interactive dimensions totally unperceived by physical sensory organs. They are, however, very active on the subconscious extrasensory levels affecting our subtle energy biological organ functions. The unconscious right-brain perception mode also accesses all types of information that influence our vital, emotional, mental, and spiritual subtle energy qualities.

Time and space as we know them are woven into the linear flow of the physical dimension. The Law of Time itself emerges from within the non-dualistic all-encompassing "Omni-dimension" that governs the creation of pulse in all levels and dimensions of Creation. In other dimensions, there are different time-space criteria where multi-directionality of time and multi-layered, multi-directional interactive space configurations are the norm. Multi-directional resonance replaces causality in those dimensions beyond linear time-space of the physical electromagnetic range. All of this exists within the harmonic multi-layered background medium behind the physical world. In our physical existence and beyond, we interact with all those dimensions with their different criteria on an unconscious level. These are the unperceived levels of subtle energy that govern all biological functions. This is the living subtle energy that we must address when interacting with the environment. Everything in Creation emerges within this living conscious cradle of life in all its forms.

The natural intelligence and wisdom of the living Earth surpasses, by far, the sensory time-space-based capacities of the human mind.

They are, however, in constant interaction and exchange with the human unconscious levels where they are at the core of all biological life functions that are mostly beyond our control. All forms of life are part of the earth's energy, forming one unified conscious living subtle energy system.

To give a simple crude example of this unity, we live off the sun's energy but, besides our skin, we have no organ to capture it directly into our digestive system. Plants do that for us. They transform the sun's energy into chemical energy which they store physically and which we can access with our digestive systems. In a way, plants are an external organ of our body. We and the plants are one biological system.

We do not live on the earth as a separate species but are part of it. Like the bacteria in our body, we must perform to the good of the whole or else we become dispensable and will ultimately be taken out to restore the health of the earth.

Although our modern mainstream science does not include subtle energy in its multi-dimensionality, quantum physics is stretching its borders into subtle energy realms of Consciousness, emotions, thoughts, and intention. Experiments have shown that intention can affect the outcome of an experiment forward and backward in time and this has been reported in the book *The Intention Experiment* by Lynn McTaggart

.

These subtle energy effects go far beyond the time-space boundaries of existing science. A new type of physics is needed to understand and effectively work with all those levels of subtle energy. The Physics of Quality in BioGeometry is such a science. Its roots go back to the Pythagorean Universal Harmonics that was an important part of the experiential temple sciences of Ancient Egypt. Pythagorean Universal Harmonics explores the cyclic resonance (e.g., octaves on a piano) along string lengths of a musical instrument. It was in a way based on musical notes extended to cover all string lengths from the smallest to the largest in a linear way. The notes on the strings expressed the proportions of Creation. Pythagorean Universal Harmonics extended the resonance to include everything in existence such as sounds, numbers, elements, shapes, plants, animals, seasons, days, planets, and so on in a unified system of sympathetic relationships or similarities. This became the expanded esoteric *universal* version of the basic Pythagorean Universal Harmonics. The attribution of Universal Harmonics to Pythagoras is based on the fact that he brought to the Western world the secret ancient knowledge he learned in the two decades he spent in the Egyptian temples.

Several previous attempts by such great figures as Kepler, Chladni, and Newton aimed to revive ancient Harmonics as a modern universal science, but they failed to find anchor in the mainstream scientific community of their day. Swiss scientist Hans Kayser revived Pythagorean Universal Harmonics again in the 1940s. His books: *Akroasis* and *Handbook of Harmonics* are available in English, but all his other works are written in German. A society bearing his name in Bern, Switzerland, houses all his works.

The Universal String Instrument

Universal Harmonics is based on the resonance between musical strings, where one is double or half the length of the other. In a musical string-based instrument, like a piano, for example, this resonant phenomenon produces sounds from different string lengths; they all have the same qualitative effect on the user. In other words, the Law of Resonance connects qualities from the shortest to the longest string in the instrument. We refer to these as octaves: the notes based on the resonance between multiples of string lengths are experienced as the same quality on lower or higher pitches and labeled as the same note. When one note is struck, all others vibrate and sound along with it, producing a background echo. The same notes are in a primary resonant vibratory communication along the whole instrument. Similarly, there are other secondary levels of resonance between different notes. For simplification, we will only use the primary resonance to illustrate the concept of the Physics of Quality.

To apply resonance as a universal law on all subtle energy levels, we will expand the musical instrument beyond the hearing range to include string lengths that cover all vibratory ranges of absolute reality (sound, color, shape, number and so on) from zero to infinity (Figure16). This will give us the possibility to connect to everything in the Universe through its resonance with an existing physical string length. This puts everything in nature (colors, numbers, angles, shapes, emotions, thoughts, etc.) in a system where they all become intercommunicative qualities to form an overall unity of Creation. All past, future, invisible, and parallel dimensions become part of this accessible interactive unified information system. From a qualitative point of view, they are connected through a multi-dimensional web of resonance.

Quality is therefore a very practical way to study and work with subtle energy in its full multi-dimensional form beyond the confines of physical time and space.

While mainstream science with its quantitative analytical methods tries to go from the physical level into higher dimensions, BioGeometry uses the Physics of Quality to work directly on any plane of nature and other dimensions in a solid scientific and practical way.

The model of an expanded string instrument to describe the resonance of qualities from zero to infinity is, however, an oversimplification as it seems to imply wavelengths are a basis for quality on all levels. As we approach higher levels of subtle energy towards the zero and infinity states the concepts of duality, linearity, and directionality of wave propagation

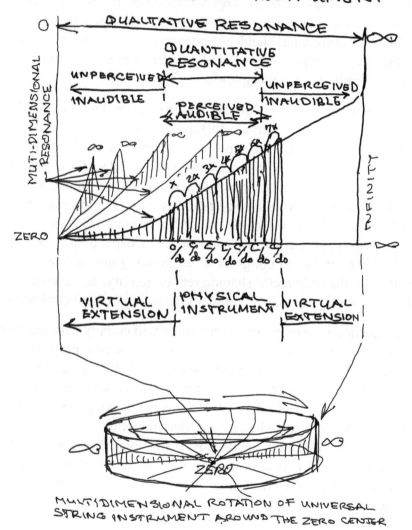

Fig.16 - Zero to Infinity Musical Instrument

in time-space—as we know it—change. The first levels beyond the speed of light are mostly multidirectional compression waves traveling faster than light; this includes some forms of scalar waves and hyper-sound, for example. The concept of physical waves or frequencies cannot describe higher levels of subtle energy within other time-space dimensions because, without the linearity of physical time and space, these levels are more like multi-directional fields simultaneously pulsating in different dimensions. Any attempt to apply the idea of physical waves or frequencies is therefore limited to the metaphoric.

When we look deeper, we will also understand the fact that an observer can find a wave or a particle in formless states of subtle energy in compliance with the observer's mental concepts. On this level, universal Consciousness interacts with our expectation to shape our perceived reality. To be clear, universal Consciousness interacts with and shapes all other dimensions and realities beyond our sensory perception. This is in a way like the experiments in quantum physics where the observer finds the electron as a particle or a wave, but not both, depending on what he or she is looking for. Let us not go as far as thinking that our thoughts and intentions are the only factor shaping reality. Reality, as we know it, is a result of a two-way resonant communication with the Universal Mind.

The intelligent universal all-prevailing mind will comply with our mental concepts, since they emerge within it, and will act accordingly, producing the effects that reflect our so-called discoveries of the Laws of Nature in modern science. The hidden reality is that the universal intelligent energy is reaching out to us and adapting itself to our quantification and measurements within a very limited sensory-based worldview to give us what we need; yet the separation between us is illusionary, just like the drops in the ocean. The all-prevalent Universal Mind, of which we are part, is giving us tools of communication to experience its omnipotence in a form of self-observation.

To sum it up, subtle energy is alive and intelligent and interacts with the observer in any dimension and will comply and reciprocate according to the properly deducted patterns of understanding. It is the background weave of the multi-dimensional reality. I refer to it as omni-dimensional because it is the cradle in which our own and all other dimensions become manifest. This background weave of life nurtures all dimensions of Creation. With such elusiveness, the Physics of Quality is a methodology of working with subtle energy that is true to its living, emotional, and intelligent nature. The Physics of Quality goes beyond our left brain sensory perceived reality to access all levels and dimensions of absolute reality. These unperceived dimensions are experienced through a right-brain mode of connection to the universal resonance of the heart. The Laws of Nature at the core of biological functions are found on the higher transcendental levels of absolute reality. Irrespective of the different types and manifestations of energy in different dimensions, the resonance of quality is the active path of information exchange.

Manifestations of Subtle Energy

Several manifestations of subtle energy have been known since antiquity and come in many forms such as qi, prana, ether, life force, and others. More recent researchers discovered it in different forms such as Reichenbach's "animal magnetism" or "Od," and Wilhelm Reich's "Orgone." Rupert Sheldrake's morphogenetic fields also show some of the attributes of subtle energy. Pyramid energy, made popular by Patrick Flanagan in his book *Pyramid Power,* is now a popular field of research. Patrick and I started on a project for a second book on Pyramid power from a BioGeometry/Physics of Quality perspective, however it did not fully materialize due to the passing of his wife, who had played an active part integrating both our ideas in the book. I would also suggest that when we know more about the nature of such things as the "Dark Energy" and "Dark Matter" that form most of the invisible background substance of the Universe, we will find that they fall into this multi-dimensional subtle energy category and that their effects, qualities, and polarities can be measured using Bio-Geometry tools.

The highly energetic state of subtle energy has been demonstrated by Russian scientists. Torsion is an integral aspect of subtle energy as proposed by Kozyrev. In the Russian experiments, the spiraling effect of torsion can be observed on the rotation of a pendulum in reaction to the change of state of materials, like melting ice or freezing water. The spiraling torsion at the core of the background subtle energy of the Universe makes it a source of powerful energy. This is a universal endless "clean" living source that can be tapped to fuel a future environment-friendly civilization. Humanity can thus have a powerful living omnipresent energy source with which it can interact. The intelligent emotional properties of this energy could bring life force in all our future products.

In most cases, the conscious, living, intelligent, and emotional attributes at the core of subtle energy are still largely ignored by modern science.

The different theories of quantum physics suggest an interaction on minute energy levels connecting the observer to the outcome. Zero-point energy at the base of electromagnetic forces seems to border on non-electromagnetic subtle energy. The zero-point field is a manifestation from higher levels of Creation during the first eruption of the electromagnetic Universe. This field is the lowest manifestation of an endless higher non-physical harmonic hierarchy. In a science of quality, like BioGeometry, this would be the border with the vast dimensions of subtle energy with all its life force attributes. Qualities emerge into awareness when one system is affected by another, so a science of quality deals with how everything affects not only the human subtle energy system but other living systems as well.

In order to go into those subtle energy levels, the Physics of Quality brings the human being as the multi-dimensional measuring instrument for all effects on all levels (physical, vital, emotional, mental, and spiritual). This includes all other dimensions and parallel universes.

In nature, the interaction of qualities is governed by laws of balance and harmony from a higher level down through the archetypal dimension. If we take the example of the perfect arrangement of qualities emerging from the center and manifesting in time-space along the periphery of a circle, a center of a circle cannot be expressed as a point because if we enlarge the point, it becomes a circle with a center and so on. The center is elusive and can only be understood as a transcendental quality; it is the multi-dimensional quality within a tunnel or a wormhole to other dimensions.

The center is therefore detected through a special harmonizing transcendental subtle energy quality through which the archetypal laws from higher dimensions emerge into physical reality and the information from physical reality is transmitted to higher dimensions. These centers are two-way wormholes connecting different dimensions.

This centering, harmonizing, subtle energy quality exists naturally in certain locations on the Earth: they have the same communicative qualities found in the centering effect of a circle. It is like the center expands to fill the circle so that the whole circle becomes a center creating a vortex in the form of a wormhole connecting multiple dimensions of the earth and the sky. In the past, such areas became areas for healing, burial, and oracles—sacred power spots around which all kinds of ritual and sacred monuments have developed.

Humanity's relationship with power spots became the most important factor that shaped history from the dawn of humanity to the present day.

BioGeometry is a language of shape that introduces this harmonizing subtle energy quality into the environment. The one central quality, present at power spots around the world, and now available through mastery of the Physics of Quality, is referred to in BioGeometry as "BG3." BG3 can be detected with harmonic instruments of measurement which track the simultaneous resonance of three subtle energy qualities. Sometimes we also refer to BG3 through its attribute as the ONE Harmonizing Quality.

The integration of the BG3 quality into all products of modern technology—whether electromagnetic or combustion-based—is the way into a healthy future. Economies that depend on fossil-fuel technology need to apply the harmonizing quality just as much as those that are dependent on electromagnetic products.

The BG3 subtle energy quality can be incorporated into all types of design to ensure a resonant communication with the Earth, as well as the forming process in nature from higher archetypal levels. Applying design principles based on the forming process of nature ensures the proper interaction of man-made products with the universal life force. The practice is based on designing centers of shape through which the laws, templates, and patterns of development emerge from higher archetypal dimensions to govern their evolution and forming. This is the cornerstone of BioGeometry, and it sets the path of interaction within the Physics of Quality.

Where Did We Go Wrong?

All types of natural energy systems in the earth have an inherent intelligent life force within them and this includes chemicals, fossil fuels, and electromagnetism, which are all part of the earth's energy system. Energy systems overall play a major role in the support of all life forms on the planet. Human beings, animals, and plants, as well as seemingly inanimate matter, are like drops in the ocean of this life force, which supports the natural evolution of the earth.

In its present form, however, modern man-made technology does not take the life force at the core of all subtle energy systems in nature into consideration. In fact, the effect on the human subtle energy system governing our biological functions is not a criterion that is considered at all in the development of the products of modern technology. As a result, modern man-made fuels, whether fossil, chemical, or electrical, are depleted of life force and are harmful to all forms of life. They were all beneficent in their original natural state as part of the Earth's energy. Unfortunately, we are largely unaware of the fact that the quality of our psyche and the narrow-minded way we have applied modern technology have corrupted the original beneficent living attributes of subtle energy in nature. "Humanizing" modern technology, through the reintegration of life force, is the only way to ensure the future of life on our planet.

Since we cannot turn back the clock, we must work within the existing situation. The only immediate solution is to change the quality of the harmful side-effects that modern technology has on living systems. To create an ideal future, a new life saving scientific paradigm is needed. The products of modern technology should be initially produced along the laws of the natural forming process to support the quality of the life force of our planet.

This approach brings the total invisible absolute reality that lies outside of our very limited time-space dimension into our grasp. These subtle energy dimensions are affecting us on a subconscious level. They contain Laws of Nature that support our biological functions.

The Nature of Paradigm-Changing Scientific Breakthroughs

What kind of new scientific paradigm do we need to save our planet? There are two types of scientific innovators that have changed the face of society. The first includes those researchers who took existing scientific achievements to new levels by traveling the road of increased specialization and evolved technological possibilities within the confines of the established educational and research institutions. This is the solid base that continuously fuels the existing scientific paradigm to new achievements. There have also always been individuals from outside the establishment who have had a visionary, multidisciplinary, generalized outlook that embraces all fields of life. They see the interdisciplinary connections that form the web of everyday life activities resulting in a unified vision in which everything has a place in a harmonious universal symphony. They look at every detail in any specialized field and seek its place in the puzzle of life in relationship to the whole. Embracing the perception of holistic unifying relationships adds qualitative aspects to the separate pieces and transforms them into components of a larger unified reality.

This holistic worldview usually leads an individual to the path of multi-dimensional right-brain perception, which brings with it a higher level of ethics, universal values, wisdom, and interest in the invisible. Ultimately, the universal geniuses who are enfolded within this approach usually encode many hidden levels of knowledge in their work, which is destined to be discovered by the illuminated minds of future generations. Labels such as "Renaissance Man" are often applied to these people. Their innovations are not step-by-step advancements through specialization, but rather they are completely out-of-the-box visionary, and revolutionary ideas. In the beginning, they usually shock the establishment, which results in fierce attacks against them. In fact, this defensive peer ego response has marked scientific, religious, and other mainstream establishments throughout history. Usually with time, however, and with the evolution of the general culture of society, those new paradigms embed themselves in the popular culture of the times where they can, at least in part, become accepted by the establishment.

This type of multi-cultural universal genius has always existed. One of the earliest examples can be found five thousand years ago in Ancient Egypt in the figure of Imhotep. He was an architect, a physician, and a philosopher at the time of King Djoser of the Third Dynasty. He built the stepped pyramid of Saqqara, the first stone-block and granite core pyramid in history. It still stands firm today, more than five thousand years later, defying the passage of time. Other people who fall into this category include:

- Pythagoras (who was skilled in mathematics, music, geometry, and philosophy)
- Avicenna (pharmacology and medicine)
- Al-Khayyam (poetry, science, mysticism)
- Gaber (alchemy)
- Da Vinci
- Kepler
- Newton
- Goethe
- Steiner
- Schauberger (water, subtle energy, gravity)
- Jung
- Jenny (Cymatics) and
- Kayser (Universal Harmonics)

The knowledge these people presented to the world was anchored in secret traditions that go back to the multi-dimensional universal temple sciences of the earliest civilizations. All great cultural revolutions in history are based on opening the rigid boundaries of the mind through alternative modes of thinking that are usually closely related to, or based upon, the ancient secret traditions. This secret knowledge from Ancient Egyptian and Mesopotamian civilizations gave the necessary impulse that spurred the great cultures of the Greeks and Romans, as well as the Islamic classical period that influenced the fifteenth century Renaissance era in Europe. Sufism and the builder guilds of the Arab world influenced all the esoteric societies of Europe. With time, they attracted all kinds of intellectual factions that replaced their practical building secrets with symbolic rituals.

Eventually, human perception lost its anchor in the powers of nature due to the slow shift of focus into the sensory analytical mode of left-brain perception which itself gave birth to modern science and technology. The ancient ways of living in universal environmental unity became estranged from people's daily lives. As unified perception edged increasingly into the unconscious levels of human awareness, the ancient knowledge came to be regarded as nothing more than a collection of old traditions based largely on superstition. What was left of this knowledge became absorbed into esoteric disciplines that were totally separated from mainstream science. Science and spirituality, which had originally been unified in the ancient holistic sciences, came to occupy opposite poles of wisdom which were now separated by the quantifying mindset of the scientific establishment. Furthermore, the ancient knowledge posed a threat to the supremacy of political and religious authorities and its adherents, fearing persecution, had to submerse it in an underground culture.

The secret sciences and traditions were put in the same category as the magical spells and herbal concoctions that were widely used and had nothing to do with the ancient temple sciences. We see this happening as far back as the early Greek civilization with the persecution of Pythagoras, who is credited with the foundation of mathematics, geometry, and music, and his school, and the persecution of other Greek philosophers of his time. Together these men became regarded as the fathers of Western science. However, the real credit goes to the ancient civilizations of Egypt, Mesopotamia, and the Far East where Pythagoras, Plato, and other Greek philosophers studied. They ultimately brought to the Western world fragments of ancient knowledge upon which the Western scientific worldview was built. Most of these seekers of wisdom went to the library and school of Alexandria in Egypt, which was the beacon of knowledge at the time, and there they found the knowledge of the ancient world. The Greek school of medicine of Alexandria from where we got physicians such as Galen (Galinos), said they based their knowledge on old yellow tattered papers that had been brought from the main school of medicine in Memphis. The papers were attributed to the god Ptah and the famous Imhotep.

Ancient Egyptian Theories of Creation

There are several Ancient Egyptian theories of Creation. In the Memphite theology, which is probably the oldest known, there were nine deities known as the "Pesedjet" in Greek. There was one creator god, Atum. He begat of himself without using a female counterpart. He spat the goddess Tefnut of the dew, breathed the male god Shu of the wind and when they married, they gave birth to Osiris, Isis, Seth, and Nephthys. Other theories include the Ogdoad or company of eight gods of el Ashmunein in Menya, the theory of the Big Cackler, and other beliefs such as those around the primordial temple mound in the temple of Ramses III in Karnak. In one theory there was nothing but water covering everything. Then the waters receded to reveal the tip of a mound. A bird like a goose landed on the tip resembling a pyramid's apex, and cackled. The sound vibrations started a series of events which brought all Creation into power. MAAT is the universal balance of order. It represents the natural order of existence and the perfect balance and harmony in a perfect world .

The secret ancient traditions, especially those of Egypt, lie hidden deep within the subconscious core of Western civilization and even today are still playing an important role in the background of human knowledge. In this context, Egypt is not just a country on a map, it is the spiritual anchor of Western civilization.

This knowledge is still today referred to as the "intellect of the heart." As a secret doctrine, a lot of this ancient knowledge has found its place throughout history into great works of art, architecture, and planning. It may be denied by the conscious mind, but it will always influence it in subtle and unexpected ways. The new universal Physics of Quality, as codified in BioGeometry, brings the unperceived levels at the core of modern science to the surface and bridges them to spirituality and the humanities in a new holistic scientific approach. It can also transform communities to play a practical beneficent role in restoring the environment.

I was lucky enough to have met and interacted with several people who fall into the category of Renaissance men and who have shaped my worldview. Such an individual was my father, who in many ways shaped my personality; people in the Middle East always refer to me as the son of this great man. Dr. Sayed Karim was a pioneer of modern architecture in the Middle East. He was an urban planner, a researcher in Ancient Egypt, a philosopher, a musician, an author and, also, in the late 1930s, he became the publisher of the first Architecture and Arts magazine in the Middle East (*Al-Emara wa Al-Fonoun*). When I was a child, the cultural elite in Egypt gathered every evening in our home and I was privileged to witness the birth of many of the famous works of music, art, film, and so on that shaped the culture of the whole Middle East. My father loved and understood all types of music. His vast art, music, and Egyptology library was my favorite place to abide. His attitude towards everything was that when you dislike something, it means you do not understand it, and when you do, you will like it. This made me study anything that I came across and formed my attitude towards the world so that I was always hungry for new knowledge. In the early years of my development of BioGeometry, he became excited with every new discovery I made and gave me correlations and topics to research in Ancient Egypt.

Although the development of BioGeometry was not derived from Ancient Egypt, it gave me the paradigm and the key to discover the subtle energy scientific knowledge of that culture. My father insisted I apply my research to Ancient Egypt and gave me important guidelines for doing so, although I never became an Egyptologist in the traditional sense. Coming from different complementary paths, we were both fascinated with our research related to Ancient Egypt. My research in Ancient Egypt is based on both my profession as an architect and my personal specialized knowledge of, and practice with, subtle energy. This has given me an alternate path of understanding not found in mainstream Egyptology.

My Multicultural Background

The concept of resonance and my interest in Pythagorean Universal Harmonics—as well as Ancient Egyptian multi-dimensional "Universal Harmonics—gave new meaning to my early musical studies at the Tiegerman Conservatoire in Cairo where I studied piano for a few years. Music and other forms of art in all forms and cultures even today play an important role in my life.

In my study days in Europe, I found that most of the great works of science, art, and music had a background in esoteric traditions that somehow connected to Ancient Egyptian culture. This spurred my interest in knowing more about the secret ancient traditions of my ancestors. The medieval scientific Islamic traditions that spurred the European Renaissance played an important role in my path as did mystical Sufism. I studied and practiced many Esoteric Spiritual Eastern and Western traditions with special interest in Ancient Egyptian and Coptic mysticism. I attended meetings but never joined any group. My goal of developing a practical scientific body of knowledge ran parallel to the wisdom of the esoteric schools with which I interacted; the task was to bring this complementary knowledge into everyday life.

From a cultural point of view that goes beyond my scientific engineering studies, my personal background is deeply anchored in Middle Eastern, European, Ancient Egyptian, Gnostic, Coptic, Islamic and Sufi traditions. My Oxford and Cambridge school upbringing and further university studies in Zurich took me into the European English, German, and French inner traditions, in which culture I am also deeply anchored. The European thinkers, philosophers, artists, and builders also had a great influence on me in my formative years.

Stations Along My Personal Journey

During my studies at the polytechnic in Zurich my open-minded professor, Walter Custer, introduced me to the revival of ancient Universal Harmonics through the work of Johan Kayser, another giant of ancient knowledge. He gave me Kayser's book, *Akroasis*, which was the best simple introduction to this complex subject anyone might have considered.

In Zurich, I became particularly interested in the work of the famous Swiss psychologist Carl Gustav Jung. The Jungian school of thought has roots in the Gnostic and Hermetic doctrines of Ancient Egypt. The spiritual history of Zurich is linked to Coptic Egypt and is under the protective wings of its Egyptian patron saints, Felix and Regula, who are buried in the crypt of the Grossmünster Cathedral.

My interest in Jungian psychology led me to meet several proponents of the post-Jungian psychology, such as those already mentioned who were affiliated with the Dallas Institute of Humanities.

Walter Odermatt (1928-2017): The Need for a New Physics

There is an ever-growing trend all around the world to search for a new Physics. In this context, I have chosen to introduce my Swiss friend, the late Professor Walter Odermatt, with whom we planned to host an international conference on new visions for a new physics in 2010.

Professor Odermatt founded the Odermatt University in Lucerne, Switzerland, and continued from where Jung left off to develop one of the most complete post-Jungian platonic paradigms. His theories of the soul are among the most complete modern interpretations of the subject. Unfortunately, they are only known in the German culture. What I find most interesting about his approach to a new physics relates to the merging of his interpretations of geometric archetypes from ancient civilizations with Pythagorean and Platonic concepts to create a new understanding of reality, upon which he based his new physics of the soul.

Walter was interested in my own vision and my practical subtle energy work in the new Physics of Quality I had developed. I had written some of my documents in German and these he studied thoroughly; I also had my book translated into German for his unique use, as he did not speak English.

In 2010, he invited me to visit the Odermatt University to discuss arranging an international conference to share a vision for a futuristic new physics. My opinion was that the new physics should be a *"qualitative expansion"* of existing physics. The preparatory meetings were confined to limited group discussions among German-speaking researchers.

We only met a few times in his home on Lake Lucerne, but we spent many hours discussing our views and planning a future collaboration. We formed such a strong bond that in his last days he asked his wife, Hermine, to keep up the strong connection we had after his passing. Unfortunately, Professor Odermatt passed away before we could hold this important conference at his university. He would have been a great companion along my journey to introduce a complementary view of the new Physics of Quality. I have since kept contact with his wife and hope to introduce his core concepts in future works.

Back in Egypt

Upon my return to Egypt, I immersed myself in the study of both Ancient Egypt and Islamic Mysticism. At that time, I was also introduced to the Coptic inner traditions by two friends who deserve the label of "Renaissance Men." Although I mentioned them in my first book, they deserve mention here again as we became inseparable friends. During a thirty-year journey of research into Ancient Egyptian medicine and the esoteric sciences they served as my guides and research companions. The first was Dr. Khalil Messiha, a medical doctor, Egyptologist, and artist. The second was Dr. Fawzi Soliman Soweiha, a medical doctor, philosopher, and director of the museum of Ancient Egyptian medicine. These two scholars introduced me to Radiesthesia and its use in different forms of healing. I then developed Radiesthesia into "BioGeometry Quality Measurement," which became an important tool in the measurement of the energy quality of sacred power spots and the development of a geometric design language to replicate it. I was at the time advisor to Egyptian Minister of Health Dr. Mahmoud Mahfouz—another example of a Renaissance Man who was interested in my new research and who was an important supporter of BioGeometry in its early development.

I have been blessed to have met several other such personalities from different fields, all of whom have shaped my journey. It would go beyond the boundaries of this book to introduce them all in a manner that does justice to their work.

PART TWO
The Origin of Life force

Life force is the animating principle of all dimensions of Creation. Life force exchange is the main criterion of integration in nature. To understand the origin of life force, we must go to the beginning of Creation before the duality dimensions of time and space arose. The challenge, however, is that the human mind is not equipped to go beyond duality and analyze what happens there. The extrasensory perception of the heart is, at an unconscious level, hidden from the left-brain sensory perception. So, if we try to understand with our inadequate minds the timeless dimensions that the intellect of the heart perceives, we will get somewhat lost in complex models and we will need to resort to unavoidable repetition. That is why the ancients used mythological stories to understand Creation. In a Physics of Quality, however, we cannot use the ancient myths and we must present proper subtle energetic qualitative models that we will simplify and present in stages as we go along.

The Universal Animating Principle

We can open the door to understanding the laws of the Universe by expressing the abstract energy measurement qualities behind the energy principles of shape. This is a challenging task, however, so to facilitate this process, we have created the terms "Ziron" and "Psychon." They describe the model of a center and a periphery in the first unit of Creation. We will briefly provide an overview of this model before going into greater detail later in this chapter.

The cornerstone of BioGeometry is the measurement of the centering energy quality found in Earth Energy Power Spots and in all centers of shapes; we have labelled this quality "BG3." BG3 is a transcendental centering principle that balances the duality in Creation from the zero state. Its effect on our biological energy system allows us to detect the manifestation of a spiritual energy quality. This discovery opened the doorway to all BioGeometry environmental solutions: they permit us to understand and interact with quantitative phenomena through their qualitative effects. In doing so, we also bring a qualitative resonant unity to all experiences, through which every experience becomes a possible doorway back to the center.

We must next understand the quality of the doorway through which the BG3 harmonizing principle emerges. We call it the "Ziron." It is a vortex tunnel, or window, to the zero state *before* the creation of time and space. It is non-localized and exists everywhere at the same time.

We call the harmoniously balanced pulse action emerging from center to the periphery (and back to center), the "Psychon." The nature of the energy begins when the pulse of the Ziron—as the "WORD"—activates the emergence of "life force" (Figure 17).

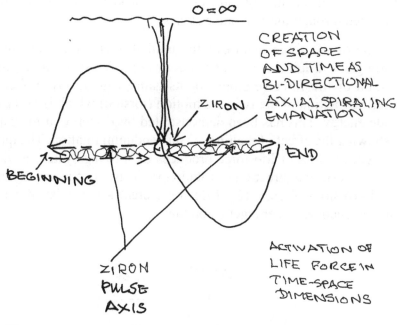

Fig.17 - Ziron Pulse

This model is based on the qualitative measurement of the energy of shape in harmonically related diagrams that resonate with the original shape archetype. The measurement of our connection to archetypal shape qualities is an evaluation criterion that is taught in all BioGeometry practical courses.

Life force is the animating principle of Creation. It is the force that activates the principle that I introduced and labeled as the Law of Time. It is the Law of Time that produces the original archetypal pattern of the pulse of duality. We will have a brief look at the Law of Time here and deal with it in more detail later, in a dedicated part of this book. The Law of Time is the intelligent principle that creates, governs, and balances all pulses of Creation. It controls the central Ziron burst to create its inward and outward "breathing" cycle. From the center, a spiraling wave-shape sets the path of the beginning and end points and keeps them harmoniously connected through the two pulse cycles.

The action of life force manifests the unified interactive Laws of Nature through the original spiraling energetic twist. A loss of order through dissipation of life force (entropy) or its gain (neg-entropy) affects the direction of rotation of the twisting motion (torsion) which is at the core of subtle energy. This has been demonstrated by Kozyrev in the experiment showing the effect of melting ice on pendulum rotation. The quality that the gain or loss of life force produces on a living system is visible through the resulting direction of rotation in the twist of its energy emission (QL-Torsion—Figure 18). Life force creates the twist of torsion, which then becomes its energetic conduit.

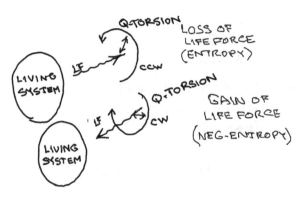

Fig.18 - Life Force Twist of Torsion

Life force also activates the emergence of infinity from the zero/potential infinity state through Divine central doorways (Zirons) from the highest to the lowest physical level; the pulse action of the Ziron triggers the manifestation of the Psychon as the first unit in Creation. The unit is formed through the outward and inward spiraling motion emerging from the expansion and contraction of the Ziron center. This occurs through the creation of the first complete bi-directional spiraling pattern of the time-space pulse. This is the blueprint for the emergence of pulsating, spiraling, highly potent subtle energy. All interactions on our physical level are built upon the pulsating breath between the expansion of the pulse emission (radiation/mental) and its contraction (gravitational/emotional) back into itself (Figure 19).

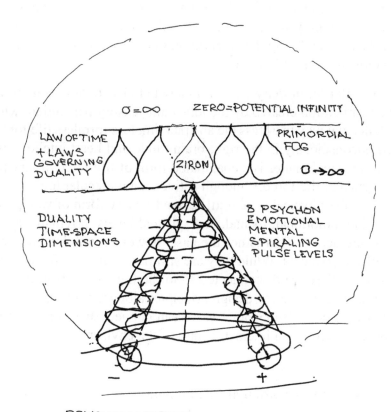

PSYCHON: FIRST UNIT OF CREATION
TIME-SPACE-GRAVITY UNIT

Fig.19- Time-Space-Gravity Unit - TSGU1

We can see the Psychon, therefore, as the original living time-space, mental-emotional unit which we will be referring to as a "Time Space Gravity Unit" (TSGU). In other words, this is the first manifestation of the life force Activation. This unit, with its emotional and mental (psychic) configuration, is an expression of the Universal Mind active within the life force, the main components of subtle energy. It should therefore be understood as the basic life force unit of Creation. The infinite pulsating emergence of the Psychons in many simultaneous dimensions creates the stability of those subtle energy existences within an overall inclusive background state. Here again, we can define the all-containing stable subtle energy background as the omnipresent intelligent life force medium from which all Creation arises. This is the true essence of what is referred to as primordial fog or waters. It can also be understood as the living Divine mind. When we communicate with it through wishes, hopes, prayer, and so on, we are just part of the self-reflection of this omnipresent life force. We can safely say that everything in Creation is a manifestation of the intelligent living life force.

What we refer to, or deny, as God in any belief with any name or figure is a personification created by the left-brain sensory perception, which is the intellectual way to access the abstract timeless formless life force perceived unconsciously in the right-brain mode and heart intellect. In this context, physical matter is a coagulated form of life force. In dry matter this coagulated life force, although active on a molecular level, becomes inactive in the physical state until revived by any form of water. On the higher vital, emotional, mental, and spiritual levels, it remains active as well as interactive. That is not the case, however, with human-made or manipulated products. While they are still part of the life force on a molecular level they are disconnected from the higher levels in the natural environment. By applying design principles along the forming process of nature, as we do in BioGeometry, we can connect those products to the life force to become an interactive part of the environment.

Science is the Observation of Phenomena

Science was originally defined as the observation of steps or factors leading to a phenomenon. If we observe the quality of any type of recurrent effect, we can expand the barriers of science to include all human experience. Unfortunately, in the age of modern technology, quantitative measurement is regarded by many as the main criterion for the definition of science itself, rather than its tool. Quantitative measurement has become the holy grail of science. This erroneous new understanding has limited us to defining energy as steam-based, kinetic, electromagnetic, nuclear, fossil fuel-based, solar, wind-generated, and so on. The original definition of energy, however, is *the ability to produce an effect*. Effects are perceived through their quality. Some qualitative effects can be quantified through measurement. The non-physical causes of energy on emotional or mental levels are not acknowledged as energy types. This has left all other non-scientific fields to use the word "energy" in every discipline and in many cases completely out of context or in a pseudo-scientific way. A Physics of Quality must therefore incorporate all phenomena in our lives in a new holistic scientific paradigm.

We become aware of quality on the mental level while its effect is felt on the emotional level. A Physics of Quality must incorporate all levels, from vital through emotional and mental, and on up to the spiritual dimensions that affect us. Those dimensions of energy lie in the domain of faster compression wave fields that are known as "subtle energy," beyond the electromagnetic range. A more appropriate descriptive label would be "life force." Qualitative restoration of life force can produce quantifiable measurable effects. For example, we have measurements showing Bio-Geometry as a solution to help restore serotonin levels, normalize liver enzymes in hepatitis C patients, and raise low platelet counts in immuno-compromised patients.

Subtle Energy

And so, we must expand our concept of energy to include subtle energy, which is a general term that comprises life force, Universal Mind, Laws of Nature, and Divine attributes, among others. It has been largely misunderstood, even though it is widely known through its many forms or components—Chi, Prana, psychic energy, torsion, and so on. But it has been excluded from the mainstream scientific worldview because our physical universe is basically created by an interaction of electromagnetic phenomena. This electromagnetic physical universe is bound by the Laws of Time and Space as we know them. The linear perception of the flow of time and space governs our concepts of energy. Energetic effects beyond the confines of time and space that are faster than the speed of light governing electromagnetic flow are not often dealt with in our mainstream scientific paradigm. Telepathic, intuitive, and extrasensory experiments, however, have shown that thoughts and emotions can travel faster than the speed of light and they are not bound by the linear flow of time. They have been shown to connect to the present, future, and past.

Perceived sensory reality is a very small part of the total absolute reality that covers all vibratory ranges from zero to infinity in countless dimensions. Physically-based energy types—such as electromagnetic or nuclear—are nothing more than leaves floating on the vast ocean of subtle energy.

Pulse and Motion

Perceived reality, which seems to be continuous, is, just like the subtle energy background, the result of emerging and disappearing pulses that arise from a deeper un-manifested Consciousness that provides a sense of stability. This is like the effect of old-fashioned film strips.

Let us analyze linear motion in connection to the pulse. It originates from a higher level, which starts from the center in the form of a vortex that emerges from the non-dualistic state. It expands and contracts in opposite directions, forming two opposing states that retract back into the center. It is the center that produces and controls the outward and inward motion of both, in a balanced complementary way (refer to Figure 17). It is the center that produces the complementarity of the opposites forming the unity of the pulse. The expansion and contraction from the center create the unit of motion where one of the opposites forms the beginning and the other becomes the end. Beginning and end are complementary time-space manifestations from the non-dualistic center. This interconnectivity of beginning and end exists in all cycles from the smallest to the largest as they are all harmonic levels created by an infinite number of Psychon pulses. This right-brain holistic model of the pulse is perceived by the left-brain sensory time space perception as a motion from beginning to end in a straight line. In this perception of a line, the BG3 centering quality is found at the center of the line pulse as well as slightly outside both extremities.

When we draw a line, we go through several pulses to form the larger pulse of the total appearance of the line. Everything in existence, from the most minute particle to the largest, is based on embedded pulses within an overall harmonic unity of Creation. All cycles in life are connected and harmonically embedded in higher levels; they contain the same hierarchy on smaller dimensions. Every life cycle has a beginning and an end; they emerge as two complementary manifestations of the pulse cycle. The moments of birth and death are two interconnected manifestations of the same thing, and they are in continuous exchange of information, with each affecting the other. They are two faces of one coin that cannot be seen at the same time. In the flow of linear time, the end is programmed in the beginning and vice versa. The connection and information exchange increases as the beginning and end move closer in the linear time of the physical dimension.

Using the example of drawing a line as an illustration of this point, we can see that its starting and end points emerge from a mental-emotional archetypal template in a higher center that governs the way we draw it. We will find the center has the BG3 quality showing its transcendental origin, while our physical starting point is in resonance with the Violet color quality and the end is in resonance with the Red color quality. The line, which seems to follow one direction on a physical level in its holistic reality, traces a bi-directional motion from its center. On a physical level, a distortion or imbalance of the time cycle can affect the harmonious unity between the beginning and end. This imbalance in the breath of time will have further repercussions in the quality of the life force functions within the overall span of the pulse and its harmonious integration in the overall stability of the pulsating pattern of the greater symphony of life. This distortion in the time cycle that governs the pulse will be dealt with in the section of this book dedicated to time.

PART THREE
The Vortices of Creation

The stability of all levels of Creation is a result of the centering balancing effect acting within the forming process of nature. These are the vortices at the geometrical centers of motion within the natural shape. They are the design centers of shape. They are referred to as energy wheels, chakras, points of rotation, acupuncture points, or any type of points of rotation or connection in joints. The process starts with the omnipresent omnipotent non-dualistic state. It connects to the duality levels through centers in the shape of bidirectional vortices. These dualistic levels of Creation include multiple conscious vital, emotional, mental, and spiritual dimensions, which include archetypal levels that contain templates of everything in Creation. As we've mentioned before, we refer holistically to the total conscious background medium in which all Creation takes place as "subtle energy" or, synonymously, "life force."

This background medium is a living conscious life force full of endless powerful spiraling torsion energies on every conceivable level or dimension. The original zero state of everything and nothing contains the undifferentiated potential of infinity. Infinity is the Divine conscious omni-dimension in which, through an act of Divine will, all levels of Creation emerge, arising from the activation and differentiation of the zero state.

We are part of one of many electromagnetic physical universes which are limited to a vibratory range around the speed of light and as human beings, it is almost impossible for us to perceive or conceive of the existence of other non-electromagnetic energy types beyond this range, such as, for example, the mental, emotional, or spiritual levels. However, the other types of energy at work within this conscious living medium are not only much more powerful than the physical universe limited to a range around the speed of light, but they are also the source of and support to all life functions, of which we are in constant energetic exchange. The holistic conscious subtle energy background of the Universal Mind permeates and animates all dimensions in a unified information system.

The multi-dimensional pulse appears and disappears, creating resonant copies across multiple simultaneous parallel realities. As we have seen in quantum experiments, subtle energy can manifest as waves or particles through the action of the Universal Mind. Just as the Universal Mind complies with our intention to create electromagnetic particles in the physical dimension, other types of compression waves or particles are created in other dimensions on vital, emotional, mental, and spiritual levels of subtle energy. This generates a large variety of materialized worlds that are unperceivable to our physical senses. Just as our physical matter is a sort of electromagnetic coagulation, compression waves on emotional, mental, and spiritual dimensions can produce "knots" of matter in any of their endless dimensions. This matter is only perceived with the relevant sensory organs of that dimension.

Our physical sensory organs limit our perception to the physical word. At the moment of death, all our physical senses will die with the body and our left-brain perception with it. The right-brain unconscious perception becomes the main vehicle of the released soul. The afterlife, or better said, the other life, becomes solid to the soul senses. From a Physics of Quality point of view, there exist purely mental-emotional energetic dimensions that are material and physical, but which are totally unperceived by our sensory organs. With our detection instruments we can, however, measure their qualitative effects on us. These materialized forms of life can include life forms from very primitive to highly advanced civilizations, that could be millions of years older than ours. They cannot be perceived, however, by our limited left-brain sensory perception. Some of them can perceive and interact with the emotional, mental, or spiritual levels that we refer to as astral bodies or soul levels.

When we try to find life on other planets, we only think of the electro-magnetic material physical life with which we are familiar. We must understand that the background omnipresent conscious living medium is the collective essence of life that animates all dimensions and gives them their own life forms. Life "on" other planets may well resemble nothing like what we are currently seeking. For that matter, life on our own planet extends far beyond our standard conception of what constitutes physical "life."

In order to avoid being like the fish in the ocean trying to find a drop of water, let us look at this from another perspective: instead of seeing life as something that exists in different locations in the physical universe, let's envision life as the background subtle energy medium that animates materialized individual life forms in an endless number of dimensions. Some of these are physical, but the majority of them exist in unperceived material dimensions.

This is a domain of subtle energy wherein new types of non-electromagnetic compression waves follow different laws beyond our perceived time and space dimensions. Our current quantitative measuring devices are not capable of measurement in the numerous subtle energy dimensions. They can only convert physical effects to quantifiable measurements.

The Physics of Quality, based on the qualitative interactions of Universal Harmonics, is the way to expand our scientific capabilities in a new worldview beyond our perceived physical time-space boundaries. Quality becomes the universal tool for measuring and communicating subtle energy effects.

The Laws of Nature

The non-manifested potentials of living attributes or qualities in the zero-to-infinity primordial state are activated in the emergence of duality. They are then balanced through the centering quality of the original zero-to-infinity primordial state resulting in the perfectly balanced archetypal patterns of the living Laws of Nature. The result is an infinite number of controlled formulas of living interactions governing all functions of the natural forming process on all planes all the way to the physical dimension. These archetypal patterns of motion govern the creative process.

All interactions in the physical universe, as well as all biological functions, are governed by laws incorporating all levels of absolute reality. This means that the Laws of Nature are building blocks that introduce life and the harmony of evolution into the natural forming process, and they do so through the special energy quality of the centers of shapes.

These centers are the active wormholes connecting the planes of nature. Each of the Laws of Nature is a manifestation of an attribute that is balanced internally through all other attributes in the original non-differentiated state. We can simply say that every attribute in nature incorporates all the others within it. It is a team project where the leader changes regularly. This is the ultimate expression of complementarity in unity.

All types of natural shapes are composite multi-level physical, vital, emotional, and mental constructs balanced by the harmonizing quality of primordial living Laws of Creation. Every physical particle in our Universe and in our bodies is a multi-dimensional manifestation of the creative values of the Laws of Nature.

The creative values, laws, or attributes are labelled differently in different cultures and beliefs. All the above scientific analysis is embedded in ancient scriptures that express this same hidden reality. All references to this completely hidden absolute source of everything that creates the duality of time and space from a state of seemingly omnipotent nothingness—whether we call it Divinity, Creator, Godhead, the Unpronounceable or something else—are essentially incomprehensible. Modern humanity's commitment to operating from the left brain makes it impossible to understand this inconceivable reality, which is ultimately the hidden presence ensuring the stability of Creation. We may try to understand it through the one center as the source of everything, or from a paradigm where everything leads to the center. But, either way, the task is to understand the truth hidden in all beliefs from the dawn of humanity to the present day: that there is a true unity behind the apparent diversity. The right-brain-focused early humanity up to the age of the great ancient civilizations did not have to bother with understanding such a concept, as they were already living it and experienced the diversity as integral components of the overall unity.

In contrast, the modern human mind, embedded in the duality of left-brain perception, cannot comprehend the hidden unity behind diversity. The unity in the worldview of ancient humanity was lost with the great shift in the focus of perception from the right to the left brain that shifted humanity from "Ancient" to "Modern" according to Jung's categorization. The American nineteenth century philosopher and psychologist

William James sets this shift vaguely around 1200 BC. We should not generalize, however, as natural on-going shifts in perception occurred at different times around the world depending on the pace of human development.

While advanced great ancient civilizations flourished in some places, human beings in other areas were still living in the environmental unity of primitive humanity. The original universal unity of primitive people developed into the more interactive analytical perception of the ancient civilizations before it became hidden in the depths of the subconscious mind of modern humanity. The natural universal wisdom that is now hidden in the depth of the subconscious mind had to be taught to modern humanity through belief systems. To comprehend and interact with this ultimate, unperceivable, unreachable source, modern humanity must bring it within the mind's personification process using an omnipotent version of human attributes to create an image of the Creator with which they can have a two-way interaction. The different names that are given to this personified Divinity in every belief system, if properly understood, are all references to the same personified principle.

In the so-called left-brain sensory mode, the unifying Laws of Nature acting on a subconscious level emerge as the conscience that brings balance in the form of ethical values into our everyday actions.

Divine Benevolence

In our modification of the principle behind the experiments of Quantum Physics, we introduced the concept of the Universal Mind complying with the intention of the observer in the manifestation of energy as particle or wave. The same principle applies to the Universal Mind acting through the subconscious levels to comply with the left-brain intention in a two-way communication. The same invisible Laws of Nature will comply through the right-brain perception and act according to the different human left-brain mental paradigms. The Universal Mind of the all-prevalent life force in nature complies with our concepts and beliefs in religion, spirituality, mythology, and all other fields just as well as our newly discovered scientific laws do. Whatever our language is, nature will use it to communicate and comply. This is a core principle in *The Hero with a Thousand Faces* written and made popular by Joseph Campbell. He found that similar myths existed in different areas of the world. He explains that the same inner reality emerges from the earth's mind in remote unconnected locations through the human subconscious mind which surfaces in the form of different myths woven from the local cultural content. The same hero in the subconscious mind wears different masks or faces to emerge into the local conscious perception giving each people their own myths.

PART FOUR
The Big Bang is Not the Beginning

Modern science is built on analysis, detail, and measurement in the physical world. As they delve deeper into matter, theories of Creation are developed from the bottom upwards; some are corroborated by measurement. One of the most popular is the Big Bang theory that scientists apply to the beginning of our physical universe. Other such universes could exist because of similar explosions. But these theories do not address the totality of higher dimensions that existed before the first Big Bang: physical matter is only a minute component of the Universe.

Creation stories as they appear in ancient cultures and modern religions take the opposite path and start from a non-dualistic Divine state from which the first conscious eruption, referred to as the WORD, emerged to create everything in existence. These stories deal with the conscious creation of many unperceived dimensions before, after, and simultaneously with the physical world. The WORD comes from the omnipresent omnipotent Divinity that is personified as God when related to human sensory perception. This worldview starts at the top and goes down the vibratory scale from infinity to lower speeds, down to the speed of light where physical dimensions are created. Science, however, takes the opposite path of starting at the bottom and going upwards from the physical dimensions into deeper energetic levels within the electromagnetic universe.

The bottom-up path of modern science, trapped in an analytical quantitative methodology, cannot cope with higher dimensions of existence and concepts of an abstract or personified Divinity. It takes the easy way of denying the existence of ideas and beliefs that are not directly measurable by mainstream scientific methods. The result is an ever-growing chasm between science and spirituality. In our left-brain mode we believe in science, while in the right-brain mode we believe in spirituality. This state of affairs creates tension on an unconscious level that paves the way for psychological disturbances that can fuel depression, despair, aggression, and other symptoms in the face of the hurdles of everyday life.

BioGeometry not only bridges and connects science and spirituality, but it also merges them together in a much greater unified worldview.

The Physics of Quality in BioGeometry is built on a scientific approach from the top downwards. This is based on a qualitative scientific approach, even when we're dealing with quantitative concepts. In this paradigm, the quantitative world is dealt with as a manifestation of quality. Quality brings the right-brain universal perception into play so that science connects to the knowledge of the heart. This path leads to the understanding of subtle energy and life force.

In the grander view of our holistic paradigm, the Big Bang is but one of many electromagnetic sparks that erupted from the compression wave background when the original infinite vibratory rate slowed down to the speed of light. As each spark erupted, it created a universe that started and ended with the spark. Through this paradigm, many universes are continuously created and ended. Parallel universes made of mental-emotional matter beyond our physical sensory perception also emerge from probabilities that exist in mental-emotional dimensions. Each universe develops in different resonant environments, and so parallel universes will not be copies of each other, although a psychic connection with common emotional and mental energy quality will exist on a higher level.

From a strictly physical point of view, the Big Bang, or other theories of the beginning of electromagnetically based "physical" creation have a certain validity. However, from a holistic multi-dimensional point of view, they represent a very temporary late stage, rather than a beginning.

Better still is to understand the cradle of the electromagnetic universe—connected to higher dimensions—as the zero-point field. It is through this boundary between physical and subtle energetic dimensions that physical life, a small temporary manifestation of the eternal life force from higher levels, manifests as an electromagnetic spark.

The Unified Field Dilemma

Scientists' inability to find a unified field theory arises from the fact that they limit their consideration of our physical dimension to four different categories—electromagnetic, gravity, and strong and weak nuclear forces; they all follow different laws. The unifying field will not be found in these four categories but rather on the higher levels from whence these laws emerge.

The unified field theory can only be fully understood from a multi-dimensional holistic perspective. The archetypal laws from a higher subtle energy level that govern the physical actions of the categories of the unified field theory are themselves governed by the transcendental centers of balance from an even higher level that governs and harmonizes the evolution of duality. The ultimate source in the zero-infinity level is the centering harmonizing stage upon which all other levels down to the apparent physical dimension take place.

This reinforces the concept that the zero-infinity level is a completely inert dimension that is potentially infinitely active. From it, the archetypal laws control evolution in all other dimensions.

The Qualities in the Zero-Infinity State

This zero-infinity state, where non-existence of the zero is the container of infinity, is a state of Omnipresent Omnipotent Consciousness. It has an inert potential for harmony, holistic qualities, and perfect balance at the core of evolution. These inert qualities produce infinity manifested in time and space as Divine Attributes, Laws of Nature, or values. Ancient cultures referred to them as personified nature powers that we erroneously call gods; in modern languages they are referred to as angels or Divine Attributes. In Ancient Egypt, they were called Neters, written as "NTRs." They were pronounced in the singular as Nether or Netjer and in the plural as Netheru; the Egyptians did not write vowels the way many Semitic languages do today. NTR is the root for "nature" in modern languages, indicating that these were nature powers and not the gods that modern interpretations have labelled as polytheism. The Neters are the different attributes of the life force. Here we must move in circles again with unavoidable repetition: no words can adequately explain this concept, as the dualistic mind does not function on the level where all the attributes of Creation or Divinity exist as a potential in a non-differentiated state, where each one is all, and all are in each one.

Each Divine Attribute, Law of Creation, or Nature Power includes at its core its opposite, as well as all other qualities in perfect balance and harmony. The seeming separation of the attributes is due to the shortcomings of the left-brain perception.

The manifestation of qualities, values, or Divine Attributes arises with the first pulsation initiating the creation of duality. It is very much like the seemingly dead seed that holds within it all the inactive attributes needed to produce the archetypal pattern for the living tree. Water is needed for the activation of physical life attributes. Similarly, the ripples of the primordial waters caused by a primordial breath activate all the attributes of life.

Like the example of a film strip, motion is composed of separate consecutive units, pulses of time-space erupting and disappearing within a background medium. At the center lies the creator of the film. We referred earlier to the singular zero balancing center from the non-duality state in each unit as the "Ziron." The Ziron is a centering spiraling pulse from the zero-infinity state that holds everything in an undifferentiated form within it (refer to Figure 2). This is the first expression of the central harmonizing principle of Consciousness. It is a wormhole connecting to the zero-infinity state. Here the primordial waters and the Ziron centers are one. One can imagine an infinite number of erupting and disappearing Ziron bubbles densely grouped in the unified whole of the primordial substance—where a Ziron contains everything and is equally at the center and is the whole. The zero-infinity state is the background container that activates the primordial ocean; it provides for the first emergence of the stage of duality where all Creation takes place. This is a state that no dualistic mind can comprehend. The following paragraphs will thus be a very crude understanding of the primordial impulse of Creation. A simple analogy of the zero-infinity state is that it's like taking a frequency and speeding it up until the sine curve is so small, with an infinitely short wavelength, that the shape becomes a straight line that can equally be zero or infinite motion.

The Psychon

We refer to the ripples created by the Ziron bi-directional spiraling pulse in the medium of the all-embracing waters of the infinity state around it as "Psychon" levels (refer to Figure 19). The eight, spiraling, pulsating Psychon ripples activated by the Ziron create the opposite forces of radiation and attraction which themselves become the wormhole centers of an unlimited number of torus-shaped fields. They appear as a formless spherical light emanating from an invisible center. The Psychon is thus the first emergence of the pulse of duality and is harmonically embedded in all levels and dimensions of Creation. The bi-directional spiraling effect radiating from the Ziron center in all directions and dimensions of the spherical Psychon, is the primordial level of spiral, vortex, twist, or "torsion." The result is a pulsating highly energetic subtle energy medium. This twist is the active manifestation of the time-law into the pulse of time. Time is therefore present as a core component of energy. In the Physics of Quality, we refer to the quality of the effect of this original twist or torsion on living systems as "QL-Torsion." Torsion and QL-Torsion are the quantitative and qualitative energetic patterns of motion around a central pulse axis (Figure 20).

QL-Torsion is the manifestation of Consciousness in the outward mental and inward emotional forces. This concept puts the primordial QL-Torsion at the onset of Creation as an integral and central component of subtle energy; it also connects it to the energetic principle of time. In this case, QL-Torsion is not a separate type of subtle energy but is a quality present in the original twist, with a harmonic reproduction in all other planes of nature. We are dealing here with a geometrical qualitative analysis of the Psychon pulse. The aspect of torsion that we present here as QL-Torsion is qualitative in the sense that we measure it through its effect on the human energy system. QL-Torsion is the qualitative reaction of living systems that can be measured through a pendulum rotation. It manifests on all levels and dimensions of Creation from the smallest to the largest. This original twist in all forms and levels of subtle energy is a potentially infinite source of untapped energy that can be harnessed in an environmentally friendly way.

LAW OF TIME → TIME PULSE

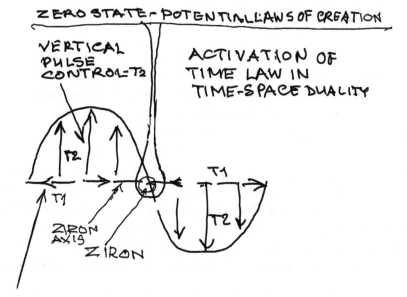

ZERO STATE - POTENTIAL LAWS OF CREATION

VERTICAL PULSE CONTROL=T2

ACTIVATION OF TIME LAW IN TIME-SPACE DUALITY

T2

T1

T1

T2

ZIRON AXIS

ZIRON

HORIZONTAL AXIAL PULSE CONTROL -T1

ZIVON AXIAL MANIFESTION

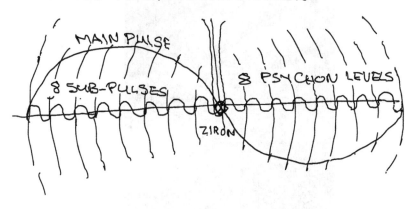

MAIN PULSE

8 SUB-PULSES

8 PSYCHON LEVELS

ZIRON

Fig.20-Law of Time Pulse

This is the other side of the coin where we look at torsion as a qualitative effect on the human subtle energy system and therefore label it QL-Torsion to differentiate it from the original quantitative approach. Russian scientists like the astronomer Nikolai Aleksandrovich Kozyrev researched it from a human-independent quantitative aspect and equated it with subtle energy in general.

In the qualitative paradigm of BioGeometry and the Physics of Quality we expand the range of QL-Torsion using the strings of a virtual musical instrument that extends from zero to infinity. This concept creates qualitative scales, to which we calibrate pendulum devices. The direction of pendulum rotation indicates either the loss or receiving of energy, and this information is evaluated through qualitative scales that put the human being at the center of measurement. The concept of a pendulum is thus expanded to become a detector and an emitter of the qualitative effects of QL-Torsion on biological systems and it helps to confirm the concept of "the human being as the measure of all things." In BioGeometry we have also developed shapes that emit a harmonizing subtle energy quality of QL-Torsion in the environment (Figure 21).

Fig.21 - Hemberg Flower

The Psychon is formed of an infinite number of tori in all directions, which makes the Psychon equally present in multiple dimensions. In our diagrams, we show only one torus section relevant to our dimension. The Law of Time in the Ziron governs all pulsating motion, producing om-ni-directional Psychon pulses. The infinitely quick pulse of each Psychon gives it an infinitesimal and very temporary presence in each dimension. The continuous pulsating appearance and disappearance of Psychons in a dimension produces a sense of continuity in that dimension like what one experiences watching a filmstrip. The Psychon appears simultaneously in different dimensions producing multiple stable parallel realities. Its two opposite spiraling forces produce mental and emotional dimensions that express the activity of an all-prevailing Consciousness from the primor-dial state. The primordial un-manifested Ziron state and the manifested Psychon duality pulse state co-exist, with the Ziron providing the spiri-tual centering at the core of the Psychon pulse of Creation (Figure 22).

The Psychon pulse is the first "living," "conscious" Time-Space-Gravi-ty-Energy Unit (TSGU) and it is the original building block of Creation, upon which everything is created in a harmonic hierarchy.

We will analyze the many aspects and levels of the manifestation and perception of time in a dedicated topic later in this book.

Activation of the Ziron

The WORD mentioned in many Creation stories represents the activation of the Ziron to create the ripples of the pulse pattern of duality in the primordial waters. The "Word" here is a metaphor describing the first activation and emergence of the centering principle of the Ziron, which created energy, motion, time, and all the attributes of the Laws of Cre-ation. The Psychon pulse is a mental-emotional pattern interacting with the background medium. The latent inactive, undifferentiated attributes of the Ziron are activated in the Psychon to become the value units that connect with other Psychons to create patterns that form the first qualities or attributes on which the Laws of Creation in nature are built.

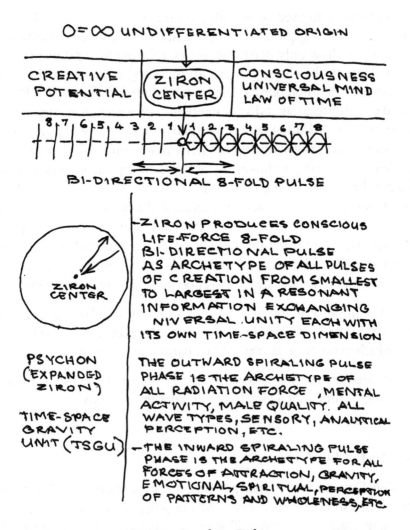

O=∞ UNDIFFERENTIATED ORIGIN

| CREATIVE POTENTIAL | ZIRON CENTER | CONSCIOUSNESS UNIVERSAL MIND LAW OF TIME |

8 7 6 5 4 3 2 1 / 1 2 3 4 5 6 7 8

BI-DIRECTIONAL 8-FOLD PULSE

ZIRON CENTER

ZIRON PRODUCES CONSCIOUS LIFE-FORCE 8-FOLD BI-DIRECTIONAL PULSE AS ARCHETYPE OF ALL PULSES OF CREATION FROM SMALLEST TO LARGEST IN A RESONANT INFORMATION EXCHANGING UNIVERSAL UNITY EACH WITH ITS OWN TIME-SPACE DIMENSION

PSYCHON (EXPANDED ZIRON)

TIME-SPACE GRAVITY UNIT (TSGU)

THE OUTWARD SPIRALING PULSE PHASE IS THE ARCHETYPE OF ALL RADIATION FORCE, MENTAL ACTIVITY, MALE QUALITY. ALL WAVE TYPES, SENSORY, ANALYTICAL PERCEPTION, ETC.

THE INWARD SPIRALING PULSE PHASE IS THE ARCHETYPE FOR ALL FORCES OF ATTRACTION, GRAVITY, EMOTIONAL, SPIRITUAL, PERCEPTION OF PATTERNS AND WHOLENESS, ETC.

Fig.22 - Psychon Pulse

The Psychon pulse can be envisaged as a spherical pulse with outward and inward moving forces in perfect balance. The outward (centrifugal) diversifying force is mental in nature while the inward (centripetal) unifying force of attraction is emotional in nature. The two are held together by the circular spherical toroidal motion of the Psychon. The two forces coil around each other in an eight-fold pattern around a centering Ziron axis.

They move in an overall multidirectional spherical motion and create the eight-fold Psychon (Figure 23). The pulsating Psychons emerge from the background medium in multiple dimensions for an infinitesimally short time, like bubbles in boiling water, giving a surface appearance of a stable absolute reality. The apparent permanency is only surface deep.

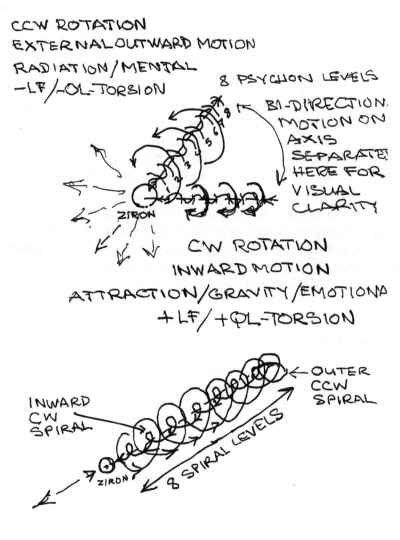

Fig.23 - Eight-Fold Pyschon

The resonant harmonic levels emerging from the all-prevailing zero-infinity state—the primordial waters or Ether—descend through the vibratory levels to the speed of light. Thus, they create the electromagnetic relationship between hydrogen and oxygen atoms to form water as we know it on the physical level.

The primordial waters are a harmonic subtle energetic presence at the core of physical water. Water in this sense can be regarded as a materialized level of life force. The higher levels within physical water activate the inert attributes within seemingly dead matter as in the case of the seed needing water to become a living tree.

To sum it up, water is a physical harmonic manifestation of spiritual, mental, and emotional value patterns that we refer to as qualities. Physical water is a harmonic manifestation of the background primordial waters, which is the activator of inert qualities that are part of the living Laws of Nature that manifest as life. In this context, we can safely say that "water is the bearer of life." As such, water is the bearer of mental and emotional qualities and is therefore a main component of the brain. The higher dimensions of water contain all the qualities (humidity, fire, air, earth,) emerging from a primordial fog. Water, in all dimensions, is also the bearer of the fire quality, as the cradle of the first sparks (Big Bangs) which created the electromagnetic dimension. Our intentions affect the quality of water and are affected by it.

The Unstable Duality

At this point it serves to go back to a geometrical model we used earlier to illustrate how the unstable duality resulting from the first impulse is transformed through a pattern of intelligent living motion into a creative principle. The purpose of a model is to use existing concepts to simplify and explain a phenomenon, and not to imply that the model itself represents the actual reality of the phenomenon. In this case we may use a rotating circular/spherical shape to assist people to visualize how the first motion or impulse creates duality in the form of multidirectional multi-dimensional ripples in the original motionless primordial state.

The outgoing force (centrifugal) created by the impulse interacts with the increasing resistance of the background medium and creates a backward reaction in the form of an inward retracting (centripetal) force towards the center. The two forces are in perfect balance and create pulsating concentric circles that expand and contract.

The outward spiraling motion is the archetype of mental creativity through analytical and fractal expression, while the inward spiraling force of attraction is the archetype of emotion, gravitation, and contraction in all their manifestations.

The perfection of the first impulse that we expressed as a geometrically perfect circular/spherical multi-dimensional toroidal motion is the result of the centering force of the Ziron. This geometric manifestation is the result of spiritual wisdom expressed in the living attributes that form the universal Laws of Nature. The first word of Creation is expressed in a meaningful geometric language that directly connects with the so-called right-brain mode of perception that is sometimes referred to as the "intellect of the heart." This represents a direct communication with the Laws of Nature governing life systems.

It should be noted that the perception of geometric shapes is a sensory manifestation in the mind of the perceiver and is projected from it into the perceived reality. These shapes express different qualities. This is similarly true with numbers, letters, and other forms of expression. It is the language that the Universal Mind uses to interact with us. The true reality, however, is formless and in the time and space of our current existence it is beyond our mental capability. The perception of patterns of motion as shapes or geometric figures is no different than qualities of sound, color, touch, and smell that are produced by the brain as reactions to external stimuli. Geometric figures are mental-emotional archetypes of motion that form the laws governing the forming process of nature.

The circular spiraling motion is the first expression of perfect balance, harmony, and the wisdom of the WORD within our perception.

The centering principle of the circular spiraling motion is therefore the basis of the design language of BioGeometry, which strives to connect to the center from which everything emanates and returns. This spiritual centering induces harmony on all levels of Creation.

The sensory mind perceives the circumference of the circle. The extra-sensory perception of the heart, however, perceives the light of the vortex at its elusive formless center. While the so-called left brain sensory perception of the circle is relating to its periphery, it creates a sense of separation from the undifferentiated wholeness of Creation. This is the outward moving centrifugal force of the creative mind. The extrasensory perception of the heart and so-called right brain consciousness are connected to the center, or Ziron, within whose seeming nothingness is contained everything in the Universe. This is the centripetal gravitational balancing, emotional pull towards the center. The defined circle is related to our separate ego while the center is a total oneness with the Universe in which the ego completely dissolves. The center is a doorway connecting to everything in the multi-dimensional Universe. We are equally perceiving our sensory time-space physical reality on a left-brain level and equally part of the total multi-dimensional timeless ever-present realities that we perceive on a subconscious level hidden from our sensory awareness.

This is what we referred to above as a dual being, with one component living temporarily in a limited sensory reality and the other immortally present as an integral part of the total multi-dimensional reality beyond our time-space boundaries.

An Elusive Relationship

Our minds cannot grasp this elusive relationship between the Consciousness of the zero state and the potential infinity of everything contained in it that can be activated by the Law of Time to produce the pulse of motion that produces the emergence of duality. In trying to use our mental faculties to explain it, the resulting sentences seem absurd and nearly meaningless. That is why the stories of Creation in all beliefs point to an unpronounceable unidentifiable source. The word Amen in Arabic and other related languages means, "safely hidden." This is the unnamable unknowable essence from which all the concepts and names of a creator have arisen to allow humanity a certain link to the source of Creation. We use the abstract concept of the Ziron centering as the doorway to the unidentifiable.

All existing forces of attraction, including gravity, implosion etc., are manifestations of the inward pull of the centripetal force. At the same time, all the forces of expansion, radiation, explosion etc., are manifestations of the outward push of the centrifugal force. We can place the analytical perception of the mind in the outward radiating force and further radiating into perceived reality. The right-brain heart perception finds its place within the centripetal force pulling towards the center. Both forces exist through the impulse from the transcendental center that radiates the mind levels into the sensory world while impelling the extrasensory unconscious pulling of the heart towards it. Both motions are pulsating manifestations of the central Ziron that on one level contains everything and on the other is the doorway connecting all levels to support everything.

We can say that unconditional LOVE is the emotional force centrally pulling the heart to the Ziron. Physical attachments will pull it away. Mental action radiating outwards is the imaginative analytical expression of the Ziron role in the forming process of nature. They are each, however, coupled within the bi-directional spiral pulses and they exist as complementary forces balancing the pulse action. This is the ultimate Law of Balance where the equality of the opposites lies in the complementarity governed by the centering Ziron.

At the crossing points where the eight-fold outgoing and ingoing spirals meet, a bi-directional emotional mental information exchange occurs, resulting in an emotional aspect embedded in the outgoing mental spiral. Similarly, a mental aspect is embedded in the inward flowing emotional spiral. On a human level, we have right-brain mode extrasensory activity referred to as the intellect of the heart coupled with unconditional emotional values. In the left-brain mode emotional and mental activities become conditioned through sensory perception and physical time-space criteria. This means that we have two types of emotional and mental activities, one linked to perceived reality and the other hidden in the veils of extrasensory multi-dimensional universality. There are moments when one feels that love has a mind of its own.

The time-space toroidal field information starts and ends with every pulse but is restored in each new pulse through resonant transmission, creating the sense of continuity. The universal timeless information and time-space sensory modes exist together in all species in nature.

On all levels of Creation, the universal order is achieved through complementarity in a higher centering order which achieves unity. This is the concept behind the universal order of the Law of MAAT in Ancient Egypt, and it is the true meaning of the term "dynamic living equality."

The Law of Trinity at the core of Creation that we introduced earlier is expressed through this circular model: It is the governing law from a higher level that keeps the opposites in a perfectly balanced pulsating circular/spherical motion so that the opposites become complementary in the formation of a new unity in another dimension. This is the Trinity in Creation where the central balancing law and two opposite reactions form a new unit on another level. This in turn interacts with another unit that in turn, through another action of the higher Law of Wisdom, creates a new unit on another level. This Trinity of interaction keeps forming units on one plane after another. The Law of Trinity is active from the primordial level—where the Ziron manifests itself through it to form eight layers—down to the speed of light where electromagnetic sparks erupt from the ripples of the compression wave that has been created.

Non-Physical Material Worlds

We perceive physical matter through our senses, which receive information from limited vibratory ranges in the electromagnetic physical dimension. The higher planes of compression waves moving beyond the speed of light, and hence beyond our time-space awareness, are totally unperceived by our sensory apparatus. The vital, emotional, mental, and spiritual compression-wave planes moving beyond the speed of light, and the limits of our time-space perception, become perceptible once we lose our limiting physical senses in death or in dream states. When this happens, we perceive the mental-emotional content of our subconscious mind as a physical reality in which our bodies and our surroundings are made of a different type of matter. This physical matter has compression wave particles in a form of physical hyper-sound or mental-emotional energy as its building blocks. As far as we are concerned, there is no difference between this and our existing physical world. It doesn't matter whether the materialized world is made of electromagnetic particles or *mental-emotional particles* as we are not aware of either; our sensory apparatus is tailored to each reality. Just as physical energy can manifest as a wave or a particle on the quantum level, we can detect wave or particle manifestations of emotional or mental types on higher levels of energy. Our perception will be the same when our consciousness moves into those levels in death, near-death experiences, or out-of-body travel.

The perception of time-space follows completely different laws in what BioGeometry refers to as non-linear "stacked time," and we will examine this in more detail in upcoming chapters. In those dimensions, the linear flow we know is replaced by completely new types of separate multidirectional time-space patterns. In this situation, the Psychons, as time-space units, form groups arranged in different patterns or molecules based on qualitative resonance. The resulting meaningful combinations form situations with their own separate time-space dimensions. Through the resonance of qualities of the content we will move in any direction from one page/molecule to another creating complete meaningful situations that will be made of a group of related pages that we will call "Experions," and we will examine these later in more detail when dealing with time. This is like the way we move in our dreams, beyond our conscious control over the situation. Causality is a left-brain translation of resonant relationships into our time-space perception and cannot exist beyond a linear perception of time. Resonance between event qualities is the governing factor in moving through time-space, which is multidirectional and multi-dimensional. To our sensory perception, resonance is a timeless spaceless background echo that is given time and space stamping by the left brain, and then labeled as cause and effect. This cause-and-effect relationship is linked to the linear time sensory perception that is replaced by mental-emotional resonance beyond our physical time-space dimension.

The Holistic Effect of Motion

The seemingly fluid flow of linear motion, as we have examined above, is based on a very quick pulsating action just like a movie strip. The Psychon pulses move out of the center along axes in all directions, creating a multi-dimensional spherical emanation. The reality of motion and shapes is always multi-dimensional. From a qualitative point of view, every linear motion creates around it a toroidal qualitative effect on the subtle energy of the environment. This motion is embedded in an infinite number of larger pulses and similarly contains endless smaller ones. Every component on all levels of Creation, from the tiniest to the largest is vibrating within a synchronized system of pulses within the grand pulse of the overall unity. When we draw a line or create any type of motion, every level in Creation enters into a two-way interaction with it. The quality of the motion is important as it has universal implications.

The 2D Energy Key in BioGeometry

In BioGeometry, we use a simplified 2D section of the Energy Key to analyze the distribution of qualities created by motion in a space. A linear flow will produce four different effects on the surrounding subtle energy, with different qualities showing up on different levels (Figure 24).

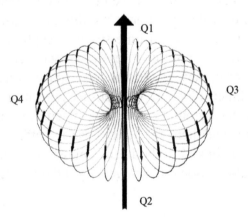

Fig.24 - 3D Energy Key

The center of the motion is on a BG3 line/axis; a Violet subtle energy quality is evident at its beginning (Q2) and a Red subtle energy quality (Q1) shows up at its end. We get clockwise rotation (Q3) on the right side, and a counterclockwise rotation on the left side (Q4). Each motion creates multiple layers of qualities in the surrounding medium on, vitality emotional, mental levels as well as vortices of connection to spiritual dimensions (Figure 25). Any physical motion will therefore, in an abstract way, affect us on all levels.

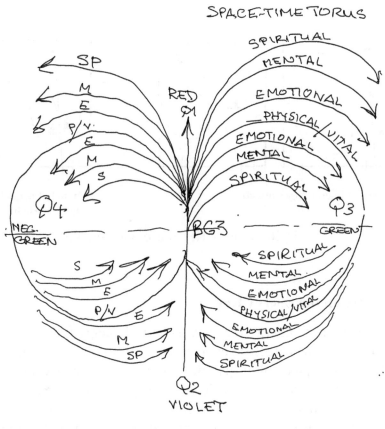

MULTI-DIMENSIONAL ENERGY KEY
OF HORIZONTAL MOTION

Fig.25 - Multi-Dimensional Energy Key

The proper balance of the Energy Key in a space is important for the well-being of the occupants. In classic buildings where the doors and windows were placed on the central axis of the space, the four energy qualities were usually balanced. In modern times however, due to space considerations, the doors and windows are usually offset, creating an energy quality imbalance that will put a certain stress on the users (Figure 26). Doors and windows are simple examples of sources of emission that create energy movements in a space. We will look some applications of the Energy Key in the design topics.

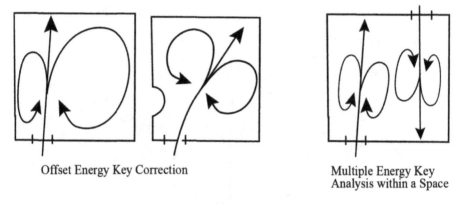

Offset Energy Key Correction

Multiple Energy Key
Analysis within a Space

Fig.26 - Energy Key Space Assessment

Life Force on the Energy Key

The BioGeometry Energy Key is a pattern of energy flow configuration that we will use repeatedly to explain different concepts; it is too complex to allow us to explore all its qualities and dimensions in one and the same figure. After covering all the different concepts of the 2D and 3D Energy Key we will provide a diagram with the combination of all the concepts to show the richness of this archetypal pattern of shape in Creation. This is a perfect example of the venerated phrase, "As above, so below," as it expresses the reality of the macrocosm in the microcosm.

The Energy Key shows the BG3 quality in the central axis of motion and the BG3 disk at the equator of the torus. The axis of motion and the spirals around it create the outward extension in time-space as a torus form containing multi-layered spiritual, mental, emotional, vitality and physical planes where the sensory time-space mind of the system manifests. (Refer to Figure 25).

When these toroidal layers are harmonized, creating a positive energizing life force quality on the whole shape, we refer to them as the "Al-Kareem Quality Fields/Grids." This quality is at the base of the energizing aspect of the life force that manifests as the living Laws of Nature, or Nature Powers. While BG3 is a timeless dimension in the form of a communication vortex to the creative forces, the Al-Kareem Quality Fields/Grids carry the enfolding time-space configured information as the Laws of Nature producing the earthly mind of the system. The BG3 quality is at the centers of the life force planes. This model of expansion of the Al-Kareem Quality is equally valid from the smallest to the largest dimensions.

PART FIVE

Perceived Reality

The nature of perceived reality is not as simple as reproducing what is out there in the world we live in, but rather it is a complex selective procedure that happens within our brain. What we perceive is not the total absolute reality, nor is it an illusion of reality. It is based on a selective process that produces the perception of a living species out of the total absolute reality.

I will use a simple visual model to explain this. Imagine having a bottle full of sand with grains of every possible color mixed together to form a homogenous grayish colorless whole. However, we need to see the patterns formed by only one color. If we want to see only the green particles from within the colorless whole, we must use special eyeglasses that filter and show only the green color. Suddenly the green pattern becomes visible and a green world manifests from the all and nothing of the background. Now, let us imagine that each color represents a whole universe, and we need a selective filter to show our own universe by separating it from the colorless background. This is what our senses do: each sensory organ resonates with and reacts to a very limited specific vibratory range. The five senses interact with different ranges that have different criteria so that a three-dimensional world is formed.

The abstract undifferentiated nervous reactions to the sensory stimuli happen in corresponding brain areas where they are decoded through qualitative scales of color, sound, smell, touch, and taste. After the different modalities are decoded in different areas of the brain—where they are given their qualitative sensory aspects—they merge in a meaning level of the brain that associates them to the contents in the brain's data bank to form a meaningful three-dimensional picture. In other words, our world is then formed as an image inside the brain. The brain then projects this image through the sensory apparatus on the background holistic subtle energy medium of absolute invisible reality to bring forth the perceived reality that forms our world (Figure 27).

Following the model just outlined, absolute reality, as well as everything emerging from it, is formed of temporary pulses emerging into being from deeper dimensions and then falling back out of reality. This continuous eruption of pulses that appear and disappear at very high speeds give the effect of the stability of the background medium of total absolute reality.

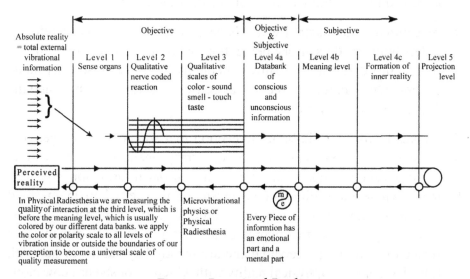

Fig.27 - Perceived Reality

In their interaction with absolute reality, the sensory organs work in a resonant information exchange mode where they receive and emit information.

Now let us take it a bit further and imagine the sand particles to be differently colored drops within the water content of the bottle. If we drink from the bottle, we will drink from the colorless grayish water where all the colored drops are diluted. So, although our eyeglasses filter out one color dimension, we are still drinking from the totality of colored drops. Although we perceive only a small part, we are affected by the totality of unperceived absolute reality.

This analogy shows us that the hidden absolute reality is affecting our being. It contains all the Laws of Nature that govern the functioning of the biological processes that enable our senses to construct and select our own perceived reality. It generates the universal life force that produces physical life and activates the senses. Our sensory ego and our perception of the physical world are part of the later stages of the manifestation of life force. On an extrasensory level, we are an integral part of absolute unperceived reality, and we are aware of its presence within us.

To recapitulate: the material world is perceived through what is referred to as left-brain mode sensory perception, while the interaction with the absolute multi-dimensional reality is in the right brain extrasensory mode perception. One can refer to the first as conscious brain awareness and the second as subconscious perception.

This takes us to the right-brain perception that sometimes emerges into awareness as intuition, gut feeling, love, ecstasy, oneness with everything, and spiritual states. This unconscious extrasensory information exchange with the whole multi-dimensional existence is referred to in mystical schools as the intellect of the heart. In other words, the human being has a subtle energy system that expresses all the laws of multi-dimensional existence that are not perceivable and are mostly beyond his or her will, and also has a sensory physical reality with which he or she has conscious interaction. We are equally the drops within the ocean as well as the total-ity of the ocean itself.

Projection of Reality

An image of the world is first created in the meaning level of the brain, and then projected outward and superimposed as a filter that brings re-lated parts together from the unperceived absolute reality. The physical appearance of our own material bodies is part of this process as well. This concept of a holistic environmental inner reality changes a lot in our understanding of how the material world we live in emerges from an unperceived reality. We are part of the projected perceived reality that we live in.

Everything we see in the world around us is really part of us as we are part of it because it all first comes into existence inside our brain and is then modeled out of the absolute reality.

Our cultural background and the image database that forms our world are inside the meaning level of the brain. It is only through the personifying action of left-brain perception that we identify ourselves with our body and feel separation from our surroundings. The different parts of the projected image manifest to each other as separate physical objects.

On a subtle energy level, we and the environment are one living collective subtle energy system in which our body has several boundaries forming our multiple different levels of existence.

The first is our physical tangible body, and the second is our perceived environment, which is the world we live in. We associate the first level with our ego; the second involves our merging with the collective perceived reality of others as well. So, with every level there is an additional shift from individuality towards collectivity. If we move further into the hidden right brain extrasensory subconscious perception—the intuitive perception of the heart—we become one with not only our own universe, but with all the multi-dimensional parallel universes beyond time and space; what's more, the past, present, and future become part of our being.

We must understand, however, that the right and left-brain modes are related to quality and the nature of perception, and they are not about a physical location inside the brain. One can alternatively use other terms such as sensory and extrasensory to describe those modes of perception.

The connection between the two brain modes plays a role in communication but has an even bigger role to play in keeping a lot of non-linear right-brain extrasensory information from overwhelming the left-brain awareness. This connection is also the place where information is given the time and space criteria needed to emerge into the duality of left-brain perception. The rest of our right-brain's unconscious content is kept hidden from us by the sensory personality mask of the ego that we wear. As this mask is our left-brain mode of perception, we can partly take it off by shifting into a right-brain mode of being. We move into this mode in altered states of consciousness when we experience spiritual and creative/artistic states. This reinforces the fact that every left-brain type of feeling or judgement towards other people or things is directly affecting us as a form of wider self-judgement on the unconscious right brain collective level which unites us all. We are also affected by all levels, even those in other dimensions that we are completely unaware of. The past is affecting us, and also the future that exists as probabilities within the absolute reality.

Fortunately, we are not helpless drops of water in the vast ocean. The drop is the ocean manifesting differently to perceive itself in a form of self-reflection. The living qualities of the drop are the same as those of the ocean. It is only the mode of consciousness that makes them seem separate; the drop's individualized mental-emotional activity can affect the whole ocean. This is based on the resonant connection of all the samples so that each contains the information of the whole. The drop carries not only the total information of the ocean, but also its omnipotence. Those are the levels of power within us that we are not aware of. We shall see the practical applications of this concept in BioGeometry as we go along.

Beyond the Third Dimension

Linear time perception adds a fourth dimension to our three-dimensional world. On the right-brain side, however, things are totally different. Without the confinement of our time-space sensory-based perception, the right-brain subconscious mind opens to an unlimited number of dimensions. Although we try to categorize them into different types of physical, vital, emotional, mental, and spiritual planes, they are an integrated holistic fluidity which has different qualitative areas dissolved within it, although each still retains its specific functionality.

Ancient humans applied the practical analytical tools of their evolving left-brain awareness to the right-brain universal dimensions where their focus of perception was sited. They used such tools as numbers, colors, sounds, motion, geometry, and so on, to navigate and interact with the universal subtle energy dimensions. These tools were empowered by the highly energetic universal dimensions that supported their practical use in everyday activities.

The only way we can achieve such a holistic state of perception is when our focus of perception is equally interacting with both types of perception and integrating them into a multi-dimensional reality; the ability to do this and the practice of it leads to the emergence of a new human category that Jung refers to as contemporary humanity. In our present state, the higher dimensions of our emotional, mental, and spiritual nature are working on the unconscious level, and we are in an unconscious connection to other material worlds on those levels. When we permanently leave our physical bodies, we will become part of the unlimited multi-dimensionality.

Consciousness from Perception to Imagination

Mental activity in general is a dynamic process that involves resonant interaction with the perceived environment, and this is true whether we are thinking, imagining, or talking. Being conscious of our surroundings is a dynamic interaction that changes the subtle energy quality of both the perceived and the perceiver; they are each part of an overall unity. In this context, time-space constraints are irrelevant, and this work allows us to take the first steps into the extraordinary world of subtle energy. Consciousness can be divided into several types: there is the consciousness within sensory-based perception (as a left-brain type of activity) and the unperceived consciousness of the extrasensory mode of the right brain. We can even go further to another level of the unperceived universal consciousness of the heart. Communication here occurs through the multi-dimensional levels embedded in the heartbeat, as we shall examine when analyzing the wave planes through which this two-way resonant information and quality exchange operates beyond the confines of our perceived universe. The unperceived consciousness of the extrasensory mode of the right brain and the unperceived universal consciousness of the heart are unperceived by the left brain and are therefore labelled as unconscious or subconscious levels. These levels are, however, different types of collective and universal consciousness that we access under certain conditions. *Consciousness itself is a primordial quality existing as an integral part of subtle energy on any level and in any form.*

Multi-dimensional Sensory Information Exchange

Let us examine the different types of multi-dimensional information exchange:

A. **Direct Extrasensory Perception**
This information exchange happens through the skin as well as a hierarchy of subtle energy vortices such as the chakras, acupuncture points and joints. The multiple different shapes of the body are in seamless resonance with all vibratory levels on all time-space dimensions. The heart and gut brain play an important role in this extrasensory information exchange.

B. **Sensory Multi-dimensional Information Exchange**
The senses capture information from very limited vibratory ranges that are channeled to related decoding areas in the brain. This is the information that is put together to form the perceived reality. Although the ranges involved in sensory perception are very limited, they are still in several types of resonance with all other unperceived ranges across the board from zero to infinity that they carry in the background of the sensory information and are transmitted to the extrasensory information level of the body. This means that sensory activity works on two levels carrying all the unlimited universal multi-dimensional extrasensory information on the limited sensory perception.

In this context, one of those two levels forms the mortal sensory soul which includes the ego personality, while the other is the domain of the immortal soul.

Our Senses Affect the Evolution of Perceived Energy Systems

The resonant information exchange between our senses and our perceived reality means that we are also causing a change in other subtle energy systems within our perception. This is more evident when we understand that perceived reality emerges within our brains making us an integral part of it. We are an agent of the qualitative evolution of all subtle energy systems in our perceived world and beyond.

Our own subtle energy quality is therefore continuously being affected in a dynamic quality exchange. This resonant exchange is not confined to the sensory information, but it involves all levels of our subconscious mind as well. We inevitably project our personality content, and the qualities of our biological subtle energy functions, as well as our unperceived subconscious content, into other living energy systems, which contributes to the quality of their dynamic evolution. Resonance is a two-way information exchange so, for example, when a person speaks, he affects and is equally affected by the listeners (Figure 28).

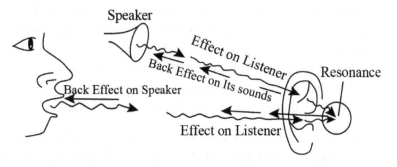

Fig.28 - Sensory Two-Way Effect

Human Subconscious Quality Transfer into Energy Products

In the physical dimension, where the linearity of time produces cause and effect relationships, our physical actions have a very powerful effect on all levels of the background subtle energy of the environment. Intent and knowledge play a main role here. This is an important consideration when we produce modern technologies that neglect to incorporate any aspect of universal life force. Modern industry's lack of a human-centered qualitative outlook is affecting the quality of emotional and mental energy inherent in the life force of the forming process in nature. This means that man-made objects depleted of life force are being produced from otherwise beneficent natural sources. As a result, all other living species are impaired and lose the balance of their natural productive state. In other words, the disturbed qualities of the modern psyche are hitting back at us through the products of modern technology. In the new holistic paradigm of the Physics of Quality, this is a scientific reality.

Once we acknowledge this fact, we can transform ourselves, as well as the products of modern technology, to have a beneficent healing effect on all life forms.

In its present form, modern technology, however beneficent to our very advanced civilization, is a disease in the body of the earth that needs to be cured.

There are only two possible outcomes. The first is to acknowledge the progress and innovation of modern technology, as well as the contributions mainstream scientific specialization has made to the understanding of the mechanisms of the material world, and we can do this without discrediting and limiting ourselves to this narrow worldview. The second path involves expanding our worldview in an integrated quantitative and qualitative way, to enable a sustainable prosperous future.

The pursuit of political and economic gains is eroding ethical values. Psychosomatic disease is just as valid on a global scale as it is on an individual level. Humanity is like bacteria in the body of the earth that transforms beneficent life-supporting chemical, fossil, and electromagnetic reactions without being aware of their subtle energy connection to the complete life force of the earth. Luckily, we have free will, which can be steered in a different direction, and the Physics of Quality can unify science and spirituality to do just that, while bringing forth the true golden age of modern technology.

Responsibility of the Senses

I always joke with my audience at this point in my lectures, by saying: "I suggest you put your fingers in your ears so as not to hear what I am about to say. If you don't, you will carry a huge responsibility beyond anything you can dream of." I then introduce them to the BioGeometry solution.

The human species has free will that comes with a certain responsibility towards all other subtle energy systems. That means that we have a responsibility to introduce balance and harmony in all levels of our own physical and subtle energy system—vital, emotional, and mental. This has a sensory effect on the evolution of other energy systems, some of which will be beneficent, and some of which will be harmful.

This is a complex matter: the human brain only perceives the limited information derived from the senses to create a very selective limited reality. The subtle energy information exchange goes much beyond this into the dimensions of unlimited absolute reality. The imperfect balance of the limited cannot bring balance and harmony into the unlimited. The only solution is to connect to the transcendental centering energy from a higher archetypically harmonizing spiritual dimension and bring its perfect balancing effect into our perceived world.

The use of the word "centering" in BioGeometry refers to a harmonizing quality active in the whole shape or figure. It is different from its conventional use as a form of connecting the periphery of the shape to its geometric center to achieve a balanced state. In BioGeometry, the center is a quality found in the middle of the vortex or wormhole connecting two or more dimensions. It is an elusive qualitative doorway that has no physical coordinates and is only accessible through resonance with its subtle energy quality (labeled BG3 in BioGeometry). The process of centering occurs through the BioGeometry design principles derived from the living forming process of nature. It is based on using resonance to open the door for this harmonizing life force to flow into the whole shape so that the whole shape becomes a qualitative center connected to its archetype on a higher dimension (Figure 29).

The Use of Samples in BioGeometry

One of the methods we use in BioGeometry to harmonize the energy quality of any object or person utilizes the principle that any part, however small, keeps a resonant holographic connection with its origin. The sample has all the information of the whole and will display all its subtle energy qualities beyond the constraints of time or space. We take a minute sample of the object to harmonize and proceed to change its energy quality by placing it in either a "BioGeometry Material Balancing Wheel" or a "BioGeometry Material Balancing Sphere." These devices use the subtle energy qualitative effect of polarized angles to harmonize the sample and

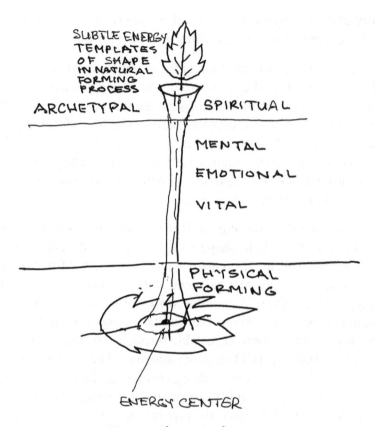

Fig.29 - Shape Archetype

through it affect its original source (Figure 30). We frequently apply them to change how existing building materials affect us. This very practical method can be used on location or remotely.

The Human Being is an Example of Perceived Reality

Based on the sample containing the information of the original whole, the individual human being is a sample of the perceived reality of which he or she is a part. When we work on bringing ourselves into harmony, we affect the whole environment. Being effective at this work entails resolving negative judgements of our own life events, as well as resolving negative judgements of others. Accepting the other is a main criterion of harmonized evolution, both individually and collectively.

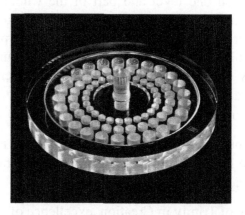

Fig.30 - BioGeometry Material Balancing Wheel

Human Being is a Sample of The Whole Multi-Dimensional Reality

The human being usually experiences their right-brain mode or heart perception through ethical values. This is a sample of the multi-dimensional existence spanning past, present, and future, as well as all other invisible parallel realities. Let's look at this physical world as a leaf floating over the vast primordial ocean of total multi-dimensional existence. It is affected by the movement of the ocean but floats in a very limited superficial dimension. To have significant in-depth effect, a change must happen in the ocean itself, and the leaf must completely dissolve in the water. It will, however, still exist as an unseparated form of the whole ocean. Likewise, we cannot affect our world unless we connect to the multi-dimensional harmonizing principles of the whole reality.

Subconscious harmony is impossible to achieve without a connection to a higher spiritual dimension beyond our dualistic time space reality, one which gives rise to, and balances, life force and includes all the Laws of Nature and archetypal patterns of everything in the material world.

This is the cornerstone of the design language of BioGeometry. The earth, as well as everything in nature, is created by a forming process that draws its archetypal patterns and harmony of evolution from the higher dimensions. When we acknowledge that we are part of our perceived reality on one level and part of the whole multi-dimensional reality on another—and, going further into the Laws of Resonance, that we exist everywhere in both realities so that the part and the whole are one—we can begin to understand that we can bring harmony to the whole system by concentrating on achieving it in everyday life through "excellence" of action. The excellence is the product of a higher connectivity that brings the harmonizing quality of BG3 into every action.

Changing the subtle energy of the whole Universe is much simpler than we think and can be achieved on an individual level through the practice of excellence of action.

Through the Law of Trinity in Creation, excellence of action results from a balance of motion or activity through the higher centering principle that creates the unity that turns opposition into complementary. It acknowledges opposites, and it can be achieved through the natural forming process of BioGeometry. BioGeometry designs empower and create resonance with a centering effect; this is a form of personal initiation along the path of excellence of action. A sample charged with the spiritual connection quality is far more potent than a collection of many samples with negative qualities. The resonant effect in this case is qualitative, while quantitative criteria have only a secondary influence.

Life on Earth is the Unique Opportunity

Some religious, philosophical, mystical, and spiritual traditions see this world as the cradle of all evil while others see nature as the beautiful manifestation of Divinity on Earth. It can be both, depending on the actions of the perceiver. Human actions that are coupled with the higher universal subconscious levels are holistic in nature; when further combined with the physical, and with all levels of subtle energy in perfect balance, the result is an excellence of action that affects the quality of life in all dimensions of Creation. The ability to actively influence and participate in the harmony of universal order is unique to the action of free will in the physical dimension. In short, our actions in the physical world influence the quality of all other dimensions. Our world is the unique factory that produces the qualities that affect other dimensions. We make our heaven and hell here and resonantly create it in other dimensions. We can view this world as a puzzle that needs a higher faculty of visualization to form the beautiful picture contained within it. Otherwise, the individual pieces are just scattered around meaninglessly. Each of us is born with a puzzle that can form the ultimate beauty, if properly understood. All the pieces are necessary to complete the picture. Discarding any piece due to negative judgement will not enable the completion of the picture needed for a happy journey. This means that self-judgment is a barrier to creating the beautiful picture.

Living in Harmony with the Laws of Nature (Accepting All Others)

To enter into full harmony with the Laws of Nature we must achieve resonance with this original Law of Creation, and in practicing it in everyday life we become an expression of it, thereby introducing harmony into the environment. How do we practice this? Through motion centered in a higher principle. In other words, when we connect to the centering principle in our conscience, we can translate the universal harmonizing connection into ethical action and accordingly connect the opposites in our life, through the centered motion, to form a complementary relationship. This requires us to move out of our fixed point of view into the harmonizing motion that connects us to the opposite, and we can do this in one of two ways. The first one is to make perceivable motion along the circular path between the two opposites, and the second is to connect to the transcendental harmonizing center.

We must change our understanding of liberty and re-evaluate the erroneous concept of being able to express the point of view that governs the perception of our reality. Clinging to this concept builds walls of protection against other different interpretations. The fixed point of view also results in judgements of others, which imprison us in a false sense of liberty. In reality, by adhering to a fixed point of view we are reinforcing opposition and disrupting the Law of Motion, and producing imbalance in the complementarity of Creation. Centered complementarity is necessary for creative evolution. Liberty is fulfilled when we keep the anchor in our point of view while moving towards a centered communication with its opposite. Liberty and ethics lead to the acceptance of and communication with ALL others. Knowledge of the other leads to appreciation and acceptance.

By accepting all others, we enter into harmony with the Laws of Creation; this communication restores the life force of the individual as well as the environment, as they are one and the same. Knowledge plays a role here: by acknowledging the fact that the center of motion in every type of particle is a transcendental harmonic connection to higher levels up to the Ziron at the core of the Psychon pulses of Creation, we acknowledge the fact that there is a creative Ziron center at the core of every material particle. By being aware of this fact, we realize that the Ziron centers hold reality together through the spiritual essence at the core of every particle. This automatically leads to the irrefutable fact that everything has a Divine creative light at its center giving it life force. Everything in Creation is sacred.

The opposite—being wrong in action—does not cancel the sacred essence. One can refuse to accept someone's wrong action and strive to correct it through leadership by example, governing laws, or corrective action—and still acknowledge that person's sacred essence. In this case the correction applies to the action and should never be levied in judgement of the person. No power can extinguish the Divine light in matter and even when eclipsed it is still there. Corrective judgement of action should never be about the person or any form of creation.

Accepting all others through acknowledgement of their sacred essence is the way to complementarity along the Laws of Creation, while opposition is the way of control, and it disrupts the life force and harmony in nature.

The practice of accepting all others has an impact on a multi-dimensional scale. Our mental-emotional make-up can cause havoc in other dimensions of Creation beyond our awareness, resulting in corrective measures to restore harmony. These measures can be subtle or harsh and in the worst cases they can lead to the demise of the human species. This is like a surgical intervention that removes a tumor to save the whole system. As the biological functions in our physical dimension are governed by the universal Laws of Nature on higher dimensions, a disturbance produced by disrupting the natural Law of Creation will result in a reduction of life force in all species on our planet.

The practice of acceptance of all others as I am expressing here is not a form of ethical or religious preaching that one can accept or deny, but rather it is a scientific reality within the Laws of Creation that works irrelevant of human choice.

We are under the false assumption that having a point of view from which we can judge others gives us power over them. The power of judgement is a holistic principle of destruction that affects both parties as well as the whole living environment. Collective judgement manifests as a form of control that is prevalent in political, industrial, religious, and economical systems. It is, in the long run, more destructive than nuclear weapons, as it spares nothing in existence. The opposite is also true: in achieving complementarity, the Laws of Creation are enforced and can thereby restore natural harmony in nature, as well as at all multi-dimensional levels of Creation.

Causality Versus Resonance

Our minds perceive everything within the duality of our time-space reality. We can perceive ourselves as separate from our surroundings and we can distinguish objects from their environment. Similarly, we must personify abstract concepts to bring them within our time and space causality and so we impose a dualistic time-space way of thinking about non-dualistic realities that are beyond our physical dimension. The concept of the timeless eternal existence of our other soul levels cannot be easily comprehended through our physical time-based existence. We therefore doubt our immortal existence in other dimensions. But once we are there, our life here will seem like a temporary stay in a place away from our permanent real home.

We impose cause and effect from our dimension on matters beyond it, and we create a personified time-space understanding of concepts like the afterlife, reincarnation, and karma. These do not necessarily comply with the Laws of Causality as we understand them. To understand the true nature of such matters, we must replace the term "causality" with the term "multi-dimensional resonance" instead.

This is easier said than done if we include all the forms and levels of secondary resonance that contribute to "the unified information system in multi-dimensional Creation." This might look complicated in the beginning, and it also might threaten to shatter your existing beliefs. Once understood, however, it will completely change your worldview and give you a deeper insight into the essence of your existing beliefs. Just imagine removing the word "after" from "afterlife." With no "before" or "after," our sensory-based dualistic brain perception would be at a loss to understand things—like causality, for example. We cannot escape the causality principles within our physical linear time space perception, but we can broaden the scope through which we understand them. In reincarnation, for example, each life has its own sensory ego created from interaction within its own dimension.

The individual's actions on the physical plane enter into resonance with the lives of other personalities in other dimensions resulting in an information exchange. It is not the same personality or sensory ego that manifests on the mortal soul level of each lifetime; however, each living person in this world attracts and steers, through his or her actions, the resonant information exchange with the other personalities in other lives.

The immortal soul exists on a higher level beyond our time-space boundaries—beyond the sensory ego and personality—and can have multiple existences. These personalities are like twins who are separated, each having their own life; we should not apply limited concepts of cause and effect to think that one pays for the other's mistakes. The common misconception that some people with disabilities or disadvantages in this lifetime are paying for what they did in a past life cannot be supported and goes against human values. There are no linear time relationships between incarnations that are in a simultaneous presence linked only by laws of resonance. Plus, the personal sensory ego, which is part of the mortal soul, is a physical time space construct with no existence beyond this life. It is the extrasensory higher universal immortal soul hidden in the depth of our subconscious level that is not constricted by sensory linear time-space flow. This multi-dimensional ever-present soul is what connects to other incarnations.

The immortal soul can be at the core of different incarnations but will not carry the guilt from one personality to others. It only transmits affinities that lie hidden until tapped. Karma can be understood as the timeless exchange of information affinities and probabilities depending on the present actions of a person. Karma does not take away free will. In hypnotic regression, for example, one can usually identify with resonant personalities in other dimensions, without ever having been them.

The Physics of Quality can even extend this concept beyond earthly existences to conceive of interacting with other forms of life in separate dimensions. The immortal soul, which is sometimes referred to as the *Self*, does not contain the personality of the sensory ego in its fullness. Yet it still has aspects of memory content and identity that are not dependent on the time-space configuration of the physical dimension. This identity is an infinitely expanded form containing a stripped-down ego whose information is rearranged such that it can exist in the different dimensions of the right brain/heart mode. This higher Self is multi-dimensional with simultaneous individual, collective, and universal levels and attributes. Some of the memories can affect other lives projected from the same central self. While the self is exchanging the masks of sensory egos of different earthly or other lives, some memory transference can occur, reinforcing the concept of reincarnation. As we go along, we will look at ways to access those seemingly unreachable dimensions to harmonize the physical environment on universal and individual levels.

The Multi-Dimensional Harmonizing Subtle Energy Quality

The quality of our perceived reality is projected from our subconscious mind and our actions. The great ancient civilizations ensured the prosperity of their world through a permanent connection of every aspect of every-day life with the harmonizing principles of the archetypal spiritual dimensions. Every action in the physical dimension followed certain principles to ensure a permanent spiritual doorway of communication with the higher dimensions.

The subtle energy quality of the spiritual doorway or wormhole I mentioned previously can be detected through three energy qualities that are based on methods of string harmonic resonance expressed through an objective qualitative color scale: The Higher Harmonic of Ultraviolet, the Higher Harmonic of Gold, and a communicative property in the middle gray range. This middle gray is referred to in the French system of Micro Vibrational physics as "Negative Green" because of its position opposite the color Green in the color distribution on a circle or sphere (Figure 31). The book, *Physique Microvibratoire et Forces Invisibles,* by Bélizal and Morel, was translated into English when we introduced their work to the English-speaking readers in our BioGeometry courses in the late nineties.

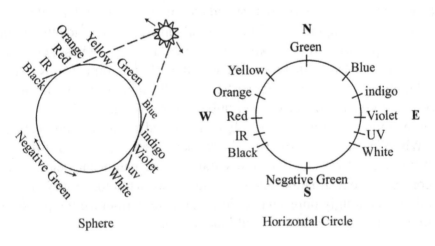

Sphere   Horizontal Circle

Fig.31 - Color Distribution on a Sphere Circle

This model of color distribution on a sphere or circle is a very simplistic means of color distribution that only shows a small part of the picture and is only adequate at an introductory level. Chaumery and Bélizal's Universal Pendulum is a more elaborate model that arranges the colors on a sphere along three meridians. The two vertical ones, perpendicular to each other, are magnetic and electric, while the horizontal equatorial one is electromagnetic (Figure 32).

The concept of the harmonizing BG3 quality emanating from the center of a wormhole is the main discovery that made BioGeometry possible. The unique design language of shape in BioGeometry creates this harmonizing energy quality.

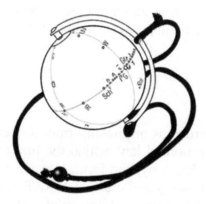

Fig.32 - Universal Pendulum Chaumery and Bélizal

PART SIX
The Origin of Time

To understand the nature of time, we will stop it and see what happens without it. The missing parts will give us an idea of what time is really made of. Let us now imagine that time has stopped. What happens? Our heart cannot beat, and we cannot take a breath, as motion seems to be linked with time. But energy is what produces motion. So, it seems that time is part of the forming process of energy. In the physical dimension, the perceived linearity of time has a direction related to motion. Beyond this dimension, the movement is multidirectional moving simultaneously into past and future directions and into other unperceived parallel realities. Time seems to be a main primordial force at the core of the creation of duality.

The Law of Time

Time was always regarded as originating from the level of the gods or Neters. Time is the primordial law behind the first creative WORD. It is the creator of order, harmony, and form. In Ancient Egypt, it was expressed through the harmony and order of MAAT and the forming process of her consort, PTAH the creator and sculptor of shapes. In the Greek pantheon, Chronos was associated with time. The Gnostics had Aion as the primordial god of time.

To understand time, we must look at its two aspects: the Law of Time that works from beyond duality to produce every pulse in Creation, and the manifestation of time in Creation within the Law of Trinity that creates the stable units on every plane of nature. We shall analyze the motion and shape of this manifestation of time in detail when dealing with the Bio-Geometry Energy Key. Everything in Creation, from the smallest to the largest, is the result of multi-dimensional pulses that appear and disappear simultaneously on many dimensions, creating the effect of stability. All pulse levels and dimensions are in a harmonic unifying information exchange, forming the overall unity. The perception of time is different within every life system as it is related to its sensory perception and evolution. We will, however, look at different modes of time related to human perception.

The Time Principle Behind Energy

The Law of Time can be regarded as the principle that governs the pulse in which the motion of the Trinity takes place. The motion governed in harmony by the Law of Trinity is active within the governing pulse of the Law of Time to produce harmony, stability, and the evolution of the natural forming process, in all dimensions of Creation. In a way those two laws of motion are two faces of one coin. The Law of Time is the governing forming principle at the core of the Law of Trinity we introduced above. The conscious living wisdom in the centering principle itself has the power of controlling the motion within duality in all its levels of Creation. This aspect of the Law of Time must act with a form of wisdom resulting from the interaction of Consciousness, intellect, evaluation, and control within a harmonious motion to produce a stable complementarity within the living process of duality. The Law of Time produces the initial Psychon Pulse extending along the central axis of wave motion, and a secondary motion forming the amplitude of the spiraling two-way wave shape of the pulse (Figure 33).

Since time produces the centering principle within all wave motions, there must be ways of using it and interacting with it. We should be able to access and use it like other forms of energy. In fact, we can store, amplify, project, and influence time, and even change the quality of its effect on us, through the BioGeometry Physics of Quality. The primordial Law of Time governs the pulse of duality and is a centering vortex that channels life force into the motion and balance of the Trinity. In other words, life force has the primordial Law of Time at its core. In this context, time can be seen as a main agent in the forming process of life force.

As a main component in the manifestation of the life force within duality, we can see how time plays an important role in the flow, balance, and harmonious interaction of biological functions in nature. The Law of Time itself is active through the center in the bi-directional axis of the wave and keeps the balance of the wave shape (refer to Figure 17).

Health problems in any living system are the result of over or underactivity of biological functions. This seems to be linked to balance and harmony in the motion of the time waves within a functioning organ function. This can be the result of a disturbance at any level of life force (vital,

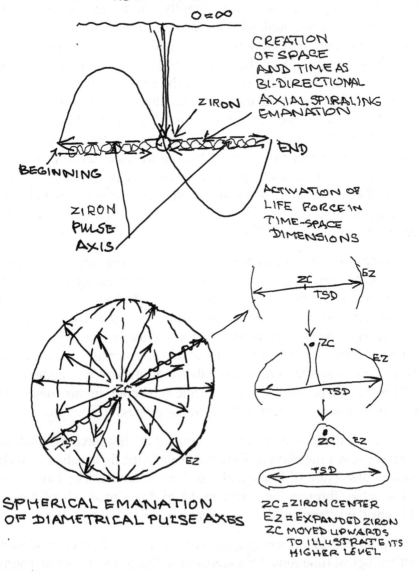

THE LAW OF TIME
GOVERNS THE FORMING PROCESS
OF THE PSYCHON PULSE

$O = \infty$

CREATION
OF SPACE
AND TIME AS
BI-DIRECTIONAL
AXIAL SPIRALING
EMANATION

ZIRON

BEGINNING

END

ZIRON
PULSE
AXIS

ACTIVATION OF
LIFE FORCE IN
TIME-SPACE
DIMENSIONS

ZC
TSD
EZ

ZC
EZ
TSD

ZC
EZ
TSD

SPHERICAL EMANATION
OF DIAMETRICAL PULSE AXES

ZC = ZIRON CENTER
EZ = EXPANDED ZIRON
ZC MOVED UPWARDS
TO ILLUSTRATE ITS
HIGHER LEVEL

Fig.33 - Time Pulse 2

emotional, or mental), which goes on to affect the balance of the higher centering effect. The spiritual dimension is the harmonizing centering principle of the other levels.

Time Waves/Fields

The Russian astronomer Nikolai Aleksandrovich Kozyrev developed a theory of "time waves." He found that although time waves penetrate everything, they are, for some unknown reason, reflected by some materials, such as aluminum and granite. He discovered this by chance while using an aluminum telescope and he went on to construct aluminum containers; people who spent time inside them would suffer complete disorientation (The full story can be found in my book *Back to a Future for Mankind*).

In our BioGeometry paradigm, the primordial Law of Time creates the axial centering time dimension within all pulse types and resulting waves. It is the main criterion in the forming process of waves. In this context, all wave types are governed by the Law of Time and can be understood as "Time Waves."

This is our modification of the concept of time waves proposed by Kozyrev: that they are to be understood as a central dimension of all types of waves, and not a separate type. In the original Ziron pulse the interaction of the outgoing and ingoing mental and emotional spirals activate living Consciousness. Projected Consciousness and life force within the spiraling torsion pulse shed light on the very potent energetic power of time in all the life force manifestations of subtle energy. In its creation of the time pulse, the Law of Time activates the potential omnipotent force from the zero-infinity state to create the core infinite energetic state within subtle energy. This is the energy inherent in the all-prevailing background cradle of Creation that we define as life force.

Dual Time-Space Dimensions

As mentioned earlier, in the 3D-Energy Key of motion we use to understand different aspects of energy quality, we find that the bi-directional central pulse of motion creates a spiraling vortex in both directions. The timeless BG3 dimension of the central axis of motion, and the spiraling vortex, manifest the time pulse archetypal unit which creates time-space toroidal compression wave fields at both ends of the central vortex. According to this model, this manifests from the smallest level of the Psychon to the largest universes. Interestingly, space-time dimensions are always created in complementary pairs, one on each end of the vortex.

This theory of interconnected universes is described by the late MIT physicist Dr. Claude Swanson in his book, *The Synchronized Universe*. Dr. Swanson supported the understanding of the vortex configuration as the connection between two universes. Qualitatively, those two time-space dimensions are of complementary opposite polarities and exchange information through the vortex. What's more, time-space is also inverted in such dimensions. This model would link another Earth and another material electromagnetic sun, as well as another galaxy—up to even another universe—to ours in an unperceivable existence. We should not imagine these linked worlds to be exact copies of everything here, but more as complementary counterparts of everything in our material universe, just as complementary colors (such as Red and Green) are manifestations of a central unity. Although they are in complete synchronized entanglement, they develop differently in their own dimensions. As the information from one of the two universes crosses the center of the vortex, referred to as a black hole, it is completely stripped of its material and time-space qualities to emerge in a new format according to the different time-space configuration of the other universe. Therefore, the information does not directly travel from one dimension to the other, as it is completely dismantled and reassembled according to new criteria.

The twin universes are not copies of each other but rather exist in synchronized entanglement. Their qualities affect each other but are not necessarily dealt with in the same manner. While we are destroying our environment, they could be regenerating theirs. Our influence could be a negative effect that they observe and harmonize while theirs could subconsciously affect our behavior towards nature.

Whether they are advanced enough to communicate and emerge into our world is a question that cannot be answered until we know how far ahead their civilization is.

Effect of Reflection on the Time Principle Within Waves

Materials that seem to reflect time waves are actually either reflecting certain frequencies or distorting the time pulse of the wave and this causes the disturbances in perception noted by Kozyrev. Looked at from another perspective, such materials cause a complete shift of perception towards the right-brain dimension. They disrupt the time-space criteria and open the door to the endless abyss of subconscious realms. This would be like the effect of psychedelic plants and drugs.

The interesting thing about the distortion of time waves within subtle energy and the life force within it is that there is evidence that the ancients knew and used it in their monuments. The "granite" chambers in the pyramids, for example, enabled the opening of the full multi-dimensional doorways of perception.

Our sensory perception of color is based on the reflection of light on all types of natural or modified surfaces. Artificial or modified natural surfaces seem to distort the centering time-pulse function. This can be verified through measurement using our living color disks and we will discuss this in later chapters; these disks detect life force on natural surfaces but not on artificial ones. The products of modern technology, in general, distort the reflected time-pulse producing a negative effect on natural surfaces or objects.

Pulse, Wave, and Time-Space
At this point, we need to recapitulate, starting with the emergence of the first Psychon Pulse, so we can better understand the relationship between the pulse and the wave. The pulse, as we have explained earlier, is a central emanation creating an expansion and contraction back into the center. This central emanation, in turn, creates the beginning and end of the linear

wave emanation. In the central expansion of the pulse, a linear motion of the wave is created from beginning to end with an embedded motion in the other direction on an energetic level. The outward motion creates time and space while the inward reverse motion of attraction happens on another dimension opposite to the time-space flow (Figure 34).

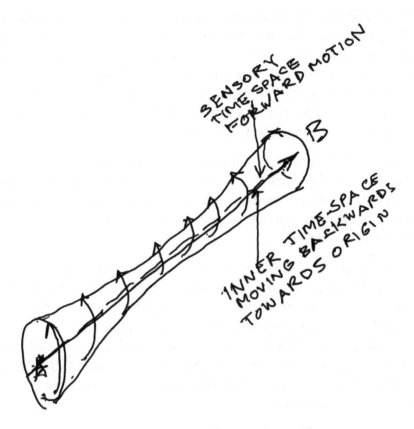

Fig.34 - Bi-Directional Time-Space Flow

The attraction towards the center creates a secondary embedded flow in the reverse direction. The secondary flow is opposite to the motion of time-space within the pulse. It is on another level beyond the time-space dimension, leading back to the central Ziron of the Psychon Pulse.

Creation is based on the harmonic multi-level resonance between all pulses from the smallest to the largest. Each pulse, in this multi-level harmonic hierarchy, has its own time-space configuration built into it, as well as the inward flow to the higher dimensions from which it is emitted (Figure 35).

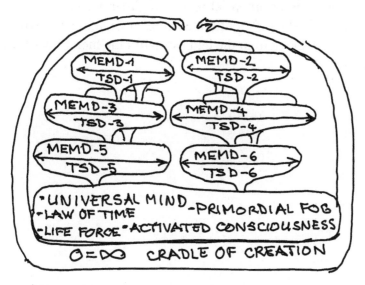

Fig.35 - Hierarchy of Pulses

The spherical multidirectional emission of the Psychon is composed of endless bi-directional vortices and their toroidal fields emanating from the Ziron center through the eight Psychon planes created by the vortex double-spirals.

We must go back to the archetypal model of the Psychon resulting from spiraling waves caused by the transcendental Ziron pulse (refer to Figure 3). The Ziron pulse is the result of the eight sub-pulses created by the eight-level spirals in all directions in a spherical form, making the Psychon pulse appear in multiple dimensions simultaneously. The same Psychon pulse emerges and creates many dimensions at the same time. All the dimensions resulting from the same Psychon pulse are not just connected but different faces of one primordial reality of Creation. This means that all existing realities in the different dimensions of Creation are built with the same building blocks within the endless harmonic hierarchy of levels and dimensions.

PART SEVEN
Time Perception

Time perception as we know it is a major aspect in our interactions in everyday life. It is a left-brain sensory activity that is laden with mental-emotional content associated with our cultural memory database. A great amount of stress results from fear associated with pleasure, sadness, gain, loss, past, future, aging, health, and all other aspects of everyday life. Fear becomes associated with time. Time can also be a motivating and healing factor in our life when associated with happy events or healing environments that we can recall. We shall examine below how this changes with every mode of time perception.

Linear Time

In our physical dimension, the lowest level of mental-emotional subtle energy is entwined in a linear flow that governs the perception of time and space within the analytical mental forces. This leads to a form of quantification. Past, present, and future are perceived like beads on a string. You consecutively hold one bead at a time while moving in one direction. You cannot untie the beads to rearrange them. You cannot break the repetitive flow of physical experience, but you can move your perception of the beads in a non-physical recalling of past events and the imagining of future ones; you can only experience the physical feeling of the bead in your fingers. Our sensory perception creates a continuous time and space perception by connecting the otherwise separate "beads."

To help understand this concept better, I will also introduce the analogy of pages in a book. We can look at the pages of a book as individual Time Space Gravity Units (TSGU). A sensory pattern attaches the TSGUs together in a linear form as we move through them, just as though they are bound into a book with numbered pages and we are reading through them in sequence, which we perceive as linear time-space. This type of time creates the perception of present, past, and future with the past as gone and the future as uncertain, creating a fear of losing and a fear of not getting. This is the time concept that shapes our lives and which we count in consecutive years. The quantitative perception carries with it the seeds of stress as we emotionally relate to it. However, quality plays a major role in the perception of time as well. Our perception of linear time and space is linked to the quality of sensory experience, and this governs the way it is stored in memory and how it is recalled.

The experience of our time and space is linear and we can visualize it as a flowing river. Imagining the future is like looking ahead: swimming with the flow poses no stress on our system unless we burden it with qualities from past experiences, which come from looking back against the current. Recalling memories is like moving upstream against the current or the flow of time. The resulting resistance when swimming against the current causes stress. Memories are therefore burdened by a form of stress that is added to the original emotional quality experienced when the event took place. We have found by several measurements based on qualitative scales that even memories of happy moments cause stress in our subtle energy system in the present moment, because we are swimming against the current of time, as well as experiencing an innate feeling of loss.

To find a solution, we must go to the work of a famous Austrian nature scientist, biomimicry experimenter, philosopher, visionary, and inventor: Viktor Schauberger. His work analyzes the motion of fish or birds against the water and air currents, and it deals directly with this problem.

Schauberger is one of the great thinkers of twentieth century German culture. His intellectual world, among others like Rudolf Steiner and Carl Gustav Jung, played an important role in my worldview of psychological and subtle energy concepts of time. He passed away in 1958, the same year I began my studies in Switzerland; Jung died three years later. Schauberger studied the shape of an egg and the similarly elongated shape of fish and birds. He showed that by hanging an egg on a string, with the larger part at the top, in a slightly angled flow of water, a spiral effect results around the egg and pushes it upward. This " spiraling push" is the same principle of how water or air flow around a fish or bird: they spiral around it and push it forward against the current. We can use a similar concept to relieve the psychological and mental stress associated with memories and visualize a similar shape effect drawn in a clockwise motion. The best way to do this is to visualize the infinity sign before reflecting on the past. This will relieve the memories brought on by the stress of looking back against the flow of time. There are some BioGeometry shapes, such as the BioGeometry "L90" shape, that produce a similar effect.

Cyclic Time

Most of us find that the quantitative aspect of linear time generally dominates over the qualitative one. There is, however, an alternative method of perceiving linear time that is mainly qualitative. Let us take our previous example of the beads on a string, but this time we will have beads of four different colors on the string and they keep repeating themselves in the same sequence. When our attention is on color, we can look at each color and discover its place in the pattern of repetition without being aware of the count. Take farmers as another example. They look at the seasons as different repetitive stages or qualities in the life of a plant. Their whole system of agronomy is based on the recurring seasonal qualities in the life of plants. For them, each seasonal quality is an ever-present repetitive part of the whole pattern. The year becomes a pattern of qualities instead of numerous months or days.

It must be emphasized here that numbers are also manifestations of qualities depending on how we perceive them, as we shall see in a later chapter dedicated to this topic. It is important to note that our perception is mainly quantitative when related to the linear passage of time. But when we are aware of the whole pattern, quality emerges to supersede quantity, and this results in a cyclic perception of time. The stress of linear time, caused by the loss of the past and the insecurity of the future, becomes insignificant with the ever-present repetition of qualities: instead of focusing on the count of each bead, the focus is on the whole pattern of qualities. The holistic perception of the Laws of Nature creates an intuitive wisdom and unity of the qualities of life. Cyclic time is a qualitative right-brain perception mode within the quantitative left-brain linear time awareness.

It must be noted here again that right- and left-brain modes are not separate physical locations in the brain hemispheres but are associated with sensory awareness and subconscious extrasensory perception. They are only vaguely associated with fixed physical locations in the brain, as brain locations can take different functions when needed.

This wisdom results from the application of intuitive qualitative perception to the analytical intellectual mode. This is the way of values, spirituality, art, sports, and other similar activities. The wisdom resulting from the perception of cycles can be practiced on any level where a repetitive pattern is perceived. Days of the week, time of day, day and night, lunar and solar phases, and feasts and holidays within the calendar year are all part of a pattern that can create a level of cyclic time. What is applied to time can also be applied to places or activities that are done repetitively but not necessarily at a fixed time. This awareness of pattern is a relaxing right brain activity that balances the stress in our sensory left-brain perception. It is a type of meditation on pure quality. Intellect is associated with sensory perception, but wisdom results from the holistic relationship of patterns and the resulting connection to extrasensory universal communication.

In this time perception mode, the TSGU pages are still arranged in a linear fashion but are read with an overview of the whole. This allows for the perception of repetitive qualities within a pattern and their connection to the Laws of Nature where they feel one with the earth.

Stacked Time

There is also a purely qualitative way of perception that takes place when the boundaries of sensory linear physical time and space are lifted. This is the foundational level of perception on which others are built. Let's go back to our example of the string of beads, but in this case, we cut the string and remove it completely, leaving the beads in a seemingly unconnected haphazard arrangement with no apparent relationship between them except the distribution of colors. When we bring our attention to one color, we become aware of the presence of the pattern that connects all the beads of that color. This results in a resonant communication between the parts of the pattern. Perception of quality is a right-brain mode that is linked to multi-dimensional "holistic pattern" recognition. It is different from the perception of a "repetitive pattern" in cyclic time as a complementary mode to linear time. It takes on its full splendor when it is free from the sensory veil of the physical dimension. In dreams and out-of-body experiences, we get a glimpse of this type of seemingly irrational jumping in time and space.

Free from the constraints of the string, the beads of the same color form a relationship through their place in the multiple possible arrangements within the overall haphazard pattern. There is no specific linear flow in this case. The result is a form of color resonance between the beads. This resonant pattern is the basis of a new qualitative time concept, where our awareness jumps between beads of the same color in multiple possible secondary patterns within the overall main pattern. This highlights two types of qualitative relationships: the first is a result of the main resonance resulting from qualitative similarity and the second is based on the resonant complementarity between all the colors connected to the overall unity. There is also a third type of resonance related to shape. This is a resonant phenomenon between similar shapes irrelevant of size. This resonance is seamless and covers all ranges from the smallest to the largest. So, all waves, for example, with the same proportion between wavelength and amplitude giving them their shape quality, will be in resonance in all frequencies from the smallest to the largest.

There is no apparent flow in this concept of time. Awareness jumps in any direction from one spot to another anywhere within the pattern. If we imagine each bead as a page containing a singular piece of information about an event, we end up with a stack of pages that can be rearranged in different ways depending on the force of resonant attraction of the qualities of each. This is what we refer to as stacked time. In pure stacked time the movement from one page to another is instantaneous and the place or time of the event within the physical time-space flow is irrelevant.

We can observe stacked time once we get out of the sensory left-brain mode of perception—such as in states of spiritual grace, dreams or daydreaming, appreciation of the arts, and so on. When this mode of right-brain intuitive perception kicks in within physical sensory time, it is not totally free of the senses and can be influenced or pulled back anytimethe senses are activated. We can, however, still move between different thoughts and emotions in an instantaneous, seemingly unstructured way. In such cases as out-of-body experiences or comas, the sensory effect is much diminished, but it is still there. Only at death when the sensory organs stop functioning and a complete separation from the physical body occurs can permanent stacked time take place.

Time-Space "Experions" Within Timeless Stacked Pages

It is very difficult to explain the perception and interaction of time and space in what to us is a timeless dimension using the tools we have in our dualistic left-brain sensory world view. We can only hope to have a very vague impression of those elusive dimensions when we translate them through our cultural and experiential dictionary.

Beyond the confinement of the physical body and sensory time perception, things look totally different. The pages are taken out of their binding and put in a stack with no order whatsoever, so that they can be shuffled and rearranged in any way. One can jump between pages. All the pages that were not bound in the book because they were un-manifested probabilities are also thrown into the stack as they might have manifested in other parallel realities. We instantly move into whichever page we resonate with through an emotional or mental action, and it becomes our reality. This movement between pages is not bound by a time-space pattern as it carries within it its own configuration.

There is no time or space linkage between the pages in their original stacked layout, but in the composition of elements that form an individual page there is an inner relationship that includes time and space data; they are needed to form the picture. These do not flow from one page to another except when a group of pages connect through resonance of qualities to form a small separate stack that we will call an "Experion" as it forms a whole situation or experience.

The word "Experion" as used in this book is a time-space molecule (TSM) composed of several pages of stacked time. It is like primary particles where different arrangements of the same particles produce different molecules. In a similar way, stacked pages arranged differently create different Experions.

Each page in a combined group contains information from preceding and following pages to become a resonant totality with the complete information of the whole group, and this manifests as the situation of an Experion. Each Experion has its own time-space configuration with a closed internal flow.

The ever-present stacked time exists simultaneously as a background right-brain perception and a linear and cyclic representation of sensory left-brain perception. It is buried within our emotional and mental subconscious levels, and we cannot perceive it with our senses. When relevant, it can manifest in the form of intuition.

Causality is a main component of interaction in the physical world because of the linear flow of time. Cause and effect can only take place when one precedes and triggers the other. If we imagine a situation with a configuration of time that lacks the linear flow that we are used to, then causality does not apply but the resonance of qualities does. In fact, this resonance of qualities will be the only thing that governs movement from one page of the timeless stack to another. Since the causality does not apply beyond our physical dimension, we must completely rethink the way many of our current concepts work—such as life after death, reincarnation, the book of records, or our subconscious relationship with the past and future.

The quality of action in the physical dimension affects the resonance between the pages of background stacked time and plays a role in the forming of that reality. We constantly affect and are affected by the relevant qualities of stacked time. Any page from the universal dimensions of stacked time with which the right-brain perception is connected can be recalled through resonance with any aspect in the left-brain sensory perception and thus influence an action in everyday life. It is usually experienced as "I don't know why but I just felt that I should do it this way…against all common sense." In a broader sense this can appear as a form of two-way causality, but it is not quite that when one of the ends is universal and timeless. We are forming and simultaneously living in the parallel life that we erroneously think of as life after death. This is difficult to perceive as the two modes of consciousness are of different types.

Causality

To recapitulate: in linear and cyclic time, the Law of Causality prevails. Everything can be translated to cause and effect. However, beyond physical existence, our sensory time-space perception fades away, to be replaced by a multi-dimensional form. If we imagine the bound pages as beads on a string, we can go through them by count as in linear time, or by color as in cyclic time, but they will always be in the same place in relation to the other beads on the string. There is always the bead before and the one after, which creates a certain relationship. Beyond the physical sensory dimension, the string falls apart leaving the beads in a haphazard order. The time-space order of the string between the beads does not exist anymore. The beads, when represented as pages, will each have an internal time-space pattern needed for the composition of the picture within it.

This time-space pattern is part of the forming process of the picture and does not flow beyond it unless it connects to other pictures in other pages through qualitative resonance of content to form a stack. The combination of pictures in the stack produces a living situation which we referred to as an Experion.

Causality falls apart with the disappearance of the string of the linearity of time. One can, however, pick up the individual beads according to any subconscious emotional or mental quality of common information. Pages are units in a state of eternal presence, with no before or after, and therefore no causality. The concept of multi-dimensional resonance applies to this non-linear time-space configuration because it is multidirectional in its quality exchange.

Causality no longer connects the pages the way it did in the physical sensory dimension. The only connection between the pages is qualitative resonance of content manifesting through timeless space-less multi-dimensional resonance. Causality is limited to the perception of linear time.

Analyzing Time and Space in Other Existences

We usually try to understand things beyond sensory perceived reality, such as reincarnation, the afterlife, karma, and the book of records, through the lens of our sensory mental-emotional construct. We accordingly attach the loose pages onto our time-space strings and apply causality to them. These are timeless realities co-existing with us as pages floating around in an eternal presence. There is no afterlife—there is just another timeless life that we are already living. At death, when the sensory limits are removed, a new type of perception opens into this other existence. We were always there but now we are aware of it. There are, however, temporary transition zones between this life and the timeless one where different configurations of time and space exist. These are the dimensions we can journey to in out-of-body travel or dreams and meet departed souls. We cannot go with them further into their dimension or we will have a complete cross-over with no return. These are the different gates inside the tunnel connecting sensory and extrasensory dimensions in the brain hemispheres.

Many doctrines translate this knowledge into a personified causality-based language that is grasped by our sensory time-space-based left-brain perception. This translation illuminates many concepts related to those other realities, but, unfortunately, it also leads us to develop them further along the logical time-space path, thus hiding their true nature. In the right-brain mode operating out of the timeless universal dimensions of the subconscious mind, the individual existence of the sensory ego is transformed into a collective universal form of consciousness that excludes the separate aspect of the left-brain personifying ego.

Multiple Existences

In the total resonant transfer of information between Experions, the subject who is part of the page contents of one Experion also becomes part of all other resonant Experions. This results in the creation of living conscious "copies" of the subject in the other resonant Experions over endless dimensions.

One subject's awareness of the copies is limited, but on a subconscious universal level, a complete information exchange takes place and exercises some effect between the different copies of the subject in multiple dimensions. These effects are like insinuations within the subconscious mind that are only activated if a physical action resonates with them. With time, however, the copies evolve differently as they interact with different situations in other Experions. They form individual personalities with a diminishing impact on the original and eventually cannot be regarded as copies. The Universe, as well as all other dimensions, are a unified subtle energy system forming a huge energy soup that is impossible to navigate through or understand with our limited physical left-brain perception. Meanwhile, on a subconscious level, the qualitative impact of those universal holistic dimensions is exceedingly vague.

Moving Through Timeless Pages

To understand the multi-dimensional impact of universal life exchange on subtle energy, let us first examine how we go from one page to another without the order of time and space. Resonance based on similar qualities is the key. This type of resonance occurs between the subtle energy quality that we experience on any level—action, movement, emotion, thought, or an effect from another system—and that of the similar quality on one or more pages. Since all the pages in that timeless dimension are in an eternal present state, we immediately find ourselves on the related page and simultaneously on other qualitatively resonating pages. This means that we can co-exist on many individual pages or Experions. We are part of every page or Experion that we have created: we exist simultaneously in a network of connected pages and Experions with a basic resonant connectivity between them that is the result of our presence in all of them through "our copies."

On another level, besides the main resonance between certain pages, there is a secondary background resonance connecting all our stacked pages and Experions of similar quality. Let's take musical notes, for example. We find the main resonance between the same notes occurring on string lengths half or double the size of the original note selected. We also find other secondary resonances between different notes. When we turn to color qualities, we find similar colors are in resonance with each other and there are also other secondary resonant relationships based on laws of harmony, complementarity, hue, and luminosity. If we take those resonance levels into the realm of connectivity, effect, and the exchange of information between pages and Experions, we end up with a multi-level multi-dimensional resonant pattern that connects every conceivable thing in existence in one endless unity of Creation. This pattern is the pathway of the instantaneous jump from one page or Experion to another.

If it is instantaneous as part of an eternal presence, then we should imagine that we exist everywhere at the same time. By jumping into different Experions, we are just shifting our awareness into different self-images of ourselves linked to the situation. We are used to having a separate, individual sensory physical existence and cannot imagine being everywhere all the time in a universal multi-dimensional existence. We still use the self-image of the personality within this universal presence to emphasize our presence in each of the pages we are in. So, there are two parts to our existence: one left-brain-created self-image that persists in our subconscious memory, and the other right-brain universal multi-dimensional presence. Individual pages exist as timeless spaceless units that can be combined in any pattern imposed by the dimension they are in to acquire time and space criteria that can be totally different in nature than in our sensory time and space. It is the pattern of combination that produces the internal time and space configuration of an Experion.

A Life Journey with Time as a Companion

Regardless of all the scientific aspects of time as a governing law in the Universe, it is how we personify, relate, and interact with it that affects us. Our everyday sensory perception works through focus and analysis in a dualistic reality of the relationship of opposites. This leads automatically to the personification of abstract ideas into linear time and space so they can be understood. This personification applies to all abstract timeless things that we need to perceive, whether it is the powers of nature, Divinity, or even Time itself. We tend to personify our interaction and experiences with linear time throughout our lives by categorizing the moments in time as a memory of the past, a material present, or an uncertain future, and we deal with time as though it were a person with three faces. Each of the three faces has two sides to it: one as a friend and one as a foe.

In a happy situation, time is our friend, but when it moves into the past, time is a friend giving us nice memories while at the same time we feel that it has taken those nice moments away from us. The seed of fear on a subconscious level is at the root of most psychological problems. Fear of losing or fear of not getting is, in a way, related to time. Time takes every present moment away from us into the deep sea of memories, from which nothing comes back. Some can emerge from the depths to float below the surface where we can see their elusive reflections. While there is a sense of loss and happiness related to nice memories, there is also a slow fading of the grief of sad moments. Time here is a friend taking the sadness where it dissipates with the years.

The Healing Effect of Memories

Going back in time against the outward perceived linear time flow produces a certain level of stress from swimming against the current. We have seen how certain geometric shapes like the infinity sign can alleviate this stress. Let us analyse the resonance of the infinity sign with the linear bi-directional flow of time to understand how it harmonizes the backward navigation. The Psychon pulse is the origin of outward radiation coupled with mental energy as the archetype of motion in the linear flow of time. The outward spiraling motion is intertwined with an inward gravitational flow of emotional energy towards the source in the Ziron center.

The inward backward flow of energy is at the core of the outward perceived flow of time giving it the centering spiritual balance, which sheds light on the inner spiritual source every step of the outward spiraling flow of time. This mode of perception brings out the wisdom in looking back towards the source, in other words, it points to how every memory is an important building block with an inherent lesson that carries the next step in the timeline. Seeing the wisdom in past events and the awareness of their carrying the present and future ones injects a healing effect into the bi-directional perception in the linear flow of time. This concept has developed into a practical exercise of "correcting the cracked steps" in the timeline of life. This exercise is explained in a coming part related to energetic time travel. The psychology school of "Logo Therapy" developed by Victor Frankl, based on his experience in the concentration camp during the second world war, uses the discovery of the positive meaning behind past life events as achievements to relieve depression in the present.

The future is in many ways like the past in that it is unreal but, unlike the past, it carries with it a sense of uncertainty that translates into hope or despair, depending on one's attitude towards life. We perceive this companion along the path of life with mixed feelings. One day as our lives end, this loyal companion that travelled with us, and towards which we had those mixed feelings, will feel its end coming and give us the key to the storage locker that holds everything it has preserved for us. We will cross the threshold to find that we have everything that we ever had. However, our linear time companion, who is bound to our physical senses, will not cross with us. There will be a difference to our memories in that they will exist without any "past" mental-emotional quality attached to them. Their quality will be added to the container of who we are through our subconscious mental-emotional makeup which in itself results from our judgement of experiences before the crossover. The qualities resulting from this judgement relate to how we judge ourselves as well as all others. The kind of eyeglasses we wear when we cross over will attach good or bad qualities to our new reality. It is the qualities distilled from our physical actions, and not the actions themselves, that will cross the threshold with us. These qualities will form the color of the eyeglasses with which we see everything in our new world.

The Immortal Soul Levels

For us to understand the make-up of the soul in what is, to us, a time-less dimension, we must look at the information connections on a sensory-based storage and meaning level. Each unit of information includes a logical arrangement of time and space data that permits its attachment to another unit. This occurs within an overall flow that the meaning level of the brain can relate to. This type of configuration forms the ego and personality that give us our physical identity. That is the "ME" as I know it, traveling through the physical time-space life journey. When we think of the afterlife or our past lives, we assume that this sensory-based self is there in a somewhat different form, but it is still a form of our current self in a different time-space configuration. Any theories we develop involving a linear time-space relationship of past and future lives must be understood in a metaphorical sense.

Reality is, however, different in many ways. If we take away the time and space "stamping" from existing memory units, they lose any sense of meaning, as the brain needs time-space duality to function. The content of the soul on unconscious levels will not provide the sense of identity, personality, or ego that we use to choose and govern our actions in physical life. When we strip the physical time and space data out of the information content, it does not follow the known laws of interaction of our world. Instead, the information rearranges itself according to resonant qualitative relationships within a different stacked time reality. We thus have no conscious control over the self in its new physically immortal state. The individual and collective causal relationships in our physical world are replaced by laws of resonance, which act in the same way as musical notes communicate and qualitatively exist within each other.

Universal resonance will produce multiple qualitative connected copies of this new type of soul in the different Experions of the other life. Through the resonant two-way information between the copies, there will be a sense of unity resulting in a composite broader soul with multiple existences in different Experion dimensions. It is difficult for us to understand this broader existence of the soul equally present in different time-space Experions, and how awareness moves within each as well as between them. Each of the copies develops differently depending on the situation within its Experion and the relationships in the environment of that dimension; they cannot be regarded as identical copies anymore, although they are influencing each other. With its own partly separate awareness, each new self is connected with others as one larger self. The boundaries between individuality, collectivity, and universality, as well as simultaneous existences, are blurred, and the sensory ego/personality dissolves and fuses with several others resulting in a new collective state. This concept sheds light on the non-localized multiple presences of the immortal soul that occur in reincarnation.

As we've already noted, this other dimension will influence this physical self or any other in the past or future, depending on the resonance of the qualitative content it initiates through physical actions in our world.

What must be clear is that what we call our immortal self does not carry our sensory-generated identity with it, just the qualitative universal content of it in many different arrangements. Being beyond physical time-space it does not carry causal relationships of linear time. This removes the existence of the same personality in different lives, as well as the transfer of responsibility through the different reincarnations we experience. To put it in a simplified way, the mortal soul is in the left-brain sensory dimension, with a linear time flow from beginning to end, while the immortal soul is in the right-brain universal extrasensory multi-dimensional presence that is free of the linearity of living in an ever-present existence. These two soul types interact in the duality of human existence. Human beings perceive the sensory causality effects of the mortal soul, while the multi-dimensional immortal soul is the universal connection to the unperceived forces of Creation animating the physical body. The information from the timeless immortal soul must undergo a translation into linear time-space as well as an association with the cultural content of the sensory database to emerge into the left-brain mode of perception.

However elusive this immortal soul seems to be, we are living within it, as our right-brain perception is a doorway into it. If we take the same personification idea that we used to perceive time as a life-long companion and apply it to the immortal soul, we end up with the concept of an invisible roommate. In this case, we live only temporarily with our room-mate, who will be staying after we leave. Imagine that the roommate is in another room, and you must traverse a short corridor in order to get to him or her, and vice versa. This is the situation between the left and right-brain modes of perception. They are connected by a subtle energy bridge or tunnel in the corpus callosum area connecting the brain hemispheres. The journey from the physical life to the other side occurs simply by crossing the bridge or going through the tunnel, and this is how it's been described by people who have had near-death experiences (Figure 36).

There are multiple gateways in the tunnel where information can either be translated or prevented from moving from the unconscious right mode into the sensory left mode. Some gates can be accessed through sensory perception while other gates can only be crossed at death. Disturbances in the way the connector between the hemispherical brain modes filters and translates information usually leads to psychological and perception problems. A disturbance can come from the misuse of hallucinogenic substances or from some forms of excessive psychological trauma. Spir-itual practices and rituals linked to the subtle energy quality of sacred power spots can, however, open safe doorways to the universality of a well-balanced connected state and these have been practiced in the tem-ples of ancient civilizations. Such practices involve many types of out-of-body experience. Natural states such as motherhood and premonitions can also produce this connection.

The Grand Pulse

The famous Hermetic statement engraved on the Emerald tablet states: "as above so below, as below, so above" and it assists us to look at the subtle energy principle of the Psychon pulse in its grandest role in the holistic motion of Creation. The emerald tablet containing Hermetic texts wisdom of Ancient Egypt was regarded by Arab and European Alche-mists as the foundation of their art. As we've seen, the eternal drop in the ocean with the Ziron at its center emerges as the eightfold spiraling pulse of the Psychon that manifests through the emotional and mental planes

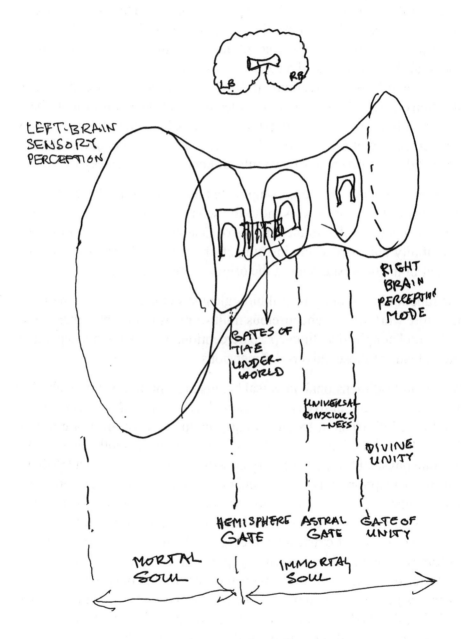

Fig.36 - The Tunnel and The Gates

down to the physical (electromagnetic) dimension. It stays for a short time and then moves back up the spiraling planes. This is the end goal in the grand plan of Creation. The harmonizing, stabilizing effect of the Ziron with its centering principle attracts everything back to the source. The total dissolving into the zero state is not a complete loss of every-thing gained in both directions of flow in Creation, it is becoming part of infinity where the information collected on all levels is brought back into the infinity of everything within the zero. This new form of totally non-personified blissful universal existence in the Divine light of the pri-mordial dimension creates new multi-dimensional universes.

Some may wonder how this complicated analysis of all those other di-mensions of Creation is relevant to the scientific approach of BioGeom-etry; the answer is that in the Physics of Quality they are part of the zero and infinity universal string instrument of Universal Harmonics and im-portant in the understanding of the origin of life force.

The functioning of our physical biological systems is based on the Laws of Nature working on subconscious multi-dimensional subtle energy lev-els beyond our physical time-space perception, making us an inseparable, integral part of those universal dimensions.

We are multi-dimensional universal beings present on several levels. The physical aspect of our lives is only a small manifestation that occurs with-in a limited dimension. Its animating principles, in contrast, are part of the life force functions within the limitless universal subtle energy. Our separate physical body is a sensory construct. Just as we have a left-brain sensory perception creating our separate ego and material presence, we have another part of us that combines individuality and universality in a limitless subtle existence. Ancient humanity had a combined perception of the two modes of existence which gave them the sense of unity with all forces of nature. The Ancient Egyptians lived by the Law of MAAT, the Neter of harmony of the universal order. This is only possible when humanity perceives the unity and beauty of the Laws of Nature as part of their individual physical being. Modern humanity can never achieve the universal natural order without the awareness of being one with the environment.

We cannot affect the quality of the drop separately while disregarding the ocean. The BioGeometry Physics of Quality revives the unifying centering concept, found in the secondary resonance between all strings in Universal Harmonics, to experience the full paradigm of ancient civilizations in its full multi-dimensional resonance. This centering unifying concept is active on all levels of Creation.

PART EIGHT
Time and the Universal Order

I am neither a professional Egyptologist nor a historian but rather a scientist researching subtle energy practices in the Ancient Egyptian civilization. I therefore do not give any official mainstream information about Ancient Egypt that can be found in the abundant literature but rather leave that to the experts in the field. My special fields, being an architect, are design and construction, and as the founder of BioGeometry, I use the Physics of Quality to uncover the subtle energy secrets behind their sciences. My research in monuments, rituals, and activities is conducted through this modern scientific Physics of Quality paradigm. I therefore share the information that relates to subtle energy at the core of the ancient beliefs and practices I've studied and leave out what is not relevant to the topic of energy quality.

MAAT in Ancient Egypt

The Ancient Egyptian civilization that flourished for thousands of years followed the "Universal Order" that was expressed as MAAT. Here are some aspects of this concept that are important for our discussion of subtle energy:

- MAAT, a Neter (Law of Nature) represents the Divine wisdom that manifests in universal harmony, order, and balance.
- MAAT, the Goddess of Truth, Justice, and Morality, generates balance within mind and heart, which in turn generates physical and spiritual harmonious integration.
- MAAT is the perfect "harmonizer of the pulse" that puts duality into motion
- The harmonizing power of the word "MAAED" brings harmony. Ancient Egyptian names were usually composed of energetic principles related to their function. They were pronounced to activate the special energetic effects associated with the power of nature (NTR). They were thus used as words of power.

This Universal Order governs, balances, and harmonizes the motion of the pulse and gives MAAT the function of the primordial Law of Time.

Weighing the Heart in the Hall of MAAT

In the hall of MAAT, the heart of the deceased was weighed against a feather. It was the quality of the higher subtle energy content in the physical heart that was actually being weighed, along with the extent to which the heart's subtle energy quality harmonized with the Universal Order of MAAT. In other words, the level of manifestation of universal values and principles of the heart in every action in life mattered to the Ancient Egyptians.

The pulse-harmonizing Law of Time manifests in the initial pulse of the human heart, from which all others in the body arise. The quality of the heartbeat expresses the harmony of the time pulse in its resonance with the universal order. In Ancient Egypt, if the time pulse were in complete harmony and balance, it would have no weight. If, however, the amplitudes or wavelength parts were not in balance, then the heart would outweigh the feather and the deceased would not cross into the spiritual realms and would be trapped in the perils of the underworld.

The Forty-Two Questions of Passage

The soul of the deceased had to answer forty-two questions to pass to the spiritual realms. The following is a list of questions that give an idea about the everyday values of the Ancient Egyptians. We have simplified them to be used as exercises in our courses. Unfortunately, the compiled translation from several sources and simplification necessary to be grasped by the modern mind takes away the depth and wisdom of the original language and meaning.

42 Negative Confessions

(Refer to http://www.blackhistoryheroes.com/2013/02/42-laws-of-maat-under-kemet-law-and.html for additional information)

1. I have not committed sin.
2. I have not committed robbery with violence.
3. I have not stolen.
4. I have not slain men or women.
5. I have not stolen food.
6. I have not swindled offerings.
7. I have not stolen from God/Goddess.
8. I have not told lies.
9. I have not carried away food.
10. I have not cursed.
11. I have not closed my ears to truth.
12. I have not committed adultery.
13. I have not made anyone cry.
14. I have not felt sorrow without reason.
15. I have not assaulted anyone.
16. I am not deceitful.
17. I have not stolen anyone's land.
18. I have not been an eavesdropper.
19. I have not falsely accused anyone.
20. I have not been angry without reason.
21. I have not seduced anyone's wife.
22. I have not polluted myself.
23. I have not terrorized anyone.
24. I have not disobeyed the Law.
25. I have not been exclusively angry.
26. I have not cursed God/Goddess.
27. I have not behaved with violence.
28. I have not caused disruption of peace.
29. I have not acted hastily or without thought.
30. I have not overstepped my boundaries of concern.
31. I have not exaggerated my words when speaking.
32. I have not worked evil.

33. I have not used evil thoughts, words, or deeds.

34. I have not polluted the water.

35. I have not spoken angrily or arrogantly.

36. I have not cursed anyone in thought, word, or deeds.

37. I have not placed myself on a pedestal.

38. I have not stolen what belongs to God/Goddess.

39. I have not stolen from or disrespected the deceased.

40. I have not taken food from a child.

41. I have not acted with insolence.

42. I have not destroyed property belonging to God/Goddess.

Today we would view this as a prohibitive exercise as it would be impossible to pass such a test by modern life standards. Jung's categorization of humanity can help us understand how the Ancient Egyptians found no difficulty in living with those principles. Ancient people were mainly sited in the right-brain type of perception. They felt a sense of oneness with the Laws of Nature and considered that their subconscious mind was part of their everyday perception. While primitive people are more animal-like and acted according to the Laws of Nature, ancient people had developed some left-brain type tools stemming from their right-brain counterparts (numbers, symbols, hieroglyphs, musical notes, geometry etc.). But he was still anchored in the right-brain mode and therefore consciously lived in harmony with the Laws of Nature and abided by the universal order. The Ancient Egyptian regarded everything in nature as sacred and lived in harmony with the archetypal dimension. The forty-two questions reflected their way of life. Coincidentally, the Greek historian Herodotus in the fourth century BC described the Egyptians of that time, who were already different from their ancestors, as "the healthiest, happiest, and most religious people he had ever seen."

The Heart and the Universal Order of Creation

MAAT was the Neter (Power of Nature) representing the Universal Order of Creation, which was the supreme law that governed the land and ensured the harmony and complementary equality of that great civilization.

Middle Eastern languages, such as Arabic and Hebrew, have several names for the heart. For example, the word "Leb" or "Lob" is found in the Old Testament and in the Quran. They refer to the complete inner being and equate the heart with the mind and the soul. The heart in Ancient Egyptian is represented by the Hieroglyph of a pot pronounced "ieb, or yieb." The reference here is not to the pot but rather to what it contains, a weightless subtle energy principle related to the universal order of MAAT, which is also the Law of Time manifesting through the primordial pulse of Creation. This puts the heart pulse in direct resonant connection with the universal order governed by the Law of Time. In this context, the different names for the heart refer to its presence in different forms on higher harmonic dimensions spanning from the physical all the way to the manifestation of the Law of Time that produces the harmonious complementary unity of duality.

The recent discovery that the heart contains brain cells gives credibility and meaning to the age-old reference to the term "intellect of the heart" that we find in ancient scriptures and traditions. The brain gets information from the sensory organs to build its perceived reality. The heart, however, is the provider of the physical pulse which brings the universal multi-dimensional time pulse into the physical dimension to govern all other sub-pulses of the organs. In other words, the heart pulse represents the harmonic presence of all dimensions of Creation in the human body. The heart brain is a doorway of the universal order governing and bringing harmony into the physical dimension. The heart brain in this role must have senses in the physical body as well as on the different universal subtle energy levels. Our research has identified some of the areas in the body that are linked to the heart brain: the top right brain area, the pineal gland, and the inner ear. They are all in extrasensory physical communication with the heart brain and bring it information about the quality of our activity in our world. At the same time, they bring harmonizing information from the heart brain into our biological functions and worldly interactions. The sensory perception that feeds the brain is limited to minute ranges from the total vibratory span of absolute reality.

The unperceived subtle energy levels and dimensions from vital, emotional, mental, and spiritual realms, as well as other parallel universes, are as much a part of our holistic being as the physical world is. The quality of these dimensions affects us in the same way our physical environment affects us. All species in nature are multi-dimensional beings but only a very small part of their being is accessible to the physical senses. The holistic quality of our actions, from intention to action, affects the heart and the harmony of its universal order. With only a minute amount of physical sensory information we cannot balance the other levels of our being that we cannot access. The heart brain brings that universal information into our subconscious mind so that we can balance our actions in a multi-dimensional holistic way and bring them into harmonious resonance with the natural Laws of Universal Order. In this sense, our physical actions become a harmonizing agent within the universal order and thus bring physical existence to its true role in Creation.

The universal information in the subconscious mind must, however, be translated into physical sensory time-space and brought into perception by the meaning level of the brain. There the harmonizing principles of Universal Order are perceived by the heart brain and emerge in our actions as meaningful values and ethics. Our conscience interacts with the universal laws within the ethical values and brings full multi-dimensional harmony into physical action. When this happens, the sensory and extra-sensory levels of existence bring forth perfect multi-dimensional balance in our actions. This is what I refer to as "excellence of action," which represents the highest and truest spiritual achievement possible. Excellence of action empowers physical action to introduce resonant harmony into all levels of Creation. All species in nature live—as did primitive humanity—by the unconscious intuitive guidance of the universal laws. Self-reflection and free will give the human being the potential to actively participate in, and empower, the universal order. The subtle energy quality content of the heart is weighed against the feather of MAAT to determine the person's level of participation in the universal order.

The Matriarchal and Patriarchal Personification of Divinity

The universal order is perceived as a holistic unifying harmony where everything in existence, on multiple levels, interacts to form the universal symphony of Creation. The connection to this universal state of evolution and Creation within an overall unity is anchored in the heart brain. It is also referred to as right-brain mode of perception. The fact that it operates on an unconscious, intuitive, instinctive level, governed by the Laws of Nature and geared towards life preservation, makes it feminine in nature. It is therefore represented by the female Neter MAAT. Her male consort, Thoth, is responsible for bringing knowledge to humanity.

The left-brain mode is characterized by analytical mental faculties. This works along the original path of outward spiraling motion in the original archetypal pulse of Creation. The right-brain/heart mode's inward spiraling motion towards the center of the pulse results in emotional qualities that have a unifying character. The two spiraling motions are interlinked through connections at every level of the spiral and are balanced by the centering action of the expanding and contracting Ziron pulse axis. This forms the inter-connected mental-emotional qualities of the active Universal Mind. This means that the two brain modes are manifestations of the components of one unity encompassing two different time-space modes. The left-brain mode with its outward radiating, dispersing, analytical and mental nature has masculine characteristics. When the holistic unity of the right-brain mode emerges through the linear sensory personification of the left-brain, the time-space dimension acquires dominating male attributes represented in a patriarchal concept of Divinity reinforced by our ever-increasing left-brain dominance. This left-brain dominance has produced all the benefits of a very efficient world of modern technology that has suppressed the unifying wisdom of the ethical values of the right-brain subconscious mode.

The forces of life preservation connected to the Laws of Nature that work on a subconscious level associate with the feminine. This concept is supported by the increased right brain function in the female that is reflected in the subconscious intuitive aspect of all her actions. We can trace the concept of the gender personification of the creative principle by looking at how humanity's development has shifted the brain's focus of perception from right to left hemisphere. The human figures people created in prehistoric times represent the mother goddess. The people who created the great ancient civilizations gave equal values to the male and female deities. The great shift in the focus of perception in the brain that produced modern humans anchored in place the patriarchal form of the creator, and we see this today in modern religions. This has led to the erosion of right-brain ethical values around spirituality, and it has increased the control of materialism. As a result, many people today seek to revive the matriarchal concept of the Deity.

We have reached a level of materialism that has no ethical boundaries, and this will produce a backlash of emergence in what Jung refers to as an emerging contemporary humanity. The personification of the Universal Mind will then move away from the patriarchal concept into a new spiritual holistic form that manifests within both genders. This is a gradual process that will not manifest in all humanity at once. Let us examine here how Consciousness is expected to move into higher dimensions in contemporary humanity.

The right-brain or heart mode is connected to our unconscious levels beyond our physical time-space perception. As such, it has a continuous presence in multiple time and space dimensions. It is equally present in all higher dimensions, and so it is simultaneously individual, collective, and universal. This means that our right-brain mode connects us to all forms of life, animate or inanimate, in all dimensions of a multi-level universal unity. We already exist in all higher dimensions. It is the left-brain sensory mode of consciousness that perceives the three physical dimensions, plus the flow of time as the fourth dimension, because it is related to motion in space. The other non-sensory dimensions are unperceived.

The female energy as an emotional force of attraction is moving towards the spiritual center and is in interaction with the outgoing male radiation at the spiral intersections. At those points of interaction, the male mental energy qualities are connected to the spiritual values of the inward female attraction. The perfect balance is when the focus of perception is properly centered between the inward and outward flows of the right and left hemisphere modes. When the great shift towards the left-brain male mode happened, and continues in its polarization towards more effective mental analytical functions, the balancing attributes of the right-brain spiritual connections were weakened. This continuous shift is happening differently in males and females, however. The male brain focus shift is much greater than in the female brain and only temporarily connects to the right-brain-mode with certain spiritual, artistic, sport-related and similar harmonizing activities. The female brain, however, is continuously connected to the wisdom of the right brain emotional, spiritual mode. The female and male are different species in the sense that the female brain still has many of the attributes of ancient humanity that created the great ancient civilizations.

The worldly male mental energies need to access the female emotional energies to find the spiritual values that are needed to balance mental actions. In other words, the male activity mode needs the spiritual gateway of the female energy to connect to the centering genderless Divine level.

It is only at death, with the complete shift out of the sensory mode of the physical body, that the immortal soul perceives all higher dimensions and moves through them, depending on its acquired subtle energy quality. In dreams and out-of-body and near-death experiences, we perceive some of those dimensions. Certain spiritual practices, rituals, meditations, visualizations, and drugs can bring our perception to some of those dimensions. However, the experience will be a physical, sensory, left-brain time-space translation through the meaning level of the brain, with its culturally related content. The movement of the focus of perception to a central position between right and left-brain modes will give contemporary humanity conscious access to additional dimensions through left-brain perception. To sum it up, we all exist on all dimensions of Creation from the physical up to the Divine center at the Psychon core of manifested Creation. Some of the dimensions within the subconscious levels of humanity will move into conscious perception through a left-brain translation. However, the direct awareness of those extra dimensions will reinforce our unity with our environment and raise ethical values from the subconscious mind, and these will be directly perceived through our actions. This new category of humanity will be counteracted by the sinking of modern humanity deeper into left-brain materialism. Hopefully this transition state will end with the emergence of a worldwide contemporary humanity taking us away from the feared end of our world into the prophesied Golden Age.

Words of Power for Time Balance

In all beliefs and cultures, we find the concept of "words of power." In modern religions, the Divine Names or attributes are the words of power, and they are believed to have very potent qualities expressed through their subtle energy combination of letters and vowels. This concept takes us back to the primordial right-brain language of humanity where letters and vowels expressed and activated energetic functions.

In Ancient Egypt words of power called "HeKaw" were used to perform energetic effects that enhanced physical activity. They were also used by adepts to perform acts of magic. There are certain words that restore the time balance:

Sounds connected to TIME

Divine pulse maker Law of Time	**MAعED**	عع ع•
Divine Time attribute of Life	**HحASIEB**	حح ح•
Divine Harmony and beauty	**AZIEZ**	Z ز•

©1995-2019 BioGeometry Energy Systems Ltd.

The Divine Names of many traditions are considered words of power provided they are pronounced in their original language—such as Ancient Egyptian, Arabic, Aramaic, Ancient Hebrew, Sanskrit, or other original forms. These words embody subtle energy qualities that resonate with and categorize the powers of nature and the Laws of Creation.

They are magnifications of the human attributes that the mind uses in its personification of the abstract Divine Laws beyond our mental possibilities. They should be regarded as a human categorization and not the actual Divine level.

The powers of the Laws of Nature are the building blocks of Creation. They can be grouped and referenced according to numerical qualities such as 1, 3, 7, 8, 9, 10, 11 or 12, depending on the attributes or function referred to, or in the spiritual qualities of 16, 19, 28, 33 as in the BioGeometry series. Their creative principle as the many Laws of Nature or attributes of the Divine can be expressed in larger numbers such as 72, 81 or 99 (with the quality of 9 reflecting action and transformation) to show their creative attributes and laws behind the innumerable powers of nature.

PART NINE
Energetic Time Travel

According to the laws of Universal Harmonics, all Creation, including its parallel dimensions from beginning to end, is an intercommunicative unified system. Past and future are parts of the equally present and connected whole. In a way, past and future exist within each other. The time pulse that manifests as the Psychon, the building unit of Creation, is harmonically present in all levels and dimensions up to the whole unity of everything in existence. The bi-directional connection, communication, and information exchange between beginning and end are equally valid from the smallest to the largest dimensions of Creation forming a universal ever-present unified system.

This system contains the information of everything that exists with all possible probabilities in an ever-present state from which all manifestations of existence in all time-space moments arise. Once we understand this multi-directional, multi-dimensional, interconnected universal unity, we can examine concepts like free will as a freedom of movement between a system of probabilities that gain weight according to resonant associations. We can also understand such concepts like the book where everything in Creation is written, or the Akashic Records, and similar beliefs in all cultures. In the Islamic tradition, the night of the fourteenth of the lunar month of "Shaaban" is considered very special in the sense that it is the time when a prayer is said to shift our destiny into better probabilities.

The simultaneous existence of probabilities in the ever-present container of universal information sets the stage for interconnected parallel dimensions and universes where copies of us exist.

We have not yet developed the ability to physically travel in time. The linearity of physical time puts constraints on the ability of material substances to travel into the past, future, or other dimensions or parallel universes. Our emotional and mental subtle energy levels, however, are not bound by the confines of linear time flow and can move in any direction in time and space. Our emotional and mental awareness can move forwards as in imagination or precognition, as well as backwards in time to recall and re-live past events through memory. Similarly, it can access other dimensions resulting in subconscious effects.

This access allows us to change a past or future emotional quality that is affecting a present-day event. The sensory perception of the ego cannot travel in time but the extrasensory awareness on the subconscious emotional and mental levels can. In other words, our mental-emotional soul can move freely in all dimensions as in dreams, near-death experiences, or out-of-body travel. In such experiences, there is a possibility of temporary materialization in other time-space physical locations. In such cases the materialization can be formed by physical matter from the surroundings or by non-electromagnetic mental-emotional particles that can be perceived by physical senses, although they are equally physical in their own dimension. This is, however, not time travel of the earthly physical body. The dematerialization and re-materialization of physical objects across time or space distances has been demonstrated by some people with special abilities. This is one of the research goals of modern science. I refer the reader to the physicist Dr. Claude Swanson in his book trilogy, *The Synchronized Universe*.

This type of instantaneous jumping to different time-space events through resonant association is the normal way of moving between the pages of stacked time. We get glimpses of this type of movement in dreams and psychic experiences. Once we permanently leave our physical body this becomes the normal state of affairs.

Moving into Different Life Stages

All the situations we create exist as Experions in stacked time dimensions, as is the case in dreams, out-of-body travel, near-death experiences, and existence after physical death. The Experions are formed of situations from all stages of physical life from childhood to old age. Resonant association with people or places at different physical life stages between related Experions can take us backwards and forwards from one situation to another. The non-physical make-up of the soul will materialize through its mental-emotional particles. In those dimensions "jumping" between different time-space stacked-page Experions with material bodies is the normal way of moving around in an ever-present existence.

Universes that exist beyond the speed of light do not have the constraints of linear time. They can be made of materialized mental-emotional particles. Based on our analysis of time-space dimensions beyond the linearity of physical existence, we can deduct that materialized life forms in those worlds of non-physical, purely mental-emotional universes—which we do not perceive with our physical senses—would have the ability to travel forwards and backwards in time directly with their material bodies or by using some modes of transportation. They could travel to any point in time or space just as we can travel between physical destinations.

In BioGeometry, we work with subtle energetic resonant laws that allow possibilities such as subtle-energetic time-space travel or simultaneous presence in multiple locations. These are resonant travel possibilities of the extrasensory mental-emotional right-brain mode. This allows information exchange between dimensions beyond our physical time-space boundaries. The Physics of Quality extends through all vibratory dimensions from zero to infinity. The laws of resonance have no boundaries and they are a main factor in forming the overall unity of Creation. We can therefore use BioGeometry qualitative measurement methods to access information from any part of this universal unity. Some of our instruments are specially tailored for such work.

Correcting the Present Through the Past

Let us take as an example one of the exercises we use in our BioGeometry courses to reduce the effects of previous situations, such as indigestion after a meal. We can imagine the infinity sign to reduce the stress of moving against the current of linear time, and then shift our awareness back to the past meal. Subtle energy moves to where our awareness and imagination go. Next, we can imaginatively place a BioSignature, L90 BioGeometry shape, or a blessing into the imagined picture to correct the energy quality (Figure 37). This will immediately reduce the mental-emotional impact of the disturbance on the physical level. This concept can be applied to more complex past situations of all kinds to correct the energy quality. The L90 shape is one of several similar shapes with different angles that will be discussed in more detail when we explore the design topic.

Fig.37 - BioGeometry L90 Shape

The emotional quality associated with any object, person, or situation in our memory bank is ever-present in our system. It is good to start with the most negative effects of people or situations and send an image of an L90 without any meaning behind it into it. Unconditional blessings in most cases carry unconscious biases with them, which is why abstract geometrical shapes work better. It is not very effective to protect yourself using any method you might commonly practice if you feel harmful effects coming from someone, as the person's image is already embedded in the databank of your memory and it cannot be erased. So, changing the energy quality in a sort of healing process using abstract shapes is significantly more effective. It is good to remember that every person is a Divine manifestation that we should hold sacred and not judge in any way. The actions and not the person should be judged. This separation of people and actions leads to a state of accepting all others, which is the highest form of spiritual initiation.

The Staircase of Life

Another BioGeometry exercise we refer to as "the Staircase of Life" takes us back in time to project our present energy into a past moment. This allows us to measure and correct any "steps" that were "cracked" through any negative self-judgements we associate with the events.

As we imagine each step in our life's timeline, we use BioGeometry shapes or Signatures to correct them. This reduces their harmful emotional and mental effect on our present-day subtle energy system. We can also extend the steps into the future beyond our present age. Different forms of this exercise can be used to work on future events.

1. Visualize your life as a staircase with your date of birth, or earlier, at the bottom and each step representing another year in your life. It is usually more effective and efficient to count forward from the start of your life than counting backward as many of the problems in the later stages of life can have roots in totally different disturbances that occurred earlier. This means that correcting from the beginning forward will resolve many later disturbances and the number of later disturbances will be reduced.

2. Counting steps backwards might be more practical if a disturbance has only emerged in recent years. This can be the case with trauma or diseases.

3. Counting forwards one "step" at a time, measure your personal wavelength on a pendulum, preferably BioGeometry's IKUP pendulum. You are seeking to detect disturbances without reference to any meaning and without trying to associate the step to a certain situation. The measurement of subtle energy quality should be totally abstract so that your subconscious mind, or any form of self-deception, does not interfere with the process by hiding problems from you as a form of protection. Once the pendulum detects a disturbance by reversing the direction of rotation, we can apply corrective measures.

4. The most effective way to correct a disturbance at a step/year where a disturbance is found is to use a BG shape such as, for

example, an "L90" or the BioGeometry "Clearing Card" and/or "Planes of Nature Harmonizing Card" (Figure 38). The "cracked" steps are a result of our own judgement of the situation.

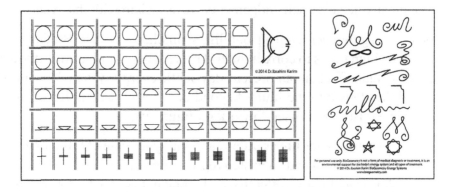

Fig.38 - Planes of Nature Harmonizing Card (Left) &
Clearing Card (Right)

We usually take our feelings during the situation with us after the situation is long gone to become a continuous judgement of the event. The way to resolve the negative judgment that causes the crack in the step is to understand that it is a building block for what we are today. This means that it was an exam along the way. Unless we learn a lesson from it, we will not pass the exam. Once we can analyze the situation in retrospect and find how it positively affected us through the lesson learned, we will start appreciating that it happened and understand its importance for the whole staircase of life. Unless we reach a level where we are thankful for how it has benefitted us for the rest of our lives, we will not repair the crack. This is easier said than done as the solution must come from the conscious as well as the unconscious level. Professionals in the field of human psychology are trained to take their patients along that tedious labyrinth. Using a geometrical shape to harmonize that subtle energy quality disturbance in an abstract way is a much easier method.

Let me give you a visual example. Imagine a person is an empty cup, and a pebble falls into it making a sound and causing the cup to shake. The shake makes the pebble move, resulting in more sound and shake. A vicious circle arises. We cannot catch and remove the pebble as it is continuously in motion. This is a very complicated situation that requires a trained professional to detect and follow the pattern of motion from its starting point so as to predict where to catch it. There is another way that does not involve detecting the complex pattern of pebble motion: if we see the cup shaking, and stop it by holding it from the outside, the pebble will stop moving. In this stable motionless state, we can easily remove it, if need be.

5. After the harmonizing intervention using a BioGeometry shape, or other method, a second measurement is needed to ensure the correction has been made. This is done by going back a step or two before the corrected one and measuring forwards to make sure it is repaired. Otherwise, the corrective measure must be repeated until the step is harmonized.

6. Once the measurement and correction of the steps reaches the present day, one can continue for a few years into the future as a future cracked step can affect the present just like a previous one can.

7. This exercise can be used to correct the effect of any location or object we have interacted with regardless of whether we know it or not, as the abstract measurement and BioGeometry correction will automatically take care of it.

8. This method can be tailored to harmonize the interactions in a collective way of small or large groups, regardless of their causes. The key here is to calibrate the pendulum or other measuring device on the collective aspect of the entity, which can be a family, classroom, school, company, or even a whole country. This correction will, however, have to be repeated whenever changes to the original entity, like additional people or change of location, occur. The application on larger continuously changing groups like a neighborhood or country must be repeated daily to be effective.

In such cases, we use Google maps of the place to perform the measurement and correction.

Creating Material Objects in Other Dimensions

Imagination into the future is a very powerful tool to change the quality of the present as well. It is like creating a goal that pulls one towards it, affecting choices and actions at every step. In our physical dimension, it can greatly enhance the quality of life. Imagination is a mental, emotionally laden visualization tool that can indirectly affect our physical life, but in a non-physical dimension it is a powerful tool to create a material reality. This means that we can build material objects in our future non-physical existence while still living in the physical dimension. One can imagine a whole building like a temple, home, spa, or even a natural landscape, and keep visiting it and adding more detail from time to time.

The physical life, although very temporary in comparison, is a unique opportunity to create the quality of the more permanent next dimension in which we will continue to live. Since it will be projected from our own subconscious content, we can create a harmonious mental-emotional state of total serenity in our inner being. The left-brain sensory perception creates the ego which will ultimately serve the senses. This is the root of all imbalances in life. This imbalance will affect the quality of interaction with the right brain unconscious content that forms our immortal soul. Accessing the right brain harmonizing aspects of the universal Laws of Nature, through art, sports, meditation, prayer, and similar activities, is important to bring universal harmony into the daily sensory experience. The right brain extrasensory perception, in its experience of the unity of Creation, will also have a positive effect on accepting all others as components of that unity, seeing the sacredness of all living species, and inducing constructive judgement of actions and not persons. Every person is a manifestation of the sacred, so our judgement and corrective measures should be geared towards the actions. With such a quality of inner perception we can construct our future heaven.

The Sky

Our sky is a very good example of the simultaneous presence of multiple time dimensions. The stars we see projected on the surface of our atmosphere are a result of light traveling from the original celestial bodies from different distances in the Universe. The light projected on the "screen" of the sky can travel millions of years from far distances or for a short time from nearby stars. However, the stars appear as if they are all present now. When we look at the sky, we see all the stars at the same time, but we are viewing a manifestation of different times. Some of those stars could be long gone by the time their light reaches Earth.

Observing this simultaneous presence of the projection of different times and spaces breaks down the sensory linear time perceived by the leftbrain and takes us into the universal bliss of the right brain dimension. The night sky is a very powerful doorway into our subconscious realms. Sky gazing enhances creativity and has a powerful healing effect. Artists have depicted it in many ways in their creations throughout history.

Words

The resonance between octaves in a musical instrument goes in both directions from the shortest to the longest string lengths. In the Physics of Quality, we have extended our string instrument to cover all string lengths from zero to infinity to express the concept of *Universal Harmonics*. This model is, however, only limited to one dimension and must be expanded to cover many string instruments intercommunicating through time and space.

BioGeometry instructor Kris Attard devised an exercise to show that during resonance qualities travel forward and backward in time and while demonstrating it one day we asked a person to pronounce a vowel forward and backward and measured how this affected the energy quality of all present. The "Aaaa" produced a harmonizing quality that raised the energy, while the "Eiiiiii" had the opposite effect. We pronounced the letter B once as in "Biiiiiiiiiiiii" and found that it corrected the quality which in turn raised the energy. We had the person place the B at the end of the "Eiiiiii" sound. Surprisingly, the harmonizing effect started in the beginning before the B was added at the end. To make sure that the intention of placing the B at the end did not affect the beginning, as many researchers had found in different experiments, we placed two pieces of paper face down on a table, one with a "B" written on it, and the other with nothing. While the person was sounding the "Eiiiiii" a third person chose one of the shuffled papers and showed it to the person making the sound with the instruction to add whatever was written on the selected piece of paper to the end of their sounding. We tested several times and find that every time the beginning showed uplifting energy quality, that paper recommended the letter B be placed at the end; when the quality was lowered, the paper was empty. This exercise was a demonstration of how the beginning and end affect each other.

Let us take this exercise a bit further to note that the letters in words we pronounce affect other people's subtle energy quality forwards and backwards in multiple ways as the number of letters grows. Experiencing different time flows simultaneously opens a gateway to the universality of the right brain unconscious universal realms. Words can take the quality of their meanings across to the right brain. The power of sounds and words puts the speaker and the listener into the universality of right brain connectivity. Critical observance can show how speaking is at the same time a way of accessing universal subconscious information and the emergence of creativity. Knowing the subtle energy quality of individual sounds and letters, as well as their combinations, was one of the most powerful secret sciences of the ancient temple sciences. In Ancient Egypt, the words of power were called "HEKAW." In modern Arabic, this word is still used in different forms in relation to storytelling.

PART TEN

The Time Pulse

The Law of Time produces and governs the pulse forming process in all levels of Creation. It emerges from the Ziron to produce and govern the bidirectional eight-level spiraling motion of the Psychon. The Psychon pulse takes place within the expanded Ziron forming the periphery. This is the primordial archetype of motion that can be represented as the dot in the center of the circle. The Ziron manifests equally as the center and the container or the zero of nothingness and the infinity of everything. The infinite number of axial emanations in all directions of the pulse are like the spherical radiation from a light source. To put it in a geometrical configuration that we can work with, we will imagine the endless rays from the source as axes of expansion and retraction in all directions.

Let's analyze the wave-forming attributes of one of those diametrical, axial pulses enclosing the internal eight-fold bidirectional, pulsating, axial spiraling motion of the Psychon (Figure 39). If we look at one single pulse from the eight levels of the Psychon we may understand how the Law of Time works within it. The Ziron at the center expands to form the radiation of an eightfold spiraling pulse that then retracts back into the center. It is the motion of a center expanding to form a sphere that retracts back into it. This axis represents a unit within a multi-axial bi-directional spherical motion. The central axis of the spirals that emanates and retracts into the Ziron with every pulse is on a higher dimension than the resulting wave shape as it contains the archetype creating the wave forms of the pulse.

Looked at it in section, it is the relationship of the transcendental center to the periphery of the circle. The axis will exert its control on the dualistic ripple keeping the two upper and lower amplitudes of the wave motion in balance as well as the two parts of the wavelength. The Law of Time creates and manifests as the unperceivable centering axis from a higher dimension containing the forming principles of the resulting wave form. The harmony at the essence of all levels of Creation is based on the correct functioning of the Law of Time from the smallest to the largest pulse. Creation rises to existence through pulse. This makes the forming Law of Time the Divine backbone of all Creation.

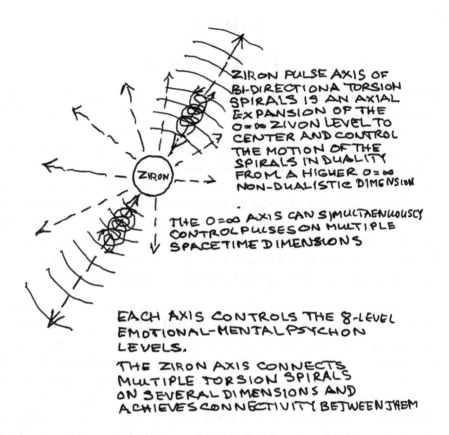

ZIRON PULSE AXIS OF
BI-DIRECTIONA TORSION
SPIRALS IS AN AXIAL
EXPANSION OF THE
O=∞ ZIVON LEVEL TO
CENTER AND CONTROL
THE MOTION OF THE
SPIRALS IN DUALITY
FROM A HIGHER O=∞
NON-DUALISTIC DIMENSION

THE O=∞ AXIS CAN SIMULTAENUOUSLY
CONTROL PULSES ON MULTIPLE
SPACETIME DIMENSIONS

EACH AXIS CONTROLS THE 8-LEVEL
EMOTIONAL-MENTAL PSYCHON
LEVELS.

THE ZIRON AXIS CONNECTS
MULTIPLE TORSION SPIRALS
ON SEVERAL DIMENSIONS AND
ACHIEVES CONNECTIVITY BETWEEN THEM

THE PSYCHON IS A SPHERICAL EMANATION
WITH ENDLESS NUMBER OF AXIS MAKING IT
PRESENT ON MULTIPLE DIMENSIONS.

Fig.39 - Bidirectional Diametrical Pulse

The ancients understood the Universe as a multifold manifestation of Divinity and perceived the sacredness of everything in their world. The concept of a primordial twist or torsion in the time pulse of the Psychon supports Kozyrev's theories connecting time and torsion. I refer the reader again to the three volumes of *The Synchronized Universe* series by MIT physicist Dr. Claude Swanson. In BioGeometry we work with the Physics of Quality to identify the primordial motion of life force that produces the quality of QL-Torsion as an integral part of the first manifestation of the duality of Creation. While torsion describes the spiraling motion in subtle energy, QL–Torsion refers to the qualitative effect of torsion on a receiving living system. QL-Torsion is therefore the result of the effect of life force in torsion on the human subtle energy system. The bi-directional torsion within the Psychon creates the mental-emotional attributes of subtle energy and therefore resonates directly with those levels in living systems.

That is the reason that the mind influences all levels of life force within QL-Torsion as well as the pulse components of time controlled by the Law of Time in the Ziron pulse center (Figure 40). In this sense we can regard the spiraling motion of QL-Torsion expressed in the rotation of a pendulum instrument held by the human body as a direct indication of the quality-of-life force. We will refer to it in our work as positive energizing or negative depleting quality of life force (+LF, -LF).

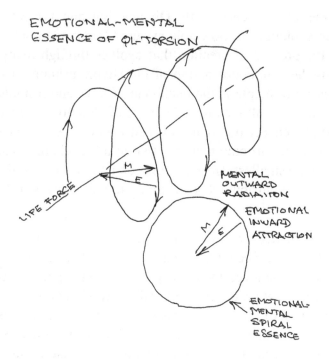

Fig.40 - Emotional-Mental Essence of QL-Torsion

Distortion of The Time Pulse

Can this universal Divine Law of Time be disturbed by any action? Yes! Any type of species exercising a limited form of free will that results in an imbalance between the entwined emotional centripetal force of attraction and the mental centrifugal emanation will affect the harmony and balance that the Law of Time exercises over the pulse. This means that the human disturbance of the time pulse must play a role in the evolution of Creation because our limited free will is a tool of the Divine mind. What we see as the disturbance of the time pulse and the problems created by the resulting imbalance creates tension, which is needed to fuel our free will and direct it towards an awareness of, and attraction to, the Ziron center. This is the drop in the ocean given just enough individuality of perception to create the amount of separation needed to create an awareness of the ocean. It is, however, a temporary state created by a temporary kind of tension.

How does the self-awareness of the Divine origin and its creative process serve in the evolution of the whole system? It serves to help us understand that the process of creation that evolves through many dualistic levels needs the continuous action of the Divine primordial level. The Ziron centering principle is the backbone of it all and it holds the continuous evolution of all the dualistic levels of Creation. The background universal subtle energy of Creation is self-aware. The self-awareness of the Universe is an attribute that is active in all levels of Creation from the largest to the smallest. Here we differentiate between self-awareness and free will as an attribute that triggers different degrees of freedom of choice of every species.

Self-awareness is triggered by a slight tension between the duality components that activate free will, which is an attribute of the original pulse. On a holistic Divine level, the duality in Creation happens within a harmonic hierarchy that produces an overall unity. Creation in this sense is the differentiation of the components of that overall unified system. It is an interplay of qualities that produces this dimension of diversity within the overall unity. Our world exists in what is at most a temporary surface-deep phenomenon.

Correcting the distortions of the time pulse is an important role that humanity plays towards the continuous evolution and regeneration of the whole system. What on one level seems to look like the wrongful actions of the human species is a Divine tool of stabilization, harmony, and the spiritual evolution of duality. Self-reflection is an integral attribute of universal Consciousness that is accessed by some species with different degrees of free will and self-judgement.

Harmonizing the Time Pulse: The BG3 Connection

Measurements show that a time imbalance in a wave will produce an imbalanced Vertical Negative Green (VNG) quality; when balanced it emits the harmonizing BG3 spiritual quality. The connection of the time balance with BG3 is very interesting. It shows that the Law of Time that governs the pulse phenomena in Creation creates two pathways of motion from and towards the spiritual dimensions. The balance of time within the pulse means that the central Ziron axis acts as a wormhole doorway to the primordial Divine. Pulses have a directional movement in their dimension as well as a multi-dimensional connection to their Divine origin. Our perceived Reality is a physical painting on an invisible Divine canvas. It is the invisible canvas that holds it all together and allows it all to appear. Human DNA, with its two spirals and unperceived central axis that holds them in perfect balance, is an example of this.

Time Pulse and Life Force

The connective axial Ziron wormhole at the center of the pulse brings life force in from the primordial level. Pulses are alive. All kinds of pulses that form the building blocks of Creation are "life units."

Let us examine the factors and actions that influence the Law of Time waves. These can be verified by harmonic resonant measurements with BioGeometry tools that we will examine in the following chapters.

- Reflection of any kind of waves, natural or not, on man-made surfaces distorts the time-wave balance

- The dark sides of unnatural objects show a distortion of time pulse
- Shadows of man-made objects of any kind on natural ground or unnatural floors show a distortion of the time-wave balance
- Shadows of natural objects on natural ground have BG3 quality
- Shadows of natural objects on man-made floors lose their BG3 quality and distort the time pulse
- The dark side of natural objects have the BG3 quality
- Unethical emotional or mental intentions or actions distort the time-wave balance

The Quality of Shadows

Shadows created by any object have qualities that can be different from those of the object itself.

- Shadows from a plant on the natural ground will have BG3 whether the plant itself has it or not. The shadow will furthermore carry the same life force as the plant
- The shadow of a plant, whether it has BG3 or not, will not have BG3 or life force qualities when it falls on artificial or modified materials
- The shadow of buildings or any unnatural products falling on a grass, ground, or a plant will cancel the BG3 and life force in the area under the shadow but not around it
- The shadow of any type of object falling on a BioGeometry-designed object will have BG3 and life force even if the object itself does not
- Sitting on the natural ground or grass in the shadow of a tree is a very effective healing energy-balancing practice. It is like being in a sacred power spot
- The shadow of the body from artificial light on a natural surface will give BG3. From the shadow's point of view the type of light is irrelevant. But the direct effect or reflection is different
- Black and white reflections of man-made objects in water have a strong BG3 quality

The Power of Shadows

The shadow of a human being will carry all the information in the unconscious levels of the person and transmit them to other people or objects. The information exchange here is qualitative so it will give the qualitative effect of the content without the actual meaning or information of the content. What is translated as content by the recipient is resonant information from the database of the receiver and not the actual content. The qualities of the receiver are also transmitted to the original person in this two-way communication.

This concept will give us a broader understanding of how the effect of other people's shadows, or any other type of shadow in the surroundings, can affect our mood and health. Choosing the right shadow environments becomes an important factor that shapes the evolution of our health and mental-emotional makeup in general. It is therefore of great importance to use any form of BioGeometry product to emit the harmonizing BG3 quality into our surroundings.

Darkness is the Shadow of the Earth

The above concept also applies at night when we are subjected to the qualitative effect from conscious and unconscious levels of the earth. The collective information from all humanity and other life forms also affects this two-way transmission.

At night, the earth is replenishing our information systems and thus regenerating our psychic and biological life functions. This regeneration is greatly diminished in modern buildings which are not connected to the life force of the earth.

Our unnatural buildings will cancel the regenerating effect of the earth at night. Neither synthetic building materials nor natural ones will solve the problem. We need to know how to connect our buildings to the life force of the earth regardless of building methods.

The BioGeometry design principles restore the connection with the earth by creating a subtle energy vortex that draws in life force with the spiritual quality of a healing Earth sacred power spot. The BioGeometry design principles are introduced in the appendix of *Back To A Future For Mankind* and will be expanded upon in upcoming chapters.

Natural Shadow Healing and Right-Brain Perception

Restoring the balance of the time pulse by reinforcing the spiritual balance of Ziron connection results in a balanced interaction between positive and negative QL-Torsion. In other words, it balances the in- and outflow "breathing" of life force. This brings harmony into the life force functions on our physical, vital, emotional, and mental levels through the restored balance of the spiritual connection. What's more, we know that the balance of the time pulse in the reflections, dark sides, and shadows in our perceived environment will activate the right-brain mode of perception and enhance all kinds of spiritual, artistic, and health-related activities. Here are some ways to interact with shadows to balance the time pulse in our biological functions:

> • Sitting on natural ground facing and looking at or touching one's own shadow. The light can be from natural or artificial sources. This shadow dimension is a very powerful gateway into multi-dimensional universal information

> • Sitting in the shadow of a natural object on the natural ground

> • Combining the above two points by sitting on natural ground in the shadow of a natural object while facing and looking at or touching one's own shadow

> • The shadow of one hand falling on the other hand or any part of the body. The type of light source is irrelevant. The hand can also be formed so that the shadow from the fingers fall into the palm of the same hand while connecting mentally to the body part you want to heal or placing/pointing the other hand on the organ you want to heal (Figure 41)

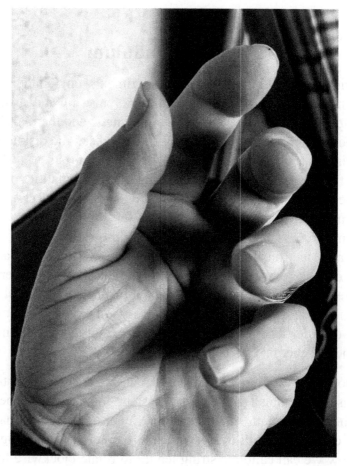

Fig.41 - Finger Shadow on Hand

PART ELEVEN
The Time Pendulum

In the original quantitative Russian experiments on torsion, scientists used a pendulum in the form of a disk hung on a string and covered with a bell-shaped glass container with electromagnetic and thermal shielding. Melting ice placed at the top of the disk then caused the disk to rotate in a clockwise direction (refer to Figure 4). It is important to differentiate this from the use of pendulums in detecting life force qualities of the body within the BioGeometry system of QL-Torsion. In the Russian torsion experiments, the disk rotation was due to the loss of energy caused by the melting process, the rotation indicating the existence of torsion. If the ice was placed in front of a mirror the reflected waves changed the direction of disk rotation. The direction of rotation or string length was not calibrated to indicate a certain quality, it just proved the existence of a spiraling force referred to as torsion. This loss of energy is accompanied by a loss of order labelled "entropy." This emanating loss of energy can be absorbed to energize a receiving system.

In BioGeometry, by contrast, we want to measure the effect that the melting ice has on the human subtle energy system. In this case, the pendulum string is held between the thumb and forefinger of the human hand. The direction of rotation will differ with each hand and with string length, as we know we can calibrate string length to rotate clockwise for either negative or positive polarity over a battery, for example. If the melting ice is placed on the top of the right hand directly above the string, we get a counterclockwise pendulum rotation. If we bring the melting ice under the pendulum, which is how we usually measure, the rotation changes direction. If we use our left-hand index finger to point at the melting ice, the rotation reverses again. In any of the methods above, the direction of the rotation indicates the quality of energy gain by the body. With further calibration of the pendulum with a color or other scale, the quality of energy gain can be assessed. The Time Pendulum is usually used to indicate gain or loss of energy (Figure 42).

Fig.42 - Time Pendulum

Due to the multiple variables affecting how the calibration of the pendulum expresses the quality of measurement, one should consistently use the same method of calibration when measuring. This can all be overcome by using BioGeometry horizontal or vertical dial pendulums, which are calibrated according to polarized angles. By calibrating a dial pendulum to a scale of quality, we can fine-tune the pendulum reaction to determine the quality of the life force activating the QL-Torsion on our subtle energy system.

In the quantitative torsion experiment it is the subtle energy emanation from the melting ice that is turning the pendulum. In the second QL-Torsion experiment it is the effect of the melting ice that affects the energy emanation of the human being which produces the rotation of the pendulum.

The Origin of the BioGeometry Time Pendulum

In order to create a resonant connection with the primordial harmony of the time-pulse quality, I designed a BioGeometry pendulum tool using the principle of resonance of shape across the universal harmony of dimensions. The resulting geometrical shape of the "Time-Pulse Pendulum," referred to simply as the Time Pendulum, expresses the bi-directional time-pulse emerging from the center into duality. The exact locations of the two holes on the pendulum body (slightly offset to the outside) are an important factor in creating the dynamic stability of the time pulse.

The Time Pendulum, held in its horizontal configuration on melting ice will rotate a few times in each direction to indicate a disturbance in the time pulse, as sensed by the body. The pendulum rotation will also restore the balance of the time pulse. In this case, the quality of dissipation of life force within torsion, as sensed by the body, is reversed indicating restored balance of time pulse even though the ice is melting. The melting ice is losing energy while giving a regenerating life force quality to the body. This reverses the direction of the body's QL-Torsion reaction. In BioGeometry we refer to this state of positive life force (+LF) as the "Al-Kareem Quality Field."

On a harmonized time-pulse, this pendulum will rotate continuously clockwise, indicating the existence of positive life force and the Al-Kareem Quality Field. If the time-pulse quality is disturbed, this pendulum will rotate a few times in one direction and reverse to rotate in the opposite direction when it is held over the object. To restore balance, we allow the pendulum to go through these opposite rotations until it stops. We then take the pendulum off the object and return it so we can check that we are getting a continuous clockwise rotation. Laying the pendulum on an object for a minute will restore the balance of its life force.

Examples of Exercises That Can Be Completed with the Time Pendulum:

1. **Testing the state of life force energy dissipation or regeneration in the environment.**
   The Time Pendulum is held at the top of the string and placed over the location or object to be measured. The other hand can also be used to point at the object or space. In either case a counterclockwise rotation will indicate negative QL-Torsion indicating loss of life force (-LF). A clockwise rotation indicates the presence of the positive QL-Torsion and the presence of the quality that we refer to as the "Al-Kareem Quality Fields (+LF).
2. **Checking the Toroidal Grid quality.**
   The Al-Kareem Quality Fields, which will be explained in detail in a dedicated chapter, enhance life force by creating a positive

QL-Torsion in the subtle energy environment. The Al-Kareem Quality fields rise in curved planes at a diagonal inclination of forty-five degrees and have a final curved ceiling above which we find negative QL-Torsion. There is a certain balance in the atmosphere as well as in all levels and dimensions of Creation, from the smallest to the largest, where negative life force/QL-Torsion is absorbed somewhere else as positive life force/QL-Torsion. This interactive balance can happen across dimensions and levels. This life force exchange can happen between physical, vital, emotional, mental, and spiritual levels. In contrast to the quantitative criteria of torsion, QL-Torsion is present in many qualities that can be detected through any of the different qualitative scales and measured through its effect on the human energy field. According to the Laws of Universal Harmonics, those QL-Torsion qualities have resonant presence in the electromagnetic physical world, as well as in all other slower or faster compression wave dimensions.

3. **Testing Materials.**
   This pendulum can also be used to test materials before and after harmonizing with BG3.
4. **Rotation Direction.**
   The Time Pendulum will rotate clockwise on the shadow of an object on natural ground and counterclockwise when the shadow falls on artificial surfaces.

PART TWELVE
The Living System of Qualities

My path to creating BioGeometry started with my studies in the history of architectural monuments and building traditions. Excavations at different depths at ancient monument sites showed remnants of sacred buildings from earlier civilizations; this revealed that the location was more important than the building. The spot would have been held sacred and used as the center of worship by the surrounding community over thousands of years, regardless of their changing beliefs and cultural traditions. The quality of the subtle energy of the place must have been identified as very special by all subsequent cultures. The energy found in those Earth energy power spots had special harmonizing, healing, and multi-dimensional communication properties that humanity obviously regarded as sacred.

Luxor Temple Upper Egypt is a very good example of the sacred role of a location throughout different historical periods. It was originally built around four thousand years ago. In later, more recent eras, a Christian church and a Muslim mosque were built inside its boundaries. Those seemingly different religions all chose the same spot as their center of worship. This, in a way, expresses the underlying unity of all beliefs that might seem different on the surface.

In choosing their building location, ancient builders used several methods of identifying the spot's quality of subtle energy. These special locations would initially be identified through simple observation: most had natural water springs or lakes that had a very special healing water quality. The plants looked healthier. Pigeons passing over those areas would break their flight formation and circle over the spot a few times before regrouping and continuing their flight. Goats and sheep would be placed in the area for a couple of weeks and then sacrificed, after which the quality of their meat would be examined. Milk and meat in these areas did not ferment. Dowsing with calibrated rods and staffs would identify the special quality of energy and water.

BioGeometry Centering and Life Force Qualities

BioGeometry has its roots in the essence of those ancient building rituals and mirrors their goal of achieving a connection to the higher dimensions that was accessible in those special Earth locations. It grew out of my research into the centering, harmonizing, and healing properties found in sacred power spots, as well as research into multi-dimensional communication.

The cornerstone of BioGeometry is this "centering" subtle energy principle that connects to a higher spiritual level to govern the motion and balance the interaction of qualities to produce complementarity and harmony of the opposites. The use of the word "centering" in BioGeometry is not based on quantitative assessment. It is based on the qualitative interaction with subtle energy to bring balance and harmony to its surroundings. This subtle energy quality is found in the centers of the composition of shapes. Simply said, it is a holistic harmonizing quality.

This centering effect in power spots is the result of underground streams crossing to produce a subtle energy toroidal vortex that communicates between the physical and the higher dimensions. The life force in the forming process of nature is accessed through such living centering vortices, and these govern the evolution and development of natural shapes. This is where spirituality and matter merge into a living unity.

The next step in the development of BioGeometry and the Physics of Quality was to include the concept of the BG3 centering principle into the resonant Laws of Pythagorean Universal Harmonics. This combination of BG3 and Harmonics facilitated our research into the action of life force in the forming process of nature. There is evidence in ancient building practices that the role of life force in Universal Harmonics existed in the temple sciences of ancient civilizations. This living resonant centering principle was at the core of their scientific worldview and permeated all their teachings. The BG3 quality criterion in the choice of proportions and locations for their monuments supports this worldview.

From Harmonics and Radiesthesia to BioGeometry

A BioGeometry system of measurement was developed by applying the harmonizing centering principle of the energy quality of sacred power spots used in ancient building rituals and the energy principles of shape of Ancient Egypt, according to the laws of resonance in Universal Harmonics, to existing subtle energy detection methods found in French and German Radiesthesia. French Physical Radiesthesia is referred to in books about the field as "Microvibrational Physics." Through their study of the energy effects of shapes in Ancient Egypt, the French researchers developed a measurement system for what they termed "shape-caused waves" (*Ondes de Forme*).

There are two different methods of dowsing and Radiesthesia: the first and most prevalent, was based on mental/psychic methods of entering a dialogue with the subconscious level. That is why some practitioners refer to dowsing as a psychic gift from God. In the Middle Ages, the church authorities labelled it as a magical practice. Some monastic traditions, like the Jesuits, used it successfully for the detection of herbal remedies and sacred water sources and kept the tradition going down to modern times. Arab dowsers from the Middle East used this skill in the survey of Earth energy patterns for the planning of sacred buildings and city layouts.

It was the Jesuits who applied a simple calibration in which they arranged colors based on string lengths or calibrations on dowsing rods and staffs. This was the basis for the second, less well-known method of Physical Radiesthesia, which was further developed in the 1940s and 1950s by some European researchers. Physical Radiesthesia was based on the detection of colors or wavelengths through an elaborate physical calibration of pendulums and rod instruments. French and German Physical Radiesthesia schools used the scientific language of their day to understand and explain this method of detection.

Physical Radiesthesia was practiced and explained using electronic wave theories, which were popular at the time. Practitioners spoke of electric/ vertical and magnetic/horizontal wave components. They detected the color qualities on the periphery of a circle in relation to the magnetic north orientation. Green faced north, with Violet to the east and Red to the west and Grey to the south. On a sphere facing the sun, they categorized colors as being reflected, absorbed, or penetrating, just as they saw it in the spectrum of visible colors (Figure 43). This mixture between quality and quantity was unavoidable as the science of universal harmonics was still being revived and had not found a place in the Radiesthesia of the day. In BioGeometry, it was necessary to have a "purely qualitative" system of measurement with dedicated tools to deal with such concepts as centering, BG3, and life force; this became possible through the integration of Physical Radiesthesia with Universal Harmonics. We therefore found it necessary to give a different name to BioGeometry methods and we now refer to this as "BioGeometry Quality Measurement."

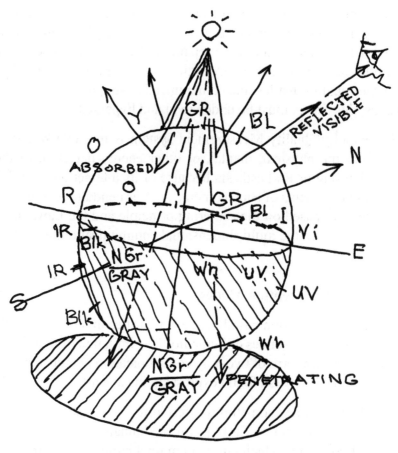

Fig.43 - Color Distribution and Wave Properties

Qualitative Perception in the Brain

Within the small vibratory ranges of the physical senses, the perceived qualities are limited to the material state. They are not grasped in their true resonant nature on all unperceived vibratory ranges of absolute reality. They become isolated qualities without a connection to the unified resonant holistic reality. They are not perceived by the senses as an information exchange mechanism in the universal unity. Simply said, they have been imprisoned by the sensory limits of a quantified left-brain perception. On the subconscious level however, the biological functions are in full interaction with the multi-dimensional levels of the Laws of Nature and are perceived by the brain cells in the heart and the gut.

In many alternative and complementary healing practices, such as frequency or color healing, perceived qualities are treated as units within a quantified range. Their quantitative separation from the unconscious universal subtle energy base has greatly limited their effectiveness. In a holistic science of quality that has the communicative support of all universal dimensions, this aspect must be understood and bypassed.

The BioGeometry Quality Measurement system is in a totally different category from the physical, mental, or other energy detection methodologies of dowsing or Radiesthesia because of its interaction with living qualities. All instruments of BioGeometry, such as pendulums, stands, and other devices, are based on the centering principle and the Laws of Harmonics, as well as on the multi-dimensional communication of qualities.

The Evolution of Perception Modes

Methods of communication based on the similarities in motion have their roots in the primitive practices of humanity. The imitation of motion, posture, and sound was a form of two-way communication practiced between humans and animals. It also found expression in cave art.

The Law of Similarities, sometimes referred to as sympathetic relationships, is as old as humanity. Early primitive humans functioned mainly from a right-brain mode which put them in total harmony with the Laws of Nature. A form of collective consciousness prevailed wherein a resonant subconscious mental-emotional information exchange ensured communication between all forms of life. Individual communication between living species occurred through the synchronization of movement patterns, postures, sounds, and so on. Any similarities consciously communicated unconscious content. Left-brain sensory awareness of subconscious interactions became the first conscious language of communication resulting from the Law of Similarities.

Humanity, according to Jung's categorization mentioned earlier, evolved from a primitive to an ancient state of perception; at this stage, letters, numbers, shapes, and notes were developed as a more sophisticated left-brain way of expressing and interacting with subconscious qualitative information.

As humankind's focus of awareness moved slowly towards the left-brain mode and its analytical capacities, the practical quantitative usage of letters, numbers, shapes, notes, and so on, became a part of everyday life, heralding the emergence of modern humanity. The total shift of focus from the subconscious mind to the external sensory reality affected humankind's worldview so much that I referred to it in my first book, *Back to a Future for Mankind,* as "the great shift." The doors to the subconscious universal information, and the personification of and conscious interaction with the powers of nature that went with them, were closed.

One can say that the great shift in perception created a new human species with a different perception of reality. This is the emergence of modern humanity that the nineteenth century psychologist and philosopher William James placed around 1250 BC, although it probably varied in different parts of the world. From this perspective, we should try to understand the culture of ancient civilizations as that of a different species.

In their right-brain mode of perception, they interacted and communicated directly with the powers of nature, which they projected into and personified in their left-brain mode. We can say that the powers of nature as Neters, angelic and other spiritual beings lived among them. It is very difficult for us to whom this dimension has been totally closed to imagine that the Neters, or what we erroneously call gods, which we see in ancient humankind's art, were real. Unfortunately, ancient history is in many ways misinterpreted from a modern psychology perspective.

The great civilizations of ancient humanity that grew within the universal unity lost their anchor and were doomed to extinction; they became imprisoned in the depth of the unconscious content of modern humankind. The Law of Similarities is anchored in the subconscious right-brain mode where the holistic unity of everything in Creation is prevalent. This holistic unifying information exchange is at the core of the ancient science of "Multi-Dimensional Universal Harmonics." It fueled the great civilizations of antiquity and was kept secret by the temple priest-scientists.

Sympathetic Relationships

The practice of imitation of movement, shape, or sound, sometimes referred to as sympathetic relationships, can be found in many old traditions of herbal and natural remedies, where similarities of shape or energetic color qualities detected through Radiesthesia were applied.

The use of this principle of similarities—or sympathetic relationships—in Radiesthesia and scientific dowsing is a way of categorizing everything according to its resonance with one of seven (or more) colors. Similarities can be visualized as seven or more differently colored containers into which everything in the Universe finds its proper place. The categorization, based on color qualities, can be completed using a pendulum calibrated to each of the colors in turn; all things that produce a rotation on a color can then be said to be in a sympathetic relationship and will produce similar effects on the subtle energy level of a person. The effect is very subtle and is similar to how we react to physical colors. This protocol was used in ancient and medieval times to help people choose plants or other remedies. The Jesuit monks in Europe kept this knowledge alive as a valuable tool that enabled their missionaries to choose remedies in faraway lands where different plants which were unknown to them grew In ancient civilizations, the sacred hieroglyphs were used according to the

.

Law of Similarities in a process whereby the concept behind the figure was transmitted to the perceiver. The perceiver exchanged information with the hieroglyph on the subtle energy level, perceived through the right-brain and heart intellect. In this mode of perception, the perceiver became unified with the hieroglyph. The perceiver with a conscious left-brain connection to the right-brain content experienced another reality. The extrasensory right-brain perception of primitive and ancient humanity allowed people to see the personified change in the person concerned. As the focus of perception moved to the left-brain mode, the different time-space dimensions perceived by the universality of the right-brain mode could not be conveyed properly to the sensory perception. We erroneously think that our present symbolic understanding of modern psychology can access the reality behind the hieroglyph. What we see is what it means to us, which is completely different from what it really is. Unfortunately, the door has closed.

In BioGeometry we use the subtle energy methods of becoming a subtle energy copy of the object of detection. This allows us to assess and analyze and induce a change in the subtle energy of the other system. We will explore this concept repeatedly in several remote applications of BioGeometry.

In the French school of Radiesthesia, Léon de Chaumery, Antoine De Bélizal, and Paul-André Morel expanded the system from seven to twelve color qualities by adding Infra-Red, Black, Grey (referred to as Negative Green), White, and Ultraviolet as measured on a sphere related to the sun or a circle in relation to magnetic north.

This color categorization system showed the sympathetic relationships in the Universe expressed in seven or twelve separate categories. The concept of resonance at the core of sympathetic relationships and color correspondences was not fully understood at the time and would have affected the accuracy of detection, which needed a separation of the colors. The concepts of subtle energy quality according to the laws of resonance, which played a main role in ancient harmonics, had not found their way into Radiesthesia at the time.

Pythagorean Universal Harmonics was being revived at the same period by the Swiss Hans Kayser. This is the reason why the early French and German researchers in Radiesthesia did not clearly distinguish between quantitative and qualitative aspects of color. In the pursuit of a scientific explanation, they resorted to wave theories and used terms like reflection and penetration of color waves, as well as electric and magnetic wave components. They also used frequency and wavelengths as quantities in scales of color qualities. They produced an extensive body of work, using instruments like the wave-length-based Lecher Antenna and the virtual cone pendulums based on color-angles, in their practical research.

In BioGeometry, we used those methods to develop the methodology and measuring devices suitable for the needs of BioGeometry, which could not be met with existing instruments. We have therefore revived some important French schools of Radiesthesia from researchers such as Chaumery, Bélizal, Morel, Turenne, and others, and we first introduced them to the English-speaking world through our courses in North America. We also introduced the earth grids discovered by Hartmann, Curry, and other members of the German school of Radiesthesia. The French and German works were translated for our courses in collaboration with the Vesica Institute in Asheville, NC.

Physical Radiesthesia is a science of detection using calibrations based on "sympathetic color affinities." This is different from popular methods of dowsing and "Mental Radiesthesia" that we have previously introduced, which are types of psychic detection. For Physical Radiesthesia to be fully understood from a scientific point of view, one must refer to the concept of quality as a repetitive effect of resonance between different string lengths of a musical instrument (e.g., piano octaves). The principles of resonance as in Pythagorean Universal Harmonics must be applied to restructure Radiesthesia according to its true qualitative essence. This is the path taken by BioGeometry to produce its own system of BioGeometry Quality Measurement.

Universal Harmonics

Universal Harmonics is very complex, so to avoid complicating things we will only look at the qualitative and communicative aspects that relate to our Physics of Quality in BioGeometry. The BioGeometry Physics of Quality used the Laws of Universal Harmonics to develop an extended multi-dimensional system of universal abstract qualities covering all vibrational ranges of absolute reality.

A clear differentiation was made between color as perceived in its sensory vibrational range and color quality, which is the abstract universal effect behind color that can be found in all vibratory ranges.

Qualitative scales were developed by using such ranges as colors or musical notes to express the same resonant abstract qualities along all vibratory ranges from zero to infinity. The different qualitative scales expressed the same universal abstract qualities across the board and were thus interchangeable. Correspondences between musical notes, colors, polarity, numbers, and shapes that have the same qualities were established. The specific laws of each became applicable to all other ranges of absolute reality to cover all planes of nature (physical, vital, emotional, mental, and spiritual) in all dimensions.

The realization that resonance of qualities connects all the dimensions and universes in an eternal unifying web of information exchange marked the birth of a multi-dimensional Physics of Quality where resonant correspondences between different planes and dimensions of nature were explored.

In the science of Universal Harmonics, the quality of a musical note keeps repeating itself through resonance with every other string double or half its length. This is the main resonance of the same quality on different string lengths. Since the resonance between the different notes on different ranges is not perceived in the case of colors, which had only one "octave," researchers in Radiesthesia did not address colors as a universal scale of qualities. The application of resonant qualities of musical notes over several octave ranges on color produces the concept of color quality across the total vibratory range.

In the ancient system of Pythagorean Universal Harmonics, the notes are derived as different mathematical proportions on a string as expressed in a Pythagorean Lambdoma chart. In the BioGeometry Physics of Quality, the fixed points of musical strings are the multi-dimensional centers of rotation connecting the notes to the higher levels at the source of Creation. This means that through the fixed points, the sound of a musical note will always contain all the other notes within its background echo. The fixed point—which is a form of central transcendental vortex connecting to higher dimensions—is the main criterion of living qualities where each contains all others. In BioGeometry, this is the same multi-dimensional doorway that produces living qualities of colors, notes, numbers, etc. In a universe of qualities, there is only unity; nothing exists separately, but only as components expressing the whole.

This is the reality in nature that is only perceived beyond the confines of physical sensory perception. Those fixed points on the body of the musical string instrument connect the quality of shape with the quality of the notes on the strings (Figure 44). The qualities of shape and material in the body of the instrument become part of the resonant qualitative information exchange of the multi-dimensional vortex. The instrument body can be designed to resonate with the different planes of nature. In this paradigm, qualities become living principles resonating with the Laws of Creation. The fixed points (BG3 transcendental vortices) of a musical string instrument transfer the different life force qualities to the body of the musical instrument where they are given further qualities; we will explore this with the "life force" dials. The concept of living interactive qualities becomes a practical transformative harmonizing force that can be used to enhance the evolution of all life forms.

To make this concept more visual, we can imagine a football or soccer team with each player wearing a different color. When we watch the player with the ball, we know that he or she expresses the action of all the players in the team. Behind every individual play, we find teamwork.

Quality is perceived through the right-brain mode. It identifies whole patterns as the expression of unity. Each part appears as a different expression within the whole and does not exist on its own. This is the complete vision of qualities in Universal Harmonics. The existing instruments of scientific Radiesthesia or dowsing identify each color, musical note, or wavelength as an individual, separate unit of measurement. Instruments of BioGeometry Quality Measurement were developed to address different levels of this qualitative unity through the incorporation of the centering principle of BG3.

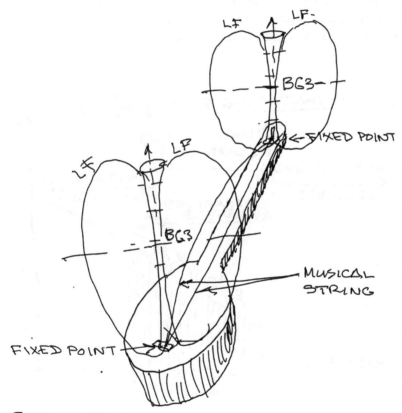

STRING FIXED POINTS ARE MULTIDIMENSIONAL COMMUNICATION DOORWAYS TO SPIRITUAL DIMENSIONS

Fig.44 - BG3 Fixed Points of Universal Note Resonance

To understand the principles of multi-dimensional Universal Harmonics behind the lost sciences of the great ancient civilizations, we will return to our simplified model of an expanded musical instrument that spans all string lengths from zero to infinity. We can thus go beyond the hearing range to cover all vibrational levels of absolute reality and reach a system where everything in existence is in resonant communication. To give a more realistic picture, the zero-to-infinity instrument should be rotated around a central axis to cover all angles and directions in a spherical form. We will, however, use the simpler model on one plane to simplify things while still giving an adequate picture (Figure 45).

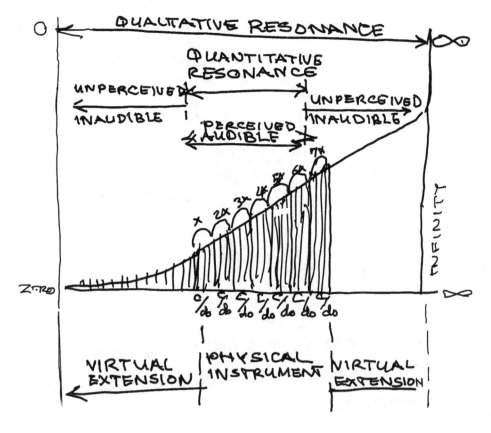

Fig.45 - Extended Qualitative String Scale

Pythagoras used the monochord to show the relationship between the proportions or tension on a string and the musical note perceived by the brain. This fundamental concept is the basis of Universal Harmonics where everything in the Universe is in a qualitative resonant interaction, and qualities can be expressed through numbers and proportions. This is an example of the conversion principle between quantity and quality. Numbers, therefore, had a living philosophical interpretation in the Pythagorean doctrine.

One can use this principle of the resonance of qualities between string lengths to make different types of instruments that will show quality affecting the human subtle energy system on an extrasensory level. These qualities can be further enhanced through the angles in the design of the body of the musical instrument (Figure 46)

Fig.46 - Sound and Shape Research Instrument

At this point, we must understand that quantitative control of any type of emission alone is only partially effective because from a qualitative point of view the resonance factor spreads the effect in an echo-like form across the whole vibrational ranges of absolute reality from zero to infinity. So, by reducing the intensity or power of an emission of any type we only take away one aspect of the harm and the smallest amount left will still cause harm to living systems according to its resonant effects on all vibratory levels.

Some of the material we dealt with in my previous books are needed here to pave the way to deeper levels, especially for general readers who have not gone through our BioGeometry courses. So, let's review it now. For the existing BioGeometry community, this unavoidable repetition is done with a new angle: to prepare for the integration of the harmonic concepts into existing methods.

The ancients had developed staffs, antennas, pendulums, and other wave-length-based instruments to detect the human perception of quality. The human being is thus the main measuring instrument, while the harmonic instrument used provides the pointer and qualitative measurement scale to evaluate the effect. To make an analogy here, let us take an example from our first book about driving a car without a speedometer. We can still drive effectively and know if the car is going slow or fast. As far as we are concerned, the lack of speedometer does not diminish the usability of the car. If, however, we add a speedometer comprised of a pointer and a scale, we get additional precise quantitative information, which enables us to calculate precise information about speed, distance, time, etc. In the case of harmonic measurement, by comparison, we want to measure the *extra*sensory qualities associated with any physical sensory information. The difference here is that our pointer or other method of indication is calibrated to *scales of quality*. The quality of any object or activity is determined as an effect on the human multi-dimensional subtle energy field.

This way of thinking must be incorporated into the modern scientific worldview that addresses practicalities but is unable to include human subjectivity in its criteria. We currently have a very advanced age of modern technology which is, however, causing chronic health problems and destroying the natural environment and polluting the earth with electromagnetic radiation and chemical products. The Physics of Quality is based on the effect on the human subtle energy field as a method of detection and evaluation of quality. This is a complementary approach to modern quantitative science that puts human health and well-being as its main criterion.

Quality is Alive

In the BioGeometry paradigm, as we explained above, energy in all its forms and interactions contains Consciousness as well as all other attributes of life. The pulse within any form of energy is a conscious living time-force unit. We are an integral part of this universal energy, and we are in constant exchange with all its levels and attributes. The human interaction with subtle energy, therefore, speaks of an integral vital, emotional, mental, and spiritual relationship which we perceive as quality. Quality is a living holistic relationship. Qualitative scales are, in contrast to quantitative scales, comprised of living attribute units. It is the universal language that binds everything in this dimension, as well as in all others, in a qualitative, unifying, living web. This is the subtle energy that forms the background carpet weave on which everything exists, including the limited electromagnetic realm we live in.

PART THIRTEEN
Qualitative Scales in the Brain

A Physics of Quality must be based on some form of objective qualitative scales of measurement. Qualities are the effects of interactions between two systems that produce changes in both. In the Physics of Quality, an effect produces a quality on the human subtle energy system. These qualities are perceived by different areas of the brain which then decode the nervous stimuli from the corresponding senses and express them through different qualitative scales of color, sound, smell, touch, and taste.

These scales translate the same undifferentiated nervous reactions in their different modes. Although they result from reactions within different vibratory ranges, they express the same nervous reactions. From a purely qualitative point of view, they represent the same quality affecting the nervous system since the nerves leading from the sensory organs to the corresponding brain locations are all similar in nature. There is thus a background resonant connection between the qualities resulting from all sensory information since they travel through a unified nervous system. Applying the concepts of universal resonance of qualities in nature, as with musical notes, each sensory quality will have in its background an interaction with all other sensory qualities.

The result is very like the resonant quality of a musical instrument where all the notes that resonate in the background of the perceived note are affected by the quality of shape resulting from the body of the instrument. This emphasizes the fact that all qualities of natural systems are an interactive and holistic unity. We should therefore understand the working of the different sensory decoding centers in the brain as an interconnected system. Thus, a disturbance or effect on any of the sensory organs will manifest as a change in the perception of the other senses. The qualitative scales express the harmonic interaction on all ranges of absolute reality, which means that the quality perceived by the brain is also present on different subconscious dimensions. This shows a certain qualitative unity between the two hemispherical brain modes of perception.

In the Physics of Quality, all qualitative scales such as polarity, color, and musical notes are used beyond their respective vibratory ranges to express the same universal qualities that repeat themselves on all levels from zero to infinity. Each of these scales has certain proprietary laws that are specific to it. In color, we have unlimited hues and tones as well as concepts of complementarity and harmony; these are different from what we find with sound or numbers. Here's an example of this: while we have only one octave in color, we can perceive the phenomena of resonance in the many octaves of musical notes. We cannot easily observe this phenomenon in color because its visible spectrum is limited to one range. In numbers, we have a lot of mathematical relationships that are much more elaborate than other scales. The interesting thing is that while each scale can be more useful in certain applications, the fact that they are interchangeable means that the laws of each scale are working within all the other scales. This opens new dimensions of research and understanding of the workings of the powers of nature, which can produce new applications.

Interchangeability of Scales

If viewed as pure units of measurement within qualitative scales representing abstract universal qualities, instead of being restricted to their own specific sensory ranges, scales become interchangeable. What's more interesting is that each scale becomes usable in any range in an extrasensory way. This complements the original sensory data with information on emotional, mental, and spiritual levels. We are therefore dealing with interchangeable living scales of quality (Figure 47). One can use colors to identify the quality of sounds—for example, the musical note "C" or "do" (depending on musical notation used) resonates with the color red. Both the note and the corresponding color have the same quality of effect on our subtle energy system.

By the same principle, this resonance is extended to all unperceived vibratory ranges, from zero to infinity, to which we can interchangeably apply any qualitative scale. In ancient Universal Harmonics, these resonances become applicable to all vibratory ranges beyond perceived reality, covering all other dimensions. In general, however, all the physical senses can, in certain cases, react to extrasensory stimuli. This sensitivity differs from person to person. People afflicted with synesthesia experience excessive cross-sensory sensitivity. A perfect example here was the famous Austrian music composer Wolfgang Amadeus Mozart (1756-91); he used to see colors corresponding to the musical notes he played. Special abilities children sometimes display such forms of cross-sensory perception.

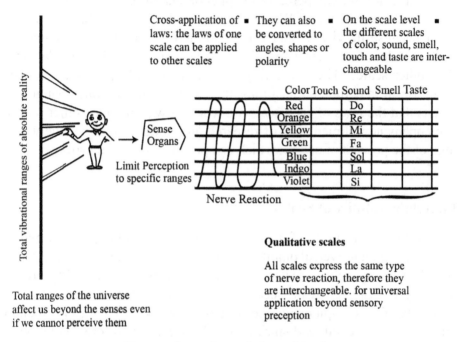

Fig.47 - Interchangability of Scales

Some people can smell the quality of energy in a place or have a skin reaction to it—like goosebumps. Similarly, in the Physics of Quality, one can develop instruments that use any sensory effect as a scale applicable to other sensory or extra-sensory ranges. Color scales are the easiest and most popular but there are instruments that use other sensory reactions as scales of measurement. Some early radionics instruments used a stretched leather pad on which the user slid his finger to assess the level of friction, which indicated energy quality. One can calibrate stringed instruments like pendulums or antenna devices on musical notes and use them as qualitative scales. Many people get different feelings or body reactions indicating the energy quality of a place. This could manifest as itching, twitching, coughing, sneezing, headaches, a change in breathing pattern, or any other physical reaction to an energy quality. Natural responses can sometimes give an indication of change in energy quality, but on their own, without qualitative scales of measurement, they do not give the necessary information needed for scientific research.

The cross application of color, musical notes, and angles on different ranges can be expanded beyond the sensory ranges to cover all vibratory ranges from the smallest to the largest, expressing a universal multi-dimensional qualitative scale. When applied from zero to infinity, multi-dimensional interactions can be measured just as simply as those within our perceived reality. With this concept, we use qualitative scales that can be applied to detect qualities and resonant information exchange on any level. This is the basis of Universal Harmonics at the core of many of the advanced sciences of ancient civilizations. They are still largely misunderstood, although they could open new horizons to modern technology. This, in a way, brings the unperceived universal knowledge of the right-brain mode into the perception of the sensory left-brain mode. We can thus experience the hidden Laws of Nature first-hand or, as I usually express it: "reading the language of the writing and drawing of the Divine hand in the nature we live in."

Types of Qualitative Scales

Based on the Laws of Universal Harmonics, a string length will resonate with other string lengths that are half or double its length and they will each have the same quality of effect on the subtle energy system of the listener. Besides this primary resonance there exist other harmonic resonances between all the different notes or string lengths, ultimately leading to a universal unity of all note qualities. This universal unifying principle of qualities is central in the BioGeometry paradigm. Other systems like

Radiesthesia and dowsing rely on the separation of qualities for precise detection. By applying this harmonic Law of Resonance to other sensory ranges, where we do not perceive several octaves as we do in sound, we can still universally apply them beyond their respective sensory ranges. We can apply the laws of universal resonance to color, number, shape, polarity, touch, smell, and so on, as qualitative scales across the board. Although we end up using the color scale that is used in Mental and Physical Radiesthesia, the harmonic concept is much broader than that of sympathetic similarity. One can equally apply the concept of complementary colors (e.g., Green-Red, Yellow-Violet, Orange-Blue etc.) to the corresponding musical notes.

String Length Qualitative Calibration Scales

In dedicated uses, such as water dowsing, gold detection, herbal remedies, and finding and mapping sacred power spots and Earth energy grids, one can calibrate the string, rod, or staff length directly on the object, regardless of the type of scale used.

When a certain length on the string, rod, staff, or wavelength setting on an antenna of a detection device resonates with an object, the wavelength setting represents a unit of quality that is applicable on other wavelengths with the same quality. Let's take the example of a musical stringed instrument: resonance is a qualitative vibratory relationship between different string lengths. In this sense, the wavelength is a scale expressing a quality repeating itself on several string lengths.

Detailed analysis of string lengths corresponding to color qualities shows us three superimposed scales starting with Violet at the bottom and Red at the top, as well as three others with Violet on the top and finishing with Red at the bottom. The fact that the six scales are interpenetrating can be confusing. These scales also repeat themselves along different string lengths based on the Laws of Harmonics. One should always calibrate according to only one scale on the string and ignore any points in between that belong to other scales. This needs a certain proficiency. In general, one should calibrate on the scale most suited to the system used.

We have to repeatedly emphasize an important fact that confuses most dowsers or practitioners of Radiesthesia, which relates to the qualitative essence of universal harmonics: there is a huge difference between wavelength and wave quality, or color and color quality, and so on—with all qualitative scales. The first is restricted to a specific vibratory range while the second applies to all ranges perceivable or unperceived.

It is important to understand that subtle energy detection devices are based on quality scales and even with wavelength calibration they do not measure the wavelength of an object. The wavelengths are units of quality scales used beyond their physical dimensions to express an endlessly repeatable quality.

Let's take, as an example, a Lecher Antenna like the H3 from Luedelin in Germany, or that of Acmos in France. There are long tables of wavelengths corresponding to all types of things that should be understood as harmonic qualities. Multiples of these wavelengths give the same quality so that the same object can be detected using any of them.

Personal Calibration

In a science of quality, the human subtle energy system becomes the base on which all other energetic effects are measured. Measurements can be done on any other living energy system, like plants, for example, but they do not have all the possibilities of the human system. The first step in measuring is to calibrate the instrument on the user's energy field. This has been referred to since the early days of Radiesthesia as the process of finding the user's "personal wavelength." Although this term implies a quantitative type of calibration, that is not the case here. The calibration is based on the individual's personal subtle energy quality. The term "wavelength" refers to the string length at which a pendulum will indicate the subtle energy quality has been identified. The wavelength is a metaphor for quality.

The personal wavelength, as indicated by string length, can be identified when the user holds the pendulum string between the thumb and forefinger of one hand while dangling the pendulum above the back of their other hand. They slowly allow the weight of the pendulum to drop. The lengths at which the pendulum begins to rotate clockwise signal that they have found their personal wavelength. There will be more than one point at which this is indicated, based on the main harmonic resonance of repetitive qualities: the personal wavelength will also exist at half or double the string length. One can choose the most convenient point. There will be points between the indicators of personal wavelength where the pendulum will rotate counterclockwise. This is due to the change of polarity of points on the string. In general, we usually use those producing a clockwise rotation for the calibration.

In BioGeometry, we typically use the "Ibrahim Karim Universal Pendulum" (IKUP) which has been designed to enter into resonance of shape with all the planes of nature (Figure 48). The personal string length setting of this pendulum is holistic as it resonates with all the planes of the human subtle energy system. As an emitter of BG3, it enhances connectivity and gives a certain level of protection from negative energies when measuring. Once identified, this personal string length indicates a holistic resonance with the user's subtle energy quality. Whatever increases the amplitude of the rotation, be it a location, an object, food, or some other item, will be beneficial for the user. A detrimental item will cause the pendulum rotation to diminish, oscillate, or turn counterclockwise.

Similarly, one can calibrate one's personal basic subtle energy quality using a staff, dowsing rod, antenna, or angle, as well as with a dial or cone pendulum or other instrument. A personal color calibration can be most accurately done with a BioGeometry Horizontal 360-dial pendulum, which offers a more comprehensive holistic approach.

THE IKUP

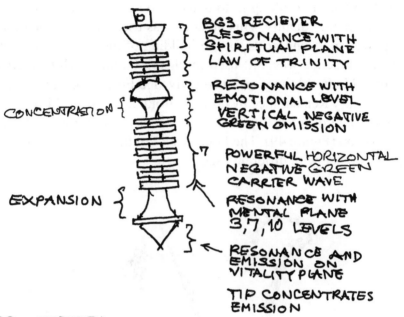

CONCENTRATION {

EXPANSION {

BG3 RECIEVER RESONANCE WITH SPIRITUAL PLANE LAW OF TRINITY

RESONANCE WITH EMOTIONAL LEVEL VERTICAL NEGATIVE GREEN OMISSION

POWERFUL HORIZONTAL NEGATIVE GREEN CARRIER WAVE

RESONANCE WITH MENTAL PLANE 3,7,10 LEVELS

RESONANCE AND EMISSION ON VITALITY PLANE

TIP CONCENTRATES EMISSION

PROPERTIES :

EMITTER AND RECIEVER ON ALL PLANES

HEALING BG3 + LIFE FORCE EMITTER

CREATES POSITIVE QL-TORSION IN UPRIGHT POSITION

CAN BE AIMED AT EMR SOURCES FOR PROTECTION

Fig.48 - IKUP (Ibrahim Karim Universal Pendulum)

The Roman Lituus

In Ancient Rome, special practitioners known as "augures" were responsible for detecting underground water sources and Earth energy grids. They used a special staff called a "Lituus," which had a spiral head and calibration markings along it, to detect underground water quality, gold, and Earth energy quality. This practice was used to detect the proper sacred power spots and grids for the building of monuments. In Christian times this practice was still used in church building. This practice was used until Medieval times and then revived in Europe again during the fifteenth century Renaissance by dowsers from the Arab world. The Ancient Egyptians had different types of staffs and scepters for energy detection and emission (Figure 49). The famous staff of the Biblical prophet Moses is such a device with different uses.

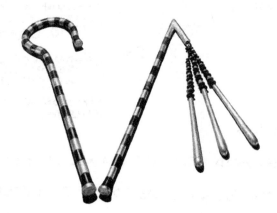

Fig.49 – Sample of Ancient Egyptians Scepters

Taking this concept further we have developed BioGeometry walking staffs and scepters with different emission properties. They have a special type of resonance with emotional, mental, and spiritual planes giving them healing and protection properties. They can also correct Earth energy grids in a person's space (Figure 50).

Fig.50 - BioGeometry Walking Staffs and Scepters

Musical Scales

Radiesthesic detection devices such as pendulums, rods, or antennas can also be calibrated on proportions of musical notes. This results in a scale that categorizes qualities of things as inaudible sound notes that also resonate with color qualities.

It is relatively rare for people to use Radiesthesia instruments calibrated with musical note scales because they are not as practical as colors, although the two are interchangeable. In any case, the harmonic laws of resonance, as found in musical notes, are applied to the other types of scales. It is, however, only in musical notes on stringed instruments that we can observe the resonance between different strings of different lengths. For example, we can see on piano keys that different octaves of a note all produce the same note but with higher or lower pitches. By looking at the musical notes, one gains the best understanding of the *laws of Universal Harmonics* that express the resonant interactions and manifestations of the abstract universal qualities behind all types of scales.

Applying the laws of one type to the others opens new paths of understanding, research, and applications. Cross-concepts like resonance of color or complementarity of musical notes, as well as their resonant correspondences with shapes, give us a new wider holistic worldview where everything is part of an overall qualitative unity of Creation.

Complementarity of notes, for example, corresponding to complementary colors such as green-red, blue-orange and violet-yellow, will connect to the centering BG3 quality. However, the musical note Fa/F, on its own, corresponds to the green color quality and produces a neutralizing, balancing effect.

Polarity Scales

Everything in Creation is based on the spiritual centering balance of dualities. The dualistic principle is expressed in the polarization of everything in Creation on the subtle energy level. Polarities are expressions of unity within time and space. They are the qualitative components of the unity. The balanced tension between polarities is a main criterion for the lifeforce in nature. Just as with musical notes, opposite polarities only exist individually as a function of each other; on another level, each exists within the center of the other. Polarity scales, like all other qualitative scales with different divisions, express the abstract universal qualities running across the board. Polarity is one of the two complementary qualities within the unity of the universal harmonic system. Polarities do not exist independently of each other. Each polarity exists within the opposite one, as the Chinese Yin/Yang diagram expresses. This is just like the original central pulse that creates the beginning and end that are interconnected manifestations of the centering force.

Used beyond their range, polarities become universal attributes, like the Yin/Yang concept of polarization and Ancient Egyptian male and female Neters expressing the duality within the unity. Although this scale is comprised of only two components of the unity, its use in a harmonic system as a universal scale becomes unlimited as we see in the universally applicable Chinese concept of Yin and Yang, which represent the interplay of subtle energy polarities in nature. One can calibrate the length of a pendulum string, staff, rod, or antenna on the polarities of a battery, to determine the polarity relationships in objects and phenomena. When using a conventional pendulum calibrated with string length, polarity plays a role in the direction of rotation. When the pendulum is held in one hand while the other hand points to the object of measurement, the reading will be different than when the pendulum is held directly over the object. The measurement should always be done according to the method used in calibration.

The French engineer Louis Turenne devised a pendulum with two magnetic needles, which enables different polarity calibrations on which he based his measurement system. With the BioGeometry dial pendulums the calibration does not change regardless of whether one is holding the pendulum over the object of measurement or pointing at it with the finger of the other hand.

In all measurements with pendulums, rods, staffs, and antennas, the fixed point of the device's movement is in the hand of the user. As we have explained previously, the direction of movement of life force in the energy field of the user produces QL-Torsion, which is visible in the pendulum rotation. The fixed point where the person holds the string is where the quality-of-life force creates the QL-Torsion/rotation and connects the opposite polarities to the center, expressing all the different living qualities within it.

In all qualitative scales, each quality is measured in a functional relationship with the others. The unified duality principle is used in BioGeometry's life force dials where the functional relationship includes the two qualities or polarities as well as their origin in the quality of the center. In this case, the two living qualities or polarities are connected to the center in an angular relationship with each other, and they manifest different combinations of all the other colors in a harmonic relationship (Figure 51). Measuring instruments based on dials show the angular relationship of the qualities emerging from the center, creating a subtle energy vortex during the measurement that connects it to the higher harmonizing, life-giving archetypal spiritual dimensions.

Fig.51 - Preset Life Force Dial Example

Qualitative Measurements with Polarity Scales

The principle of polarization exists not only in the measurement of electromagnetic polarities, but also on the emotional and mental subtle energy planes of every living system in nature. We find polarities in the human body manifested in the eyes, ears, nostrils, hands, feet, fingers, toes, and so on. We can use them to restore balance to organ function. Disturbances in any organ function can generally be restored by emphasizing one polarity through posture, and this can also be achieved, without measuring polarity, by alternating the movement of any of our dual organs. The simplest way to balance polarity is simply by walking, as any alternate repetition of polarities will restore balance in all organ functions.

Some schools of nutrition, like macrobiotics, are based on polarity. It is possible to accurately detect the polarity of food and drink using a calibrated pendulum in order to classify them in the macrobiotic system. One can also detect the polarities of colors, musical notes, letters, numbers, orientation, and so on. The digital age is based on just two digits—zero and one—with which we can access unlimited information. So, using just this scale can give us limitless qualitative information, just as the other more elaborate scales do.

Instruments based on the Quality of Numbers

Several BioGeometry emission and measurement devices—rods, staffs, stands, scepters, and pendulums (e.g., the IKUP and BG16 pendulums)—are designed to use numerical qualities in specific groupings of elements with other geometrical elements. We have designed several pendulums with repetitive elements to express certain number qualities (Figure 52). Some are based on number qualities from the BioGeometry series that produce BG3: 16, 19, 28, 34, 43, 54, 68, 72, 83, 89, 99. These numbers all have the BG3 quality. They will be dealt with in detail in a relevant part below.

Fig.52 - Disk Number Quality Pendulums

We also developed several types of pendulums with number-based dials that can be calibrated to detect and emit numerical qualities. These pendulums will be introduced when dealing with the subtle energy quality of numbers.

BioGeometry Stands

Using the principles of the qualities of shapes and numbers we have developed stands. Some can be used for emissions into a specific space, and others for large-scale regional solutions (Figure 53). In the latter case, the stands are put in tubes and buried in the ground. We used this method for many years in military campsites that had a lot of electrical cables buried in the ground to which a lot of equipment was connected. The resulting electromagnetic fields created a lot of stress on the occupants of the mobile units and tents.

Fig.53 - BioGeometry Stands Group

As we had a lot of experience with this type of solution we applied it in Hirschberg, Appenzell-IR, Switzerland. We usually test our products with every new development in mobile communication (e.g., 3G, 4G, 5G and so on).

BioGeometry Attachments

We also used the quality of numbers to develop small strips, some of which can be attached to or placed on electrical boxes and cables as well as on water pipes. The strips have proprietary BioGeometry L-shapes at the ends and numerical codes on the sides. There are always notches (16, 19, or 28) on one side and a function-specific number of similar notches, ranging from 3 to 15, on the other side. The basic strip leveraging the number 9 is generally used for electricity (with secondary 7, 8, and 12 strips used for smart meters, wireless devices, metal construction, and so on). The number 11 is generally used for water pipes, and the numbers 3 and 7 are placed on doors, starting with the building's main entry (Figure 54). The quality of numbers can be used along with the BioGeometry design principles, and we will discuss this later in the relevant topic.

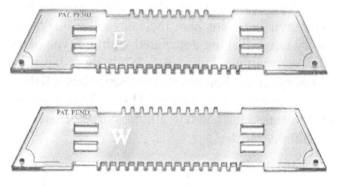

Fig.54 - Electricity and Water Attachments

Touch Scales

Radionics instruments usually have dials that are set to numerical rates that correspond to the quality of objects to be detected or emitted. Some of those devices use touch as an indication of energy quality. A stretched leather, synthetic, or digital membrane is used so that when the user slides his or her finger along it, they can identify different levels of friction. We can experiment with this by sliding one finger along a smooth surface while pointing a finger on the other hand at different objects. The level of friction we experience will differ. We can feel a similar body reaction by placing a palm or some fingers about a centimeter above a person's skin and slowly moving our hand up and down. In this case, we will feel a change in resistance or temperature.

Color Quality Scales

The resonance between multiple octaves, as on a piano, for example, can be perceived as audible sound. When we apply this concept to color, we only actually observe one octave, while the other octaves are invisible color qualities that are repeated on different levels. Color scales are the most commonly used scales of quality. A pendulum calibrated on a visible color will rotate on different objects, herbs, stones, numbers, etc., that have the same abstract subtle energy quality but do not necessarily have this color. As an example, iron that is black in color has a Red color quality. The invisible color here indicates color qualities outside the visible vibratory range that are associated with the type of units (sound, shape, number, etc.) in the other ranges. While those units are applied to their own vibratory range, their resonant presence beyond their respective ranges can be expressed as color quality. This is the concept of color quality scales applied across the board to all vibratory ranges and it applies to all types of qualitative scales.

On a visible level, objects that are similar in color are in resonance with each other. In a similar way that musical notes are in primary resonance with similar notes on different string lengths in higher or lower octaves, as well as in a secondary background harmonic resonance with all other notes, objects of one color are in resonance with those of the same color as well as in secondary background resonance with objects of all other colors. This can be understood when looking at invisible white light being refracted on a glass prism giving different colors in different angles. All the colors are projected components from the same unified source, and as such have a resonant connection between them. The secondary harmonic resonance in its coverage of all vibratory ranges beyond sound ranging from zero to infinity connects the object's color to similar colors, as well as through a secondary background connection to the overall unity of all other colors, shapes, sounds, fragrances, and types of motion.

Radiesthesists and dowsers calibrated their pendulums, strings, rods, and other devices on the seven colors (Red, Orange, Yellow, Green, Blue, Indigo, and Violet). These were expanded by the French school to twelve colors (they added: Ultraviolet, White, Grey—referred to as Negative Green—Black, and Infra-Red). Some pendulums were designed with a sliding disk on a rod to calibrate virtual angles with colors as well (Figure 55). Chaumery and Bélizal even devised a ruler to measure the intensity of each color. BioGeometry rulers with added color dials can be used for this purpose as well.

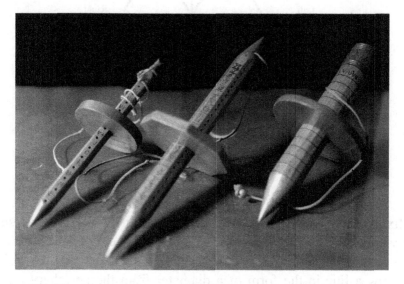

Fig.55 - Chaumery and Belizal Virtual Cone Pendulums

Polarization of Shapes

When we draw a line, we always get the Violet quality at the beginning, indicating a positive polarity of the line, and the Red quality at the end, indicating a negative polarity. Between them we will find all the other color qualities with Green in the middle. We will also find BG3 in the middle where the pulse producing the line is connected to a multi-dimensional vortex. The motion of the line creates a torus-shaped field around it. We use a 2D section of the torus in the BioGeometry Energy Key to analyze energy qualities in a space (Figure 56). The simple drawing of a line creates a form of polarization at its extremities and becomes the centerline of a torus shape.

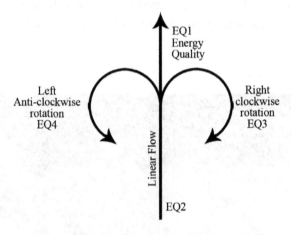

Fig.56 - 2D BioGeometry Energy Key

The fixing of polarity allows us to create measurement tools and subtle energy emission devices calibrated to a specific energy quality irrelevant of orientation. The simplest way to fix the polarity of a sphere or circle, is to draw a line in the form of a diameter from the periphery moving through the center to the opposite periphery. Lines are always polarized based on their direction of motion. The starting point of the line will have a Violet quality while the endpoint will be Red. The shape will have a fixed polarity of Violet and Red at the line ends independent of orientation to the magnetic north. A subtle energy torus-shaped field will be formed. A second virtual axis passing through the center perpendicular and rotating

CCW to the first one will have Green at one end and Negative Green (Grey) at the other. This will form a BG3 disk at the center of the original line (Figure 57).

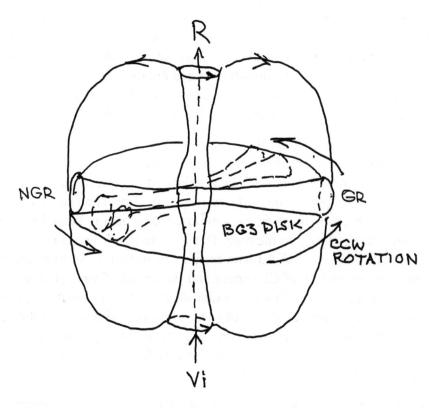

Fig.57 - BG3 Plane at Center of Motion

Dial Polarization

There are other ways to fix the polarity besides using a central diametrical line as explained above. To fix the polarization of a circle, we can place a battery, a magnet, or a geometric polarizer in a radial position on the diameter of the circle. Geometric shapes that have fixed polarities can be used as polarizers. Geometric polarizers are generally based on one or more superimposed hemispheres or semi-circles, with a shape modification or additional shapes added to cancel the harmful vertical Negative Green quality (Figure 58).

To develop a calibrated measurement instrument that does not have to be oriented to the magnetic north or the sun, so that it can be used in any direction, at any time, we need to arrange and separate colors on the periphery of a circle or sphere and fix their position regardless of orientation. The sphere shows a vertical distribution and polarization of color quality so that the Green is facing towards the sun. On a horizontal circle or on the equator of a sphere, the Green is in the north direction.

In researching Ancient Egyptian shapes, Chaumery and Bélizal discovered that cutting the sphere or circle in half fixed the polarity. Thus, the top of the hemisphere or semicircle always showed the Green quality while the base had a Negative Green (Grey range) quality. The beauty of this discovery is that a hemisphere or semi-circle creates a polarized axis of emission from the center of the base. This knowledge allowed the creation of polarized spheres and disks with fixed color qualities. As an example, the universal pendulum of Chaumery and Bélizal has four superimposed hemispheres embedded within a wooden sphere to fix its polarity. Caution should be taken while charging objects or people with this pendulum, however: this concept of amplification of emission by superimposing several hemispheres upon each other can be very harmful due to excessive Vertical Negative Green emission.

In creating a polarizer for BioGeometry devices, we used hemispheres or semicircles with certain additions designed to cancel the harmful effect of both hemisphere and semicircle.

A three-dimensional geometric polarizer is based on the geometric shape of a hemisphere or a pyramid, while a two-dimensional polarizer is based on a half-circle. We have created a special geometric polarizer for the Bio-Geometry dials in the form of a hemisphere engraved with seven stroke marks and a BioGeometry L66-shape. This empowers the axis of polarization and corrects the harmful emission from the base of a semi-circle or hemisphere. The dials usually have a second smaller polarized pointer

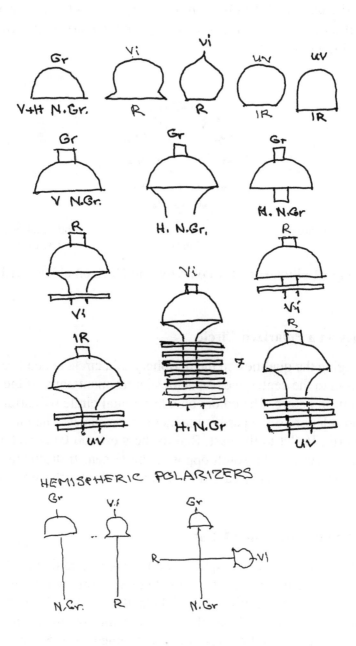

Fig.58 - Dome Pendulum Solutions

on an axis, like clock hands, from the periphery to the center, while the base dial face has a polarizer on a complete diametrical axis from top to bottom (Figure 59).

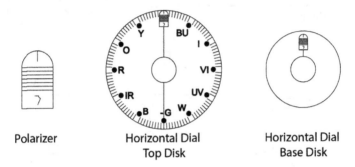

| Polarizer | Horizontal Dial Top Disk | Horizontal Dial Base Disk |

Fig.59 - BioGeometry Polarizer and Horizontal Dial Disks

Qualities on a Polarized Circle

By arranging the qualities on the periphery of a circle to achieve a certain connection to the center, we can achieve a resonant unity of the colors as they occur in nature. The colors on a horizontal circle will arrange themselves in relation to the earth's magnetic coordinates. The Green will be to the north, Violet to the east, Red to the west and Gray (referred to as Negative Green) to the south opposite the Green. Instruments based on this phenomenon must be carefully oriented to the North using a compass.

Fixing Polarity with an AA Battery

The polarity of a circle or a sphere can be fixed by setting an AA battery along its access. In this case the Violet color quality will be fixed on the circle in front of the positive pole of the battery and the Red on the negative side. The Green will be on the right side opposite the Negative Green on the left. This would express the arrangement of the vertical/electric color components. Most of the settings on this type of disk have harmful vertical/electric components of the colors. In such configurations, they should usually be avoided. An exception to this rule, are the "Living Color" settings on a vertical disk, which will be introduced below.

Geometrical Fixing of Polarity

Some geometric shapes (e.g., hemisphere, semi-circle, or pyramid) have a fixed polarity that can be used to fix the polarity of a circle, sphere, or any other shape. By arranging the colors around a circle with a geometric polarizer on a central axis we can create a circle with horizontal magnetic color qualities independent of the earth magnetic coordinates. These would be beneficent color components that are needed for detection. By adding a second disk with a pointer and a polarized axis on the lower color disk, we create a dial that emits the color on which the pointer is set from the main axis opposite the pointer of the color disk. The BioGeometry Dials are used on a free-standing basis or on pendulums and stands. The dials can be calibrated to color, number, or other qualities.

PART FOURTEEN

The BioGeometry Horizontal and Vertical Dial Pendulum

The centering effect of qualities in BioGeometry is achieved by using dials on the instruments where the qualities on the periphery are connected to the center through the polarizer design on the main axis, as well as through the secondary half-axis of the hands. By using a circular dial tool with an adjustable polarizing axis—whereby every angle creates a different color quality—the dial tools allow the expansion of the color quality scale into as many divisions as needed to cover subcategories of color or other qualities, simply by varying the gradation size of the disk.

The Quality of the Center in BioGeometry

Some quality settings on the periphery are more strongly connected to the center, manifesting the full BG3 quality within the color setting. The multi-dimensional BG3 connectivity gives the color the living quality found in nature. These settings are strongly connected to the center, which gives them their unified harmonic qualities (Figure 60). These settings will have BG3 in horizontal as well as vertical dial positions. All the other points have a lower BG3 intensity within each quality range; they do not manifest the full harmonic unity of a living quality and are better suited for accurate detection.

In all dial designs using polarizers whose axes pass through the center, the emission of Negative Green along the polarizer axis is harmonized with a small amount of protective BG3 to balance the vertical Negative Green effect, while still preserving detection accuracy. In general, all pendulums that have a hemispherical polarizer to increase emission should include some way of cancelling harmful emissions. Not all dome solutions, however, can be used on pendulums, as we need design solutions to keep the Horizontal Negative Green emission of the hemisphere while cancelling the harmful vertical one.

Green

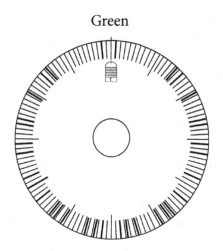

Living Color Base Disk (BG3 points on polarised circle)

Fig.60 - Living Color Disk

Color Quality Versus Living Color Quality

Let us examine in more detail the concepts that are used in the dial-based instruments. In general, horizontal color qualities (which are in resonance with the magnetic wave plane) are used for detection of any element through its quality. In the vertical position (which is in resonance with the electric wave plane) the color qualities are harmful, except those living colors with full BG3. When measuring vertical colors on man-made products, especially vertical Negative Green, we are detecting their unbalanced harmful effect. These need to be avoided or harmonized. This does not mean that when measuring natural objects and not detecting the vertical color qualities, that the natural products only have the horizontal ones. It only means that they cannot be detected with a basic color setting and only appear when using living color settings. In nature, we detect living color qualities with horizontal and vertical components that are balanced through their BG3 centering quality. These exist in nature and can be measured with the living color quality settings. This is not the case with conventional color settings.

A special configuration of living color quality settings using two polarized pointer hands on an upper disk sitting on top of a lower disk with full polarized axis allows the detection of different life force components. We will deal below, in detail, with the different dial and disk configurations.

The concept of living colors in nature is a holistic phenomenon. Living colors are a manifestation of the universal unity of Creation, with a strong BG3 connection, where each individual quality carries all the other qualities in its background arranged according to the main color. This background cradle of unity only manifests in living color and life force settings. In a basic dial color setting the BG3 is not strong enough for the background colors to appear.

With a polarized dial, we find that when we move the secondary polarizer to a color on the main dial, all the colors on the upper dial move with it creating new color combinations within the background behind the main emission. So, each dial movement produces new secondary color combinations between upper and lower disks. Every setting produces a new combined holistic quality represented by the color setting of the pointer.

In summation, BioGeometry, with its Physics of Quality and centering principle (BG3), achieved the integration of Universal Harmonics and Physical Radiesthesia to form BioGeometry Quality Measurement. This is a new scientific harmonic form of qualitative life force (LF) measurement that is not just a method of detection: it is a science of resonant emission of shape that provides solutions to the environmental problems of modern technology and provides an advanced path of practical spiritual initiation.

The Physics of Quality in BioGeometry is a modern practical science that holds a key to unlock the secrets of the sciences of the great ancient civilizations. Universal Harmonics is very complex, so to avoid complicating things we will only look at the qualitative and communicative aspects that relate to our Physics of Quality in BioGeometry.

Dial Calibration of Instruments

BioGeometry dials are used with several types of pendulums. The dial systems are based on calibrated disks where the colors are in a relationship with the BG3 quality which is the main criterion in the BioGeometry harmonic measurement system that differentiates it from all other systems of subtle energy detection. The basic pendulum set is comprised of a horizontal dial pendulum with one dial on top and a vertical pendulum with two dials on the sides (Figure 61). These two pendulums have different attachments for fine tuning their resonance with different types of Earth energy gridlines, planes of nature, underground streams, and so on. We created separate pendulums for the detection of horizontal and vertical energy because combined pendulums and detection instruments often confuse their readings between the vertical and horizontal components. Some aspects of the vertical energy quality components are harmful. For advanced research, however, there are cases where the calibration must be done equally on horizontal and vertical dials. We have therefore designed special pendulums for such purposes with four and six dials.

Fig.61 - BioGeometry Horizontal & Vertical Dial Pendulums

Color Dials

In BioGeometry Quality Measurement, we use different types of dials (Figure 62):

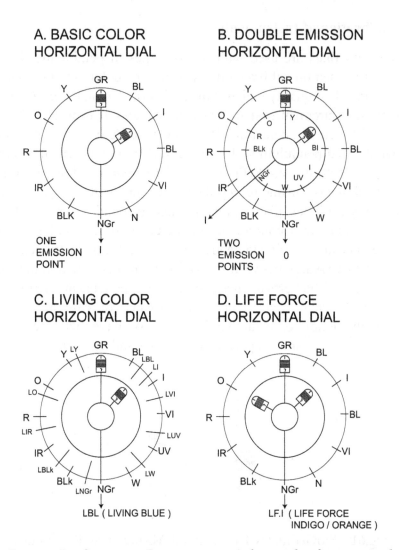

Fig.62 - BioGeometry Basic, Living Color and Life Force Dials

An upper disk with an axis from the center ending in a geometrical polarizer to act as a pointer, rotating on a polarized base disk that displays different qualitative scale units. We calibrate the dials by rotating the polarizer of the upper disk to point to the desired calibration marked on the lower disk. The polarized axis of the lower disk is a full diameter with the polarizer on one side and the other extended to the circular edge (in contrast to the upper disk which stops at the center and does not extend across the circle). This is the point of energy quality emission of the dial used to calibrate the pendulum which is a subtle energy quality detector and emitter at the same time, referred to below as the Basic Horizontal Dial. At a standstill, the emission of quality is only through the polarized axis, but during pendulum rotation, the emission is in a cone form under the pendulum corresponding to the angle of the string in motion. For emission purposes one can set the dial by moving the upper polarizer to any quality marked on the base disk. The pendulum can then be rotated to start emitting under it. Without rotation, it emits only from the dial axis (Figure 62A). To detect the energy quality, one must try the different settings until one creates a pendulum rotation. An initial straight push to overcome pendulum weight is helpful. Otherwise, no intervention of the user through questions or mental suggestions should be used, as it will affect the calibration. The resulting pendulum rotation indicates the quality of QL-Torsion in the body's reaction to the object of measurement.

There are also pre-set disks with the pointing polarizer axis engraved into the base disk. This is mainly used for "living color" or "life force" settings that would need a lot of precision when set on a conventional two-disk dial.

Here is an overview of some of the BioGeometry Dial Configurations and their uses:

1. The Basic Horizontal Dial (Figure 62A)

This dial has the basic arrangement of color qualities based on their corresponding resonant location with respect to the magnetic coordinates on a horizontal circle. In this case, the polarizer fixes the quality of the north direction. The Green color is centered upon it with the Violet on the right and Red on the left. When the dial is in a vertical position, its polarity changes in relation to the horizontal position. In this case, the Red shifts to the right of the main polarizer axis and the Violet is on the left. This is because the two planes of motion in electromagnetic waves, whether at ninety degrees or any other angle or even parallel, are of opposite polarities. The labeling of horizontal and vertical here relates to the opposite polarities of the electric and magnetic planes regardless of their configuration or the rotation of the wave. This is the standard configuration that comes with the horizontal and vertical pendulums and the included manual.

In general, any line (or calibration strokes) on the circle pointing in the direction of the center will have some degree of BG3 quality. In this basic configuration, the colors on the periphery have some degree of connection to the center. The BG3 quality of the center is not very strong in the individual colors on the periphery. This has the advantage that the colors are not interconnected harmonically with all the other colors, and the emission from the main axis shows only the color chosen by the secondary half-axis pointer of the smaller upper dial on the lower dial. It will still show the secondary centered Negative Green qualities of the axis, which acts as a carrier wave. This is the basic configuration, used in Radiesthesia and basic levels of BioGeometry Quality Measurement, that keeps the secondary colors dampened and out of the way. This is just like playing the piano where the pedals are used to suppress the other strings and keep them from resonating with the selected note. If the pedals are used to lift the dampers on the strings, the other notes will all sound in harmonic resonance creating a holistic echo.

2. Double Emission Dials and Disks (Figure 62B)

These are used on stands and emitters that we use in BioGeometry. The upper pointer has a complete diametrical axis just like the main one on the dial face below it. When two full-length diametrical axes are involved, they can both be drawn, or both omitted with the same effect, because they are virtually present as an emission from the polarizers. The stand-alone dials in this configuration emit two main colors instead of just one and are therefore more suitable for emission than detection.

3. Living Color Dial (Figure 62C)

The measurement and emission of full living color qualities requires devices that are specially calibrated to the points of maximum BG3 in each color range. We refer to this as "living color." Only the points of full harmonic unity manifest the full BG3 centering that properly balances the horizontal and vertical components. These points are marked on the Living Color Dial. The Living Color Dial or disk type has a distribution of colors like the basic disk but the marked color quality points on the periphery have a full connection with the center manifesting as BG3 within the color. They are marked with longer strokes. They can also be set on a normal disk as they show a high intensity of BG3 along with the color setting. The distribution of the harmonic colors here is not equidistant as in the basic dial/disk. Also, in addition to the chosen single color, the emission from the single full diametrical axis will have all the dual color combinations resulting from the rotation of the upper and lower polarized disks as a background emission.

In the dial, whose polarizers include two full diametrical lines, we see that two main colors are emitted from each of the full axes, with all the other color combinations in the background. Each color here is a quality reflecting a resonance with all the other color combinations through their communication with the center. The center here with all its transcendental qualities and life attributes is manifested in all the colors. The result is a holistic multi-dimensional living color. This type of disk is the basis for a full harmonic measurement system suitable for research in the living powers and attributes of the Laws of Nature. The disks in this case emit a double combination of main and harmonic colors in the surroundings. The harmonic color pre-calibrated disks can be used with the same effect in vertical or horizontal position although the color distribution will flip horizontally.

The BG3 points in each color range indicate the full living color quality setting. These are the main points of calibration of the living color adjustments in which the horizontal as well as the vertical components are beneficial to life. In those settings, the Vertical Negative Green quality component is in full balance and harmony with its horizontal counterpart as it occurs in the forming process of nature. In this case, the harmful dehydrating Negative Green quality found in electromagnetic radiation is balanced through the BG3 centering harmonizing quality of life force of the living color.

We have also produced preset Living Color Disks to ensure the accurate settings that achieve the full BG3 connection with life force.

4. The Life-Force Color Dials (Figure 62D)

The life-force components are attributes of the powers of nature and as such are endless. The Ancient Egyptians had around one-and-a-half thousand personifications of different nature powers in the form of their Neters. Some were single powers while others were composite. Placing so many attributes in different combinations on calibrated dials can give us more insight into their interactive qualities.

In order to ensure the accuracy of the life-force calibration of the dial, we have created preset color disks for each Life-Force component, that do not need any calibration (Figure 63). This disk has two preset secondary polarized pointers connecting two living colors in a configuration that resonates with qualities of the life force in nature. These disks show two half axes and a main full axis.

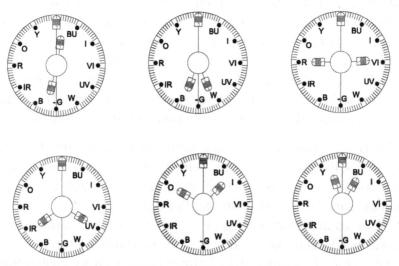

Fig.63 - Preset Life Force Disks

The full carrier-wave polarized axis emits a combination of two harmonic colors that manifest as a component of life force calibration, and which are in harmonic resonance with all other harmonic colors.

We have devised sets with a group of life-force calibrated dials that cover the endless attributes of life-force. The basic set is comprised of six dials (preset disks) which are used to check for and restore life force attributes in living systems and thus restore their biological functions. Each one is usually put on a horizontal pendulum to detect and emit a single life force component. We also produce a pendulum with six dials that can take the basic set of components simultaneously for a complete holistic life force emission (Figure 64). Although we are only producing the basic six-disk set at the moment, larger sets with more disks can be used for calibrations to differentiate more sub-levels of life force qualities. Some sets are also combined into a single disk for use with the horizontal pendulum. Each set is a holistic group of life force qualities showing different aspects of the whole unified interactive group. Disks or calibrations of one group should not be mixed with other groups.

Fig.64 - Six Disk Life Force Pendulum

The BioGeometry Pendulums with four or six life force disks are designed to detect several life force components simultaneously. BioGeometry pendulums with one life force dial are used to detect and separate the individual components of life-force so as to separately detect the presence and strength of each of the life force components in an object. The single-dial life force pendulum is then used to restore the specific component. One can also use the multiple dial life force pendulum to restore the balance of all life force components. In our practical online or on-site courses our instructors teach the protocols of use for the BioGeometry pendulums as well as for our other tools.

For a complete life force emission and measurement, we use our life force pendulum with six dials. It achieves a certain resonance with the primordial waters which carry the life force. In general, any form of balanced complementarity expressed in connection to the center will resonate with some attributes of life force. We therefore have several sets of life-force disks for different uses. The disks in each set should not be used in combination with disks from other sets. In our system of six disks, each disk can be used separately on a horizontal pendulum to detect each of the six life force components and to find the weak or missing ones. They should be used singly or as a set of six.

Using the six life force quality disks separately on a horizontal pendulum we can detect and emit each of the six qualities on natural living things. When every biological function is in balance it will resonate with all six disks. If one of the disks is not in resonance, it is an indication that an organ is not functioning properly. In this case, the disk function can be emitted by suspending the pendulum directly over the organ and letting it rotate until it stops. Alternatively, the pendulum emission can be centered on the heart chakra to resonate with the main pulse of the heart, which affects all other pulse types in the body. This can be done with the six-disk pendulum or the combined disk on the horizontal pendulum where all six life-force functions can be detected or emitted simultaneously as a unified holistic group. The life-force disks can be used in vertical or horizontal position. We must, however, take into consideration that the color labels are reversed (from one side to the other), which does not affect the emission. This means that the same living color and life-force dials can be used vertically or horizontally without inverting the calibration, due to their strong BG3 centering effect, which is not the case with basic color dials.

The life force dial, with its two harmonic living color pointers on the upper disk set on Ultraviolet and Infra-Red, reminds us of the configuration of the DNA where we find an Ultraviolet and an Infra-Red quality of two spirals around the invisible BG3 Ziron-pulse axis; it's also represented in the Hermetic tradition by two serpents around a central winged staff. The life force components are endless, like the drops of water in the ocean. It is a unified system of endless qualities that can be expressed in any number of components depending on the system used. Regardless of which component is addressed, it will contain all others in a special arrangement in its background. As we explained earlier, in regard to this context, every component expresses the overall unity containing and governing all systems of Creation.

The Hermetic staff expresses the unified Divine attributes manifested in the Laws of Nature through the number three, while other systems divide it into 4, 5, 6, 8, 9 or 12 components; other traditions group them in the numbers 72, 81 or 99. The choice of number for the group usually harbors a certain numerical secret quality. In Ancient Egypt for example, some of the Creation myths had eight Neters, referred to as Ogdoad. In the Abrahamic religions we find reference to eight angels carrying the throne of God. All myths of Creation are based on some sort of numerical quality analysis expressed as a mythical story. We can experiment with the quality of eight by turning a glass of water eight small movements to express the subtle energy quality of the number eight which can be measured on the content, which will have the Al-Kareem and the BG3 qualities because of the additional circular rotation of the number. In BioGeometry, we work with all of them to shed light on their respective systems.

5. Life Force Space Dials/Disks

These have three full axes, each of which emits three colors as well as all the other combinations in the background. These are used in the harmonization of spaces.

We manufacture several sets of dials/disks that are designed for different life force attributes.

6. Dial Divisions

The standard dials and disks with 120 divisions are the most suitable size for use on the BioGeometry devices but we also use larger dials and disks of 180, 360, 720, and 1440 divisions. They have additional secondary living color points for advanced research purposes.

The 360-degree dial is a special case, which we will deal with in more detail in an upcoming section. All the 360 calibration strokes on the periphery have the BG3 quality. This means that each of the 360 strokes pointing to the center will have a higher BG3 quality. Each setting will have the BG3 level of a living color quality.

Using the harmonic color calibrations in BioGeometry Quality Measurement, we find that all of them can be detected when reflected, absorbed, or penetrating natural forms. This is not the case with basic color calibrations used in all other methods of Radiesthesia. We can use BioGeometry's harmonic color calibrations to detect all harmonic color qualities on both the light and the dark sides of objects and extend our research to their shadows on different surfaces. This aspect of living harmonic qualities shows us the multi-dimensional nature of the compression waves of subtle energy. The subtle energy background is a multi-dimensional communicative living information system encompassing all of Creation. The complexity of these measurements is the reason that we developed the basic color dials, which have a straightforward simple color calibration.

7. The BioGeometry Non-Polarized Disks

BioGeometry offers several non-polarized disks where a number of radiating lines work as a unit. Each disk expresses different attributes of the emanation from the center. An emission from the center in several directions can be detected on the periphery of the disk. The radial lines marking these emissions act as a unified system with specific angles and connections between them. A special type of BG3 quality from the center manifests on the periphery at each point when all the radial lines are in the right place in relationship to each other, as they act as a closed group with a fixed arrangement. Any shift in one of the angles changes the quality of emission of the whole system. One of our non-polarized disks has twenty-eight radial connections and is therefore referred to as a BG28 disk (Figure 65). If needed, a polarized pointer dial can be used on it for certain types of special research.

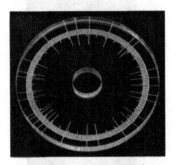

Fig.65 - BG28 Disk

8. The BG28 Quality on a Non-Polarized Disk

BG qualities are usually accessed through settings on polarized dials that connect to the central vortex. There is, however, another way of directly detecting the BG3 emanation from the center onto the periphery. It is a very delicate process, but it produces very powerful emanations without the need for any adjustment. It does not require a polarized dial as the divisions work together in unity. The disk we currently have for this uses twenty-eight unequal divisions of a circle, through which the BG28 emanation arises. This is a very potent disk that spreads its BG28 quality in its environment and it is used with several BioGeometry devices and pendulums (Figure 66). This pendulum will also resonate with BG3 quality like all other BG3 numbers. Each BG3 number also resonates with additional numerical and color qualities showing the different secondary resonances giving each BG3 number its distinct personality.

The BG28 disk pendulum will automatically rotate on a disturbed part in the body or place until the subtle energy quality is adjusted. Or one can be placed on different types of BioGeometry stands to harmonize an area. It can also be worn as a pendant on the body to harmonize its energy quality.

Fig.66 - Space Harmonizer with BG28 Disk

The BG28 disk is in resonance with the Al-Kareem Grids and Fields of mental-emotional information without any adjustment or calibration. We will explore the uses of this disk in harmonizing spaces when dealing with the toroidal Energy Key.

There is also a BG 28 number quality pendulum compromised of 28 superimposed disks (refer to figure 52) which have similar properties to the BG28 disk pendulum. This pendulum also works on non-physical extrasensory dimensions beyond our time space confinement. It is useful in detecting the energetic remnants of past eras, such as monuments, cities, people and so on, that are present on other dimensions. This process is akin to reviving holographic three-dimensional images. It can also be used to detect the presence and location of those other dimensions in the energy fields of the body, such as the location of the astral body above the physical one during sleep.

PART FIFTEEN
The Centering Qualities

Qualities usually have a certain amount of polarization. Looking at the horizontal polarized color disk arrangement, we find the colors Blue, Indigo, and Violet grouped on one side of the central axis with Yellow, Orange, and Red on the other. The two groups have opposite polarities. The positive polarity starts with the Blue and reaches its fullness in the Violet color. The negative polarity starts with the Yellow and reaches its fullness in the Red color quality. One can use these two settings of Violet and Red on the horizontal pendulum dial to detect the polarity on a battery. The Green color quality in the middle is the neutral center. The middle Grey quality on the opposite side, labeled Negative Green, is the centering quality on the other end of the central polarized axis. This central polarized axis passes through the center of the circle where the multi-dimensional centering vortex manifests the BG3 quality. The three qualities of Green, Negative Green, and BG3 have a balancing effect on the other polarized qualities. The BG3 has the additional centering effect that connects to higher harmonizing dimensions. While the Green and Grey/Negative Green qualities offer a certain level of centering, the full outflowing multi-dimensional harmonizing effect is achieved when the BG3 quality manifests.

The Neutralizing Effect of the Green Color Quality

In many ancient traditions, we find certain rituals of protection and healing related to the neutralizing effect of the Green color quality. Green tea, green light, and vegetables emitting the Green quality are used against cancer. In Nubia, Southern Egypt, palm branches and embalmed baby crocodiles are placed on top of doors for energetic protection. They show the Green quality. Salt is another substance used in many traditions that radiates the Green neutralizing quality. In some rituals, salt is placed in room corners for protection against psychic disturbances. Things placed in a corner create images spreading the protective Green quality in the whole space. Swimming in a saltwater sea or ocean has a cleansing effect. Walking in the forest where many plants radiate the Green quality has a cleansing and energizing effect.

The Negative Green as a Group of Qualities

Let us start here with an important definition to clarify the confusion that some authors have caused due to their quantitative interpretation of Negative Green as a color frequency found somewhere on a very high vibratory level within the grey range between black and white. This can perhaps be explained by the fact that radio wave theories were popular in the 1940s and 1950s at the time Negative Green was discovered. Negative Green was therefore understood as a frequency on the color spectrum. In reality however, it is a repetitive resonant quality beyond the color range that can be identified with the appropriate instrument.

I must unfortunately repeat this important point that is largely misunderstood. Let us be clear: color qualities repeat themselves beyond the visible spectrum across all vibratory ranges according to the laws of resonance from zero to infinity. In the science of musical harmonics, the notes repeat themselves on every string length half or double the original one. In the science of universal harmonics of ancient civilizations, the resonance is extended to string lengths (wave lengths) from zero to infinity connecting the repetitive qualities to all ranges such as color, smell, touch, number, shapes, and so on, to include everything in existence. The laws of harmonic resonance become applicable to all ranges to connect colors, smells, numbers, shapes, and the sense of touch through universally applicable interchangeable qualities. One of the basic questions we ask new BioGeometry students is: what is the difference between color and color quality? A very simplified answer would be: "The first is the effect looking at a color will have on the sensory as well as extrasensory subtle energy of an organism and the second is the extrasensory effect the organism will experience when a color is placed behind it. The color quality scale is based on this secondary extrasensory effect and it applies beyond the color range on all vibratory levels.

Negative Green is the label we give to a certain subtle energy quality that can be found on all vibratory levels of all types of waves. The Negative Green quality is also one of the three main components within the centering quality of geometric centers of shape.

As mentioned earlier, the French researchers Chaumery and Bélizal invented and applied the term "Negative Green" to the gray area on the shadow side of a sphere opposite the Green color which faces the light. It lies between the white and black colors marking the boundary between the light and dark side of the sphere. The qualities on the dark side cover a wide range of colorless shades from white all the way to black. It must be clear to us that colors, in this context, had no harmonic resonant unifying qualities and were used as separate units of categorization. The instruments of conventional Physical Radiesthesia were calibrated to detect the colors on the light side as reflected waves, and the colors on the dark side—the blacks and grays—as penetrative waves. This is a simplification that has many benefits when accurately detecting a single specific color quality without the intrusion of other collective or holistic levels. The Negative Green band is the quality of the gray range between Black and White. This Gray range can be divided into as many shades as an instrument is configured to detect.

We now know that some components of the vertical component of Negative Green are extremely dangerous and can lead to many types of cancer while the horizontal component of Negative Green is extremely beneficent and can be used to heal.

The Russian researcher Scariatin, who lived in Egypt and wrote several books under the pseudonym "Enel," used horizontal Negative Green for healing and found that its concentration was unusually high in the bodies of several saints he measured. While researching this fact, we also found that in some cases, this beneficent energy quality was found in an entire location. We also found this energy quality in several types of sacred buildings, and we detected this beneficent Negative Green quality in all sacred power spots.

In nature, we find color qualities with full life attributes. They can be measured with dial pendulums marked with living color locations. With living color settings in BioGeometry Quality Measurement, both horizontal and vertical Negative Green are beneficial when measured in living systems because they additionally have the BG3 quality. In nature, these two components are usually balanced. The harmful aspects are always the result of human intervention in the environment—for example, in all types and frequencies of man-made electromagnetic radiation.

Negative Green on the Sunny Side of a Sphere

We already know that the horizontal component of Negative Green exists in every energy center and sacred power spot as well in our body's chakras. As a component of BG3, the Negative Green quality has a healing communicative potential. In nature, we usually have a balanced state of vertical and horizontal Negative Green, and we can detect the balanced vertical and horizontal components found in nature using harmonic color settings on living colors. In the case of harmonic measurements, we detect the full integrated harmonious vertical and horizontal components in natural balance.

With harmonic color settings on the living colors found in nature, we can also detect the beneficent Negative Green vertical qualities in both the dark and the light areas, regardless of any reflective, penetrative, or absorbed properties that might be in play. This gives us a completely new understanding of Negative Green in nature. The harmonic living Negative Green has all the other color qualities in its resonant background weave of qualities.

When working with living color measurements in nature, we can detect the beneficent aspects of both vertical and horizontal Negative Green as part of natural objects, and this is also true of shapes harmonized by BioGeometry design principles. In this context, the presence of vertical Negative Green will not indicate a harmful side-effect. The presence of vertical Negative Green quality in Earth energy gridlines in a building that we harmonize through BioGeometry solutions can be detected with the vertical dial pendulum. When using living color disks to measure grids on natural surfaces, the living vertical Negative Green quality alone will not indicate whether it is harmful or not. The IKUP set on the personal string length can indicate whether the effect on the body is good or bad.In such a case both the vertical and horizontal Negative Green qualities will always be present. For this reason, the use of the IKUP calibrated to one's personal wavelength will give a proper indication if an object is beneficent or not.

The Use of the Centering Qualities in Healing

Besides the use of Green for healing (e.g., in the case of cancer) which we mentioned above, some BioGeometry practitioners have used the other color qualities for healing, as they connect to higher dimensions to restore the balance in organ function through their centering effect. Some highly adept practitioners have even used Living Vertical Negative Green to mummify cancer cells in the body. I would not advise this practice as it needs very careful calibrations to avoid the harmful effects associated with this quality if not perfectly balanced. The other centering qualities are much safer to use.

The French Virtual Cone Pendulums

Chaumery and Bélizal developed several types of Virtual Cone pendulums which have several cones superimposed upon each other that function as one. They are all based on an ingenious idea: a disk with a hole in its center slides up and down a wooden rod that has holes along its length which are placed according to the calibration of different colors. Using a fixing pin, the operator can place a disk at a specific height, thus creating a virtual cone whose angle resonates with the chosen color quality. Chaumery and Bélizal also developed eight- and sixteen-sided Virtual Cone pendulums. The IR-UV virtual cone with eight sides could be calibrated to sixty-four different Negative Green settings (Figure 67). They used this tool to differentiate between different types of cancer and other diseases, cavities, underground cracks and streams, and so on. The sixteen-sided pendulum is the most elaborate and complex virtual cone. This pendulum, however, which I acquired in France in the early 1970s, was not included in their publications.

Within the divisions of the Negative Green Grey range, we find some beneficent settings on an angle a few degrees from the Vertical under the apex

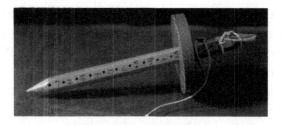

Fig.67 - Chaumery and Belizal Basic Virtual Cone Pendulum

of the great pyramid in Egypt. Different researchers have given them different names such as the Omega Ray and the Pi Ray. There is also a point in this range that we refer to as the universal point in BioGeometry. We refer to this setting near the center of the Negative Green range as the universal setting on the BioGeometry dial (Figure 68). A small warning: these Negative Green settings are delicate, so one might mistakenly calibrate on harmful vertical Negative Green settings if not careful. The BioGeometry dials do not have this problem, as they include solutions to cancel Negative Green as discussed earlier. What's more, this applies only to manmade shapes, as in nature most of the Negative Green range is beneficent and found as part of all living systems. BioGeometry's design principles aim to follow the natural forming process and produce living colors that show this phenomenon.

Fig.68 - BG Dial Universal Point

The problem with all virtual cone pendulums is that they use vertical angles for both horizontal and vertical color components and differentiate between them with a small ring on one side of the disk. When used upside-down, the ring can raise the disk a little bit (about 1 mm); if the operator makes any shift while holding the string they can change the calibration, making these instruments inaccurate for critical types of detection. For that reason, BioGeometry instruments use separate disks in their respective positions for horizontal and vertical quality component measurements.

Unfortunately, Chaumery's experiments with superimposed hemispherical and pyramid shapes emitting Negative Green led to his death: he was found totally dehydrated in his lab. We therefore do not advise the use of Chaumery and Bélizal's elaborate "Universal Pendulum," although it is one of their best calibrated devices for charging as it is polarized using four embedded hemispheres that radiate vertical Negative Green. Today we know that the laws of resonance and impregnation mean that avoiding this harmful quality by just keeping out of its linear emission is not possible as it will spread through the secondary fields around the main radiation. This is the exact principle whereby electromagnetic radiation produces a background electro-smog in its environment as well.

We must not forget that the labels "vertical" and "horizontal" should be understood as two planes with opposite polarities—one electrical and the other magnetic—regardless of what the angle between them is, or even if they are parallel in some cases.

The BG3 Group of Qualities

We can detect the general quality of sacred power spots and two- or three-dimensional centers of rotation using a BG16 pendulum through the resonance with its hemisphere radiating through this number of disks. The horizontal dial pendulum detects the BG3 quality through the separate individual measurements with its three main components|: Horizontal Negative Green, the higher harmonics of Gold, and the Ultraviolet settings. The Gold is detected through two settings—Indigo and Orange—making it four measurements altogether.

Together, these qualities represent the BG3 centering quality and it manifests in different forms with additional secondary qualities. For example, in BioGeometry, transcendental numbers with a BG3 quality, such as those in the basic BioGeometry qualitative series (16, 19, 28, 34, etc.) and irrational numbers such as Phi, Pi, the square root of two, and others, create a vortex that connects to other dimensions. BG3 also occurs with additional qualities in living colors and in living musical notes. This represents the original manifestation of the infinity of living attributes arising out of the primordial zero state.

As the BG3 quality is an emanation from the multi-dimensional connective vortex of the center, it will have all the qualities and attributes of all the living creative forces of nature. To make the general detection of BG3 simpler, especially for designers without any knowledge of BioGeometry Quality Measurement, we developed a pendulum with a special emitting design that includes sixteen disks as this is the lowest number that resonates with BG3. This BG16 pendulum (Figure 69) is based on resonance of shape and therefore needs no specific string length to function correctly. It will automatically rotate on the BG3 quality, and it will resonate with the general BG3 quality. The BG3 label refers to the calibrations used for detection and not to the components of the central multi-dimensional energy quality which manifest as a single non-polarized quality. The addition of the qualities will not produce BG3.

Fig.69 -BG16 BioGeometry Pendulum

All harmonic qualities, as well as the components of life force, are found within BG3, but they manifest differently as sub-categories of BG3 and can be used for differentiation within the vast BG3 centering realm of qualities. To research and differentiate between them, we can use the harmonic color settings on specially calibrated dials, either the complete harmonic dial showing all settings on which the pointer axis can be placed, or pre-calibrated dials for each setting, which is more accurate. The preset life-force dials with two top dials to calibrate to two qualities simultaneously can be used for the detection of certain attributes within the totality of life force. The advanced teaching and practice of BioGeometry deals mainly with the numerous harmonic and life properties found in the vast BG3 realm. Using devices such as the Human Archetype Ruler (which has geometrical calibrations on the different planes and sub planes—i.e., the physical, vital, emotional, mental, and spiritual planes), we can expand our research into the levels of BG3 in those dimensions. We will discuss those devices as we go along.

Reflected, Absorbed, and Penetrating BG3 Color Qualities

The shape, motion and other properties of all waves are governed by a BG3 multi-dimensional central axis that sets the time-space pulse. This axis is the result of the activation of the Ziron center in the time-space duality levels of the Psychon. The BG3 central range of qualities can be detected in all horizontal and vertical components of all wave types.

The frequency/wavelength of a wave, as well as its angle of incidence, determine its reflected, absorbed, and penetrating properties. From a qualitative point of view, the shape of the wave plays a role in the final quality produced in the environment.

Wave shapes with an overall BG3 quality, have a Psychon-like multi-dimensional resonant existence and are therefore not affected by time-space quantitative constrictions of reflection, absorption, and penetration. In dealing with the BG3 harmonic qualities, it is important to understand their simultaneous resonant presence in multiple dimensions. This qualitative resonance across the board of holistic absolute reality opens the door to understanding concepts of parallel dimensions or universes. It also allows us to understand biological systems through their multi-dimensional energy exchange.

The shape of a wave, therefore, plays the most important role in the final quality produced in the environment. The correspondence of frequency to quality practiced by most researchers in the subtle energy of shape does not reflect the full qualitative effect. This can be understood by measuring the qualitative effect of the same frequency with different amplitudes using the personal wavelength method to assess how the body reacts to it.

Every color setting on any of the BioGeometry dials includes some level of BG3 due to their basic harmonic centered configuration. However, the intensity of BG3 is different in each dial type. In the basic dials, the intensity of the BG3 quality is kept very low, just enough to balance the Negative Green components of the polarizers in the emission without affecting the separation of colors needed for detection purposes. The living color settings on the basic dials are an exception to the rule as they show a higher BG3 level in horizontal or vertical dial position. The living color and life force dials/disks have a higher BG3 intensity in any setting as they include a higher level of all the background colors as they are found in nature and are suited for research into life force occurrence and intensity. Basic color settings in instruments of Radiesthesia that are not based on dials do not have all the other colors in the background. The full background colors appear when using dial systems of calibration. In the basic color dial the background colors are at a low level, which increases with living color and life force dials.

This concept is the same as what we find in musical harmonics, where we can detect several levels of resonance between different notes, in addition to the main resonance between one note played in different octaves. This points to the emergence of qualities as components of a unity, where each color has an underlying BG3 connection to all others. The living color calibration can be verified and fine-tuned on the BG3 and Human Archetype Rulers.

This is also expressed in the Law of Samples where any small sample, however minute, contains all of the information of the original. A similar phenomenon can be seen in holograms where each part of a divided beam contains the information of the whole. The physical individuality of living species has an underlying, if unperceived, unity.

Penetrating BG3 Color Qualities on the Dark Side and Shadow of a Sphere

With settings between the white and black, we can detect the different shades of gray settings or Negative Green as practiced in Physical French Radiesthesia. Some virtual cone pendulums, introduced earlier, are calibrated to detect sixty-four sub-divisions of Negative Green. If we use the harmonic color dial, however, we will detect color qualities on the dark side, as well as on the side facing the light.

This goes beyond the basic concepts of Physical Radiesthesia as we know them. Our harmonic dials, however, have properties that are needed for the detection and differentiation of certain types of water, like those found in sacred wells, where we need to differentiate the different types and qualities of underground water streams.

The BG3 Centering Effect Cancels Dosage

The BG3 centering quality creates a state of harmony through the vortex connection to higher dimensions that will restore the ultimate natural balance and complementarity between opposites. All mainstream and complementary types of treatment work through the principle of balancing opposites to reduce over-activity or increase-under activity of an organ's function. To achieve the right balance, one must determine the correct dosage. In sacred power spots known for their general healing effects, however, the amount of time spent in the healing environment is not relevant. Body functions are balanced regardless of a problem being related to over or under activity. The balancing effect is a state of being which improves with time. The introduction of the BG3 quality into any form of treatment can balance dosage and reduce side effects while achieving a higher level of healing with an increased mental-emotional harmony. We therefore introduce the BG3 quality to everything we consume. Pointing or rotating a BioGeometry emitter like the BG16 or the IKUP on what we consume or just rotating our cup or plate eight small increments clockwise will activate the Al-Kareem Field quality and add BG3. Stirring liquids 16, 19 or 28 times will also add the BG3 quality. BioGeometry trays are also used to charge pharmaceutical drugs with BG3 to make them more effective and reduce potential side effects. There are many other ways to bring the BG3 harmonizing quality into any activity such as through prayers, as we usually repeat before a meal, or simple rituals or hand postures.

BG3 Versus Life Force

Life force as a combination of living color qualities will always have BG3. Life force is the result of a balanced energetic activity between absorption and dissipation of the surrounding environmental energy on all levels (physical, vital, emotional, mental. and spiritual). These multi-level qualities are taken in and tailored through specific shape qualities of the organs to perform their biological functions. They are then sent out to perform environmental functions. During the in-take, the shaping increases order within subtle energy (negative entropy, positive QL-Torsion). In the out-going direction, there is a loss of original order (entropy, negative QL-Torsion) that is tailored to a new order relevant to the absorbing energy system in the environment. Looking at the simplified Energy Key model of the Psychon pulse, we find BG3 at the center of the vortex on a BG3 central plane, as well as on a ring at the top of the vortex. The secondary qualities—Q3 and Q4—of the compression wave fields forming the torus are forms of negative QL-Torsion where energy dissipates and then regroups again into positive QL-Torsion towards the central BG3 disk. Those toroidal fields are formed by the action of the time-space spirals around the center. The vital, emotional, and mental levels in the toroidal fields are the result of the Universal Mind and Laws of Creation acting on the central BG3 disk plane and creating the multi-level qualities (Q3, Q4) of the time-space torus. The central BG3 disk connects to the archetypal universal source that creates the life force within the environment of the time-space toroidal fields. There is a continuous translation within the information exchange between the central universal dimension and the limited toroidal field dimension. The negative QL-Torsion of the toroidal field interacts with the environment giving it energy with every pulse. When the central BG3 expands into the toroidal field, we get positive QL-Torsion with BG3 in the whole toroidal field, a state we referred to as the "Al-Kareem Quality Field" (Figure 70). There is a complementary balance in nature between negative and positive QL-Torsion. Sacred power spots and connecting paths and ley lines, mountains, valleys, rivers, lakes, springs, as well as natural oases, all have the energizing Al-Kareem Quality Field positive QL-Torsion. Bird nests, beehives, sea shells, and other forms of natural habitat also have the BG3 quality of the Al-Kareem Quality Fields.

Life Force Measuring Separate from and Within BG3

Everything in nature has life force with BG3 manifesting at the centers of shape where the communication with the archetypal dimensions controls the physical evolution. In the human body, for example, you will find BG3 at the centers of energy vortices referred to as chakras, as well as at any other centers of rotation (e.g., joints) or energy line crossings (e.g., acupuncture points). Life force is measured on the fields surrounding those centers and the lines of communication between them.

Color and Object Balancing of Space

There is a place where every object in a space becomes part of the natural forming process and creates a vortex at the center of the area. The vortex brings in a harmonizing quality of life force. This natural connection will manifest as the BG3 quality. There is also one, or more, specific points around the periphery of a space where every object or color creates BG3 in the object as well as in the whole space around it.

Here's a very simple procedure for creating the harmonizing BG3 quality in a space: take a color dot or object and move slowly around the periphery of the space while measuring the BG3 quality around the center of the space. Fine tune the placement, by moving in small increments, to expand the BG3 quality to cover the whole space.

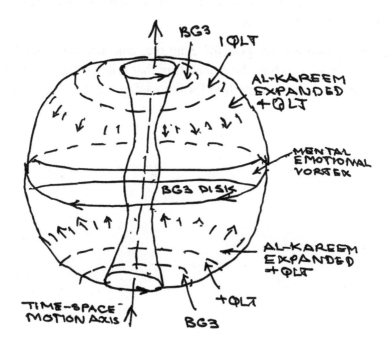

THE AL-KAREEM QUALITY
IS ACHIEVED THROUGH
EXPANSION OF +QLT
OVER THE −QLT FIELD
RADIATING THE
ENERGIZING QUALITY
FIELD INTO THE
SURROUNDING AREA.

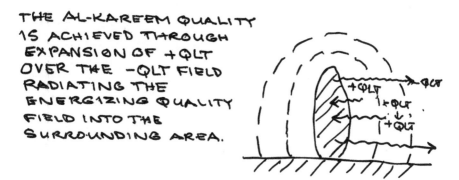

Fig.70 - BG3 and Life Force

This method can also be used to harmonize any object with the BG3 quality using color. After the place is found where the color dot induces the BG3 quality in the object, continue fine tuning through incremental movements in all directions while measuring to achieve the highest level of BG3 quality. One can further fine-tune so that the BG3 quality remains when the object is moved.

An object, like a plant pot, for example, can also be rotated clockwise around its center to find the orientation that creates the highest BG3 in it. This is a very effective method for increasing the life force in the plant.

PART SIXTEEN
Impregnation

There are many misconceptions about the impregnation of the subtle energy fields of all objects so let us set the record straight. Everything in the Universe impregnates. Impregnation simply means new information acquired in any level of the subtle energy field. All energy systems in the Universe are in continuous information exchange on all levels through universal resonance. The Universe and everything in it is in continuous evolution. Our interaction with perceived reality exchanges information with all its contents on the sensory level, as well as on all unconscious levels.

Impregnation of Qualities

Everything in the Universe is continuously absorbing and emitting information and evolving accordingly. Some of this information causes the imbalance and disruption of multi-dimensional harmony and must be cleared from time to time. The disturbance may be on the physical, vital, emotional, or mental plane. The spiritual planes do not get out of balance; connecting with them clears the disturbance and restores the communication that creates harmony. A disturbance on the physical level can result from any form of chemical, electromagnetic, or sound, input, or any form of pollution or imbalance.

Electrostatic impregnation resulting from friction with clothes, air particles, and motion on any surface forms a field like a coating on objects, disrupting their subtle energy exchange with the environment. This can usually be felt as discomfort with jewelry, eyeglasses, clothes, hats, etc., that have been worn for some time. The urge to stroke the hair or skin indicates impregnation has occurred. Due to the universal phenomenon of impregnation, healing stones, jewelry, and all types of remedies gradually deteriorate over time. Electrostatic impregnation has the Vertical Negative Green Quality through which its disturbing quality can be detected. Shaking the container of a remedy you might be taking—as well as those

277

containing foods and drinks—can disperse the harmful Vertical Negative Green. Shaking clothes and tapping or stroking surfaces, especially beds and sitting areas, also clears impregnation. Hand clapping usually clears impregnation after large gatherings. Some people clap in the corners of a room to clear it.

Before we look at some clearing methods, we must first understand that however we design or produce healing products, they will lose their efficacy with time unless clearing methods are applied. Impregnation cannot be prevented, it can only be balanced and harmonized.

Clearing Impregnation

The color qualities that are most efficient for clearing impregnation are BG3, Horizontal Negative Green, UV, and Green.

1. The easiest way to apply BG3 is to point the BG16 pendulum or rotate it clockwise.
2. You can also rotate a multiple life force dial pendulum clockwise.
3. Prayers and blessings produce BG3 and are very efficient in clearing emotional and mental impregnation.
4. The UV effect present at dawn is also helpful for clearing, which is why many rituals are performed at that time. The higher harmonics of Ultraviolet are linked to the angelic dimension in many cultures.
5. Walking and sports clear impregnation through their alternating polarity.
6. Salt has the Green quality and is therefore used in many ways to clear impregnation. Swimming in salt water has the double clearing effect of water and salt. Rituals like putting salt in the four corners of a space are also effective.
7. Placing green light bulbs in lighting fixtures in every room and turning them on has a good balancing effect and can help cancer patients.
8. There are so many cleansing rituals linked with water, movement, posture, and places that we would need a separate book to go through them all.

Geometrical Clearing

Using BioGeometry BG3-emitting shapes in stands, as well as pendulums and scepters that emit BG3, can greatly reduce impregnation. Emitting shapes like hemispheres and pyramids have the full vertical and horizontal Negative Green quality and can be very harmful with extended exposure if not corrected. I have already shown some ways to correct hemispheres and am also including pyramid corrections because so many people who include them in products, solutions, and architecture are not aware of the importance of correcting them (Figure 71).

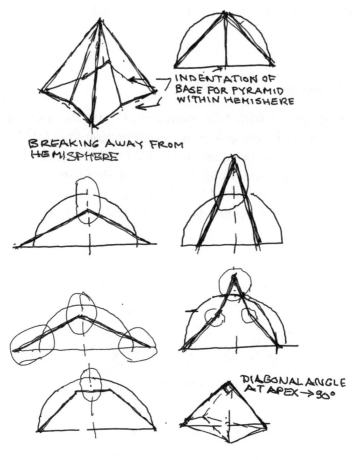

Fig.71 - Pyramid Solutions

A few years ago, at an international conference on pyramids, I explained the dangers-and solutions-to this problem and found that none of the representatives of companies offering pyramid solutions were aware of the issue. Several members of the BioGeometry community in attendance began educating the exhibitors and showed them how to correct their pyramids.

Over the years, we have tested many pendulums on the market that have hemispheres and pyramids in their designs and found that most emit the harmful vertical Negative Green quality. One can make corrections to the hemisphere shape or add a certain number of rings or other shapes related to the functions of the pendulum design. Usually shapes that have emission properties, or a linear flow of energy through them, will be less prone to impregnation.

Numerical Clearing

Design configurations with BG3 numbers (16, 19, 28 etc.), as well as irrational numbers like the golden mean proportion Phi (1:1618...), and others like Pi (22/7) or the square root of 2 (1.4142...), can be used for clearing. Certain numbers along with certain BioGeometry shapes are used in the BioGeometry clearing tray designed to clear impregnation, on all levels (physical, vital, emotional, and mental) of objects placed on it (Figure 72).

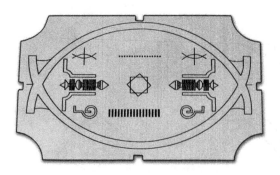

Fig.72 - Clearing Tray

The clearing trays supplied with all BioGeometry products are specially designed to clear impregnation on all planes and levels. Putting pendants, rings, and the cubes of the BioGeometry Home Kit on the clearing trays daily will maintain their efficacy.

Clearing can also be targeted to certain subtle energy levels more than others, as with the corrective resonant diagrams of the sub-planes of nature that accompany The BioGeometry Human Archetype Ruler which will be introduced in an upcoming chapter.

Clearing Symbols

Every culture has many symbols that have shown a clearing effect. The cross in its many forms, from Ancient Egypt and Mesopotamia to Christianity, is very potent for clearing. The modified Vesica shape, with line extensions on both sides radiates the BG3 quality, from inside it, to the immediate space around it (Figure 73). There are many other such symbols and plants used in many traditions.

VESICA SHAPE CLEARING PROPERTIES

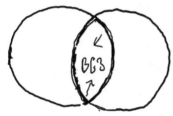 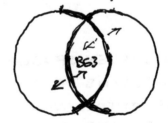

BG3 CLEARING
ON INSIDE

BG3 CLEARING
EXTENDS AROUND
VESICA SHAPE

Fig.73 - Extended Vesica Shape for Clearing

Some geometrical patterns used in Sacred Geometry, religious art, and decoration also achieve connectivity and clearing. Islamic geometrical patterns are good examples of this property (Figure 74). Four- and eight-pointed crosses also have a clearing effect. The five-pointed star clears emotional levels while the six–pointed double-triangle star and the eight-pointed double-square star clear the mental levels.

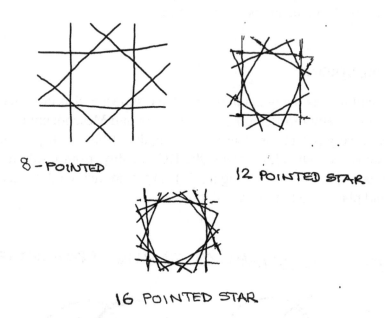

8 - POINTED

12 POINTED STAR

16 POINTED STAR

EXAMPLES OF ISLAMIC GEOMETRICAL
PATTERNS DEVELOPED BY ROTATION
OF CENTRAL SQUARES
THE NUMBER OF CENTRAL ROTATION
GIVES THE QUALITY OF THE DOORWAY
TO HIGHER DIMENSIONS

Fig.74 - Islamic Patterns

Personal Calibration

To assess the effect of any substance on someone's personal subtle energy system, we need to calibrate our pendulum on the individual's personal energy quality. This is the subtle energy quality resulting from all environmental factors in place at the time of birth, when the umbilical cord was cut. It is determined by the time and place of birth as well as the planetary pattern in the sky at the time. The mental-emotional quality of the family or other people, and the quality of place, at the exact moment of birth, might also have a temporary or permanent effect. The final energy imprint is unique for every person, just like a finger or voice imprint.

The most accurate way to determine how something affects a person's subtle energy system is to hold a "witness" from the person in the hand holding the pendulum, or to place a witness inside the pendulum itself, like famous French dowser Abbé Mermet did. This will provide complete data regarding the person's personal code. The witness can be a skin fat sample (obtained by rubbing a piece of tissue on the forehead), a drop of blood, some saliva or anything the person has used.

With use, a pendulum's string becomes impregnated with fat cells from the user's fingers which gives a person's pendulums an additional personal calibration.

For personal calibration, calibrate your pendulum by finding the point of strongest resonance by holding the pendulum above your free hand. This will give the strongest rotation. You can use a neutral ball pendulum—or better yet, the IKUP, as it resonates with all levels, and gives a holistic resonant connection. The point on the string where the pendulum begins to rotate in a clockwise direction indicates a harmonic resonance with the personal wavelength, which repeats itself on different octaves on the string. One can choose the most sensitive or convenient point.

It's important to know that measuring and emitting subtle energy with any type of instrument or tool means that all the conscious and subconscious qualities in one's personal subtle energy system are also being emitted and, at the same time, those of the object are being received. This is the same principle as the energy quality exchange in sensory perception. For this reason, it is best to do any emission using an IKUP or BG16 pendulum as the fact that they emit BG3 qualities will cancel any imbalance or harmful side-effects in the information exchange.

Dedicated Remote Work in BioGeometry

Working with the BioGeometry methodology along the principles of the Physics of Quality provides new possibilities of remote work beyond the restrictions of time and space as we know them in the physical dimension. Many types of witnesses and samples can be used to achieve the resonant connection necessary for remote work. We usually use remote measurements in order to pinpoint the areas on the target site where we need to conduct the detailed final work. We also use satellite images to complete the initial subtle energy analysis of large areas, which makes site work on predetermined qualities of a location much easier.

Using Witnesses and Samples in Remote Work

The paper BioGeometry emitter is the simplest tool to use for remote work (Figure 75). The emitter has seven BioGeometry L shapes in each of the four corners to generate a carrier wave of Horizontal Negative Green and BG3 near the center of the paper. Any combination of witness and remedy placed in the center of the paper will enter into resonance and exchange information. We can enhance the connection between the two by drawing two lines from the remedy to the witness. The emitter functions at any distance.

We must repeat the fact that when we work with subtle energy, the body is regarded as an open energy system in constant exchange with the quality of the environmental energy. In this context, the term "remedy" is not used as a form of treatment but rather as a method of harmonizing the energy exchange with the environment through the energy quality of the remedy. Harmonizing the biological subtle energy exchange reinforces the body's own natural healing ability and supports all other forms of treatment.

We must emphasize that one ought not to depend on the energetic effect but to physically take any prescription as recommended by one's medical physicians We advise however, that all treatments including pharmaceutical drugs be placed on BioGeometry charging trays to give them the BG3 quality, which will reduce undesirable side effects.

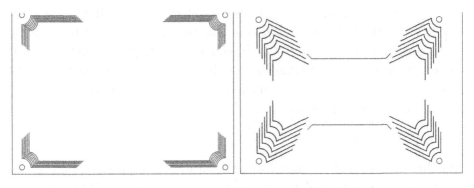

L90 Emitter   L66 Emitter

Fig.75 - L90 & L66 Emitter

The emitter is not just used in remote work: it has numerous applications. For example, it can be used to:

1. Send the energetic quality of remedies—such as from herbs, minerals, stones, homeopathic medicinals or BioSignatures—to a person at a distance without worrying about the dosage.
2. Radiate the effect of BioSignatures to babies, children, or animals, when it is not practical to make them wear BioGeometry products.
3. Bring the quality of a location into the subtle energy field of a person. You can do this by placing a picture or Google map of a place with a witness from the individual in the emitter. We use the term "bi-location" to describe this method as the personal wavelength of the person will be detectable at the location itself.

When using emitters, one must consider the effect of electrostatic impregnation from dust particles in the air. The static fields created on the paper will reduce its power of emission. One can pass a hand, cloth, or duster over it once a day to keep it effective.

The Use of Anatomy Charts

It is a common practice in many forms of distant energy quality work to use a witness or sample to make a resonant connection with drawn charts, maps, anatomy charts, acupuncture charts, or architecture plans for detailed navigation, detection, and harmonization. In these cases, the pendulum is held over the witness or sample while a pointer in the other hand is used to navigate through the diagram. This enables the diagnosis of energy imbalance in all diagrams of the chart all the way down to DNA or sub-atomic levels, or up to very large dimensions. Detailed methods of use are practiced in BioGeometry courses.

Google Maps and Pictures

Satellite images and pictures can be used to locate people, objects, and minerals at a distance. We use satellite images in our architecture projects, to survey Earth energy gridlines on a large scale. We also constantly monitor our animal farming and electro-smog projects, and carry out any needed adjustments, through remote work, which is then implemented as a permanent sustainable physical solution on site.

To detect the location of a sacred power spot on a satellite image, move a ruler vertically over the map with your left hand while holding the calibrated pendulum (BG16) over it. When BG3 is detected, draw a vertical line. Then place the ruler in a horizontal position and repeat the process by moving vertically down the page. There will be one or more BG3 positions. The crossings of the vertical and horizontal lines will pinpoint the BG3 locations with great accuracy.

To locate objects or people, we do the same thing by holding and calibrating a pendulum over a witness prior to following the protocol described. This is an accurate method of remote detection, but additional variables of connectivity may interfere. For example, we will detect the spot if the person might have left the location or if they are thinking of it. One can measure the occurrence on the physical level using a planes-of-nature strip on the Archetype Ruler, to make sure we have the body and not a mental-emotional impregnation. Once a lost person or animal is located, we can use an anatomy chart to check for any disturbance such as injury or anxiety. It takes some training and experience to get good results with this method.

The Material Balancing Wheel

We can also change and harmonize the subtle energy quality of materials by placing a tiny sample in the appropriate hole in the BioGeometry Material Balancing Wheel where it will have the BG3 quality. The sample is a resonant copy of the whole and can be used to reduce the harm of building materials. A paper titled "Protective Role of BioGeometry Against Indoor Pollutants of Some Egyptian Building Materials in Adult Male Rats" was published published in the *World Journal of Medical Sciences* by Drs. Nevin Sharaf, Mohamed El Sawy and colleagues (2014). It confirmed the efficacy of BioGeometry in reducing the harmful effect of modern building materials, including those with radioactivity.

PART SEVENTEEN
Gray Scale Qualities from Black to White

When using color quality as a qualitative scale, it becomes important to study the different concepts and theories of color, just as we did with harmonics in sound.

In the 1960s, during my architecture studies in Switzerland, I was very interested in color theories and systems, and I studied every color system I could find. The famous German researcher, philosopher, and poet Johann Wolfgang von Goethe developed one interesting color system. Another color system in the Germanic culture was developed by Aemilius Müller. As I researched that system, I found out that Müller was still alive and that he lived in Winterthur, an hour from Zurich. He was already retired by then, so I called his home and visited him. We chatted for hours, and he showed me one of the few color cone systems with 720 colors that he had made by hand. One had to use tweezers to handle it. He had developed color cones with 1440 and more colors, which were used by the textile industry. He only had one or two systems left. I was excited to have met him in person as he received very few people. I was happy that he welcomed my visit and let me have the set he showed me at a very nominal price.

Black and White and Gray Levels

The importance of this system in my work appeared later with the development of BioGeometry. As a photographer, it also gave me a new perception of the black and white dimensions at the core of the colored world. In the configuration I received, Müller had placed a central column with white at the top and black at the bottom and all the gray levels in between, and he had placed the colors around them on multilevel disks based on the degree of luminosity through the corresponding gray level in their mix. The basic colors and their many combinations on the circle were put on the central gray level and their lighter or darker hues on their corresponding gray levels. In this system, he clearly separated the luminosity aspect from the color combination. This configuration showed the black and white with their gray levels as the luminescent backbone behind visible color.

Let us examine how this concept relates to the BioGeometry Physics of Quality. The sensory organs of vision transform a nervous reaction from a specific range into colors. The colors differentiate each part of the visual field by the type of reaction they produce in us, creating a colorful and more differentiated three-dimensional experience. In Müller's model, these would be the concentric disks of the conical configuration around the black and white backbone that is now hidden from perception. On the extrasensory right-brain level, we directly perceive the Black and White Gray scale at the center containing all the color qualities. This is the luminosity dimension perceived by the holistic right-brain perception. As a holistic multi-dimensional image, it contains the higher levels of all the color qualities in multiple colorless interconnected dimensions. This also means that all other colors exist at the central essence of every color, and together they form the holistic BG3 gray dimension. This expresses the fact that every differentiated perception is basically the unified whole expressing itself through one of its attributes. My meeting with Müller had a much deeper significance for me that revealed itself years later. His model showed the importance of the grayscale at the center of all colors as the doorway to the BG3 in the living colors of nature.

In our earlier discussion of the Negative Green quality, we explained that the early French and German radiesthesists placed the gray spectrum on the shadow area of a sphere facing the light between the Black and White as penetrating color qualities; they placed the visible reflected color qualities on the light side of the sphere. This is too simplistic, but it works fine in basic levels of Radiesthesia. However, when we go into the detection of living colors as they appear in nature, things are different. The transcendental connection in the natural forming process adds an extra life force dimension to the luminosity level of the gray scale that exists at the core of every color. In this case, the central gray column is the vortex that gives BG3 to the colors on the horizontal circle. The gray levels, as active in nature, contain the BG3 life force of the natural color. That is why living colors in nature, whether horizontal or vertical, have—through their BG3 content—a positive energizing QL-Torsion effect that is not found in artificial colors. However, this is only the case when the environment is not polluted by human intervention which leads to a dissipation of life force. Another point to consider is that even though the defense mechanisms (poisons, etc.) of some species in nature have living color qualities, they should still be measured with one's personal wavelength to determine their effect on one's human biological system.

Black and white therefore comprise the soul that exists inside the colored appearance of the world. In color perception, it is the sensory sight organs and visual centers in the brain that clothe a very small range of the gray reality in color garments. Therefore, each species in nature with a different sensory range will perceive the colored world differently.

Black and White Photography

Colors are a result of the reflection of light on the surface of an object. If the different frequencies of light waves did not reflect off the surface of an object, it would be invisible. In a color photograph, we see only the reflected frequencies of color. Unlike the audible sound range, the visible color range is limited to only one "set." In the case of colors, higher or lower frequencies of visible colors that correspond to musical octaves are invisible. Those invisible background harmonics of color appear as a black and white picture does when the colors are stripped off. While the color picture represents the limited one-level color range, the black and white tones here represent several harmonic levels, or octaves as in sound. There is a multi-level resonant effect in both black and white that is obscured by color and only felt on a subconscious extrasensory level. The color qualities in Black and White tones in a picture can be detected using the horizontal dial pendulum on the Black and White tones. This demonstrates the difference between color perception and the invisible effect of the color quality scale units on the subtle energy of the perceiver. It is the same as with all other sensory scales.

Black and white photography is often said to bring out the soul in people and the belief that it represents a philosophical artistic description of an item is based on a truth not everyone comprehends. Colors address the perceived reality of the sensory left-brain mode with their beauty of composition leading into the right brain unconscious mode. Black and white, however, are perceived directly in the subconscious extra-sensory dimension of the right brain and in the heart-mind levels. Does that mean that the other extrasensory dimensions are all in black and white?

Color in the Afterlife

The afterlife, or other world, is not necessarily black and white, as the subconscious mind can, on occasion, revive it with color, just as the brain does in our sensory perception. We see that dreams and out-of-body experiences can also be represented in color, but in both cases the body is still alive: the sensory experience in the visual cortex is active and it colors the perceived world. If the body is not alive and the sensory perception is completely disconnected from the subconscious mind, the different color qualities can exist in a non-sensory mode that can be translated into either color or black and white luminosity. This is because the visible color range is sensory-related and limited in range while the transcendental color quality present in all vibratory ranges is found in the gray colorless multi-dimensional levels.

Perceiving the afterlife or astral dimension through clairvoyance or out-of-body experiences is still, in the end, translated by the living left-brain mode. Any out-of-body perception is linked to the visual cortex of the living brain and cannot give us color-related information as color perception and color quality measurement are totally different. The latter is a harmonic quality relationship without expression in any specific color range. After the complete permanent separation of the soul from the physical body, however, other senses will be at work that might give reality in that other dimension a different color appearance. For example, it may be more or less vivid with different transparency and boundary qualities resulting in a new form of materialization.

Gray and Negative Green

Returning to the model of the colors on the sphere, the gray levels exist on the shadow side as well as within the background of the colors on the side facing the light. This contradicts the French radiesthesists' labeling of the gray spectrum as the Negative Green and their placement of central gray on the shadow side of the sphere directly opposite the Green quality, located at the top of the sphere, directly under the light. As discussed earlier, this confusion resulted from the fact that the French color system was anchored in the quantitative scientific wave theory paradigm of the day. In that same period, Universal Harmonics was being revivedby Hans Kayser in the Swiss-German culture and was not yet known by Radiesthesia practitioners of the day. Kayser's work led to the application of quantitative concepts from the popular wave theories to the methods of Radiesthesia, giving them a scientific explanation. Practitioners began speaking of the scientifically correct reflective or penetrative properties of visible colors, as well as their vertical and horizontal wave planes. Since their system was based in ancient similarities and affinities between colors, planets, minerals, and so on, it served well as a method of detection.

Universal Harmonics is a science where quality is seen as a universal expression of effects with a resonant repetition on several vibrational ranges. This fact has been used in musical instruments through the ages where the same note appears on all ranges like the octaves on a piano. In BioGeometry, we differentiate between the visible color as a wave with a specific frequency, and the invisible color quality as a unit of a universal repetitive scale beyond the color range. Similarly, the units of the gray range known as Negative Green are repetitive color qualities within all vibratory ranges. As qualities, they exist in all frequencies and in all vibratory ranges. In other words, the Negative Green quality exists as a certain wave-shape configuration in all frequencies. Many authors making their way through this confusion lack the knowledge of universal qualitative resonance and then incorrectly claim to have discovered the frequency of Negative Green.

The crucial difference between all schools of Radiesthesia to date and BioGeometry Quality Measurements is that the latter is a pure multi-dimensional universal science of resonant qualitative communication.

A simple illustration is the fact that one can use the BioGeometry pendulums with a Living Color Dial set on any Gray/Negative Green living color calibration and we can find it in any natural object of any color. All frequencies and types of electromagnetic radiation have a harmful excessive vertical Negative Green quality that we will examine in more detail when discussing electromagnetic radiation.

Vertical Negative Green

In nature, the occurrence of Negative Green in both horizontal and vertical components is always beneficent, and it has a balancing, harmonizing, centering quality. It is found in all BG3 centering vortices and it can be measured with the living color quality dial. In this form, it has healing properties. In human-made products—as well as in some forms of disease—we detect a harmful increase in vertical Negative Green setting outside the living color calibration.

PART EIGHTEEN
Mental Radiesthesia

There are many ways to enter communication and dialogue with the sub-conscious mind using instruments to evaluate information. However, we must understand that the unconscious mind is in permanent background interaction with our daily actions. In many ways, it steers our decisions towards future goals. It will use "gut feelings" to protect us by trying to take us away from harm lurking in the future. Those constant autosuggestions are important in steering us through life. The communication from the subconscious mind, with its different time-space configuration, with the conscious mind, will have to be associated and translated by our memory bank to be perceived. Our perception of the world is a result of this mechanism. We will usually react to this information based on repetitive actions forming into habits. People will perceive and interact with everything in their lives according to the cultural content of their data bank with its personal and collective aspects. Each person lives in a world they have created. In a broad sense, this is a form of autosuggestion playing a major role in the perception and interaction with our daily life.

Dowsing and Mental Radiesthesia

There is another process at work that does not go through the database and is totally unperceived by sensory perception because it is related to the action of the universal Laws of Nature within the subtle energy organ functions. The translation of the Laws of Nature into action within the biological functions takes place on an unconscious extra-sensory level beyond the interference of the conscious mind. Communication with the subconscious mind and the universal unperceived dimensions is a natural phenomenon that is referred to as a right-brain mode of perception or the use of the "intellect of the heart." All Laws of Nature at the core of biological functions act in that background mode, and they ensure the operation of all life functions without the meddling of the sensory left-brain ego.

A physical activity in resonance with harmonious subconscious information will bring it out into awareness through a situation, object, or person.
This is what Jung called "synchronicity" The information can sometimes
come out as a form of intuition to warn, protect, or illuminate a situation.
The left brain, in its time-space sensory mode of perception, will personify the information from the subconscious extrasensory source through its
database of cultural belief content. Some will identify this as channeling
an entity, a spiritual guide, an angel, the Akashic Records (also referred
to as the "hidden tablets" or the "mother of books") or Divine message.
In any case, the message is very real, and its emergence means that it is
needed.

Whenever we want to access dimensions within our vast unconscious
realms that lie outside sensory time-space, we cannot perceive it without
the process of translation. A form of autosuggestion is necessary to bring
the information into our world view.

The problem here is that associating the information with one's personal
interest could lead to the rise of further information from one's intentions,
in a form of autosuggestion that will change the original information and
interpret it according to one's beliefs. Usually, the first information that
appears before autosuggestion kicks in is the purest. In many cases, the
process starts with information that seems illogical. The more a person is
detached and selfless, the more authentic the information will be. This is
the case when the information has no relevance to the seeker. The moment
a personal association arises, autosuggestion from the ego is triggered, as
well as telepathic interaction with other people.

Things become more difficult if we are consciously asking a question
which we want the subconscious source to answer. The subconscious mind
is very literal so a question cannot have more than one variable in it. A
question like:

Shall "I"..."go into"..."this"..."venture"?

has four variables and must be split into four separate questions to get a separate reaction for each part. This involves a form of self-hypnosis where

one can develop the technique of automatisms, in the form of physical reactions, to access the information through a set of one-variable questions. There are several ways to achieve hypnosis in oneself or others: in order to enter into the extrasensory unconscious dimensions. Focusing the attention on a monotonous rhythm in the form of sound beats or repetitive motion (movement of a pendulum) or focusing on an object (e.g., a candle). Speaking in a slow monotonous tone can sometimes induce a hypnotic state in others. In this state a person is highly suggestable and can be steered into extrasensory dimensions beyond the confinements of physical space time. The subconscious reaction will resort to different ways beyond the control of the conscious mind to communicate.

Automatisms can take many forms and any change in the subconscious emotional or mental levels of subtle energy will produce a physical effect. Muscle testing can be used without any need for training. Similarly, one can develop automatisms in the form of a twitch of a finger or eyelid by linking the body reaction to either a "yes" or "no" answer. With time, these automatisms will work on their own when the subconscious mind wants to relay information. In such cases the automatisms become a sort of omen. We would need volumes to explore the methods of dialogue possible with the subconscious mind, so I refer the reader to the extensive work of the French psychologist Emile Coué de la Châtaigneraie (1857-1926), who dealt extensively with this subject. Coué founded the Lorraine Society of Applied Psychology and was known for his discovery of what became later known as the Placebo Effect.

As we mentioned earlier, dowsing and Mental Radiesthesia are psychic activities based on a form of self-hypnosis, that assists one to work with one's own subconscious mind, or even that of others. One can use it as a form of self-hypnotic movement of consciousness into past lives or even future ones, to reinforce new habits, or to reduce existing ones.

We explained earlier how the spiraling rotation effect is a basic principle in subtle energy as illustrated by torsion pendulums. The direction of the flow of life force determines the direction of rotation in the pendulum reaction, based on the calibration of the instrument. When we measure the effect of any object, situation, or environment on the human subtle energy system, the life-force direction on a pendulum resonates with the mental-emotional twisting effect, as in the archetypal Psychon pulse. The pendulum indicates the quality of dissipation or absorption in the balance of subtle energy created by the mental-emotional forces. When the mental and emotional spiraling forces are in perfect balance, we get a positive energizing life force quality. Any imbalance in the mental or emotional spiraling will produce a dissipation of life force. We will therefore deal here only with using a pendulum to enter into a dialogue with the subconscious mind, as it is directly linked to the quality of torsion in the body that we refer to as QL-Torsion; we will also be mindful that there is also the possibility to calibrate a pendulum to any type of qualitative scale. Body automatisms and other devices can also be used to indicate the direction of life force, but they do not allow the same level of resonant scientific differentiation needed for research.

Let us recapitulate some of the points explained earlier that are relevant here. We have examined the spiraling relationship between emotional and mental directions in the Psychon pulse. This form of primordial Psychon torsion (twist) is measured in the Physics of Quality through its effect of the human subtle energy system as the qualitative effect of Psychon torsion (QL-Torsion) that produces the rotation of a pendulum. The clockwise rotation of a simple pendulum, held in the hand, indicates the energizing effect of the subtle energy reaction in the body, while the counterclockwise direction shows a depleting action. The mental and emotional spiraling forces in QL-Torsion respond to the quality of effect on the subconscious mind of the user.

The human-independent Psychon torsion is linked to the activation of radiating centrifugal mental force and retracting centripetal emotional energy. The effect of torsion on the body produces the quality of QL-Torsion as a mental-emotional reaction which moves the pendulum. This is in a way giving the soul a language of communication. We can therefore consciously enter into a training mode where a positive energizing mental-emotional effect producing clockwise QL-Torsion will be translated as "yes" and the opposite direction as "no."

One can use diagrams or charts to map the question, or perhaps writing dates or locations on a piece of paper and then testing the subtle energy response through the rotation of the pendulum. One can also use scales on any ruler or paper to indicate intensity or number of years, for example. Many charts arrange the objects of information in a linear, semi-circular, or circular pattern. These can be used as mental dowsing tools to guide the focusing activity on a question. The arrangement is arbitrary and irrelevant from the energy quality point of view. For details and research, we ideally should use Physical Radiesthesia charts that use polarized circles or semi-circles on which each item can be properly placed according to its color quality. If the samples are properly placed on a Physical Radiesthesia chart according to their subtle energy quality, they should also contain some BG3. Unfortunately, we find that many instruments of Radiesthesia on the market today mix up the physical and mental modes. Most charts available arrange the samples in a haphazard manner and work as mental guides. In this case, they should be regarded as solely psychic aids for Mental Radiesthesia, in which case, their location will not correspond to their energy quality.

We have explained the basic principles to be used in this psychic form of dowsing or Radiesthesia. With the right basics, we can engage in many practices, based on a dialogue with the subconscious, that could be very difficult to attain with Physical Radiesthesia or even BioGeometry Quality Measurement. In contrast, the Physics of Quality uses instruments developed according to the laws of universal harmonics that enable research into absolute reality from zero to infinity using qualitative scales, which are perfect for scientific research and developing multi-dimensional solutions.

Visualization can be a very useful tool in producing mental environments to guide navigation in formless dimensions that we can move through in out-of-body and near-death experiences. We can also use BioGeometry instruments calibrated with shapes that can be set to enter into resonance selectively with the different planes and sub-planes of nature. In this context, the IKUP pendulum has been designed to resonate, emit, and receive subtle energy qualitative information from all planes and sub-planes, and can be used to measure and interact with their quality. BioGeometry sub-plane strips and the Human Archetype Ruler, which we will introduce later, can be used with the IKUP for this practice.

Checking the Source of Channeled Information

It's very important to determine the source of information when dowsing or channeling extrasensory information, or when connecting with entities in other dimensions. Entities with a separate existence, or those personified by the sensory perception, can be very deceptive and can fulfil the expectations of the person channeling them. It is therefore important to know from which sub-plane of nature the information is derived, regardless of whether you are connecting with a separate entity or one of the levels of a person's subconscious mind. One must then determine the effect of the quality of information on the personal energy field. In Part Twenty-One we examine a shape's resonant connection with the sub-planes of nature.

There are also several ways to use a geometric shape that resonates with the desired sub-plane and navigate to it. A few examples, from our practical courses, are given below:

• In meditation or imaginative processes, place the shape that is in resonance with the desired sub-plane directly in front of you, preferably in your hand or on your body. If you are working with your eyes open, the shape can be placed in your direct field of vision. It is recommended to use the general sub-plane shape for detection and the corrective sub-plane shape for emission.
• Alternatively, you can place your witness in a "BioGeometry paper emitter" and add the geometric shape that connects to the desired sub-plane (as given in Part Twenty-One), beside it and connect them with double lines (Figure 76).
• Place your witness on the Human Archetype Ruler, in emission mode, with the shape that connects to the desired sub-plane level of measurement on the centerline (the Human Archetype Ruler is introduced in part 21).

• With this method, one can check the level of energy on the ruler before and during the communication to see if there is an increase in the positive rotation of the pendulum as well as the presence of BG3 on the selected sub-plane.

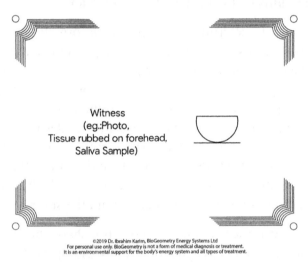

Witness
(eg.:Photo,
Tissue rubbed on forehead,
Saliva Sample)

©2019 Dr. Ibrahim Karim, BioGeometry Energy Systems Ltd
For personal use only. BioGeometry is not a form of medical diagnosis or treatment.
It is an environmental support for the body's energy system and all types of treatment.

Fig.76 - L90 Emitter with Spiritual Subplane

These same methods can be used in order to pinpoint the center of psy-cho-somatic disturbance on a specific level:

• Using the ruler and sub-plane strips, one can also find the origin of the communication by checking to see if there is a sudden increase in the lower astral levels without an increase in the desired higher plane. The ruler is also used to pinpoint the source of disturbance of any weakness in the system.

• If vertical Infra-Red is detected with the vertical basic dial pendu-lum, an additional check with the personal setting on the IKUP will indicate the quality of effect on one's own subtle energy system. How-ever stressful the effect is, one should not straight-away jump to the conclusion that there is a form of a harmful entity with the detection of Infra-Red quality, as the Vertical Infra-Red and Vertical Negative

Green qualities, causing stress on emotional and mental levels, are found in electromagnetic radiation, prevalent everywhere as the carrier-waves of our modern age of information. However vertical Negative Green and Infra-Red on a living color dial are part of nature and cause no problems.

Protection

A word of caution here: when doing any psychic work such as channeling, healing, dealing with possession, astral travel, and other similar forms of communication, or when doing archeological work in tombs and cemeteries, we advise wearing a BioGeometry L90 or placing one's witness in a BG paper emitter with the seven L90 shapes in each corner. This is very powerful psychic protection that works against the most harmful types of entities. As a rule, however, after each dowsing one should do some form of cleansing with water: simple washing of face and hands, sprinkling water drops over the head and elsewhere on the body, taking a shower or bath, as well as swimming, especially in salt water, will wash away harmful impregnation. Rituals involving water in sacred power spots are very effective. Raising the arms to the sky, walking in green areas, making the sign of the cross, and clapping one's hands, will also have a cleansing effect. There are countless rituals that can be used, and your choice may depend on the situation as well on your cultural background.

Mental Calibration Methods

There are ways to help focus the mind using physical charts, such as those used in Physical Radiesthesia, as well as pictures, samples, calibration, ruler scales, handwriting, and so on in a mental "Yes-No" interaction with the subconscious mind.

Visualization

The ability to visualize objects is a powerful tool that finds its application in the psychic method of mental Radiesthesia and dowsing as well as in the scientific method of physical Radiesthesia and harmonic detection methods. This fact, just like the use of pendulums and rods, causes a lot of confusion and blurs the boundaries between these two distinctly separate activities. One crucial difference between both methods is that any meaning or questions associated with the visual image, will automatically trigger a dialogue with the subconscious, which is the basis of all psychic and mental methods. In the physical scientific approach using instruments calibrated to qualitative scales, the images are visualized as samples to guide the measurement without any questions or meaning attached to them. Unless a person can clearly separate both methods, some degree of autosuggestion will affect the results of physically calibrated instruments and affect their scientific validity.

In the case of Physical Radiesthesia, one visualizes people, places, or future or past timelines (as used in the BioGeometry staircase exercise, for example) to navigate to the object of measurement. The pendulum calibrated on the personal wavelength will indicate the disturbed step in the timeline. One should not try to look for meaning or relate the disturbance to an event, as the disturbance can be caused by sources totally beyond our perception. In order to be effective, one must interact in an abstract way by 'throwing-in' a visualized corrective shape (usually L90 or a sub-plane corrective card).

Visualizing physical solutions and projecting them remotely is usually coupled with meaning, and even if totally abstract like placing a visualized BioGeometry object to work according to the physical method, the effect will be temporary unless followed by the placement of an actual physical solution.

Projection

In purely mental methods, when asking the questions one can mentally project in any situation in time and space. One can move into other related lives, where the higher impersonal self (not the ego/personality) has a resonant connection. Interaction with the other life dimension, where we see our departed family and friends, is also possible through projection. One can build a mental virtual future that will influence our physical future.

One can also indulge in the above practices without any pendulums or other devices, as in clairvoyance, clair-audience, intuition, and other forms of psychic activity which are beyond the scope of this book.

The Net

There is an Ancient Egyptian practice referred to as "Masters of the Net" that has found its way into many beliefs in the form of the "fisherman" or "fisher of souls" using a net. We will introduce a visualization physical method here that has been simplified and tailored to daily use. This method is very effective in clearing negative psychic (mental-emotional) impregnation from a person, building or larger areas.

We start by imagining a net with four BioGeometry "L-90 shapes" in the corners. We can hold a paper emitter with a grid pattern on it, which forms a kind of a net, to aid visualization and extend it mentally to include the body, room, house, neighborhood, and so on. There is no limit. We start from below the ground and move upwards through the space gathering all the negative energies. Some will feel the net getting heavier or "see" imaginary shadows that can take any shape. When you reach the top of the area to be cleared close the net and burn its contents and throw it into the salt water of the ocean. It is a good practice to do this every night. It can be used to clear a space or person before healing sessions. This type of clearing will have a healing effect.

PART NINETEEN
The Subtle Energy Quality of Numbers

This is an introduction to the vast world of the subtle energy quality of numbers and it serves as a door opener into an understanding of total reality through their unlimited interactions and dimensions. This subject would need several volumes to explore in detail. I therefore plan to delve deeper into it in a future volume of the Physics of Quality series, to further explore the interaction of the energetic mathematical qualities in nature and apply them in BioGeometry designs, based on nature's own forming process.

A New Holistic View of Mathematics

The awareness of the wisdom behind the flow of seasons, the sunset and sunrise, and the moon phases, all give the soul the stability of eternal presence through their representation of a unified cycle. The beauty behind the unity of the opposites connects to the multi-dimensional central vortices of nature, giving a feeling of the eternal presence. In ancient times, numbers were related to qualities of the time of day, days of the month, and seasons of the year, perceived as qualitative components of an overall unity. Quantitative aspects of number were secondary to their qualitative significance. The shape of the hand with five fingers was worn as a protective amulet. This practice is still used in the Middle East today. Similarly, five-pointed stars were mounted on the ceilings of temples and tombs for protection and passage to higher dimensions. The Divinity of Creation was directly experienced.

Let us delve into the core of this chocolate-coated problem: the continuous shift of the focus of perception from the right to the left brain results in an ever-increasing analytical quantification of time and space. When this took place, the purely quantitative linear time perception completely eclipsed the qualitative cyclic time awareness at the core of natural phenomena.

Modern science has made measurement the main criterion in the evaluation of phenomena. Mathematics became a tool to "authenticate" reality

.

Mathematics is the backbone of modern science and as an engineer most of my work relies on it, one way or another. It has taken the world of modern technology way beyond anything imaginable by the great ancient civilizations. We have, however, lost the living essence of numbers and proportions within the forgotten paradigm of qualitative mathematics, which was central to the knowledge of ancient civilizations.

The same restrictive quantified paradigm that was placed on science, generally, was also applied to the definition of energy. If we cannot measure something in "numbers" we do not now accept it as a form of energy. This thinking led to a split between science and the humanities. Feelings and thoughts were not accepted as resonant interactions with subtle energy levels. Emotional, mental, and spiritual levels, and other types of subtle energies, are not accepted by mainstream science today. Although the psycho-somatic effect on biological functions is widely acknowledged in modern medicine, we find mainstream science is struggling to accept that those subtle energy levels have a direct influence on the functions of our genes. The original scientific definition of energy, which is the "ability to produce an effect," was set aside, otherwise emotions and thoughts would have had to be treated as forms of energy, even though they cannot be quantified by modern instruments.

In the current mainstream scientific paradigm, the notion of the qualitative energetic effect of numbers on the human psyche is also generally not recognized. This is understandable as the quantitative world of mathematics has evolved to a very high level, giving all branches of modern science possibilities that were unimaginable prior to the computer age. Quantitative artificial intelligence is not only satisfied with the simulation of life but dares to assume that it would be possible to create it with its current state of lifeless numbers.

Life force is accessed through the interactive resonant communicative process with the living background medium of the multi-dimensional universe from which everything emerges. In this form, the quantitative processes are nothing more than a manifestation of higher-level qualitative sources.

To enter the world of numbers from a qualitative point of view, we need to shift into our right-brain mode and focus on the perception of patterns and relationships within an overall holistic unity. Our worldview will never be the same again when we start to measure the quality of a number by its subtle energy effect on our organ functions, or when we analyze its effect on our emotional and mental levels. We are dealing here with living units that can have a profound healing effect if they are properly understood.

The prevailing systems used to address the quality of numbers do not address the qualitative essence of numbers; rather they rely on giving philosophical interpretations arising from using numerical methods metaphorically as models to explain elusive natural phenomena. Here is an example of this way of dealing with numbers: *The Pythagorean Tetractys* has ten dots arranged in a pyramid shape with one at the top then two followed by three and then four (Figure 77). It can be read as the proportions 4:3 (a perfect fourth), 3:2 (a perfect fifth), 2:1 (an octave). This can also be read as Unity (Monad), Power (Dyad), Harmony (Triad) and Cosmos (Tetrad). The Pythagoreans used the Tetractys to symbolize the four elements: Fire, Air, Water and Earth. It also symbolized zero, one dimension as a line, two dimensions as a plane or triangle, three dimensions as a square. The four rows add up to ten, representing the higher order.

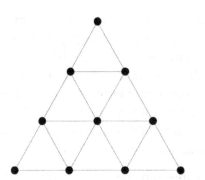

Fig.77 - Pythagorean Tetractys

There are many symbolic uses of number to express reality, such as the trinities of gods in Creation, the ten points of the Jewish tree of life of the Kabbalah, and the five and six-pointed stars of David and Solomon.

The list of numerically based symbols is endless. There are systems of assigning numeric values to alphabetical letters like the Jewish Gematria or Arabic Abjad numerals.

Mathematical models are sometimes applied in solving problems related to complex systems of a philosophical nature. As such, they have proven to be of great value in imposing a certain order, creating patterns, or showing trends. Such mathematical models are, however, still used symbolically, and do not express the full essence of natural phenomena. Quantification is not universal. It has two levels of boundaries. The first is the limit represented by our sensory perception and our quantification ability. The second is the quantification limits of our instruments of measurement. These instruments have greatly expanded our limits of quantitative measurement, from the smallest to the largest in the Universe, way beyond the natural possibilities of sensory perception and quantification. The quantitative paradigm does not, however, include the natural universal multi-dimensional communication ranging from zero to the infinity of absolute reality that the harmonic resonance of qualities has. Quantification is an analytical tool of diversity while quality, properly understood through the Laws of Universal Harmonics, is a unifying communicative principle.

Numbers can easily take us into the analytical quantitative left-brain mode. We must therefore deal with numbers very carefully and concentrate on the subtle energetic qualitative effects. There are many disciplines that are based one way or another on the qualitative interpretation of numbers and geometry—numerology and astrology being two of them. We will not deal with them here, and only refer to them when necessary. In BioGeometry, we use the abstract scientific methods of the Physics of Quality, as we have done throughout this text, whenever we want to access some specific aspects or examples in other disciplines without engaging the doctrines or philosophies behind them.

Number and Psyche

Marie Louise von Franz, who worked with Jung and ran the Jungian Institute in Zurich for some time, analyzed the psychological background of the quantification process in the brain that produces numbers. She introduced the idea that numbers, just like colors and sound, are a result of sensory stimuli to which the brain uses a qualitative scale (color, sound, touch, etc.) to denote the type of effect on the nervous system. This means that numbers are primarily a way of expressing the quality of effect on our sensory system that the brain evaluates through a numerical scale. The numerical scale is an expression of quality through quantity. So, while we are aware of the quantitative aspects of number because they are processed in a left-brain mode, the qualitative aspects perceived in the right-brain mode are beyond our sensory perception, but still affect all living systems on several subtle energy levels.

To further understand those dual modes of perception of number, we will resort as we did in our first book to Jung's categorization of humanity through the location of the focus of perception between the right- and left-brain modes. Repetition is unavoidable here, as we arrange those previously explained building blocks differently in the analysis of other topics. Whenever we discuss primitive humanity or the builders of ancient civilizations, we must first understand that they were different from each other and more so completely different from us, otherwise we are looking at them with our own criteria, which do not apply to them. Primitive, ancient, and modern humanity are three different species of human beings living in three worlds that are perceived completely differently. Since we project our inner perceived reality on the fabric of the total unperceived reality, if the mode of perception in our brains changes or shifts, we become a different species and our whole world and the way we interact with it changes.

The perception of primitive and ancient humanity was essentially based in what we call the right-brain mode (refer to Figure 15).

Primitive humans had very little left-brain analytical perception. They had a collective herd consciousness, and they experienced very little separation from an environment in which they were part of a universal unity that governed their actions in a way that was similar to the experience of animals, where the right-brain perception dominates over left-brain actions. They had very little personal sensory ego, and they perceived their world through what we refer to as their subconscious intuition; theirs, however, was a fully conscious extrasensory perception that led them to live according to the Laws of Nature. Their conscious mind was anchored in the extrasensory subconscious mind, and as such was governed by their senses. Sensory perception was totally subordinate to the Laws of Nature. This human species unconsciously felt the unity of Creation as they were part of this unity.

With the slow development of sensory perception and the exercise of it in the development of tools, the focus of perception started moving to the sensory world and created the individual ego. The emergence of a stronger, practical, left-brain sensory perception was secondary to the main extrasensory perception as the focus was still centered in the right subconscious mind. Ancient humanity developed from their primitive ancestors as a new species that stood with a foot in each world. They developed a multi-dimensional ego that we cannot even begin to comprehend in our present mind state. We are going to keep referring to the brain state that categorized ancient humanity as one pertaining to a different species whenever we discuss the qualitative side of the physical, sensory world. This will assist us to discover what lies behind the quantitative veil obscuring the qualitative reality of numbers, mathematics, proportion, geometry, shape, color, posture, sound, music, and so on. This differentiation of qualities was the bridge connecting ancient man's left-brain sensory perception to his or her inner reality while at the same time it assisted the development of the analytical aspects of the left-brain mode of perception.

The isolation of number in its purely quantitative form is at the core of the modern analytical worldview and its practical achievements. But number in its dual mode of simultaneously anchoring in quality and quantity opened the path to understanding the laws of motion, geometry, sound, and so on, through their energetic interaction. These two conscious realities operating in a complementary interaction, produced a unique species of humanity far superior to either its predecessor or the one which followed. Ancient people interacted consciously with the environment and the absolute multi-dimensional reality under the umbrella of the universal order of "MAAT" and the wisdom of "Thoth." Ancient people lived and communicated with the other dimensions through the right brain/heart connection emerging in the perception of the left brain. The differentiation of quality components of the overall unity of Creation—in which the right brain lives and in which the focus of perception resides—reinforces the notion of being part of one universal Divinity.

The universal uncreated Divine mind imagines everything in Creation within itself. In this sense, everything in Creation is a Divine manifestation and is regarded as sacred. Self-reflection, and the materialization of ethics and universal harmony, were the guiding lights of the world of quality in Ancient Egypt. There is an unconscious longing in modern humanity for such a state, one where heart consciousness emerges with equal power into the highly evolved left-brain perception and produces a new species on a higher level in the spiral of evolution.

The Origin of Numbers

To recapitulate, the different quality components emerged out of the qualitative differentiation within the unity. They took different forms to communicate with different senses, and to navigate the universal unity of Creation with left-brain sensory faculties. Different languages of communication between sensory and extrasensory worlds arose in the form of numbers, color, music, shape, and the resulting mathematics, proportion, geometry, posture and so on. Those tools of communication with the other dimension were developed further, in a more quantitative way, by the analytical faculties of the brain so they could have practical uses in everyday physical activities. The languages were developed in a way that allowed the quantitative and qualitative aspects to work seamlessly together, unifying both worlds. In our way of thinking, a unification of left and right-brain perception, would be the invisible working through the visible world to bring the Laws of Nature into everyday activities and produce what I usually refer to as "excellence of action."

We shall deal with numbers in this universal multi-dimensional dual mode where each number is a quantity and represents a qualitative aspect of the universal unity. In this sense, all numbers have a powerful effect on the subtle energy level and are inter-connected as a unity in a form of resonant communication. This also applies to musical notes and colors, as well. When worldly activities reach a certain level of perfection, they resonate with the related harmonizing principles of the Laws of Nature in the universal unperceived reality and then they emerge as intuition, feelings, ideas, premonitions, and artistic and mystical states. This can also occur as a preservation of life action in the relationship between mother and child, for example, or as an intuitive warning to an eminent danger.

Modern humanity resulted when the focus of perception—through the further development of the analytical faculties of sensory perception—was completely pulled into the left brain, where the sensory ego became the master of perception. The ego, which is a sensory creation, must ultimately serve the senses. The doors to the unconscious mind were closed.

Time and Number

Returning to the model of Creation, we know the zero-state contained everything in a latent primordial state. Everything in the zero state was, however, active at an infinitely fast vibratory state that reached "the other end of zero," as it was still a non-existent potential. Before the creation of time and space zero has no beginning or end but is equally both. The Law of Time, existing in this zero state, produces the first pulse. This is like the first Divine breath, which is a pulse, creating ripples activating the primordial waters into existence. The first pulse is a two-way multi-dimensional motion governed by the multi-directional expansion and retraction of the central Ziron creating an axis on which the two opposing forces of the pulse manifest for an infinitesimal time unit.

To produce the pulse, the Law of Time produced the quantifying aspect of the one as the first quantifying principle within the pulse of duality.

While the zero contains everything in an un-manifested inactive potential state of UNITY, the ONE arises from it with a dual nature; it contains everything in its un-manifested inactive state and reproduces everything in the manifested dualistic dimensions through self-regenerative actions of multiplication and division, and thus produces the other numbers.

In this quantitative manifestation lies the fact that the one, existing within all numbers while equally containing them, produces a resonant harmonic communication between them, creating a qualitative unity behind the quantitative diversity. The left-brain perception will use the diversifying quantitative aspect of numbers in an ever-increasing analytical way. In the right-brain perception, numbers become humanity's way of understanding, connecting, and interacting with the Laws of Creation within the overall unity of the ONE.

This is the first emergence of number forming the governing Law of Motion. It produces the duality of Creation within the first mental-emotional activity of number as it emerges from the spiritual primordial dimension of the Ziron. Earlier we introduced the idea that the Law of Time, in the spiritual dimension of the everything in the nothing of the zero-dimension, activated the first breath of Creation. Here the "Universal Mind" emerges as the primordial state at the beginning of Creation. It contains the universal intelligent living fog or waters of life and the fire of primordial light from which all the Laws of Creation arise. Within this universal mental state of living forces, the Laws of Number play the major role in harmonizing the motion of all Creation. Within the primordial waters of the Universal Mind, all Creation takes place through the interaction of infinitesimal two-way pulses that produce Creation.

Living Numbers

Let us look at the number qualities we explored previously, but from a different angle. From the energy quality point of view, the term "Living Numbers" expresses both their quantitative and qualitative subtle energetic life force aspects, resident as they are in the forming process of nature. In the natural forming process, living numbers, as components of the original unity, are part of the geometrical configurations of the archetypal templates behind the forms in nature.

Living numbers, as they are found in nature, have an additional BG3 quality as a result of the transcendental connection with life force that accrued to them in their forming process. In addition to its main quality, each number, as a component of the original unity, contains all other number qualities in its subtle energy background configuration. This results in a perfectly balanced harmonized state. The centering principle manifests through the presence of all number qualities in the background from which the living number emerges. Our earlier discussion of living colors applies to other qualitative scales, such as living number quality, and its effect on us must be tested with our personal wavelength. Numbers used in modern science in a purely quantitative way are not connected to the centering life force and therefore cannot interact favorably with biological functions of life. This is a main criterion to consider in the evolution of artificial intelligence to run life processes.

The BG3 number series, that we will deal with later, is a special case of living numbers, because these numbers, in any form, are a direct manifestation of the BG3 quality.

The natural forming process is governed by centering communications with higher archetypal spiritual dimensions. In nature, the numerical geometrical configurations of shape are therefore connected with the BG3 quality vortices channeling life force. The center projects and contains all the information of the periphery in a continuously evolving two-way communication process. The periphery itself is in constant energy exchange with the environment. This results in the center and the environment being one qualitative unity connected to all higher dimensions of Creation. All dimensions on the periphery of a shape exist equally in the center. Living numbers are projected from the center, which contains BG3 and qualitative aspects of all other numbers. Creation, from a numerical qualitative point of view, is a unified system where all numbers interact in the musical proportions of the grand symphony of Creation.

In addition to the BG3 series and number quality manifestations in nature, the life force of all numbers can be identified using a BioGeometry polarized 360-degree dial horizontal pendulum in the same way as colors, sounds, etc., can be.

The Living Quality of Numbers in Nature

The quantification of objects is a qualitative aspect of sensory information, and the qualities in nature, in whatever sensory form they are perceived, represent different manifestations of the endless array of life force attributes. All life force manifestations are an activation of certain attributes from within the unified whole. In that sense, quality in nature is based on the activation of an attribute with all other attributes in its holistic background. This applies to all the qualities of our sensory perception—color, sound, touch, smell, and number.

In BioGeometry, we have developed two systems of identifying the subtle energy quality of numbers. The first arrangement is on a horizontal dial which shows the color correlations of numbers. Just as with color arrangements, the numbers are placed on the dial where they manifest the BG3 quality alongside their color correspondence (Figure 78). In this arrangement, we find that the odd numbers fall on the right side of the dial from Green through Blue, Indigo, Violet, Ultraviolet and White into Negative Green. In contrast, even numbers fall into the left side of the dial from Green through Yellow, Orange, Red to Infra-Red and Black into Negative Green. In this arrangement, odd numbers have a positive polarity, while even ones have a negative one.

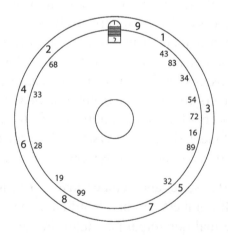

Fig.78 - Number Qualities on a Disc

The second arrangement, on a disk graduated from 1 to 360, emits the living qualities of all numbers (Figure 79).

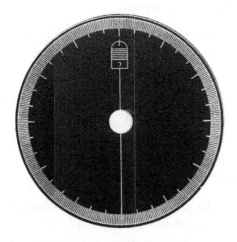

Fig.79 - 360 Base Disk

We therefore have two dial systems to generate or measure two different aspects of natural living number qualities. We have developed a 360-degree polarized dial for the horizontal pendulum and a stand-alone version for emission in space. Every number emitted by this dial will contain the BG3 centering quality connecting all natural living numbers. The 360 divisions reflect the diversity as components of unity. So, in a way, the 360 and the ONE are the same. The quality of the number 9 can be detected in both, giving us an extra dimension of this number in relation to its transforming active quality within universal unity. The number 9 has an Ultraviolet living color quality that is in resonance with the BG3 centering quality as well as the source of the physical manifestation of a line. By using a 360-degree dial, we get the centering effect, where the BG3 of the center extends to the periphery. In any design product using the BioGeometry principles, numerical configurations should resonate with living numbers from the 360-dial.

BioGeometry Numerical Qualities (BGN)

We will briefly introduce here the idea of numbers as units of a transcendental qualitative scale, and we will deal with them again in later chapters related to shape, number, and design.

Numbers have different color qualities depending on the way they are produced, whether through different mathematical operations or geometrical configuration.

Number qualities on a conventional color dial, without graduation strokes, will arrange themselves with the odd numbers on the right and even ones on the left, as previously mentioned. The numbers are thus points placed on the circle's periphery where they show BG3, and they are synonymous with the color qualities in corresponding areas.

The disk/dial can be divided into as many numbers as needed to go into deeper differentiation of qualities (4, 6, 8, 12, 24, 60, 120, 180, 360, 720, 1440 etc.). In this case, the location of the number on the graduation degrees/strokes will differ, as will the color quality of the numbers. The color quality emission of the numbers will depend on their location on the disk. While the location of the number changes depending on the division of degrees/strokes, the color distribution on the polarized disk will not change. The dial will always emit the color quality but the attribution to the numbers will change.

The division of the disk into 360 parts qualitatively manifests the unity *expressed* as the circle. This is the "Unity" dial expressing diversity as components of an overall unity. In this case, the BG number layout on the dial is not just quantitative but qualitative as well. On this disk all the numbers have strong different levels of BG3 giving all the numbers the living qualities. The number emissions from this disk are similar to living and life-force colors. The number 360 expresses the unity of ONE. The 12 divisions on the 360-degree disk are also expressing the relationship of this number to the unity. The calibration on any of those 12 points gives a higher intensity of BG3. In Ancient Egypt, they divided the year into 360 days and once the unity was completed, the remaining five days were sacred days of the Neters. These were derived as the mean between the

11-day difference between the solar and lunar year. This is expressed by Pythagoras as the Comma, doorway to the Divine, which was the difference between the perfect mathematical music note arrangement of Creation and the human note arrangement (Figure 80).

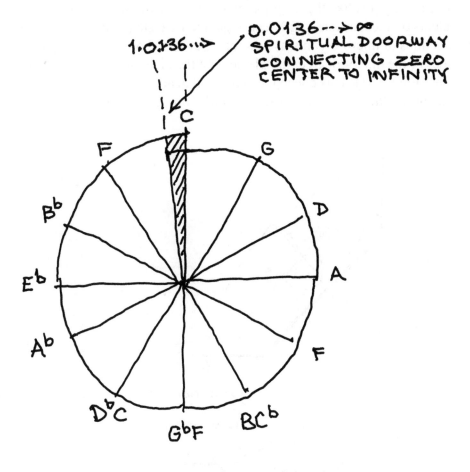

Fig.80 - Pythagorean Comma

BG Irrational and Transcendental Number Qualities

Irrational numbers like the square root of two (1.41421..), Pi π (3.1428..), and Phi Φ (1.61803…) are endless and create a vortex into higher dimensions, each with a distinct BG3 quality. The 90-degree triangle with equal sides has a diagonal equal to the square root of two. The diagonal has a BG3 quality just like the diagonal of a cube. One of the first BioGeometry patents on the harmonizing effect of geometrical shapes on biological life functions of micro-organisms was for a tray based on the extension of the sides of the ninety-degree triangle beyond the diagonal to extend the BG3 zone (Figure 81). This concept can be used in architecture and design, but one must adhere to certain criteria in order not to lose the BG3.

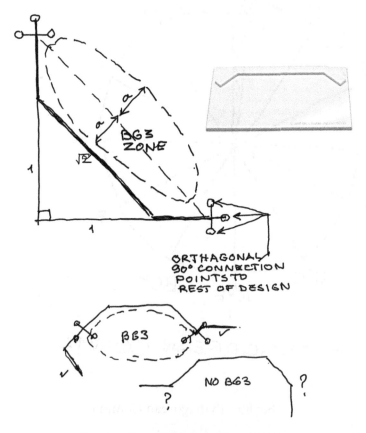

Fig.81 - BioGeometry Tray Design

The 360-Degree Unifying Quality Dial

The 360-degree divisions on a circle express a unity and each degree manifests a BG3 quality component of the whole. This disk configuration, which we introduced earlier, is a perfect expression of the "centering" concept, where the quality of the center fills the whole shape to become one big center.

The number 360 expresses diversity in unity. It is the one and the many in a coherent harmony. For example, it expresses the unity behind the number of days in the year. The Ancient Egyptians added five days at the end of the year, that were known as the *Epagomenal days*. These five days expressed the mean (the halfway point) between the number of days in the solar year and the number of days in the lunar year. They thus connected the year to the unity while maintaining its 365 number of days. The 12 divisions on our Unifying Quality Disk have a powerful emission reinforcing the subtle energetic quality behind the division of months in a year. The 12 divisions are therefore marked on the 360-degree disk/dial.

According to the Physics of Quality and the Laws of Resonance in Universal Harmonics, all quality scales are interchangeable. So, whether we put the numbers, or the corresponding color distribution, or other type of units in their place on a 360-degree dial, the life force in every color setting will emerge as BG3 and become a living color that can be detected or emitted. What's more, all the degrees within a color range will show the BG3 living quality.

Adding any existing disk/dial layout with a quality scale distribution (which might be based on color, notes, etc., or elements, stones, herbs, or other remedies in the appropriate places) to the 360-degree disk/dial, causes all calibrations to come alive. Living quality scales allow us to do research based on the natural forming process. With this dial, we can emit all kinds of remedies in their holistic, connected, perfectly balanced living form by connecting to their resonant quality location on the 360-dial/disk, giving each a personal living number. We can find the ultimate location, on a specific day of the year, of any remedy, plant, or object. On this day, the remedy will have a holistic effect incorporating the qualities of all other remedies in the system to give it the ultimate balance and effectiveness.

In a way, it is like celebrating the "Healing Anniversary" of each remedy. This is the way qualities exist in nature, where each one includes the rest in its background, expressing the perfect balance and connection to the spiritual archetypal forming dimensions. This means that each number will have BG3 as the anchor of the individual quality emitted from the main axis of the disk.

The 360-degree dial can be configured to emit numbers greater than 360, by using two polarizer pointing disks above the base one. Each polarizer is set to a number on the lower disk. The numerical quality emitted will be the result of the multiplication of both numbers.

Living numbers, like all other living qualities, are not affected by dosage and can be applied for any length of time—or even permanently, as in design and architecture. Without the BG3 anchoring, any type of healing with numbers, colors, frequencies/wavelengths, and so on, must adhere to a specific dosage in order to ensure proper balance.

All settings on a 360-degree dial emit living qualities in vertical as well as horizontal positions. Vertical living colors and numbers in nature are usually not harmful. In human products, however, most color qualities, as measured through existing methods of Physical Radiesthesia, are harmful. Vertical qualities measured in monuments erected on sacred power spots are all beneficent; in some cases, natural phenomena such as radioactivity and Earth energy gridlines are harmful. Earth shifts, cracks, or anomalies, as well as natural or other pollution, will also have harmful vertical color or number qualities.

A stand-alone 360-dial will have a main axis from top to bottom on the lower disk. The upper disks however, come in two versions; one with the axis all the way from top to bottom like the lower disk, while the other comes with a half axis from periphery to center only. The first disk will emit two sets of numbers from both axes just like the color stand-alone dial. The second one will emit only one number quality; it is the one used on a dial pendulum for detection or emission of an object's specific numerical quality of an object. This pendulum can be used to check the significance of certain times or days in a year.

Here are some interesting exercises one can undertake with this pendulum:

1. Correlate number qualities with chakras.
2. Correlate number qualities with planes of nature.
3. Correlate number qualities with organs.
4. Correlate number qualities with medicinal plants.
5. As a personal wavelength tool by setting to date of birth.

In all the above exercises, we determine the day of the year with maximum subtle energy effect life force balance of the remedy or object in general. Everything in existence has a time and place in this holistic system.

The Life Force-Based Lifestyle

The horizontal 360-dial pendulum is the most accurate and practical way to set your personal energy quality for all types of measurements. One does not need any measurement for this setting, just the day of birth in the year. The setting for December 26-31 is on the 360-degree point, as it applies to the five extra days, which are sacred days beyond the regular count. This should give the maximum rotation of the pendulum on the top of the palm. One can also use this dial to find the day of birth of any person.

We start by setting the pointer of the 360-dial disk on the number corresponding to the day of birth in the year. We can then use this setting to test remedies, herbs, stones, foods, drinks, and so on, or even places, to find the ones in full resonance when the pendulum rotates maximally. Using this method, one can build a personalized life force-based lifestyle.

This setting on the pendulum will not indicate what is generally good for you at the moment, like, for example, checking which food to eat. For such measurements, it is better to use the IKUP with personal wavelength setting on string.

As mentioned earlier, dial types with different number systems show us that numbers have different color quality associations depending on the system of quality measurement in use. They usually have a place on a color dial disk (as in the horizontal pendulum) expressing some qualities like odd and even, as well as secondary placements deriving from their components or combinations. On a 360-dial, the numbers are arranged from 1 to 360 around the dial and therefore have an additional and different color quality association to the basic arrangement of the color disk. This is outside of the fact that all living color qualities have all the colors in their background.

Life Force Quality Emission

Living numbers are life force qualities. One can use the 360-dial to impregnate an object with any desired subtle energy quality while at the same time restoring its life force. One way to do this is by setting the dial to the desired number and pointing its emission axis towards the object. The setting can be in accordance with that of the object or any other quality needed to correct a situation. One can change the horizontal 360-dial pendulum's settings until it rotates to find the numerical quality of an object. This allows finding its place in the unified system or day of the year as well as recharging it with its original energy quality. The dial can also be placed on or next to a person to emit a specific healing living number quality. It can be calibrated to harmonize electro-smog or environmental and psychic disturbances using the BioGeometry Human Archetype Ruler for verification on all sub-planes of nature.

The Forming Process of Numbers

There are numerous factors in the forming process of numbers that play a role in their final quality, such as the time and place of forming and this is especially true in alchemical processes. For example, the time of day starts with the Violet/UV quality at dawn and goes through the color spectrum up to the Red/IR in the evening. Location and orientation can also affect the quality of numbers. This phenomenon is applicable to all measurements in general regardless of the qualitative scale used.

For research purposes, we will look at some of the criteria in the forming process of numbers while putting aside the time-space effect for the moment so as to avoid complicating the issue. The world of number qualities is very rich with criteria, and it is in constant dynamic exchange of qualities with the environment, as well as with all dimensions of Creation. Subtle energy is a potent universal multi-dimensional life force background medium that is in constant dynamic interaction and evolution.

Numerical Even and Odd Qualities

The main even and odd quality of a number is determined by whether it can be divided into two equal halves or not. There is however a secondary odd or even quality resulting from the sum of its components. There are odd numbers with a secondary even quality based on the sum of their component digits such as 19, and there are even numbers with a secondary odd quality such as 12 or 16. Odd numbers usually have a positive polarity when measured with a pendulum. The pendulum string can be calibrated on an AA pen battery. Polarity can also be measured with the Violet and Red settings on a horizontal dial pendulum. Even numbers have a negative polarity when measured with a pendulum calibrated on an AA battery and they resonate with the Red range on a horizontal dial. Numbers showing odd-even, or even-odd qualities (e.g. 16, 19, 34) have a balanced neutral polarity and resonate with the Green range and have some level of BG3 in them.

The Basic Color Number Correlation Dial

We previously mentioned that numbers arranged according to their basic qualities on a polarized circle color quality dial express other properties of numbers. Here we can see that odd numbers have their place on the right half of the polarized circle while the even numbers are on the left. This arrangement will often show the same number resonating with additional positions on the polarized circle. This is because the number can be in secondary resonance with the components of another number in that location (Figure 82).

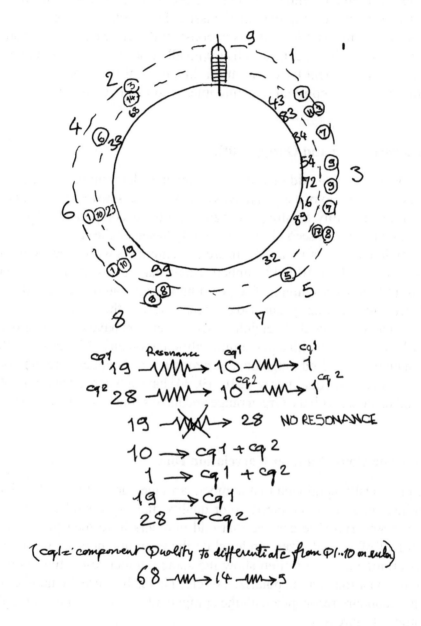

Fig.82 - Primary and Secondary Number Quality Interaction on a Disk

The Time Pendulum and Quality of Numbers

The Time Pendulum has a use in numbers, where we differentiate between the energy qualities of odd and even numbers. In its vertical configuration, the pendulum will resonate with odd number qualities while the horizontal position resonates with even number qualities.

Mathematical Creation of Number

The mathematical processes between the components in the creation of a number also play a role in its quality. This is a world where the energetic effect of the number four, for example, is different when it results from adding two plus two than it is when it results from multiplying two by two. In general, numbers resulting from the multiplication of their components will have the BG3 quality of living numbers and positive QL-Torsion (QT+). Numbers resulting from the addition of two numbers will have negative QL-Torsion (QT-). The addition of three numbers gives positive QL-Torsion. The quality of those components will be present in the quality of the number, and it will be different each time an operation is completed. The following examples are an oversimplification of the real number-forming process to illustrate this point. The mathematical combinations and formulas behind the manifestation of any number are far more complex.

$1 + 1 + 1 = 3$	Violet (Green), QT+
$1 + 2 = 3$	Red (Green, Orange) QT-
$1 \times 3 = 3$	BG3 Red (Green, Violet) QT+

The above examples should not be taken for granted, since multiple variables within the forming process affect number and shape quality. One should always verify through measurement. This is done using the dial pendulum on geometrical combinations of number components (Figure 83). The color is measured with the horizontal dial pendulum while QT polarity is measured with the IKUP.

In the natural forming process, however, although all numbers show different qualities, they will have BG3 regardless of the way their components were combined. For this reason, they are referred to as "Living Numbers."

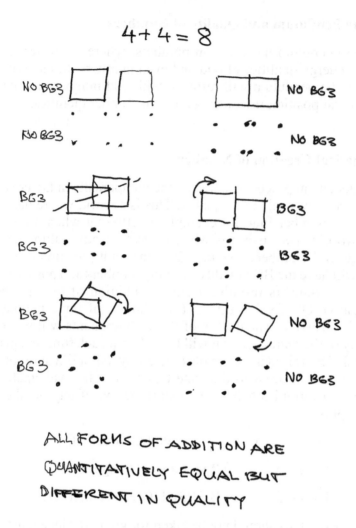

Fig.83 - Addition of Number Qualities

The Effect of Forming on Number

The pattern of arrangement of units (e.g., dots, strokes, etc.) of a number will influence their subtle energy quality. Numbers that do not have BG3 can be shaped into a figure to produce this harmonizing connection (Figure 84). Any degree of rotation in the arrangement will produce a centering vortex with a BG3 quality that will expand the resonance to connect to the spiritual planes. The geometrical arrangement of 10 dots in the triangular shape known as the Pythagorean Tetractys that we discussed earlier is an example that gives the number 10 the additional BG3 quality not present in a different arrangement. In this configuration, the number 10 expresses all the levels of Creation.

Fig.84 – BG Formed Numbers

Emission of Numerical Qualities

We earlier introduced two methods of determining the emission of number quality using a basic color-number dial and a 360-dial but there are also other methods used in design to emit the quality of numbers. For example, rows of columns will do this, as will the placement of windows or chairs. The quality of the total number will be emitted in certain directions and each place in a row will have a different quality. Thus, the numerical rhythm in any arrangement plays a role in the quality and this is especially useful in design. We will show some examples of how this can be used later.

Number Qualities in BioNumerals and BioSignatures

The concept of BioNumerals is based on applying a desired number quality through strokes, loops, waves, spirals, or other geometrical forms to any type of design. This concept relates to the Use of Number qualities in the forming of Pendulums, Stands, and BioSignatures.

The following is an example where 7 loops have been applied as a modification of the BioSignature for Pituitary to target subtle energy function in some cases of Dyslexia (Figure 85). For more information, please refer to our book dedicated to the subject of BioGeometry Signatures. In any adjustment to the BioSignature, we must ensure that the proper function of the BioSignature has been enhanced while still allowing it to be effective in its resonance with the biological function.

In the design of pendulums and stands, we use specific numbers of disks to give additional numerical qualities to the shape or to enhance resonance with the corresponding levels of mental planes.

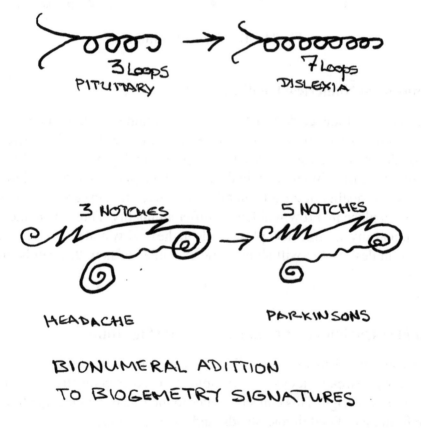

Fig.85 - BioGeometry Signatures with BioNumberal Qualities

Number-Based Instruments of Quality Detection

We also use the numbers 6, 8, 9, 10, 11, 12, as well as 16, 19, 28, 34... in the design of pendulums, scepters, stands, and staffs to activate BG3 and the Al-Kareem Quality Field. This concept has been used to develop several pendulums, stands, and staffs where the disks have been added to hemispheres which point downwards for emission, or upwards to connect to spiritual dimensions. Examples of these pendulums were shown earlier. The quality from the number of disks cancels the harmful effect of Vertical Negative Green emitted from the base of the sphere, cone, or pyramid shape and adds extra quality and plane connectivity to the emitting device.

A typical example here is the BG16 pendulum. By adding sixteen disks under the hemisphere, we retain its emission properties, cancel any of the harmful effects of the vertical components, and enhance the BG3 property of the number 16. In this case, we also have resonant communication with the higher mental and causal spiritual plane. This pendulum is therefore a powerful emitter and detector of BG3.

Healing with Numbers

There is a very simple exercise that we do in our introductory courses to show the qualitative aspect of numbers. Take a pendulum calibrated to the sample, wavelength, or living color of a person, and then find an area of disturbance on the body where the pendulum reverses direction from clockwise to counterclockwise. This indicates a disturbance in one of the organs in the area. Use objects that you know are harmful to the body—like cigarettes, for example. One by one start putting them in the person's hand while measuring with the pendulum on the disturbed area. The pendulum will turn counterclockwise. Keep adding more cigarettes, one by one, until your pendulum turns clockwise on the disturbed area. Add one more to see if the clockwise rotation of the pendulum will increase or not. If it reverses, then take off one cigarette and you now have the needed number quality.

We might also complete this type of exercise using a pen while drawing the numbers as dots or strokes on a piece of paper and maintaining awareness of the imbalanced area in the body. Every time you place the paper on the body the problem will correct. This is a proof that numbers have a qualitative effect that can be used directly or added to any type of treatment if possible. To add the BG3 Quality, and override directionality effects, we always include a BG3 number such as 16 in addition to the measured corrective number. Alternatively, one can measure the needed BG3 number. Below are examples of BG3 numbers and their effect related to subtle energy organ functions (note that multiple numbers can be related to certain aspects of a biological function).

16: Liver, throat, throat chakra, third eye

19: Eyes, migraine, solar plexus chakra

28: Migraine, heart chakra

34: Heart, knees, colon, heart chakra, root chakra

43: Small intestine, stomach, solar plexus chakra, reproductive chakra

54: First chakra above crown

68: Arthritis, joints, thyroid, sinus, lower back

72: Platelets, third chakra above crown

83: Kidney prostate, reproductive chakra, crown chakra

89: Second chakra above crown

99: Heart, Sinoatrial node (pacer), throat chakra

Here are some tips to apply the quality of numbers in everyday life

- Stirring drinks 16, 19 or 28 times
- Rotation of cups and plates 8 small increments clockwise will enhance the contents with the BG3 coupled with the Al-Kareem Quality.
- Seat and row numbers like 3, 7, 8, 12, or any number with dual polarity in its components will have a balancing effect without necessarily being a BG3 number. In this case the number itself has a polarity while the addition of its components will give a

different polarity. The number 12, for example is even but its components add up to 3 which is an odd number.

Electromagnetic Generation of Number Qualities

All devices that use electromagnetically generated frequencies have a disturbance resulting from electromagnetic or scalar fields. These reduce or completely cancel the living quality of the numbers within the frequencies generated by the device. The application of BioGeometry solutions to those devices reduces the electromagnetic stress effect and restores life force into the numbers within the frequencies generated by the device through the centering effect of BG3. This is a cornerstone criterion for healing practices and we will be dealing with it in more detail in the relevant part of this book.

Applying the Quality of Numbers in Design

We can use numbers to introduce certain qualities in design in many ways. As a rule, we want to make sure that we have the numerical quality coupled with the BG3 quality of natural living numbers. A BG3 number in the dimension of a line or object (e.g., 16 inches or centimeters) will not produce the quality, because the scale of measurement cannot be read by nature. If, however, the length of the strip and its width are in a BG3 proportion it will work The subtle energy quality is affected by the number of similar objects or the proportion between any two of them. The proportion between two numbers produces a subtle energy quality. One can use different proportions to produce any color quality. In BioGeometry, we are concerned with the BG3 quality that is produced through a proportion between the numbers 1 (or 10) in relation to any number from the BG3 series: 16, 19, 28, 34, 43, 54, 68, 72, 83, 89, 99. Alternatively, one can also create a proportion using any two or more numbers from the BG3 series, to bring harmony into the design and its environment.

We went further by using numbers from the BG series to create proportions and these are shown in the BioGeometry proportion tables which follow. They show two systems using BG3 numbers to create the proportions (Figure 86).

BioGeometry Modulor

Base unit: 1   Scale = 0,1

BG No.	0,10	1,60	1,90	2,80	3,40	4,30	5,40	6,80	7,20	8,30	8,90	9,90
1												
16		25,60	30,40	44,80	54,40	68,80	86,40	108,80	115,20	132,80	142,40	158,40
19		30,40	36,10	53,20	64,60	81,70	102,60	129,20	136,80	157,70	169,10	188,10
28		44,80	53,20	78,40	95,20	120,40	151,20	190,40	201,60	232,40	249,20	277,20
34		54,40	64,60	95,20	115,60	146,20	183,60	231,20	244,80	282,20	302,60	336,60
43		68,80	81,70	120,40	146,20	184,90	232,20	292,40	309,60	356,90	382,70	425,70
54		86,40	102,60	151,20	183,60	232,20	291,60	367,20	388,80	448,20	480,60	534,60
68		108,80	129,20	190,40	231,20	292,40	367,20	462,40	489,60	564,40	605,20	673,20
72		115,20	136,80	201,60	244,80	309,60	388,80	489,60	518,40	597,60	640,80	712,80
83		132,80	157,70	232,40	282,20	356,90	448,20	564,40	597,60	688,90	738,70	821,70
89		142,40	169,10	249,20	302,60	382,70	480,60	605,20	640,80	738,70	792,10	881,10
99		158,40	188,10	277,20	336,60	425,70	534,60	673,20	712,80	821,70	881,10	980,10

BioGeometry Lambdoma

Base unit: 10   Scale = 1

BG No.	10,00	6,25	0,53	0,36	0,29	0,23	0,19	0,15	0,14	0,12	0,11	0,10
1												
16	100,00	8,42	5,71	4,71	3,72	2,96	2,35	2,22	1,93		1,80	1,62
19	118,75	10,00	6,79	5,59	4,42	3,52	2,79	2,64	2,29		2,13	1,92
28	175,00	14,74	10,00	8,24	6,51	5,19	4,12	3,89	3,37		3,15	2,83
34	212,50	17,89	12,14	10,00	7,91	6,30	5,00	4,72	4,10		3,82	3,43
43	268,75	22,63	15,36	12,65	10,00	7,96	6,32	5,97	5,18		4,83	4,34
54	337,50	28,42	19,29	15,88	12,56	10,00	7,94	7,50	6,51		6,07	5,45
68	425,00	35,79	24,29	20,00	15,81	12,59	10,00	9,44	8,19		7,64	6,87
72	450,00	37,89	25,71	21,18	16,74	13,33	10,59	10,00	8,67		8,09	7,27
83	518,75	43,68	29,64	24,41	19,30	15,37	12,21	11,53	10,00		9,33	8,38
89	556,25	46,84	31,79	26,18	20,70	16,48	13,09	12,36	10,72		10,00	8,99
99	618,75	52,11	35,36	29,12	23,02	18,33	14,56	13,75	11,93		11,12	10,00

Fig.86 - BioGeometry Harmonic Tables

The first uses multiplication to further enhance the BG3 Quality. It is labelled Modulor as a tribute to the Swiss architect Le Corbusier, one of the pioneers of modern architecture. He created two scales labeled Red and Blue, based them on the "Golden Mean," and gave them the name Modulor.

The second table uses both multiplication and division (fractions) to further enhance BG3. I've named it *Lambdoma* as a tribute to Pythagoras's original arrangement of numbers to create musical proportions. Any two proportions from either table create BG3 in the design. They both have a base unit that one can change into a common dimension in all parts of the design. As an example, we can input the ceiling height into this cell to enter it in as a multiplier in all cells so that all chosen proportions will take the common ceiling height into consideration. In this case, any single dimensions from the table can be used and will automatically become a proportion with the ceiling height. The second cell to set the size of the base unit is a scaling cell which moves the decimal point right and left in all the numbers of all the cells. This allows working with different design sizes. These two "scaling" cells are found in both the Modulor and Lamb-doma to tailor them to all dimensions of design.

Irrational Numbers

The transcendental properties of some irrational numbers create a motion or vortex to an endless dimension. This vortex will connect to the BG3 quality. This has made them play an important role in the mathematical approach to geometry.

- Pi (π=22/7=3.14......) used in the calculation of the circumference and area of a circle.
- Phi (Φ = 1.618033988749895...) used as a main proportion in Sacred Geometry
- Square root of two $\sqrt{2}$ = 1.414213562373095-...

A 90-degree triangle with two equal sides will produce a diagonal with the irrational square root of 2 that has the BG3 quality.

The BG3 Tray

We used this principle in the development of a BioGeometry tray shown earlier. This was one of our first BioGeometry patents (No.23/1992). The tray is very useful in enhancing and balancing life force and reducing side effects from any products placed on it for a few minutes. The side effects of medicinal drugs were reduced after they were set on the tray before ingestion. We even tried the tray on chemotherapy drugs with good results. We have designed several food trays along this principle as we have seen a reduction in allergic reaction with the use of the tray. (refer to Figure 81)

The BG3 Ruler

We used the same square root of 2 principle in creating a ruler to measure the intensity of BG3 using a scale of BG3 triangles (Figure 87). This ruler uses the quantitative aspect of the number of triangles to indicate the intensity of the BG3 in any object without having a real quantitative measurement. The associated numbers indicate intensity of quality and not its quantification.

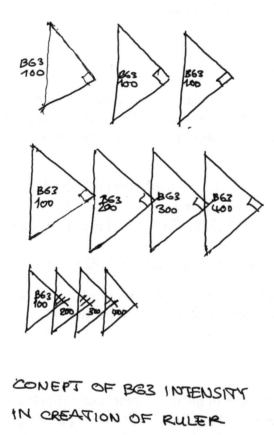

CONEPT OF BG3 INTENSITY
IN CREATION OF RULER

Fig.87 - BG3 Ruler Concept

The angles at 45, 90, and 135 degrees of a triangle and its side extensions are part of a system and will not produce the same quality if used separately. As an example, a simple individual octagon with the 135-degree inner angles as used in the BioGeometry tray will not have BG3. In the design section, we will explore the activation of the octagonal shape.

The BG3 Quality Scale

This is a scale developed to measure the level of BG3 in any object. This scale is an indication of the intensity level of the BG3 quality and is not a quantitative scale measurement. It is a valuable tool to fine-tune BioGeometry designs or check the subtle energy solutions in a space. The unit of this ruler is based on a 90-degree equal-sided triangle with a diagonal equal to the square root of two. This is a method of producing the BG3 quality of an irrational number. A sample is placed on the ruler and a BG16 pendulum is held over the scale to check to see how far it will detect the BG3 resonance on the triangular scale. As the ruler is measuring BG3 one can also calibrate to the wavelength of the object to assess its BG3 level. Instead of the sample one can place a sphere to measure the BG3 level of a space (Figure 88)

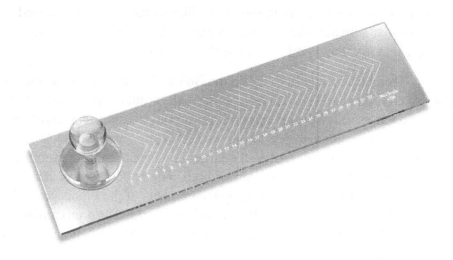

Fig.88 - BG3 Ruler with Space Attachment

This ruler cannot be used to evaluate a person's level of BG3 using a witness, as this depends largely on the location, activity, and interaction of the moment. What a person is consuming or wearing at that specific moment will also affect the measurement. This is, therefore, a continuously changing measurement that cannot be used for a general assessment of the development of a person. It is therefore not our business to judge others as we can never get a correct stable measurement. The ruler is very useful in developing body postures that can be combined into a movement, however, and we can use it to develop exercises, and dance, sitting, and standing postures. We can study and develop the postures by measuring on a person or on a flexible wooden human figure used by artists for drawing.

For the emission of BG3, however, we use the more sophisticated possibilities of the Human Archetype ruler.

BioGeometry Versus Sacred Geometry

Sacred Geometry and BioGeometry form an integral part of the design language of nature. At face value, they are totally different in nature, like apples and oranges. Their similarity, however, lies in their complementarity. In a way, each exists in the other. BioGeometry can be viewed as the heart that activates the spiritual energy at the center of the shapes of sacred geometry, that is referred to as the centering effect.

Sacred Geometry is largely based on the Golden Mean proportion labelled Phi, which is equal to 1:1.618. So, it is basically a quantitative mathematical approach to design with a spiritual/philosophical interpretation of geometrical patterns. This proportion divides a line into two parts where the proportion of the smaller part to the larger one is equal to the proportion of the larger part to the whole sum of both. The pattern keeps repeating itself across the board as expressed by the numbers of the Fibonacci series 1, 2, 3, 5, 8, 13, 21, 34, 55, etc. It is therefore regarded as a proportion of evolution. It can be used to create elaborate systems with endless levels of complexity.

The use of this proportion in simple configurations creates the BG3 subtle energy qualities. With increasing complexity, it keeps the design harmony of the evolutionary process but loses the BG3 spiritual vortex, which is not its main goal. Aside from its use in proportion, the number 16 on its own has the BG3 quality.

BioGeometry, on the other hand, is the measurement of life force through its qualitative effects on biological energy systems and it reproduces the centering subtle energy quality—such as that found in sacred power spot vortices—through design principles of shape.

Sacred Geometry uses a mathematical and philosophical perception to express spiritual concepts, while BioGeometry is a purely qualitative science rooted in both universal harmonics and the energy connectivity of sacred power spots. BioGeometry is a practical application of the subtle energy quality of spirituality.

The difference between the two bodies of knowledge can be seen in the numerical series of each discipline. The Fibonacci series from Sacred Geometry is a series of numbers based on a mathematical formula where each two consecutive numbers in the series are added. As we noted previously, they give the following number sequence: 1, 2, 3, 5, 8, 13, 21.... When each number (beyond the first few) is divided by the previous one we get the golden mean proportion of 1.6. This is a typical quantitative series where a mathematical formula is consistently expressed throughout. In the BioGeometry series, however, we find no repetitive mathematical relationship whatsoever between the numbers: 16, 19, 28.... This is not a quantitative series but a purely qualitative series that is based on the same quality of effect of each number on living energy systems. The only connection is that all the numbers have the same centering subtle energy quality of sacred power spots—labeled BG3, as it is detected using three subtle energy qualities.

The Golden Mean proportion, when used according to BioGeometry principles, will produce the BG3 spiritual harmonizing quality. In Sacred Geometry, it will give this quality in some configurations and lose it in others while still retaining its proportional harmonious properties.

Ancient civilizations used musical proportions to resonate with the Divine Laws of Creation. They therefore used all the musical proportions to "compose" their works of art and architecture.

The Ancients used to combine the proportion of eight-fifths with other musical proportions to achieve full spiritual harmony through resonance with the Laws of Creation to bring in the creative life force and invite the Neters into their work. Hans Kayser in his book *Akroasis* quotes Goethe, who in turn quoted the Ancient Egyptians, to say that "architecture is frozen music," as it contains all the musical proportions needed to connect to the universal Laws of Creation. Music was used in all moments of change or turning points in every activity of life (birth, death, celebrations, war, temple rituals, and so on) to bring a blessing through the spiritual connection.

One can expand Sacred Geometry to contain all musical proportions and become the harmonious "other side" of BioGeometry. Some authors have expanded it in this direction and combined it with spiritual activities like the creation of mandalas, while others have gone into ever-increasing quantitative detail, producing the BG3 quality through fractal principles found in nature's language of creating living communicative boundaries.

The synergetic integration of BioGeometry and sacred geometry is a form of alchemical marriage that gives a deeper understanding of ancient knowledge that was lost in the great shift of the focus of perception from the right to the left brain, closing the door on all the universal knowledge.

PART TWENTY

The Living Energy Qualities of Shape

Shapes, as we perceive them through our physical senses, are only a small physically materialized part of their full multi-dimensional holistic presence in absolute reality. They manifest in different forms of materialization in other dimensions that are beyond our physical senses. Those other dimensions remain "formless," without shape to our physical awareness.

Perception of Shape

Our interaction with physical shapes occurs through our five physical senses, where the left-brain faculties of perception create the time-space-based duality, personification, and separation which in turn produce the physical boundaries that characterize shapes. In the forming of physical shapes in our perceived world we find some projection of our own subconscious emotional and mental qualities.

Resonance of Shape: The Third Type of Universal resonance:

We have already introduced three types of resonance: the first occurs between wavelengths of the same, double, or half dimensions from zero to infinity with the same musical note quality. The secondary resonance happens in the background between different musical notes. In this sense every note exists within the background of all the other notes. This is like every color existing out of the other colors of the light. These two types of resonance are based on qualities related to wavelengths or frequencies. The third type of resonance is related to the shape of a wave, as a proportion of its wavelength to its amplitude (height). The shape of a wave gives it an additional quality regardless of wavelength or frequency. All waves of the same shape (proportions) are in resonance and have the same quality regardless of their wavelength or frequency. This phenomenon has to do solely with quality of shape that is present seamlessly in all its sizes. We can therefore understand how all species in nature are in communicative resonance through their similarity of shape, regardless of size. Physical shapes are in communicative resonance through all time-space dimensions of Creation. In other words, the shapes of our material world are in a two-way information exchange with all dimensions beyond our limited time-space perceived reality. Shapes are therefore the most potent universal language.

The Human Body

The shape of the human body is a very elaborate design composition resonating with all the shapes in Creation. It is in resonance with all the planes of nature (physical, vital, emotional, mental, and spiritual) and is therefore the perfect container for all those levels. The human body in this resonant context is a microcosmic manifestation of the macrocosm. All humans are in a background unifying resonance of shape regardless of any secondary differences. Different species with similar shapes are also in resonance. The relationships between plant and organ shapes in herbal remedies are such an example. Body organs of similar shapes, like the ears and kidneys, are in resonance, and so on. Natural shapes are life force qualities. BioGeometry allows us to design products with the natural life force qualities.

The Archetypal Dimension

The resonance of shape connects physical shapes with all shapes in all planes of nature across all time-space dimensions. A shape's resonance originates in the primordial fog dimension at the core of the activation of the duality of Creation. The perfect shapes in this dimension can undergo slight changes or imperfections through interaction in the different dimensions but are held in control through the resonance with the perfect shapes of the primordial dimension. These perfect shapes act as archetypal templates for all other dimensions.

The Inaudible Sound Waves

The interaction and motion of shapes in the living subtle energy background produces compression waves. These are a form of inaudible sound wave that can be scaled down by division to the audible level as the sound of shape. This phenomenon has been described by Pythagoras as the music of the spheres of celestial bodies.

The Sound of Shapes in Motion

Shapes in motion produce compression waves whose quality is the result of the shape of the moving body interacting with the shape of pattern of motion. The resulting compression wave patterns can be scaled down to audible music levels.

Energy, Shape, and Function

There is also a relationship between motion and shape. From a qualitative subtle energy point of view, the concept of shape goes beyond the physical appearance of objects. To find the quality behind function we must look at the pattern of energy behind it. In other words, the shape of energy flow determines quality and function. This trifold relationship gives us a totally new outlook wherein shape is frozen energetic motion.

To understand the quality of material shapes we must regard them as a form of motion. Geometry in this sense is a study of the quality of motion. While the concept of shapes as motion looks frozen on the physical level, the subtle energetic levels of the shape on vital, emotional, mental, and spiritual levels are much larger. Even at the material level shape is composed of atoms and smaller units that are a form of energetic motion.

Let us take a closer look at the subtle energy effect this has on us and how we perceive quality. A resonant exchange of information occurs when any objects interact, which happens on all subtle energy levels. Quality is felt as an effect on the emotional level, and it is interpreted on the mental level. The quality of an interaction is felt and perceived on the emotional and mental levels even if it is based on function in the physical dimension. BioGeometry solutions produce a change in the quality of an object by shaping its emotional and mental subtle energy patterns and introducing the harmonizing BG3 life force attributes through a connection with higher dimensions. This is the principle at work when we harmonize electromagnetic radiation and chemical side effects without applying change to the physical aspect of an environment or object.

Angles as Living Qualities

Let us examine more deeply the concept of shapes as frozen subtle energy qualities. A light beam passing through a glass prism produces the colors of the spectrum, each with a different angle radiating out the other side. This phenomenon, where each frequency band comes out at a different angle, correlating colors to angles, is called refraction. Colors are qualities produced in specific areas of the brain as reactions to the effect of light wave frequencies in a certain range. The corresponding angles, therefore, produce color qualities, as in the case of light through a prism. According to the principles of harmonic resonance, those angles produce those same qualities on all ranges beyond the color range, covering all vibratory levels from zero to infinity and extending to other dimensions.

In this sense, angles become a qualitative scale that can be used in all invisible dimensions. The dial concept uses the quality of "polarized" angles in connection to the centering BG3 quality.

The separate colors emerging from the whole colorless light have a qualitative link to their unified origin and are in harmonic resonance among themselves. This is in addition to their main resonance with similar qualities on the invisible ranges. One can correlate angles to colors, sounds, touches, tastes, or smells so they become interchangeable. Some laws, like those of resonance, can be better understood if expressed as sound, while other qualities might be more apparent if expressed as color, touch, or smell. On a secondary level, however, all the components of the different qualitative scales are in secondary resonance with each as part of a universal unity.

To Sum It Up:

Since colors are produced in the brain and play a role in forming a meaningful perceived reality, they have emotional and mental quality content. These psychic color qualities are affected by the perceiver, others in the field of perception, and by collective and universal qualities. Light refraction on a prism shows the unified source of colors as well as their correlation with angles. They both arise and are in resonance with their BG3 source. Colors and angles are living qualities in their own way and can affect the vital, emotional, mental, and spiritual quality of their surroundings. Based on the laws of resonance in Universal Harmonics, all shapes are in resonance with similar shapes, and they are also in secondary resonance with all other shapes. Similarly, they are also in resonance with other types of subtle energy systems in existence, with which they are interchangeable. In short, every shape affects the life force quality of the environment, as well as that of all the other shapes around it.

Quality of Shape

Angles are the components of shape, and accordingly shapes are qualities that affect their environment. In BioGeometry, shapes produced according to the principles of the natural forming process interact with life force. Those shapes become an integral part of nature connected to the multi-dimensional levels of the life force of the earth.

The Physics of Quality has introduced a new dimension to shape, seeing it as a frozen living subtle energy quality that affects the environment. As we explained earlier, the concept "multi-dimensional resonance" in Universal Harmonics shows there is information exchanged between shape, color, sound, smell, touch, and taste. Solid shapes, however, have an advantage over the other manifestations of quality, in that they fix the qualities achieved through their physical presence and exchange them through their presence on all their other levels with the surrounding subtle energy. As long as a shape is intact and not impregnated by other energies, it will continue exchanging its qualities with the environmental subtle energy. Emotional and mental disturbances can affect the related invisible levels of a shape and distort its qualitative effect on the surrounding environment. All forms of electromagnetic impregnation from modern technology can disturb the emotional and mental levels affecting the total shape quality and the way it in turn affects the environment.

Shape can store, amplify, diffuse, or emit several types of subtle energy qualities on multiple levels. The evolution of natural shapes is linked to their full interaction with life force. The quality of their evolution is directly linked to the number and balance of life force components, as well their harmonious exchanges with the environment. The natural forming process is based on the interaction with higher planes of nature from which the archetypal living patterns are accessed. These centers of communication in the shape take the form of vortices communicating with the higher planes of nature.

Human products, in contrast to products of nature, are not connected to the higher dimensions of Creation and do not interact with life force.

BioGeometry design principles produce shapes that create the quality of BG3 as a multi-dimensional portal for the harmonizing principles from higher dimensions to manifest. BioGeometry shapes are formed to produce their own power spot with a wormhole energy vortex at their centers that harmonize environmental subtle energy quality. In this way, life force is brought into the shape, which then enters a harmonious exchange with the environment. These concepts of integration into the forming process of nature echo the paradigms of the great ancient civilizations.

The Living Angles/Life Force Angles

The angles in the composition of the shapes of nature, as well as their surface structure, affect the quality in the process of life force exchange. The surface of any shape that reflects light and makes it visible to our perception also has the exchange and storage functions of boundaries. The boundary is the resonant exchange layer of information between the inner levels of the shape and the outer levels in the environment. Therefore, our skin, for example, contains a copy of the information of the sensory, as well as the extrasensory, soul levels.

Energy Quality of Boundary

The energy qualities in a shape's boundary layer are related to the material properties, the surface color, and the structure. The boundary is a quality information communication layer between the inner and outer subtle energy systems. It will always have the communicative, penetrative, Negative Green. The harmonious fractal configuration of the boundaries of natural shapes, such as seashores or plant leaves, for example, creates a double-interface situation giving a transition layer between the two seemingly separate parts, and it creates the BG3 subtle energy quality. This is, however, only the case with natural boundaries. From a subtle energy point of view, boundaries are not only information exchange layers between the outer and inner environments, but they also play a protective harmonizing role in the exchange process.

The Skin as an Information Layer

The process of bi-directional information flow through the boundary leaves a copy of the resulting harmonized mix from the interaction between inner and outer states in the structure of the boundary, which acts as a storage layer. The boundary, therefore, contains a copy of the living soul with its individual and collective levels. The storage function of the boundary layer makes it a secondary living soul layer. The quality of stored information will ultimately affect the structure and appearance of the boundary itself—which reflects the quality of mental-emotional states and general health of the body, as well as of the environment. The number of additives to our food and drink, for appearance and preservation, as well as food-processing methods, also have their toll on skin appearance.

The dehydration effect of electromagnetic radiation causes a dryness of the skin that plays a major role in its appearance. Dehydration means a loss of life force. The skin is a layer of life force exchange with the environment. Through its material, structure, and color, the skin acts as a harmonizing protective filter in the exchange mechanism of subtle energy quality with the environment; if clogged, it will greatly affect our well-being. Moisturizing and revitalizing the skin with all kinds of products, whether applied or ingested, has become an important part of our efforts to restore health and appearance.

A person's world view and mental-emotional attitude also affect the skin, which is our body's largest organ. Living according to the Laws of Nature through the introduction of ethical values in all action has a harmonizing effect on all the levels of exchange of the boundary and it has an influence on the skin's appearance. The skin is therefore equally a mirror of the soul and its environment. The harmonizing treatment should address the physical health and balance the vitality through activity in energizing natural healthy environments.

The German psychologist and holocaust survivor Viktor Frankl developed Logo Therapy where a person reflected to find a hidden wisdom behind their experiences to cure depression and other psychological problems. The most effective way to thrive, however, is to live in harmony with the Laws of Creation by accepting all others, as we have explained above. This "excellence of action" is achieved through the integration of universal ethical values of the heart intellect, and it will ultimately reflect on the skin's appearance. There are many examples in history of mummified corpses from ancient times, laid in sacred power spots, that had the skin appearance of a sleeping person, and which only deteriorated when they were moved to other locations. In relatively recent history, there are in many parts of the world similar stories of holy people who were found in this preserved state many years after the death of their physical body.

Shapes as Living Entities

The above criteria apply to our interaction with all kinds of objects of any shape as well. All natural shape boundaries are, by the analysis just shared, part of living entities with their own mental-emotional personalities interacting with us on all levels and exchanging emotional and mental information and life force components with us. This does not apply to human products devoid of life force which are causing disturbances in the living fabric of the earth.

Forming the Energy Quality of Shape

Shapes are living qualities expressing frozen moments in time-space. The designer, being an architect, or someone practicing in any field of design, should become the foremost expert on practical modeling of time-space perception to achieve specific mental-emotional qualities. Every activity involves some aspect of design in one way or another, which can be used to introduce harmony and enhance life force. Most natural environments are *energizing* with the balance of QL-Torsion slightly tipped towards the positive. There are of course depleting or even harmful areas in the natural environment, that have become so without human intervention. The harmful effects of such areas can result from natural radioactive materials or gases, cracks, shifting, and so on. The quality of water of underground streams and their angles of crossing can produce harmful Earth radiation.

Modern technology has introduced new types of electromagnetic and chemical pollution that tip the scale of QL-Torsion on our planet towards the depleting negative side. The Physics of Quality is born out of this practical holistic multi-dimensional design paradigm that restores the balance of life force in the environment using a design language of shape that produces positive QL-Torsion.

Motion and Shape

The apple is a good representation of the hidden secrets of the subtle energy effect of motion and shape in the environment as represented in the shape of a torus. This is the original building unit of shape that works on all levels of existence from the smallest to the largest. A vertical cross-section of the apple represents the Energy Key used in BioGeometry. The Energy Key is an important tool in the subtle energy configuration of space and the balance of QL-Torsion qualities within it.

Geocentricity and the Shape of Motion

In my first book, *Back to a Future for Mankind*, I briefly touched on Geo-centricity. This perspective, from a qualitative point of view, puts Earth at the center of both the solar system and the whole Universe, but it contrasts with the scientific physical reality where the planets of the solar system revolve around the sun. In this book, we will examine the qualitative effects of the movement of celestial bodies on human biological functions, including emotional and mental subtle energy levels. The effect on the-human being is what concerns us here. This effect is related to the shape of motion around the observer. In this paradigm, the earth becomes the center of evaluation of the qualitative effect of the surrounding motion.

There are two aspects to this qualitative human-planetary geometrical re-lationship. The first relates to the actual position of celestial bodies in the surrounding space, and the second relates to the position and motion in the image created by the light from the celestial bodies as it falls on the earth's atmospheric boundary. The first of these effects is a very complex distribution in a multitude of time-space configurations, and the second is a composite projected image on the canvas of the earth's atmosphere. The latter is a projection of the pattern of motion in the former on a single time-space dimension related to life on Earth. Present, past, and future ex-ist simultaneously in an eternal present. It is therefore this celestial image that has the most effect on living systems on the earth.

This is a perception of the pattern directly affecting the quality-of-life force on Earth, and the one that has a certain effect on all our subtle ener-gy measurements.

Let us imagine several interactive paths and shapes of motion in space, where the pattern of each motion has a qualitative effect on the others. The effect is, however, different at different points within the collective pattern of motion. The qualitative effect is different at each point of perception because the shape looks different from different angles. So, any motion at the point of the perceiver changes the quality. Taking the perceiver as the point at which the quality is measured means it becomes the fixed center, even when it is moving. Relating all movement to a fixed center means any movement of that center becomes part of the forming factors of the overall collective pattern of movement. In the world of quality, the human being is the measure of all things. In this qualitative concept, the earth is the fixed center around which the effect of the shape of motion of all celestial bodies in the whole Universe, and not just the solar system, is measured.

On a multi-dimensional level, I can even take you further into the sub-conscious dimension of the human perceiver to relate that the effect of all motion in absolute reality, beyond our very limited sensory perception, will affect all forms of life on Earth. Those dimensions are extrasensory and therefore lie beyond the limitations of our physical time and space perception in a form of eternal presence within the overall time container. Shape, however, exists and is affected by all those unperceived levels beyond what we perceive as a material shape. This concept has several implications, one of them being that the impact of what we perceive as past, present, and future equally affects us at every moment of our lives. The physical universe that we perceive is the visible material part from a huge number of unperceived equally solid material universes built of emotional or mental particles. They are not accessible to our limited senses. The mental-emotional information in our memory, as well as our self-image, have a main role in forming the shapes that we perceive on the higher levels.

Once we leave our physical existence, we will be in bodies made of emotional matter with a different unlimited perception in a different non-linear time-space configuration. The mental-emotional bodies of our immortal soul exist simultaneously alongside our sensory-based ego, which is in complete mastery of our physical perception. This is the left-brain mode of sensory everyday perception of our world, which cannot access the subconscious unlimited universal information of the immortal soul. We are two different beings living as roommates in this physical body, one temporal and the other permanent and timeless. They cannot communicate directly, as the information from the roommate in the right-brain mode of extrasensory perception must go into a time-space culturally associated translation to rise into our daily consciousness.

That means that we can only perceive the patterns of motion of physical objects to assess their effects on our lives, although motion within the unperceived absolute reality, which produces all the functions of the laws that govern all forms of life in nature, eludes our senses. The ancient qualitative science of astrology deals with the effect of the planets in our solar system on our lives. From the point of the perceiver on Earth, our standpoint affects the shapes of visible or invisible motion that in turn affect the quality of our lives. If we change our standpoint to another planet, all those patterns of motion will acquire new shapes affecting life differently.

Through the application of the resonant principles of Universal Harmonics, we can access the quality of shapes and functions on any unperceived dimension through resonance with physical shapes. This interaction is present in all the natural shapes, as they are in resonant communication with life force through centering subtle energy vortices in the forming process of nature. By applying the design principles of BioGeometry to human-made products, we connect the shapes to the centering multi-dimensional life force, giving the communication and existence to all planes of nature. This connects the shape to its source in the archetype on the spiritual dimension. Any object on the periphery will have a qualitative counterpart in the center and vice versa.

To understand the manifestation and evolution of shapes in nature, we will examine the centering principle of the forming process. Shapes are formed with one or more geometrical centers. These centers are subtle energy vortices connecting the shape's form and evolution to a center within an archetypal dimension beyond our physical time-space configuration. This center is, however, a multi-dimensional connection with all the planes of nature and has a spiritual Ziron doorway at its core. Pulses emanating from the Ziron in the form of bi-directional spirals in all directions create the eight-fold levels of the torus-shaped Psychon. The vortices at the shape centers are a result of multiple toroidal pulses emerging and vanishing at infinitely high speeds. These pulses create the stable-shape of the vortex from which all shapes are formed in a bi-directional information flow that brings out the archetypal pattern while bringing in the environmental information. The physical shape exists in the material world with a counterpart at the center. The shape has an existence on all planes of nature in the center as well as in those of the surrounding environment. In the analysis of the Energy Key of motion in relation to the Psychon, we can see how the linear flow is formed by bi-directional emanations from the center of motion of each pulse. The linearity is within the resulting time-space dimension within the pulse (Figure 89).

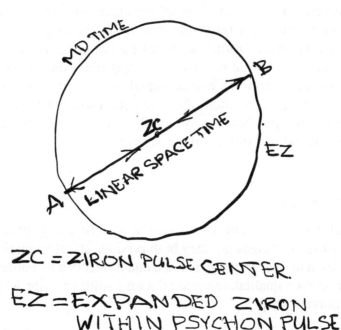

ZC = ZIRON PULSE CENTER.

EZ = EXPANDED ZIRON WITHIN PSYCHON PULSE

THE LINEAR TIME-SPACE FLOW CREATING A BEGINNING (A) AND END (B) OF A MOTION. MANIFESTS WITHIN THE MULTI-DIRECTIONAL (MD) TIME OF THE PSYCHON PULSE

Fig.89 - Linear vs. Multidimensional Time

The Geocentric Human Subtle Energy System Contains All Information of the Multi-Dimensional Universe

From the above analysis, the human being as the center of perception contains, on an unconscious subtle energy level, all the invisible information of the physical universe as well as all the other multi-dimensional levels of Creation in a two-way resonant information exchange. Unfortunately, this information, which forms the major part of our existence, is hidden from our limited left-brain sensory perception and is only available to our unconscious right-brain mode of universal unity. When the veil of limited sensory perception is lifted when we permanently leave our physical body, we will not just have access to all the hidden dimensions, but we will be an integral part of them in a resonant unity.

Sound and Shape

Sound and shape are two manifestations of a subtle energy pattern on two different vibratory ranges but they both produce an effect on the nervous system related to a sensory organ. Each one is decoded in a different brain area with its own qualitative scale of sound notes or color which create the perception of shape.

This process of sound frequencies creating shapes because of sound interacting with a medium or matter is a main Law of Creation that is expressed in many scriptures as, "In the beginning was the Word." This expresses the beginning of Creation from a higher timeless spaceless subtle energy level on a much higher dimension than the resulting material creation referred to as the Big Bang.

The principle of sound as a main component in the forming process of nature can be found in many cultures. Such examples are found in|:

- Ancient Egyptian Universal Harmonics.
- Pythagorean Universal Harmonics relating proportions to sound, expressed as the Lambdoma. revived in modern times by Hans Kayser.
- Cymatics of Hans Jenny, which shows creation of shape through sound.

- Dr. Masaru Emoto's use of intention and sound to produce frozen water crystals, reviving the ancient principle of monuments as a frozen form of music.
- Similarly, one can use shape to affect the quality of sound, such as in concert hall architecture or the shapes of musical instruments.

An architect is a sculptor of space using shapes to introduce harmony into the quality of life and affect both sensory and extrasensory ranges. The same concept applies to all the arts.

In BioGeometry, the Physics of Quality builds on a vast field of knowledge that has existed on an esoteric level since early civilizations, fueling innovations in mainstream science. Pythagoras, Kepler, and Newton are only a few examples of people who have walked that path. The esoteric background of Isaac Newton, made public many years after his death,-disclosed that Newton had a vast library of esoteric and occult works and was a practiced Alchemist.

Alchemy is a practice where one combined different metals, salts, and other substances in a holistic way, where the power of words, planetary movements, hours of the day, days of the week, month, or year, as well as the purity of the practitioner, played a role in the outcome. The visible goal of Alchemy was to create gold out of other non-precious metals. The grain of gold indicated the presence of the higher harmonic quality of gold that indicated the spiritual transformation of the practitioner. It was not about the creation of physical gold, but the spiritual attainment of the Alchemist himself.

BioGeometry in this sense is often described as "Geometric Alchemy."

As an example of many great people who have opened new doors of scientific knowledge for humanity, Newton was simply showing us the tip of the iceberg that only floated because of the huge hidden part carrying it. The worldview of his time was not ready to understand or accept what lay beneath.

Holistic subtle energy-related design must address the effect on all levels (vital, emotional, and mental) achieved by a connection with the spiritual dimension. This way of looking at architecture is the only way to truly develop holistic living harmony in building spaces. The built space should achieve this holistic subtle energy balance and radiate this harmony into its surroundings. This environmental harmony will balance all life functions and restore life force. Environmental energy quality is the way to rearrange the subconscious patterns governing our outlook on life. This in turn has a harmonizing effect on our genetic make-up. Several authors like Bruce Lipton, for example, in his groundbreaking book, *The Biology of Belief,* and Dawson Church, in *Genie in your Genes*, have shown how intention and attitude can reprogram our genes.

In BioGeometry, the Physics of Quality gives us universal qualitative scales to interact with qualities and a design language of shape with which we can interact with universal qualities through resonance; this gives us the possibility of reproducing, amplifying, storing, and emitting qualities. The true definition of energy is "the ability to produce an effect." An effect is perceived through its Quality. Effect is a form of free energy that can be accessed through shape. It is usually referred to as the "Energy of Shape." Shape's interaction with the subtle energy background produces effects on multi-dimensional levels, especially when harmonized through BG3, the centering communicative quality of BioGeometry. This is the way of the forming process of shapes in nature.

Compression Waves Related to Shape

Physical shapes in their interaction with the subtle energy medium of the environment affect the living qualities within their surroundings. Subtle energy is the general term we use to refer to all levels of non-electromagnetic compression wave background energy. Every type of movement on the physical or higher levels will create some type and pattern of ripples in the subtle energy background medium; this will affect the life force and quality of QL-Torsion. The life force balance and quality of QL-Torsion influence individual and collective vitality and will have an impact on the emotional and mental levels. The emotional and mental state of a person also affects QL-Torsion, resulting in a seemingly unbreakable vicious circle. This makes it difficult to generate the necessary balancing effects on the environment. Although creative and compassionate activities produce positive QL-Torsion, their balancing effect is reduced by the excessive pollution of modern technology.

The act of procreation of all species in nature enhances life force and positive QL-Torsion, but it can be affected by strong negative QL-Torsion that depletes life force. We've seen this show up in our research projects as infertility problems in areas with excessive electro-smog. Geometrical shapes have a stable permanent effect and can be formed using the design principles of BioGeometry to keep emitting positive QL-Torsion in the environment to reduce the harmful effects of modern pollution. We have the knowledge and ability to create a future where every designed object from the smallest to the largest (e.g., from a button to city planning) can restore the natural healthy quality of the environment and neutralize the quality of modern technology that disrupts QL-Torsion: this is the positive attitude we need to restore the environment in our modern civilization.

The earth's rotation, the movements of the planets, and all background compression waves interact with all shapes whether in motion or not. Material shapes are also forms of motion. This makes the unperceived background in which everything takes place a highly active multi-dimensional living energetic medium that extends to all levels of Creation. All levels and dimensions of this subtle energy medium are harmonic octaves of the original primordial background at the emergence of duality, which is sometimes referred to as the primordial waters. This is where Consciousness creates everything from the potential in the zero-to-infinity state that manifests in the formless subtle energy dimension.

On every plane of nature beyond the physical, from the lowest vital levels through emotional and mental up to the higher spiritual planes, we can identify many types of compression waves that influence biological life functions in our physical world. These are extrasensory unconscious activities that are influenced by the quality of our physical actions, emotions, intentions, thoughts, and so on as explained above. That is why our receptivity to information from the holistic background medium depends largely on the quality of our own subconscious mind. The formless takes form based on the universal conscious exchange with the sensory perception of each dimension.

At this moment in human history the information age has put a lot of stress on the physical as well as all the subconscious dimensions, from the individual and collective up to the universal. Electromagnetic stress is a universal pollutant. We have therefore become sensitive to the subtle energy activity in the background medium related one way or another to electromagnetic pollution. We will look at this phenomenon in more detail when dealing with geopathic stress. This applies also to emotional and mental forms of pollution that will affect the future of humanity. The only solution is to restore the life quality of human-made forms of electromagnetism, so they are in harmony with their counterparts in a nature that supports all forms of life.

BioGeometry aims to reinforce this subconscious spiritual unity on the understanding that it will automatically lead to the discovery of new interactions between beneficent compression waves and existing types of electromagnetic radiation. In this case, the harmonizing process on the subtle energy levels—of which the electromagnetic waves are only a very small part—will greatly reduce their stress on living systems. This can also be achieved by shaping the physical electromagnetic wave, for example, by fixing the proportion of its wavelength to wave height, or through other design principles. In Ancient Egypt, this concept was applied in the proportions and materials of the central chambers in temples that shaped the quality of the standing waves emitted from the doorway. The BG3 quality of the sacred power spot, on which the temple was built, harmonized the emission and connected it to the higher spiritual dimensions.

This shift in our scientific paradigm will extend to our subconscious resonant quality and restore the health of the planet and all types of life on it.

Through the paradigm shift in BioGeometry, we steer discoveries towards more beneficent types of compression wave patterns, through the creation of specifically harmonized shapes, movements, postures, and sounds. Music, ritual, and sacred architecture have a very potent harmonizing effect on the multi-dimensional levels of the environment. This harmonizing effect results from continuous harmonious interaction with the forces of nature manifesting in human consciousness as Divine attributes, or the Neters, as they were known in Ancient Egypt.

Before the age of modern technology, many traditions discovered and worked with beneficent subtle energy types such as prana, chi, and so on, and we still access these through certain motions and postures such as religious rituals, Yoga, Tai Chi, and other similar disciplines. These in themselves affect the quality-of-life force with which we interact. Many types of sports, games, and martial arts performed with subconscious harmony enhance the subtle beneficent energy qualities in their environment, making them more effective.

We work with our colleague Georg Gaupp-Berghausen to add the harmonizing BG3 quality in the forming process of musical instrument body design. The compression wave quality of shape resonates into the musical notes giving them the living harmonizing quality that enhances the life-force of the listener. These are capable of harmonizing electro-smog effect when transmitted by electronic means. (Figure 90).

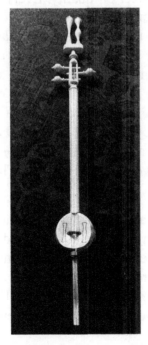

Fig.90 - BioGeometry Rebab by Georg Gaupp-Berghausen

Shapes and QL-Torsion

Using the horizontal Time Pendulum one can detect the quality of QL-Torsion affecting the body's subtle energy system. All natural shapes produce a positive energizing QL-Torsion from which we can restore our well-being. Human-made shapes usually create negative QL-Torsion around them, and they deplete our subtle energy on all levels because they lack the life force present in natural shapes. BioGeometry introduces design principles that bring life force into the shapes we produce and create an energizing QL-Torsion that restores the life force in their surroundings. There are several BioGeometry pendulums that directly detect the quality of QL-Torsion—such as the Time Pendulum, the 12-Disk Pendulum, and the IKUP.

The Fundamental Ray

Materials also have an effect on quality. Every element radiates a compression wave with a specific quality at a specific angle to magnetic north. French Radiesthesists in the 1940s, such as *Abbé Mermet,* refer to this as the Fundamental Ray. One can analyze the chemical composition of any substance in terms of the number, quality and direction of the fundamental rays emanating from it. This method can give an indication of the existence of traces of harmful material in a substance, which in any case must be confirmed by chemical analysis. For environmental effects of substances, these rays also show the direction in which the element is affecting the quality of everything in its path. This effect can be detected at larger distances.

Other qualities of objects affecting the environment are generated through the effect of compression wave fields produced by the shape and linear motion of any object, whether solid or wave, on its surroundings. This is an important phenomenon that is dealt with in detail in the different applications of the BioGeometry Energy Key. In BioGeometry design, this phenomenon is used to induce harmony in the environment.

Shapes and Pattern of Motion

Another aspect of the energy quality of shape results from the overall pattern of motion resulting from a flow along a shaped path. This is where energy is shaped to produce function. By shaping the flow of heat from the fire to reach an even distribution of heat resulting from the shape of a cooking pot, the function of cooking is achieved. Similarly, the shaping of the air in the lungs supports the organ's biological functions.

The direction and the shape of every curve within the flow plays a major role in the resulting function. The patterns of motion can flow internally, or flow along the periphery of the shape. It is, therefore, of great importance to the designers of shape to form the pattern of the whole layout in order to produce the desired quality in its surroundings. The patterns of shape of the BioGeometry Signatures, sometimes referred to as BioSignatures, fall in this category.

BioGeometry Signatures

The energy quality produced by the shape of movement is applied in the creation of BioGeometry Signatures. We have already introduced the fact that subtle energy flows through open-ended lines. The beginning, where the subtle energy flows in, has a Violet quality while the end is Red, with the other color qualities in between, so that the Green is in the middle. The central axis along the line, as well as the mid-point, have a BG3 quality. This basic straight-line configuration can be formed into an open-ended shape or pattern that give it additional qualities to resonate with similar shapes or energy functions. BioGeometry Signatures are based on this phenomenon to bring harmony and balance body functions on different levels (physical, vital, emotional, and mental) balanced by spiritual connection.

In BioGeometry, there are several ways that these Signature patterns work: one is to create a resonant connection with the subtle energy flow patterns of the organs. There are several super-imposed patterns of subtle energy, each with a different quality, on which the physical shape of an organ is based. BioGeometry Signatures mimic those patterns so that the energy flowing through them creates a subtle energy motion that resonates and achieves communication with the related organ patterns. In this case, the entry and exit points are tweaked to introduce the BG3 quality into the function. There are two other methods used to create BioGeometry Signatures that harmonize, through resonance, energy functions not directly related to organ shapes (e.g., vital, emotional, mental, and spiritual): the first is in the form of a "corrective" open-ended linear pattern that corrects the energy disturbance (e.g., the depression and immunity Biosignatures— see Figure 91). while the second achieves a resonant "communication" with the higher harmonizing principle (e.g., the Angelic Biosignature). We have dedicated a book to this subject, and it includes a list of Bio-Geometry Signatures for personal subtle energy balance (*BioGeometry Signatures: Harmonizing the Body's Subtle Energy Exchange with the Environment,* available at Amazon.com*). A BioGeometry Signature can be used as a subtle energy harmonizing support for any type of treatment. In themselves, BioGeometry Signatures are not a form of medicine of any type.

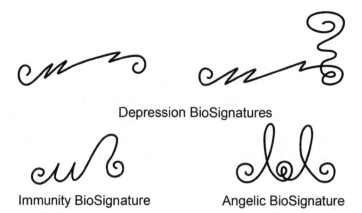

Depression BioSignatures

Immunity BioSignature   Angelic BioSignature

Fig.91 - BioSignatures

Shape of Body Organs

In the cycle of energy exchange with the environment, each type of energy intake is shaped by the relevant organ, where it is given additional qualities to perform the biological function. The relationship between organ shape and biological function is a main criterion in the development of the basic type of BioGeometry Signatures.

BioGeometry Signatures Motion Exercises

There is a very effective way to bring the effect of BioGeometry Signatures into the body's subtle energetic functions that has gained popularity in BioGeometry in our BioGeometry Special Topics international events. We sometimes refer to it as The BioSignature Dance. We project or hang a group of BioSignatures on the wall in front of us. We have been using groups related to different energetic systems of the body, e.g., digestive, respiratory, cardio, endocrine, and spine (Figure 92).

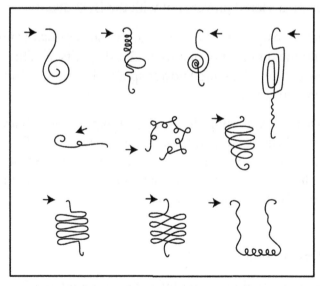

Fig.92 - Digestive BioGeometry Signatures Movement Set

We can tailor our choice of BioGeometry Signature to our needs. We usually play the BioGeometry music titled, "The Sirius Odyssey." And we move our body along the flow of each BioGeometry Signature, to resonate with it and bring its harmonizing qualities into our bodies' energy systems. In this way we can target the harmonizing effect to any area or function needed.

We also used BioGeometry Signatures to develop games for children with special abilities (Autism, ADHD, etc.), a practice that has been the topic of a Ph.D. thesis.

Shapes and Life Force

In our multi-dimensional energy system, we find all the attributes of life, the living Laws of Nature. So, whatever form energy takes, it will still contain all those attributes of life. In architecture, the musical proportion of five-eighths known as the Golden Mean, used along with the other proportions of musical notes, will bring life force into a building, which is ideally placed on a sacred power spot with the BG3 quality.

In BioGeometry design, however, we use the proportions from the BG3 series to create the power spot quality in the shape itself. This allows the creation of the quality of a sacred power spot and brings the life force into the shape in any location.

The Pythagoreans, expressing the Ancient Egyptian worldview, showed that musical proportions were in resonance with the Laws of Creation. Architecture, in this sense, became a central point in the universal symphony of Creation. The universal laws found a home in the building that became the home of the living powers of nature.

Shape and Orientation

The distribution of qualities along the external boundary of the shape, in relation to its orientation to the magnetic axis, is another type of qualitative interaction between any shape and its surroundings. So, the shape will have a secondary Green quality to the north, Violet to the east, Red to the west, and Negative Green to the south. This type of distribution can become fixed if the shape is geometrically polarized (through hemispheres, pyramids, cones etc.) to overcome the effect of orientation (as seen in polarized BioGeometry tools such as the Dial Pendulums and the Material Balancing Wheel).

Shape and Number

Another type of energy of shape that we have discussed earlier, and which we repeat here to complete the picture, relates to either the quality of number of repetitive components in a shape or the position of the shape in an arrangement of similar shapes, such as the location of a column in a row of columns. In any repetition of elements, each one would have an additional number quality related to its position in the whole, besides that of the overall number. This plays an important role in the functions of spirals, BioSignatures, and BioNumerals mentioned earlier.

The Effect of Shapes on the Quality and Functions of Subtle Energy

Geometrical shapes are a way to interact with the quality of compression waves (e.g., sound, air, water, etc.). As we have previously mentioned, we can see these concepts applied in the acoustics of a theater where we use shapes and materials to interact with sound waves. We also shape musical instruments to give the desired sound quality.

The same concept is used when we want to affect the quality of the background weave of inaudible sound waves that act as a universal symphony. All types of motion, from the largest to the smallest, create compression waves moving at speeds faster than light that form a sort of background weave or echo in the environment. We constantly bathe in this background weave of compression waves. This resonating weave produces a form of unperceived echo that contains emotional, mental, and spiritual levels of subtle energy; this all affects and is affected by our own subtle energy systems. Geometrical shapes can change the quality of this background weave for better or for worse. By incorporating the BioGeometry design principles into shapes to produce BG3, we bring harmony into the whole weave and everything interacting with it. The BG3 quality is the centering harmonizing quality in the forming process of nature.

Shapes and Scalar Waves/Field

Some early researchers used the term Scalar Waves to cover all non-electromagnetic compression waves that would cause some confusion with subtle energy or torsion. The term today refers to fields generated by a special configuration of electromagnetic flow. Scalar waves differ from electromagnetic fields in that they are non-electromagnetic compression waves resulting from the original electromagnetic motion, and they travel for long distances beyond the boundaries of the electromagnetic field. As non-electromagnetic fields, they are not bound by the speed of light and can decelerate or accelerate depending on how they are generated. In the fifteenth century, Leonardo Da Vinci demonstrated how the way he stirred water in a bucket created accelerating or decelerating wave speeds either from or to the center. We will deal with them in detail later when we discuss the electro-smog phenomenon.

Although scalar waves in general are not electromagnetic in nature, they are still in resonance with their electromagnetic origin, with which they have a two-way information exchange. They therefore carry the stressful quality of their origin for large distances in the environment and cannot be measured by conventional electronic devices. Some experts in the field, like Konstantin Meyl, consider electro-smog and Earth energy grids as scalar wave phenomena. Although Earth energy gridlines are naturally produced scalar waves, they can enter into resonance with artificial sources and produce electro-smog. *The fact that electromagnetically produced scalar waves create electro-smog in the environment should be addressed in the growing use of scalar wave devices in energy healing.*

Because they are compression waves, scalar waves can be qualitatively modulated through interactions with shapes. BioGeometry shapes entering resonance with scalar waves or fields can balance the stress and intro-duce harmony through the BG3 quality, which can be resonantly transmit-ted back to the waves' original electromagnetic source.

Shapes resonate differently with different planes of nature. The resonance between a shape and the subtle energy level of each plane seems to differ in intensity, which indicates certain affinities. We will examine this con-cept in more detail in the next topic.

PART TWENTY-ONE

The Planes of NatureAnd the BioGeometry Human Archetype Ruler

In this chapter, we will categorize the relationship between shapes and planes of nature to allow us to read new information in the shapes around us. We will examine the use of geometric shapes as a way of entering into resonance with the planes and sub-planes of nature, which are equally the subtle energy levels of the soul. This focus on abstract interaction with soul levels can be used to harmonize many disturbances. This abstract system is not different in concept from the functional approach to the soul components; rather it simply separates levels with different energetic types of perception according to the collective planes of nature in which the multiple levels of the soul components are located.

Geometrical Resonance with the Planes of Nature

The functional approach to the holistic human existence usually divides it into living entities with several subtle energy components. The concepts here range from the most basic three-fold division into body, soul, and spirit—which is one of the most commonly dealt with subjects in literature—to the complex group of living entities in the configuration of the soul in Ancient Egyptian and other ancient doctrines. Some of the Eastern doctrines use a straightforward division of levels composing the soul. We can see an example of this division into plane levels in the theosophical doctrine which brought Eastern spiritual traditions to the West, through Helena Blavatsky's ground-breaking books, *The Secret Doctrine* and *Isis Unveiled,* as well as through other works of literature by Annie Besant and Krishnamurti. These had a great influence on Western spirituality; in fact, many European thinkers like Rudolf Steiner and others were influenced by theosophical doctrine.

In BioGeometry, we divide individual, collective, and environmental soul levels into abstract universal planes and sub-planes of nature in our work with subtle energy. In this diagram, we can see the geometric shape that is in resonance with each plane (Figure 93).

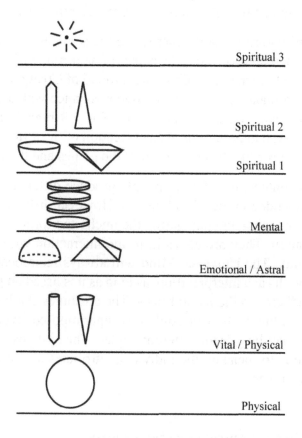

Fig.93- Geometrical Resonance with Planes of Nature

The Perception of the Planes of Nature

Subtle energy is a formless all-encompassing living background medium, from which everything arises and is animated. Let us go back to the model of the bottle full of sand particles containing many colors mixed together that we applied earlier to sensory perception: it also applies here. No color is visible in this dynamic mixture. It appears as a medium gray until the senses filter out a specific color to manifest its pattern from the gray background. This model, which we applied to explain the relationship between perceived and absolute reality, also applies to subtle energy as they are one and the same, although examined from different perspectives.

The planes of nature in subtle energy are the same as the formless attributes that we perceive as color. The planes of nature are different attributes of the unified whole medium of the background of Creation. The different planes and sub-planes are in a qualitative resonance with all other levels just as sound, shape, or color quality are. The left-brain perception process creates a system or pattern of classification of the different attributes, like a map to allow the differentiation of the planes and their attributes.

The cultural contents of different people produce different systems with doctrines embedded in their local beliefs. However different, all systems are tools for mapping and navigating the uncharted formless absolute reality of Creation. They are all valid in the interaction with the absolute formless reality. The Universal Mind will always reciprocate and act in accordance with each interpretation, as long as it is based on proper observation and adheres to the natural laws. The attributes can be categorized as functions within the holistic soul or as superimposed levels. They both look at the same thing from different angles. The systems of categorization enable one to focus on the individual attributes to achieve selective resonance with them.

The Planes in the Natural Forming Process

The forming process in nature is based on this selective resonance between material shapes and immaterial subtle energy functions. To contain a material object, the container must be shaped accordingly, like the shape of a cup for containing water. In this case we are dealing with straightforward physical attributes. What if the cup must contain an immaterial subtle energy attribute? Physical methods do not apply here. We must apply a transcendental method that is active on all ranges and spans all absolute reality beyond the physical. Resonance is a multi-dimensional communicating process that connects qualities in all ranges of Creation, including the physical. It is also the ideal means of generating information exchanges with all the attributes of subtle energy. In nature, shapes are formed according to a process of multi-dimensional holistic subtle energy resonance that brings in, connects with, and contains the attributes collectively in the physical shape.

To achieve a selective resonant connection with the differentiated attributes and subdivided planes or levels, we use simple geometric shapes that resonate with them. This selective differentiation is necessary for the functioning of a dualistic mind in a holistic dimension.

Let us examine this process in more detail taking the example of breathing. The intake of breath adds life force to the body creating an energizing positive QL-Torsion and putting more order into subtle energy; this is referred to as neg-entropy or negative entropy. The exhaling process produces a dissipation of life force and loss of order in subtle energy and produces negative QL-Torsion, which we refer to as entropy. The balance between both is essential to the healthy functioning of biological organs. Biological organs are living entities functioning collectively as part of the total body and in their own individual existence. As individual forms of life, each organ must interact with all the attributes of subtle energy. In our example of breathing, the shape of the lungs plays a resonant communication role in absorbing all the levels of life force from the air flow in the lungs. If we go deeper into an analysis of composite shapes, we find that some shape components interact with relevant sub-planes. In the Physics of Quality, we decipher that language of shape to find the relevant relationship between shape components and sub-planes of nature. We use the differentiation between the attributes of subtle energy through a simple layering system with levels, also known as planes, ranging from the physical through the vital, emotional, mental, and spiritual in an abstract way. In this simple differentiation into levels/planes we avoid going into their composite functions (e.g., body-soul-spirit) as these manifest as living entities with a focus on one level and components stretching onto several other levels.

The Living Dimensions of the Planes of Nature

There are many systems for interpreting the unperceived subtle energy planes of nature and they cover several dimensions–from the vital through emotional, mental, and on up to the spiritual levels. The first plane which is strongly linked to the physical world is the vital plane. The theosophical system refers to it as the "etheric" realm and considers it a part of the physical dimension. Other spiritualist traditions use the word etheric as a general reference to all levels of subtle energy. This plane is of great importance in esoteric traditions as it is linked to the physical level of life force.

The Ancient Egyptians identified two intelligent functions of the soul on the vital level, which worked within the physical body. The Khaibit and the Shoot are two shadow entities inseparable from the physical body that dissipate upon death. There is another vitality-related principle that we are concerned with here, because under the right conditions it can continue living, around the mummy, in the tomb.

At this point I would like to recommend to the reader, one of my favorite books on the subject written by Enel (Scariatin) and titled *Les Mystères de la vie et la mort* (*The Mystery of Life and Death According to the Teaching of the Temples of Ancient Egypt*). It can probably be found in antique bookshops.

Mortal Soul

The mortal soul is better described as the sensory ego/personality soul. It is the sum of sensory information within physical linear time and space that contains background qualitative mental-emotional patterns of mixed sensory and extrasensory origin. This soul level is sensory bound with the physical body and slowly dissipates with death. However, on a vital subtle energy level, with some emotional and mental physically-bound remanences, it will usually outlive the physical body for a few days.

The KA and the BA were two components of the soul that we find depicted in Ancient Egyptian tombs. The KA, which can be referred to as the mortal soul, is centered mainly on the vital level and is symbolized by two hands raised from the elbow upwards (Figure 94). On a higher level we have the immortal soul called the BA, represented as a bird with the human head of the deceased that continues its journey in the spiritual dimensions. There are other components of the soul in the Ancient Egyptian tradition, each representing a function or aspect of the person, that we will not deal with here.

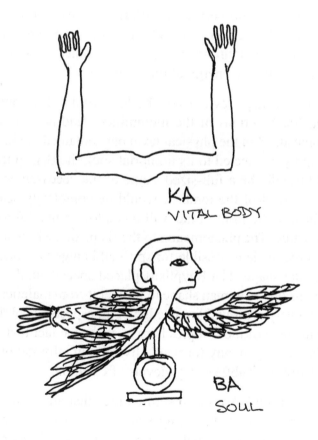

KA
VITAL BODY

BA
SOUL

Fig.94 - KA & BA

The KA was very much an invisible part of the physical body, and it was engaged in a two-way energetic exchange with it. It fed off the subtle energy of the food and drink consumed by the body. To keep it alive in the tomb as a protector for the body, it had to be fed directly through food offerings from which it could replenish its existence; otherwise, it would dissipate in a few days. The Ancient Egyptians found a way to revitalize the KA from specially formed archetypal images which were painted, engraved, or embossed on the walls and which radiated energy into the tomb. The figures on the wall had a permanent life force charging effect on the KA.

The same concept would be used in offering tables with the images of food and drink embossed on them. Water would be poured into the tray at one end and collected through a nozzle at the other. It would then have become charged with the energy of the offerings.

As long as it was kept revitalized, the KA would also connect to the non-physical life functions of the mummified dead person. The person did not become alive on the physical level but contained the life force that kept the mummy connected to its immortal soul, the BA, in the afterlife. There would usually be a full-sized statue of the deceased enclosed in a chamber in the wall of the tomb. It would be completely sealed except for a small hole in the front of the wall that allowed the KA to come and reside in the statue. The phenomenon of the shape of the human body containing life force made it possible for spiritual beings to connect with, or even inhabit, the shape. The Egyptians placed special amulets, symbols, and hieroglyphs on the human shape to protect it from maleficent entities. This showed a very profound knowledge of all aspects of subtle energy. I am going into some of those topics here to stress the fact that all components of subtle energy in any form are alive and in information exchange with all the harmonic subtle energy levels of Creation.

Both the KA and the BA refer to soul entities that are each focused on a level of the planes of nature (physical, vital, emotional, mental, and spiritual), but they are functionally connected to several other levels. As a very primitive entity, the KA can be easily influenced and programmed to perform certain tasks, such as protecting the mummy. The protection here must relate to physical effects generated from a subtle energy level.

There are many types of elemental spirits on the vital level, just as there are life forms on the physical level, that are beyond the scope of this book. These entities are linked in many ways to the physical dimension and can occasionally materialize. There are some types of such entities in the Infra-Red vital and lower emotional/astral levels that are very close to our physical dimension and can also occasionally manifest into it. Such entities are referred to in the Middle East as the "Jinn." Communication with them, even if they sometimes seem helpful, is always depleting to all levels of our energy. Their energetic constitution is not compatible with ours. Magical practices that use the Jinn to achieve goals are mostly harmful. The most important part of the channeling ritual is the anchoring to a sacred power spot to ensure the connection to proper sources and to avoid being deluded by the many tricksters of the astral world. As we repeated several times, the BioGeometry L90-shape is a very potent psychic protection. Using the BioGeometry Home Kit or wearing BioSignatures medallions create a virtual protective environment for such practices.

Energetic Principles of Ancient Egyptian Hieroglyphs

The Ancient Egyptians used hieroglyphs to symbolically express an idea based on its full energetic functions. The multi-dimensional resonant effect of shape was used to recreate the full living energy functions involved in the idea it represented. To understand this concept in a practical way in which we participate and experience the true meaning and function, we shall present some practical exercises involving the KA and BA soul principles.

The KA Subtle Energy Effect

We will use BioGeometry methods to explore the energetic possibilities of those two potent principles of the soul. Let us start by practicing the individual components of this very powerful exercise. Each one by itself is very effective. Once we experience the effects of every step, we can combine them together.

KA Exercise 1

Pronouncing the word KA, while breathing in and out, will activate positive QL-Torsion (QL+) and activate the energizing Al-Kareem Quality in the body and surroundings. The correct pronunciation and effect can be verified with the IKUP held at any string length.

KA Exercise 2

Raise your arms in horizontal position and bend your elbows to raise the lower arm vertically with both palms facing forwards, in the same way as the symbol of the KA. This is the most potent energizing physical posture. It will activate and remove blockages in the flow of the body. This activates the immune system and has many other benefits. Anytime you feel depleted or tired, you can imagine this posture and benefit from its energizing effect, discreetly, anywhere. A word of caution, however, do not imagine doing exercises when doing any activity that needs attention.

KA Exercise 3

Combine the sound of KA with the hand posture, facing east.

KA Exercise 4

Repeat the sound of KA eight times, while breathing-in, as well as when breathing-out. The IKUP will show the Al-Kareem Quality in both directions. Usually it is only present when breathing-in.

KA Exercise 5

Rotate clockwise in eight small increments, while in KA position.

KA Combined Exercise 6

Combine all the above exercises into one complete exercise.

This exercise that activates the energizing (QL+) Al-Kareem Quality in the body, has a healing effect on all body organs. It should be practiced several times a day for a few minutes.

The BA Subtle Energy Effect

The KA is centered on the vital level as connected to the physical dimension, with some connection to higher levels if empowered with the AL-Kareem quality. On the other hand, after the BA leaves the body, it

is centered on the spiritually connected mental-emotional level. The BA exercises will therefore enhance the BG3 centering, spiritual connection, that harmonizes all other levels.

BA Exercise 1

Pronouncing the word BA will activate BG3 in the body and surroundings, which can be verified with the BioGeometry 16-disk BG3 pendulum.

BA Exercise 2

The BA is centered on higher levels beyond the physical and vital and resonance with the BA is enhanced by visualizing feathered wings spreading from the shoulders. To facilitate imagination, one can stretch the arms and do a wing flapping motion.

BA Exercise 3

Pronounce the BA twelve times while breathing in as well as out. The BG3 quality which is usually only found in the centered phase between them, will also be found in both directions of breathing. As mentioned above, the presence of BG3 quality can be verified with the BioGeometry 16-disk BG3 pendulum. There are many ways to achieve the BG3 centering quality, which is at the core of the science of BioGeometry. Here, however, we are examining it in relation to the KA principle of the soul.

BA Combined Exercise 4

After mastering the above exercises separately, we combine all of the above BA exercises into one.

The frequent practice of this visualization exercise, especially before going to sleep, will make the wings a permanent part of your self-image and soul body giving you spiritual serenity and protection.

The Planes of Nature as Stacked Levels

Most systems look at the levels of the soul as multilevel functional entities, simply differentiated according to body, soul, and spirit. For more complex entities with different functions or attributes, such as were known in Ancient Egypt, we divide the subtle-energetic part of our being into universal levels or planes of nature. To understand the effects of modern technology on the quality of subtle energy levels and their effect on afterlife dimensions, and to do something about it through actions in our physical existence, we will envision an abstract model of soul levels as a stacked system of planes similar to the theosophical model.

We subdivide the emotional levels into twelve subdivisions for measurement purposes although they are fluidly interconnected. The lower levels deal with instincts and biological aspects while the higher ones are more related to emotional activities; at the highest level we are dealing with spirituality and altruism. These levels are affected by the motion of the planets in a human-centered, Earth-centric relationship. They are therefore also referred to as astral planes.

The afterlife dimensions of the astral planes are much like our physical one, although materialized mental-emotional particles have a different time-space configuration that we have referred to earlier as stacked time; it is free from the linear constraints of our sensory perception. The soul of the deceased moves into those dimensions according to the quality it brings with it: the soul's mental-emotional qualities are a result of the person's actions in life in the physical world. Moving into a higher spiritual heavenly quality of environment is achieved in earthly life through "accepting all other" that we have mentioned previously.

The Resonant Plane Shapes

The sphere equally represents wholeness and unity. The motion of the spheres in the sky and their gradual appearance on the horizon creates an interplay of living qualities that Pythagoras referred to as the "music of the spheres." The gradual emergence or vanishing of the spherical/circular shape over the horizon creates different qualities in the environment that resonate with the different planes of nature. We therefore analyzed the quality of the different sections of the sphere and their resonance with the planes of nature. We started with the form of the sphere and found it to be in resonance with the physical material dimension, and a resonant container, of all other levels. The center of the sphere does not exist in time and space, as every center has a center creating a multi-dimensional vortex. The elusive formless center of a point resonates and connects to the highest level of the spiritual dimension. This shows clearly how the physical dimension is the full manifestation of the spiritual center and contains all the levels in between. We cut the sphere on several horizontal levels to get sections that resonated with the individual planes of nature (Figure 95). Using this process, we could develop a geometric language to communicate with each plane.

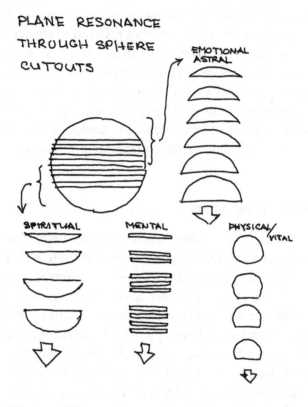

Fig.95 - Planes of Nature Resonance with Sphere Sections

The Corrective Resonant Plane Shapes

Using the same method that we applied above to find the geometrical shapes that are in resonance with the sub-planes of nature, within the sections of a sphere/circle, we then applied certain modifications to those shapes to correct and harmonize any disturbance on those planes. We measured the quality of energy in the different sphere sections, as the shape changes, during sunset and sunrise to find the moments of disturbance and we used vertical and horizontal lines as tangents that corrected the energy quality.

We have produced such corrective shapes on strips to be used with the BioGeometry Human Archetype Ruler. We also produce clearing cards that contain all the shapes that can be used to swipe over a disturbed space or body area (Figure 96). These are also very potent chakra harmonizers to restore connectivity with all planes of nature.

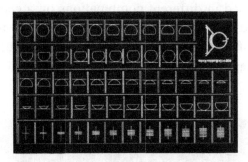

Fig.96 - Subplanes Harmonizing Card

The planes of nature shapes are used in the form of strips that are added to the BioGeometry Human Archetype Ruler (Figure 97) to fine-tune measurement and emission to the individual sub-planes. This allows for

Fig.97- Subplanes Measuring & Corrective Strips

better detection of the level of disturbance in any biological subtle energy functions, and for better application of the corrective measures. The next section discusses the use of the BioGeometry Human Archetype Ruler for different applications as a dedicated topic.

We usually develop pendulums, stands, staffs, and scepters with resonance to all or specific planes of nature using individual plane shapes that can be superimposed in different combinations on a central axis. Along the same lines, we have developed a special pendulum for sensitivity of detection on specific planes on which we can add and combine the relevant geometric shapes (Figure 98).

Fig.98 - Pendulum Set with Plane Additions

The BioGeometry Human Archetype Ruler

In BioGeometry we address a certain forming aspect of the archetypal dimension, an information source that contains the subtle energy patterns of everything as original templates of the emergence and evolution of all forms, concepts, and laws active in dualistic dimensions, regardless of whether they are in electromagnetic physical form or in purely mental-emotional dimensions. This forming aspect is the geometrical manifestation of subtle energetic pattern templates on a higher mental level of the information in the zero-infinity state upon which material Creation is built. It manifests all the Laws of Creation as perfect geometric templates for the creation of shapes through the natural forming process in different dualistic dimensions.

We repeatedly resort to the geometrical model of a vertical section through the Psychon to explain many concepts of Creation. Through it, we can follow the path of information from the origin in the archetypal dimension and through the mental-emotional vortex connecting to the time-space motion vortex. Through the action of the Law of Time, this information produces the bi-directional pulse forming the double spiral motion of the central vortex (Figure 99).

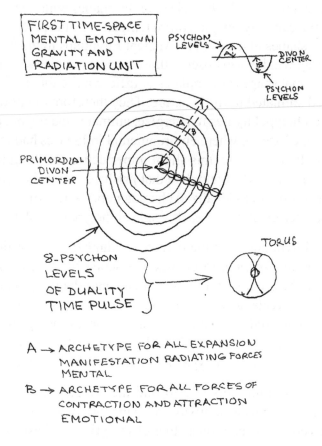

A → ARCHETYPE FOR ALL EXPANSION
    MANIFESTATION RADIATING FORCES
    MENTAL
B → ARCHETYPE FOR ALL FORCES OF
    CONTRACTION AND ATTRACTION
    EMOTIONAL

Fig.99 - Time-Space Motion

The resulting toroidal planes created by the spiraling vortex translate the timeless archetypal information into the time-space toroidal plane dimension, and back into the archetypal disk plane, where they are stripped of their time-space imperfection and stored back in their origin. The existence of the toroidal plane of time-space is as infinitesimal as the pulse unit itself. The myriad pulses emanating from the eternal spiritual plane exist harmonically, through resonance, from the smallest to the largest dimensions; they create a sense of the continuity of the toroidal plane. The seemingly material permanency of any reality is the result of the film strip effect of the bubbling surface of the plane of that dimension.

The connection to the higher dimension through a BG3 vortex does not give a window through which to observe the shapes within the archetypal dimension. We can only imagine those templates as the perfection behind the imperfect shapes in nature. The Ancient Egyptians found an ingenious way of creating windows to observe those perfect templates. They saw the perfect archetypal shapes as templates of different life force combinations that produced animated forms in nature. They therefore found ways of accessing the archetypal figures to energize, animate, and restore perfection in the physical existence where environmental influences had led to slight imperfection. It is, however, this slight imperfection resulting from small deviations from the perfect template that produces some dynamic tension and provides for the individualized character and beauty of the innumerable different interpretations of each single archetypal template.

The Ancient Egyptians used the quality of numbers, one of the primary manifestations in Creation, to enlarge the scope of the connective vortex and create the quality of a multi-dimensional doorway. The doorway was created as a rectangle on a 10 x19 or 10 x16 grid. These are BG3 numbers that are used to create the connection to the spiritual dimension. They could use this doorway to achieve resonance between a natural shape and the original archetypal template to which it was connected.

Their first step in doing this was to find the template by projecting the physical shape through the doorway and using the connective points where it crossed a vertical or horizontal line of the grid as a basis to construct the archetypal template. The dimensions of the archetypal window would be based on the proportions of the numbers 16, 19, and 28. The first two were the most common numbers used, with the 10 as a base to create the proportion. In BioGeometry, any combination of two numbers with the BG3 quality will produce the archetypal window frame. This grid was used as a guiding pattern on which the figure was placed as a relief or drawing (Figure 100).

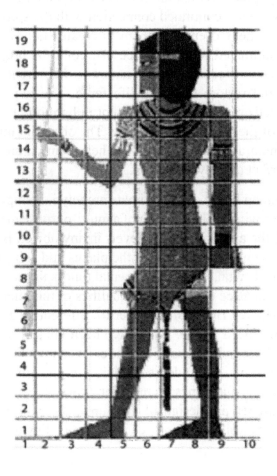

Fig.100 - Human Archetype 10x19 Grid

The numbers used to create the window depended on the size and configuration of the natural shape. By laying the natural shape in the BG3 grid and plotting the points on the grid, the Egyptians constructed the archetypal templates of everything in nature. Those templates were kept secret in the temples and given out to the sculptors and artists who created the physical archetypes. Each animated statue, relief, and drawing carried the life force within it and transmitted it to its counterpart in nature.

The Ancient Egyptian civilization flourished in the harmony and perfection derived from their continued connection with the spiritual archetypal dimension. This method enabled them to create statues and reliefs and wall paintings animated with life force that could be projected to living humans. They connected all forms in nature to their archetypal templates to harmonize and restore their full life force. The imperfection of the physical materialization in nature was kept in harmonious limits through the perfection of the archetypal template. The slight harmonic tension in the imperfect natural form produced the beauty in nature, in contrast to the stylized perfect archetypal shapes.

We used the human figure as the ultimate archetypal template in a 10 x 19 grid to develop a window in the form of a multi-purpose measurement ruler that allowed the analysis of BG3 levels in any object. By adding strips that contain the geometrical codes of the planes and sub-planes of nature from the physical, vital, emotional, mental, and spiritual levels, we can measure the occurrence of the ten BG qualities of the ruler on every level (Figure 101). The ten BG qualities refer to differentiated qualities of the BG3 group introduced above. They have been chosen from the endless number of BG3 secondary qualities that exist within all living colors in nature. As an example, a 360-degree dial detects and emits 360 additional BG3 qualities to the main ones. In the ruler, however, we use ten qualities related to the archetypal design of the human body. They relate to the planes of nature as well as the body chakras. depending on the calibration.

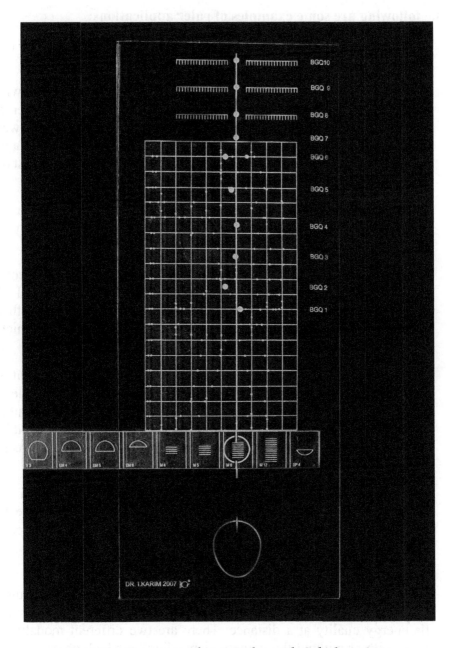

Fig.101 - Human Archetye Ruler with Subplane Strip
Measuring Mental 12 Level

The following are some examples of ruler applications:

1. Placing a witness on the ruler to find the strength of each of the BG3 qualities in the system.

2. By adding the "Homunculus" (a human body shape) to the witness, we can correlate and measure the 10 BG3 qualities of the ruler to the chakras in and above the body. We did not include the three lower chakras between the legs as they are too much posture dependent and are adjusted through the heart chakra as well as through the highest of the three centers located within an arm's length above the body.

3. Adding body organ diagrams, body meridian charts, reflexology zones, or any other type of navigation to the above method, we can diagnose the energy status in them.

4. Using the strips with diagrams of the geometrical resonant connection to the planes and sub-planes, one can pinpoint the level of concentration of any disturbances. There are also strips and cards that contain diagrams of the harmonizing shapes for each sub-plane which can be used with the other methods of emission.

5. To use the ruler as an emitter, we've provided an extra strip that is to be placed horizontally on the fourth, sixth, or tenth BG3 quality level depending on the plane of emission we use. By using the horizontal emitting strip, the full perfection of the archetypal pattern is emitted in our dimension. It is important to note that for measurement, diagnosis, and choice of remedy the emission strip must be removed.

6. One can add a dial calibrated to achieve the needed correction as a remedy. The adjustment can also be done by adding a live sample or picture of a remedy which also applies to locations and stellar objects (Figure 102).

7. In all the above examples, a resonant connection is achieved between the ruler and the person through his or her witness. The ruler acts as a powerful resonant emitter to harmonize and balance subtle energy quality at a distance. There are two different modalities here, with or without the witness, depending on which object, body, or space is targeted.

8. The witness area of the ruler can be left empty, or the addition of a small sphere without the sample, and homunculus can be used to measure or emit the ten BG3 qualities in the space.

9. By leaving the horizontal emission strip on the Human Archetype Ruler when not in use, it introduces the harmony of its ten BG3 qualities into the space, whether the sphere is on it or not.

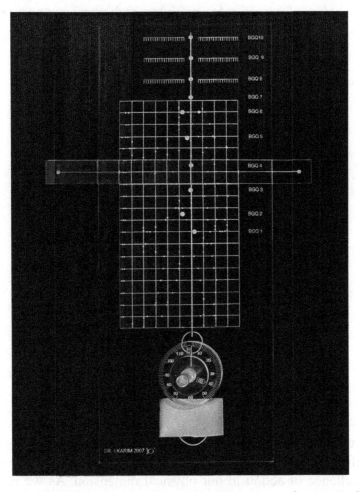

Fig.102 - Dial Emission to Witness on Human Archetype Ruler

We use mainly the IKUP and BG16 pendulums on the ruler. For special applications, however, one can use calibrated horizontal dials or BG28 disk pendulums, as well as the Time Pendulum. Placing the horizontal Time Pendulum with the emitting strip on the ruler is a way of activating the energizing QL-Torsion quality of the Al-Kareem Quality Fields.

There is also the small Human Archetype Pendant based on the emitting archetypal ruler diagram (Figure 103). It has the emitting horizontal line on the heart level that is taken off for measurement and placed on for emission. It reinforces the harmonizing archetypal connections of the body with its subtle energy template.

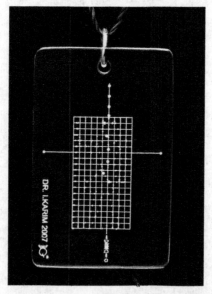

Fig.103 - Human Archetype Pendant

Reinforcing the connection with the archetypal level brings in its natural laws, life force and mental-emotional harmony to achieve holistic health and excellence of action in our physical dimension. As we have stated earlier, "Excellence" is the goal of all doctrines.

PART TWENTY-TWO

Chakras and the Shape of the Human Body

The shape of the human body can be studied in its full multi-dimensional subtle energy configuration through the resonant relationship between shapes and the levels of the planes of nature. The body energy centers, usually referred to as chakras in the Indian systems, are subtle energy vortices that connect multiple dimensions, just like the ones connecting parallel universes (Figure 104). Within this multi-dimensional existence, health and disease must be reviewed with a completely new holistic approach.

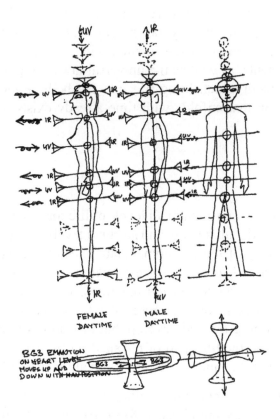

Fig.104 - Chakras

The Multi-Dimensional Human Body

While health in nature is partly within the reality of cause and effect, on the subtle energy level it is also affected by multi-dimensional resonance beyond causality. The Laws of Creation and the powers of nature that manifest as life force in our physical reality are in the extrasensory dimensions beyond the reach of our daily sensory perception, although they activate these and bring them to life. This resonant relationship with the universal multi-dimensional reality takes us into a new paradigm of understanding the shape configuration of human body.

In analysis, we must approach the human body from two angles. The first is related to the perceived physical, anatomical aspect of a hierarchy of basic shapes with mobility through posture and motion. The second relates to the unperceived subtle energy anatomy that expands the body into several boundaries reaching beyond the physical time-space dimensions of our sensory perception. These include vital, emotional, mental, and spiritual components, as well as the universal laws and powers of nature acting through them which bring life into the body. Every moment of physical evolution that enfolds with time already exists in its invisible envelopes.

The Goal

The archetypal statue can contain all levels of life force in their full activity on the vital, emotional, mental, and spiritual levels, but not on the physical level. The body of the archetypal statue has all the external design features of the natural forming process, making it the holistic resonant container of all life force levels and functions. The material body of the statue, however, lacks the other features of natural shapes like motion and growth to allow it to grow and develop, but instead has other features of permanency beyond the life span of physical forms. The statue becomes the eternal house of the human life force with all its higher levels.

It now contains the harmonizing multi-dimensional subtle energy attributes of life, carried by the physical form. However, the body does not manifest the natural forming process needed for growth and motion in the physical world. Luckily all is not lost as there is another solution to this problem that is not perfect but still works: a human surrogate, in which the harmonized and empowered levels of life force can act to complete the excellence of action and be brought into use. In other words, the archetypal statue is empowering the community to produce the excellence of action that will in turn, bring harmony into the multi-dimensionality of Creation. In all this, the human being remains the center of action while the statue is the connective tool.

The Boat

I will use the following story to give a visual metaphor to show the unperceived holistic picture of the human journey through life. The body is sailing on a boat in the river of life from birth to death within its world. It perceives the boat, but not the flow of the river and its surroundings. In the boat, we do not look forwards or backwards at the beauty of Creation. We can, to a limited extent, steer the boat right or left within the general flow of the river to interact with other boats, and this gives us a sense of free will that defines the path we take within the governing flow of the river. The boat is, however, connected through multiple strings to different points in the sky and the surroundings, which is how the Laws of Nature keep it going and stable. The invisible captain controlling the strings is in the higher dimension. We do not see as he takes into consideration the effect of all the actions in the boat that he senses through the strings. This is a two-way interaction where the universal affects and is affected by the activity of the individual.

This a topic that has deluded philosophers through the ages. If we detach the strings to take control of the boat the currents will sink it immediately. Luckily, our free will is limited to what we do inside the boat with all its contents, and we are free to enjoy them in any way we want during the journey. The physical body is in the boat which represents the perceived physical reality of our world, sailing in the invisible dimensions. Once we get off the boat, leaving all its contents behind, we are back where we were before taking the journey, and can now move in any direction in the whole landscape and enjoy the scenery. We become free from restricted movement of the physical time and space within the boat. The boat, however, continues its journey along the river. We should not think that the time will come for us to cross the river and reach the other side as we have been sailing it from the beginning.

We perceive the movements inside the boat, as well as its linear flow along the river, as being of continuous forward movement because our sensory perception is confined to the time-space dimension inside the boat. Outside the boat, where there is no physical linear time-space, we move according to the resonant principles of Stacked Time of the afterlife, as explained above. It is like a film strip made of separate individual pictures that can be arranged in different ways. Our physical linear time-space perception is based on a very limited sensory perception optimally tailored to life in the physical existence. It cannot function on higher dimensions where linearity and causality are not the norm. When the string that binds the frames in a linear flow is cut, stacked time becomes the way to move in the multi-directionality of time-space. The Laws of Nature that animate us must therefore convert from stacked time to linear time. This happens through a communication string at the center of a multi-dimensional vortex that can connect the stacked pages in a linear time-space form, giving us the seeming continuity of physical existence in our physical world. These strings are the vortices at the centers of physical shape, to which they bring the archetypal templates and their animating life force from higher dimensions. These vortices are those referred to as energy wheels or chakras.

Identification with the Body

The way most perceive our life journey is more limited than the above story. It was, however, necessary to expand the boundaries of the story to enter the universal scientific paradigm of the Physics of Quality. Our main sensory perception regards the skin as the primary boundary that separates us from our environment. It makes us identify ourselves with our physical body, reinforcing our sense of individuality and separateness from our surroundings. As we discussed in the earlier section, all the conscious and unconscious levels of action on individual as well as universal levels are stored and reflected in our skin's total subtle energy quality (beyond the limited perception of appearance) making it a holistic physical representation of the soul, which reinforces our total identification with it. The skin also deludes many materialistically inclined scientists to regard the physical body as the beginning and end of our existence and the source of all emotional, mental, and spiritual phenomena. This prevents us from perceiving our eternal existence.

The seemingly perfect skin we have in our youth is like the beauty we see in the basic color of a blank sheet of paper. With time, the beautiful background gives way to the information placed on it through our life experience. Instead of lamenting the loss of the background, by shifting the focus out of preconception, we can find the splendor in the work of art covering it. The skin is the canvas on which the values of life's experiences are painted. The older the skin is the more stories it has to tell.

The continuous drift of focus of perception deeper and deeper into the left-brain sensory mode reinforces the ego in a vicious circle relationship with the increasing materialism of the consumer society and the products of modern technology. Materialistic scientists think they can push nature aside and recreate it with artificial intelligence. They are under the illusion that they can even create future environments that don't need nature anymore. They view the material body as if it is separate from nature and simply interacts with it, without realizing that humanity and nature are one and the same. Many people have had practical experiences of out-of-body travel, the materialization of their own subtle energy body, encounters with spirits and deceased people, remote healing and surgical interventions, near-death experiences, premonitions or travel into the future, and many other examples of the existence of some form of conscious life independent from the physical body. Reputable scientists have conducted wide-ranging, serious, and credible research into these phenomena. Yet they cannot be acknowledged in a world where materialism is the beginning and end of everything.

Although I am a scientifically minded engineer, I have personally had first-hand experiences in all the fields that support the practical multi-dimensional paradigm at the core of the great ancient civilizations.

Through these experiences, I have been able to expand the boundaries of physics to include what used to be called metaphysics and have brought it into the world of subtle energy.

Returning to the boat metaphor above, instead of following the Ancients' example in preparing oneself for the wonderful unlimited journey outside the boat, we tend to hold tight to the boat and refuse to leave it. Seeking immortality of the physical body, while we are immortal beyond it, is absurd. Longevity should be a quality of life and not a quantity of years. We do not want to be like an egg refusing to hatch, or a worm refusing to leave the cocoon and become a butterfly. So, let us expand the boundaries of science into the multi-dimensionality of existence through the available tools of qualitative research.

There is another aspect to our boat metaphor, which has to do with our experience viewing the scenery on the banks of the river. The perception of this separate environment is based on a projection on the unperceived fabric of absolute reality of an inner image of the world created in the brain as a reaction to vibrational information received by the sensory organs. So, it follows that from a subtle energy point of view, part of us exists in the perceived environment that we project in the left-brain mode. This is the secondary boundary of the other senses: it includes all aspects of living information from our brain data bank and meaning levels. This second level is shared with others "seeing" the same thing and projecting their information within it. This can be understood as the sensory based, first perceived, collective level of our soul.

On the extrasensory level of the right-brain mode, we interact with several levels of subconscious information patterns that affect the way we see our world through the left-brain mode of perception. There is also a universal level of communication with the whole multi-dimensional reality on a subconscious level. By expanding our knowledge of subtle energy, we become aware of the different modes of our multilevel existence.

To Sum It Up:

We are an inseparable part of the whole multi-dimensional universal symphony. This is an important fact to consider as the part contains the information of the whole and is in resonant communication with it. While the part is affected by the whole, it can also affect the quality of the whole. This means that the multi-dimensional qualities affecting the human and other living subtle energy systems can also be changed and harmonized by working on the individual part. This gives us the new hope that we can each become a universal multi-dimensional harmonizing agent. If you work on the living subtle energy qualities of the drop, you will change the whole ocean!

The Chakras and the Shape of the Body

Subtle energy wheels or vortices in the body, widely known as chakras, are very popular in all complementary and subtle energy practices. Their presence and activity bring life force and multi-level vital, emotional, mental, and spiritual activity into all shapes of nature. As centers of shape, they are defined by the physical shape through the natural forming process to become the holy grails receiving the higher dimensions. Their presence in any seemingly inanimate natural object, or the products of humanity, is an indication of the life force being captured through the design of the physically lifeless shape. In this case, the inert object becomes animated on the higher levels while on the physical level it is only a carrier of life force that can be transmitted to any human, animal, or plant.

The origin and detection of chakras in the body are widely misunderstood. As we have explained earlier, chakras are the vortices of communication between the archetypal plane and the physical body. They are the doorway of the archetypal templates into the forming process of nature. They ensure the communication between the shapes in nature and all the subtle energy planes. The archetypal templates govern the forming process in the evolution of all shapes in nature. As such they are geometrical centers of the physical shape. For the physical shape to manifest those communication vortices it must be in resonant relationship with each of the planes. On the physical level an object must have a concave shape to contain water. Similarly, as we discussed with the shape of the lungs in relationship to life force and QL-Torsion, for any object to contain subtle energy from any level, it must be shaped to contain it through a specific resonance with it. Natural shapes, therefore, are formed to enter into resonance and exchange subtle energy from all the planes and their sub-plane divisions where different subtle energy life force functions are located (vital, emotional, mental, and spiritual).

When a natural shape is formed accordingly in a two-way communication it will manifest the BG3 vortices. If we examine copies of natural shapes, like a wooden human statue for example, it can be possible to detect the BG3 centers of the chakra vortices resulting from the shape. Although the natural shape, in this case, holds no possibility of evolution on the physical level, it will still contain all levels of subtle energy and life force without physical evolution, as we explained earlier in the introduction. We can detect all chakras on a human statue and even increase the radiation of one or more chakras by changing the position of the hands on an artist's wooden statue that has movable limbs. In this way, we can emit any chakra quality into the space for subtle energy healing.

I usually take one of those wooden figures with me in my courses and introduce him as my trusted assistant who does healing and space harmonizing for me. In (Figure 105), I show several posture and related chakra activation. Placing the wooden figure on a BG diagram (paper emitter) will enhance the healing emanation. This practice revives the old practice of erecting archetypal statues on sacred power spots to perform healing and give oracle readings. Positioning oneself in front of such a statue in its original location harmonizes the body's chakras and activates the multi-dimensional right-brain/heart perception. That is why the practice of moving statues from their original location cancels their whole concept of being.

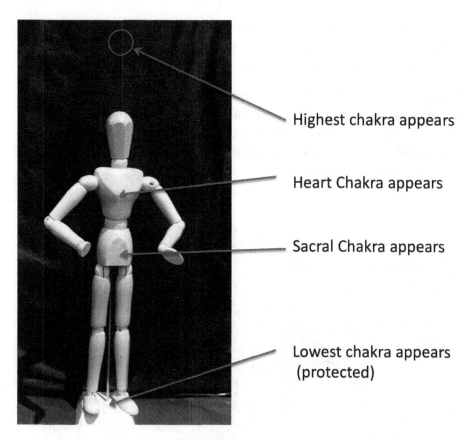

Highest chakra appears

Heart Chakra appears

Sacral Chakra appears

Lowest chakra appears
(protected)

Fig.105- Mannequin Chakra Activation

Chakras and the Planes of Nature

Chakras, as we have seen, are the vortices connecting the planes of nature from the lowest to the highest. The chakras are part of a hierarchy of vortices in the body, such as those at the joints, that are anointed in many traditional practices as well as the Chinese acupuncture points which are like windows connecting the meridian subtle energy to the environment. They are therefore connected to archetypal levels beyond our time and space. In the pulsating reality, they keep our physical, seemingly permanent, reality floating on a pulsating base of interconnected physical appearances which are connected in time and space through the chakra vortices. This is just like the filmstrip effect, a model that we use repeatedly to explain different aspects of our multi-dimensional pulsating experience. The chakras also connect us to other copies of us in other dimensions (Figure 106).

Some sub-planes will have an increased affinity for biological functions, but all levels are active within each sub-plane. One cannot relegate each chakra to a specific plane of nature. As we have seen in the analysis of living qualities, nature works through the holistic balance of every quality with all the others in the background.

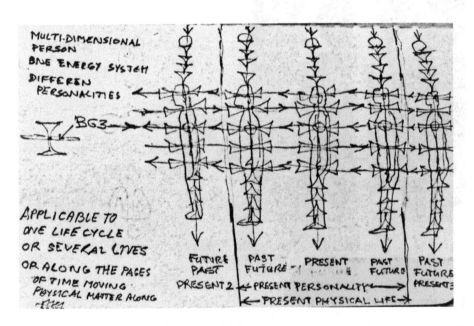

Fig.106 - Chakras Multidimensional Connection

Interaction of Chakras

The level of activity of every chakra is continuously changing in relation to the biological functions, activity, surroundings, time of day, lunar phase, mental-emotional state, and many other environmental factors. Just as the body's organ functions are interlinked and work within an overall unity, so are the related chakras. The chakras work as one system, just like a piece of music where each note is part of the whole and affects, and is affected by, its quality and the order of activation. Each chakra will take a leading role supported by the others, depending on the related organ functions in which they all participate on different levels. At any given moment one can restore the BG3 quality of all chakras and let them play out their dynamic roles with ever-changing levels of activity. We give some examples of how to interact with the chakras below.

If we could listen to the chakras' dynamic activity during the day, we would hear one of the most beautiful symphonies in Creation. In fact, this is possible if we listen to the higher heart consciousness in the right-brain mode. We can check how each posture that activates a certain chakra affects the others using a BG3 or any of the life force pendulums.

Shapes and Chakra Interaction

Because chakras are multi-dimensional centers of shape configuration, they can be affected by any changes in the shape such as in motion or posture. The shape and material of objects worn on parts of the body can also affect the relevant chakras.

All shapes influence the quality of compression wave fields around them, and this results in a qualitative communication and information exchange between separate shapes. This also goes for the shape quality of the chakras. Their shape is affected by the biological, emotional, and mental qualities related to an activity. All forms of environmental pollution produce a change in the shape of the vortex ends of a chakra, like a flower opening or closing, and influence its functioning. Let us examine some examples of taking the opposite path of changing the shape of the chakra to positively affect its functioning on biological, emotional, and mental levels, and on its surrounding environment. To do that, we can use any of the following methods:

1. We move our arms so that the palms are on the level of the chakra we want to activate. In Figure 105, shown earlier, we see a wooden mannequin in postures activating the relevant chakras. We can use the statue to radiate its chakra quality to affect all in its surrounding space. We can do the postures ourselves without the wooden

figure. The postures can be combined in a sequence to harmonize all chakras. The postures on the wooden statue can be used to study the relationship between the chakras and their interactive relationships. When we work with the BioGeometry ruler, we activate the ruler emission through either the heart chakra or the third chakra above the head as they help to activate all other chakras. When the highest chakras are harmonized, this is reflected in the three lowest chakras that connect to the earth, creating the BG3 quality of a protective sacred power spot.

2. When we place a bowl on the fire, its shape is imposed on the flame. Similarly, we can take a cup or bowl and place it on the chakra (concave side out) to activate it. This takes only a few seconds to work. It is an immediately effective, lazy way to activate it.

3. Visualizing any shape will produce a mental-emotional counterpart that has the same effect as the physical shape. One can visualize a cup of any size and mentally place it on one or more the chakras. An easy way to do this is to visualize it in one's hand and physically place the shape on the chakra.

4. One can speak a vowel to open a chakra. Pronouncing "Hou," as in "Whooo," activates the third highest spiritual chakra above the head and will open all the rest.

5. One can tap each chakra with a certain corresponding number. There are several complex systems of number, geometry, or color correspondences with chakra functions in the different traditions. The simplest way to do this is to start from the base chakra with one tap, then the reproduction chakra with two taps, the solar plexus three taps, four taps on the heart center, five on the throat, six on the forehead, and seven on top of the head. The three higher spiritual chakras above the head, although not convenient for tapping, will respond to eight, nine and ten respectively. The BG3 Numbers e.g., 16, 19, 28 etc. can also be used on the chakras.

6. One can imagine basic colors starting with red at the bottom for root chakra, orange for sacral, yellow for solar plexus, green for heart, blue

for throat, indigo for brow and violet on the crown chakra over the head.

7. The Ancient Egyptians used to place amulets on the chakras, comprised of related gemstones.

8. Walking for some time will open all the chakras as it produces an alternation of polarities that will restore balance to all organ functions.

Sacred Power Spots and Chakras

The subtle energy vortices in sacred power spots can be referred to as the chakras of the earth due to their multi-dimensional configuration. As primary chakras, each one is in a resonant relationship with all other secondary chakras within the subtle energy fields of the body of the earth. It is all a multi-level resonance between all dimensions of spiraling subtle energy vortices within the earth's life force. Ensuring the strong harmonious unity of the human subtle energy chakra system with all other components of the earth's life force is the only way to a healthy future of our species. Restoring the lost awareness of the need to harmoniously integrate ourselves into the life force of the earth is the first step. It need not be in the full grandeur of the elaborate rituals of the great ancient civilizations, which ranged from the smallest activity to the location of important buildings and city planning. Just being in a power spot from time to time is already a first step towards better health and enhanced creativity.

Finding the nearest power spot in your area and "owning it in your heart" is the beginning. A further step would be making it the center of community activities. You will probably find that collective centers of community activities in older towns are already on such power spots. In most cases, historic monuments and sacred buildings will be located on power spots. There are many types of rituals that can be performed, like prayer, meditation, chanting, postures etc., to enhance your connection.

This is what made spiritual power spots the most important factor in the history of humanity. They are the primary spiritual fountains of life. All the great ancient civilizations understood this and tailored every aspect of daily life around this concept. The best way to reintegrate with the earth is to restore the forgotten role of sacred power spots in the earth and sky to everyday life through planning, building, the creation and use of everyday products, rituals, pilgrimages, and awakening it in all forms of artistic creativity. All human activities are thus transformed into rituals of initiation. The return of humanity to Mother Earth through the sacred power spots will restore the energizing healthy positive QL-Torsion layer and stop the depletion of life force in the environment that has been visited upon it by modern technology. This human-Earth reintegration will create a healthy co-existence of all life forms with modern technology. Human civilization is a delicate state that has been shown to be very volatile throughout history. Many great civilizations have developed to a very high level and then disappeared while at their peak. This time we have the knowledge to survive provided we let the natural wisdom of the heart prevail. This way, humanity can become an environmental harmonizing agent.

The Protective Role of Chakras

The multi-dimensional BG3 quality in the vortex configuration of a chakra creates the transcendent spiritual conversion into our time-space mental-emotional time fields (Figure 107). When the chakras are harmoniously active, they create the harmonized centering quality on their toroidal planes producing a positive QL-Torsion energizing effect. This creates a protective layer that keeps the life force of the body from dissipating into the negative QL-Torsion surroundings. In upcoming chapters, we will be discussing how the Al-Kareem Quality Field shows the centered harmonizing quality on all the layers of the toroidal plane.

The Chakra Tunnel

In the following examples, a permission from the person on which the experiment is performed, should be sought. Chakras are wormhole-shaped tunnels leading into multiple other dimensions (Figure 108). The vision of the tunnel going into the light in near death experiences is related to the

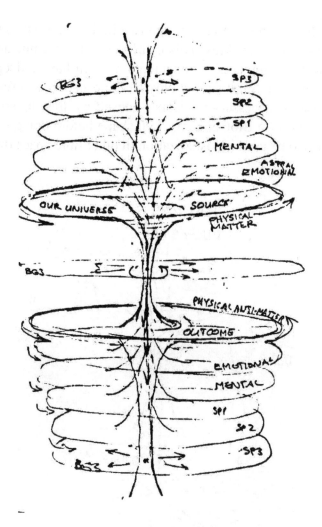

Fig.107 - Chakra Vortices

travel through a chakra vortex. In out-of-body states we find the point of entry and exit through one of the chakras. The associated chakra can vary, so we need a form of measurement to detect it. You can take a BG pendulum with twenty-eight disks, which is specially configured to detect objects in other dimensions, and try to find the astral body above a consenting person in deep sleep. You will detect it around twenty centimeters above the physical body. Between the two bodies you will find the connection to one of the chakras. This is, however, not a game and must be taken seriously as any action—or intention—will have a deep effect on the sleeping person. So, it should only be done as part of a research protocol. It is always necessary to cleanse oneself by drawing an imaginary five-pointed star or a BioGeometry L90 shape before doing this. Chakra tunnels can also be used in visualization in other time-space dimensions.

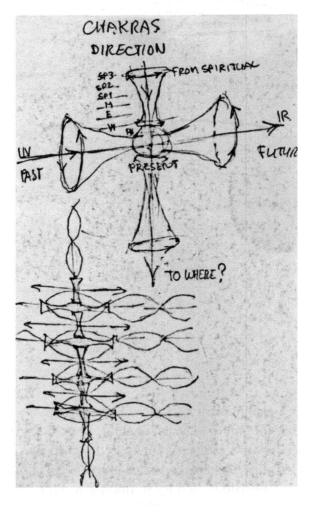

Fig.108 - Multidimensional Chakra System

PART TWENTY-THREE

The BioGeometry Brain Stands

The 3D Energy Key of the Brain

The brain, like all other body organs, is an open energy system constantly exchanging emotional and mental subtle energy with the environment. The communication is done through the exchange of abstract qualitative information as a bi-directional effect. All body organs are immersed in some form of physical water. In the biological systems of nature, the water is in full harmonic communication with all the higher resonant harmonics of water, all the way up to the primordial state at the onset of the duality of Creation where universal Consciousness is activated. This is the dimension of the emergence of the attributes of the Universal Mind at the center of the life force that travels through all the levels of water from the highest primordial fog to the physical level. Even dry matter that seems inert is only an outer shell containing all the higher levels of water that form most of its invisible existence. The physical brain in this context is a manifested part of the Universal Mind that the sensory perception masks in favor of a more efficient physical action. The sensory mask, however, contains the free will needed to produce qualities on the higher dimensions.

Brain Subtle Energy Configuration

According to the Laws of Universal Harmonics, the Psychon geometrical configuration that we analyzed earlier is a repetitive resonant model from the smallest to the largest dimensions of Creation. We will use this model to analyze the subtle energy qualities of the human brain. The shape plays a major role in the subtle energy configuration. We can therefore study it on a human figure.

The human head can be analyzed through the qualitative measurements of BioGeometry as a spherical toroidal shape to which we can apply the Psychon model in the form of the BioGeometry 3D Energy Key. The first thing we learn is that there are different complementary qualities on the right and left of the central vertical and horizontal axes of motion. This subtle energetic analysis supports the research in the different yet complementary perception modes of the brain hemispheres.

We also find that the BG3 plane passes through the center of the head on the level of the pineal gland. This is where a connection to qualitative universal information from beyond our physical sensory time-space occurs. This BG3 plane is found on the level of each chakra at the center of the vortex perpendicular to the direction of motion creating the time-space vortex (Figure 109).

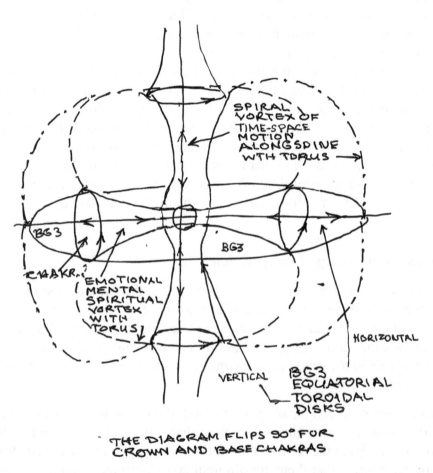

Fig.109 - Brow Chakra Subtle Energy Configuration

The translation of the qualitative universal information occurs through the spiraling effect of time-space and an association with the pre-existing content of our sensory databank, where the universal meaning is re-configured according to existing cultural and belief systems. The information creates the toroidal mental and emotional fields in the hemispheres. Those fields arise from the depth of the unconscious into perception, in a resonant communication with the higher universal dimensions into the lower individual and collective dimensions within the brain in the pineal gland area. They remain as subconscious information in the toroidal fields of the brain. This kind of information does not rise into everyday sensory perception, due to its lack of time-space coding. It stays as an unperceivable quality in the subconscious mind.

As already discussed, the brain has the left-brain and right-brain modes of perception. The first is the receiver of sensory information that the brain uses, stores, and gives meaning to; it then forms a three-dimensional image and projects it outwards on the medium of absolute reality as our perceived world. This is where the ego and the personality reside.

To find the true self, we must go further into the extrasensory right-brain mode and understand how the brain is a receiver of information about the rest of the ranges of absolute reality beyond the limited sensory ranges. The brain here acts as a universal antenna through which the Laws of Nature manifest into the biological functions of life. These laws, as we have explained earlier, are pre-requisites for the functioning of the sensory organs. They are embedded in the total life force of the Universal Mind. As we have explained, life force moves from the first level of the creation of the Psychon pulse through endless levels of harmonic resonance, carrying the primordial form of Consciousness into all dimensions of Creation tailored to their respective time-space configurations. The medium in which this resonance takes place starts from the original background fog through the primordial waters connecting the endless levels down to the physical water in our world.

The primordial waters exist as the unperceivable backbone within physical water. Water is a carrier of Consciousness and life force into all levels of Creation and, as such, it communicates information on all levels and dimensions. The water in the brain, and in the rest of the body, is not just a bearer of life force, but as a multi-dimensional medium, it is the antenna receiving universal information. The pineal gland situated on the timeless BG3 plane in the brain is in direct resonance with all the universal information of Creation. It is like the seat of the universal Divine mind in the brain.

There are geometrical shape resonances between the pineal gland, the shape of the eye, and the shape of the heart resulting in a two-way exchange of information so that the heart becomes a storage space for unconscious information. This quality puts the heart in resonance with the universal planes and spiritual dimensions. It becomes a very strong emitter of the BG3 and Al-Kareem Quality Field qualities. That is why many traditions have several names for the heart. As an example, in Arabic we call it *Al-Qualb, Al-Lobb, Al-Fouad, Al-Gaash, Al-Gannan, Al-Tamour, Al-Roa, Al-Eyab*, etc., with each name expressing a different level, attribute, or concept. Recently, it has been discovered that the physical heart has its own brain cells which take their information directly from non-physical levels of subtle energy. This leads to the concept of the intellect of the heart that we introduced earlier.

Light Behind Colors Produced by the Brain

Colors are produced in special areas inside the brain as a reaction to physical vibratory stimulation of the sensory organs. Light includes the full spectrum that produces all colors. Colors cannot exist without light, so the brain must be producing its own light to give each color its specific luminosity. Each color is a manifestation of an attribute of luminosity. We have examined earlier the Müller theory of colors, which places the colors around a central gray scale between white and black, expressing the degrees of luminosity at the heart of the colors.

It is also evident that the brain produces its own light when we dream in color. So, the light that projects the colors of our perceived reality into the world is produced by the brain. The light of the world is your own light. By now, this should be a normal fact as we have established that on one level, we are our perceived environment, and on another, we are the multi-dimensional invisible reality.

The Inner Eye and the Light of the Heart

Our scientific approach based on the Physics of Quality seems to affirm the teachings of the mystical schools of many spiritual traditions that see the pineal gland as a third eye in the brain that is sensitive to the vibrational range of external light and produces melatonin to induce sleep. It is also receiving a form of inner light. This light, in the water of the brain, is a resonant harmonic multi-dimensional manifestation of endless levels of light all the way to the beginning of Creation, where light is part of the primordial fog. These spiritual traditions identify the inner light as coming from the heart.

From the qualitative point of view dealing with subtle energy, the heart is the largest fiery center of the subtle energy body and as such it is the center of light contained in the water medium of the blood. This light of the heart is of a higher spiritual dimension with several resonant harmonic levels, each connecting to different dimensions. It gives off the BG3 quality. The light on the higher dimensions of the heart resonates with all the other harmonics of light in a bi-directional resonant communication with the pineal gland that, in turn, creates the light behind the colors in the brain. So, even the light that we see in front of us is in a resonant communication with all the multi-dimensional levels of invisible light.

Intellect of the Heart

All types of energy have all the information of the whole Universe encoded in them. Only what falls within sensory ranges is decoded by the brain through left brain perception. The rest of the information, due to its non-dualistic spaceless and timeless nature, is unperceived by the physical senses and remains at a subconscious level. Information beyond the confines of sensory perception is coded differently and accessed through different types of brain cells distributed in several areas of the body. The brain cells in the heart and gut have a resonant connection with the universal levels and the Laws of Nature that activate our biological functions.

There is, however, a holistic perception of patterns in the right-brain perception that is communicated to the left-brain enabling the sensory perception of physical forms. The formless qualities unconsciously perceived by the right brain are communicated to the sensory perception of the left brain to be personified into shapes. The awareness of the form and quality of shapes is a bi-lateral brain activity. The contemplation of physical shapes activates and synchronizes both left-brain and right-brain activity. This practice is based on the multi-dimensional resonance of shapes.

Some of the information that is perceived and digested by the intellect of the heart needs to surface at certain times into a person's conscious awareness. This translation involves the conversion from multi-dimensional time-space into sensory linear flow of perceived reality, then given shape and meaning in the brain's database. In a simplified form, the information in the subconscious mind creates a question in the conscious mind in the form of a symbolic interpretation of an object, thought, or action. This draws the question into context and surfaces it into Consciousness. In many cases, the information stays in symbolic form if it is not directly resonating with an obvious action. This could also be the mechanism of it surfacing in a dream. This is, in a way, the answer creating the question to bring the information into our attention.

The 3D Energy Key of the Brain

When applying the BioGeometry 3D special configuration of the Energy Key, we place the left-brain sensory time-space axis horizontally in the direction of motion. The higher levels of emotional and mental energy, as well as the parallel timeless multi-dimensional subtle energy dimensions connect through another vortex to the present moment at the center of the time-space dimension and move around it in a counterclockwise direction (Figure 110).

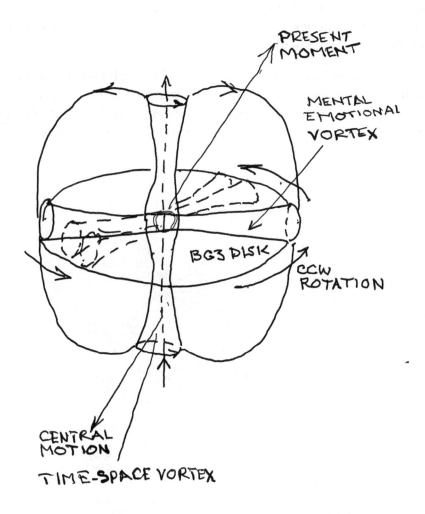

Fig.110 - 3D Energy Key of the Brain Showing
Multidimensionality of Present Moment

At the point of connection, the effect of the emotional, mental, and spiritual information exchange with the perception level of the personality in the second vortex produces a sort of a bulge in the center of the first time-space vortex. As a result, the left-brain LB time-space vortex has a bulge in the center, while the right-brain RB wormhole rotating in a vertical BG3 plane circling around the center does not.

The motion in the Energy Key can be viewed through two different forms of perception (Figure 111). On the right-brain vortex that connects to the center of motion, there is a bidirectional time pulse at the center of motion with the BG3 quality; this creates the inter-connected beginning and end of the linear motion.

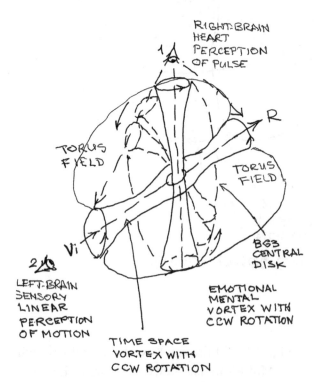

Fig.111 - Perception Modes

This pulse manifests as a linear motion in time and space, with the Violet quality indicating the beginning at one end of the left-brain horizontal vortex and the Red quality at the other end. The line of motion expresses the qualities of the Energy Key on the resulting torus field, around the time-space left-brain vortex, while the counterclockwise rotation of the right-brain shape along the disk around the time-space axis connects to the harmonic universal time pulse of Creation. The resonant connection with the Psychon time pulse creates the spiraling counterclockwise motion with another clockwise subtle energy spiral at its center.

This holistic 3D Energy Key configuration of the brain shapes has the most potent effect on the quality and balance of subtle energy in the brain hemispheres. Both the centering BG3 and the energizing (QL+) Al-Kareem qualities are activated in the brain hemispheres and the body organs, as well as the surrounding environment.

This brain stand configuration connects perceived reality to emotional-mental dimensions so that we get the full effect of both in one. This is achieved through the central ring at the point where the vortex connects to the timeless BG3 planes (Figure 112).

Fig.112 - Interaction of Brain Stand Perception Modes

This stand activates the pineal gland in the brain and harmonizes the pituitary functions, activating the crown and brow (third eye) chakras in the process. It also activates the BG3 and Al-Kareem qualities in the body and its surroundings. This stand will create a harmonizing quality that will make all kinds of subtle energy rituals more effective.

The BioGeometry Brain Stands

The BioGeometry brain stands (Figure 113) are derived from the multi-dimensional version of the Torus Energy Key, but it is split so the stands can be used separately and thus independently interact with the hemispherical functions of the brain. These stands can be used to separately research the subtle energy link between hemispherical brain modes and biological organ functions, as well as the psychosomatic effects of environmental stress.

Fig.113 - BioGeometry Brain Stands

Our research has shown a resonant communication between the geometric shape of the mental-emotional wormhole represented by the right brain (RB) stand and the right brain; and a similar resonance between the time-space left-brain (LB) stand with the bulge at its center with the left brain. These shapes have been found to activate and harmonize the activity of their corresponding brain hemispheres and can be used in many forms of healing, meditation, and spiritual practices.

We offer the stands as a set of two, one for each brain hemisphere mode, and we have fixed a polarized BioGeometry dial to each stand. The stands are separated from their original configuration in the 3D Energy Key and placed vertically side by side so they can be adjusted and used separately. The LB shape works directly on the vitality of the organ function. The RB works on the mental-emotional aspects related to the organ function. The two shapes can be calibrated individually and then used together.

To ensure their communication they are placed on a base plate to create a synergetic unity and the BG3 centering energy quality between them. The distance between them on the base plate is fine-tuned to work with the shape of both stands, including the dials and the screws used to fix them to each stand. If the stands are used without dials or screws the space between them must be adjusted without the base plate to give maximum BG3. This is also the case when using a BG28 disk or any other addition instead of the dials and their screws. The BG28 is an effective general body and space harmonizer that does not need any calibration.

An interesting observation that confirms the activity of the brain stands, is that the effect of the LB bulged shape can be seen on body functions when medical diagnostic devices are in use. The RB shape produces an effect only when combined with the LB shape beside it.

The Unity of Body and Environment

Harmonizing the environment with the BioGeometry brain stands is another example of the fact that the perceived world is synthesized from sensory information and projected from the brain onto the invisible fabric of absolute reality. This makes the human being and his or her reality one unified energy system and not two separate things. This emphasizes the BioGeometry axiom that "We are the Environment."

As we explained earlier, the brain creates and projects our perceived sensory world out of the absolute unperceived holistic reality. The brain interacts in a two-way communication with perceived reality. We are affected by the quality of our perceived reality on vital, emotional, mental, and spiritual levels, however we also project our quality on all those levels into our perceived reality. So, we can say the total quality of one person's perceived reality is slightly different from another's. The individual qualities we project onto the collective and natural realities, color our world. We see the world as brighter and more colorful when we are happy and healthy, and we experience it differently in times of distress.

We have therefore developed BioGeometry experiments to change the quality and bring harmony into our perceived reality, and we can verify our results through the presence of BG3 and Al-Kareem qualities.

We have shown repeatedly in such experiments that a BG3 or Al-Kareem emission from an IKUP, Djed-Wadj or BG16 shape aimed at or placed on the visual cortex, for example, will create those qualities in the surrounding space and will harmonize biological functions, as well as electromagnetic and geopathic stress, etc. The eyes must be open when we place the BG shape on the visual cortex. When the eyes are closed, the harmonizing effect stops. The same process can be observed with the other sensory centers in the brain. If the BG shape is placed on the auditory center, the person must speak or listen to others speaking to project the effect.

The Use of Brain Stands

The Brain Stands can be used in the following ways, and these are covered extensively in the BioGeometry courses:

A. **Brain Stands with Polarized Dials**
   The distance between the brain stands is set by the positioning holes in the base plate.

1. The left brain stand (LB) works alone on the left hemisphere of the brain with a polarized dial for fine tuning.

2. The left-brain shape works alone on the left hemisphere of the brain as well as on the right brain hemisphere with the polarized dial on the left shape set from UV to Negative Green. The right brain (RB) shape can be set to neutral with both polarizers facing each other, or the whole stand can be taken off completely.

3. Both stands with dials, with their distance set by the positioning holes on the base plate, can be set to certain functions in body or space (organs, grids, electromagnetic radiation, chemical toxicity, radioactivity, etc.). Adjust the LB stand dial first and then proceed to adjust the RB stand dial.

B. **Brain Stands with BG28 Disks**

Use two BG28 disks without numbers, with screws on top of both disks. Place them the distance apart that's been set by the base plate. If dials are placed on top of stands without vertical screws, then the stands must be adjusted off the base plate in order to generate the maximum amount of BG3 between them.

1. Both stands with BG28 disks on them work on both hemispheres. They harmonize body organs and space.

2. The LB stand with the BG28 disk alone (without the RB stand) does not harmonize all organs.

3. The RB stand with the BG28 disk must be used alongside the LB stand. On its own, it does not work on the body or the environment.

C. **Brain Stands without Dials**

This solution works when it is within the visual field of the person.

1. The LB stand works alone without the polarized dial.

2. The RB stand alone, without a polarized dial, does not seem to work on either the right or left hemispheres when tested with bio-feedback or other devices. The effect on the right or left brain or organs can, however, be detected by specially calibrated pendu-lums.

3. Both stands together, without dials, work on both hemispheres (the distance between them must be slightly closer or wider than on the base plate to get the best BG3 results).

In a BioGeometry Special Topics seminar hosted by the Vesica Institute in Asheville, NC, Dr. Michael Maley introduced us to some of his tech-niques for left and right brain activation and he asked me if we had some-thing in this field. This was the beginning of an interesting journey that led to the addition of the Brain Stands into our teaching curriculum. Dr. Maley has done some interesting research with the Brain Stands. With his permission, I have included one of his relevant articles here, which he pre-sented at the Special Topics conference hosted by the Vesica Institute in Asheville, NC in 2012 following our discussions and work with the brain stands in the previous year (appendix).

PART TWENTY-FOUR
Earth Subtle Energy Grids

The quality of subtle energy in Earth locations has played an important role in building patterns, city planning, and architectural design since early historical times. Subtle energy power spots and their connective paths set the pattern for the layout of human dwellings: community leaders would place the important buildings, starting with the temple, on the most powerful power spot in a location and other important buildings, like hospitals, monuments, palaces, and the marketplace, on the secondary power spots. The power spots then served as central hubs from which the main roads radiated: the main avenues would be placed along ley lines connecting the power spots and creating the basic pattern of the town plan.

In some ancient town plans and historical monuments, we find a slight shift in the angle of the roads or building plans. In many of those cases there seems to be no reason for the change in direction. We noticed, however, that in all such cases there is a shift in the subtle Earth energy gridlines. The most common causes for such shifts are underground water streams or cracks in the earth's underground rocky strata.

There is a very prominent example of this phenomenon in the Mosque-Madrasa of Sultan Hassan in Cairo, which was built in the fourteenth century. We made a grid survey of the area outside the mosque and found a shift in the whole area both outside and inside the mosque. This indicates the shift was not caused by the building structure but rather was the cause of the building's shift in design (Figure 114).

Examples of such slight change of direction in the grid pattern are also found in the street layout of many European medieval towns of Roman origin (refer to Mettler's book, *Atmosphaerische Reize Streifen,* meaning *Atmospheric Stress Strips*). There are several theories behind the causes of the grid pattern change of angle: some believe it's a superposition on the original grid, others feel it's a deflection resulting in a change of direction. What interests us here is the fact that town planning and individual buildings took them into consideration.

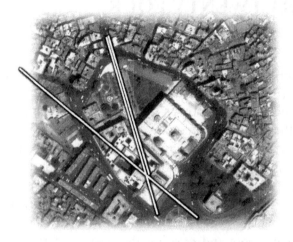

Two Main Grid
Directions

Change of Direction of
Grid lines

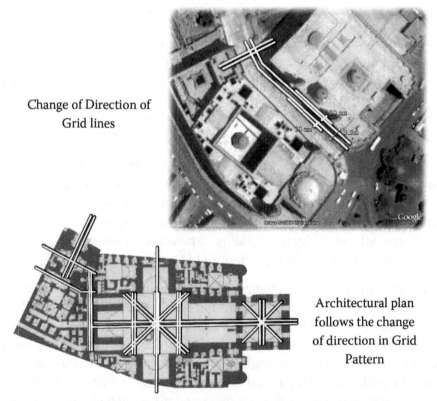

Architectural plan
follows the change
of direction in Grid
Pattern

Fig.114 - Sultan Hassan Mosque, Cairo, Egypt Planned on
Earth Energy Grid Pattern

These traditions were applied in more recent history in the planning of Washington, Paris, Rome, and Cairo. The book *Talisman* by Graham Hancock and Paul Bauval is a good reference on this subject. Many of the towns of Europe that have Roman origins also display a knowledge of power spots and subtle energy patterns. Zurich in Switzerland—originally a Roman garrison called Turicum—is one such example (Figure 115). Town planners detected Earth subtle energy patterns through dowsing methods, using tools based on the harmonic resonance of wavelengths. The Roman Lituus or shepherd's staff, which we see depicted in the hand of saints, and the dowsing rods in the hands of Arab dowsers in the Middle Ages, are such examples. Those ancient dowsing methods were based on underlying scientific principles and could be depended on for subtle energy site surveys.

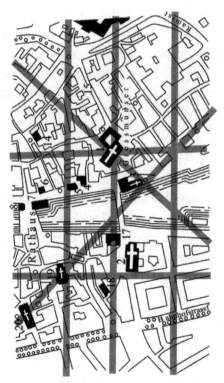

Fig.115 - Zurich Plan Showing Earth Energy Relation
Location of Churches

As human interest shifted from nature to technology, this type of dowsing was forgotten. Today, most popular modern methods of dowsing rely on the mental or psychic method we dealt with earlier in this book, and it is prone to autosuggestion, which can make it unsuitable for scientific research. Aside from the ancient ways of water dowsing, which is still practiced, modern dowsing was basically used for channeling, oracle reading, premonitions, healing, and similar interests. For the mapping of Earth energy gridlines, however, this popular and prevalent type of dowsing gave mixed results, with different dowsers affecting the credibility of dowsing methods and discrediting all forms of Radiesthesia.

Earth subtle energy radiation and electro-smog are subtle energy non-electromagnetic compression wave phenomena (scalar, torsion, hyper sound, etc.) which cannot be detected with mainstream electronic devices. So, without the forgotten ancient harmonic wavelength-based tools, it was impossible to differentiate between the different types of Earth radiation patterns. These tools have become irrelevant in modern town planning and architecture, which completely ignores our connection with the subtle energy anatomy of the earth. Instead of integrating into nature, planners have become invasive to it. All the modern planning criteria of interfacing open and closed spaces cannot achieve a complete natural life force circulation to firmly plant the buildings in nature and transform them into living natural components of the earth's living system.

The modern epidemic increase in the incidence of cancer is shedding new light on the impact of geopathic stress with regards to diseases. The growing list of carcinogenic products includes chemicals used in food, drinks, household cleaning products, and sprays; building materials containing lead or asbestos; cigarettes, cellphone radiation, and Wi-Fi devices, and many others. Although they have been identified as culprits, the primary causes remain largely elusive.

Geopathic stress was clearly identified and statistically proven as a main cause of cancer and other immune diseases as far back as 1929, when Gustav Freiherr von Pohl did a survey in the town of Vilsbiburg in Germany. It showed that the occurrence of cancer was concentrated in areas of high geopathic stress resulting from the crossings of underground water streams, compounded by harmful patterns of subtle energy Earth radiation. This fact was long known by farmers who had observed this phenomenon in plant and animal health. These facts have all been written up and published in Pohl's 218-page book (with 71 drawings and illustrations), titled *Earth Currents - Causative Factor of Cancer and Other Diseases*.

German literature is abundant with information about harmful energy grids, although the theories and practices used to correct them may differ from one author to another. The H3 Lecher antenna is the most prominent detection tool used in Germany and the Acmos antenna is more common in France. Both are derived from the Lecher microwave double antenna (Figure 116). This is a very precise detection and emission tool that produces good results; although it is only explained through quantitative wavelength theories, it is a tool based on qualitative principles of harmonic resonance.

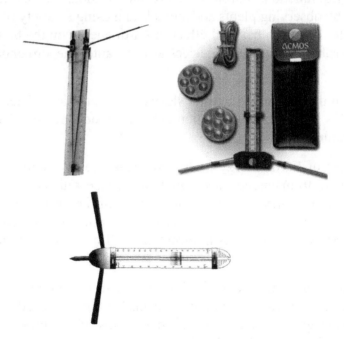

Fig.116- Top Left- Original Lecher Antenna. Top Right- Acmos Antenna.
Bottom- Luedeling H3 Antenna

I personally got to know Helmut Luedelin, who manufactures the H3 Lecher antenna, and I've found his instrument to be very precise in the detection of Earth grids and minerals. I lectured at his conference several years ago as participants were interested on how I solved the electro-smog problem in Hemberg, Switzerland. I will not go into all the German theories and practices related to Earth radiation discovered by German researchers and available in their abundant literature, but it is considerable.

Geopathic Stress

Geopathic stress is the name given to harmful Earth radiation resulting from underground Earth anomalies (cracks, shifts etc.), water streams, or Earth energy linear patterns (referred to as grids). Geopathic stress is a widespread phenomenon that is at the root of many health problems. Several patterns within the earth's energy fields have been identified. The only way to detect and identify Earth energy grids is through their effect on biological functions. Farmers usually find locations with harmful Earth radiation by observing plants and animals and using a variety of dowsing methods to detect the harmful effect of Earth energy on the body, which is made visible through such devices as rods, antennae, or pendulum devices.

The reason that modern electronic devices are not able to detect or measure Earth's subtle energy radiation is because they are non-electromagnetic in nature.

Some types of Earth energy grids, like scalar fields resulting from the motion of electromagnetic waves, are in resonance with their electromagnetic source and carry its harmful qualities to further distances in the environment. The stressful quality affects the emotional and mental levels of compression waves and is transmitted to all living systems in its surroundings.

Subtle energy includes the total vibratory ranges of absolute reality with all its different dimensions. Vibratory levels beyond the speed of light are not electromagnetic waves, but different forms of compression waves. On higher, faster vibratory levels they are not bound by our physical time-space constraints. Emotional, mental, and spiritual energy are among the types that fall in this category.

Any motion on the physical or subtle energy dimensions produces compression waves that are multi-dimensional in nature with all levels of life force. These compression waves will carry the resonant qualitative effects of the original motion on all subtle energy levels. Scalar, hyper-sound, and other waves that move beyond the speed of light fall into this category and can affect our vitality, as well as our emotional and mental well-being, before the problem manifests on the physical level. We might also speak about torsion here as it is a state of twist in the subtle energy configuration energy present in all its categories.

As a recapitulation at this point, let us analyze how in BioGeometry we measure the quality of external torsion in the subtle energy (energizing neg-entropy or depleting entropy) through its effect on the body. The body reacts to the quality in a spiraling emission of positive QL-Torsion (QL+) or a negative one (QL-), and these produce, respectively, the clockwise or counterclockwise rotation of a pendulum indicating the quality.

Compression waves are of the longitudinal type moving along the direction of motion like the ripples created by a moving object in water. Hydraulics, aerodynamics, and acoustics deal with compression waves in their respective domains. Electromagnetic waves, by contrast, have inner movement that runs vertical to the direction of wave propagation that is described as transversal (Figure 117).

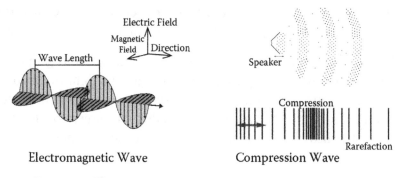

Fig.117 - Electromagnetic Wave vs. Compression Wave

We cannot harmonize environmental quality without addressing the complete wave nature of subtle energy in all its dimensions.

Once this phenomenon is understood and acknowledged by mainstream science, then a new type of advanced compression wave measurement device, similar to those for sound waves but sensitive enough to detect minute levels of inaudible sound, will surely be developed.

As we explained earlier, chronic diseases are on the rise. This category of disease can usually be managed but not completely cured. In most cases the causes can be found in the environmental, chemical, and electromagnetic pollutants, compounded by geopathic stress, which are still largely ignored by modern medicine. In the German literature, the occurrence of cancer is usually attributed to the geopathic stress people have been exposed to for several years, mostly in the area where one's bed lies. If after being cured one returns to the same bed, or to a similar situation in another location, the disease can recur in a few years.

Grid Types and Human Perception

The subtle energy of the earth is the background multi-level weave of all types of compression waves that include multi-level information in its holistic vital, emotional, mental, and spiritual dimensions. Accordingly, it interacts with all levels of biological life forms. Human actions, whether conscious or unconscious, can amplify, diminish, or affect the qualitative interaction between the earth's subtle energy and related resonant patterns. This can steer people's interest towards either beneficent spiritual interaction with Earth energies, or the harmful effects of geopathic stress.

In early historical times, before the age of modern technology, humanity was in resonance with the spiritual harmony of our right-brain focused consciousness. This led to interactions with sacred power spots that became the center of our activities. This quality of perception led to the discovery of spiritual energy paths connecting power spots (ley lines) as well as other beneficent energy patterns, and it led to connections to spiritual power spots in the sky, such as Sirius. People also discovered underground water streams running in the rocky strata of the earth that produced healing water springs arising within energy vortices in the crossings. These all played important roles in bringing spiritual harmony to people's lives.

In the age of modern technology, the increased electromagnetic radiation activity in the environment is affecting every biological system, triggering a shift in perception and mental-emotional health. The EMR within the natural Earth fields that are supporting physical life has become polluted and manipulated by human-made products.

Before the age of modern technology, the compression wave Earth energy fields had a natural origin and produced a balanced positive QL-Torsion state that supported all life functions on Earth. Human-made electricity caused those fields to lose their energizing quality and acquire a depleting negative QL-Torsion quality. The result was the superposition of a stressful quality on several types of Earth energy grids that have been affected by modern technology. The grids identified by the German researchers Ernst Hartmann (1915-1992) and Manfred Curry (1899-1953) are the most well-known. The Benker cube system is super-imposed on the Hartman grids. Many other lesser-known grid types have been identified but the Germans and Swiss are the only ones who have dealt with them in depth. We have given a few references in the bibliography.

Earth energy grids are sometimes referred to in German texts as "atmospheric stress grids." This is a term coined by architect Matthias Mettler (1923-2017), who was for many years head of the Radiesthesia organization in Zurich and it refers to the fact that the grids rise from the earth's surface like walls, giving a subtle energy structure to the atmosphere. I highly recommend his books (see bibliography) for all those interested in going deeper in this subject. We will not cover the abundant theories and research in the field, as it would be beyond the scope of this book.

Our constant exposure to the electromagnetic radiation of modern technology makes us more sensitive to related stressful Earth energy compression wave patterns than to other types of waves within the background medium. Since the body reacts more to this type of Earth energy pattern than to others, they were the first to be detected, and this was done through observations of plant and animal health that showed certain linear patterns of stress areas. Ultimately, special scientific instruments were developed along dowsing methods that used calibrated qualitative scales to detect different types of stressful Earth energy grids.

While in ancient times the relationship with Earth's subtle energy was focused on the healing spiritual quality connecting people with the earth and the sky, in modern times the focus and sensitivity has shifted towards the increasingly harmful effects of Earth radiation that is a main part of geopathic stress. Even so, the connection between harmful Earth radiation and the ever-increasing electromagnetic radiation is unfortunately still widely ignored.

Most people who are dealing with the issue of geopathic stress focus on protection through shielding from Earth energy grids, underground water streams, and Earth anomalies. Farmers will observe plant health to detect harmful subtle energy patterns and will avoid placing their animals in those areas. They will also follow the lines of the harmful patterns they observe outside into a building and avoid placing their beds in areas where the lines transect the space. Today, the scientific dowsing methods of Physical Radiesthesia represent the only accurate way to survey the patterns of Earth energy grids inside buildings or in open areas.

The Hartmann and Curry grids discovered in Germany in the last century have become more harmful with the ever-increasing man-made electromagnetic radiation with which they are in resonance. There is a lot of variation in the literature concerning the dimensions of grids and the phenomena affecting them. We will therefore not go into too much detail here but rather leave that to our practical courses. In general, we advise BioGeometry practitioners to do the detection work in every case, without preconceptions. It is helpful to know at this point that the Hartmann grids (around 20 centimeters wide) run in a square pattern of around 2.00-2.40 meters in an east-west and north-south orientation with a wider strip in both directions every 10 meters that are synonymous with the Benker cube grids. The wider north-south strip is sometimes detected as a double strip. Further analysis of the Hartmann grid system by Benker showed them as a three-dimensional cubic system with horizontal planes between the vertical ones. The Benker Cube system is superimposed on the Hartmann grid system. (Figure 118).

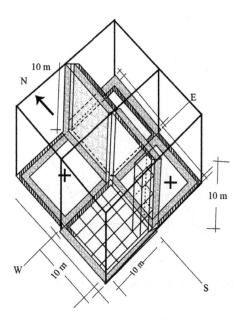

Fig.118 - Benker Cube System

The Curry grids are similar in width with a square pattern ranging from 2 meters to 3.5 meters. They run in a diagonal direction with a wider strip in both directions every 10-12 meters (Figure 119). These spacings can vary due to the associated resonant harmonic energy quality that gridlines share with EMRs.

There are also lesser-known types of gridlines like the Schneider grids that are related to lightning activity and limited to certain spots, as well as several other types of Earth subtle energy patterns linked to products of modern technology. There are also much wider strips that can be found on a larger scale in the grid pattern that we identify in surveying large scale regional areas.

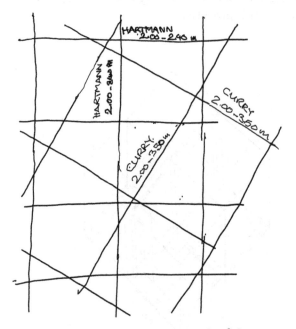

Fig.119 - Hartmann & Curry Grid System

BG3 Centerlines of Grids

The discovery of the transcendental BG3 harmonizing quality at the onset of BioGeometry has become the main foundation of the centering process applied in all harmonizing activities and solutions. This has enabled us to understand and apply the principles of the natural forming process which is at the core of the BioGeometry design language.

We will refer here to the existence of BG3 grids that can be accessed to introduce harmony in the environment. There are several types of BG3 Earth energy grids that have different BG3 qualities.

Ley lines are an example of wide strips manifesting the BG3 quality. In many cases, they connect the sacred power spots and were used as pilgrimage roads, funerary paths, or as the main avenues connecting center points in city planning.

There is also a secondary BG3 grid system at the centerlines of Hartmann and Curry grids that can be detected with a BG16 pendulum and used to map them without doing substantial detection or measurement on the harmful grids. Once the BG3 grid is detected, its direction and spacing will indicate its type. Further measurements can be taken with the dial pendulums relevant to Hartmann or Curry Grids in the mapping.

The 45-Degree Grid

There is another original BG3 grid system running in planes at 45-degrees from the earth's surface. This can be used to access the BG harmonizing quality through resonance by design principles, motion, or posture along that angle.

Al-Kareem Quality Fields/Grids

There is another special type of BG grid that we refer to as the Al-Kareem Quality Grid or Field that we activate in our projects through special BioGeometry stand configurations; these are measured with a specially configured pendulum. The Al-Kareem Quality Fields/Grids refer to the state of positive QL-Torsion and energizing life force of the environment. The Al-Kareem Quality Fields/Grids are different from other grid systems in that their planes are curved. They rise at 45 degrees and curve upwards to a certain height where they start curving downwards. They are found around natural objects and move in different directions. These different types of BG grids will be dealt with in a coming dedicated part in the context of Earth geopathic stress and radiation patterns.

The Origin of Gridlines

There are many theories in the German literature about the origin of the Hartmann and Curry gridlines. Most researchers agree that they are related in some way to the earth's electromagnetic patterns, especially the flow of the magnetic meridians between the poles. Some authors regard them as secondary non-electromagnetic compression waves resulting from the flow of the magnetic meridians in the background subtle energy medium. Konstantin Meyl in Germany identifies Earth radiation grids and electro-smog as scalar wave phenomena.

One fact that some researchers have found confusing is that the spaces between the gridlines remain constant with little change in different areas on the globe and they do not converge as they approach the poles. They are therefore probably secondary or tertiary interference patterns resulting from interactions with other flows and patterns created by all types of motion in their surroundings.

Horizontal Grid Planes

Most types of grids have been identified to have components in the form of vertical and horizontal planes, in a similar way to how the Benker cubic system is superimposed on the Hartmann grid. We can detect horizontal planes with the same qualities as Curry grids as well as other types running at different heights from the ground. The Ancients used them in the horizontal leveling of their monuments.

These horizontal planes, however, can be very harmful, as they pass through our body's organs. Fortunately, they can be addressed and harmonized with direct or indirect placement of BioGeometry solutions. Placing one of our solutions where a vertical grid crosses a horizontal one, or on points of maximal disturbance, serves as an effective solution for both, and delivers a wide harmonization.

In sacred power spots, the vertical and horizontal planes of all grid types usually have the BG3 quality and it's interesting to note that the original builders used them to level either the horizontal building components or the base platforms on which the monument was built.

Any pendulum calibrated to someone's personal wavelength will react if the gridlines affect the body negatively, but once the stress is mitigated the pendulum will no longer react. In BioGeometry, we always strongly advise that one should harmonize the space by placing a BG harmonizing shape, such as the BioGeometry cube or space harmonizer, prior to detecting gridlines to ensure that the interaction with the gridlines is always a harmonizing BG3-based interaction.

The BioGeometry horizontal and vertical dial pendulums are some of the most accurate instruments available for the detection and differentiation of all types of Earth energy grids. These instruments are calibrated through the subtle energy qualities of resonant angles. They have the advantage of detecting a grid even after it has been harmonized by a BioGeometry solution that removes stress on the body.

An alternative method for surveying gridlines is based on the observation that parallel lines of any sort create a fine BG3 central line between them, which represents a geometric center. This phenomenon produces a grid shifted at half phase in both directions (Figure 120). One can detect this grid pattern and through it map the Hartmann or Curry grids by their relative shifted orientations, without entering into resonance with their harmful qualities. The BG3 pendulum in this measurement should be moved up and down perpendicularly on the BG3 lines to check if they rise vertically, and to thus determine if they are related to the orthogonal grid walls. If the BG3 detection does not rise vertically then we are dealing with a totally different BG3 diagonal grid whose planes are at a 45-degree inclination. (Figure 121). To avoid the confusion and increase mapping accuracy, we have introduced the first method of detection in our basic teachings and kept this one for advanced levels, although its basic principles have been dealt with in the design principles of BioGeometry.

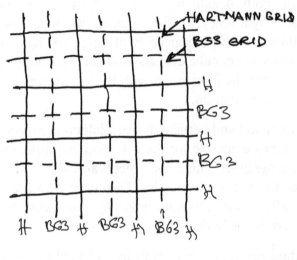

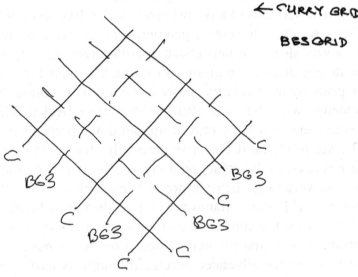

Fig.120 - Hartmann-Curry BG3 Grid

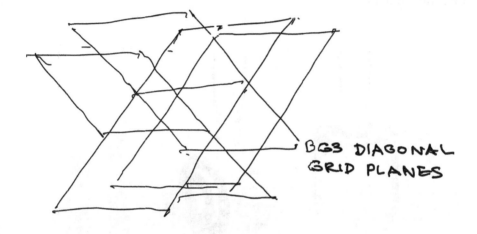

BG3 DIAGONAL GRID PLANES

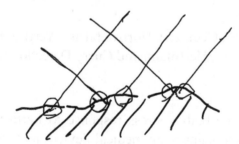

IRREGULAR GRID PATTERN ON EARTH SURFACE

Fig.121 - BG 45 Grid

The BioGeometry horizontal dial pendulum and the BG16 pendulum are the best detectors of the beneficent energy quality of Earth power spots. We can use the vertical dial pendulum with two additional wavelength rods, calibrated to Hartman or Curry grids, to detect stressful locations and Earth energy grids (Figure 122). When used with the living color dials both pendulums can also be used to detect and emit the beneficent qualities in nature.

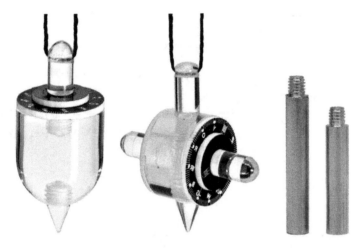

Fig.122 - BioGeometry Horizontal and Vertical Pendulum Set
with Hartmann and Curry Detection Rods

We can detect the body's stress response to Earth radiation and electro-smog through mainstream medical devices and tests such as electroencephalograms (EEGs), electrocardiograms (ECGs), and blood tests. It can also be assessed through energy diagnostic devices based on gas discharge visualization, Chinese medicine, and other modalities. These methods are, however, better suited to assessing the overall subtle energy effects of a place than for mapping its gridline patterns.

Shielding Solutions

Trained practitioners in gridline detection are not widely available. There are, however, complete or partial floor covering solutions available on the market, and these do not require homeowners or office managers to do any work around grid detection. The most common form of this type of protection is through shielding using cork mats or complete coverage under the flooring material itself. Dinkel, a common plant in Germany, provides some protection when used in pillows and bedding fillings but it is necessary to renew the filling periodically. There are also different types of composite or synthetic Earth energy shielding materials on the market. Building biology uses electromagnetic shielding on walls and windows to protect from EMR. This can, however, make matters worse if any electromagnetic devices are used within the shielded space, as it would trap the radiation and increase the stress.

BioGeometry solutions, which use resonant harmonizing shapes and attachments to electric and water systems, address the quality of energy in a space and do not involve any shielding. Their action is based on the quality of numbers and angles, and where they are most active, they also support the mental-emotional well-being of people within the space. The science of BioGeometry is aligned with the same paradigm as that of Ancient Civilizations and it deals mainly with the detection and reproduction of the energy quality of sacred power spots—which we call BG3, referring to three of its quality components. BG3 is the resonant harmonic configuration of the center of balanced geometric shapes. The higher the intensity of the resonant harmonic energy quality found in a space, the more it will harmonize and balance geometric energy patterns, resulting in more balanced environments.

Our main solution lies in the application of the BioGeometry principles to the design of new buildings, or in modifications and additions applied to existing ones.

Specially designed BioGeometry shapes, of which examples were shown earlier, are placed in a building to radiate the beneficent energy. For regional solutions, larger versions of those shapes are buried in the ground. BioGeometry Solutions, in general, have proven they are efficient environmental solutions for disturbances arising from geopathic stress, as well as shape-caused disturbances. They also reduce harm caused by building materials, they harmonize EMR, and they increase water vitality.

There are also simpler solutions in BioGeometry that are easier to use and widely available. Our plexiglass cube, on which a specially arranged number and pattern of figures are engraved, can be placed on a table or shelf in a building. We can then place extra attachments on windows and doors, electrical panels and cables, and water pipes (Figure 123).

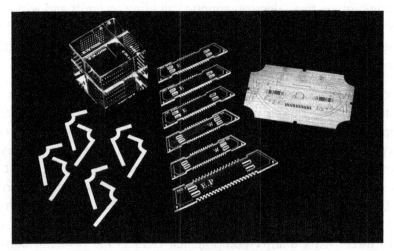

Fig.123 - Home Kit

Some electronic devices produce Earth energy patterns of disturbance in a building that should not be mistaken for the Hartmann or Curry Gridlines as they appear only when the electronic device is on. They are sometimes referred to as Technical Grids and are often superimposed on the Hartmann or Curry grids or strips. Wireless electronic devices such as Wi-Fi routers or wireless phones can amplify the harmful effect of gridlines in a space. In some cases, they produce technical grids or strips that disappear when the device is shut off or disconnected. They also have the Vertical Negative Green and Infra-Red (IR) quality. Attaching either the 9-notch electrical strip included in the BioGeometry Home Kit or two mobile phone stickers will solve the problem.

It's interesting to note that mirrors can reflect and change the quality of energy in a space, and they have therefore been used in many traditions at the entrance of a building, facing outside, to reflect and diffuse harmful energy quality coming from outside. In bedrooms however, the situation is different, as mirrors will reflect the good energy in the room as an inverted image that creates a stress in the brain. They should be covered at bedtime or a BioGeometry L90 shape should be placed in a corner.

PART TWENTY-FIVE

Earth Energy Quality and Psyche

There is a resonant relationship between the grids in a house and the emotional and mental levels of its residents. In general, negative emotions or actions can amplify and increase the resonance with the harmful quality of gridlines, especially, as we mentioned earlier, in the bed area where one sleeps.

Mental-Emotional Interaction with Grids

The negative emotions associated with disease can influence gridlines and create a vicious cycle between disease and grid effect. There is abundant literature on the mental-emotional memory content of houses. The building material itself can also be impregnated with different energy qualities which can be amplified and carried along the earth's energy patterns.

The Human Archetype Ruler

To measure the emotional and mental effects of the earth energy grids we use the Human Archetype Ruler with a personal witness and a planes of nature strip. We can do measurements on the twelve sub-planes of each level (vital, emotional, mental, as well as the three spiritual levels). The subtle energy quality of the eighth mental sub-level (M8) is usually a good indication of the effect of gridlines on the body. If this sub-level is balanced, then the grids are in a positive QL-Torsion state; otherwise, the grids are harmful. We can also do the above measurements by placing the ruler on the line itself without a witness.

Multiple Floors

In multi-story buildings, the grid system rises through all floors and a correction on any level can affect other levels above or below it to varying degrees, depending on the level of environmental stress in the building. This must not be taken for granted and must be measured each time, and it does not apply to horizontal grid planes, where the correction will more likely spread out horizontally than vertically. But again, in this case we must check how far the harmonizing effect extends.

Grids Transporting Qualities of Locations

Grids transport information through places or people and solutions that use stones, rods, and other objects must take the direction of flow into consideration. The BioGeometry concept of the Energy Key can be used to measure the quality on each side of the grid to determine its direction of flow: the Green quality is usually to the right and Negative Green to the left when we face the direction of flow (Figure 124). By contrast, BioGeometry solutions work through resonance throughout an entire gridline, and they are not affected by a grid's direction of flow; we can harmonize grids simply through placing appropriate BG corrective solutions in the space, which could be in the form of a Home Kit Cube, or a BioGeometry stand or attachment.

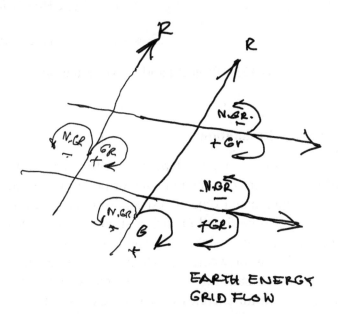

Fig.124 - Earth Energy Flow

Subtle Earth Energy Surveys in Large Areas

Gridlines are usually around 20 centimeters wide but every 10 meters we find strips around 75 centimeters wide; at larger distances of 75 and 100 meters we find even larger strips that can be up to 2 meters in width. For large area surveys, we use wider Hartmann and Curry strips. On this level, too, we find a grid of BG3 strips between the Hartmann and Curry strips. The following map shows a large-scale survey from one of our projects (Figure 125.)

Pueblo Del Sol
BG3 Beneficent Grid, Wider Strips, and Power Spots   Harmful Earth Energy Spots, Strips, and Grids

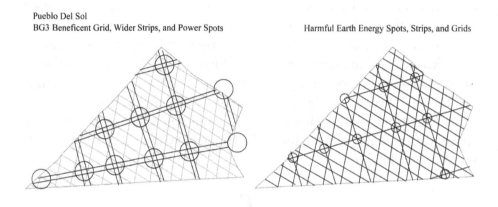

Underlaying Land Satellite Image Removed Due to Copyright

Fig.125 - Project Land Survey Analysis

Harmful Energy Emanations

German studies point to another type of harmful energy flow, one which is emitted from sources of contamination or pollution, or one that results from certain impregnated objects, especially those from ancient burial sites. Mold can also be found in such a situation, and certain spots in a house where a previously sick or psychologically disturbed person was accustomed to being, or where an extreme violent action occurred, can be impregnated with harmful energy flows that can affect other people. Those types of harmful energies flow from their source towards people living in the area, usually towards the bed location, whether a person is sleeping on it or not. BioGeometry solutions will usually take care of such problems. In all cases like this, however, if a physical source of disturbance exists, it should be removed. The final solution should be verified by measurements of the space on the emotional and mental levels of the Human Archetype Ruler.

We encountered such a case in Hirschberg in Appenzell Innerrhoden, during the installation of our BioGeometry solution for electro-smog. There were many cases of psychological disturbance and suicides in the area and the electro-smog solution we provided did not seem to help the situation. We still detected a strong energy disturbance emanating from three empty areas in the grass fields. We installed specially configured BioGeometry emitters and pointed them at each of three circular centers of disturbance in the area. An immediate deep relief was felt by everybody in the area. The stress was reduced, and the affected people started sleeping better and feeling a new joy in their lives.

A few hours later, my friend Sepp Mazenauer, who played a major role in raising community awareness and forcing the authorities to provide solutions to environmental problems, gave me, as a present, a book about the historical castles of Appenzell. In it, I found drawings of three round castles that no longer existed. They were located on the same circular areas of disturbance I had detected. They had been destroyed when an army from neighboring St. Gallen massacred four thousand people who had been living in those castles. They were never rebuilt, and the locations were left as empty fields. This was the most painful event in the history of Appenzell, and it affected the descendants of that massacre for generations, causing a large part of the psychological distress we were seeing in modern times.

Stressful Grid Patterns Produced or Increased by Wi-Fi and Other Electric Devices

It is important to switch off all wireless devices in the bedroom and adjacent spaces before going to bed. A television set located in the bedroom should likewise be unplugged at night. The reason is that all these electric devices will increase the activity of harmful Earth gridlines. The BioGeometry solutions will take care of such problems, but, as a principle, we always advise people to continue with protective practices, as a matter of awareness.

Negative Emotional and Mental Effects on Harmful Gridlines

As we have explained earlier, all types of energy systems in nature contain some form of active life force. This life force gives all types of Earth subtle energy grids vital, emotional, and mental attributes. There is therefore a continuous communication between all life forms and the grids on all levels. In this sense grids, like everything else in nature, are living systems in their own dimension. BG3 grids produce positive QL-Torsion that replenishes living systems on all levels, hence their healing properties. The amount of life force is greatly reduced but not totally absent from products of modern technology. Grid types with electro-smog have a depleting negative QL-Torsion effect and create stress on the emotional and mental levels. They cause a depletion of life force that results in reduced immunity and vulnerability to disease.

BioGeometry Perception in Measuring Earth Energy Grids

The term "Radiesthesia" means sensitivity to radiation. The practices of dowsing and radiesthesic detection increase one's sensitivity to the quality of radiation or subtle energy fields in general. Repeated measurement of the qualities one is most interested in detecting increases one's sensitivity. As a result, the body gets programmed through a sort of impregnation process by the subtle energy quality being measured and, in a way, becomes a copy of the object of detection. As the intensity of the programming increases, the individual becomes more proficient in detecting the object of their specialization. With time the person's emotional and mental awareness becomes so coupled with the specific subtle energy quality in which they specialize that they are in a sort of continuous connection with it. They may pride themselves on the fact that they don't need any instruments of detection; they can independently perceive and influence the subtle energy quality of a situation.

Unfortunately, the general fear from the effects of geopathic stress made the detection and surveying of Earth energy grids a main activity among dowsing and Radiesthesia practitioners, not the least due to its being financially rewarding. This is very dangerous because with time mapping will affect a practitioner's health and distort their emotional and mental-make-up. People impregnated with a certain energy quality tend to seek it out, as it provides the most comfortable environment for them. This why such people will always seek or return to places with harmful Vertical Negative Green quality.

This level of focus is ideally applied mainly to beneficent qualities and is preferably concentrated on the detection and measurement of BG3 qualities in nature, or through the production of them in design.

This type of programing of the human instrument leads to spiritual initiation and good health and allows one to become an unconscious but powerful harmonizing factor on a collective level. This is the real goal of BioGeometry. Early humanity and people living in the great ancient civilizations were always drawn to sacred power spots because their focus of perception was anchored in the right-brain mode connecting them to the harmonizing Laws of Nature.

The important role that sacred power spots played historically has eroded due to modern humanity's shift into left-brain consciousness. Our connection to the Laws of Nature was lost and the birth of modern technology polluted the subtle energy quality. This caused us to lose our unconscious connection to the spiritual energy quality of power spot locations. We also lost the direct resonance of the body's chakras with the sacred power spots in their role as chakras of the earth, and our experience of being bathed in the unity of nature. Modern humanity became an enemy of nature. In a broader sense modern humanity is in the awkward position of being an enemy of itself. By opening up our awareness to the subtle energy of power spots we can begin restoring the vital connection with the life force of the earth, and we can bring our era of modern technology into harmony with nature.

However, there are many situations where a BioGeometry practitioner must survey the grids in a home or map larger project areas. We offer the following guidelines as a form of general protection that applies to any form of subtle energy measurement or practice. BioGeometry students are taught to only work with the grids in the home after having brought the home to a high BG3 level.

1. Harmonize the place with a BG3 solution, then detect with a vertical dial pendulum. You can measure the space using a BG3 Ruler or a Human Archetype Ruler to verify the environmental subtle energy quality. Complete the following steps after your measurements to make sure that there are no harmful residues left in your energy system.

2. As a rule, always look for occurrences of BG3 in nature. The more times one measures BG3 every day, the better one is protected from harm.

3. Look for BG3 in spiritual practices and rituals.

4. Introduce BG3 into your actions and activities through BioGeometry practices and design principles.

5. For every gridline measurement make four BG3 ones, through BioGeometry activities.

6. Clear the harmful energies by walking in nature and raising your arms above your head. An effective procedure would be to synchronize your footsteps, heartbeat, and breathing.

7. You can also raise one or both hands stretched above the head, palms in, to activate your highest chakra and protect the lowest one, while harmonizing all the chakras.

8. After any form of healing clear the impregnation through washing and walking (and in extreme cases take a saltwater bath for its clearing effect).

9. After every healing activity, check yourself directly or on anatomy charts and clear any areas of your own body that need it before doing further healing for other people; do this also before going to sleep every night.

10. Maintain a positive life attitude, free of judgement and accepting yourself and all others; empathy, love, benevolence, charity, protection, and nurturing of the natural environment are important

factors for holistic harmony. Living in healthy environments, following a proper diet, and getting exercise are obvious things that most people do not follow.

BioGeometry Quality Measurement Techniques

As highlighted in the above section, if the detection of Earth energy grids is not carried out safely and in an energetically harmonized environment, the process can be quite detrimental to our health and our energy systems.

For this reason, I will not delve into the BioGeometry methods of detection, which should be taught practically in class and not merely through books. All BioGeometry tools and devices come with specific instructions and are dealt with in more depth with practical exercises in our courses. However, people with a background in Physical Radiesthesia and who already practice grid detection can use the BioGeometry Horizontal and Vertical Dial Pendulums set, which comes with an instruction manual. Prior to working with these pendulums, we advise placing a BioGeometry Home Kit Cube in the area to benefit from the protective benefits of BioGeometry; the pendulums are designed to detect grids even when the space has been harmonized.

We continue to stress to our students and practitioners the importance of ensuring the environment they are practicing in has been fully harmonized with BG3 prior to commencing any form of gridline detection. This way, they are always approaching the gridlines after their detrimental qualities have been harmonized. In the BioGeometry Environmental Home Solutions (BG-EHS) protocols, all Earth gridlines are fully harmonized before they are mapped. This makes the process beneficial for the person doing the mapping, and so the only purpose for mapping those gridlines would be to use their energetic momentum to add extra levels of environmental harmonization.

The Cube Development in Hirschberg

In the electro-smog solution, we applied in the Swiss area of Hemberg in St. Gallen, Switzerland, we attached the BioGeometry emitters, which we had developed specially for this purpose, pointing to the antenna body from a distance of twenty centimeters (Figure 126).

Fig.126 - Hemberg Emitter Pointing at Antenna Body

We now refer to those special emitters as the Hemberg emitters. We also attached them on some of the houses and aimed them at the antenna in the church tower and other distant sources. This carried the harmonizing BG3 quality on the mobile communication waves and spread them throughout the area, addressing electro-smog issues, as well as gridlines and other forms of geopathic stress. This solution proved to be successful and very economical as regards the number of shapes installed. The health and well-being of humans, animals, and plants was restored.

The Mobile Communication Authority and Swisscom, the government provider, wanted to test a second solution independent of the mobile communication network with the goal of running it as a pilot project for a total country solution. The area of Hirschberg on a small hill at the center of the Appenzell IR valley was chosen because it represented an urgent situation: the residents, suffering from ill-health symptoms that affected humans, animals, and plants, were threatening to dynamite the mobile communication towers. For this project, we used a solution from our projects in desert camps in the Middle East that involved an elaborate underground electromagnetic network. We used special types of BioGeometry stands as space harmonizers, putting twelve of them into plastic pipes and burying them vertically in the ground. We buried the tubes in a central location on a pattern of beneficent Earth gridlines. The subtle Earth energy patterns carried the BG3 quality of the stands in all directions up to the mountainous borders of the valley covering an area that was around six or seven kilometers in diameter. We also added a central solution in each project to activate the Al-Kareem Quality Fields (Figure 127).

Fig.127 - Central Solution in Hirschberg

The first project in Hemberg was completed in 2003 but by the time we went through the negotiations for the total Swiss solution, of which the second project was to serve as a model, four years had passed so that Hirschberg was not started until 2007. The first projects had made a huge impact and the electrosensitive people all over Switzerland were waiting for their turn. This success created the need for an individual home solution, not only in Switzerland, but all over the world. We tested groups of stands in different arrangements engraved by laser on Plexiglas strips and small cubes. We had the cube ready that same year as a harmonizing solution for an individual home. The cube was introduced as part of the BioGeometry Home Kit pictured earlier that included strips (based on number and angle qualities) that were to be attached to electrical and water systems. The Home Kit included a clearing tray that addressed all levels of impregnation of the cube body. We advise the use of the clearing tray for cubes, pendants, rings etc. The pendulums, emitters, and stands do not need clearing as they are constantly cleared through their emission properties.

BioGeometry Environmental Home Solutions

A main premise of BioGeometry, as a modern environmental science, is to provide effective and sustainable environmental harmonization solutions to enhance the quality of our home environments.

My son, Sayed, who has been working with me for more than twenty years on BioGeometry projects and research, has dedicated his journey in BioGeometry to the development of BioGeometry Environmental Home Solutions (BG-EHS) protocols and applications, as well as the development of a training and licensing program for BG-EHS practitioners. He continues to move forward in that regard with research and development of BG-EHS protocols and applications, as well as with the BG-EHS Independent Licensees Program to spread the availability of the BG-EHS offering with independently licensed Associate-Practitioners and Practitioners worldwide. Here is what he has to say about our environmental solutions:

BG-EHS services are evidence-based applications that aim to turn our modern home environments into environments that are actively perform-ing to positively contribute to our well-being and quality of life. These applications are based on the objective quantitative findings of decades of scientific research that show a significant correlation between BioGe-ometry environmental solutions and the balancing of bioelectrical activi-ty, the reduction of physiological stress markers, improved quality-of-life indicators, and improved immune function with different biological sys-tems, across various high environmental stress conditions. Collectively, these quantitative findings provide the applied proof-of-concept for the BG-EHS offering as an effective and sustainable means of achieving a healthier home environment.

The development of effective and sustainable BG-EHS protocols was from the beginning based on the achievement of several key criteria:

First, the basis for the BG-EHS offering had to be grounded in scientific research with objective quantifiable metrics and results, not simply on subjective feelings or testimonials (unless these testimonials were based on structured qualitative feedback metrics within a research framework).

Second, those objective quantitative results must show sustainability over time (at least ten years), especially within higher environmental stress conditions than those in homes (e.g., aircraft, telecom centers, automo-biles, and ships), and also across different biological systems (human be-ings, cows, chickens, rats, agricultural areas, lake ecosystems, and mi-cro-organisms).

Third, BioGeometry tools, methodologies, and work processes included in the BG-EHS protocols were to be based on those applied in BioGeometry research to achieve those quantifiable results.

Fourth, any widespread offering of BG-EHS to the general public had to be based on the implementation of BG-EHS protocols to achieve the BG3 centering levels associated with the quantitative research findings, based on BioGeometry Quality Measurement. Therefore, BioGeometry Quality

Measurements, within the scope of BG-EHS applications, must be replicable by different BG-EHS practitioners. Replicable BioGeometry Quality Measurement results must be demonstrated within the scientific gold standard of a double-blind and controlled context. This is the current standard for assessments within the BG-EHS Program to license practitioners. This applied assessment benchmark within the BG-EHS Program highlights the modern-day scientific distinction between BioGeometry Quality Measurement and all other forms of Physical Radiesthesia.

PART TWENTY-SIX
Sacred Power Spots

A subconscious attraction to the spiritual harmony and healing effect of power spots led humanity to the location of those connective portals on Earth. Through the portal one dissolves in the bliss of oneness resulting in a timeless multi-dimensional communication. This was based on a subconscious right-brain guidance that the Ancients shared with animals and birds. Once the portals were identified the sensory apparatus, in a left-brain type of activity, slowly went into action through observation of phenomena that identified those spots. The interaction with transcendental information and multi-dimensional beings in those spots led to the development of the earliest rituals of connection and communication. They became sacred to humanity across the ages. Sacred power spots from then on became one of the most important factors of development in the history of mankind and played a huge role in every aspect of life from town planning to religious ritual.

Perception of Sacred Power Spots

This shows us the way to the solution of our dilemma so that we do not carry the burden of harmful effects on natural energy systems. This very special subtle energy quality that we have identified as BG3 is the cornerstone of BioGeometry. This quality should be restored at the core of all human activity. It should become the core of our scientific paradigm as an integral part of every activity. It should play a central part in the development of all products of modern technology. It existed at the core of every endeavor in ancient civilizations. It was the thread that held the beads of everything together, bridging seemingly opposite activities like science and religion to form the harmonious unity that produces great civilizations.

A proper holistic connection to sacred power spots is essential to health and well-being through an integration with the life force in nature. The modern separation from and destruction of the environment will ultimately lead to the demise of the human species. Some spiritual, emotional, or mental activity can cause stress if not properly connected to the BG3 quality of a power spot through ritual. This can be measured as a disturbance in the frontal lobe. Rituals connected to spiritual activities (e.g., postures, affirmations, symbols, motion, etc.) are needed to overcome this stress. We do not go into specifics because we are trying to highlight an abstract vibrational system that can allow the unification and understanding of spiritual and vibrational practices

The Power Spot in the Harmonic Symphony of Creation

The geometrical model of the power spot vortex and toroidal field is a harmonic geometrical manifestation of the original Ziron-Psychon pulse template of everything in Creation from the tiniest to the largest reflecting what we stated earlier, and which the Ancient Egyptian Hermetic texts expressed thousands of years ago as:

"That which is above is like to that which is below, and that which is below is like to that which is above."

This expresses the fact that the macrocosm and microcosm are two dimensions of the same thing. It is an endless hierarchy of harmonically resonant communicating pulses bringing everything in all dimensions of Creation into a living unified system within the universal Consciousness. Communicating with any part of this unified holographic system emphasizes a harmonious unity with the universal symphony. This is where the individual note becomes self-aware of its place in the symphony, which in turn acknowledges its presence and place within the note. William Blake expresses this in his timeless poem:

> *"To see a World in a Grain of Sand*
> *And a Heaven in a Wild Flower,*
> *Hold Infinity in the palm of your hand*
> *And Eternity in an hour."*

As children of the earth, our communication with its sacred power spots puts us into resonance with all levels of Creation from our DNA through the millions of subtle energy vortices on different levels of our body up to the chakras and into the higher harmonic levels of all energy systems in Creation. Every molecule or atom of anything we see has a vortex at its center in resonance with the universal symphony on multi-dimensional harmonic levels. We can imagine the vortices as holes in leaves floating on the surface of the ocean. Standing on the leaf, we see them as tiny black holes, although they are the ocean that will always be there when the wind blows away the leaves. The shift of awareness from the leaf to the tiny hole and ultimately the ocean is a qualitative resonant journey where the material quality is harmonized by the whole becoming a center.

The centering process dissolves the material quality into the eternal harmony of the ocean. This qualitative harmonizing journey starts with the connection to the power spot that will enhance the BG3 in our body chakras and all other vortices in our subtle energy system to achieve a universal resonance with all toroidal levels of all Creation. Connecting an Earth power spot to one in the sky amplifies the qualities of both and enhances the qualitative universal connection. The power spot is the ultimate key to the Divine that has been given to us since the dawn of humanity.

Modern science, with its extreme left-brain focus, has severed this relationship and we should bring it back into all our products so that they connect to the life force and become an integral part of nature. This can be done easily through the BioGeometry design principles that create BG3 quality in our products, echoing the forming process in nature.

Seeing the BG3 Centers Everywhere

The detection of sacred power spots on any dimension from the smallest to the largest requires focusing at the desired level. This can be tricky. If we want to find the BG3 power spots in the grains of sand in the desert or the molecules of the air, we must be able to visualize the endless spots of light within the perceived pictures or project a word of prayer onto them to manifest their centers. Once the perception is successful the whole area of sand or air becomes a large mass of BG3. The centering effect will have expanded the BG3 quality of the center to cover the whole area. The projection of Divine light from within will have created the color luminescence of perceived reality. The Divine light is, however, still present in the essence of the colors. By turning our attention to the light at the essence of the colors we resonate with it. This resonance is a two-way amplification of the BG3 quality. This process is summed up in the following three lines I wrote in my first book. I put them together several years ago to address the Divine light of Creation that equally expresses the scientific aspects of perceived reality and the spiritual reality of the Ziron presence as the centering principles in the harmonic multi-level pulsating units of Creation.

> *You make me see everything*
> *I see you in everything*
> *You see me through everything.*

Connecting with Sacred Power Spots in the Sky

Connecting with large sacred power spots in the sky is a straightforward matter of BG3 detection pointing at the sky. One should, however, discern if the star we are looking at is the center of BG3 or if the location itself is the sacred power spot.

We must seek to achieve a continuous resonance with a sacred power spot in the sky at the time of its heliacal rising above the horizon. Any action at the beginning or end of a cycle, where BG3 doorways are found, will prevail through its whole duration. This is applicable to points of change in time cycles as well as motion between different spaces units, as well where the entry and exit qualities affect the whole area.

We start connecting our home to sacred power spots in the sky by finding an existing BG3 spot in our home or create it using a BioGeometry solution. This will help us either ensure the resonant BG3 connection in the sky or create a 3D grid. We then make a paper tube with a diameter and length in any convenient BG3 proportion. We can then create a tube out of a more durable material that is also in a correct BG3 proportion. By using the BG16 pendulum to scan the area above the horizon for BG3 quality, we can select a point where it exists and point one end of the tube to it, while pointing the other end of the tube at the BG3 spot in the house. The permanency of the solution can be checked by measuring the level of BG3 on the ruler, to indicate the beginning of a cycle. To connect to a specific star like Sirius, for example—which was regarded as the spiritual center of our Universe by many ancient cultures—then we can find the time and position of its heliacal rising after its disappearance from the sky for seventy days. This is usually sometime around the end of July and beginning of August. In Ancient Egypt when the heliacal rising of Sirius coincided with the beginning of the Nile flood, the result was a very prosperous year. The spiritual quality covered all aspects of life for the whole year.

The Al-Kareem Quality and the Sacred Power Spot

The subtle energy configuration of the power spot, as mentioned above, is that of the archetypal Psychon in the form of a central vortex and surrounding torus. It is used in a simplified form in the BioGeometry 3D Energy Key. At the vortex extremities, we find a positive energizing QL-Torsion that changes, away from the vortex, along the toroidal fields, to a negative quality of QL-Torsion creating a loss of life force. BioGeometry methods create a positive QL-Torsion energizing life force along the multiple layers of the whole toroidal field. This positive toroidal life force is referred to as the Al-Kareem Quality and we have dedicated an upcoming part of this book to it. The energizing positive QL-Torsion quality gives the area around it emotional and mental harmony, which affects the health and well-being of everyone in the area, as well as all activities of community members. The Al-Kareem Quality Fields enhance the quality of plants, agriculture, and animal farming. Ancient people found ways of enhancing the BG3 quality of the power spot vortex to reinforce and expand the range of those Fields to cover the whole community, as well as activities in the surrounding area. Through observation, intuition, and a sense of environmental unity they identified stones with high density and quartz content that resonated with the BG3 energy and then amplified and radiated this quality into their surroundings. They would quarry megalithic granite stones and bring them to the power spot location, sometimes from faraway places. To achieve their goal, they erected megaliths—which weighed an average of forty tons—on the exact center of the BG3 subtle energy vortex. The power spot became the activator of the Al-Kareem Quality on the toroidal fields. This became the main planning concept for towns and cities throughout history as it achieved the energizing quality on all levels, from the individual home to the whole city and its supporting surrounding environment.

This concept of subtle energy planning to achieve the Al-Kareem Quality is needed today more than at any time before because we have entered an age of modern technology that creates a depleting negative QL-Torsion in the environment which makes us vulnerable to all types of diseases; further, it is taking us into an age of pandemics which will destroy the health and psychological make-up of humanity. Restoring the role of sacred power spots becomes a life-saving necessity in the present situation. The science of BioGeometry creates the BG3 quality through design, irrespective of location, which means that it can be incorporated into every product of modern technology. Every building becomes its own harmonizing sacred power spot with the Al-Kareem Quality Field. Birds, as an example of all creatures in nature, innately build their nests or other types of homes to become protective energizing environments.

Ley Lines

Power spots are usually connected by straight paths. These paths are sometimes referred to as "leys," or "ley lines." Their harmonizing BG3 subtle energy quality is similar to that of sacred power spots and it has played an equally important part in human activities throughout history. Up until very recently people travelled along those paths from one power spot to another. Even today, we find ancient traditions still practiced in rural areas in Egypt. The power spots were traditionally used as burial sites for saints, to whom a sacred monument would be dedicated. Travelers time their visits to those power spots to attend the birthday festival of the saint—called "Mouled" in Arabic. This tradition is followed by all Sufi sects. Those paths became pilgrimage roads to the shrines as well as funerary roads to burial sites which were, again, usually in power spots. The Romans built their roads to reach all parts of their empire along those paths, so their armies would be energized as they walked along them. With the same concept of activating spiritual energy through motion, they also became the main avenues connecting the power spots in city planning, as we have seen above.

Primitive Humanity's Right-Brain Perception of Power Spots

The way early human beings perceived power spots is totally different from how we perceive them today, and it would be totally incomprehensible to the modern mind. By going back to Jung's categorization of humankind and the shift from right-brain to left-brain perception that we have been discussing and referring to as "The Great Shift," we can view modern and ancient man as two different species. If animals could speak, they would tell us a lot about our earliest ancestors. They had a primitive budding of the sensory ego and an active perception focused in the right-brain unconscious mind, and they had an intuitive interaction with an environment from which they felt no separation. The very weak and primitive left-brain sensory perception was not strong enough to inhibit at least some form of sensory interaction with the subconscious realms. People would have used the left-brain personification process to visualize the subconscious world in which their focus of perception was actively located. The multi-dimensional vortex of the power spot was a bridge to many dimensions with different life forms and powers of nature. People could communicate with those entities through conscious telepathy as well as through sounds and postures. The power spot was a bridge for intelligent life forms from other dimensions to come and interact with humans. The power spot BG3 subtle energy quality protected this doorway from intrusion by any malignant entities.

Dealing with all the types of encounters that occur in sacred power spots can take volumes on its own. My own experiences, measurement, and research in this subject would fill a whole dedicated book. I will, however, describe some of the categories and types of activities and encounters in sacred power spots below.

Miraculous Healing

There are many types of miraculous healing that can occur in sacred power spots. Most of the time the healing happens spontaneously in the area, or when a person drinks from the sacred water that is usually found there. Before the healing occurs, an individual may sometimes experience short-term loss of consciousness, convulsions, or cleansing effects in the form of temporary ill-health symptoms before the healing occurs. Some people also report that angelic or spiritual entities performed the healing. Lourdes in France is a famous area for miraculous healing, which sometimes occurs along with the appearance of the Virgin Mary.

Angelic messengers play an important part in the three Abrahamic religions and most of the biblical prophets have had such encounters. I will not delve into this much-explored topic, but only show the fact that most of these messengers are linked to sacred power spots. The "Tor" mountain in Sinai, the temple mound on the Jerusalem plateau, the valley of Mecca and the nearby mountain caves of "Hiraa," are examples of locations of angelic encounters with the three main prophets of Abrahamic religions.

Teachers of Humanity

The personified powers of nature that we refer to as deities, as well as angelic and higher beings from other dimensions, have brought a lot of knowledge that spurred the development of the human species. Restoring the connection to sacred power spots will open the channels to ever advancing universal knowledge. The BG3 quality of a sacred power spot will ensure the communication with higher beings and protect from lower ones.

Dedication of Temples to Deities

In ancient times, temples were built as earthly homes for the deities. They were the meeting places where humans interacted with the personified powers of nature, the Neters. They put an archetypal statue in the innermost sanctuary of the temple—the holy of holies—for the deity to inhabit. The presence of the personified Neter was accompanied by miracles, oracles, healing, and so on.

The deities are the personification of forces of nature that are components of a holistic unity. In this context, each force of nature contains within its undifferentiated background all the qualities of the others resulting in a perfectly balanced manifested force. In this concept, each deity is an attribute of the whole. Dr. Konstantin Meyl connected each wavelength emanating from the central chambers of Greek temples to a specific Deity. As an example, he found that the central chambers of temples built to honor the god Apollo had the same dimensions, while those of Athena had different ones specific to them. Some temples might be dedicated to a certain deity because of the subtle energy quality of the area. In many cases, the subtle energy quality was "fine-tuned through a resonant stellar connection that had been attained through the placement of specific openings, shafts, or other architectural elements.

Healing Practices

Many of the alternative healing practices of ancient times were performed in the sacred power spots within religious buildings which became places of health pilgrimage. Many thermal water spas in Europe are located on sacred power spots. The water that emerges there from underground streams running in the rocks is of a special quality. Besides its healing qualities, it has the low surface tension of structured water. This type of water has a UV quality along its flow and BG3 at crossing points. It stays fresh through thousands of years, as we can observe in the temples. Water wells drilled on underground water reservoirs do not have this quality and increase in salinity with time. Oases usually have the quality of healing water, which stays fresh over time as it originates from underground water streams running in the rocky strata. We have dedicated an upcoming chapter to sacred water detection.

Visions

The visual cortex and pineal gland are situated in the central BG3 plane of the brain's toroidal hemispheres. In the absence of sensory stimuli, the visual cortex receives extrasensory information from the pineal gland along the BG3 plane. In a sacred power spot, the resonance between the toroidal configuration of the skull and the vortex of the earth sacred power spot increases the BG3 quality and enhances multi-dimensional communication producing powerful prophetic dreams and visions. The temples were places of oracles and the priestesses in ancient times were known to practice the art of prophetic visions.

Dreams

Sacred power spots open doorways to prophetic and healing dreams. In antiquity, there were dedicated temples in which dream therapy was practiced. There is evidence of healing dreams in temples from the Ptolemaic Period related to spots such as a Chapel in the Deir el Bahri temple of Hatshepsut, a chapel in Dendera temple, and a place in Memphis which has not been uncovered. Those are places where dream incubation therapy was practiced where the sick person would sleep in a spot in the temple overnight and would either be healed or would receive knowledge on how to be cured. This practice was also found in ancient Greece, where it was related to the Asclepius, the Greek god of healing they equated with the Egyptian, Imhotep. This was known as dream incubation or dream healing.

There is a story carved on a stone slab erected between the paws of the great Sphinx in Egypt, which is itself erected on a power spot on the Giza plateau (Figure 128). It is called the Dream Stele, and it was erected by the Ancient Egyptian King Thutmose IV of the 18th Dynasty in the first year of his reign in 1401 BC. It tells the story of a prophetic dream that he had when he fell asleep while resting in the space between the paws of the Sphinx. He was told in the dream that he would become pharaoh. This was not probable as his older brother was the successor to the throne. However, the prophecy was realized, and he became ruler of Egypt.

Creativity

In a sacred power spot, one becomes not only a spokesman for the earth, but also for the whole Universe through the vortex connection. Artistic creations were created in caves and buildings on sacred power spots. Many of the world's greatest known works of art are found in ancient temples, churches, and mosques. The wonderful multi-dimensional worlds that are only accessible in the right-brain mode and heart intellect emerge into the physical world as involuntary artistic expressions that usually have many layers of universal information hidden behind the material expression and these can take the observer's consciousness down into the vast abyss of the unconscious dimensions.

Fig.128 - Ibrahim Beneath Sphinx Dream Stele

Oracles

The ancient temples were places where people received oracle messages through the priests and priestesses. Today, the practice of channeling is gaining a lot of popularity. We must not undertake such activities without the proper ritual, otherwise we are mixing autosuggestion, telepathy, and personal beliefs into the messages. The vortex in a sacred power spot is a form of tunnel connecting different universes. We can use those doorways in out-of-body journeys to other dimensions, as well. It is therefore a two-way doorway through which beings from other universes can cross time-space boundaries and emerge onto our planet. Angelic encounters are often linked to those places. Such encounters must be conducted in the proper BG3 power spot and with proper rituals of protection from unwanted intrusions.

Out-of-Body Travel

Sacred power spots were also places of initiation where out-of-body practices were performed. Astral projection, as it is sometimes called, was performed along ley lines connecting to other power spots in the earth or sky, where the BG3 quality mapped the way to spiritual dimensions and gave protection from astral entities. In the sarcophagus within the pyramid chamber, the soul of the dead king travelled in the solar boat to his final abode in the heavenly Sirius. He travels in the solar boat as the sun god so he will continue the cycle of the sun, until the end of time. The form of the serpent symbolizes the beginning and the end of the world.

"The text on the second gilded shrine of the king Tutankhamun, where Nephthys addresses the deceased saying: "Your soul will go to the sky with Re Your body will go to the earth with Osiris Your soul will be in your body every day." When the sun god (ba) leaves the Underworld in the morning, and ascends to the sky, the body remains in the darkness and will be as "the manifestation of Osiris who is in the darkness". Osiris remains the lord of life and the lord of the Underworld even after Re leaves him. He waits for Re in the following night to renew the life by their unification

*again. 2 The texts upon the shrine of Thutankhamun express this mean-
ing." Chapter 175 of the Book of the Dead expresses this end clearly,
when everything returns to its beginning: "I will destroy what I have created, this land will sink in primeval ocean, (and) it will be primal water as
it was in the beginning" Another text explains that the end of the life does
not mean only destroying of what has been created, but it means also the
return of the creator God to his beginning. "It is I who will stay with Osiris,
after I turn into a snake, whom the people don't know, and the gods don't
see" In the former text, the form of the serpent symbolizes the beginning
and the end of the world, it represents the first unit, which is divided into
many creatures, and at the end of the world comes back to the unit again."*

(Research paper by Dr. Nehad Kamal El Deen, URL: https://cguaa.jour-
nals.ekb.eg/article_37714_011edd33d5d6d4ed205340c80192f4e2.pdf).

This out-of-body journey was also performed as a form of ritual of initiation. In the out-of-body journey to a sacred power spot, the strong energizing positive QL-Torsion makes the materialization of the traveler into
a physical form possible. The person appears in a temporary solid material or semi-transparent form and interacts with people from a certain
distance.

Harmful Doorways

Not all spots labeled as "power spots," however, are beneficent. Many
people use this term for places with a strong energy quality, but they lack
the knowledge of how to identify and verify the centering effect which
would signify it as a beneficent location. Power spots that do not have the
BG3 quality can be harmful and can produce nightmares, headaches, nau-
sea, convulsions, and, over a prolonged period, they can cause sickness.

Those power spots that do not have BG3 can still have strong energizing
qualities wherein an initial empowering feeling is followed by a harmful
impact due to the Vertical Negative Green quality of the area. Vortices in
these areas are doorways for the emergence of lower astral entities such
as the harmful Jinn in our dimension.

A word of warning here for those who promote their own rituals in power spots without the knowledge of how to measure subtle energy quality or detect BG3. The label power spot is sometimes used loosely to describe any location with a powerful energy vortex, irrelevant of its subtle energy quality. I, however, consider the BG3 quality to be the main criterion of a power spot. Interactions with so-called power spots without the BG3 quality can sometimes be dangerous. On several occasions, I have seen respectable researchers promote power spots that when tested proved to be very harmful.

Any power spot with an ancient monument erected on it is usually good, which can be verified by the presence of the BG3 quality, as the Ancients used many methods of subtle energy quality assessment. They used observation methods, of which we gave some examples earlier, such as the flight pattern of birds that circulate over the spot before returning to their original traveling formation. Before building, they tested the energy quality of the location, by putting sheep in the area for a week or two and then examining their livers for anomalies. Hanging meat to dry or putting pots of milk in the area to check the degree of fermentation was also a common practice. The lack or slowing of fermentation indicated a good spot.

PART TWENTY-SEVEN
The Pyramid

When discussing the energy qualities of shape, the most prominent shape that comes to mind is the pyramid. No other shape has intrigued and perplexed researchers as much through the ages as this one. The Egyptian pyramids play the leading role in this archeological saga. Their purpose and construction have eluded researchers for hundreds of years. The Physics of Quality sheds light on the subtle energy configuration, effects, and purpose of these intriguing megalithic monuments that stand defying the passage of time.

The Emilia Roberts Award

In 2019, the Global Pyramid conference was held in Chicago. I was invited as the key-note speaker and was honored with the Emilia Roberts award of the Egyptian Exploration Society for my research into the subtle energy of pyramids. In my first book, *Back to a Future for Mankind*, I dealt with the development of the pyramid concept from prehistoric megalithic construction as well as the solutions applied to cancel the harmful effects of the pyramid shape when not located on a proper power spot. With the detailed knowledge on the Physics of Quality presented in this book, we will deal with the subject with a slightly different and more holistic approach.

Let's first look at some foundational concepts relating to the evolution of human perception, sacred power subtle energy configuration, Earth-linked city planning, the energy of shape, and resonance with the planes of nature to understand and analyze the world-wide phenomena of ancient pyramids. There are many theories about the pyramids' mathematical proportions and their relationships to the earth and the solar system. We will not go into such quantitative mathematical theories, as our work deals with the qualitative subtle energy measurements of the Physics of Quality that can be replicated by anyone with enough experience with the tools of BioGeometry.

The First Buildings' Interactions with Power Spots

The interaction of shape and space play a major role in all eras of architecture and the first forms of buildings on power spots were intuitively linked with the two complementary forces in the pulse of Creation: radiation and enclosure. These became the first two expressions of humanity in the form of large, high density megalithic stones that contained quartz, such as is found in granite or other similar stones. The single standing stone, referred to as a "menhir," amplified and radiated in all directions the special subtle energy quality of the spot upon which it stood. The second early shape, which we discussed previously, was referred to as a "dolmen." It took the form of two upright megalithic stones with a third one placed horizontally on top of them forming a gate or chamber. This would be erected on a sacred power spot to enclose and amplify the subtle energy quality. This gate form was oriented along East-West coordinates. In this orientation, the energy of the spot was projected on a straight path in both directions and connected the dolmen to the cycle of life from sunrise to sunset.

The dolmen chamber on a sacred power spot above underground water streams became a subtle energetic expression of the universal multi-dimensional resonant connection that we discussed earlier. The dolmen is a megalithic subtle energy expression of the forces of Creation in the heart and it developed into the holy of holies found in sacred buildings throughout history. The origin of this resonant manifestation lies deep in the subconscious archetypes that arise as creative expressions of humanity emerging from the earth in those power spots.

From Dolmen to Sacred Mound

Dolmen were later covered with Earth to form a mound with the chamber at its center. The hemispherical mound unconsciously resonated with the multi-dimensional perception of a sky dome as well as the human skull, with the chamber connecting to the pineal gland at the center of the brain. These mounds became sacred places for humanity and with time sacred monuments and buildings were erected on them.

The Pyramid at the Heart-Mind Core of Humanity

With the advent of ancient civilizations and the birth of mathematical and geometrical sciences, stone pyramids over the central megalithic dolmen chamber replaced the earth mound. The shape of the pyramid became the heart-mind connection to the Divine creative center, not only in a symbolic, psychological form but, more importantly, as the subtle energetic reality affecting the heart-mind core of humanity. The pyramid acquired its place at the spiritual core of human consciousness.

The Dating is Only Valid for the Final Stages of the Pyramid

Understanding the origin and development of the pyramid concept makes the dating of the building of any pyramid totally irrelevant as it would only apply to the final stage of a journey which is as old as humanity. As we go deeper into the underground levels of pyramids, we find stages of human activity going back to the early stages of human existence. The underground chambers carved out of the bedrock below the great pyramid of Giza provide one such example. So, if we date the final stages of the pyramids as they stand, we will still not have discovered the sophisticated technology in their building, some aspects of which elude us even to this day.

The Pyramid and the Power Spot Vortex

The megalithic stones of the menhir and dolmen became the core of several types of sacred buildings in history. Their placement on power spots and their underlying water stream crossings create a multi-dimensional subtle energy vortex. The multi-dimensional subtle energy configuration of the pyramid includes the special properties of the location and cannot be separated from it. In modern times, we completely lost the right-brain heart connection to the unperceived subtle energy dimensions that formed the multi-dimensional configuration of sacred monuments; we started to research their secrets solely with regard to their physical shape. Using an unmodified pyramid shape without placing it on a sacred power spot brings with it many dangers. Pyramids and hemispheres emit a communication wave that can have harmful effects with prolonged use if not balanced by the BG3 quality. There are several ways to harmonize their energy quality (refer to Figures 58 and 71).

The Astral Portal

The pyramid and dome, in their simplest form, are in resonance with the astral plane. The astral resonance of the pyramid, and its spiritual connection, make it an ideal portal for initiation rites through out-of-body travel or the soul journey of the deceased to a sacred location in the sky such as the constellation Orion.

As we showed earlier, the different angles of a pyramid's sides, as well as the sections of a hemisphere, are in resonance with the astral sub-planes (Figure 129). These shapes can be used to connect to the related astral sub-planes and can be configured to emit their energy quality. The shape can be modified to extend its resonance with the spiritual planes by configuring them to connect with the transcendental BG3 quality. This can be done in many ways. The most pertinent one is to follow the age-old tradition of erecting this shape on a sacred power spot. Another method would be to introduce geometrical modifications to the pyramid shape to connect with and emit the BG3 quality. Example modifications discussed earlier include changing the angles of the side, with the height or indents in the square base splitting the sides to form an eight-sided pyramid. If the corner angle is 45 degrees, the triangle base forming the diagonal of the base will become the square root of two and the crossing at the center of the base will form a BG3 vortex, giving the pyramid shape its sacred spot, irrelevant of its location.

The Pyramid Effect on Consciousness

The pyramid connection to the heart-brain will enhance the right-brain mode of perception and provide an ideal location for all kinds of astral and spiritual ritual. What's more, the universality of coupling with the

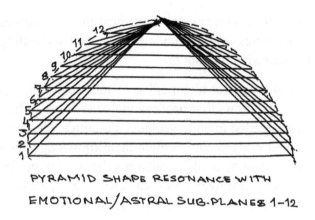

PYRAMID SHAPE RESONANCE WITH

EMOTIONAL/ASTRAL SUB-PLANES 1-12

IN GENERAL PYRAMIDS IN ANTIQUITY

WERE LOCATED ON SACRED POWER SPOTS

WITH MINOR GEOMETRIC MODIFICATION

(SIDE OR BASE INDENTS) TO ACHIEVE

ADDITIONAL RESONANCE WITH SPIRITUAL

PLANES

Fig.129 - Pyramid Shape Resonance with Emotional-Astral Subplanes

energizing life force of the Al-Kareem Quality that the pyramid radiates in the environment produces the magical effect that we feel in the pyramid's surrounding environment.

Building Rituals in Sacred Power Spots

Rulers regarded all types of sacred buildings or city plans as acts of initiation, and they even regarded them as a form of talisman—an object designed to bring good fortune and protection. In order to maintain the buildings' spiritual connection at the highest level, the emotional and mental quality of interactions in any part of the building process needed to be safeguarded. This was achieved by performing certain rituals.

The ruler would order that rituals of purification be observed before any interaction or activities could be undertaken—such as healing, oracles, or burial—on the sacred power spots.

We know from the earliest historical accounts of building rituals in the great ancient civilizations that professionals involved in building on sacred power spots needed to undergo special practical teaching to bring the life force into their craft to complement their knowledge and expertise on the material level. Just as in alchemical practices, they performed certain prayers, used words of power, and connected every part of their work to certain times and planetary configurations. This was needed to connect their practice with the higher spiritual dimensions of the sacred vortex.

They formed closed guilds that guarded the sacred practices. It was a great privilege to join such guilds: members had to be free men with a very pure ethical background that descended from a specific lineage. The masters of the trade guarded the secrets and taught other professionals. In Egypt, members of these guilds built the sacred monuments. The workers who did other jobs in the pyramid and temple buildings would be recruited during the flood season when they were not working in agriculture, and they were properly compensated.

The very ancient traditions and secret knowledge of the workers in building professions who worked on sacred buildings and monuments continued within professional builders' guilds up to modern times. These ancient guilds are the origin of many Sufi orders and closed societies. As an example, the Freemasons recreate the story of Hiram Abiff, the master builder of the Solomon temple, in their rituals; he was killed because he refused to reveal the building secrets he held. The names of every person who placed a stone in the rebuilding of the holy mosque of Islam in Mecca—which was demolished several times in history by floods and fires—are kept in records which delineate each person's name, position in the tribe, and genealogy. It's also interesting to note that the Islamic practice of Sufism dates to those professional builders.

The ancient traditions and knowledge applied in the building of these sacred ancient monuments show a knowledge of the subtle energy quality of building materials and its interaction with the human subconscious mind.

The origin of the building materials, the tools used, and the accompanying rituals were an important part of the holistic building process. The building represented the forming process of a living entity.

PART TWENTY-EIGHT
Al-Kareem Quality Fields

Let us start with the introductory explanation we gave at the beginning of this book in our "Note to the Reader." We are particularly interested in the discussion of breathing cycles introduced in "New Concepts Introduced by the Author".

In the breathing cycle, the energizing quality of the inhalation phase has an energizing effect that is coupled with positive qualitative torsion (QL+): the inbound energy gains order that is labeled Negative Entropy (or Neg-entropy) as it is entering the body.

In the exhalation phase, the loss of energy is coupled with a negative qualitative torsion (QL-). The exhaled air is accompanied by a loss of order; the loss of order is referred to as Entropy.

After each of the two phases of the breathing cycle we have a state of neutral balanced bi-directional torsion. These are the two states of stillness between the active phases of the breathing cycle. As turning points this centering state between the two phases of the cycle has the BG3 quality.

The Al-Kareem Quality is a state where the energizing quality of the intake phase extends to a part of the exhaled energy before it starts losing order. The shift of the qualitative balance in the cycle to extend the energizing quality in the immediate surroundings is a state that we refer to as the Al-Kareem Quality. In this energizing state, the BG3 quality manifests in all four phases of the breathing cycle.

The Toroidal Time-Space Fields

Once we have introduced the essence of the Al-Kareem Quality through the simple example of the breathing cycle, we can further explore it in the context of the energy key.

Let us start with the toroidal model we analyzed earlier. The BG3 pulse creates a central vortex with a spiraling time-space configuration: the time spiral twists around the central axis of motion in space creating a time-space dimension in the toroidal fields around it. As we have noted earlier, the information from the timeless BG3 archetypal dimension on the central plane is converted into the time-space dimension on the walls of the central spiraling vortex. This produces a multi-layered compression wave field in the form of a torus. The spiraling central twist produces torsion in the toroidal field. This torsion field can have a negative energy dispersion or a positive recharging effect. The multiple bubble eruptions forming the plane of that time-space dimension might have either torsion properties, depending on the type of interaction and the spread of the central BG3 quality in the environment.

The BG3 area around the central vortex will have a positively recharging QL-Torsion quality slowly turning into a negative QL-Torsion until it reaches the central disk and moves into it to show BG3 again. This QL-Torsion change of quality happens on both ends of the central vortex which is composed of two bi-directional spirals around the central axis of the bi-directional pulse. Furthermore, each toroidal manifestation of the central pulse is replicated on endless harmonic levels from the smallest to the largest forming a multitude of toroidal time-space planes (Figure 130). The Al-Kareem Field quality usually extends up to the height of the natural object and can be extended beyond that using BioGeometry Al-Kareem Field emitters.

The environmental interactions on the toroidal plane can increase or decrease the spread of the positive QL-Torsion along the field. All living species interact with the ingoing and outgoing life force. There is usually a balance between both, in a process like breathing. The immediate environment around a living entity shows a slight bias towards the ingoing action. This results in a state of energizing life force and positive QL-Torsion, which separates it from the life force dissipation and negative QL-Torsion which surround it. In our current world, the negative QL-Torsion effect in the subtle energy around our bodies is continuously increasing due to the combination of electromagnetic and chemical pollution from modern technology and the quality of humans' psychic makeup. The Psychons, which are the primordial units that produce the bi-directional mental-emotional spirals, have become unbalanced, creating more outward than inward motion. This in turn has pulled the Law of Time in the pulse out of balance, causing a negative depleting life force state and producing negative QL-Torsion in the environment. This state of reduced immunity can be observed in the environment leading to a vicious circle of ever-increasing parasites and thus the necessity to use more pesticides.

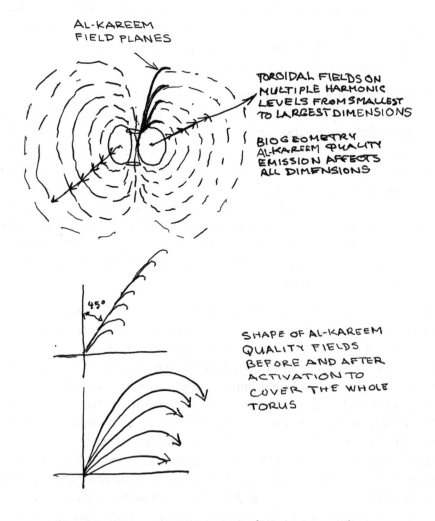

AL-KAREEM
FIELD PLANES

TOROIDAL FIELDS ON
MULTIPLE HARMONIC
LEVELS FROM SMALLEST
TO LARGEST DIMENSIONS

BIOGEOMETRY
AL-KAREEM QUALITY
EMISSION AFFECTS
ALL DIMENSIONS

45°

SHAPE OF AL-KAREEM
QUALITY FIELDS
BEFORE AND AFTER
ACTIVATION TO
COVER THE WHOLE
TORUS

Fig.130 - Harmonic Extension of Time-Space Planes

The QL-Torsion Effects of Toroidal Fields

As we have explained above, the quality of QL-Torsion indicates the gain or loss of living subtle energy from the environment. This has a direct effect on the life force and immunity of all forms of life in nature on that plane. The toroidal time-space fields are composed of multi-layered planes of existence, the vital, emotional-astral, and mental planes, which repeat themselves above and under the outer plane (as shown earlier in the multi-dimensional energy key model in Figure 25). The pollution of the fields on the main plane reverberates on all other levels of life force. This means that as life moves from one plane to another, it will still be affected by the main QL-Torsion quality. In a healthy natural environment, this problem does not exist, as the QL-Torsion quality is kept positive by healthy life forms in nature.

BG3 Grids and Al-Kareem Quality Fields

Many ways of increasing the spread of the positive QL-Torsion in the toroidal fields rely on amplifying the centering effect of the BG3 quality. This turns the whole toroidal shape into a multi-layered center where the toroidal fields and the central vortex become a unified qualitative positive QL-Torsion system. We refer to this state of the torus as Al-Kareem Quality Field. The term, "Al-Kareem Quality Field" refers to a state of positive QL-Torsion of energizing life force on the total surface of the multi-level layers of the time-space toroidal plane. It is the state where the positive energizing life force aura is extended to the surrounding space of energy dissipation.

To sum it up in a simple way, we can say that the Al-Kareem Quality is a BG3 state where the dissipating life force has an initial energizing effect and does not start its depleting effect straightaway. This results in an expanded Al-Kareem Quality Field around the person or object.

In other words, the Al-Kareem Quality is achieved when the BG3 extends into the surrounding life force creating an energizing harmonized zone where the balance of the "breath of life" has a slight shift towards the in-going energy.

Al-Kareem Quality Series

The Al-Kareem Quality Series are the numbers, besides the BG3 series, such as 3, 6, 8 and 12, that resonate with the positive life force quality of the toroidal Al-Kareem Quality Field planes. These numerical qualities can be used in the configuration of the shape of detection devices, like the number of disks of a pendulum or numerical calibration of 360-degree dial pendulums. They can also be used in any type of design as the number of elements to create the expanded energizing Al-Kareem Quality Field around the object.

Here are some general rules which can enhance this life force energizing state in our environment:

1. All types of prayer, spiritual activities, and rituals.

2. Interaction with sacred power spots

3. Truthful, benevolent emotional and mental attitudes.

4. Pursuit of universal beneficent knowledge.

5. Morals, values, and acceptance of all others, manifested in excellence of action.

6. Protecting nature.

7. All creative activities and sports in a harmonious connection with the subconscious realms produce the Al-Kareem Quality Field.

8. Music played on non-electronic instruments and not diffused through electric-based media, will enhance the life force. However, BG3-harmonized music will enhance life force even when played through electronic media.

Living by the 42 rules of the Ancient Egyptian Judgement in the Hall of MAAT described above will cover all aspects that produce life force harmony. Although living by those rules seems difficult today, it was natural to the Ancient Egyptians who were, as we explained earlier, a different, right-brain-centered species that directly perceived and lived by the ethical values in harmony with the Laws of Nature. Unfortunately for us, the age of information technology is causing great disturbance in the emotional and mental structures of individual and collective subtle energy quality. This disturbance has a detrimental effect on morals and ethics, which reduces the effect of the above practices. The BioGeometry design language is geared to extending the centering BG3 quality along all surrounding toroidal fields. This design language programs shapes with a continuous positive effect on QL-Torsion in all products of modern technology, from town planning to small utensils. Its most important application should be in the design of electronic products. Using BioGeometry principles will achieve a more permanent sustainable general solution.

In our BioGeometry electro-smog environmental projects we use special shapes we refer to as "flower emitters" as a supportive addition to the basic harmonizing solution to create the Al-Kareem Quality Field. The flower emitters are designed to emit in multiple angles and directions, and they resonate with the spiraling motion of the toroidal fields. In the Swiss electro-smog projects, the effect is still sustained more than nineteen years later. The solution has proven to be effective even with the introduction of 4G and 5G.

The total BioGeometry solution has proven to have such a positive psychological impact that the mayor of Hemberg, Switzerland, expressed his thanks to me and my team for our solution in a documentary aired on the National Swiss television channel (SF1). Residents had previously been suffering from prevalent states of aggression, pessimism, melancholy, weakened will, and antisocial and other behavioral problems. After the administration of the BioGeometry solution the quality of life was restored. In this interview, the mayor expressed his gratitude with the words "thank you for bringing peace to our community."

The Other Worlds

We have examined previously the multi-layered toroidal planes of the Psychon. The Psychon pulses are simultaneously active on all planes giving them all a sense of continuous presence. Every plane on the upper half, above the central disk of the torus, has a counterpart on the lower half. Every plane in nature has a two-fold existence in time-space, one at the beginning and one at the end of the vortex. They interact dynamically to form a motion within time and space (Figure 131). These two physical dimensions, at the entry and exit of the vortex, are in a complementary resonance as they emanate from the center of the pulse and retract back into it, creating all the physical moments of an expanding and contracting life span between them. This applies to the emotional-astral and mental layers, which form complementary planes of emotional and mental particles that give them a material existence in their own dimension. All those dual complementary planes of existence have a continuous resonant qualitative information exchange so that the quality of actions in each plane affects all others. This pattern of the multiple interconnected existences of every Psychon pulse repeats itself on every dimension from the smallest to the largest, as is expressed in the ancient Hermetic principle "As above so below." They connect all Creation in harmonic resonance.

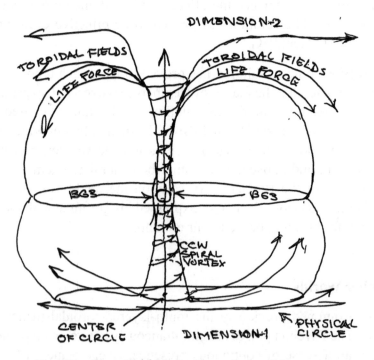

Fig.131 - Two-Fold Time Space Pulse Dimensions

The Planes in the Toroidal Fields

These planes rise within the shape of a curved toroidal field starting at forty-five degrees from the earth's surface and curving slowly towards a horizontal level under which the spiral rotates inwards. These planes are related to the size of the subtle energy torus (Figure 132).

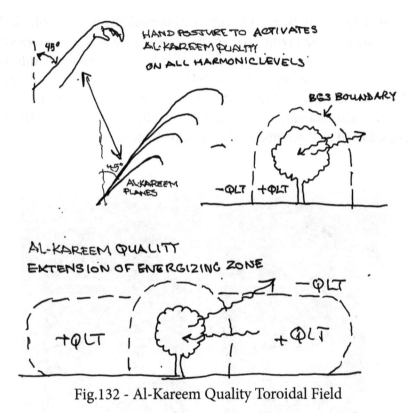

Fig.132 - Al-Kareem Quality Toroidal Field

The energizing (QL+) fields exist around and slightly above all natural objects, from the smallest to the largest. They form a vitalizing charging zone that borders on the energy-dissipating space. The harmonized Al-Kareem Quality expands the original field to approximately double its size. Activating the Al-Kareem Quality Field expands the revitalizing life force direction to a higher level above the earth's surface. Its height, intensity, and permanency depend on the solution applied. BioGeometry solutions, just like their sacred power spot counterparts, are the most effective in this respect.

Al-Kareem Quality Activation Through Posture

The sounding of the word Al-Kareem (benevolent) or the syllable KA, will activate this energizing shift in the breath cycle or any pulse in general. The KA arm position with arms extended out and bent upwards at the elbows (as shown earlier in Figure 94) will also activate the Al-Kareem Quality and the brow chakra. Postures and sounds which activate the heart chakra will also activate the Al-Kareem Quality (Figure 133). The letter M, pronounced as "mmmmmm" will activate the heart chakra.

Fig.133 - Laila Karim in KA Posture Left and
Heart Activation Posture Right

Al-Kareem Quality in Fitness Exercise

To properly benefit from any type of fitness exercises one must activate or enhance the Al-Kareem Quality Field in the space to benefit from the energizing properties of positive QL-Torsion. The harmony of motion and proper breathing during exercise will have a positive effect on changing the life force direction. This will counteract the harmful effect of electro-magnetic radiation, which produces the depleting negative QL-Torsion. It is important to add the BioGeometry electrical attachments to electronic fitness equipment to counteract their depleting effect and get the full benefit of the exercise.

Pendulums to Detect Al-Kareem Quality Fields

The following instruments that we've shown earlier, can be used to detect the Al-Kareem Quality Fields:

- The IKUP
- BG pendulums with 3, 6, 8 or 12 disks,

These other instruments detect both Al-Kareem and BG3 qualities

- The horizontal life force dial pendulum,
- The 6-dial life force pendulum,
- The 360-degree dial pendulum,
- The BG28 disk pendulum

The IKUP (Ibrahim Karim Universal Pendulum)

As the name implies, this is my personal pendulum which I developed in the early 1970s and have been using ever since. This pendulum is a very complex and highly effective pendulum that has been specially designed to resonate with very strong emission and reception on all planes. Its seven disks strongly emit beneficent Horizontal Negative Green quality that acts as a perfect carrier wave further enhancing the emission of the hemisphere above. The inverted hemisphere at the top is in resonance with the spiritual planes.

Below the sphere, we have three disks that resonate with the original Law of Centering in a geometrical circular manifestation governing the complementarity of opposites in the Law of the Creation of Stable Dualities.

The total of ten disks expresses the qualities of the one and the zero and the quality of completion following the final transformation through the nine.

This pendulum resonates and emits BG3 as well as the Al-Kareem Quality. It can be used to detect the Al-Kareem Quality through its shape quality without any string length adjustment. It emits BG3 as well as the Al-Kareem quality, which gives it a holistic quality of emission.

As a universal emitter and receiver on all planes, the IKUP pendulum is a very effective subtle energy healing tool. As a harmonizing subtle energy emitter, it can be used in many healing modalities. It can be pointed or rotated as a pendulum, on parts of the body, chakras, acupuncture points, reflexology, iridology and so on to balance the related biological functions. Pointing and moving it along the ears is a very simple way of harmonizing all the biological functions through the acupuncture points in the ear that cover all body functions. Some people like to wear the small IKUP (metal or wood) around the neck or use them for general harmony.

As a form of protection, the IKUP can be aimed at external sources of electromagnetic radiation, just like the Hemberg emitters we used in our electro-smog harmonizing projects in Switzerland. We produce the IKUP in different sizes and materials. As a stand the IKUP will radiate the Al-Kareem Quality energizing positive QL-Torsion in the environment.

Simple Methods to Create Al-Kareem Quality Fields

Let us explore some simple techniques, for those who are experienced with the use of BioGeometry tools, of detecting and working with Al-Kareem Quality Fields.

The shape of the central vortex of the torus will have BG3 on its central axis and on the circle around the center where the horizontal BG3 plane radiates. As we go up on the surface of the vortex, we can use the horizontal Time Pendulum to measure the time-space field on which the pendulum will go into a clockwise rotation. As we reach the top or bottom curvature into the horizontal plane the rotation weakens and as we move sideways horizontally on the surface of the toroidal field the pendulum will reverse direction indicating the negative state of subtle energy dissipation. As we move down the surface of the torus towards the central plane, we can use the BG16 pendulum to detect BG3 emanating horizontally along that horizontal plane. The same qualities are mirrored on the lower half of the torus (Figure 134).

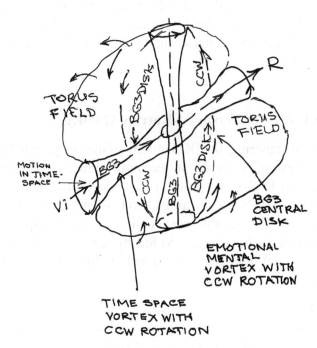

Fig.134 - Torus BG3 Horizontal Plane Perpendicular to Central Time-Space Motion Vortex

Once we have completed the subtle energy quality analysis of the shape and the invisible torus around it, we can proceed to create the Al-Kareem Quality on the whole toroidal field. To do this we place a dial set to a living color quality in the UV range on top of the vortex shape. Alternatively, we can use a BG28 disk. We can also find a BG3 spot or crossing in the space and place the space harmonizer on it. Those three methods will amplify the central BG3 quality and expand it over the entire toroidal surface to create the Al-Kareem Quality Field Quality we can measure using the BG12 or BG28 pendulums. The Al-Kareem Quality will initially cover an area around the stand roughly the size of the invisible torus and radiate the quality further into larger surrounding areas due to the emission principles of the design. The IKUP and the BG28 pendulum, and the BG28 horizontal disk pendulum, all emit the Al-Kareem quality. The brain stands can also be used with the above dial setting or BG28 disk to create the Al-Kareem Quality Field.

BG3 Versus Life force Versus Al-Kareem Quality

In the process of centering, the BG3 quality of the center extends along the time-space vortex and vertically in the multi-dimensional vortex with its horizontal central BG3 disk resulting from the mental-emotional vortex rotating CCW with the torus creating a circular BG3 disk. The whole disk becomes a center. The Al-Kareem Quality extension expands the BG3 spherically into the whole torus. Within the centering effect, the whole space of the toroidal field has BG3 as well as life force moving inwards and outwards.

This wave-like centering process produces a peripheral BG3 tube around the wave (Figure 135). The BG3 centering principle in the Psychon pulse, with its infinite number of tubes in all directions within the sphere, extends the central Ziron across the eight layers to the periphery. This is the spherical three-dimensional centering quality that the Ziron produces in the Psychon. All the dualistic levels of the Psychon are within the extended Ziron. This is the three-dimensional configuration of the centering process where the periphery of the circle becomes the center.

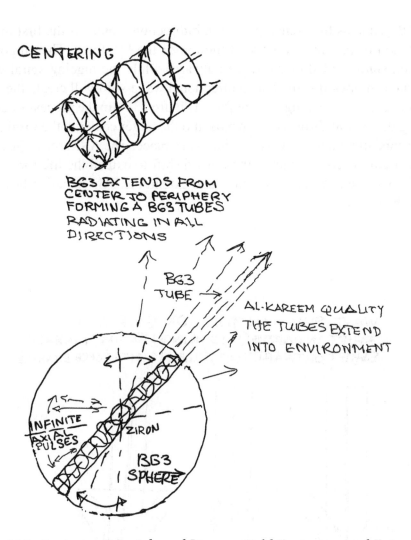

Fig.135- Centering Principle and Kareem Field Environmental Extension

This process activates the harmonizing principle to become the backbone of the background subtle energy in which duality takes place. In other words, it is the presence of the Divine initial zero within the duality of Creation.

The Psychon as the archetypal Ziron bidirectional pulse is the first manifestation of the inward-outward motion of the life force. The outgoing torsion spiral will shift the wave outwards while the ingoing spiral will produce an inward shift. This bidirectional wave-shift will create the dynamic tension activating the life force (Figure 136). In the process of centering the central Ziron axis expands into the larger center in the form of a BG3 tube in which the wave motion takes place. The Al-Kareem Quality further empowers the energizing inward shift to extend the life force energy intake zone around the object and extend the BG3 radiation beyond the tube periphery and length.

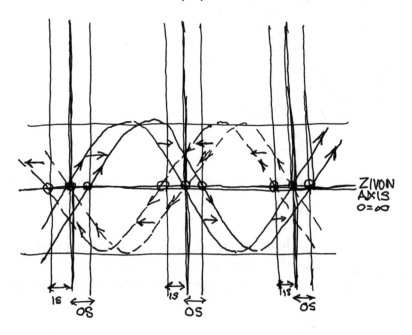

Fig.136 - Wave Shift and Life Force Direction

The Apple

All the above concepts can be illustrated on the surface of an apple and the central vortex measurement can be done on a vertical slice through the center of one (Figure 137). The apple on a tree will have the Al-Kareem Quality Fields over its entire surface as well as a measurable surrounding halo which disappears when the apple is removed from the tree. For this reason, there are prayer rituals practiced in many indigenous cultures that are performed when gathering fruits or plants, as well as when digging in the earth.

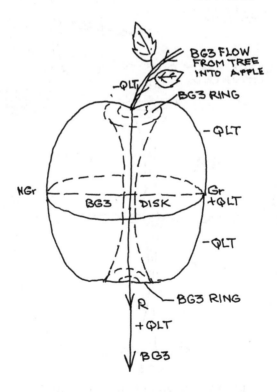

APPLE ENERGY QUALITY ANALYSIS

Fig.137 - Apple Expresses Toroidal Shape

Al-Kareem Quality Field Research Using Diagrams

The methodology we use in BioGeometry to examine these concepts is based on the Physics of Quality, where information exchange based on the resonance of shape, color, sound etc., allows us to examine and correlate any concepts through measurements in nature and on diagrams that are used as samples of all shapes in the multi-dimensional Universe. All students of BioGeometry, trained in the measurement of subtle energy qualities, can use the diagrams in this book as tools for researching the energy of the shapes. In the attached diagram, I have shown what and where to measure in the drawing (Figure 138).

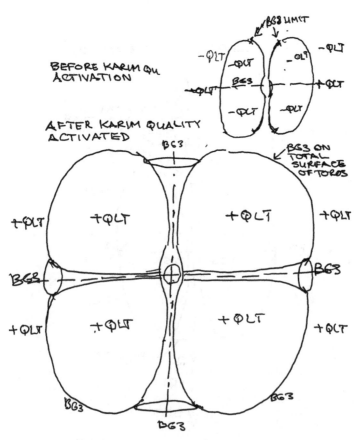

Fig.138 - Karim Quality Energy Key

PART TWENTY-NINE
The Subtle Energy Quality of Waves

As we have mentioned previously, in the BioGeometry Physics of Quality we deal with the qualitative effects of all types of waves and fields on the biological functions. This qualitative approach is based on the science of Universal Harmonics, and it allows for information exchanges on all levels and dimensions of absolute reality. Subtle energy from this point of view is the totality of effects on the biological energy systems of life on Earth from the perspective of multi-dimensional absolute reality. This is a unique holistic approach that mobilizes qualitative measurement tools which enable research beyond the possibilities permitted by the quantitatively based measurement devices of mainstream science.

In many vibrational healing methods, waves are mainly categorized according to their frequency. This quantitative approach shows only the connection between frequencies and biological organ function. Several diagnostic devices also use frequencies to communicate with an organ's subtle energy functions and, when a wave passes through the organ it can also show any excessive noise around the frequency, which denotes energy dissipation that must be corrected. But this purely quantitative methodology does not take into consideration any qualitative interactions with an organ. As we have noted earlier, any electromagnetic method of producing a wave frequency produces stress and electro-smog in the system; this will reduce the wave's healing effect.

Another issue relates to the subtle energy quality produced by the frequency itself. From a subtle energy quality point of view the effect of a wave depends upon its shape. It is the shape of the wave moving through a medium that determines the resulting pattern in its surroundings. If we build two wave shapes of similar lengths but different heights (amplitudes), and run them through a water current, they will produce different effects in the pattern of turbulence created around them, even though they have the same frequency. The same shape produces the same pattern of turbulence, in other words, it will create the same effect, regardless of its size. The shape of a wave can be expressed as the proportion between the wavelength and its amplitude, regardless of size. It can also be expressed as the angle at which the wave crosses the central axis (Figure 139). So, to achieve a desired subtle energy quality with any frequency we can change the amplitude in any device to reach a specific proportion for the quality we are aiming to reproduce.

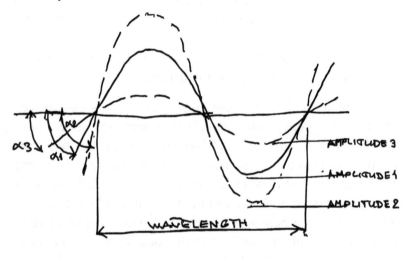

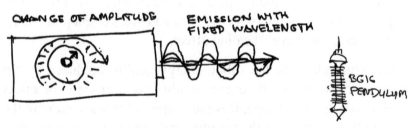

Fig.139 - Wave Shape & Quality

Our bodies perceive subtle energy effects through their quality. A science of subtle energy quality is vital at this critical phase of the age of information that is threatening life on our planet. The Physics of Quality shows us that we are one with the environment we are destroying. We need to know that the "separate existence" we believe we have in our environment is an illusion. Environmental health and personal health are one and the same.

The Multi-dimensional Planes within Electromagnetic Waves

The cross-section of an electromagnetic wave as we understand it is basically a ripple pattern moving along two orthogonal planes, a vertical electrical plane, and a horizontal magnetic plane. This configuration is stable whether the wave is rotating clockwise or counterclockwise, giving a three-dimensional spiraling effect, or just propagating with no rotation. As we know, the vertical or horizontal description of the two planes only indicates their orthogonal position of 90 degrees to each other. Waves move through the subtle energy background medium filling what was thought to be empty space, which is not a vacuum, so the cross-section cannot be cross shaped with four empty quarters. The electromagnetic planes move along the two orthogonal planes of the cross shape within a background subtle energy medium that fills the four quadrants between the vertical and horizontal planes. The movement effect on the medium creates compression wave patterns moving along other planes filling the voids between the original cross section. They have not been identified till now as they are non-electromagnetic in nature. The waves move along the two electromagnetic planes at the speed of light. The compression waves are not bound by the speed of light and move faster. The further those planes are angled from the two electromagnetic planes the faster their speed.

The Eight-Fold Plane Configuration in the Torus

The qualities of the embedded emotional, mental, and spiritual planes in the four quadrants of the wave section are related to the qualitative complementary-balanced geometric relationships of those levels in the four quadrants of the torus (Figure 140).

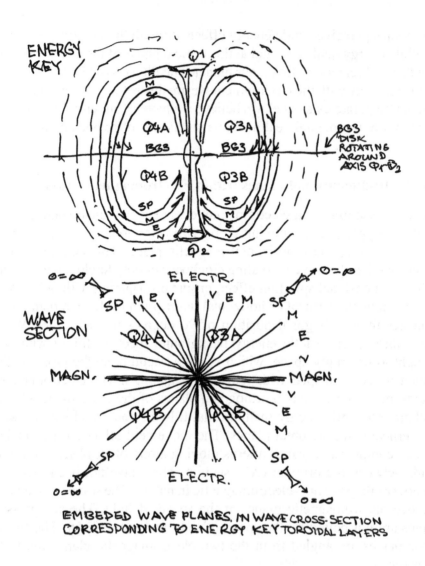

Fig.140 - Eight Fold Plane Configuration in Torus

The Flower Section

Through the detection of resonant harmonic qualities on different planes of nature through the Physics of Quality we can detect the shape of those wave planes having a wider leaf-like section. By placing a person's witness in the center and using the planes of nature connecting shapes, we can trace the coordinates and determine the shape and size of each plane section (Figure 141).

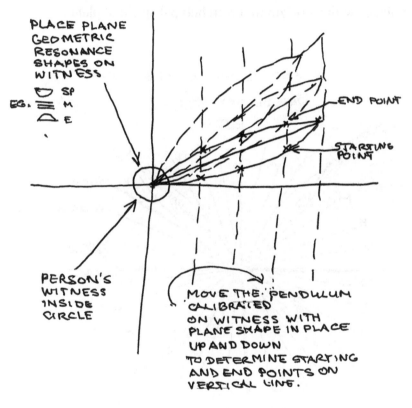

Fig.141 - Embedded 'Flower'Planes

Starting from the closest to the orthogonal electromagnetic planes we find vital, emotional, mental, and spiritual plane levels moving faster as we move away from the electromagnetic planes. Around 45 degrees we find the spiritual range with speeds reaching infinity. The center connecting all the planes is a form of straight-line wormhole with timeless spaceless zero-infinity speed (Figure 142). The diagonal spiritual plane is timeless in the sense that it is beyond the time-space boundaries of our physical dimension and cannot therefore be produced or caused by the electromagnetic components of wave propagation within physical space time. In that sense, it exists before and after the wave itself. The electromagnetic wave floats on the faster non-electromagnetic compression wave planes with its origin in the archetypal spiritual plane.

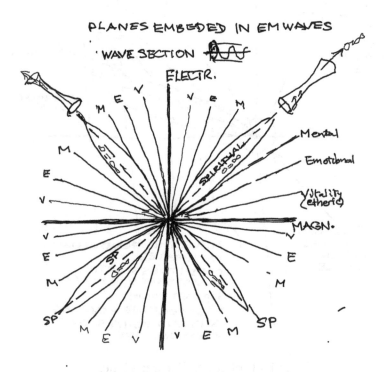

Fig.142 - Embedded Spiritual Planes

The actual multi-dimensional section of a wave is more fluid, and the planes are ranges that are more like interacting interpenetrating petals, giving a flower shape, which keep changing shape with every activity. The shape and size of the petals of the flower shape reflect the vital, emotional, mental, and spiritual balance of the person. The petal shapes are in a fluid dynamic relationship constantly changing with the person's activity, body posture and motion as well as external environmental factors. The flower shape changes when moving through different spaces in a building. This shows how the sections of the waves passing through the body, at any given moment, indicate the quality of information vital, emotional, and mental levels. Dr. Michael Maley has done some research to correlate flower shape with psychological conditions of test subjects.

PART THIRTY
Electromagnetic Radiation Versus Electro-smog

I have not missed an occasion in the past forty years to make people aware of the hazards to human, animal, and plant health electromagnetic radiation causes through global warming and climate change, and yet I remain frustrated about the lack of public awareness. I will therefore keep repeating myself, again and again, until the situation changes.

"Within electromagnetic radiation is a hidden time bomb that threatens global life extinction when the EMR saturation in the atmosphere reaches a tipping point."

The natural environment has always played a major part in the evolution of life on Earth. For many millions of years, the survival of a species has always been dependent on adaptation to changes in the environment. In modern times, however, the man-made environment is taking over as the main factor affecting life on our planet. Modern technology provides major advances in all fields of life but with every step forward unacknowledged harmful effects on the environment and life within it arise. It took a hundred years of dependence on coal and fossil fuels to acknowledge their environmental pollution and global warming effect. Now we are moving into the age of information with the fantastic promise of a digital future of a world becoming one communicative virtual entity, providing the ultimate level of services in every sector of life. The advances in the age of information are overloading the earth's atmosphere with an ever-increasing level of electromagnetic radiation. A major factor contributing to the increase in chronic diseases is the fact that modern medicine does not wholly consider the environment an integral component of the human biological system. Although, we are aware of other types of environmental pollution, the harmful effects of electromagnetic radiation are not acknowledged as such.

Industry is downplaying the harmful effect of electromagnetic radiation (EMR) and keeping it from spreading into public awareness. This is partly understandable, as doing so will only create an uncontrollable scare from a situation to which they had no solution, until now. Mainstream science has offered up a technology without enough knowledge of its subtle energy effects on living systems. Modern science does not yet fully acknowledge all the levels of subtle energy affecting our lives. The dramatic increase in electromagnetic hypersensitivity (EHS), now at epidemic levels, is starting to make the public aware of this eminent danger. There is a huge amount of scientific research on the harmful effects of EMR out there that we will not go into as it is widely available. Unfortunately, a huge cover-up exists, and both the independent- and industry-financed research are at a stalemate.

Experts at the Building Biology Institute (Bau-Biologie) are developing methods of shielding from EMR worldwide, but only in a limited way as the use of any product of modern technology (e.g., cellphones, Wi-Fi routers, etc.) will usually diffuse it into the environment. All transportation modes, for example, are highly saturated with EMR. The seat of a modern car contains more than a dozen live electromotors and many more are hidden behind the cladding for every function in the car. While we move towards hybrid and electric cars, and the increase of electromagnetic radiation communication devices within the car environment, we must be aware of the harmful effects this has on the users and the environment. While we support the reduction of electromagnetic field exposure, it will still overwhelm the minute activity within the biological system. Smart cities will be so saturated with EMR that people will not be able to live in them. The simple fact that EMR propagation has a microwave-type heating effect on the atmosphere, which is a factor in global warming, is totally ignored.

People with epilepsy, autism, and many other brain problems have an increased sensitivity to EMR. Some psychological problems such as depression, aggression, ADHD, and others are also affected by environments with excessive EMR. Parents in many countries are worried about the installation of wireless devices in kindergarten and primary school classrooms.

Bau-Biologie

Bau-Biologie (Building Biology) is another aspect of my Swiss education that is connected to my architectural studies. It deals with the effects of modern technology on our health. Building Biology made me aware of the chemical, bacterial, and electromagnetic pollution in our modern buildings.

All species in nature build homes in a way that protects them from the surrounding environmental hazards and restores health and well-being. The homes of every species are an integral part of the natural environment in an energizing interaction with its life force. The choice of material, the construction, shape, and location are in total harmony with the environment. This is a manifestation of a connection with the archetypal level of each species over time and space. The collective subconscious right-brain interaction with the universal Laws of Nature and the inherent wisdom of the Universal Mind guides their actions to ensure the harmonious life of the species. In contrast, we humans have created an advanced civilization with countless possibilities and comfort, and a modern architecture which produced buildings and modes of transportation that are slowly killing us. As an architect, it became my goal to find a way to restore this knowledge into the design of our built environments. I also realized the limits of the solutions at hand, especially with the information age's ever-increasing amount of electromagnetic radiation. A new paradigm was badly needed to deal with this pollutant we are increasingly turning to with the false assumption that we are saving the environment.

I always used Bau-Biologie (Building Biology) principles as a base level of protection in my architecture projects while using BioGeometry to achieve the environmental balance on vital, emotional, and mental levels, and introducing the harmony of the spiritual component.

Around the turn of the millennium, I commuted between Cairo and Florida, where my children were enrolled in a prominent tennis academy and school north of Tampa. In her search for a source of Bau-Biologie books in English, Rawya, my wife, found the Institute for Bau-Biologie and Environment (IBE) close by in Clearwater. Helmut Ziehe, the founder, was a

German who introduced Bau-Biologie to the US. With my German background from studying in Switzerland, we became friends very quickly and he hosted BioGeometry courses at the Institute for many years, initiating the beginning of BioGeometry in North America. At IBE we got to know Paula Baler-Laporte, an architect and building biologist, and the author of several books on healthy houses. She also studied BioGeometry, and we have a good collaboration with her to this day.

In the first joint Building Biology and BioGeometry courses hosted by the IBE at Schiller University in Clearwater, I met architect Bosco Büeler, head of The Bau-Biologie Information Corporation in St. Gallen, Switzerland, who was also lecturing there. Our paths crossed again several years later in Switzerland. At the time we were doing several BioGeometry architectural environmental harmonizing projects in Europe and the Middle East. As we integrated Building Biology into our projects, Helmut Ziehe and electro-biologist Larry Gust joined our team, which included my son, Sayed, and Dr. Mohammed Al-Sawy. Dr. Thomas Haumann also joined us as we worked on applying BioGeometry solutions to aircraft.

With the expansion of the BioGeometry and Building Biology joint work abroad, we delegated the teaching in the US to able instructors. Dr. Robert Gilbert, director of the Vesica Institute in Asheville, North Carolina, was the first instructor in North America, and he also graciously hosted several years of the BioGeometry "Special Topics" events that I taught.

In Montreal, we collaborated with André Fauteaux, editor of the magazine *La Maison du 21ème Siècle*, who has a worldwide network of Building Biology information and a significant number of resources about electromagnetic radiation. BioGeometry was featured in two articles in his magazine.

BioGeometry Electro-smog Projects

Our information on the problems related to Electromagnetic radiation and electro-smog are based on first-hand experience in the field. BioGeometry has successfully reduced the symptoms of different types of health problems in areas with increased EMR activity. In this context, I would like to refer back to our first European electro-smog research project, in 2003, in Hemberg, Switzerland. We were commissioned by the main government telecom provider, Swisscom, and the official mediation authority for telecommunication and environment. This project achieved remarkable results in reducing harmful EMR symptoms by around 60% and was hailed by the media as "The Miracle of Hemberg." When the authorities saw the results, Claude Georges, the director of Swisscom Environment, acknowledged on a television documentary on the main Swiss channel the reality of electrosensitivity as a chronic disease. This only happened because he now had a solution in hand (https://www.youtube.com/c/BioGeometry - Playlist "Swiss BioGeometry Electrosmog Project").

An independent study done by the Building Biology Information Organization of St. Gallen, headed by MP Bosco Büeler, included a medical quality of life survey done by MP Dr. Yvonne Gilli. Dr. Gilli had no knowledge of the BioGeometry intervention, yet her study confirmed the results. The chart we showed earlier (Figure 15) as well as the Hemberg Report in the appendix show the impressive reduction in health symptoms which was sustained over two years. In fact, nearly two decades later, the solutions are still effective.

The psychological effects were much more pronounced than the physical ones. People's main complaints were in such areas as: loss of the joy of life, lack of motivation, depression, disputes and intolerance among family members, and increased aggression between neighbors and in the community generally. To everybody's surprise, these psychological states were greatly reduced, and the mayor described in the TV interview how the solutions had restored peace in his region. Moreover, epileptic seizures that had plagued many children in the area were dramatically reduced if they stayed in the region of Hemberg. The parents of the children noticed that when they left the region, particularly when they visited the game arcades in the neighboring towns, they experienced seizures once more.

This promoted us to research and develop protective BioGeometry bracelets they can wear wherever they go. In the study an article was published by Engineer Jurg Studerus of Swisscom confirming our results and supporting our scientific approach of the Physics of Quality. In the same documentary, on the main Swiss TV channel, Dr. Jungi, the chief medical surgeon of the state of St. Gallen, acknowledged our success in solving this complex environmental health situation and recommended its use for other areas. In 2007, a second successful electro-smog project was done in Hirschberg as a preparation for a total country solution. In this project, the main Swiss television channel accompanied us in the work from the beginning to produce a full documentary that was aired primetime following the news.

Electromagnetic Radiation Versus Electro-smog

There is some confusion regarding the term "electro-smog." Most people, including many experts in the field, regard electro-smog and electromagnetic radiation as the same thing. This leads to an erroneous understanding of the cause of electrosensitivity or electromagnetic hypersensitivity. Moreover, virtually no scientific research has been completed in the field of subtle energy and, as a result, the cause of electrosensitivity remains largely misunderstood.

To use an analogy, electromagnetic radiation is like the motion of rain while electro-smog is more like fog. Fog, unlike rain, is a standing or slow-moving state.

Let us use another visual analogy to show the difference between the strong motion of electromagnetic waves and their related subtle electro-smog compression waves (Figure 143). A moving boat produces visible waves around it, and we can avoid their impact by getting out of the boat's path. There are, however, secondary ripples which somebody in the water at a great distance can still feel. Similarly, any motion produces those two wave effects, the primary direct effect within a limited distance and the secondary subtle effect spreading out over great distances. These two types of waves represent two levels of non-electromagnetic compression waves. These are longitudinal waves, meaning that their inner motion moves in the direction of flow, in contrast to electromagnetic waves that are transversal in nature; their inner movement runs perpendicular to the direction of flow.

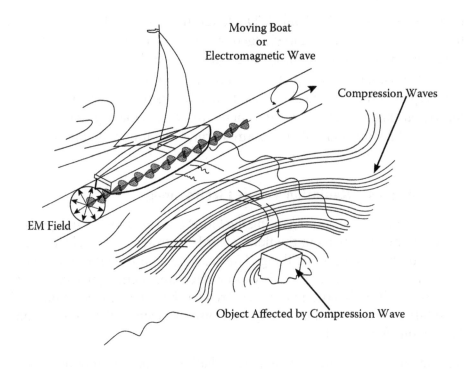

Fig.143 - All Motion Creates Secondary Compression
Waves in the Environment

Compression Waves

In the BioGeometry multi-dimensional energy analysis of electromagnetic waves, we show the emotional, mental, and spiritual dimensions as compression wave planes embedded within the two orthogonal electric and magnetic wave planes. These compression waves are traveling at speeds much faster than light. The waves on the emotional, mental, and spiritual planes are not the only ones traveling faster than the speed of light, as there are more compression waves of this type in the Universe than there are electromagnetic ones which are confined to a limited band around the speed of light.

In general, any motion of any type produces compression waves in the environment, like a boat produces waves in the water. The compression wave patterns resulting from any motion are played on the Psychon torsion pulses of the subtle energy background. The motion of an electromagnetic wave also produces compression waves in its surroundings and these fall in the domain of scalar waves. Scalar waves are non-electromagnetic in nature but, but when produced by electromagnetic waves, they carry with them the qualities that produced them, resulting in electro-smog.

Electromagnetic waves of any wavelength travel at the speed of light, while compression waves can decelerate or accelerate even beyond the speed of light. If a motion is electromagnetic in nature it will produce, as a primary effect, an electromagnetic field around the motion. The secondary effect, however, will always be in the form of non-electromagnetic compression waves that spread over great distances in the environment. They interact with other compression waves and produce interference patterns or a background echo, as they are similar in nature to sound waves. This background non-electromagnetic subtle energy pattern, or background echo, forms the standing state of electro-smog. When the primary motion is electromagnetic, it is referred to as "electro-smog" as it will carry with it the original stressful quality of the electromagnetic field. The harmful effects of electro-smog are much subtler than those of electromagnetic fields or radiation, but they subsist in the environment for a long time and cover large distances.

In a conference in Germany hosted by Helmut Luedelin, developer of the popular H3 Lecher Antenna, which is widely used by German radiesthesists, I got to know Dr. Konstantin Meyl, an authority on scalar waves. He defines electro-smog as a scalar wave phenomenon. Our measurements showed that scalar wave generating devices increased the electro-smog in the space and raised the stress level on those present. I acquired from Dr. Meyl a research set that I needed to develop scalar waves that did not produce electro-smog in the environment. In further experiments, we completely canceled the electro-smog effect by shaping the wave using harmonizing proportions (amplitude to wavelength) such as, for example, the golden mean or other irrational numbers.

As we mentioned earlier, our measurements have confirmed the existence of stress from electro-smog in scalar devices. This problem can be overcome by BioGeometry methods, such as the BioGeometry electricity attachment. It uses shapes and number quality to interact with compression waves and it has the additional benefit of adding BG3 to the scalar wave quality. We are also working with several manufacturers of scalar devices to develop built-in solutions to enhance their effect.

There is another important point in Dr. Meyl's work that sheds light on the nature of geopathic stress from Earth energy grid systems. He defines the earth radiation grid patterns as a scalar wave phenomenon resulting from the magnetic flow lines of the earth. This puts Earth radiation in the same category as electro-smog.

BioGeometry studies the relationship between electro-smog and geopathic stress through their shared Vertical Negative Green quality and its life-force-depleting effects on the biological subtle energy system through the increase of negative QL-Torsion in the environment.

The fact that electro-smog and Earth radiation, as well as other scalar wave phenomena, are non-electromagnetic compression wave phenomena puts them in a domain which is outside mainstream science. They are, however, easily detected by instruments measuring harmful effects on living energy systems.

There is a point to understand when discussing compression waves: just as electromagnetic radiation generates compression waves, as we explained earlier, similarly compression waves, under certain circumstances, generate low levels of electro-static, as well as electromagnetic, fields.

Multi-Dimensional Smog

The concept of electro-smog as secondary compression waves, carrying the qualities of the source in a subtle dimension over large distances, is a universal phenomenon resulting from any motion spreading the qualities of the source multi-dimensionally in the environment. This concept has wider implications affecting the quality of the universal background subtle energetic medium. The wide-spread multi-dimensional effect of the SMOG phenomenon applies to all types of objects and their pattern of motion and affects the vital, emotional, mental qualities of the environment, which cannot be directly measured by our modern electromagnetic instruments. It can be detected by its effect on living systems.

Smog has a thousand faces some beneficent and some harmful: Electro-smog, technology-smog, human-action-smog, human-psychic-smog, nuclear-smog, viral-smog, disease-smog, and so on, affect the Universal Mind and life force at the core of the background subtle energy. These negative effects are constantly harmonized by the spiritual connection of the Universal Mind and life force. Similarly striving for the excellence of action on all levels in resonance with spiritual virtues, creates the harmonizing smog on all dimensions.

Harmonizing by Mental-Emotional Wave Shaping

Compression waves are a form of non-electromagnetic inaudible sound waves. As scalar wave phenomena, they exchange qualitative information on vital, emotional, and mental levels with their surroundings, as well as with their electromagnetic origin. We refer to the multi-dimensional nature of waves model where we find the subtle energy on all those levels embedded within the main levels of compression as well as electromagnetic waves.

Using special shapes that resonate with each of the levels of the planes of nature (vital, emotional, and mental), we can detect the planes of motion of compression waves on each of those levels. When electromagnetic waves move through the background medium of space in their two orthogonal planes configuration, the empty spaces between them are full of embedded planes of vital, emotional, mental, and higher energy levels. These travel at speeds faster than light and they move faster as they move away from the electric and magnetic planes.

This pattern gives us a multi-dimensional subtle energy wave configuration and shows that all types of waves are in themselves living energy systems.

They are imbued with all attributes of life such as Consciousness, and emotional and mental attributes that enable them full multi-dimensional resonant communication with other life systems. The products of modern technology do not follow the forming process of nature in their design and philosophy, which prevents access to the all-prevailing primordial Consciousness inherent in life force. The subtle energy quality of any space or environment is in constant quality exchange on all levels with all living systems within it so they become one with time. As an energy system moves from one space to another it is carrying information with it from the previous environment into the new one and connecting them together.

Electro-smog is therefore a subtle energy phenomenon that affects us, not only on a physical, vital level, but even more on the emotional and mental levels of our consciousness. The non-electromagnetic nature of scalar waves makes them undetectable by modern electronic devices. Now we can understand how electrosensitivity produces psychological and mental disturbance symptoms as we saw in the electro-smog projects in Switzerland. We also know that if the EMR sources cannot be removed, we can use BioGeometry shapes to harmonize the emotional and mental subtle energy levels with the BG3 quality. The result is that the symptoms will no longer be felt as the EMR passes through people's bodies without disturbing their harmonized emotional or mental subtle energy levels. With our present paradigm, it is very difficult to understand that the effect is reduced even though the cause is still there. We need the new paradigm of the multi-dimensional Physics of Quality to deal with such subtle energy phenomena.

One can use shielding methods of Building Biology to protect from EMR, but in the case of electro-smog and Earth radiation which amplify each other, and which are not detectable using electronic devices, shielding can only provide temporary relief. An important point that we raised earlier is that if electronic devices are not properly earthed, they can raise the stress of electromagnetic radiation and electro-smog within the shielded areas.

We must remember we are dealing with living subtle energy manifestations that cannot be easily suppressed. BioGeometry, however, takes a completely different path by infusing those subtle energy patterns with the harmonizing energy quality of BG3, a quality that has been regarded as spiritual and sacred throughout human history.

As discussed earlier, we can form the complete wave shape (not just the frequency) to achieve a BG3 wave quality that is harmonizing to biological systems. Alternatively, we may also superimpose the BG3 quality by placing shapes such as a BioGeometry Hemberg Emitter and the BioGeometry Electricity Attachments directly on cell tower antennas.

The Living Forming Process of the Quality of Electromagnetic Radiation

Electromagnetic energy in its natural form as found in the earth is not harmful to life functions. It is an important component of the vital force of all forms of life on Earth. How, then, can electromagnetic fields in our modern civilization have such a harmful effect on life?

Electricity and magnetism, like any other form of energy, have components on all subtle energy levels (physical, vital, emotional, mental, and spiritual) and in their natural form they support the harmonious evolution of all life systems. All the subtle energy levels of electromagnetism resonate with and exchange qualities with those of human beings. Modern science, with its quantitative mathematical precision that seeks objectivity, has always kept subjective human interactions out of the development of industrial products. The human life force is not part of the formula. The benefits of Earth's electromagnetic fields and chemical interactions that support life have been neglected, as they are part of the life force which works on a subtle energy level (vital, emotional, mental, and spiritual); they are excluded from the mainstream scientific way of thinking. By neglecting the effect of the products of modern technology on the quality-of-life force, we end up with an increasingly harmful imbalance on all forms of life on Earth.

The increased use of electromagnetic radiation in the information age will slowly tip the scale away from all its benefits towards a deterioration of life on Earth. The slowly increasing contribution of electromagnetic radiation to global warming has a harmful effect on the harmonious natural balance in nature; it has resulted in an increased use of harmful chemicals, such as antibiotics and pesticides. When we use solar or wind energy to produce electricity, the life force in the sun and the wind is cancelled out, resulting in harmful electromagnetic fields. With the move towards electric cars and smart cities, as well as the increased use of electronic and wireless devices in transportation methods, we badly need to bring the life force and natural harmony back into our products to avoid the rise of chronic conditions which will erode all the great advancements of modern medicine.

In BioGeometry, we provide practical solutions to this dilemma. Our solutions are based on practical experience in environmental, electro-smog, and animal farming projects. When BioGeometry solutions are used in chicken farms, for example, the life force is harnessed through geometric shapes that emit this free natural energy to the chicken; it is possible to remove all chemicals, antibiotics, and vaccines and still get healthy chickens.

The Weapons Industry and Global Warming

The industry of weapons, in the name of defence or otherwise, is another type of radiation that pollutes the environment. Besides its economic benefits for the industrial countries, it carries with it electromagnetic, radioactive and chemical pollution of the environment. A far more dangerous aspect lies in the contribution of explosive weapons to global warming. On a multidimensional level, it is disturbing the emotional-mental subtle energy quality of the environment and harmonically affecting all other dimensions of creation as well. The war industry is in essence a declaration of war against the earth. This is a war that humanity cannot win. To save the human species from annihilation we need a peace treaty with the earth. We must not let economic greed lead to self-destruction.

Tips to Reduce the Harm from Electromagnetic Radiation

There are several ways to reduce our exposure to electromagnetic fields from home wiring in our walls. The most efficient is to run the horizontal wiring just above door level and going down with a vertical connection to switches and outlets from there. This keeps the electromagnetic fields away from the body. This is very important behind beds where the wiring in the wall runs at the sleeper's head level.

Another method of reducing exposure to electromagnetic fields is to separate the bedroom circuitry from the rest of the house and use a switch to shut off all bedroom circuitry. Any devices plugged in to charge overnight should be in the living areas circuitry. (This is, however, not practical when using air-conditioning.)

We have already referred to the protective BioGeometry numerical strips that attach to wiring and water pipes and add the BG3 quality to the electromagnetic fields. These are part of the BioGeometry Home Kit.

Revisiting Hemberg and Hirshberg After Fifteen Years

The success of the electro-smog projects in Switzerland was based on a proper understanding of the resonant interaction of compression waves produced as secondary effects from all electromagnetic sources in the environment.

Many years later Swisscom engineer Jurg Studerer sent a long email to the French-Canadian magazine *Maison 21ème Siècle*. They were publishing an article on the Swiss electro-smog projects and had contacted him for information. He explained the Swiss government's "support and satisfaction with our solutions" and added that "they had offered me a contract for a total country solution that I had to decline due to personal reasons." The residents who were part of our pilot project with Swisscom still ensure we are contacted for any changes in Hemberg or Hirschberg that need intervention. This happened again lately when a fire broke out in the electrical installations leading to the church tower where the BioGeometry shapes were installed. We went and re-installed the shapes in the church tower. By then the residents working with me were proficient in manufacturing the metal attachments for the BioGeometry emitters that were produced in the workshops of the Keller family. The Kellers, as well as Ruth Schaad, Susanna Rehmann, who had worked with us in the BioGeometry installations, helped with the installations in the tower in the presence of, and with the support of, Swisscom engineers.

PART THIRTY-ONE

The Multi-Dimensional Nature of
Disease Holistic Healing

The human energy body, like everything else in nature, is part of a harmonic resonant system spanning different embedded dimensions of individual, collective, and universal nature. As we explained earlier, what we see and feel as a physical separate body is a construct of our limited sensory perception. The other energetic dimensions are unperceived by our physical sensory organs. Our sensory information data bank forms our ego, with which we identify ourselves. The physical body, from an extra-sensory type of perception that is hidden in the depths of the unconscious, is not a separate solid object but a fluid dynamic system with many interconnected embedded levels that are not separable by boundaries, but rather which flow and exist in each other. The individual appearance melts into the collective and universal levels. From this perspective, we are part of a universal unity that we share with everything in Creation.

This is the first concept of the embedded hierarchy of all living systems. In a sense, we are referring to higher levels of ourselves that blend into collective and universal life forms. This is in a way similar to the cells and micro-organisms living in our body, which itself is living within the earth, which in turn is part of the solar system, and so on.

There is, however, another embedded system that is related to the quality of cycles. Time cycles are subtle energy qualities within the universal life force that animates everything. The cycles of time, from the smallest to the largest, are living entities. They exchange life force qualities that are amplified by our perception of them. The days of the week are different time cycle entities with individual qualities that interact with our emotional and mental levels. We somehow perceive each day of the week or each hour of the day differently. We relate their qualities to the planetary qualities. However, they are much more than that. They are living intelligent life forms without a physical body as we know it. We are interacting as an integral part of these embedded cycles from the smallest to the largest. They have different effects on our psyche and life force quality. Farmers who are aware of the seasons would generally be aware of time cycles and cultivate a relationship with them.

Our relationship with time cycles, whether conscious or unconscious, is a two-way street. Not only do they affect us, but we affect them as well. They can become our friends or enemies depending on how we relate to them. They play a role in our health and our interaction with them plays a role in the health of the earth. Friendship starts with understanding their individual qualities and living in harmony with them. With time this type of qualitative perception of natural cycles becomes embedded in the unconscious and enhances the activity of the right-brain mode and the perception of the heart, leading to a state of relaxation and a feeling of unity with nature. Creating harmony with the time cycles in nature is a holistic multi-dimensional path for the health of humanity, as well as for the environment. All non-human species live in that level of integration. They lose it, however, through their interaction with humans. When humans reach that level of harmony with the living time cycles, nature will reciprocate with benevolence.

Mental-Emotional Pandemics

Let us examine the question of whether pandemics can start or be propagated on non-physical emotional or mental levels and then have the psychosomatic effect of creating vulnerability to physical viruses. Quantum physics has shown us how Consciousness can influence the manifestation of formless subtle energy from a non-physical dimension into the physical electromagnetic dimension to appear as a mass or a wave. It should be noted, however, that a person's intention is not directly producing the effect, but rather it is reciprocated by the forming process of the Universal Mind whose greater omnipotent Consciousness is the creator of all phenomena. These phenomena are produced through the action of the Universal Mind on the "formless" life force, subtle energy background. Waves can condense into mass and mass can produce or disintegrate into waves. Unfortunately, mainstream modern medicine only acknowledges the particle transmission of disease and not the wave form. The wave transmission of disease might not directly cause infection in the same way as particles, but it still transmits the information of the disease into a person's energy field producing a resonant connection to the related particles resulting in a vulnerability or a sort of invitation to the disease.

Let us re-examine the information exchange on higher levels such as the emotional and mental planes of nature. These subtle energy levels move beyond the electromagnetic dimension in a multidirectional and multi-dimensional wave form.

This is a type of non-electromagnetic compression wave form moving in all directions in a different space/time configuration than our sensory physical one. It is equally moving and resonantly spreading information in past, present, and future dimensions. This kind of resonant information exchange happens on emotional and mental levels and moves across time-space dimensions and parallel universes.

Universal Consciousness is a creative force that produces particles and wave forms in other dimensions just as it does in the electromagnetic physical world. Many other material worlds are made of mental-emotional particles. Those other worlds or universes are material and solid in their own dimensions. Although material in their own dimension they remain elusive and unperceived by our physical sensory perception. Similarly, we remain unperceived to them. However, in a right-brain type extrasensory subconscious perception, there is a continuous information exchange. Under certain conditions, however, some of this information surfaces into our daily sensory perception whenever a synchronous relationship occurs. It is usually perceived as a form of intuition. It is sometimes confused with autosuggestion.

This mechanism of multi-dimensional information exchange is the basis of exchange of the life force qualities in all dimensions of Creation. This information translates into the universal laws governing all functions of life in that specific dimension. The quality of our actions in the physical world, resulting from their level of harmony with the Laws of Nature, affects the multi-dimensional subtle energy cradle of life in all Creation. The quality we impose on the subtle energy of our environment affects past, present, and future life everywhere in the endless dimensions of Creation. We are not the only physical electromagnetic life form in the Universe. Besides the numerous physical civilizations that inhabit other planets in the Universe there are many others on other higher non-electromagnetic dimensions that are also affected by our actions and they, in turn, affect us. Some of those could be present on Earth in higher unperceived dimensions and could be aware of the effect of our actions on their world. I am not indulging in science fiction but explaining in simple terms the resonant information exchange affecting the quality-of-life force within subtle energy.

The best way to interact with this seemingly complex situation is ultimately very simple: the solution lies in the practice of "Excellence of Action" on the individual level. It all starts by infusing our personal everyday actions with ethical values. This simply means listening to Consciousness in all our actions. When the individual musical note is perfectly tuned, it affects all the other notes and exists within them through different levels of resonance. The beauty of the Symphony comes to life with the fine-tuning of the individual notes. On all levels of Creation, however, we find vortices connecting to the spiritual dimension that brings the BG3 harmonizing quality into subtle energy. These vortices are part of the natural forming process in all dimensions. There are also harmonizing centers in the energy of the Universe, like the star Sirius, which radiates very strong BG3. Sirius was regarded as sacred by most ancient civilizations. The Divine Universal Mind is constantly centering and rebalancing the quality of subtle energy in all dimensions to ensure the harmonious evolution of life force.

Sacred Connective Unity with the Earth

We are an open energy system constantly exchanging energy with the environment. Our sense of individuality and separation from the earth is a material sensory illusion. On all other levels from the vital, through the emotional and the mental and on up to the spiritual, the separation is an illusion created by awareness and identification with our physical body. Our interaction within the environment of this global unity determines our health and that of the earth. Environmental electromagnetic and chemical pollution of the earth—as well as its pollution through collective actions such as warfare, excessive demineralization, and deforestation—have their resonant counterparts within our body.

Introduction to Holistic Environmental Healing

We are already aware of the physical solutions to healing the earth that are basically centered around the reduction of all forms of pollution. One of the positive side-effects of the Covid-19 pandemic was the dramatic reduction of pollution. This pandemic seems to be a remedy to heal the sick Earth. Will we learn from it to reduce the pollution from our modern technology by revising our production methods? Although we can produce electricity through natural environmentally friendly methods such as solar or wind power, we still produce harmful electromagnetic pollution.

The solution is not by moving from fossil fuels to electricity, which will prove even worse in the long run, but on how to work with new efficient methodologies to make fossil fuels and electricity, as well as all other forms of energy, more environmentally friendly by restoring their depleted life force. BioGeometry, through the activation of the Al-Kareem Quality Fields will restore this life force in all forms of energy we use.

Perception of Immune Responses as Disease

To be more effective, our interactions with disease through all kinds of treatments need to be supported on the emotional and mental levels. So, let us examine what happens on those levels. The mind will usually perceive disease through its personification process. The mind is an agent in forming the disease as an entity with which it interacts. We then form an emotional relationship with it. This is usually a negative relationship to which we bring animosity; we aim to get rid of the disease as quickly as possible. We use a form of aggression towards it, which leads to a reciprocation, making it cling more to us. So, let us analyze this process of personification of the disease. What we identify as the disease, when we are perceiving it, is the work of our immune system using whatever methods necessary to fight the disease. These might include fever, diarrhea, coughing, pain, etc. These are usually uncomfortable to us and indicate that we are sick. This is the good part of our body doing its work, but as we cannot perceive the disease itself through our sensory apparatus, we identify our sensory perception of our own weapons as the disease. Our emotional and mental aggression will be directed against our own soldiers who we wrongly identify as enemies. There is a form of self-betrayal here that although aimed at the disease is directed at our own body.

Now let us start by acknowledging the fact that the disease is partly us and partly foreign. On the physical level, we should consider the foreign part. Our physical remedies can protect and support the immune system, and our mental-emotional attitude towards the disease should do something similar. The disease is usually the result of our environmental pollution. As we have shown earlier, this is why chronic diseases are on the rise. The disease as an entity is partly us, so it should be perceived as a child we are raising to let go on its own into the world. Throwing it out is not a solution, as part of it is our own immune system. The only solution is the raising of the immunity of all natural living systems through the activation of the Al-Kareem quality. Changing our lifestyle is a holistic approach that is only effective within a harmonious energizing environmental quality.

The acceptance of all others is not something we should apply only to human relationships; we must include a holistic embrace of the environment as the main other. Lifestyle changes in diet, exercise, and attitude cannot be effective in a depleting environment.

BioGeometry is not a treatment modality, it is a way of restoring the life force through communication with higher harmonizing BG3 principles to activate the Al-Kareem energizing quality that introduces a state of positive QL-Torsion in the environment. In this energized state of the environment, all medical treatments can reach their full potential.

The Revival of Earth Sacred Power Spot Culture

BioGeometry solutions create the harmonizing BG3 and the energizing Al-Kareem qualities which energize the environment regardless of location.

This allows their integration into all products. However, this must be accompanied and supported by the age-old connection to the earth by bringing the sacred power spot into all activities of humanity. Environmental awareness is the vital, emotional, mental, and spiritual foundation for a reintegration of humanity into the unity of Mother Earth. BioGeometry and similar world views need to be received by an open-hearted humanity to unleash all its possibilities as a path of initiation on both individual and collective levels. This is the healthy lifestyle that through unity with the natural environment gives better prevention and protection than any remedy. All creatures in the wild had this lifestyle before human intervention. Let us bring the paradigm of the wild animal into our lives instead of imposing our way of life on them.

Al-Kareem Quality Field Quality in Holistic Healing

As we have seen above, when we introduce the Al-Kareem Quality Field quality into the toroidal fields to prevent the dissipation of life force through a negative QL-Torsion environment we energize living systems and protect them from absorbing the pollution from the environment. Activating the Al-Kareem Quality Field globally allows us to bring down the age of pandemics to normal levels of disease, and perhaps even below that benchmark. This can be done by bringing the sacred power spot back into human consciousness, something now nearly impossible in our consumer-based global society. The only applicable path is the activation of this healthy state. By paving the way to the necessary change in consciousness to achieve the sacred spot revival, we hope BioGeometry can be one of the disciplines that helps us succeed in this.

Harmonizing Electromagnetic Radiation

We have achieved great advances in the information age and should be able to find solutions to diffuse the hidden time bomb in it that threatens global life extinction. BioGeometry offers a possible beneficent solution to the problem.

Controlling wave shapes (wavelength:amplitude according to BG3 pro-portions) of all Electromagnetic Sources through some form of Harmo-nizing Algorithms is one of many ways to reverse their negative effects on immunity. This can lead to an immunity-supporting information age.

Freedom and Depression

There is an individual and collective form of depression that results from the stripping of freedom resulting from being imprisoned in one's own opinion and not accepting that of others. People wrongly understand free-dom as the ability to speak and exercise their opinion and they fail to see that this paradoxically strips them of their freedom, as they become pris-oners of their own opinion. Applying judgement gives power individually or collectively to those who are insecure. True freedom lies in being able to move from our fixed point of view to embrace those of other people. The fact that we are all far from that state gives rise to a general state of depression and aggression. The creation of the Al-Kareem Quality Field quality over large areas to cover whole communities will introduce a men-tal-emotional harmony that can introduce a general change of behavior where peace, positive attitudes, and collaboration prevail. These results have been observed in several projects we have completed in people's workspaces. it is therefore an important factor for areas where people with special abilities are integrated into their surrounding communities.

PART THIRTY-TWO
Sacred Universal Waters

Many ancient traditions, as we explained earlier, refer to the initial medium of Creation as primordial waters or fog. To understand the qualities of this primordial medium, we must go to the first level of emergence of duality from the zero-infinity state of the Ziron center generating the Psychon pulse as the first unit of Creation. The Law of Time activates the Ziron pulse. Meanwhile, the mental and emotional properties of the Psychon pulse manifest the activation of Consciousness and all life attributes. The endless eruption of Psychon pulses produces a continuously "bubbling" medium. Due to the infinitely fast bubbling speed, this primordial medium will have an inert multi-dimensional presence. The spiraling "life force" components of the Psychon pulse produce bi-directional torsion in this medium, making it infinitely energetic. This multi-dimensional life force background—this primordial medium—contains the archetypes of all the Laws of Nature. They interact to produce all dimensions of Creation from this background life force medium. This life force cradle of Creation in which everything emerges is the essence of what is referred to as primordial waters or fog. The term water or fog is used metaphorically here because they are physical manifestations that do not exist on the primordial level. From a harmonic qualitative point of view, however, everything we see on a physical level is only a thin outward manifestation of endless harmonic resonant layers.

Primordial Waters

Water in its full harmonic levels is in a unified connection with all its higher vibrational levels—all the way to the primordial medium from which it emerges. Primordial Water, as referred to in ancient traditions, is a holistic all-encompassing conscious background medium. This primordial medium contains everything in Creation. The four energetic elemental qualities of Water, Air, Fire, and Earth all arise within the consciousness of this all-containing medium we refer to as a primordial fog.

The term primordial waters or fog that is used in many Creation myths is a bit confusing as in this state it contains all four qualities embedded in a state of active consciousness, sometimes referred to in ancient doctrines as the fifth central element of "ether." This active consciousness is a central principle within the four qualities of this primordial state.

The Double Role of Consciousness

Consciousness is a result of the Law of Time activating and governing the emergence of duality in the initial Psychon pulse. Let us go back to our model of the Psychon pulse, where the activation of Consciousness and its interaction at the center of the eight-fold bi-directional spiraling motion creates mental radiation and in-going emotional/attraction forces. In order not to over-complicate things in the earlier analysis of the Psychon, we did not go into the double nature of Consciousness. So, let us now go deeper into the role of Consciousness as the main player in the Psychon pulse.

In the outward radiation of the Psychon pulse, as we explained above, we find the manifestation of time circulating in the out-going spiral with space as the out-going motion in the center. This is the creation of "conscious time-space" and "mental consciousness." The in-going direction of attraction is the redirection of Consciousness to the Ziron center. This is an inner retraction of time-space and an emergence of emotional activity. Consciousness here has two faces, one manifesting outwards in the activation of sensory perception within the dimension of manifestation of the Psychon pulse, while the other relates to emotional consciousness redirected inwards as self-reflection of the source. The two aspects of Consciousness interact together in a complimentary Yin-Yang fashion at each of the eight crossings of the spiral.

The pure water sources we find flowing as veins in the rocky strata of the earth, and identify as a main criterion of the energy quality of sacred power spots, contain all four qualities within the active state of Consciousness that we refer to holistically as "life force." This is what is commonly referred to as "living waters." Pure physical water is the carrier of life force. Following the example of the bi-directional double nature of Consciousness, the same criteria apply to the same four primordial qualities (Water, Air, Fire, and Earth) within life force. Life force must be understood in its bi-directional double nature of manifesting life as well as connecting and directing it back to the source.

Looking at it through this holistic paradigm, it follows that all physical matter is, in one way or another, a manifestation of primordial water, containing all the other elements. Even dry matter contains life force on a higher non-physical state. In this sense, we can say that everything is a form of life force manifestation. From a multi-dimensional harmonic point of view, everything arises from higher harmonic levels of holistic water. The true nature of the subtle energy background is the conscious intelligent life force which fuels every type of motion in all dimensions of Creation from the tiniest particles to the growth and motion of every species. It is the mental-emotional energy that animates all souls. This is the omnipotent, omnipresent, infinitely energetic subtle energy from which all dimensions of Creation arise. This has been acknowledged by the intellect of the heart in many traditions as Divinity, but it is totally elusive to modern mainstream science. It is this most potent natural intelligent living energy source, which fuels all dimensions of Creation, to which humanity must revert in order to create a truly timeless civilization that is totally integrated with the life of Mother Earth. This is the energy source that will allow humanity to have a positive effect on all other dimensions and become an active harmonizing part of Creation.

Water as the Ultimate Communicator of Living Information

Water is the bearer of life force, the cradle of the manifestation of the Universal Mind in earthly dimension. It is a harmonic manifestation of the primordial waters at the source of the life force of the living Universal Mind. In its pure unpolluted form, it will contain and transmit the vital, emotional, and mental components of the life force in its perfect spiritually centered balance. Water is the highest form of spiritual being living among us and within us. Water is a doorway to Infinity, containing all the information of what was, what is, and what will be.

The human ego, in total separation from the environment, has failed to see water as a universal living spiritual being. The water we have on Earth—whether in the natural oceans, streams, or the atmosphere—has been polluted by modern technology and contaminated by human beings' emotional and mental residue. This has weakened Water's harmonic connection with its higher life force levels and distorted the way we perceive and interact with the environment.

Restoring the harmony of universal waters in multi-dimensional biological systems is the only path to a healthy survival of the planet.

Modern technology has a detrimental effect on the life force in water. Electromechanical systems drain the vital force from water and disturb its mental-emotional quality. Our research showed that when the BG3 energy centering quality of BioGeometry was introduced to the water, it regained the full life potential of its original natural state. This is the quality of water we find in springs and lakes in Earth power spots. Besides the presence of the subtle energy quality (BG3), measurements show that the surface tension of the water decreases, which indicates structured water.

We worked with Rasmus Gaupp-Berghausen, head of the late Dr. Masaru Emoto's European Hado Life Institute in Liechtenstein, Switzerland, and showed the effect of BioGeometry shapes on frozen water crystals (Figure 144), as per Dr. Emoto's work. We collaborated with Dr. Emoto for many years, and he spent some time with us in Egypt. Our connection assisted us to doing a lot of research on the effect of BioGeometry shapes on frozen water crystals.

Aside from being a music professor and builder of musical instruments along BioGeometry principles, my colleague Georg Gaupp-Berghausen, mentioned earlier, is a well-known energy quality water researcher. Using the Hofer "Spagyrik" Method (Von Asche der Phoenix, Hofer, 2018), he demonstrated resonant mental-emotional interactions with water: drops of water observed under a very powerful microscope showed a clear effect on their structure when exposed to electromagnetic radiation. This was corrected using BioGeometry harmonizing shapes. In another experiment conducted in our center in Egypt, water drops viewed under a microscope manifested one of our BioGeometry shapes that was not present in the lab, showing an information exchange with us on a subconscious level (Figure 145).

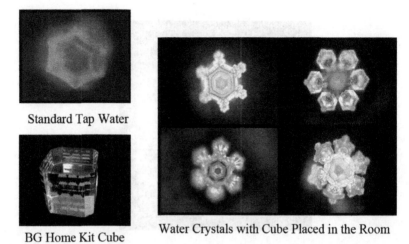

Standard Tap Water

BG Home Kit Cube

Water Crystals with Cube Placed in the Room

Fig.144 - Effect of BioGeometry Cube on Water Crystals by Hado Europe

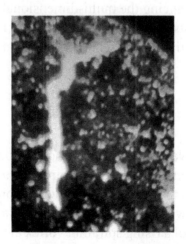

Fig.145 - BioGeometry "L" in Water Drop

Using a powerful microscope, Georg was able to produce water drops containing beautiful natural life images. They show a natural environment with plants and flowers. Nature seems to exist in its fullness in a drop of water. (Figure 146)

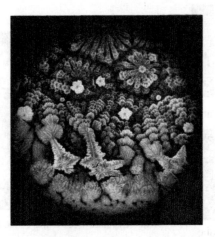

Fig.146 - Nature in a Drop of Water

Primordial higher dimensions of water carry the archetypal templates of all types of life. By enhancing the multi-dimensional resonant connection of physical water with its higher dimensions, which lead to the primordial life force origin, we activate the archetypal energy pattern of the natural forming process.

Sacred Water Wells

The water in sacred power spots has a holistic harmonizing effect on users that occurs through a multi-dimensional communication with higher levels. This water contains the complete holistic life force and has full communicative resonance with the Universal Mind. Natural wells, streams, and lakes are the result of a rising spiraling vortex at the crossing of underground streams. These streams flow through channels in the rock giving them a special water quality that is in resonance with higher harmonics of the living Ultraviolet (UV) quality. To detect this type of rock water we recommend the use of living color dials calibrated to UV. This water quality is sometimes referred to as "primordial water." This water plays a central role in the sacred power spots that have played a major role in the history of humanity, and which are part of religious rituals all over the world. All the sacred monuments in history are located on sacred power spots that have underground water streams that sometimes erupt over ground as natural springs, streams, or lakes.

In the Karnak temple complex in Luxor, we find the sacred lake still intact. When not polluted, oases in the desert, like the one in Siwa in the Egyptian Western desert, usually have the sacred water healing quality. In Oman, people would go to a lot of trouble to bring the sacred waters from the mountain sources down to the villages through channels they carved out of the rock. I myself used scientific dowsing methods to locate and excavate the twelve wells of Moses in Egypt's Sinai Peninsula. My goal was to build a very special project that would serve the three main religions. Unfortunately, it did not materialize, and the wells were soon buried back in the sand. In the picture, we see the remains of one of the wells (Figure 147).

Fig.147 - Dr. Ibrahim at the Moses Wells

In the holy Mosque at Mecca, we have the famous Zamzam well that is renowned for its healing properties. The renowned water source at Lourdes in France has attracted people from all over the world because of its healing properties.

Water dowsers usually detect this type of rock water to locate the best spot to erect sacred buildings and drill the wells. They are not concerned with underground water reservoirs used for agriculture that show increased salinity over time. The rock water wells stay fresh for thousands of years without any increase in salinity.

Water Dowsing

I worked for some time with the late renowned Swiss water dowser Hans-Anton Rieder, who detected and drilled more than eight hundred rock water wells. I visited one of the towns in Switzerland where he drilled four such wells that have served six thousand local residents for more than thirty years without any intervention required to correct the natural water quality. He theorized there were water streams about 80 centimeters in diameter running through the rocky strata at a depth of around one hundred and twenty meters in a grid approximately 150 meters in both directions that runs N-S and E-W. His theory seemed to be validated by his numerous successes over the years. He pointed out that he needed special drilling machines with a drill head of 8 centimeters to avoid cracking the water veins. For that reason, he also never drilled directly over stream crossings that might be found on different levels. When a clean hole of the right size was drilled into the center of a water vein, the water would erupt with a lot of power to the surface. However, if it was offset or larger in size, the vein would crack and most of the water would dissipate in the ground resulting in a weak flow on the surface. If the drill reaches a water reservoir instead of a vein, we get normal underground water that will show more salinity over time.

Rieder's method was purely psychic, and he believed in his God-given natural ability. Nevertheless, there is a scientific explanation to water dowsers' psychic ability: more than two thirds of our weight is comprised of water and therefore a dowser enters into resonance with water flow when he or she is directly above it. People with increased sensitivity can feel this resonant communication as a tingling or vibration in their body. In addition to their extreme sensitivity to underground water, they tuned-in much better with the flow of water streams than with underground water lakes that were not in motion. The friction between the moving water and the rocks created the necessary energy patterns emitted above ground that the dowsers reacted to. All the successful water dowsers I have encountered who detected rock water had a special kind of sensitivity to the subtle energy quality of sacred power spots. Their consciousness reacted to the spiritual quality, which put them in a state of grace that they attributed to Divine intervention.

I accompanied Rieder during his dowsing using my BioGeometry horizontal dial pendulum to determine the proper calibration. The rock water streams we encountered had the "Living UV" quality with BG3 at the crossings. The water also had the Al-Kareem Quality that indicated its vitality. I cross-checked Rieder's detection on the Google maps he used for remote detection before going out on location and came up with the same mapping of the streams. Unfortunately, our collaboration ended when Rieder passed away last year. He was the greatest water dowser I have ever encountered.

BioGeometry Technique for Water Detection

Although the method we propose here will allow readers to detect underground rock water streams it should be noted that success here requires experience in detection, drilling, and using proper instruments of detection, otherwise, one risks spending a lot of money without success. Water drilling with the needed precision for rock water streams needs proper machinery and is costly. One has to find the right quality of water as well as the proper flow pressure.

In general, water wells drilled in Earth locations with a BG3 quality will have some BG3. It will not, however, be the same as water from the rock water veins.

Here's how the BioGeometry technique for water detection works:

First, we must calibrate the horizontal dial pendulum on the living color UV setting, as well as the 360-degree dial pendulum on the 43 setting. We usually use both pendulums and cross check with the BG3 pendulum and IKUP for Al-Kareem Quality.

We can then use a Google satellite image (not a map) and go with the pendulum over a ruler in both horizontal and vertical directions. Where you find a response, in the form of a pull and a rotation, you can move the pendulum around that point to find the next one, and then connect them all to find a path. You will detect a few lines in both directions. The points at which they cross will indicate a water vein.

Once this work is done it is important to continue the work on location; never start drilling based only on the work you've done on a map.

So now, the next step is to go on location to the spots found on the Google map. The paths will usually have a natural-looking flow. If the paths show straight lines, you could be detecting a BG3 grid. In this case it is better to use a pre-calibrated living color disk or calibrate a 360-dial calibrated to the number quality 43 and second check with the number 80 setting on the horizontal dial pendulum.

By moving the pendulum higher or lower along a stream you can detect the angle of emanation, and this must be taken into consideration as this will shift deeper in the ground. Aside from the detection of the UV in the stream you will also find a thin BG3 line at its center and a Horizontal Negative Green emanation at the side borders of the vein. This is caused by the friction of the water moving over the rocks. There are secondary emanations on both sides that rise at an angle and can be used to calculate the depth (Figure 148).

To increase your accuracy and chances of success, it is important to raise your sensitivity and program it, through a lot of practice. Before dowsing for rock water, one should have completed many measurements on sacred wells, streams, and lakes using pictures or preferably on location, so the body's subtle energy system can synchronize with this resonant quality. This will improve the efficiency of detecting and differentiating rock water

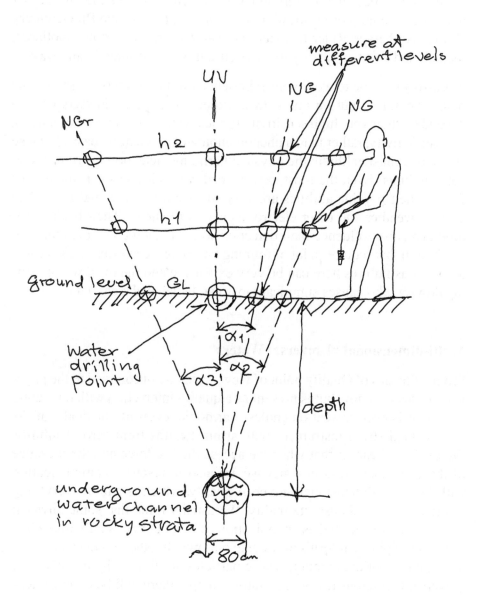

Fig.148 - Water Channel

from other types of underground waters. After completing the proper mapping on a map or on location it is important to use the BioGeometry Human Archetype Ruler to check the water's vitality, and its emotional, mental, and spiritual quality to make sure it is not polluted in any way.

It is also advisable to work with experienced water dowsers for some time before venturing out on one's own. Experienced water dowsers usually depend on their very high sensitivity to rock water, which they explain as a psychic activity, rather than a phenomenon with a scientific basis. In these cases, one must calibrate the physical harmonic detection instruments on their findings. Even the most experienced water dowsers can sometimes fail, as their psychic abilities are very susceptible to external influences such as weather and other electromagnetic pressures . Their health condition can also influence their detection work. It should be noted this is a profession that requires a lot of training before one can offer one's service to others as failures here can be very expensive and the most well-meaning dowser who causes significant loss can be labeled a charlatan.

Multi-dimensional "Universal Waters"

From a Physics of Quality point of view, water is not confined to the physical phases we know but is present as a quality interacting with our subtle energy. It is ever present on endless harmonic levels of our model of the hypothetical string instrument with string lengths from zero to infinity. We explained earlier that when we access the life force and the presence of the Universal Mind in water we are also in resonant communication with its multi-dimensional universal quality, which is within everything in the unperceived absolute reality. We usually think that some physical form of water is needed as an indication of life, but that is only true when speaking of physical forms of life like our own. In other dimensions based on mental-emotional matter, whose particles are formed by the action of universal Consciousness within subtle energy, there will be other dimensions of water just like ours. Those higher harmonic dimensions contained in physical water will not be made of electromagnetic components but from other conscious compression wave life force on the vital, emotional, and mental levels.

From our perspective as Earth beings, we should be aware that dry, solid seemingly inanimate matter that does not contain any form of physical water can still be full of life force with its full conscious, intelligent, life giving and spiritually harmonizing properties from higher harmonic dimensions of water quality.

We will use the term "universal waters" when referring to the multi-dimensional totality of intercommunicative harmonics. It is the omnipresent life force of the Universal Mind. This is important to know as everything in nature that we think is inanimate matter contains this intelligent life force. Unfortunately, human manipulation of natural materials depletes them of life force. It was not like that in the great ancient civilizations as we repeatedly pointed out earlier. The Ancients connected every product, event, and monument with the total life force on the higher dimensions of water and channeled the powers of nature that were an essential part of bringing spiritual harmony into every activity. Humanity lived in the harmony resulting from the integration of the material and the subtle energy worlds. They lived with the personified powers of nature we erroneously refer to as gods

The Conscious Living Creative Force of Primordial Water

Primordial water or fog, as we have explained earlier, is synonymous with subtle energy and life force. It is the stage on which the levels of conscious mind in the universal water background medium imagine Creation. In a way "all is water." It is the living collective universal multi-dimensional being in whose oceans we exist as the fish in the ocean. Our intelligent but ignorant modern technology closed the door on the universal perception of the heart, and all the other dimensions of absolute reality, and is leaving us to dry on the shore. With the possibilities of BioGeometry, we have the knowledge to revive the universal water and restore the life force of our planet.

Restoring the Life Force of Water

Let us start with some very simple methods, that have been well researched and applied in BioGeometry:

A. **Using the Quality of Numbers to Revive the BG3 Quality in Water**

1. Stir drinks such as water, tea, coffee, juice, soup etc. with any number of clockwise rotations from the BG3 qualitative series (e.g., 16, 19, 28…).

2. There is however another simpler way with wider use. Turn the holder such as glass, cup, bottle, plate, plant pots etc. eight small increments clockwise. The motion can be minimal. They can be used on any objects you can easily rotate. The number eight in rotation is the result of multiplication of two by four as found in the rotation of two squares.

3. There are physical solutions based on the quality of numbers that are more permanent such as the water strips included in the BioGeometry Home Kit along with other electrical strips. They include the number 16 for BG3 on one side and the number 11, which is in resonance with water on the other, and both ends have additional BioGeometry L shapes. You can also attach two wire coils, one with 16 and the other with 19 coils, with some space between, them on water pipes, or engrave parallel strokes with these numbers on the pipes.

B. **Restoring Water Quality with Color**

1. The universal water connection can be achieved by applying UV and Horizontal Negative Green (HNG) through a horizontal dial.

2. Pointing or Rotating the IKUP or BG16 pendulums over the water will restore its life force.

3. Applying a clockwise rotation of the combined four or six life force dial pendulums on the water will restore it. One can use each of the separate life force dials separately to check for their independent occurrence and find the weak one and the apply it.

C. Clearing of Lakes

1. BioGeometry color balancing techniques, which involve inserting different colored pegs into the ground around the lake to create the BG3 quality in the water, can be applied. In the case of larger lakes, you can start remotely on a Google map and pinpoint the correct spot for each color before going on location to do the final measurement and placement. In several projects we've tried in the past, the water became clearer in a day or two. This is a very popular practice in the BioGeometry community, whose members have shared many diverse success stories with one another. The lake becomes your sacred power spot.

D. Using Intention to Revive the BG3 in Water

1. Say a blessing, prayer, or words of love to your food or drink, or plants, animals, and so on.

2. All beliefs use water in sacred rituals and the rituals are usually based on sacred water sources that have the natural BG3 quality. In general, any kind of water used in a spiritual pratice will acquire BG3 through intention.

E. Activating the Earth Energy Grids/Fields

1. The Al-Kareem Quality Fields and Grids are the harmonized toroidal grids and fields resulting from motion. In our world of modern technology, however, the depleting negative quality of energy fields usually shows up in the form of negative QL-Torsion (QL-), which causes a *loss* of life force (i.e., the IKUP will turn negatively). In contrast to natural environments, seashore locations, sacred power spots, or shapes benefitting from some aspect of BioGeometry design will usually have an energizing positive QL-Torsion. When harmonized through BioGeometry devices these fields are referred to as "Al-Kareem Quality Fields/Grids," in which case they become a state of positive life force as previously explained. The activation of the Al-Kareem Quality Fields/Grids restores

the life force in water in all its forms in the environment, including in all living systems. As it resonates with its universal levels it is revived as universal water.

2. The crossings of BG3 Earth energy grids running at the center of Hartmann and Curry grids, or any other types of BG3 spots, can revive the water above it. The water within a plant on such a spot or crossing will also acquire the universal connection that will be visible in the plant's quality of health.

After applying any of the above methods to restore the connectivity of the universal water levels, you can check for positive resonance with all the planes of nature (physical, vital, emotional, mental, and spiritual) on the Human Archetype Ruler using an IKUP pendulum and the strips with the shapes that resonated with the different sub-levels of the planes to make sure you have done the full universal water restoration.

Body Water and Multi-dimensional Connectivity

All body organs have some form of "universal water" in them and depend on it for proper functioning and for communication with the archetypal dimensions. The quality of sensory perception of perceived reality, as well as the extrasensory perception of the brain and heart, depend on communication with the higher dimensions to access the forces of nature's functions and harmony with which the Ancients kept a sacred relationship. The heart and brain carry a large amount of universal water through which they, as well as other organs, regulate the multi-dimensional functions they perform in communication with the universal harmonic octaves. Our quality of perception depends largely on the presence of the multi-dimensional communication of universal waters.

Restoring the Life Force of Water (UV) M8, M12

The harmonizing methods to restore the universal water quality can be verified by the balance of the emotional and mental levels. The measurement on the eighth and twelfth mental levels measured on the BioGeometry Human Archetype Ruler are a good indication of the resonant quality of universal water in the brain. The brain's fluid quality affects sensory perception. Its universal quality enhances the right-brain perception and heart consciousness as both heart and brain contain large amounts of water in different forms.

PART THIRTY-THREE
Life force: The Ultimate Energy Source

The evolution, motion, and growth of all forms of life is fueled by the living conscious life force which is in an interactive unified state with the earth, and the whole Universe, as well. There is a point where other more advanced civilizations in the Universe will become aware of the benefits of using energy sources based on the living intelligent natural life force. Such civilizations could be millions of years ahead of us and using forms of life force as the main energy that fuels everything in their technology. This kind of energy interacts with the psyche. It leads to the harmony of interaction and to a subconscious drive to "excellence of action." This future fuel is driven by thought and emotional patterns. These advanced civilizations would be truly living in a Golden Age. Any civilization that wants to avoid self-destruction and achieve a healthy permanent state of human environmental integration can only do so by converting to life force as its main energy source.

There are two stages to the implementation of a life-force-based civilization:

The first is the creation of a new generation of human products that contribute to the immunity and health of all species. This can be achieved through the implementation of the BioGeometry design language to create products that create the BG3 and Al-Kareem Qualities to harmonize the energy exchange of all living systems of the environment.

The second stage involves the direct use of life force as the main fuel of the mentally controlled functions and motion of new environmentally friendly vehicles and machines.

Water as the Life Force Container at the Core of Products

Water as we know it is a precondition for the action of life force in living organisms. It contains and channels life force into every natural species in a pulsating multi-level open energy exchange system. Life force, as we explained earlier, emanates from the first eruption of duality in the form of the Psychon pulse created through the action of the Ziron doorway into the zero-infinity state. Life force encompasses the total flow of living Consciousness dimensions through the harmonic levels of water from the primordial fog through the spiritual, mental, and emotional levels down to physical water. The simultaneous harmonic existence of and communication with "all" those levels is a precondition for life. This means that the water in all living systems is multi-dimensional. Physical water in all its forms, in this context, is only a very small part of the total water that carries the life force, just as our perceived world is a very small part of absolute whole unperceived reality; this is the same for all natural material objects. To be able to contain life force the water must exist in its whole harmonic multi-level form with the primordial state present in its core. This is the only way it can contain the vital, emotional, mental, and spiritual dimensions that it transmits as the pulsating life force to all species in nature. We must work on all the steps in water storage, purification, transport, and so on, to restore and prevent the depletion of its life force. BioGeometry provides effective solutions that can be applied on all those levels of interactions with water to preserve its natural life force.

Al-Kareem Quality in Nature

The important thing in designing products fueled by some form of life force is that both directions of subtle energy exchange with the environment produce the Al-Kareem Quality. This is how natural species create the enhancing life force quality in their immediate surroundings. Instead of smart cities producing negative QL-Torsion and depleting the life force and immunity of the residents, the new buildings and homes of humanity will have the same life force restoring Al-Kareem Quality found in the homes of natural species. The beehive, seashells, and birds' nests should be our raw models of the future.

The Global Life Force Environmental Solution

The creation of the life force enhancing quality of positive QL-Torsion is the only way to restore the health of our planet and change the mental-emotional make-up of all humanity. A global BioGeometry solution can achieve this, for example by distributing Al-Kareem Quality Stands in as many locations as possible around the globe. These stands can be small (e.g.,10 centimeters tall) and can be formed as candlesticks or other household objects of any size, so they can be placed in every home. Some of our stands include a container for water. They can also be larger, free-standing artistic elements in any type of landscape, or buried underground in tubes. This could be the turning point and the first step into a new golden age where life force becomes the new energy source fueling a transformed human civilization.

Electromagnetic Radiation as a Carrier of Life force

The harmful aspects of electromagnetic pollution in the age of information can be overturned and made to act in the service of humanity. BioGeometry solutions have shown that electromagnetic radiation and electro-smog can carry the BG3 and Al-Kareem qualities into the environment. It can be done at the source by enforcing BioGeometry proportions on wave shape, using controlling programs based on values from the BioGeometry Modulor or Lambdoma tables to enforce *"wavelength to amplitude proportions"* on all types of electromagnetic radiation. The same effect can also be achieved by working on the environment, independent from the sources of electromagnetic radiation, through the use of special BioGeometry shapes as direct solutions, or indirectly through all types of design.

These solutions can be applied on any level from the smallest to the largest dimensions. Mobile phones, electric cars, airplanes, and smart cities, for example, can become healing environments. Universal harmony can be achieved step by step.

Artificial Intelligence (AI) Infused with Life Force

The use of the Harmonizing BG3 and Al-Kareem number qualities in the mathematical formulas and algorithms used to create artificial intelligence can produce intelligent life force on two levels. Artificial intelligence can be used to project the harmonizing intelligent life force into the user's subtle energy fields to achieve a human-AI or human-machine integration. In this case humanity will play an integral role in all AI activities. The outward-radiating mental analytical activity governed by AI will be balanced by the inward-moving emotional conscious human values. Humanity will thus be the conscience governing the use of the machines and devices.

A much more elaborate second step would be to infuse the qualities of the inward-moving emotional/spiritual direction directly into AI to have an imbedded bi-directional qualitative interaction with humanity. At this level the AI products will have the conscience that can have a balancing effect on human conscience. This is an important step in the development of all kinds of teaching methods.

Those two levels of Human-AI interaction will not, however, create life in the physical product unless the natural design process and water integration into the physical design and materials is used in a way to achieve evolution involving growth and motion connected to intelligent life force. This third level, however, carries its own dangers as it takes humanity out of the driver's seat, and should be avoided. The second level of Human-AI integration is the ideal way to build a life-force-based utopian civilization.

PART THIRTY-FOUR

The Living BioGeometry Design Language

In this chapter, we will examine how the different aspects of the harmonizing subtle energy quality we discussed previously are used to develop the BioGeometry design language, whose goals include the achievement of the BG3 and Al-Kareem life force qualities. The presence and level of those qualities is our new standard of evaluation of any human achievement. This is the way to integrate our designs into the life force forming process of nature.

In the paradigm of BioGeometry, we bring the human being, in full multi-dimensional subtle energy qualitative existence, to become the measuring instrument of all energetic effects. The human holistic natural health quality should be added as an important "life force variable" in every scientific formula. Here we will examine the potential for the BioGeometry design language to transform modern technology, through the connection to life force, and become a holistic environmental savior to shape our future.

The Use of Shapes to Create Quality in BioGeometry

Let us summarize here the mechanism by which shapes affect the quality of the environment that we have dealt with in earlier topics of this text. As expressed in the two-dimensional BioGeometry "Energy Key," which is a section through a three-dimensional torus around a linear motion, secondary compression waves are created by any type of motion. All kinds of motion create non-electromagnetic compression waves that affect the quality of vital, emotional, and mental levels in the background subtle energy medium. In this context, the background subtle energy life force medium is a conscious, intelligent, living carpet weave of compression waves.

One way to interact with compression waves is through material shapes that are formed to support or produce any function needed. The use of shapes to produce effects is used in aerodynamics, hydraulics, or theater acoustics, for example. If, however, we go into vibratory dimensions faster than the electromagnetic range of the speed of light, we will encounter other types of compression waves that are not bound by the constraints of linear time and space. As we have shown earlier, even electromagnetic waves interact with all levels of compression waves embedded between their electric and magnetic planes. This is the domain of emotional and mental energy that is a higher form of multi-directional compression waves. The quality of emotional and mental energy levels can be influenced and harmonized through material shapes. All living systems are in an open energy exchange with the environment. BioGeometry solutions use specially designed shapes that produce the BG3 harmonizing quality.

Since everything interacts and exists within this compression-wave subtle energy medium, we can design shapes to create certain qualities within the background medium that in turns transmits them through resonance to all living or inert systems in it. By applying the BioGeometry design language, we program the shapes to produce the harmonizing qualities in the compression-wave environment.

The Living Forming Process of Nature

To integrate our modern technology as an enhancing supportive factor of the life force of the environment, we need to "plant" our products into the life force of the earth to become a living part of the "Earth Being." To achieve that we must follow and become part of the living forming process of nature. In other words, we must follow the Laws of Creation all the way from the Divine level of Creation—where the potentiality of all the natural laws exists—through their manifestation in the duality of mental-emotional forces in the Psychon pulse forming the initial time-space harmonic unit of Creation. Multiple Psychons combine in different ways to produce the Laws of Nature that interact together holistically in different ways, on all harmonic levels, to produce all the dimensions and the forms of life within them.

The communication between the higher levels of Creation that bring the life force into all the levels of the soul down to the biological functions is based on the vortices that connect between the different planes of nature from the smallest Psychon level to the largest harmonic levels. In the toroidal section of the Psychon configuration we have the spiritual archetypal plane around the center of the Ziron pulse from which it emanates into the eight Psychon layers. The archetypal templates and creative forming Laws of Nature flow along the spiraling time-space motion of the pulse to be manifested as the life force along the toroidal field information patterns according to the time-space duality of that specific dimension. All geometrical centers in nature are vortices of connection between different planes. From these, the forming laws from the archetypal dimension control the manifestation of shape.

It is important to repeat the above from a design perspective because it helps us understand that *the solid and static appearance of shape is the result of a limited physical time-space sensory perception.* The numerous unperceived superimposed multi-dimensional levels of shape boundaries are in constant dynamic change and evolution.

Designing along the natural forming process is based on achieving a "centering" connection with the primordial state that breathes all levels of the life force into the material dimension. We can access this source using the principles of universal harmonic resonance. This resonant connection can be achieved in many ways. For example, we can rotate the geometrical configuration of shape to enter into resonance with the circular/spherical motion of the toroidal Psychon pulse. We can also connect to the zero-infinity state through the BG3 number qualities that create a multi-dimensional spiraling vortex.

The emergence of infinity from the zero state is through the ONE that contains everything in a unified state. The ONE, as the first all-containing numerical expression, produces all the other numbers through energetic processes of division, multiplication, addition, and subtraction. In design, we can use numbers and proportions in a resonant way to access their source.

Let's examine the essence of the different methods of communication with the source arranged as the nine pillars of the BioGeometry design language:

1. BioGeometry Earth Energy Design
2. BioGeometry Sky-Linked Design
3. BioGeometry Qualitative Harmonic Numbers and Proportions
4. BioGeometry Design Principles
5. BioGeometry Motion in Design
6. BioGeometry Qualitative Global Scaling System
7. BioGeometry Archetypal Design Codes
8. BioGeometry Material Energy Quality Balancing
9. BioGeometry Signatures (BioSignatures)

1. **BioGeometry Earth Energy Design**

   a. These principles were introduced earlier in relation to sacred power spots and Earth energy grids as main factors in the location and design of monuments, buildings, and cities. Erecting a building or monument on a sacred power spot will put it directly in the vortex of communication. This method has been used throughout history in town planning. In modern times, those principles were revived in the original planning of Washington, Paris, Rome, and Cairo. Using this principle, major buildings and hubs of circulation were placed on the power spots and the main avenues were placed on their connective lines. The Freemasons, who played a role in such planning, adhered to Ancient Egyptian principles and brought obelisks from Egypt, erecting them on main power spots to enhance the BG3 quality of the whole city. These concepts have been dealt with in the book titled *Talisman* by Graham Hancock and Robert Bauval, which I mentioned earlier.

   Beneficent BG3 centers are like sacred power spots with which we can interact in different ways and thus spread their subtle energy quality throughout a building. One way to do this is to use radiating connective underground wiring made, for example, out of non-deteriorating plastic. In some projects, we have bundled seven wires together to increase connectivity. The wires radiate from the power spot to different areas of the house, such as the bedrooms, the living, dining, and study rooms, the kitchen, the workshop, and so on. In other types of buildings, one would lead the wires to the most important rooms. We can also point any other architecture or decorative elements towards the power spot. As a rule, in the main design we try to locate the most important part of the building, such as the master bedroom, the main family living room, and other areas of importance or prolonged stay, on the power spot if possible. With more than one power spot we must additionally connect them together to achieve a powerful BG3 pattern.

Harmful power spots should be avoided when locating any important spaces or those used for a long duration. Bedrooms should never be planned on such spots. In general, we use layered solutions to take care of all subtle energy disturbances, but we still recommend avoiding them for important spaces.

Following the prehistoric example of erecting megalithic menhir and dolmen shapes on sacred power spots, one can place sculptures, East-West gateways, fountains, garden sitting areas, pyramids, domes, or conical BG3 elements on external power spots.

b. To activate communication with the centering BG3 quality in the land, your building should be planned to take into consideration the direction of BG3 lines on the site. One or two of the directions can be incorporated into the pattern of main design axes of the building, or in secondary design elements such as pathways, flower boxes, built-in furniture, etc.

c. The main entry to a site or a building is a point of change in space. Points of change in space and time are multi-dimensional connective centers of life force. Any action taken at this moment will affect and prevail through the whole cycle from the beginning to end as in the line pulse. It is therefore important to locate the site and building entrances on BG3 areas if possible or otherwise design this harmonizing quality into them.

d. Using inclinations at a 45-degree angle on any level of design, can enter into resonance with the BG3 atmospheric grid system. Due to the diagonal inclination of the planes as shown earlier in Figure 130, this system will not show specific grid dimensions on ground level. The use of a 45-degree inclination can be applied in many ways within architecture and interior design. We have used this concept in a horizontal wall strip in the interior design in an apartment in New York with our late colleague the designer Michael Keith. The effect was so impressive it was featured in *Veranda* magazine in an article written by its chief editor, Charles Ross, titled "Calm," and a segment about it aired in a program on the television channel NY1(Figure 149). We have designed glass doors with this strip in a diagonal layout (Figure 150). This method was also used to produce the BG3 quality in a building through the use of vertical and horizontal strips, with diagonal strokes on walls, corners, and arches.

e. The energy qualities of a line, which we dealt with earlier, show the Violet quality at its beginning and the Red one at its end. We can thus tell the direction in which the line is drawn. Subtle energy will always flow along a line in the direction it is drawn. This is an important point when drawing BioSignatures as it affects the quality and function of the whole diagram. We further detected a BG3 point before the beginning of the line and another one after it with the line repeating itself in different subtle energy copies before and after the physical line. This analysis shows the flow of a line along the sensory-perceived motion in time and space. This sensory-based left-brain perception is based on another universal pulsating holistic reality beyond the confinements of time and space.

Fig.149 - BioGeometry in Veranda Magazine June 2001

Fig.150 - Diagonal 45 Degree Sections Door

The linear sensory perception of a line shows BG3 points as vortices before the beginning, in the middle and after the end. These are manifestations of the linear bidirectional motion of the pulse that produces the linear time-space flow. This is connected to a higher archetypal dimension, from where it manifests and retracts back into. The beginning and end in this context are beyond physical time and space and are not separated by sensory perception. This takes us back to the archetypal pulse configuration of the line based on a harmonic of the spiraling vortex emanation in the Psychon toroidal model. The seemingly linear flow is the result of the archetypal pulsating action of Creation.

The Psychon pulse is at the center of the two-way spiraling bi-directional motion on the projected Ziron axis. The pulse produces the beginning and end at the turning point before it retracts into the Ziron center. The beginning and end points on this level are the turning points of the outward-inward moving spiral. These turning points manifest as temporary opposite unified complementary qualities before retracting back into the center, just like the end points on a stretched elastic band. In this mode of perception, the two BG3 points at the beginning and end of the linear flow of a line are one and the same as they are not within the linear flow of physical time-space. Following this concept, we will always detect the BG3 point at the center of the line where the line originated as a bi-directional pulse. A pulse therefore always originates from the vortex at its center. Beginning and end are always connected through their unified origin and continuously affect each other in their manifestation as a line of motion. Any motion is composed of endless such pulses emerging and disappearing in and out of several dimensions giving the appearance of permanency in each dimension. This is like the film strip effect where separate images project as a continuous reality. Every line drawn in the physical dimension is therefore a manifestation of the spiritual archetypal Psychon pulse creating a time-space Energy Key producing the time-space movement of the line in the physical dimension.

This concept applies to all living systems in nature where the beginning and end of every life are interconnected and affect each other; their interaction activates a higher spiritual connection. To understand how the end affects the beginning within the direction of linear time, we must look at the mental-emotional dimensions. These are not confined by physical time-space as they are multidirectional non-electromagnetic wave fields. Let's return to the experiments we mentioned earlier where a person produces the sound of the vowel "e," and ends with another letter he or she is only shown at the end of the sound experiment. The effect of the quality of the letter that has not yet been chosen will always show at the beginning. The change in quality from the beginning will indicate the effect of the letter that will only be introduced at the end. It can be measured from the beginning to predict what will be introduced at the end.

The quality of action at any moment in a lifetime will affect both its beginning and its end. It will not change the beginning in the physical sense, but it will affect the quality of the whole span of the life, as well as that of the end. Through the Laws of Bi-Directional Information exchange in universal resonance, the harmonizing qualities of the excellence of action resulting from the practice of free will in the physical dimension will have a stronger effect on higher dimensions. Bringing the qualities resulting from the universal powers of nature in the heart into our perception—in the form of ethical values—produces the "excellence of action" that affects the quality of a beginning and an end. The physical world becomes better connected to the higher dimensions, from which it draws its life force.

Let us, however, go back to the practical use of the directionality of a line in design, to see how we can use it to bring harmony into the environment. First, we must examine another property of lines. Two parallel lines will enter into resonance and exchange qualities and create a central line between them with the BG3 quality. We will use this concept detect the central BG3 lines between the Hartmann or Curry Earth energy grids, so that we can map them without directly measuring them. However, in order to harmonize the environment through design, we need to find the BG3 spots and patterns on the site.

An Earth subtle energy survey will show the BG3 grids and larger strips. This will allow us to align one or more of the underlying design axes, or design components, parallel to them (Figure 151).

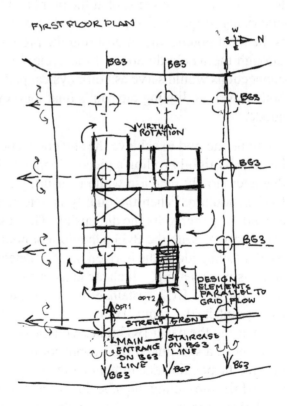

Fig.151 - JW Malaysia Site BG3 Design Axes

2. BioGeometry Sky-Linked Design

a. In general, sacred power spots are connected by straight invisible pathways created by points that emit similar qualities of BG3. In certain cases, these pathways are referred to as "Leys" or "ley lines." In ancient times, they were used as pilgrimage roads. The generals of the Roman Empire moved their armies along them, so the soldiers would be energized on their way to battle. The same concept was applied to connecting the sacred power spots on Earth with those in the sky. Certain building elements would be aligned in a way to connect with the heliacal rising of a specific star above the horizon; in fact, building activities would start at the time of the heliacal rising, and openings or shafts with certain proportions would be aligned to the sky sacred power spot at the point and time of the star's first rising. A qualitative effect introduced at the starting point is the most potent way of ensuring the presence of the quality through the whole duration of the cycle. In this way, the sky connections would serve as non-physical pathways for out-of-body travel facilitating the soul's final journey to its heavenly abode.

b. A simple method to achieve the sky connection in a home can be done by tightly rolling a piece of paper and then letting the diameter slowly increase while measuring at the ends with a BG3 pendulum. When the quality is detected, a tape is used around the paper to fix the dimension. The next step is to point at the horizon with the BG3 pendulum or point with the empty hand. Moving along the horizon one can detect a BG3 location at its rising or setting, which are ends of a cycle that will serve the purpose of BG3 sustainability. One should also find any BG3 point in the room. By connecting the BG3 spot in the room, using the paper BG3 tube, with the point on the horizon, we achieve a sky-linked BG3 connection that will endure. We then fix the position and direction of the paper tube and test the area while fine-tuning the tube direction to achieve the highest level of BG3 in the space. This method can be applied in open spaces as well and can be used in small orchards and animal farming.

c. The connection to a power spot in the sky can be achieved by applying BioGeometry design principles to music. Omar Raafat, my son-in-law, is a music composer, so we took the opportunity to introduce BioGeometry proportions into a composition that connects with the planet Sirius, which is a powerful sacred power spot in the sky. It was regarded by ancient civilizations as the spiritual center of our sky. Many Ancient Egyptian rituals were connected to Sirius. In out-of-body initiation rites as well as the afterlife journey, the soul was carried in the solar boat to its heavenly abode in Sirius. By direct energy quality measurements in the sky, as well as testing on pictures of Sirius, we then developed a basic proportion to be used as a rhythm throughout the whole composition. In that way, we created the same subtle energy quality of Sirius. This resonant connection with Sirius through music replicated the Ancient Egyptian ritual. We named this musical composition "The Sirius Odyssey." We then proceeded to add other proportions of notes and intervals, to harmonize electro-smog and Earth radiation as well as balance biological functions and achieve emotional and mental harmony.

3. **BioGeometry Qualitative Harmonics**

a. Applying any of the proportions from the BioGeometry series or the Modulor and Lambdoma, tables (shown earlier in Figure 86) to any of the design principles will enhance the harmonizing quality of the design.

b. There are endless ways of using numbers and proportions to introduce the BG3 quality into design. Using numerical positions in a row or array can also be a method of connection. One can use BG3 numbers (e.g., 16, 19, 28…) for the seats in the rows of, for example, a theater or a sports stadium, so that they interact together proportionally creating the harmonizing quality in a space.

c. The numbers 4, 8, and 12 have the Al-Kareem Quality. The 28, 34, and 43 have both the BG3 and Al-Kareem qualities. This gives us the possibility of designing with proportions to produce each quality individually or a combination of both. We have the proportions based on 16 and 19 to produce BG3, or those based on 4, 8 and 12 to produce Al-Kareem Quality as well as 28, 34 and 43 to produce a combination of both qualities.

4. **BioGeometry Design Principles (Figure 152)**

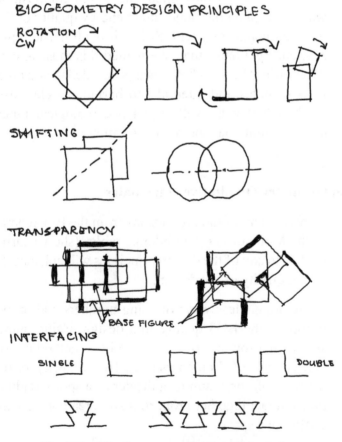

Fig.152 - BioGeometry Design Principles

a. **Rotation**

Creating some form of virtual rotation of the design will induce a connective vortex on the subtle energy level. The rotating bi-directional spiraling life forces of the Psychon pulse create torsion effects in the subtle energy medium. The spiraling pulse activates the life force in the subtle energy background medium. The life force in the subtle energy medium is in perfect balance through the outgoing counterclockwise energy dissipating action and the inward, clockwise, energizing action. The first produces the entropic quality while the second is the energizing, ordering, neg-entropic function. By recreating this second clockwise rotating action, we enhance the resonant communication with the energizing aspect of the life force. This interaction brings in the life force to integrate the design into the forming process of nature.

External Rotation: We can add elements that create a virtual clockwise or bi-directional rotation to our building plan. The main clockwise rotation connects to the energizing positive QL-Torsion (QL+). A secondary counterclockwise rotation can be added to achieve a balanced pulse. Virtual rotation in the design of any shape will produce an actual rotation in the surrounding subtle energy, which already has the spiraling effect at its core, that will react to the rotation of shape and produce a state of positive QL-Torsion and energizing life force around the building. This effect can be achieved through a slight modification to the external shape of the plan or the addition of simple small external elements that produce a virtual clockwise rotation. One can imagine the building shape placed in a flow of water to better visualize this concept (Figure 153).

Internal Rotation: The concept of subtle energy rotation can also be achieved through the rotation of internal elements, whether fixed or part of the furniture. The addition of internal elements to promote rotation are also used to balance the Bio-Geometry Energy Key in a space to achieve the proper balance of QL-Torsion (Figure 154).

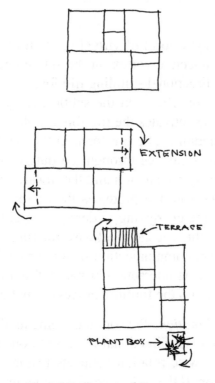

Fig.153 - External Rotation.

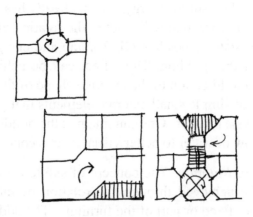

Fig.154 - Internal Rotation

The Egg Shape as a Life force Container: Elliptical shapes, such as the egg shape, rotate around two centers creating a duality that produces a special form of dynamism. The two unequal centers of the egg shape (within certain proportions) create a pulsating energetic dynamic stability that produces an ideal environment for the evolution of life. This concept has been used in the design of the BioGeometry bottle for the Sekem Biodynamic agriculture group in Egypt (Figure 155). They used it to prolong the shelf-life of milk. It is based on the interaction of three egg shapes that induce the BG3 quality into the liquid to give it health-supporting energy balancing properties and a longer shelf life. While the circle and ellipse have BG3 around the centers, the egg shape has the centering effect measured as BG3 in the whole shape, combined with the energizing Al-Kareem quality.

Fig.155 - BioGeometry Bottle Designed for Sekem

BG Interaction of Curves: This is a way of creating interactive centers that are in a resonant connection. Any curvature in design will create one or more virtual centers and produce a directional rotation in the subtle energy of an internal or external space (Figure 156). Multiple interactions of curves create several centers which can be used to create a strong BG3 quality as they will combine the BioGeometry principles of rotation, shifting, and interfacing. The direction of the first curve, at the entry point, is important in reaching a high intensity of BG3. This is an extremely important point to take into consideration when drawing BioSignatures.

CENTERS OF ROTATION

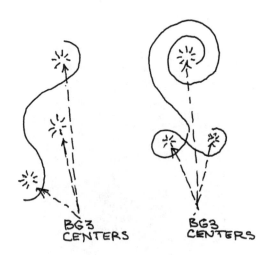

Fig.156 - BG3 Curvature Centers in Design

The BioGeometry L Shapes: Lines "rotated" at different angles around, but not connected all the way, to a center to emphasize its multi-dimensionality, produce different levels of BG3 emissions as can be seen in this example (Figure 157).

The "BG-L" is a very potent figure that creates and amplifies a central vortex through the circle segment while radiating a specific quality defined by the angle of the two radiating arms of different lengths. The 90-degree L is a very effective protection from all types of psychic disturbances, attacks, and possession. The 66/90/102-degree BG-L shapes protect from EMR and are used in pairs on wireless routers and other electronic devices.

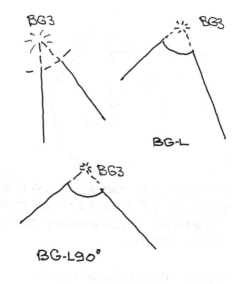

Fig.157 - BioGeometry "L" Shape Concept

The Tangent Quality: This is the quality of a dynamic angle. The tangent on a circle produces a dynamic angle ranging from infinity all the way down to zero at the connection point. This can be used in architecture, landscaping, furniture, and product design to generate harmony through multi-dimensional connections (Figure 158).

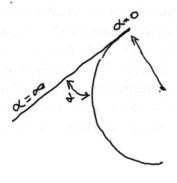

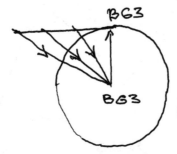

CONNECTIN BG3 OF TANGENT
TO BG3 OF CENTER OF CIRCLE
CREATES RESONANT BG3
RADIATION

Fig.158 - BG3 Tangent Quality

Color Placement: This is a BioGeometry method of creating the BG3 centering quality in a space. One takes a small color sample (e.g., a colored paper dot or object, etc.) and moves it around the periphery of a space while measuring for the emergence of the BG3 quality in the whole area, not just the center. The placement must be fine-tuned in small increments of motion in all directions to get the most powerful effect. One can keep fine-tuning to get the combined BG3 and Al- Kareem qualities. A second color can be used to increase the effect. In some cases, a wall can have the same color as the chosen sample placed to create BG3, but it still needs the sample to activate the centering axial connection. When properly placed, the dot or object used should itself have the BG3 quality. The same exercise can be done using any object in the space.

This concept of placing a color or object to create the centering BG3 quality in a space can also be used in design. The colors used on the periphery in BG3 placement can then be expanded into larger areas or used as small elements to harmonize the whole space. Reviving the BG3 dimension in living colors (e.g., using living color settings or 360-degree calibrated dial emissions) will raise the BG3 level in the space. Additionally, color placement techniques can be applied to create BG3 in the whole space.

b. Shifting

This is another principle that resonates with concentric planes of the Psychon pulse. This creates a centering axis like the Ziron axis of the Psychon pulse. Shifting can also be combined with rotation. The principle of using shifting as a form of layering is a way to create depth in motion into the third dimension. It is in alternative to using perspective to create the third dimension of depth on a two-dimensional surface. It was used a lot in wall drawings of ancient temples, where the layering was also a way of creating a hierarchy of importance of the figures. It is also used in the school of "Cubism" in art e.g., Braque, Picasso, and others. This principle is also used in modern architecture to draw the surrounding environment into the building.

c. Single, Double, Multiple, and Fractal Interfaces

Other methods that resonate with the Psychon pulses include the interfacing of boundaries, starting with single and double interfaces and including more elaborate fractals that produce arrays of centers in complementary relationships.

All boundaries of natural shapes have some form of minute fractal interfacing that creates the BG3 quality that enhances the bi-directional communication with the environment. Interfacing walls with the sky has been used in architecture, to achieve the earth-sky connection and bring life force into the building, as well as for functional reasons (e.g., the protection of archers on castle walls).

d. **Transparency**

This is a BioGeometry design principle that introduces a multi-dimensional layering to produce a background order and create BG3 in the design. Here the design is based on the subtle energy quality of an underlying geometrical order. In discussing the archetypal design codes below, we will also deal with another form of transparency that combines the concept of an underlying geometrical pattern with the connective archetypal figures.

5. BioGeometry Motion in Design

There is a first level of motion in design created by virtual rotation, shifting, interfacing, and transparency. There is also a secondary type of motion related to the circulation flow within a building. A straight corridor linking the entrance to the exit should best be placed on a BG3 line connecting power spots. Planning staircases on BG3 lines will move the BG3 quality between floors.

In the design of spaces in modern buildings, it is not always possible to center entrances, windows, and furniture. The doors and windows are usually offset, to one side or the other, creating an imbalanced Energy Key of motion with one side dominating over the other. In such cases, we must introduce some deflection in the plan, or in the furniture layout, that moves the energy flow from the entrance towards the center of the room to restore balance (Figure 159). Every motion of subtle energy in the room, such as air or light from windows, air flow from AC units, or irregular motion due to furniture layout, creates its own Energy Key resulting in a superposition of several Energy Keys. While deflecting the main flow from the door into a centered position, we must also address all the other super-imposed Energy Keys. The best way to do that is by fine-tuning the deflection to produce BG3 in the whole room, which will bring harmony into all the energy flows in the room.

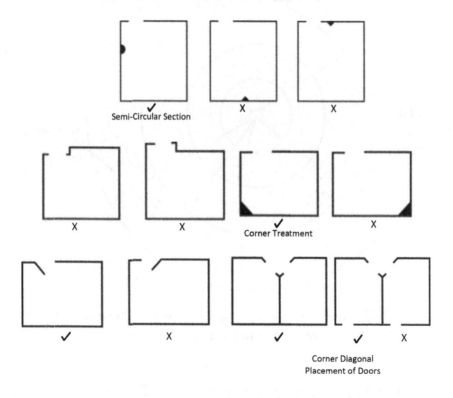

Fig.159 - Example Energy Key Corrections

6. BioGeometry Qualitative Global Scaling System

The interaction of shapes with compression waves creates BG3 patterns in the surrounding area which are related to the dimensions of the shape. The compression waves created will form BG3 points at the wave intersections. A column, for example, will create BG3 rings around it in multiples of its height (Figure 160).

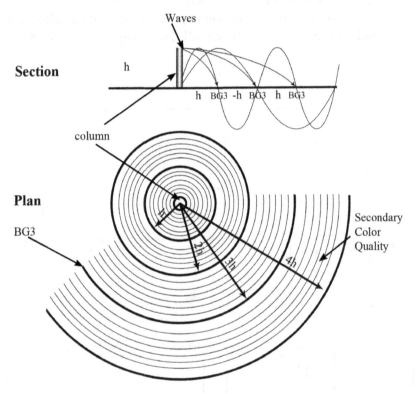

Fig.160 - BioGeometry Qualitative Scaling System Showing Gold Zones (BG3) Around Vertical Objects

A wall slab will create wave patterns with BG3 points based on its height and length. A rectangular block will create wave patterns with BG3 points based on its height, length, and width (Figure 161).

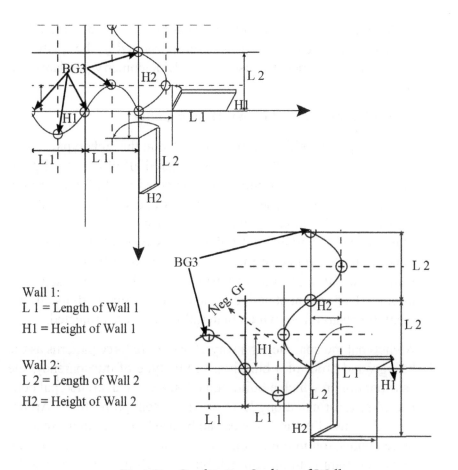

Wall 1:
L 1 = Length of Wall 1
H1 = Height of Wall 1

Wall 2:
L 2 = Length of Wall 2
H2 = Height of Wall 2

Fig.161 - Qualitative Scaling of Walls

We can detect this BG3 pattern and use it in our planning. We can create shapes whose dimensions create BG3 patterns resulting from their exterior dimensions. The interior dimensions of shapes can be tailored to create standing waves of BG3 proportions that are radiated through the opening into the surroundings. This concept was used in the dimensioning of the central holy chambers of temples throughout history. This is like the Lachovsky principle of cutting a metal ring at any point to create a resonant emitter of a compression wave quality with a wavelength equal to the diameter of the ring and its higher and lower harmonics (double or half the diameter). The size of the ring is proportioned to the quality of emission. This concept is used in the BioGeometry pendants and rings.

7. BioGeometry Archetypal Design Codes

This is a special field of design connected to the archetypal source of form that was widely used in the sacred art of Ancient Egypt. This type of art in the tombs was connected to life force through resonance with the archetypal templates that we have introduced earlier in its role in energizing the KA principle of the deceased. The Ancient Egyptians had a deep knowledge of the archetypal dimension, the source of the forming process of living shapes in nature. The harmony and prosperity of everyday life was achieved through the permanent active resonant connection with the archetypal dimension from which material forms were projected.

Archetypal transparency is a way of using life force patterns as the background order of a building. In this type of transparency, the base pattern on which a building is designed is an archetypal connected grid formed along BG3 or Al-Kareem proportions. Archetypal designs of natural shapes can be used to bring their own life force connection into the building. The archetypal shape can be a flower or plant pattern. Animal, bird, or fish patterns can also be used. Geometrical patterns that create BG3 or Al-Kareem Quality (e.g. two squares rotated to form an eight-pointed star), can also be used as a background pattern. The most common pattern is the human archetype pattern, as used in the Luxor temple in Egypt.

8. BioGeometry Material Energy Quality Balancing

The quality of materials and how they affect us is an important part of design. We explained earlier the BioGeometry material balancing solutions: based on the law that a sample of any material contains the total information of the whole, we have developed solutions to harmonize the materials used in all our design products. Using the BioGeometry Material Balancing Wheel, or the more powerful sphere, we can add BG3 to change the subtle energy quality of a minute material sample to induce BG3 into the whole original material (Figure 162). The efficiency of BioGeometry solutions in this field is demonstrated in the paper by Drs. Sawy, Sharaf, et al. (2014) Protective Role of BioGeometry Against Indoor Pollutants of Some Egyptian Building Materials in Adult Male Rats, published in the World Journal of Medical Sciences, 10(3). The BioGeometry design principles introduced earlier can be fine-tuned to change the quality of harmful materials.

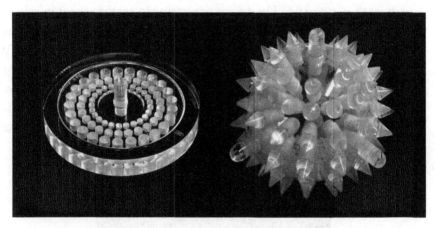

Fig.162 - Material Balancing Wheel (Left) &
Material Balancing Sphere (Right)

9. BioGeometry Signatures

Following the concept of Chinese subtle energy meridians flowing along the periphery of the body, we mapped the flow of subtle energy patterns in the organs of the body. We used those patterns to create open-ended linear diagrams that resonated with each organ's energetic functions. We developed a whole system of BioGeometry Signatures (BioSignatures) to interact and bring the harmonizing, centering, energy quality of sacred power spots into the body's energy functions. Through the uses of BioSignatures and special numerical codes, the energy balance can be specifically applied. They can be worn on the body or used in any form of design. We developed a large number of specific BioSignature patterns. Relationships exist between the internal organs and other parts of the body because of the layout of the meridians. For example, a person with an elbow injury may need a BioSignature of the colon because the large intestine meridian runs through the elbow. Other relationships may exist because of similarities found between some of the shapes of parts of the bodies and the organs, such as the kidneys and ears. BioSignatures have endless possibilities: they were used in decorative strips to restore serotonin levels in the brain as part of a PhD research project, and in another thesis on hyperactivity they were used on textiles worn by children. We produce bed sheets, curtains, cushions, carpets, mugs, caps, and many other products. My daughter, Doreya, published a book with BioGeometry Signature Mandalas for coloring. In the following figure we show pictures of BioSignatures as used in architecture (Figure 163).

Fig.163- BioSignatures Stairs Railing

Recording the Energy Quality of Shape

In 1992, we completed our first digital experiments around recording and preserving the energy quality of shapes and reproducing them by playing the CD on which they were recorded. We collaborated with Hank Kouji in Holland, working in a special recording studio. The result was, as can be expected, a silent CD that did not produce audible sound. In several tests it was found to have the same effect on the surrounding space as if the actual material shape were present. Once the phenomenon was established, we took it further by recording body postures, BioSignatures, tongue movements, thoughts, and so on. The result was our first "Silent Sound CD." We found that if the CD were placed on a table or wall facing out, but not played, the effect was the same as when it was played. We used this concept in BioGeometry solutions in our research with Professor Peter Mols on the apple trees at the parasite research center at the University of Wageningen. We used it successfully in animal farming with sick cows. We also used the CD on the electrical panel of the mobile communication tower in the church tower of Hemberg we mentioned earlier. The silent sound CD has several tracks on it with different energy harmonizing solutions. It is a very efficient way of leveraging multiple BioGeometry solutions on a CD that is very practical to use when traveling. It is a way of taking your environment with you wherever you go.

BioGeometry Alchemy

In explaining how the forming process in nature introduces the life force into matter, we have also uncovered the real essence of the esoteric practice of ancient alchemy. The real goal of the original form of this art was the spiritual transformation of the alchemist through the connection with his or her source and it was not actually a method specifically designed to create gold. That is why certain rituals related to planetary configurations, spells, symbols, and numbers accompanied the chemical processes. The emergence of a grain of gold from lower metals was taken as proof of the spiritual initiation of the alchemist himself.

Alchemy in this context would be a parallel path with the same goal and possibilities as the creation of the BG3 spiritual quality in BioGeometry. In fact, the application of BioGeometrical design principles to chemical processes would bring life force into the products being manufactured. Products enhanced with BioGeometry support the health and bring subtle energy harmony into the environment. With this view, we can understand why the great Isaac Newton had a secret alchemical lab with a library containing all the alchemical treatises known at the time. This part of his life was hidden by his family so his reputation in the scientific world would stay untarnished.

Understanding the essence of the alchemical paradigm could allow modern chemistry to follow the forming process of nature and bring in the much-needed life force. The spiritual preparation required by the alchemical process is not different from the cleansing rituals that all building professions in sacred buildings practiced: the goal was to apply excellence of action, through the incorporation of the universal values in the powers of nature, into the work. This knowledge was transmitted from the master of the building profession to his disciples. This is the real definition of the master who taught the secrets of bringing life force into human activity. Secret worker guilds developed through the ages into modern times, however the essence of Sufi traditions and societies like the Freemasons have all tried to preserve the original secrets of the building professions.

The builders of sacred monuments, from those who erected prehistoric menhirs, down to those who constructed ancient monuments and temples, all adhered to cleansing rituals before touching the stones of the building or the area to preserve the spiritual communication properties of the location and monument. The use of forced labor or slaves of unknown lineage was completely prohibited in any sacred building activity. We noted earlier that in the building, restoration, and rebuilding of the holy mosque in Mecca the records show the lineage and position in the tribe of everyone who worked on the project. These records go back over a thousand years and give detailed accounts of every worker, as well as the location of the stones he worked on. The workers' villages discovered around the pyramid sites in Egypt, show a well-structured community, with all the services we find in a modern-day community. Even the meals recovered in their kitchens, show a healthy diet. In modern times, we find that the famous Spanish architect, Antonio Gaudi, underwent a 28-day cleansing fast, in preparation for his work on the basilica of "La Sagrada Familia" in Barcelona, Spain.

True design is a spiritual interaction with the conscious life force of Creation. As such it must be regarded and practiced as one of the most sacred rituals that must be approached with the proper preparation. In partaking of and integrating into the forming process of nature, through human design activities, a very high level of respect and knowledge is of highest importance.

PART THIRTY-FIVE

Application of BioGeometry Design

The main design criterion of all BioGeometry products is that they include subtle energy, life force-enhancing and health-supporting properties. Below, we can see selected examples from our large selection of BioGeometry design products.

The BioGeometry Tangent Centering Concept and Reverso Chair Collection

The angle formed by the tangent and periphery of a circle moves through all the degrees from zero at the contact point to infinity at the outer end. Connecting the BG3 quality at the contact point on the periphery with the center creates the amplified centering effect that radiates harmony in the surrounding subtle energy environment. The Reverso design concept adds the functionality of tri-fold positioning to create a low lounge chair, a higher seating chair, and a table. The first collection of the Reverso concept uses the tangent to center the connection and achieve the BG3 quality (Figure 164 and Figure 165).

Fig.164 - Reverso Tangenet Chair Manufactured by Sherif Aly Khalil

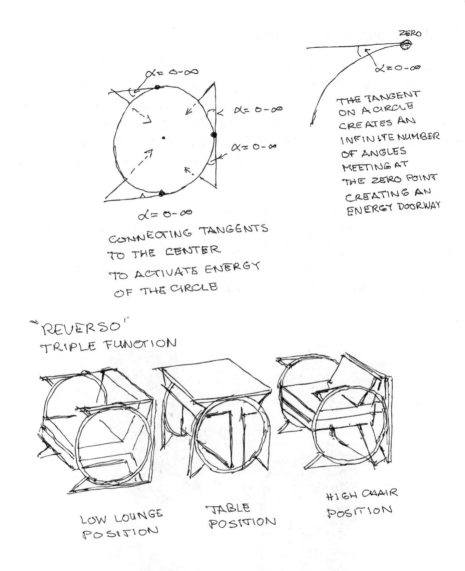

Fig.165 - Reverso Tangent Sketch

We have developed several BioGeometry patterns that can be added, on the sides or back, to give the chairs an extra level of BG3 as well as design styles and characters to suit different uses and tastes.

The BioGeometry Cube System

This cube is designed to provide for the dynamic multi-directional rotation of six virtual energetic cubes superimposed upon each other through the multiple slight angular tapering of the elements. The BG3 harmony inside the cube radiates into the surrounding spaces, resulting in a very powerful harmonizing BG3 cube. It can be used in many types of cubical spaces, for example, in all types of pergolas for terraces or gardens, or cubicles in office spaces.

The cube concept can be used in the design of chairs and tables and other pieces of furniture where the cube shape can be applied (Figure 166 and 167). This chair has the tri-fold functionality of the Reverso concept as well as the dynamic and harmonizing multi-directional rotation of six virtual energetic cubes created by the main cube.

Fig.166 - Reverso Cube Chair with Virtual Rotation

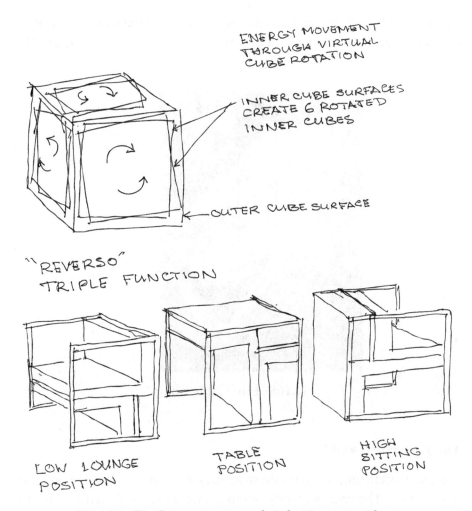

ENERGY MOVEMENT
THROUGH VIRTUAL
CUBE ROTATION

INNER CUBE SURFACES
CREATE 6 ROTATED
INNER CUBES

OUTER CUBE SURFACE

"REVERSO"
TRIPLE FUNCTION

LOW LOUNGE
POSITION

TABLE
POSITION

HIGH
SITTING
POSITION

Fig.167 - BioGeometry Virtual Cube Rotation Chair

The Half Cubic Chair combines the BG3 concept of the square root-of-two diagonal with the virtual rotation of the BioGeometry cube (Figure 168).

Fig.168- Half Cubic Chair

The Perfect Pyramid

In ancient civilizations, pyramid structures were always located on sacred power spots. The energy quality of those spots emanated a natural spiritual quality that harmonized the harmful effect of the Vertical Negative Green at the center of pyramids and hemispheres. Furthermore, certain geometric solutions were used to cancel the harmful effect of Vertical Negative Green. Stepped pyramids, bent pyramid faces and indented sides were among the changes applied to the pyramid shape for this purpose.

In BioGeometry, we used a ninety-degree connection of the diagonals at the apex to create the square-root-of -two quality in the diagonals of the base. In that way the shape of the pyramid created its own harmonizing power spot at the base (Figure 169).

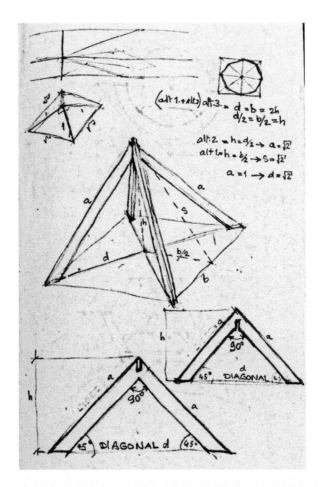

Fig.169 - Square Root of Two Pyramid Creating its Own Power Spot

This concept of integrating the power spot into the pyramid opens endless possibilities of location and design. As an example, it can be used as a pyramid-shaped roof of architectural spaces (Figure 170). In such design configurations, the pyramid energy is not only harmonized, canceling any harmful effects, but creating a power spot with a healing, multi-dimensional communication, which is very useful for spiritual activities, spas, spaces for elderly or special abilities, restaurants and many other activities where an energy-balancing quality is needed.

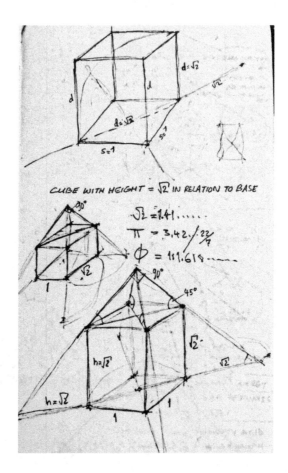

Fig.170 - Cubical Chamber with Harmonizing Pyramid Roof Design

Creating the BG3 Effect Through Interacting Curves

We experimented with several materials to create interaction of curvatures. We experimented with the bending properties of the DuPont Corian material, when heated, to create the world-first one-piece chair that was displayed on the DuPont stand in several exhibitions (Figure 171). We further experimented with bending wood sheets in special mold presses at Meuble El Chark furniture company (Figure 172). This interaction of curves is used in the design of swimming pools creating the BG3 quality in the water (Figure 173).

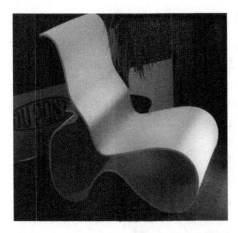

Fig.171 - BioGeometry Corian Chair Manufactured by Karim Fahmy and Exhibited by DuPont

Fig.172 - Meuble El Chark "Flow" Chair

Fig.173 - BG3 Pool

BioGeometry Carpets and Textiles

Several BioGeometry patterns were used in carpet designs produced in Egypt by Mecca Carpets, Oriental Weavers and Prado Carpet company who displayed them at the international Domotex Exhibition in Germany in 2019. (Figure 174). We also designed textiles, curtains, bed sheets, cushions, designed using BioGeometry patterns and BioSignature combinations (Figure 175).

Fig.174 - BG Carpets in Collaboration with Prado at Domotex 2019

Fig.175 - Sample of BioGeometry Curtains

BioGeometry Flooring and Wall Cladding Designs

The Caimi company in Italy, in collaboration with BioGeometry Europe, has produced a Harmonic Shape Design collection of wood and marble flooring, as well as wall claddings and partitions, using BioGeometry brain-shape, modulor, and circle-radii patterns (Figure 176). The inauguration took place in Milan in November 2021.

Fig.176 - BioGeometry Patterns Used in Floor and
Wall Cladding by Harmonic Shapes

PART THIRTY-SIX
Designing for Special Abilities

Around twenty years ago we participated in the Comparative Hepatitis-C Project at the pharmaceutical faculty of the Azhar University in Cairo, Egypt. Scientists were comparing the efficiency of alternative, herbal and pharmaceutical drugs in the reduction of elevated liver enzymes, which are usually high in people with this infection. Each remedy was given to a group of three hundred people. As we were invited at a late stage, we were given the data from other groups, members of which had suffered immune problems with the pharmaceutical drug, which had made their liver condition even worse. We had two hurdles to overcome: the first was the virus's effect on the liver and the second was the side-effect of the earlier treatment which had caused the immune system deficiencies. The best results had come with use of the drug Interferon; it achieved results for half of the patients, but the other half had dropped out because of immune problems. The overall success rate was therefore about 25%.

For the BioGeometry testing, we gave each patient participating in the test an aluminum 5x5 centimeter "chip" to wear with about 200 BioSignatures engraved on it. The first test after twelve days showed a success rate of 90%. Around seventy-five of the three hundred test subjects were willing to pay for an additional PCR test for viral clearance. More than sixty of them showed a negative result indicating total viral clearance. Although the first phase of the project was a success, the second phase was cancelled due to lack of funds. The results achieved through BioGeometry solutions, however, made a huge splash in the media when the dean at the time, Dr. Taha Khalifa, disclosed the results (video on the BioGeometry YouTube channel: www.youtube.com/@biogeometry).

Relevant to our topic here is the notable change in the psychological attitude of the patients treated with the BioGeometry solution. The usual depressive state that resulted from liver disturbances, which is present in people even after a total cure—seemed to have been greatly reduced. This was brought to our attention by Dr. Abdelrahman Alzayyadi, the Head of Cairo's National Institute of Liver Diseases, who could tell which of his patients were wearing our medallion just by looking at them as they came through the door.

Epilepsy in Hemberg

A few years later, in 2003, when we completed the Swiss electro-smog solution in Hemberg, we noticed a marked change in the psychological state of the residents. This showed up in the life quality bar chart in the official study—which we introduced previously—in which the mayor noted there was peace in his community. The aspect most related to our topic was the complete disappearance of epileptic seizures that had plagued many children in the area. However, when they went outside the harmonized area of Hemberg and surroundings, the seizures returned. This was noticed even more in areas with high electromagnetic radiation, like the electronic game area in the mall of a neighboring town. We prepared special bracelets with BioSignatures engraved on them for the children to wear when they went outside Hemberg. The BioGeometry BioSignature bracelets, rings and pendants have proven over the years to reduce epileptic seizures.

Related Postgraduate Research

In the postgraduate theses I supervise I have also noticed an increased interest in electromagnetic stress, as well as the effect of design, from architecture and industrial products, on psychological states and related cognitive challenges. The following is a small selection of such research topics that we have been referring to throughout the text:

The PhD thesis by Dina Howeidy (2013), *A Design Approach Using Bio-Geometry in the Interior Architectural Spaces with Reference to Heal Attention Deficit Hyperactivity Disorder (ADHD)* at Cairo University was done in a special abilities center in Saudi Arabia, that was linked to the university of Riyadh where she worked. The intervention was applied in three stages: stage 1 was an initial analysis, stage 2 included the introduction of the BG Cube from the home kit in the space, attachments on the electric panel and the selection of colors for interior spaces, stage 3 included balancing windows and doors using BioGeometry design principles and BioGeometry tools such as the Dial. Stage 3 also included the use of the Material Balancing Wheel. The table below (Figure 177) shows overall mean score improvements in children's' behavior across the following tested variables: focus and attention, communication, dynamic behavior, behavior, teamwork, independence, hyperactivity, social skills, and academic skills.

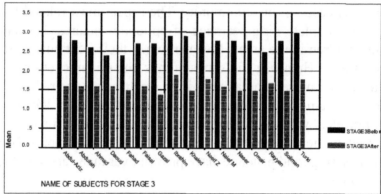

Graph (6): Bar Graph shows a comparison of mean score before and after on stage 3, it's evident from the three graphs that the mean ratings had improved more in stages 2 & 3 than in stage 1.

Fig.177 - BioGeometry Solutions Applied in Special Abilities Center

Another PhD thesis in interior design by Lobna Shaker (2014) of Cairo University, *Modern Technologies Utilizing Energy in Spas,* dealt with the success of BioGeometry Signatures (BioSignatures) as a solution for depression. She chose a BioGeometry Signature for depression used in our pendants to design a decorative strip for the wall (Figure 178). The effect of the design strip was tested on mice, as per the university's recommended protocol. The comparative results shown in the table (Figure 179) indicate that the BioSignature strip restored the level of serotonin in the brain of depressed mice. This result was only matched by one of the three other drugs tested. This was solid proof that brain chemistry can be affected by design in the surrounding environment.

Fig.178 - Decorative BioGeometry Signature Strip

"Depression" BioGeometry Signature Helps Restore Serotonin Levels in the Brain

Number	Control	Depressed Rat	With BioSignature	With Sildenafil	With Sildenafil & Atropine	With Atropine
1	80	45	70	63	57	45
2	75	42	60	64	59	39
3	74	38	65	69	60.5	38
4	76	40	62	71	59.5	43
5	82	41	63	68	58	45
6	88	38	60	60	59	48
7	85	43	58	61	60	39
8	87	39	59	66	55	40
9	79	40	60	67.5	62	39
10	92	43	69	57.5	61	41

*BioGeometry Energy Treatment Vs. Pharmaceutical Drugs Regarding Seratonin Levels

- BioGeometry restores serotonin levels in the brain and compares favorably to drug treatments

- Testing done at Mansoura University medical department, Egypt.

- Ph.D. awarded to Lobna Shaker March 2014 by Cairo University

Fig.179 - Comparative Results of BioGeometry Signature Design Strip

As part of another PhD thesis in Applied Arts Department of Textile and Knitwear, *Usage of BioGeometry Engineering to Obtain Advanced Woven Designs for the Treatment of Depressed Children*, by Nashwa Naji (2016) the same BioGeometry Signature was used in the design of several textile patterns that were tested on hyperactive and aggressive children in the Abbasiya Mental Institution in Cairo. The doctors observed that the group wearing the BioSignature shirts improved markedly in comparison to others wearing similar non-BioGeometry patterns.

Another interesting application of BioGeometry Signatures, as part of a PhD thesis titled *Designing Artistic Activities Depending on BioGeometry to Reduce the Sharpness of Some Child's Negative Behavior*, was done by Doaa Barakaat (2021), at Helwan University in Cairo. She runs a center for special abilities children, to whom she devised several very interesting games using BioGeometry Signatures, some of which were used to evaluate their cognitive faculties. Behavioral observation showed a very positive effect on the children while they played, as well as for some time after.

Architect Ahmed Wafik, designed a special computer chair and keyboard pad, as part of his PhD thesis: Cairo University in 2022, which showed the beneficent effect on the users. The study was conducted on 21 participants in an office environment in New York over two stages. The 1st s

Dr. Mohammed Al-Sawy and Dr. Nevin Sharaf, with a group of scientists from the National Research Center, published the 2018 paper in the journal *Bioscience Research*: "Bio-geometrical Shapes: A New Option for Protection Against Neurodegenerative Insult of Wi-Fi Radiation." used BioGeometry solutions to assess neurological effects of Wi-Fi radiation on rats and the protective role BioGeometry shapes may offer. Results showed that exposed groups experienced a drop in serum melatonin, an increase of serum HSP-70, and an increase of oxidative stress, with BioGeometry shapes able to offer a protective effect evidenced by an increase in serum melatonin, decrease in serum HSP-70, and restoration of oxidative/antioxidant homeostasis.

In his 2019 doctoral thesis titled *Experimental Study on the Effect of Bio geometry Design on Electromagnetic (Wi Fi) Waves In Architectural Spaces*, Khaled Youssef used BioGeometry design principles to develop architectural plans for apartments that protected from the effect of electromagnetic radiation. Several tests were done with architectural models of the apartments, in which wireless routers were placed. Models of apartments without BioGeometry design were used for comparison as well as a control model. Behavioral tests showed that the improved cognitive faculties of mice within the BioGeometry models indicated the effectiveness of the BioGeometry design in comparison to conventional design.

Egyptian Center for Re-integration of Special Abilities

Egyptian President Abdelfattah Al-Seesy asked *"Kodorat"* an Egyptian Autism foundation, headed by Dahlia Soliman CEO and co-founder with Ingy Mashhour, to design a Special Abilities Community Integration Center to be replicated in several regions in Egypt. These founders of *Kodorat* approached me to design the project using BioGeometry principles. We formed a project group with Somaya Bahy and Raef Fahmy who owns a successful architecture firm and who had worked with me for many years.

I introduced the group to our research in the field and we identified additional criteria to be applied with the BioGeometry design principles introduced here earlier. We discovered that 90-degree angles on the inside or outside created stress in sensitive children. We tried circular shapes with similar results. So, we resorted to our well-tried square-root-of-2 principle created by the 90-degree triangle used in our tray to produce the BG3 quality. This generated a 135-degree angle, which allowed us to form an octagon. This angle proved to have the most relaxing beneficent and stress-lowering effect on the children we tested. Architect Raef Fahmy, who worked with me for many years, joined the team and together we started the architecture design along those energy quality concepts. We created an upward rotating energy movement that stimulated brain functions by creating an upward positive spiraling torsion effect. (Figure 180)

Fig.180 - Roof Design Generating Upward Torsion Effect

This reminded us of the beneficent subtle energy effects of teepees, domes, and pyramids. These shapes were originally used according to subtle energy principles that produced harmony and which attracted life force through a multi-dimensional connection achieved through the inherited knowledge of design principles.

It is important in such projects to design a gradual change in space flow and configuration, in light and shade, and in temperature, air circulation, colors, textures, sound, and so on. Long straight corridors and pathways are avoided as they produce a stressful movement of subtle energy.

Special Abilities Reaearch Pavillion

In preparation for the project, we developed the classroom design and built a full-scale version as a wooden frame pavilion in the garden of the

BioGeometry center in Maadi, Cairo, Egypt (Figure 181). We then invited the representatives from *Kodorat* to do the testing on their children. They observed them and used muscle testing, Gas Discharge Visualization (GDV) with electrical finger discharge analysis, and other bio-resonance tests on them both outside and inside the shape. What impressed us the most was how quickly the behavior of hyperactive and autistic children significantly improved. Some parents reported that after two hours of play time inside the pavilion their children showed an improvement in coordination, relaxation, and attention that lasted twenty-four hours.

Consequently, upon the parents' request, we developed a miniature shape of the pavilion in the form of a lampshade to be hung in their child's room (refer to Figure 181). We also designed carpets for the same purpose. Based on our research and experience in this field, we have modified all our products to cater to the needs of this group as we have come to know that these solutions are needed by everybody due to the increased emotional and mental disturbance resulting from electromagnetic radiation and electro-smog.

Fig.181 - Minature Pavillion Shape in the Foreground with
Full-size Research Pavillion in the Background

The Space Program for the Center for the Re-Integration of Special Abilities

One of the main goals of the project is the re-integration of the special abilities children into the community. The space program included medical, commercial, and entertainment services to serve and attract the community. The re-integration also leads to a change of society's outlook towards those with special abilities.

The center in this configuration plays an important role in the transformation of society and this was a main goal in putting together the project components, which included:

1. Classrooms for those of all ages with special abilities and needs.
2. Activity workshops for people with special abilities.
3. Common rooms and meal areas for people with special abilities.
4. Commercial areas serviced by people with special abilities.
5. Entertainment areas, movie theaters, playgrounds, clubs, etc., for people with special abilities and the broader community.
6. Community services, including medical clinics, a pharmacy, maternity services, etc.
7. Hotel facilities for families.

Areas to facilitate the interaction of people with special abilities and members of the broader community was a key element in this project. The goal was to enhance community acceptance so those who were ready could be re-integrated into the community.

EPILOGUE

By Rawya Karim

Many new revolutionizing directions in science that have changed the course of humanity were initially ridiculed and attacked by the mainstream authorities of their time. The Pythagorean School and the Plato Academy suffered extensive persecution in their time and their value was only understood centuries later.

From time to time an outsider, as labeled by Colin Wilson, arises who thinks he can shake the pillars of society. Out of conviction and pure innocence he tries to achieve the "Impossible Dream" of Cervantes' Don Quixote de La Mancha with his humble spear going out to fight the windmills and save the world. Viktor Schauberger in his final despair said: "I hope the whole world is right and I am wrong, otherwise it would be a disaster."

This, however, will not stop us from hoping in pure naivety that this book with a life's work and convictions will coincide with a magic moment in time to achieve the change to a better world. A world where the sacred BG3 quality of life force induces a universal harmony.

About the Author

Dr. Ibrahim Karim (PhD, D.Sc.) is a graduate of the prestigious Federal Institute of Technology (ETH), in Zurich, Switzerland. He heads the family architecture firm "Alemara Consulting House" founded in 1939 by his father, Dr. Sayed Karim, pioneer of modern architecture in the Middle East. He joined the firm he currently heads since 1967.

He is the founder of the qualitative science of BioGeometry: the new architecture and industrial design movement that uses the subtle energy effect of geometrical shapes to induce harmony in our modern technological or natural environments. He currently supervises postgraduate studies on the applications of the science of BioGeometry at several universities.

Dr. Karim is recognized and honored by several institutes for his work in the environment and was chosen as man of the year by the Swiss magazine *Anzeiger* in 2005 for his success in reducing the effect of electro-smog in several regions in Switzerland. These projects were done in collaboration with the Swiss Mediation Authority for Telecommunication & Environment, Swisscom, the main cellular provider, and the local governments. The results received wide media acclaim and were officially documented and featured in several documentaries on Swiss National Television.

Another documentary on Dr. Karim was aired in a Swedish television program where he was chosen one of the hundred most innovative designers of the twentieth century.

For many years, Dr. Karim held advisory positions to the Egyptian ministers of: Health, Culture, Tourism, and Scientific Research, where he headed a research unit at the National Research Center to study the effect of geometric shapes on the life functions of micro-organisms; this latter distinction came after the acknowledgment of his success and the patenting of his research.

Milestones in my Professional Life

The Industrialization of Egyptian Tourism

I have always thrived on challenges, a trait I inherited from my father. One joint journey I am proud to have shared with him in his later years related to the changes we helped make to how tourism was considered in Egypt. In the 1950s and 1960s, my father planned most of the large cities and capitals of the Middle East in his capacity as a consultant to the United Nations. I graduated from the ETH in Zurich in the 1960s and by the early 1970s I had earned a PhD in tourism planning. Upon my return to Egypt, I tried to convince the Ministry of Tourism that by promoting international beach tourism— which had a market that was ten times bigger than the cultural tourism market—we could make tourism the number one industry in Egypt. With a pride derived from our Ancient Egyptian monuments—they are, after all, part of the world's heritage—ministry officials could not embrace the idea that the sand on the beach could bring more tourists than our monuments.

This is understandable: I had come with tourist planning concepts that catered to mass tourism and these were not understood in the early 1970s. We had more than a thousand kilometers of beach on the Red Sea mainland and as much again in the Sinai Peninsula; they could be used twelve months out of every year. This was a unique situation for Europeans who could come to sunny beaches all year long. My father and I approached the Governor of the Red Sea, General Yousef Afifi with our vision to turn this area into an international beach haven. Some people in the government refused our plan as the area had been regarded as a strategic military zone since the war with Israel in 1973. We convinced the governor we could achieve our goal without government support and financing. As a top military general who had received a medal of honor in the war, he convinced the military we could achieve a happy coexistence and got their cooperation.

Within five years, there were more tourist beds in the Red Sea area than all of Egypt combined. Based on this achievement, I was appointed as a consultant to the minister of tourism to officially apply and supervise further implementation of the idea. Later, Governor of Suez General Tahsin Shanan and South Sinai Governor Nour Afifi joined the plan to cover all the Red Sea regions. Tourism became the number one industry in Egypt. None of those involved got the official recognition they deserved, but we did accomplish our mission.

The Original Museum of Civilization

There is another dream I shared with my father, who spent the last years of his life researching the everyday culture of the Ancient Egyptians. Today's Egyptians look at our ancient monuments and relics as artifacts of great achievements of a civilization in Egypt, but they do not fully understand the ancestral links to them. So, together my father and I came up with the idea of a museum of civilization to bring our ancestral culture into our everyday life. In the mid-1980s I was appointed as a consultant to the minister of tourism. This gave me the opportunity to materialize our dream. Officials at the United Nations Educational, Scientific and Cultural Organization (UNESCO) were very supportive of the new concept and invited twelve museum consultants from different countries to work with me on the program. We developed the program in such a way that one could follow every profession and activity in modern society back through history up to its roots in history. One could link our daily activities in the fields of engineering, chemistry, physics, journalism, music, administration, and in our teaching establishments and our medical institutions to their ancient roots and re-construct every aspect of everyman's life. This would help us understand the culture behind all factions of Egyptian society that led to the establishment of their great civilization. All irrelevant small artefacts and tools from the museum's storage vaults would become important in shedding light on related professions. The information to create those backward channels into history was not all available. The museum program therefore included a university teaching and research center that would give out scholarships to professionals in the relevant areas under study. We created the preliminary designs and laid the cornerstone with the head of UNESCO attending an international ceremony and launching an international appeal. Some people within the department of antiquities thought I had made the project too complex, and more, beyond the objective of a traditional museum I was turning the project into a university. Unfortunately, with the death of Mohammed Radwan, minister of culture at the time, as well as that of the prime minister, Dr. Fouad Mohyeldin, the project was buried. A smaller museum of civilization was built thirty years later bearing the name but not the heart. At any rate, I continue in my talks and writings to restore links between our belief systems and to establish our lost connection to our forefathers.

The Integrated Health Projects

In 1970, I was appointed as a consultant to Minister of Health Dr. Mahmoud Mahfouz. In his twelve years as minister we put together a very advanced integrated health plan surpassing anything else in the world at the time. I built a system of linked hospitals, polyclinics, and neighborhood health centers. I used many new concepts, such as assuring functional growth of the projects, in an economical way, which ensured they would start small and grow with time. Several expansion methods were used for the different components. Unfortunately, the whole plan was shelved— before it had even started—with the change of government. The buildings are functioning with traditional methods while all the futuristic concepts were not understood. The whole Integrated Health Plan, devised by a Renaissance man, was too futuristic for its time. I mention it with pride as a milestone of intellectual achievements.

The Last Milestone

This is the most important milestone in all my life. I mentioned the above milestones to show the present one is a much greater endeavor than any of them. The creation of BioGeometry is in many ways, even at its present budding level, the most important of my achievements. The previous milestones are of a local nature. This one is global and urgent, as it restores our lost relationship with the earth at a time when our behavior could cause our demise as species. How this milestone plays out is still uncertain in this material civilization.

Acknowledgements

I would like to start by expressing my deep gratitude to my wife Rawya and as well as my children Sayed, Laila and Doreya who each played a vital role in producing this work. Furthermore, I must mention the important contribution of our staff at BioGeometry Consulting in Egypt for the manufacturing of instruments and tools mentioned in this book. I also thank our instructors and MA/PhD graduates, in Egypt and abroad, for allowing us to print excerpts from their work that has contributed to the academic acceptance of BioGeometry.

I must also acknowledge the support and collaboration that led to the completion of this work.

My friend Robert Sardello, the author of several books in spiritual psychology, reviewed and gave me valuable guidance.

Kris Attard, BioGeometry Instructor for many years, reviewed the manuscript and gave important input.

Susan Crossman, played a vital role in editing and guidance during the journey that brought forth this book.

Randa Baligh, PhD, professor of Egyptology has overseen and offered guidance and information on the parts related to Ancient Egypt.

Yasmeen Morsy, who has been part of our BioGeometry team in Egypt and Canada for many years, has been doing the layout and final form of the book.

Zeinab Hamdy, head of the BioGeometry center in Egypt, and office team, were responsible for background support.

Graziella Zanoletti, director of BioGeometry Europe in Geneva, who is responsible for the translation of my previous books in several languages.

These are only a few of those who collaborated to bring this work to light. The projects presented in this book were done through BioGeometry Consulting, Egypt, BioGeometry Europe, Switzerland, and BioGeometry Energy Systems, Canada, who each gave their support and coordination.

Dr. Robert J. Gilbert, head of Vesica Institute in Asheville, NC, and the first BioGeometry Instructor in North America, hosted the BioGeometry Special Topics events in which several of the topics in this book were first presented to the BioGeometry community.

Thanks to Dr. Michael Maley for allowing us to publish his emails and articles related to his research in BioGeometry.

Georg Gaupp Berghausen, member of BioGeometry Europe and research colleague for many years, has gratefully contributed with an article about his subtle energy research in music and water.

I must again mention, with a lot of gratitude, my daughter Doreya, my wife Rawya, and Yasmeen Morsy, who played the major role in bringing this book to light.

Glossary

Terms and concepts first introduced by Dr. Ibrahim Karim

Al-Kareem Quality Fields—This denotes the expansion of the positive QL-Torsion quality created by the central BG3 at the vortex transition into the whole torus surface. This is done by empowering the central BG3 quality. The Al-Kareem Quality Field induces positive QL-Torsion creating a life force energizing-space time environment. The label Al-Kareem comes from the Divine attribute Al-Kareem, meaning the benevolent in the Arabic language, which activates this state in the toroidal fields.

Basic Dials have all the color qualities on the periphery but are not directly connected to the center. It is important to limit the connectivity to the center to have a complete separation between the colors to improve their detection by the pendulum.

BG3—This is a label for the centering energy quality of the sacred power spots of the earth that BioGeometry reproduces through a geometric design language. It is detected through the scientific method of Physical Radiesthesia through three subtle energy qualities. These are the higher harmonics of Ultraviolet, Gray/Negative Green, and Gold, but they are not its components, as all these colors merge into its one colorless aspect. We refer to it in BioGeometry as **"the ONE energy quality."**

BioGeometry integrates the concept of the transcendental doorway of the ONE quality into a multi-dimensional extension of the science of Universal Harmonics. Here the fixed string points become transcendental doorways accessing a range from zero to infinity. This is the cornerstone of BioGeometry and the Physics of Quality. We believe similar concepts must have been at the core of the great sciences of ancient civilizations.

BG3 Number Series—In contrast to mathematical quantitative series where all numbers are mathematically related, the numbers in a qualitative series have no mathematical relationship between them. All the numbers in the series have the same subtle energy quality. Expressed in a color scale, for example, all the numbers would resonate with the same color. The BG3 series contains numbers that all have the BG3 quality.

BG28 Disk—This is a non-polarized disk showing the BG3 radiation from the center on the periphery in the form of twenty-eight inter-related radial angular emanations. It expresses the BG3 creation of life force in its surroundings. It does not have a second overlaid pointer disk as there is no polarization involved.

BioGeometry—This refers to the measurement of the life force of the earth.

BioGeometry Brain Shapes—These are two shapes derived from the motion in the vertical vortex of a torus showing a slight bulge at the center where it intersects with the central BG3 plane. This vortex with a central bulge is the one connected to the toroidal space-time dimension, which puts it into resonance with the left-brain sensory perception mode. The other vortex expresses the horizontal movement from the periphery to the central vortex at the crossing point where the bulge is. It expresses the extra sensory dimensions beyond space-time perceived in the right-brain mode. The brain shapes are used in different ways to enter into resonance with the two hemispherical perception modes respectively.

BioGeometry Color and Object Balancing—This is a process of placing a color or an object in a certain position in the periphery of a space to create a BG3 quality in the whole space. This is also the position where the color or object will have the BG3 quality in it indicating a centering effect and life force connection.

BioGeometry Design Principles—Creating a BG3 multi-dimensional vortex using design principles of centering, rotation, shifting, interfacing, transparency, and proportion.

BioGeometry Dial Instruments—The BioGeometry dial concept arranges the different qualities on the periphery of a polarized circle, so they are all related to a BG3 center with a second overlaid polarized disk as a pointer for calibration to a certain quality on the lower disk.

The BioGeometry Energy Key—This is a horizontal section through the torus created by a horizontal linear motion. It is used in architecture to analyze the balance of energy qualities in a space.

BioGeometry Harmonic Scaling—All shapes interact with the surrounding subtle energy medium to create compression wave patterns. There are recurring nodal points in those radiated patterns that are related to the dimensions of the shape. These are BG3 patterns. The simplest example of this qualitative geometrical phenomenon is found around a simple column, where we find concentric BG3 rings with horizontal radii in multiples of its height. The more parameters a shape has the more complex the BG3 pattern becomes. This concept can be used in architecture, and interior and landscape design, as well as for the placement of objects to enhance the BG3 quality in a space.

BioGeometry Material Balancing—The same concept as color balancing is applied in the material balancing wheel where a small sample of a material is placed in one of the holes in the polarized circular disk where it shows maximum BG3. The source where the sample was taken will also show BG3. This is especially useful with materials with harmful qualities. There are two versions of this tool, one is disk shaped and the other more complex one is in the form of a sphere; this allows fine tuning of the sample by movement in all directions.

BioGeometry Modulor and Lambdoma—The living quality of numbers is dependent on their forming process and the mathematical relationship of their components as well as their qualities. Numbers resulting from multiplication or division have a stronger connection to the centering quality. We have therefore used this concept to enhance the existing connectivity of numbers with the BG3 quality. The first table is based on multiplication and its title is an homage to Le Corbusier, a main pioneer of modern architecture who used the multiplication of the golden mean proportion to create two scales he called *"Modulor."* In another BG3 table of proportions we used division in the form of multiplication with fractions— like the way Pythagoras produced musical notes through mathematical proportions—in a pattern connecting numbers arranged vertically with their fractions arranged horizontally; this is referred to as *"Lambdoma."*

Pythagoras spent twenty-two years in the temples of Egypt and is considered the father of modern Western music, mathematics, and philosophy, which together represent one of the foundations of Western science. As an homage to this great man, we have used the label *"Lambdoma"* for our second table of BG3 proportions enhanced by division.

BioGeometry Qualitative Harmonic Measurement—BioGeometry methods of physical qualitative measurement differ from all those of conventional and physical types of Radiesthesia. BioGeometry puts forward a complete coherent holistic science of quality with its own measurement system referred to as *"BioGeometry Quality Measurement."* It is based on the Physics of Quality, which has BG3—the ONE quality—as its cornerstone and it takes Universal Harmonics to a higher level of qualities merging in a complete unity. BioGeometry is all about accessing life force from spiritual levels to achieve the forming process of nature. The BG3 multi-dimensional vortex where BG3 translates into life force is the main domain of work in BioGeometry. Detection instruments of conventional dowsing and Radiesthesia are not designed or conventionalized for this type of work. BioGeometry has developed special tools and instruments to serve its research and practical use of BG3 and life force.

BioGeometry Quality Measurement—BioGeometry Quality Measurement aims to put an end to the confusion caused by different paradigms where the detection of subtle energy is regarded as a sensitivity to radiation. This led to the use of radio wave concepts, which were popular in the 1950s to describe a scientific form of dowsing that was labeled Radiesthesia, meaning extending the sensitivity of the senses to include radiation. This takes us into a controversial understanding of the quantitative sensing of waves. BioGeometry does not measure life force quantitatively but rather through its quality of effect on the human subtle energy system. In BioGeometry the Physics of Quality is a pure science of universal qualitative interactions beyond the quantitative vibratory confinement of the senses. BioGeometry must be looked at through its universal multi-dimensional qualitative nature. Now that we are taking the path into the deeper scientific understanding of the Physics of Quality, we have coined the new label "BioGeometry Quality Measurement," which stresses the sensitivity to quality. Quality is the mechanism of the universal multi-dimensional harmonic exchange of information. It is the unifying principle in Creation.

BioGeometry Signatures—This refers to special linear open-ended diagrams that enter into resonance with subtle energy flows in the body and organs. These diagrams are fine-tuned to introduce a harmonizing quality to restore the proper subtle energy function.

BioNumerals—Refers to the application of numerical repetition qualities in the forming of BioGeometry Signatures.

BioSignatures—When used in context with BioGeometry this is a shortcut referring to BioGeometry Signatures.

Centering—This concept goes far beyond the usual concept of the center of balance of a geometric figure. This is a main concept in BioGeometry, which expresses the flow of the BG3 quality of the center as a transcendental multi-dimensional vortex to fill the whole shape. The whole shape becomes qualitatively a multi-dimensional center that we refer to as centered. When a shape is centered, it has the quality of a sacred power spot.

Geometrical Resonance with Planes of Nature—The discovery of a resonant connection between the planes of nature and their sub-planes and certain geometrical shapes.

Law of Time—The manifestation of duality through a Ziron pulse is based on the Law of Time governing the pulse to put the opposing polarities into a balancing motion ensuring their complementarity in the stability of Creation. It is the pulse-forming law around a central Ziron axis. This law governs all forms of pulses in all dimensions of Creation from the tiniest to the largest. This is my concept of Joseph Campbell's "hero with a thousand faces," where time emerges with a different personality in endless modes of perception as life's inseparable companion.

Living Color Dials show the specific point within the color range that is strongly connected to the center and manifesting BG3 in its peripheral position. These points will have the main color balanced by all the others in the background. In nature, this is how living colors are an expression of a quality attribute within the overall unity.

There are also **Life Force Dial** sets. Each dial is calibrated simultaneously to two living colors to measure life force components.

The Physics of Quality—This label has been introduced to denote a new type of physics to study the effect of objects or actions on the human subtle energy system. Here, the human being is at the center of measurement. As a science of quality, it is based on a combination of Ancient Universal Harmonics and the centering harmonizing quality of sacred power spots. The Physics of Quality introduces a practical spiritual harmonizing quality at the core of ancient universal harmonics.

Primordial QL-Torsion—This refers to the Psychon torsion. It is the primordial QL-Torsion measured in the original spiraling pulse of the Ziron to form the eight levels of the Psychon. In the primordial spiraling effect, we identify the outward and inward directions of motion as mental and emotional attributes.

Psychon—This is the archetypal geometric configuration at the core of Creation that manifests in a harmonic resonance from the smallest to the largest dimensions. It is the result of the bidirectional Ziron pulse enfolding as two eightfold spiraling motions around the central Ziron axis. The outward radiating spiral is the mental archetype while the inward movement is the emotional one. This results in eight psychic space-time.

QL-Torsion—The original concept of torsion is a twisting motion resulting from the effect of a change of state—like in the melting of ice—on an isolated pendulum hanging under it. This describes objective subtle energetic effects excluding human intervention. In BioGeometry, where the human being is the instrument of measurement of the quality of effects, we place the human hand between the melting ice cube and the pendulum. The body as an open energy system is continuously affected by the torsion within the external subtle energy that affects the quality and balance of the body's own torsion that we refer to as QL-Torsion. The torsion in subtle energy affects the body, which in turn produces its own spiraling reaction causes a rotation of the pendulum which indicates the quality of torsion as sensed by the human subtle energy system. The mental-emotional aspects within the QL-Torsion of the body express the quality-of-life force.

Qualitative Scales of Measurement—It is important to distinguish between color and color quality. A science of quality must have scales of measurement to detect the different qualities through resonance. In all systems of Radiesthesia the use of colors was based on sympathetic categorization of things into colors. The concepts were a vague mixture of quantity and quality. It was not until the revival of Pythagorean Harmonics in the 1950s and 1960s by the Swiss Hans Kayser that a pure science of quality could be developed. This led to the development of a pure Physics of Quality in BioGeometry. When using a quality scale like color, for example, we use the quality measured on color in the visible range and use it as an abstract unit in a qualitative scale applicable in all ranges beyond the original visible range. In the visible color range, we can quantitatively measure its frequency.

Beyond the visible range it becomes an abstract quality that can be found in any frequency. As an abstract quality it is interchangeable with units in other scales, like musical notes, and angles. The frequency of a musical note is different in every octave with a different string length. A unit in a qualitative scale does not have a specific frequency but can exist in any frequency as a proportion between wavelength and amplitude. Wavelength is a quantity, but the quality is in the wave shape. This concept is unfortunately misunderstood by practitioners of Radiesthesia and subtle energy sciences, and manufacturers and users of vibrational healing devices.

Time Pulse—The seemingly present subtle energy in the background of Creation is the result of infinitely fast pulses emerging from the nothingness of the Ziron on countless dimensions simultaneously forming stable realities on the different planes of nature from the physical, the vital, the emotional, the mental and the spiritual.

Toroidal Fields of Time-Space Dimensions—These are the fields in the form of a multi-layered torus created by a linear motion in the form of a central vortex in a background medium. These are always compression wave fields in nature regardless of the type of central linear motion, which could be electromagnetic or compression in nature.

Ziron—This is the Divine center beyond duality or time and space, a doorway to the zero state from which infinity the ONE emerges as the first number that contains infinity and from which it enfolds. The Ziron as a vortex tunnel or window to the zero state before the creation of time and space, is non-localized and exists everywhere at the same time. The Ziron contains the essence of all the Laws of Creation. It is in a way the light that projects Creation so that by reflecting backwards on Creation, we find only this light that carries all the information that manifests as Creation.

General Concepts and Terms Used in this Book

1. **Archetypal Dimension**

   We are here concerned with a special category of archetypes behind the forming process in nature. These are the subtle energy patterns on which physical shapes form. They can be

   regarded as the perfect templates of physical shapes. The interaction of the evolution of shapes with environmental effects produces slight imperfections that result in individualization. The slight dynamic tension of imperfection creates a certain attraction we feel as the natural beauty of life. The archetypal templates of perfect shape do not radiate the beauty of imperfection but instead they create the harmony and balance that will keep the individuality within natural limits.

2. **Categorization of Humanity**

   I will here examine this categorization of humanity based on the perception of inner and outer worlds further, because it enables the differentiation of human beings into different species that perceived and interacted with their world differently. Some scholars have categorized humanity based on the slow shift of focus of perception in the brain hemispheres. The famous Swiss psychologist Karl Gustav Jung categorized humanity according to the location of the focus of perception in the brain hemispheres. We have elaborated and evolved his analysis to serve within the Physics of Quality. "Primitive" humanity was totally focused in the right-brain mode, which made people live within a subconscious interaction governing their everyday life. The collective herd mind dominated over individuality. Sensory-based interactions were governed by intuition. People lived in unity with the environment as part of the forces of nature.

As the focus moved towards the left-brain mode, but remained anchored in the right-brain perception, tools of sensory quantitative interaction were projected from the right brain into the left brain enabling it to consciously perceive and navigate in the vast subconscious realms. The personification process of left-brain perception created a subtle materialization of the subconscious dimensions. People personified and interacted with the Laws of Nature, which became living entities in their perceived reality. Those new left-brain tools also had quantifying functional practical applications in their everyday life. Hieroglyphs, numbers, letters, colors, and musical notes were imbued with a double existence: one served the birth of civilization and the other served in internal communications with the personified Laws of Nature.

This double aspect of the new tools provided the quantification of qualities in the sensory mode of left-brain perception and empowered everyday actions through their connection with higher harmonizing qualities of Creation. The sense of the sacred was born. This marked the rise of a new human species Jung labeled "Ancient" humanity.

In the Physics of Quality, we have seen the brain projects the perceived sensory reality we live in. It therefore follows that a dramatic change in hemispherical focus of perception will cause a complete shift in the external perceived reality. The world will not be the same anymore. This happened with the complete movement of focus of perception into the left-brain mode. Humanity lost a large part of its holistic perceived reality. Humanity also lost one of its consciously perceived dimensions and became secluded from the Laws of Nature—separated from the environment—and lost its unity with the forces of Creation. The direct perception of the sacred in their world and the Divine order of Creation was lost. This great shift heralded the appearance of modern humanity. This new species created a very advanced material and technological civilization, while closing the door to confine the right-brain extrasensory dimension to the subconscious levels. Modern civilization has thus cut itself off from the conscious perception of life force. Modern humanity created an advanced material civilization at its own cost.

Jung sees a new category slowly budding which he refers to as contemporary humanity. This category relates to a small fraction of modern humans trying to open the door to the other side. Unfortunately, this group that provides a new hope has been polluted by the materialistic greed of modern society. Innocent people wanting to tread this path are pulled onto false paths full of delusion and false gurus. BioGeometry introduces a practical scientific path leading to the placement of focus of perception at the center between the brain hemispheres. Achieving a true "centering" creates the spiritual doorway that expands Consciousness into universality through a qualitative language of communication.

3. **Compression Waves**

Any mechanical impulse or motion produces ripples in the surrounding medium that are referred to as compression waves. They move in a form of compression and rarefaction when traveling through a medium. They are also referred to as longitudinal waves because their inner motion is in the direction of their propagation. They are also called pressure waves because they produce increases and decreases in pressure. They can move in one plane or in a spiraling rotation. Compression waves are not electromagnetic in nature, so they are not bound by the speed of light. They can be slower like audible sound, water, and air waves or faster—like inaudible hyper sound. Slower compression waves within the physical dimension follow the linear flow of space-time. Compression waves moving faster than the speed of light are not bound by physical time-space criteria.

All waves outside the boundaries of the speed of light are some sort of compression waves. From our point of view, they can travel forwards or backwards in time and can be simultaneously present in different dimensions. In that context, they are also not bound by the linear flow of compression waves as we know them. They can be multi-directional and multi-dimensional. This means that we regard compression waves as a broad category with many different configuration patterns. In this sense, emotional and mental subtle energy can be regarded as different forms of compression waves and fields. Whatever the configuration of compression fields they are all connected through a resonance of quality resulting in an overall unity.

4. **Electromagnetic Waves**

Electromagnetic waves come in many types. From highest to lowest energy, we have gamma rays, X-rays, ultraviolet radiation, visible light, infrared radiation, and radio waves that also include microwaves. These are a form of wave moving at the speed of light. Electromagnetic waves are composed of oscillating magnetic and electric fields. The electric field and the magnetic field of an electromagnetic wave run perpendicular to one another. They also run perpendicular to the direction of propagation of the wave. The inner movement shaping the wave is referred to as transversal. Waves can move along their two planes or in spiraling rotation. We live in an electromagnetic universe and the atomic particles are manifestations of electromagnetic charges, a sort of coagulation of waves into matter. The electromagnetic universe moves in a thin band around the speed of light. It is therefore a very limited vibratory dimension of the absolute reality of Creation.

5. **Left-Brain and Right-Brain Modes**

This seeming localization in the brain hemispheres is a way of describing the two modes of perception in the brain. Each mode is dominantly present on one side but functions in a bilateral way where different parts of the brain are involved. The left-brain perception refers to the sensory, analytical, interactive, quantifying, space-time restricted, personifying, ego-centric, conscious perception in the waking state. The right-brain mode refers to an extrasensory, holistic, unifying, patternmaking, non-space-time restricted, universal unconscious perception. The left-brain perception is materialistic and induces identification with the body and separation from surroundings, while the right-brain creates a sense of universality and unity with the environment.

While the left-brain everyday awareness seems to be localized in the sensory parts of the brain, several parts of the body are active in the unconscious perception of the right-brain mode. Brain-type neurons are found in the heart and intestines. In contrast to the brain in the head, those secondary brains do not seem to be connected to sensory perception and do not rise into our everyday conscious awareness. They work more on a sub-conscious extra-sensory level, giving rise to such concepts as the "intellect of the heart" and "gut feeling."

6. **Life Force**

Life is an animating composite force emanating with the first pulse of Creation. It is the enfoldment of the latent potential attributes in the state of undifferentiated nothingness and everything into the dualistic time-space dimensions of Creation. Its universal omnipresent primordial components include Consciousness, time-space, mind radiation, attractive forces of love and gravity, and all the other endless attributes that emerge as life as we know it on different levels and dimensions. In its omnipresence, we describe it as the background subtle energy.

7. **Scalar Waves**

Scalar waves are produced by the flow of two electromagnetic waves of the same frequency that are out of phase with half a wavelength shift in relation to each other so that the amplitudes cancel each other out. This produces a scalar wave or field in the surrounding medium. Scalar waves are not electromagnetic in origin; they are a form of compression wave. Scalar waves are in resonant quality exchange with their origin and carry the stress produced by electromagnetism on all forms of life in their fields. This phenomenon, which travels for large distances beyond the boundary of the original electromagnetic field, is called "electro-smog."

According to Dr. Konstantin Meyl of Germany, an authority in this field, electro-smog, as well as harmful Earth energy grids, are scalar compression wave phenomena. BioGeometry can therefore reduce the harmful stress of electro-smog by placing shapes designed to emit BG3 into the compression fields. This is the method that has produced successful results in the Swiss regions of Hemberg and Hirschberg. Swisscom, the government mobile communication services provider, has acknowledged our scientific explanation of the phenomenon as we proved its efficiency in solving the health problems in those regions.

8. **Subtle Energy**

This term refers to the unperceived background living medium in which all Creation takes place and from which everything materializes in different dimensions of Creation.

9. **Torsion**

This term is applied in many disciplines in different ways. In general, it describes a twist resulting from an external action affecting a system. What concerns us in this book is the twist that is found in subtle energy resulting from changing states of objects within it. Nikolai Aleksandrovich Kosyrev in Russia has shown that melting ice causes a completely isolated pendulum in a glass jar underneath it to rotate. The pendulum rotates in the opposite direction when water freezes to form ice. The first is a state of energy dissipation (entropy), while the second represents energy gain (negentropy). The energy dissipation from one system is regained in other systems. This experiment shows that subtle energy is in twisting states in both directions. The effect of the direction of twist on subtle energy on the human subtle energy system produces QL-Torsion as a rotation of a pendulum held in the hand. In BioGeometry, the Time Pendulum or the BG12 pendulum can be used to indicate the quality of QL-Torsion.

Bibliography

The development of the science of BioGeometry and the Physics of Quality is based on fifty years of research within practical applications, environmental solutions, and post-graduate work. It is not based on references. In my library—which contains thousands of books—as well as in my studies and multi-cultural upbringing, I stood on the shoulders of giants who formed my worldview and brought me to where I am today. When picking up a few books as suggested reading, I had to be selective, but the others are all well and alive behind every word I write. So, here are a few book suggestions from my personal library. Some are referenced in the book and the rest are suggestions for further reading. My library contains books in English, French, German, and Arabic. I concentrated in this bibliography on those in English, only mentioning others when directly related to the topics of the book.

1. Basalama, Hussein Abdullah. *The History of the Holy Kaaba.* Saudi Arabia, Tihama, 1982
2. Bauval, Robert, & Hancock, Graham. *Talisman, Sacred Cities, Secret Faith.* Doubleday, Canada 2004.
3. Bélizal, Antoine de, et Morel. P. A., *Physique Micro-Vibratoire et Forces Invisibles.* January 1, 1991.
4. Blavatsky, Irena, *The Secret Doctrine.* The Theosophical Society, 1888
5. Blavatsky, Irena, *Isis Unveiled.* The Theosophical Society, 1892
6. Budge, E.A. Wallis. *The Gods of the Egyptians.* New York: Dover Publications; 1969.
7. Buehler, Bosco, *Hemberg Harmonization with BioGeometry.* GIBB, Information Organization for Building Biology, 2004 ISBN: 3 033 00391 5.
8. Chaumery, Léon, et Bélizal , Antoine De, *Radiesthesie Vibratoire*
9. Corbin, Henry, *Alone with Alone.* Princeton University Press, March 2,1998.
10. Cott, Jonathan. *Isis and Osiris.* USA: Doubleday, 1994.

11. Coué de la Chataineraie, Emil, *The Essential Writings*. Kessinger Publishing, LLC, October 2005.
12. Church, Dawson *Genie in your Genes* https://www.amazon.com/Genie-Your-Genes-Epigenetic-Intention/dp/1604150114

13. De Lubics, Schwaller, *The Temple of Man*. Simon Shuster/Amazon.
14. De Lubics, Schwaller, *Esotericism and Symbolism*. Simon Shuster/ Amazon.
15. De Lubics, Schwaller, *Symbol and Symbolic: Egypt, Science and Evolution of Consciousness*. Simon Shuster/Amazon.
16. Devereux, Paul. Earth Memory: *Sacred Sites-Doorways into Earth's Mysteries*. Llewellyn Publications, 1992.
17. Devereux, Paul. *Stone Age Sound Tracks*. Vega. Brewery Road, London, 2001.
18. Devereux, Paul. *Shamanism and The Mystery Lines, Ley lines, Spirit Paths, Shape- Shifting and Out of Body Travel*. Great Britain, Quantum 1992.
19. Enel, *Premiers Pas en Radiesthesie*. Dar El Maaref Publishing, Cairo.
20. Enel, *Radiesthesie Thérapeutique*. Dar El Maaref Publishing, Cairo.
21. Enel, *Le Cancer*, Dar El Maaref Publishing. Cairo.
22. Enel, *Trilogie de la Rota Celeste, trois traités d'astrologie et de cabale*. Editions Paul Derain, 1960, Lyon, France.
23. Enel, *Origines de la Genese et l'enseignement des temples de l'ancienne Egypte*. Maisonneuve et Larose. Paris, 1985
24. Enel, *The Mystery of Life and Death, According to the Teachings of Ancient Egyptian Temples*. Amazon. (Originally *Mystères de la vie et de la mort d'après les enseignements des Temples de L'Ancienne Egypte*) translated by André Guy and Lucie Guy, Paris Editions G.P. Maisonneuve et Larose, 1966.
25. Flanagan, Patrick, *Pyramid Power, The Science of the Cosmos*. Amazon.com, Publisher Phi sciences, March 2, 2016
26. Fulcanelli, *Les Mystères Des Cathedrales: Esoteric interpretation of the Hermetic Symbols of the Great Work*. (French), Ethos, Amazon. com

27. Gebbensleben, R.: *Hyperschall (Hypersound)– Universeller Informations- und Energieträger.* Teil 1: *Entstehung und Eigenschaften.* raum&zeit, Nr. 190/2014, S.62 - 66, Teil 2: *Auswirkungen auf den Menschen.* raum&zeit, Nr. 191/2014, S.64 – 69, Teil 3: Gefährdungspotenzial und Nutzen. Raum & zeit, Nr. 192/2014,Guthrie, Kenneth Sylvan and Fideler, David. *The Pythagorean Sourcebook and Library: An Anthology of Ancient Writings Which Relate to Pythagoras and Pythagorean Philosophy.* Michigan, USA Phanes

28. Ivanovics, Milena, *Memento 13 Memento 13: Remembering the Self Through the Geometry of God's Love*, Amazon.com

29. Karim, *Ibrahim, Back to a Future for Mankind*, BioGeometry Energy Systems, CreateSpace May 5, 2010, Amazon.com

30. Karim, Ibrahim, *BioGeometry Signatures*, BioGeometry Energy Systems, CreateSpace, September 20, 2016, Amazon.com

31. Karim, Doreya, *BioGeometry Signature Mandalas*, CreateSpace, May 18, 2016, Amazon.com

32. Kayser, Hans, Akroasis Kayser, Hans. *Akróasis: The Theory of World Harmonics* Boston: Plowshare, Press,1964.

33. Kayser, Hans, *Textbook of Harmonics.*, Published by Sacred Science Institute, Idyllwild, CA, 2006.

34. Lüdeling, Hartmut. *Handbuch Der Radiaesthesie: Schwerpunkt Grifflängentechnik* (German), Drachen Verlag, January 1, 2006

35. Levi, Eliphas, *Le grand arcane, ou l'occultisme dévoilé* (*The Great Secret, or Occultism Unveiled*), Chamuel Publishers, Paris,1868 (French), Amazon November 15, 2012.

36. Lamy, Lucie, *Egyptian Mysteries New Light on Ancient Knowledge*, Thames, and Hudson. 1981.

37. Maes, Wolfgang, *Stress durch Strom und Strahlung*, Fuchs Druck. GMBH. Miesbach 2000.

38. McTaggart, Lynn, *The Intention Experiment*: Attria: reprint edition February 5, 2008.

39. Mendes, João and Mendes, Ramiro, *Sound—The Fabric of Soul, Consciousness, Reality, and the Cosmos*, Quantum World Enterprises, LLC, January 1, 2017

40. Mermet, Abbé and Clement, Mark, *Principles and Practices of Radiesthesia*, Watkins Publishing, January 1, 1959,Amazon.com.
41. Mettler, M.A. *Atmospharische Reizstreifen*, Metaphysik 2000. Zurich: Moser Verlag, 1986.
42. Mettler, M.A., Das Globalnetzgitter. Eine Darstellung und Untersuchung der in der Atmosphäre vorkommenden Reizstreifen, Verlag RGS, Sant Gallen 1981.
43. Mettler, M.A., *Atmosphärische Reizstreifen. Das Maß-System antiker Völker*, Moser Verlag
44. Mettler M.A., *Das Netzgitterhandbuch. Eine umfassende Darstellung der tellurischen und atmosphärischen Reizstreifen und Zonen*, Moser Verlag, Zürich, 1990.
45. Mettler's Grid-Handbook. *Fundamentals and basic Research in Geobiology*, Zürich, 1995.
46. Merz, Blanche *Kraftorte der Schweiz* AT Verlag, 2000.
47. Meyl, Konstantin, *Scalar Waves*, meyl.eu, 2003
48. Mueller, Aemilius, *Aesthetik der Farbe*, Chronos Verlag, July 1, 2018, Amazon
49. Odermatt, Walter, *Die Wissenschaftstheorie*, Odermatt Walter Universität, Anthropos AG, Stutzring, Luzern, Switzerland.
50. Ramachandran, V.S., Blakeslee, Sandra, and Sacks, Oliver. *Phantoms in the Brain: Probing the Mysteries* 1999.
51. Sardello, Robert, *Facing the World with Soul, The re-imagination of Modern Life*, Steinerbooks, February 1, 2004.
52. Sardello, Robert, *Silence: The Mystery of Wholeness*, North Atlantic Books, November 25, 2008.
53. Scott, Walter, *Hermetica, Introduction, texts and translation*, Shambala Publications, Boston. 2001.
54. Thomas, Gail, *Healing Pandora,*
55. Schaad, Ruth, The Miracle of Hemberg, St.Gallen 2007.
56. Von Franz, Marie-Louise, *Time, Rhythm and Repose* ISBN 0-500-81016-8

57. Von Franz, Marie-Louise, *Number and Time* ISBN 0-8101-0532-2 (1974).
58. Von Pohl, Gustav Freiherr, *„Erdstrahlen als Krankheitserreger – Forschungen auf Neuland"* in 1932, republished in 1978. The new title also has the wording *"Erdstrahlen als Krebsursache und Krankheitserreger"*, meaning Earth radiation as cause of cancer and other illnesses- The English title is *"Earth Currents - Causative Factor of Cancer and Other Diseases"* [ISBN 3772494021] - published in Munich in 1932.
59. Reich, Wilhelm, *Orgone Energy*
60. Reichenbach, *Od Energy*
61. Segal, Robert A. *The Gnostic Jung*, Mythos. Princeton, NJ: Princeton University Press, 1992.
62. Shauberger, Viktor, & Coats, Callum, *Eco-Technology 1: The Water Wizard - The Extraordinary Properties of Natural Water* (1998, Gateway Books, ISBN 9781858600482)
63. Schauberger, Viktor & Coats, Callum: Eco-*Technology 2: Nature as Teacher - New Principles in the Working of Nature* (1999, Gateway Books, ISBN 9781858600567)
64. Schauberger, Viktor & Coats, Callum: *Eco-Technology 3: The Fertile Earth - Nature's Energies in Agriculture, Soil Fertilisation and Forestry* (1999, Gateway Books, ISBN 9781858600604)
65. Schauberger, Viktor & Coats, Callum: *Eco-Technology 4: Energy Evolution - Harnessing Free Energy from Nature* (2000, Gateway Books, ISBN 9781858600611),
66. Sheldrake, Rupert. *The Hypothesis of a New Science of Life: Morphic Resonance.* 4th ed. Rochester, Vermont: Park Street Press, 1995
67. Steiner,Rudolf, Theosophy: *An Introduction to the Spiritual Processes in Human Life and the Cosmos* (1904) ISBN 0-88010-373-
68. Steiner, Rudolf, *Goethean Science* (1883–1897)
69. Steiner, Rudolf, *Theory of Knowledge Implicit in Goethe's World-Conception* (1886)
70. Swanson, Claude, *The Synchronized Universe*, Poseidia Press, Tucson, AZ (2003-2005), ISBN 0-9745261-0-X, LCCN 2003097147 AZ, 2003

71. Swanson, Claude, *Life force: The Scientific Basis*, Poseidia Press, Tucson, AZ (2009),
72. Swanson, Claude, *Science of the Soul, The Afterlife and The Shift*, Poseidia Press, Tucson, AZ, 2018.
73. Thomas Gail, *Healing Pandora, The Restoration of Hope and Abundance,* Steinerbooks, September 29, 2009.
74. Turenne, Louis, *De la Baguette de Coudrier aux Détecteurs du Prospecteu*r, Vol. 1-11, Editions Louis Turenne, Paris 1942.
75. White, Michael, Isaac Newton: *The Last Sorcerer*, London: Fourth Estate 1997.

Appendices

A Future Vision for BioGeometry

Acknowledgement by Ruth Schaad

Hemberg Report

Nutrinor, Raising Antibiotic Free Chicken Project

Florida Lake Restoration Project

BioGeometry Shapes and Brain Balancing by Michael J. Maley, Ph.D.

Music and Water Subtle Energy Research by Georg Gaupp-Berghausen

Appendices

A Future Vision for BioGeometry

Over the past fifty years BioGeometry has developed into a holistic subtle energy science based on a Physics of Quality and a design language that can be applied in many fields to create harmony in all living systems in the environment and bring-in life force into all products. It has many practical applications in all environmental fields, as well as in architecture, product design, agriculture, animal farming, and more, and it has achieved government and academic acceptance.

Today, BioGeometry activities worldwide are managed through a group of three companies: BioGeometry Consulting Ltd., Egypt. (Incl. Alemara Architecture Consultants), BioGeometry Europe A.G, Switzerland, Bio-Geometry Energy Systems Ltd., Canada. Under the umbrella of these three companies we have our educational arm, which includes the teaching of the BioGeometry curriculum, supervision of post-graduate research in BioGeometry, and Environmental Home Solutions Practitioner licensing, headed by Sayed Karim. BioGeometry design applications, include both in house architecture, furniture, and industrial design as well as design and architecture consultations worldwide. We are also currently underway in the curriculum for our design licensing levels which will pave the way for designers and architects worldwide to incorporate the BioGeometry Design Language into their work. Our research and development department and projects department work together to provide environmental solutions in numerous fields as well as research and development and production of BioGeometry products available through our companies as well as independent retailers worldwide.

A realistic future vision of BioGeometry must be based on the evolution of the existing BioGeometry activities into a multidisciplinary experiential activity-based all-in-one teaching, service and production complex.

When Pythagoras went to Egypt to study in the Egyptian temples he was told that they did not offer any teaching, as knowledge must be gained through experience. We share this ancient worldview and present BioGeometry through practical experience.

Our vision is centered around having all the existing BioGeometry activities as a base on which the concept of a whole new kind of project integrates into and positively changes the surrounding communities. The choice of location, architecture concepts, building methods, landscape design, as well as all interior details, will be designed and built according to the BioGeometry design methods in harmony with the forming process of nature. It will be totally integrated as a life-force-enhancing beacon in the environment. All the activities in the center will support these natural life-force-enhancing functions to produce a change in human perception and behavior creating a modern Utopia that has been the vision of many philosophers throughout the ages.

Acknowledgement by Ruth Schaad
Author of 'The Miracle of Hemberg'

After a long dark night, the light rose over the residents of Hemberg, through the harmonizing of the environment by Dr. Ibrahim Karim.

The church, in which the cellular communication antenna was installed, which had lost its sacredness and became a biggest health hazard for humans, animals, and plants, has regained its position as a sacred place.

All the people, me included, regained their health and joy of life. The wild animals are back again in our forests, in a bigger variety than ever before. The healthy plant life is evident to all uninitiated tourists who come to the area.

The people have become more receptive to the subtle energy quality of the place. Most important are the peaceful and hearty human relationships that have become evident.

The people of Hemberg have dedicated themselves to help other regions in Switzerland through BioGeometry.

There are no words that can express what Ibrahim and his family have done for us. The whole village has become part of a BioGeometry family.

It is for us a pleasure and an inner drive to work with Ibrahim on a second project in Appenzell, where ten years ago, an 80 meter high multi-function cellular tower was erected near the residential houses and stables, resulting in a fight for survival.

"Ibrahim has given us back the good quality of life. Thanks to his BioGeometry method we can now have the human life we deserve".

"Our cows are healthy again, and we can live again without the constant headaches and have a good regenerative sleep".

"My depressions and life misery are gone".

"Our trees growing much healthier than ever".

"Our dogs and cats have healthy offspring that we did not have for the past ten years".

"If it was not for Ibrahim we would have moved out of this area".

These are only some of the comments from the residents of Hirschberg in Appenzell that only give us a small idea of what really happened through BioGeometry.

With a lot of gratitude

Ruth Schaad

Excerpts from the Study of Mobile
Radiation in Hemberg (Transleted from German)

Phenomena are the Precursors of Science

Since ages phenomena accompanies humanity. Decades ago the natural radio-active radiation was challenging the spirit of research; today the technical emissions, electrical currents and fields are the challenges. Have we reached with that the end of development? I think this is not the case. The creator of this world and the universe has thought about a lot of things, and we discover constantly new aspects.

Dr. Ibrahim Karim has discovered with the BioGeometry an interesting new way. Many unfavorable influences could be changed to biological neutral or favorable influences through harmonization of forms, shapes and mathematical relations. The basis of applications possibilities are always getting wider and more open with his projects in many countries.

I first heard about BioGeometry when I met Dr. Ibrahim

Karim for the first time in 1998 in USA.

We organized together a workshop at the International Institute for Building-Biology in Clearwater, Florida. It seemed for me, that Karim's idea of BioGeometry will have an enormous future potential. Then each of us went along, and we just kept written contacts.

A surprising telephone call from Dr. Ibrahim Karim in the summer of 2003 led to a renewed contact. He has been asked, whether he could carry out an examination/investigation in Hemberg SG. Some of the residents were at the end of their strength and energy, after a new mobile phone antenna was installed on the tower of the catholic church. In a few weeks time, Dr. Ibrahim Karim was able to improve the situation to such an extent, that most of the affected persons were able to "live" again, and do till today.

The sensitivity of humans varies from one person to another. (Electro sensitive persons react stronger. The reaction of animals is always interesting as well. They hardly suffer from "imagined" disturbances. Here the BioGeometry effected a surprising change:, for example birds and bats returned back to their grounds after elimination of the dis-

turbance.

Based on the mobile phone antenna example in Hemberg, the preliminary results are evident enough to support the spread of this way of harmonization. Based on this first pilot practical project, the mode of effectiveness and influences are to be scientifically proved in a further research project.

The earth is definitely not completely explored. We have to give it a chance, to study these new phenomena! We would like to express to all, who assisted and supported us in the project of Hemberg our gratitude and thank. Their engagement was for the well-being of humans, nature and environment. Further researches should aim now to cure other affected persons.

Bosco Büeler,
Architect, Building
Biologist SIB
Managing Director
GIBB, Flawil SG

Initial situation–Press conference of OMK on August 28, 2003 in Hemberg

The Mediation Authority (OMK) Intiates the BioGeometry Experimental Project

What happened in Hemberg?
On November 3rd, 2002, the mediation Authority for mobile communication and environment (OMK) was informed by a resident of Hemberg, that he suffers from sleeping disorders, headache and concentration deficiencies since the mobile phone antenna was put into operation. Furthermore all brooding song-birds have left. An appointment on siteon December 18, 2002, was agreed upon with this resident. Ten other persons, who suffered from similar complaints, participated at this meeting.
Following this meeting, the OMK made inquiries, collecting information from the municipality of Hemberg, Swisscom, the parish of Hemberg and from the state physician of St. Gallen, who has dealt as well with this problem.The investigation revealed that the process of antenna instillation was correctly performed and that the values were clearly below the limits for non-ionising radiation. Furthermore, Swisscom has only installed antennas of 900- frequency, whereby it would have been allowed to put into operation a 1800 frequency, according to the construction license and the norms of the permissible set values.
Despite that OMK carried out different investigations and evaluated possibilities for solutions, the situation was very tense between vthe affected sick persons in the district and the Mediation Authority for

Mobile Communication. The situation was in every aspect very difficult.
At this point the contact with Dr. Ibrahim Karim was established, through a recommendation from a responsible in the Swiss Economy sector. Karim explained, that he is able to eliminate the peoples problems through his personally developed BioGeometry. During the first long session with OMK, Dr. Ibrahim Karim explained BioGeometry and the successes he achieved in the different universities and state authorities. He agreed to demonstrate his method precisely and without charge during his vacation in Switzerland.
At the request of OMK, Swisscom announced its participation in this research project, as they are in supports to all that could release the tense situation in Hemberg. On August 6, 2003, the affected persons and the district were directly informed through Dr. Karim about his plans. The residents explained their willingness to participate at the project as well. On the same day Dr. Karim started his work in Hemberg.
Here the OMK carried out a pilot project in agreement with all participants. The OMK solely holding the responsibility. We decided to start this project, after we have recognized, that it was very difficult to find a solution for this case.

We had to realize on one hand that the life quality was very bad for several persons. On the other hand it was clear that the construction of the antenna was carried out completely legally and the set value limits were kept. At this point we came to the conclusion, that we will not achieve anything without venturing anything.
At the same time the risk was not that high, as we were convinced, that we will benefit in any case. We are of the opinion that the main objective of OMK is, to offer transparency. Accordingly we are of the opinion, to inform the residents as well, if the method, which was offered for the influence of non-ionizing emissions, was not successful.

What is BioGeometry ?
BioGeometry is a relatively new science, which had been developed through Dr. Ibrahim during the last 30 years. Aim of BioGeometry is to create a harmonic energy quality in the surroundings of human beings, animals and plants.
Because the natural energy fields are more and more disturbed through the many new constructions and installations on earth, an increased negative influence on human beings, animals and plants is the result, according to Dr. Karim's statement.

Special designed geometric forms and beams, which spread energy quality, producing a balance of energy function were used. According to Dr. Karim, this will lead to the strengthening of the immune system and at the same time will reduce the disturbances. The application possibilities of BioGeometry are many. The Mobile Communication Network, electrical cables, high tension installations, all kinds of electro-magnetic waves and water could be used as transmitters for the harmonization of energies in the surroundings

What is gained through this method?

The findings and knowledge of BioGeometry were applied in different projects, as stated by Dr. Karim. This was done in cooperation with Universities of the Middle East, USA and in the Netherlands. Thus, and for example, the BioGeometric treatment of agricultural areas – as apple trees and potato fields – led to a reduction of parasites, a better harvest and a longer shelf life of products in comparison to those products of non-treated parcels.

Architecture is an important field for the application of BioGeometry. According to the statements of Dr. Karim, constructions which have been built under consideration of the BioGeometry findings from the very beginning, do have already harmonized energy-fields inside the building.

Dr. Karim emphasized, that BioGeometry should not be understood as Alternative Medicine, even if the resulting balance of biological functions and strengthening of the immune system lead to an improvement of well being and for instance positive achieved results in Hepatitis C researches. BioGeometry as a mean for the qualitative energy exchange with the surrounding can only support a medical treatment, but could never replace it.

What has been done in Hemberg?

Quiet obviously a lot of environmental problems existed in Hemberg. A lot of earth emissions, many electrical installations in the low-frequency level were found. According to Dr. Karim's opinion, with this multitude of stress affection, it is not possible to find the reason for disturbances of the well being.

Through the different stress affections, qualitative resonance features are developed between the different types of electro-magnetic waves. According to Dr. Karim, the trigger of such phenomena is not necessarily the last stress, which had been added. Thus, the project aim was not to find the reason. Main emphasis was put to help the people.

After situation analysis and discussions with the affected residents, Dr. Karim installed on the electrical cables of the antenna as well as at the houses of the affected persons, geometrical forms. The antenna has been chosen as the main bearer of the BioGeometric energy, as a great effect could be achieved with it. The works accomplished in the houses under consideration of the individual situation improved the result of the antenna furthermore. The works required an effort of about 6 days.

First results were according to the affected persons positive: they sleep better, have less headache, are less aggressive and have more energy again. The affected residents found the birds and bats coming back again, after their disappearance for over a year.

These are first results. Now we have to observe the effectivity over a longer period of time. Dr. Ibrahim Karim will follow up the project within the next 3 months, to guarantee the efficiency during different climate situations through fine tuning. He will later install specially designed figures as well for Hemberg, hoping to improve the situation furthermore, or at least to achieve a simplification of the present installations. The Mediation Authority for Mobile Communication will in future report again about the results.

Mediation Authority for Mobile Communication and Environment, August 28, 2003

More information about BioGeometry and a CV of Dr. Karim are found under www.biogeometry.com .

Experience report by Regula Keller-Frei

"On some days we left the flat hastily"

We are a family of five members with 3 children in the age of 14, 12 and 9 years. Since 14 and half years we live in Hemberg – a little village in Toggenburg with approximately 900 residents-. My husband and myself, together with 2 employees and a trainee, lead a workshop for the repair of agricultural machines and cars. During our time off we enjoy the nature with walking during the summer time and skiing during the winter. For the children and for us this living in the countryside is something very beautiful. We cannot imagine ourselves to live in a city.

But late summer 2002 our peace was massively disturbed.

"We almost had forgotten about the Natel-antenna"

At this time we accidently learned about the Natel-antenna of Swisscom, which was going to be installed on the tower of the catholic church – which was in distance of 100 meter to our house. This led us to give it pensive thoughts because of the emissions. We consulted the electro-biologist Urs Hafner from Degersheim SG and wanted to know from him, to what extend such an antenna could be harmful for us. Urs Hafner informed us immediately, that the location could not have been better for us. The angel position of the antenna

is harmless for us. Nevertheless, Swisscom could change the angel position in such a way, that the electro-magnetic fields would be directed over our house roofs and thus being absolutely problem-free for us.

We discussed this issue together with the district president, the Swisscom and Urs Hafner. After several weeks, we were informed, that the angel position could not be changed and that the construction license has been given through the municipality.

What could we do? "We have to live with it" we told ourselves. "Perhaps everything is going fine and our fear and concern about health problems were in vain". And we were ok and al-

most forgot the whole subject.

Suddenly my husband got pneumonia

After 3 months my husband felt exhausted, as if he would get a cold. He was hardly getting through daily work. At the same time I had frequent headache, dizziness and severe neck muscle pain down to the shoulders.

This sleeping area of the Keller-Frei family in Hemberg SG is protected effectively with a shielding cloth from electro-smog

As we had a lot to do in the workshop, we thought, that our complaints are the result of this work-stress.

But the condition of my husband got worse. He became hoarse and finally his voice failed completely. He got an appointment at the physician, who immediately examined his lungs. Further investigations and moments of fear were following this first visit. Finally we got the results. He was suffering from a hidden pneumonia. Only after several weeks of medication with antibiotics he started to feel better.

Meanwhile I felt more and more sick. The muscles became tenser. At some days I had to interrupt the office work, had to lay

down and massaged my neck. I needed always a longer time to be able to get back to work. In the evening I was so exhausted that I was happy when the children were in bed, and I was able to go to bed too. More and more we had the suspicion, that the reason for our complaints is the Natel-antenna on the church tower.

We discussed the issue with my parents in law, who live opposite to us. I was informed by my mother in law, that she was suffering at this time from health problems, but thought, that this was due to her age. We went together to the district president and talked to him about our health problems. We expressed our wish to transfer the antenna to another location. I mean, an

antenna does not belong to a church tower in the middle of a village. He listened to us, and promised us to discuss the matter with the municipality.

Our Kids could not sleep any more

After a while our second daughter could not sleep as well, she had never before suffered from sleeping problems, she used to stand up in the room crying at 22:30 because she could simply not sleep, and the next morning she had to skip school.

In the beginning I used to suggest that she reads a few pages so that she can get tired but that did not help, we were also wondering whether she had problems in school or else where but that proved not to be the case. Then she switched sleeping places with my husband and Sara found sleep in his bad within a few minutes, on the other hand my husband could never found sleep in Sara's bed and next morning he said I will never sleep in that bed again. It was amazing what a bad night that was for him, his eye lids where swollen and his eyes tired.

Next night I tried my luck in Sara's bed. I was as well restless. All night I was cold, then it was too hot and I woke up every few minutes.
It was obvious that we had to find another solution. We have noticed, that we do not feel unwell to the same degree in all places of the house. It was extremely bad in the kitchen. We were only able to stay there for a short period of time.

The family escaped to the basement, because this part of the house was less exposed to emissions. Here the basement, which was almost cosy.

Experience reported by Regula Keller -Frei

We felt head pressure, tense musculature and our energy was really drifting away.

In the ground floor, where our workshop is positioned, we felt sometimes better. And in the basement our complaints were reduced obviously. So my husband moved to the basement for several months. Sarah slept with me in the parents bedroom. Thus our sleeping condition had improved finally a little bit.

Only here in the basement the husband was finding some sleep. To move to another place was not possible due to the business situation.

But then my eldest daughter and my son started to have sleeping problems too. My daughter woke up every night and sat in the middle of her room on the floor. My son woke up sweated every night. We found a sleeping place for my daughter in the bathroom. She slept on a mattress a mostly was able to sleep through all night.

With expensive foils we tried to protect ourselves against the electro-smog

After a certain while we heard about an enterprise, which produces construction foils for shielding purposes and who deals with shielding material. We covered the ceils with construction foils in different rooms, and with special shielding material we made a kind of tent around each bed, in order to be protected against the emissions.

This was costing us a lot. But at least we were able to sleep again in our usual beds- with the exception of my husband. During summer time it was too hot for him under this tent. But the aggressions among each other, initiated through the massive loss of life-quality and the energy loss during the day, they all remained and we needed a lot of strength and nerves.

We often asked ourselves the question, whether to search for another living place. But due to business and financial reasons it was not possible. So we just had the chance to avoid our house as often as possible. Some days we felt better. On other days, especially on weekends we left our house hastily, because we couldn't stand it anymore.

Especially bad was Christmas. We hoped for good snowy weather conditions, so that we could ski a lot. Unfortunately this was not the case. We will never forget Christmas 2002. Our family life was very disturbed and difficult. Everybody tried to keep by himself, and to act the best way possible under the given circumstances. All day we were in a bad mood, rarely that somebody laughed. We all were tortured by the fear, how everything will go on.

Additionally we were suffering, because only very few persons understood our problems. We became outsiders. The issue of Mobile Communication antenna was not appreciated by our community. The sum of all stresses and burdens were hardly to be beard. And we just wanted one thing: to get our previous life back.

A scientist from Egypt helped

During the summer vacation we travelled for 2 weeks to the Caribbean. There we had no complaints and were able to gain back some of our strength. Back home we slept the first night well, and were all very happy about it. But already the next day complaints and problems started all over again.

Then – a few days later – we were informed that the OMK would interfere. Dr. Ibrahim Karim, an Egyptian scientist, would try to bring our suffering through BioGeometric elements to an end. We were awaiting this day desperately, on which he will start in this village with his pilot project.

About 4 months have passed since that time. Dr. Ibrahim Karim has helped us through his work and through the use of BioGeometry to get back a worthwhile life. Our family is intact again. For this we would like to express our deepest gratitude.

Hemberg, November 2003
Regula Keller-Frei

The experiences of the affected person: Rosemarie Keller

Electro-sensitive persons feel the emissions of electro-smog and mobile communication antennas very clear. Dr. Karim coordinates with precision his protecting elements in the winter-garden of the family.

Dr. Karim had to install BioGeometric elements in the church tower. Finally the acess was arranged August 20. The effect of these elements was like a relief. We were able to breath and our heads were at last clear again. The same night and as well on the following days we observed bats coming back again.

4 days later we experienced a major drop back and we started to search. We felt that "something" was coming toward us from another side. We noticed that the antennas on Saentis, Hochhamm and Schoenegrund were influencing us negatively.

Now Dr. Karim had to deal with this new problem. He installed immediately provisional BioGeometric elements. We felt better and the birds came back.

Dr. Karim sent his son back to Egypt, for the production of the specially designed elements for the Natel-antennas. Dr. Karim had to get back to the church tower, to install near to the antenna a stronger element. On September 19, he got the permission for installation.

With this holding device it was possible, to harmonise mobile disturbance sources.

"We had to protect ourselves as well against the military radio transmissions"

Now we had a good time. We heard in the village, that people were sleeping better. But at the end of October we faced a new problem. We frequently experienced bad times – actually only for some hours, but very severe in effect. When we searched for the reason, we found out, that each time of our ill feeling, the military had positioned the radio-transmission stations in the area of Saentis.

It was difficult to handle, as the military radio-transmission stations were always repositioned in another location, so that we always had to change the direction of our elements. Upon Dr. Karim's wish, my husband prepared a special holding device. On this device we mounted BioGeometric elements pointing to all directions. Thus we were "armed" against all emissions.

The project Hemberg was a fruitful time for us, we learnt a lot and we valued the close cooperation with Dr. Karim, his wife and their son. Dr. Karim had foreseen 1 week work for the Natel-antenna project, but it was extended to 4 months. We are all very thankful for his efforts. We felt all the time, that he was taking us serious and that we were in good hands.

Hemberg, November 2003, Rosmarie Keller

Questionnaire among the affected residents: Dr. med. Yvonne Gilli

Questionnaire Revealed: Complaints Have Been Massively Reduced

Conditions for the subsequent questionnaire

On October 6 and 12, 2004 a detailed questionnaire was distributed among the residents of Hemberg, concerning their complaints.

According to a scale, which included 4 intensity grades, the participating residents marked the present complaints and compared them with the condition before putting the antenna into operation and after the BioGeometric installations done by Dr. Karim.

The asked persons were a group, who were positive about Dr. Karim's pilot project. The number of persons who were asked is statistically not significant.

The subjectively mentioned complaints were structured according to a head-feet scheme. Complaints, which were not fitting into to this scheme, were noted down under a column "other complaints". Under this column disease diagnosis were noted, which were subjectively influenced by the mobile communication antenna.

Head and Concentration suffered the most

In general an increase of complaints was revealed in regard to number and intensity after putting the antenna into operation. This was followed with an obvious improvement after the biogeometric installations through Dr. Karim. Some of the persons questioned were not able to remember exactly, which complaints already existed prior to putting the antenna into operation.

In the head to feet scheme, the head complaints were clearly dominant. Under these complaints in turn, the psychological status and the cognitive performance were of main complaint. The psychological complaints could be categorized in a wider sense under depressive symptoms. The cognitive complaints concern especially the concentration ability.

Rheumatic complaints increased

Organic wise, the affected persons in Hemberg complained mainly of headache, next to eye and ear problems.

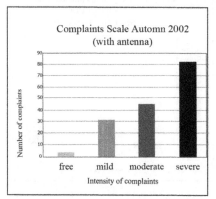

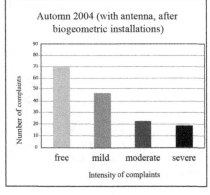

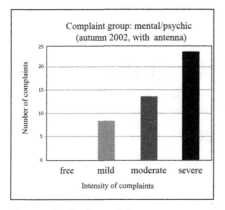

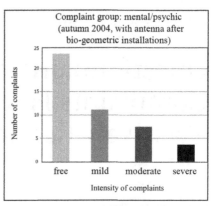

Next to the head complaints an increase of rheumatic complaints and temperature sensitivity was revealed.

Not all react similar to electro-smog

Despite of the low number of cases and the subjective statements, the questionnaire is of interest. It reflects the known symptoms, which were already described in other studies under the term biological or nonthermal effect of GSM mobile communication emissions. As most of the felt complaints are medically not objective, it is difficult to record them scientifically.

Furthermore it is difficult to record the cases, because of the large scale of complaints and the obvious different individu-

al reaction to the emission. Not to forget the individual variable exposition, even for persons in the same household.

It has been noticed in case of a family, who has been asked, that the complaints were intensified after putting the antenna into operation, despite that the family members were exposed to a 10-times stronger "house-made" electro-smog (through a microwave device, a wireless telephone, as well as other equipment in stand-by-position. One of the family members felt especially unwell in a certain room, which was proven to be subjected to more electro-magnetic emissions.

Larger scale examinations would be of outmost necessity

For future questionnaires the questions should be adapted to new findings. To be enabled to argue scientifically, the following criteria should be considered:

• A larger number of persons (100 persons) should be asked who live in a quantitative known geographic sector, which is exposed heavily to mobile communication emissions. No selection should be carried out. The persons should be chosen prior to the installation of the antenna.

• Measurements of the locations are to be done first. In flats the different measurements are to be carried out as well in regard to

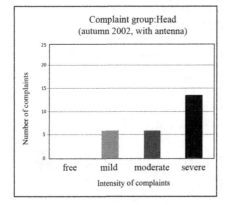

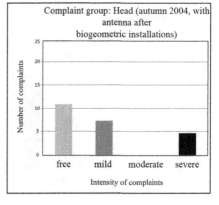

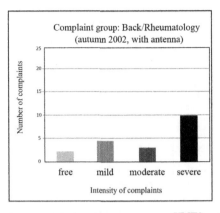

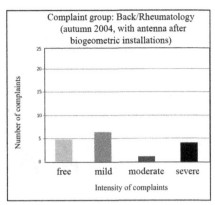

longer stays in the relevant room, e.g. bed room. The additional electro-smog must be known and quantified as well.

• A minimum of 4 different phases of questionnaires should take place: before putting the antenna into operation, 4 months after putting the antenna into operation, 1 month after the installation of BioGeometric devices and 1 year after the installation of these devices.

Neither the persons who are asked nor the persons who put the question should know the actual situation of the antenna – whether in operation or not.

UMTS – supply increases the health emergency situation

It is hoped, that epidemiological studies are financed in future. Due to the present study situation and the results of this minimal number of questioned affected persons, we may speak of an actual health emergency situation, contrary to the so called installation emergency, given by the Federal Advisory Council prior to the enactment of the NISV-decree. This is now increased due to the present provision with UMTS.

Wil, Automn 2004
Dr. med. Yvonne Gilli

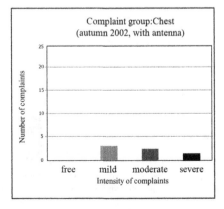

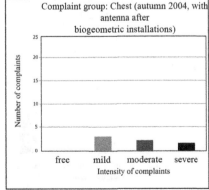

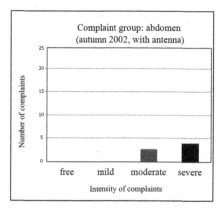

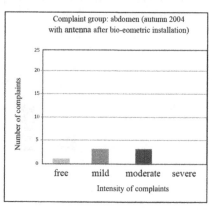

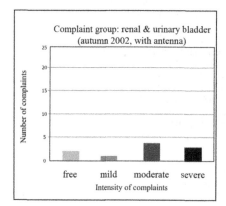

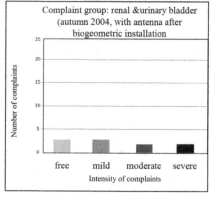

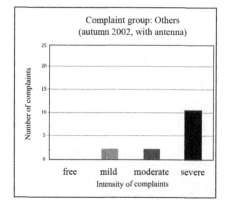

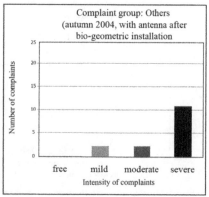

Questionnaire among the affected residents: Dr. med. Yvonne Gilli

About 60 % (58,6%) of all complaints are distributed among the below listed 15 terms:	Autumn 02, with antenna				Oct 02, antenna & bio-geom. Installations				
	none	mild	mod-erate	severe	none	mild	mod-	severe	
1. Nervousness		4	2	4	2	4	4		
2. Sleeping disorders		1	4	4	5	2	1	1	
3. Difficulty to get to sleep			1	6	3	4			
4. Exhaustion, Loss of performance		2		5	5	2			
5. Weakness of memory		1	2	4	4	1		2	
6. Irritability			3	4	3	2	2		
7. Headache, migraine,		2	3	2	1	3		3	
8. Allergies (against medications, food, rhinitis)		2	1	2	1	3	1	1	
9. Heat flushing and sensation	1	1	2	2	3	1	2		
10. Skin problems (eczema)		1	1	3		2	1	2	
11. Neck- & shoulder pain, tenseness			1	4	1	2		2	191
12. Back pain		3		2	1	3		1	
13. Vision disturbances, eye-pain		2	2	1	1	3		1	
14. Sexual problems	2		1	2	3	2			
15. Hyperactivity, concentration problems			2	3	2	1	1	1	
Total complaints	3	19	25	48	35	35	12	14	

Mental and Psychic Complaints	none	mild	mod	severe	none	mild	mod	severe	
1. Nervousness		4	2	4	2	4	4		
2. Memory weakness		1	2	4	4	1		2	
3. Hyperactivity, concentration problems			2	3	2	1	1	1	
4. Depression		1	2	1	3			1	
5. Irritability			3	4	3	2	2		
6. Moodiness, loss of energy			1	3	3	1			94
7. Nutritional disturbances, loss of appetite		1	2		2		1		
8. Exhaustion, performance weakness		2		5	5	2			
Total complaints	0	9	14	24	24	11	8	4	

Head	none	mild	mod	severe	none	mild	mod	severe	
		2	2	1	1	3		1	
1. Vision disturbances, eye pain				1	1				
2. Cataract		2	3	2	1	3		3	
3. Headache, migraine			1	3	2	1		1	
4. Ear problems (Tinnitus)		1		2	2	1			
5. Loss of hairs		1		3	3				
6. Vertigo, nausea				1	1				
7. Head browsing		2		5	5	2			49
Total complaints	0	6	6	13	11	8	0	5	

Back, Rheumatology	none	mild	mod	severe	none	mild	mod	severe	
1. Neck-& shoulder pain, tenseness			1	4	1	2		2	
2. Back pain		3		2	1	3		1	
3. Joint-problems		2	1	2	3	1			
4. Rheumatic complaints	1			2	1	1	1		35
Total complaints	1	5	2	10	6	7	1	3	

Press Conference from October 22, 2003 in Hemberg – Christoph Zweili

The Mediation Authority for Mobile Communication and Environment

Tagblatt

Thursday, October 23, 2003

Karim from Wonderland?
In Hemberg the electro-smog was tackled in an unconventional manner. Critics speak of swindle and hocus-pocus.

Hemberg: For critics the BioGeometry is mere swindle. Electro-sensitive persons call the method of the Egyptian Ibrahim Karim a blessing. The Mediation Authority for Mobile Communication and Environment summed it up after a three months field-project.
In spring the young birds returned from the warmer south, but migrated after three days again. Parents of swallows abandoned their brood, which starved to death miserably. Wagtails did noot like it either in Hemberg anymore.

That was in June 2002, when Swisscom put their new 710-Watt mobile communication antenna into operation. All at once, a farmer had bad luck in the cowshed. There were a deformed calf and two abortions. Two dozen electrosensitive people complained of headache, vertigo, exhaustion, sleeping disorders, fear and depression, down to inexplicable aggressive conditions. They felt that neither the family doctor nor the community authorities took them seriously. A dispute between the residents, authorities and Swisscom blazed up and stayed on for months the operators refused to switch off the legitimate antenna, which

broadcasts under the set maximum limiting value.

All's well that ends well
This was the case until 3 months ago. "Now we enjoy life again" says the 64 years old Rosmarie Keller, spokes-person of the residents, on Wednesday in front of the media. She and the President of the community, Walter Fischbacher, could look into each others eye again. A blessing, that the Mediation Authority for Mobile Communication and Environment, established by Mobile communication providers; Swisscom, Orange and Sunrise had the Egyptian Ibrahim Karim, graduated ETH- architect and Doctor of Sciences flown in by air? Karim installed his created BioGeometric shapes and figures made from wood and plexi-glass, which remind one of well-turned chair legs, at 6 families as well as inside and outside the church. The Egyptian, who supervises worldwide serious research programs, that can be looked up on his homepage, ordered further production of area covering shape components for Hemberg, which were to be produced in Egypt and to be sent to Switzerland. Karim transformed twelve different sources of interferences outside of Hemberg and seven in the church tower into positive energy. Enough to finalise the project. And hope for a continuation at another place – with a budget to male it possible for medical accompanying examinations and documentation through a university or laboratory.

"Hemberg is no individual case"
The Swisscom representatives at the Media-conference seem satisfied. "We have an interest that our installations are acceptable for mankind and environment" says Claude Georges, Swisscom leader for Mobile Communication and Environment. Hans Ulrich Jacob expresses himself extremely critically against the Mediation Authority of Mobile Communication providers, represented by Erika Forster. Jacob acts in the name of the Mediation mobile Communication and Health of the Swiss community of interests of electro-smog affected persons who suffer. He speaks of the "plot of Hemberg" and calls Karim a charlatan, who works with cheap plexi-glass shapes "which are available in every oriental bazaar".

More articles about this subject in Tagblatt:

July 14, 2004:
No miraculous remedy, scientifically implausible
June 24, 2004:
Is the project BioGeometry going on?
June 11, 2004:
Karim contra Swisscom
August 29, 2004:
A village resorts to self-help

The ones participating in the experiment contested vehemently during the press conference of any foul play. The transmission power has not been lowered during the experiment, as it has been claimed" says Claude Georges. To prove that, the data provided by Swisscom have been scrutinized by the Federal Authority for Communication. The supervising authority saw both, transmission power as well as limiting values complied with.

"Hemberg is no individual case", Erika Forster says and refers to the antenna at Hirschberg. Here also the Mediation Authority searches for solutions. Is she herself convinced of Karim's method? "When I see the results, then something has to be behind it" she admits diplomatically. "I stand up for further field experiments to be accompanied by scientific research."

Catchword Electro-Smog
Mobile phones and basis-stations transmit and receive electro-magnetic radiation in the range of high frequency radiation between 900 and 1800 MHz. The installation in Hemberg has been approved for 1800 MHz – transmitted so far was only 900 MHz. The spectrum of frequencies of the electro-magnetic radiation is subdivided in ionizing and non-ionizing radiation (heat, UV radiation, light and electro-smog). There are only a few scientific secure perceptions about the impacts and effects of mobile communication installations. According to the Federal Authority for Health, some impacts have been proved: Thus the mobile telephone radiation can disturb sensitive appliances, as hearing aids, instruments in the intensive care in hospitals or electronic devices in airplanes. Persons who frequently telephone with a handy, complaint more of headache, than those who uses the telephone less.

Mrs. Erika Forster had invited the press conference in her position as Mediation Authority representative. Many residents of Hemberg made use of this chance to exchange information.

Dr. Ibrahim, left, explained the details of the BioGeometric effects of his method.

Clear up Statement of the Mediation Authority

The reproaches, according to which before Dr.Karim's intervention the transmission power was increased and afterwards lowered, has caused the Mediation Authority to check this claim.

The Federal Authority forCommunication has attested in writing on October 16, 2003, that during the experiment in Hemberg the transmission power has not been raised first and then afterwards lowered again.

Signed by Mr. Philippe Horisberger, Chief of the section "frequency planning".

Mediation Authority for Mobile Communication and Environment, November 25, 2004, R. Lüthi.

NZZ am Sonntag

Edition August 31st, 2003,
Peter Traxler

"The immune system of electro-sensitive persons could be strengthened, Karim explains. This is not happening just by chance, but according to the science of "BioGeometry", which has been developed by Karim himself during the last 30 years. He has been guided by the conclusion, that even the sun has good and bad rays, but that only the good rays reach the earth. This protection is due to natural geometric forms and colours, which are a kind of God's design language.

Among his research works there are projects for the protection of fruits and vegetables against parasites. His field of work is extended from Cairo and the Middle East to half of Europe and USA.

Karim, who studied in Zurich, did the work in Hemberg free of charge. "Switzerland gave me a lot, now it is time for paying back", the father of 4 children said.

Edition June 10, 2004,
Andreas Schmid

The shapes and glass bodies produced miracles in Hemberg SG. With his BioGeometric method the Egyptian Ibrahim Karim has harmonized the emissions of the mobile communication antenna of the church tower in the village in Toggenburg.

Rosmarie Keller does not know, what happened to her. Karim changed with his shapes, which were directed to the transmitters, the harmful rays into harmless ones. Obviously with success. "The result is unbelievable". The complaints are gone, her body has regenerated continuously. An obvious indicator supports her subjective sensation: " Since Karim was here, we have martens again in our garden. And so many birds as never before". For Keller this is the proof, that BioGeometry is no esoteric hocus-pocus. "Animals do not imagine things." Keller does not want to leave it with her regain of well-being. She fights on for electro-smog harmed persons and demands the application of the BioGeometry project all over Switzerland. Meanwhile interested persons from 6 other districts asked for explanations of the unexplainable.

Baubiologie

Reader's Brief
From an interview with Dr.Ibrahim Karim issued 01/2004, page 11

BioGeometry in Hemberg:
Mobile communication is not the only cause!

In "Baubiology" Bulletin, April's issue, Dr. Ibrahim Karim was asked about the science of BioGeometry which he developed and its potentials. Reading through the introduction, you will know that Dr. Karim managed to relieve the inhabitants of Hemberg SG " from the harmful side effects of the mobile communication antenna" Moreover, the article described BioGeometry as "a technique to harmonize the mobile radio radiation" and
"to help victims of mobile radio radiation".
The readers tend to believe that the mobile phone antenna in Hemberg is causing health problems.

On the contrary, Dr. Karim has a different perspective regarding the situation in Hemberg. Moreover, he suggested from the beginning that the electrical appliances and earth radiations could be the reason and the electromagnetic fields of the mobile phone antenna-as in the saying-" the drop that spilled out the water from the glass". This point of view was announced by Dr.Karim and repeated in every meeting. And through handling the problem Dr.Karim confirmed his thesis that electrical appliances and earth radiations are the cause of the disturbances in addition to mobile phone communication. Dr.Karim - Architect by profession; graduate of the renowned F.I.T. Zurich, Switzerland; announced this in most of his press interviews like " Toggenburger" (issued in 29 August 2003), "Linth-Zeitung" (issued in 28 October 2003) and also in public meetings.

What brings happiness is that by the help of Dr.Karim the complaints of the affected persons lessened. It is important to understand that the reason of the disturbances are due to a combination of various bad effects arising from different electromagnetic waves.

Translation from German original
file:///Users/ibrahimkarim/Desktop/Appenzell%20o8%20Articles/
Swisscom%20BG%20Appenzel.webarchive

Ibrahim Karim harmonized radio waves with "BioGeometry". Karim Ibrahim, used his method called BioGeometry to harmonize the effect of the radiation of a Swisscom antenna in Appenzell with success: The cows have no more miscarriages, the residents no longer complain of headaches and may are getting better sleep again.

Picture: Keystone
Archive image of October 2003: Ibrahim Karim shows his device at the mobile communication antenna inside the tower of the Catholic Church of Hemberg.

Picture: Keystone
Archive image of October 2003: Ibrahim Karim shows one of the objects, which he installed at the mobile communication antenna in the tower of the Catholic Church of Hemberg.

According to an official release from the government commission of Appenzell Innerrhoden on Tuesday, the feedback from the public was extremely positive. The Egyptian Architect donated fee of 20 000 francs that he received for the success of the project, to the Steig Foundation for the workshop and the dormitory of the handicapped.

Plexiglas Shapes

The work of Karim Ibrahim is approved and supported by the Mediation Authority for Mobile Communications and Environment (OMC) since 2005. Two years earlier, Karim, had already harmomonised the radiation from the antenna inside the bell tower of Hemberg in Toggenburg when he installed his plexiglass shapes and freed the residents of the village of Hemberg from headaches and sleep disturbances. The architect and developer of the "Biogeometry" was contacted at that time through the Chief Mediation Officer and St. Gallen FDP member of parliament Erika Forster, to come to Hemberg. Although Karim was successful in Hemberg successful, he received a lot of criticism. The private "Mediation for Mobile communication and health" called Karim a "charlatan". He was named a "radiation guru", a "magician". The town president of Hemberg, however, gratefully thanked the Egyptian. Now the Appenzell Innerhorrden government is also doing the same - without knowing exactly what Karim actually did around the 79-meter-high antenna Hirscherberg. "We are waiting for his report," says Markus Dörig, the government spokesman.

Radio Transmission

Swisscom is the owner of the antenna erected in the mid-nineties. In 2002, it was established that the FM antenna was illegally radiating in that area at 156 percent of the limit. Swisscom promptly reduced the transmission power. In Innerrhoden they had previously suffered miscarriages in cows, they also had udder and mouth problems. Many people who live in the vicinity of the antenna in Hirschberg had complained of headaches, insomnia and fatigue. The cause was initially suspected to be due to mobile radiation and not from radio transmission.

Complaints Are Gone

In 2005 the local residents complained again from problems, which they attributed to radiation exposure. Then Karim came to Appenzell. According to Markus Dörig are the complaints of the residents not only diminished, "they have disappeared," as he, the government spokesman said. The effect of Karim's scientific method cannot be measured by conventional scientific methods. He himself says that he can influence the quality of negative energy fields with his shapes to produce positively harmonize the environment. Whether he can or whether they have fallen under the so-called placebo effect, is completely irrelevant to those that have been healed.

(Government spokesman)

Rate

(Translation from German Original)

KANTON
APPENZELL INNERRHODEN

Governor and Commissionary Board
Ratskanzelei
Marktgasse 2
9050 Appenzell
http://www.ai.ch

Prof. Dr. Ibrahim Karim

Appenzell, 24. October 2007

Hirschberg Antenna / Protection from Radiation Stress / in Gratitude

Dear Esteemed Professor

After different discussions and explanations, you have accepted to undertake the protection from radiation stress in the area of Hirschberg as a research project, in which you would test your latest development in BioGeometry, the Home Kit.

In the letter of 31. August, Ms. Ruth Schaad informed us that project completion is scheduled for the end of October 2007.

The Commissionary Board would like to take this opportunity to express to you it's hearty gratitude for the execution of the environmental harmonizing project in the area of Hirschberg, Appenzell I. Rh., Switzerland, in the period from November 2006 until October 2007.

The Commissionary Board of the Kanton Appenzell I. Rh. Appreciates very much and is thankful for the great effort you have done in harmonizing the health of the residents as well as the animal and plant environments, which has proven to have a good effect, as the survey of the residents of the area of Hirschberg has shown.

With another expression of our hearty appreciation, we extend to you our friendly greetings.

In the name of the Governor and Commissionary Board

The Governor   The Secretary of the Board
Signature   Signature
Bruno Koster   Franz Breitenmoser

Excerpt from an email from Jürg Studerus, Swisscom, to Adré Fauteaux, Maison 21 Sciecle Magazine, Montreal, Canada, and Dr. Karim:

Swisscom acknowledgement of Swiss BioGeometry Projects

Excerpt of Studerus report.

Dr. Karim was commissioned by the Ombudsstelle Mobilkommunikation und Umwelt to apply his Biogeometry in order to solve health problems from some inhabitants in the villages concerned that they attributed to the electromagnetic fields emitted by mobile communication antennae.

The Ombudsstelle Mobilkommunikation und Umwelt was founded by the mobile communication operators in Switzerland so as to give people, facing problems with the infrastructure of mobile communications, a neutral contact-point for their concerns. The organization was managed by Madame Erika Forster, Council of States of Switzerland. The foundation board of the organization was completed by four national counselors and a CEO of a mobile operator. The organisation was under supervision of the Federal Department of Home Affairs.

Dr. Karim's installation of geometric objects near the antennae concerned had the approval of Swisscom's top management.

It's a fact that people in Hemberg and Hirschberg suffering (according to their opinion) from electromagnetic fields from mobile communication antennae felt considerably better after Dr. Karim had installed his objects.

After that, the bodies involved looked for a solution how Dr. Karim's Biogeometry could be used for whole Switzerland. A first contract was prepared. The underwriting failed however, since Dr. Karim could not agree to some points of the contract.

Thank you for your attention and kind regards,

Jürg Studerus
Leiter Strategie & Entwicklung
Swisscom AG

nutrinor
COOPÉRATIVE

Saint-Bruno, 21 octobre 2014

BioGéométrie Canada
2001, Université, bureau 1700
Montréal (Québec) H3A 2A6

Fondation Ecologia
925, De Maisonneuve Ouest, #207
Montréal (Québec) H3A 0A5

Sujet : **Projet expérimental de production de poulets sans
antibiotiques et anticoccidiens avec la méthodologie de la
Biogéométrie. Poulailler expérimental # 1868 d'Avinor**

Au Dr Ibrahim Karim et à toute l'équipe du projet de recherche sur les
poulets sans antibiotiques et sans anticoccidiens.

Nutrinor tient à reconnaître le franc succès de l'expérience d'élevage de
poulets sans antibiotiques et sans anticoccidiens pendant une période
expérimentale qui s'est étendue du 23 août 2013 au 10 octobre 2014 soit
sur neuf lots de production couvrant plus qu'une année complète.

Grâce au service minutieux de l'équipe et au balancement des bâtiments,
nous avons pu produire une série de neuf lots consécutifs d'élevage de
poulets et ce sans aucun antibiotique et anticoccidien c'est-à-dire avec
zéro intervention médicale.

Le projet de recherche était de réaliser six lots consécutifs d'élevage de
poulets sans antibiotiques pour démontrer la validité et la pérennité des
solutions.

Avec la production de neuf lots consécutifs, la preuve que nous voulions
faire est très concluante.

1/2

Dans notre poulailler expérimental (#1868), d'environ 9 000 poulets par lot, la moitié était nourrie avec seulement de la nourriture et de l'eau sans aucun antibiotique ni vaccin anticoccidien alors que l'autre moitié était nourrie avec notre recette habituelle de nourriture additionnée d'antibiotiques et d'anticoccidiens en mode préventif.

Tous les lots d'élevage de poulets sans antibiotiques se sont maintenus systématiquement dans les mêmes taux de mortalité que les poulets élevés avec antibiotiques et à plusieurs reprises avec des taux de mortalité légèrement meilleurs et ce avec des poids et des durées de croissance tout à fait comparables aux productions avec antibiotiques.

Or, après sept lots dans le poulailler expérimental, deux lots ont été produits dans un poulailler régulier (#3172) de 45 000 poulets avec les mêmes résultats. Ce résultat exceptionnel se continue d'ailleurs pour un lot supplémentaire dans le poulailler régulier.

Nutrinor considère le projet de recherche terminé et confirme donc une réussite sur toute la ligne et nous recommandons sans hésiter la valeur de cette méthodologie.

Nutrinor est extrêmement fière d'avoir participé à cette première mondiale d'élevage de plus 150 000 poulets avec la méthodologie de la Biogéométrie telle que développée par le Dr Karim et son équipe.

Avec nos plus sincères remerciements!

Robin Boudreault   Chantal Bélanger

2/2

Camelot Homeowners Association

Canoe Creek Road, St Cloud, Florida

October 31, 2016

BioGeometry Canada Inc.
2001 Boulevard Robert-Bourassa, Suite 1700
Montreal, QC H3A 2A6

Subject: Lake Harmonization at Camelot, St Cloud

The Camelot Homeowners Association would like to thank BioGeometry Canada Inc for their support, time and effort for harmonizing Lake Guenevere with BioGeometry (BG) and enhancing the overall health and well-being of the lake and associated eco system.

I, Russell Brach, a board member of the Camelot Homeowners Association, got involved with the Camelot lake in November 2014 because the old water fountain was in need of replacement. We replaced the old 1.5 hp fountain with a 3 hp fountain but we found that there was over Three (3) feet of decomposed organic material on the lake bottom from years of chemically spraying weeds, algae and lily pads. The smell from this decomposing material was quite strong and I decided to try to clean the lake without the use of chemicals and try a natural approach. I mentioned this to my business partner Susanna Rehmann and she informed me of BioGeometry and introduced me to Sayed Karim. Chemical spraying of the lake was stopped in December 2014 and shapes were placed in and around the lake. In June of 2015 alga and lily pad growth became extreme and it was found that the main shape in front of the fountain was removed by a fisherman causing effect of the BG tool to be out of balance. Then in July of 2015 the main shape was again disturbed by a kid in a boat, the shape was recovered and replaced. In October of 2015 Page's Landscaping was contracted to remove lily pads and muck from the front of the fountain area, approximately 1.5 acres, utilizing scuba equipment and water jet.   Over 35,000 pounds of muck and lily pads were removed that enhanced this area of the lake.

 Over the next several months I walked and surveyed the lake's health and appearance. Lily pad growths excelled but the alga growth seemed to dissipate, the water clarity was much better and the foul smell disappeared. Without the monthly spraying of the lake the community saved over $8,000 over a two year period.

Much to my dismay a few residents complained about the lily pads, it seems they want a lake surface clear of any lily pads. I tried to explain to them that lily pads actually filter the lake and are very beneficial for the overall health of the lake as mentioned by SJWMD personnel and also Lake Doctor personnel. In October of 2016 Lake Doctor started spaying the lake again for lily pads, weeds and alga.

The overall health, water clarity and smell has drastically improved with the introduction of BioGeometry and the Camelot community, fish and ducks are very thankful to Sayed, Susanna and all team members for naturally cleaning lake Guenevere by application of BioGeometry. Based on our observations, this project has been a great success and we entirely recommend the application of BioGeometry.

Sincerely,

Russell A Brach
Vice President

BioGeometry Shapes and Brain Balancing

Michael J. Maley, Ph.D. BioGeometry Instructor Wayzata, Minnesota, USA

At Dr. Ibrahim Karim's Advanced Topics seminar, in November of 2011, the conversation at dinner with the instructors and other colleagues wandered into the topic of BioGeometry and Personal Development and the role that hemispheric balance might have on that activity. Ibrahim mentioned that he had discovered some shapes that would balance the two hemispheres, and he proceeded to draw them on a sheet of paper. We began testing these shapes on ourselves and each other, first testing the 'openness' or 'shutdowns' of each side of the brain with the Personal Wavelength (PW), and then exposing each other to the shapes. Our interest increased as we found that even brief exposure to the shapes opened the hemisphere that had been shut down (changed the personal wavelength/PW from counter clockwise/CCW to clockwise/ CW). Out of that initial exposure, came some ideas about how to further work with these shapes, and in the paper that follows, the results of these initial explorations are described. Ibrahim generously shared the shapes that he had manufactured as wooden statues and Figure 1 below illustrates how we began and what we used as our original test pattern. OL and OR refer to whether the shape 'opens' (restores and/or strengthens a CW pattern) the left or right hemisphere.

Early testing on many different subjects supported what we had experienced in Asheville—when a hemisphere is shut down (showing a reversal of the PW), exposure to a shape for that side of the brain will correct the reversal and bring the hemisphere online again. This effect was seen in everyone we originally tested. Individual differences began to emerge when we looked at how long the effect would last. For some people, it lasted for many hours and for others only a short time. Hemispheric activation is a very fluid process anyway—some individuals operate with both hemispheres online all the time; others seem to have a dominant hemisphere with the opposite side of the brain permanently shut down; and others, when engaged in a hemispheric specific activity, will somehow render the other hemisphere inactive, but it will come online when their attention shifts or the activity changes. Just like your breathing pattern, the activity you are engaged in will begin to shift the pattern, but it may or may not be a permanent change. This is quite like what occurs with the organ balancing BioSignatures, in that immediate exposure will correct a CCW reversal in the organ, but there is often a need to reinforce that with other kinds of corrections as well to support the organ continuously. To fully correct an organ imbalance, often a consideration of other energy pathways affecting the organ is required (e.g., supporting meridians that move through the area). Other similar BioSignature shapes may also help; other organs may need to be balanced; and it often helps to add other supports (nutritional, homeopathic) as well [1]. These procedures represent the effective use of both polarity balancing and Centering for healing physical imbalances.

Our next step was to begin looking at how to make the effect of the shapes more permanent and how to determine the effect of the balancing on the individual's energy system, subjective experience, and behavior. In this report, we look at preliminary explorations of three different aspects of shape exposure – length of exposure, other supporting interventions to deepen the absorption, and the effects of the shapes on organ imbalances. In Appendix I there is a short summary of the functions of the two hemispheres and how important hemispheric balance is to effective physical, emotional, mental, spiritual, and cultural harmony.

Suggested Exercise: See if you can replicate the phenomena of the shapes balancing the hemispheres. Find some subjects, take their PW with a neutral pendulum or the IKUP, place your hand close to the side of their head or point to the side of their head, and notice whether or not their PW stays CW or reverses into a CCW response. Then expose them to the shapes for some time and measure again. Note whether the shapes correct the CCW pendulum response. If you are able, test after some time to see how long the balancing lasts or ask them to look at the shapes frequently and see what happens.

One of the first things we tried was to see what happens when we prolonged exposure to the shapes. Exposure time is an important variable in many therapies, and it seemed to be a variable with BioSignatures. We made copies of the shapes for ourselves and others and taped them in locations where we would be looking at them often—on the corner of the computer screen; on their desk; on the refrigerator, etc. It was apparent that longer exposure times affected the outcome— that is, the 'hemispheric balance' as measured by both hemispheres showing a CW rotation lasted longer than short one-time exposures. Those individuals that continued to look at the shapes for days or weeks reported a shift in their awareness of their cognitive experience. One person reported thinking more clearly, another found it easier to study and recall academic material, and another reported some differences in how they related to their own internal experience. Some individuals whose left brains were more shut down and who looked at the shapes often reported some remarkable shifts in attention, cognitive processing, and the ability to focus— "it's like a light went on" one person reported..." I could think more clearly and focus my attention and not be so distracted." The effects reported when the right hemisphere opened seemed to be more subtle and harder to describe, but they did "feel different." In some younger subjects, there was a marked shift in emotional states in the direction of more stable emotional moods. These are all anecdotal reports, but suggest that exposure time is important for allowing the balancing effect to take hold. Some teachers are placing the photographs of the shapes on their student's desks to see if daily exposure can affect test performance. It is a simple thing to print a photo of the shapes and place it in a plastic holder and put it on the desk. Exposure time had one other interesting effect—as the person learned and could feel the difference between times when both hemispheres were online and those times when one went offline, there was an increased awareness of the emotional states and cognitive abilities that came and went with the balancing. When right hemisphere shutdown was accompanied by more unstable emotional states, the individual more frequently chose to look at the shapes and bring the errant hemisphere back on line. It is likely that this phenomenon is a phase of the rebalancing that comes before the hemisphere shifts permanently, but that hypothesis awaits more data. Increased emotional awareness, by itself, is an important quality associated with right hemisphere functioning.

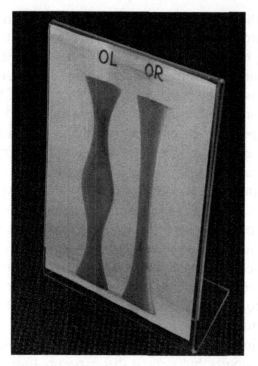

Figure: Display Stands for the Shapes

There are several other procedures we tried to increase the amount of attention the person paid to the shapes. One of the issues here is that hemispheric imbalance (e.g., a poorly functioning right hemisphere) is hypothesized to be the basis of many attention disorders (e.g., ADD, ADHD) and paying sustained attention to anything is a problem for these individuals. To increase the attention factor, we explored some ways to make the experience more physical by involving the whole body. Movement patterns that aid in hemispheric activation on both sides include walking, doing the cross – crawl exercise, and the butterfly hug (crossing the arms as if to give yourself a hug and gently and rhythmically tapping yourself on your upper arm alternating sides). We had some people look at the shapes and simultaneously perform the movements to see if it increased their attention to the shapes. It did, and that experiment is ongoing. When using these procedures with children, we explored just taking some short intervals of looking at the shapes while doing the butterfly hug several times a day to see if it would reinforce some hemispheric changes. It would be interesting to be able to do some EEG assessments of hemispheric activation to see what effect these interventions have on brain states.

In the clinical treatment of hemispheric imbalance there are many sensory motor exercises and assessments used to retrain the brain. Involving the whole body in sensory experience, movement patterns, neuroanatomic exercises, and emotional stimulation is the usual way marked hemispheric imbalance is addressed [2]. In this project, we are exploring the ways in which the BioGeometry shapes and their subtle energy emissions can contribute to this outcome. Like BioSignatures, the shapes themselves and the accompanying BG3 from their placement next to each other appears to provide the necessary stimulation to the deficient hemisphere to bring it back online. How that immediate correction makes it[s] way into more permanent changes in cognition, perception, behavior, and emotional expression is the data we are seeking.

Many organ imbalances accompany imbalances in the hemispheres. Direct causation is difficult to establish, but even temporarily restoring functioning to the deficient hemisphere can change an organ response from a CCW to CW pendulum measurement. In the literature on hemispheric imbalances, many disturbances in digestion and food sensitivities accompany right hemisphere dysfunction.

In the Foundation Training seminars, we have been using the shapes to assist students in the practicums. BioGeometry training is an interesting mix of conceptual left-brain knowledge and right-brain immersion in the Radiesthesia/dowsing experiences. Skill sets are needed in both universes. Students in the classes have the usual mix of hemispheric dominance, with some being 'right-brained' and others 'left-brained'. We have begun to use the shapes to open the less active hemisphere and see how they can contribute to better learning in both areas. Students that have taken the shapes and tried them with their family and friends have reported interesting results and we are looking for more data from those of you reading this report. Several students have reported how stunned they were to see how few children show dual hemispheric activation, and how often the left hemisphere is the only one consistently functioning. This is also consistent with the theme of one of the finest books on the issue of hemispheric balance – The Master and his Emissary by Iain McGilchrist [3]. McGilchrist traces the changes in hemispheric dominance through the history of western culture, and his ideas mirror the discussions in the Foundation Trainings on the evolution of the brain and the gradual loss of right brain integration with left brain functions.

One further intervention is being tried, and that is broadcasting the shapes using the Human Archetype Ruler. You can broadcast the qualities into the environment by leaving the circle blank or you can use the targeted person's witness or photo along with the photo of the shapes. The line strip is then placed on the ruler to make it a broadcasting instrument. This is a new intervention so we do not have a lot of reports yet, but it is a way to send the information and energy of the shapes more continuously and does not require the person to be looking at the shapes.

We welcome your participation in this experiment. If you have had some experience with the shapes; have tried them personally or with others and have some results to share, please post them on the BioGeometry Forum.

(1) Recall the discussion in the Foundation Training about the creation of the Hepatitis-C medallion. The BioSignatures for other organs were on the chip as well as BioSignatures that resonated with those for the Liver.
(2) Melillo, Robert. Disconnected Kids (New York, Perigee Books, 2010).
(3) McGilchrist, Iain. The Master and His Emissary: The Divided Brain and the Making of the Western World. (New Haven, Yale University Press, 2012)

Appendix A Short Summary of the Importance of Hemispheric Balance

In doing my research for this project, three books were extremely helpful to me. Two of them are referenced above in the report on the project. Disconnected Kids describes how hemispheric imbalances create so many clinical conditions like ADD, ADHD, Autism, Asperger's, and Dyslexia. These conditions affect families and children every day in their lives, and are responsible for serious problems that limit the individual's ability to fully develop their potential. Iain McGilchrist's book[1] brought the phenomena of hemispheric dominance into a larger social and cultural context and described how the issue of hemispheric dominance affects cultural development and it's emotional and spiritual evolution. The third book is a fascinating and inspiring account of a neuroscientist who experienced a stroke rendering her left hemisphere non- functional and placed her in a totally right brain state for several years. The story of her stroke and her incredible recovery is told in her book "My Stroke of Genius" [2] and offers a first-person account and exploration of the worlds the two hemispheres experience.

Both McGilchrist and Bolte provide excellent descriptions of the two different universes that each of the two hemispheres connect to and create in our personal perceptual world. There are two minds inside each of us and many people are aware of those dichotomies—our thinking and feeling selves; our mental and intuitive/somatic selves; our judging and perceiving selves; and the choices we make from our head and our heart. How do you find a balance between these different abilities and choose which qualities to express in any given situation?

Our left-brain controls fine motor skills—so we can play the piano, tie our shoes, and speak clearly. It is involved in every conscious move we make, and when we talk to ourselves. It's the linear, logical brain, the thinking brain, and mediates pattern recognition, working with numbers, computer games, multi-tasking, and finding the meaning in things. It takes all the energy and information of the present moment, all the possibilities sensed by the right brain, and tries to shape it into something manageable—it can categorize, organize, describe, judge, and critically analyze anything. It is one of the finest tools in the universe for organizing information[2].

McGilchrist describes the overall functions of the left hemisphere as follows: "The left hemisphere is always engaged in a purpose; it always has an end in view, and downgrades whatever has no instrumental purpose in sight...The world of the left hemisphere, dependent on denotative language and abstraction, yields clarity and power to manipulate things that are known, fixed, static, isolated, decontextualized, general in nature, but ultimately lifeless......The knowledge that is mediated by the left hemisphere is knowledge within a closed system. It has the advantage of perfection, but such perfection is bought ultimately at the price of emptiness, of self-reference."

When the left brain is offline early in life, language skills suffer and processing words and sound may be difficult. Reading, spelling, and speaking are affected, and conditions like dyslexia, processing disorders, and learning disabilities can result.

When the right hemisphere is offline early in childhood, the losses include difficulties in emotional relating and empathy for others; poor skill sets in emotional regulation; difficulties paying attention; disturbances in sensory motor functions like balance and grace; food intolerances; and a less resilient immune system. An even larger view of what is lost comes from McGilchrist's description of how the right hemisphere contributes to our experience of the world... "empathy and intersubjectivity as the ground of consciousness; the importance of an open, patient attention to the world, as opposed to a willful, grasping attention; the implicit or hidden nature of truth, the emphasis on process rather than stasis; the journey being more important than the arrival; the primacy of perception; the importance of the body in constituting reality; an emphasis on uniqueness...". Bolte's experience was similar...." My right mind is open to the eternal flow whereby I exist at one with the universe. It is the seat of my Divine mind, the knower, the wise woman, and the observer. It is my intuition and higher consciousness. My right mind is ever present and gets lost in time. Its most fundamental trait is deep inner peace and compassion."

The right hemisphere is deeply involved in the development of our personal and intimate attachments to others, and relational attachments to our earliest caregivers both develop our brains and are able to manifest through right brain systems. Allan Schore, a developmental neuroscientist (with a very developed left brain), summarizes the role of the right brain in relationships this way..."attachment transactions are critical to the development of structural right brain systems involved in the nonconscious processing of emotion, modulation of stress, self-regulation, and thereby the functional origins of the bodily based affective core of the implicit self that operates automatically and rapidly beneath levels of awareness."[3]

There is an increasing emphasis on teaching and emphasizing right brain functions and 'right-brain-to-right-brain' interactions in many fields of healing, especially psychotherapy, and a deepening understanding of how important this hemisphere is for mediating those energy qualities that provide a deeper, more emotional and spiritual experience of the world.

All of the above descriptors show how each hemisphere creates a different view of absolute reality, and it becomes so clear that we need both hemispheres online and available to us to fully experience what it is to be a human being. When they work together, our deepest desires can become manifest, and we can articulate and share the subtleties of our inner experiences with others and co-create a richer life. The integration of polarities in our emotional and spiritual life depends on our ability to see the world through both hemispheres and develop skill sets and excellence in both universes. In many of the exercises that we have done, our current impression is that the right brain in young people is more often offline than the left. Whether the excessive use of modern technology is contributing to that, or because current educational approaches favor the left

---

(1) McGilchrist, Iain. The Master and His Emissary: The Divided Brain and the Making of the Western World. (New Haven, Yale University Press, 2012)

(2) Taylor, Jill Bolte. My Stroke of Insight. (New York, Penguin Books, 2006)

(3) Schore, Allan. The Science of the Art of Psychotherapy. (New York, W.W. Norton & Company, Inc., 2011)

hemisphere, the outcome is troubling. Our hope is that these simple, but powerful shapes developed by Dr. Karim can make a difference in these trends. We still do not know the long-term effects of shape exposure, but our initial explorations have been exciting and fruitful. We do invite students of BioGeometry to explore these patterns and share them with the community through the Forum.

The following is an excerpt from a follow up email from Dr. Maley:

I wanted to update you on my work with the hemispheres and dials. They are quite potent. Here is what I have been experiencing

1. The two together feel and test as much more powerful as either one alone and seem to demonstrate that the activation of the hemispheres plays a strong role in the centering of organ systems. I have experiences much more strengthening of organ systems when tested while using the dials and the hemisphere shapes together...It seems like a more complete way to approach organ balancing compared to just the dial alone...

2. Here is the protocol I have been using...

Have both hemi-dials lying down...

Find an imbalance in an organ (reversal of PW).

Show one shape first, put it down, show the other...see which one harmonizes the imbalance the best....

Lie them down again......

Take the strongest one first and find the dial position that created the strongest CW response in the organ....

Lift the other shape, and set the dial to see if a still stronger CW response is possible (often there is a slight improvement)

Take a photo of the result and suggest that they look at it often......Talk to them about 'letting' the shapes in' and working with them intentionally and consciously for the next time period and make some notes about their experience....

3. I have done lots of people, some with chronic illness, and am still asking them about their experience. I have worked with a stroke victim on the paralysis in his arm, a blind client with macular degeneration, and several people with everyday physical problems. I am starting to look more carefully at mood (emotional) shifts and plan to find an assessment questionnaire to help with that....I have noticed that the harmonizing seems to quiet people down a bit and how they emotionally feel sometimes shows a more rapid response than the alleviation of physical symptoms. Chronic illnesses and long-term problems seem much more resistant to change even though the person might report feeling body sensations when exposed to the hemi-dial settings.

Music and Water Subtle Energy Research
By Georg Gaupp-Berghausen

The Physics of Quality is based on a special aspect of Universal Harmonics where the phenomenon of resonance is expanded from zero to infinity covering all dimensions of creation.

"Exploring the connections of the BioGeometry Physics of Quality with the development of musical instruments – whereby the tones on the strings create a multi-dimensional centering vortex, bringing harmony and life force – has constituted a large part of my collaboration with my friend and research colleague, music professor Georg Gaupp-Berghausen.
Through this centering process a connection to the higher dimensions is formed, enabling the instrument to produce conscious living sounds. This sheds light on new vibratory phenomena like the seamless (not related to frequency) resonance of shapes from the smallest to the largest in creation. I have included the following excerpts from an article in his own words, translated from the original German." – Ibrahim Karim

During my teaching activity at the Vorarlberger State Conservatory, my friend Dr. Oruç Güvenç, a Turkish Sufi master who was also a gifted musician and music therapist, advised me to contact Dr. Ibrahim Karim. This resulted in a journey into the science of BioGeometry that has been ongoing since 2005, as well as a warm friendship that followed, for which I am very grateful. My encounter with Dr. Ibrahim Karim and his science of BioGeometry was, for me, a long-awaited continuation and an unknown component in understanding the mysteries of creation experienced earlier in my life.
The International Harmonics Center/Institute for Basic Research on Harmonies, at the University of Music and Performing Arts, which in terms of content was largely identical to Hans Kayser's harmonic Pythagorean theory, but which, according to Prof. Dr. Haase, ought to have been reformed to meet the new scientific

requirements of a university (based on epistemology, empiricism and exoteric basic research), existed in Vienna for 50 years.

During my music studies, I was lucky enough to be able to study at this institute as well, which was unique in the world, and which unfortunately closed a decade ago.

Pythagoras, who underwent a 20-year training in Egypt, studied a secret doctrine whose core was not disclosed in antiquity. As a definition, what we may consider to be the core of harmonic Pythagoreanism, based on today's knowledge, is the identity of laws in nature, in the psycho-physical disposition of the human being and in music.

According to Plato, the world soul is a musical scale. Paracelsus viewed the human body as an unrolled zodiac whose 12 fields corresponded to the regions of the body. In his book „Paragranum" he explained how all of nature is subordinate to the heavenly forces, i.e. the microcosm (man) to the macrocosm (universe). Healing spagyrically means strengthening the celestial body in the human being and likewise the sphere of action of the 7 planets (the sun and the heart etc.). This could be interpreted as being a self-ordering system of the world (as a scaled system).

Vibrant cymatic[1] sound images can open up to us the procreative power (formative forces) behind all forms of the cosmos, nature and life, and show the recurring aspect of the creation of the universe in all its forms in space and time, as an expression of sound, number and movement.

In 2010, I completed a holistically designed master's thesis on the super-ordinate subject Energy Medicine with the title „*Changes in one's state of being through the 'Dhikr' mantra practice and ancient oriental music therapy*", with the accompanying support of Dr. Ibrahim Karim, Dr. Oruç Güvenç and Dr. Arno Heinen.

---

[1] Cymatics – (in German Kymatik, from the Greek word Kyma=wave) is an artistic/scientific research area which Dr. Hans Jenny (1904–1972), a medical doctor, natural scientist and artist established as a new science in continuation of the work of Ernst Chladni (1756–1827) on sound patterns which is continued today in further research by Dr. Gabriel Kelemen, Alexander Lauterwasser and others. See as well: www.internationalcymatics.org

The following is Dr. Ibrahim Karim's foreword to my master thesis on BioGeometry: "Initially, the research consisted of two steps, the first of which concerned the relationship between form and music. The shape of the wave (proportion of amplitude to wavelength or angle of incidence) is decisive for the subtle energetic effect and just as important as the direct influence of the frequency. It is thus possible to achieve and increase the quality of sacred power spots (called BG3 here) at each frequency.

The second step concerned the desired goal of achieving this BG3 quality as the main harmonization quality in all applications. The energy of the form is the result of the interaction between the form and the background as a longitudinal (sonic) wave. In our technologically influenced electromagnetic environment, there are scalar waves (Meyl) and on the atomic level torsional waves. Shapes and sounds move in longitudinal compressional waves in the same way, hence the close relationship."

BioGeometry also opens up a completely new scientific/artistic approach to cymatics by including energy quality. In Masaru Emoto's Hado Life Europe water laboratory, headed by my son Rasmus Gaupp-Berghausen, I examined, together with him and Dr. Ibrahim Karim, the energy quality/form of the crystal images created by sonication with music or by the transmission of a vibrational quality, for example the „Divine Names of God" (Divine Attributes) to water. Here the research showed that looking at the resulting crystal pictures produces a similar effect in a human being as reciting the Divine Attribute.

Images with the vibrational quality of the Divine Attributes

Furthermore, in the foreword, Dr. Ibrahim Karim wrote among other things: "As an architect, my main criterion is the use of the biogeometric design language, which is composed of angles, proportions, numbers, etc., to reproduce the energy quality of sacred places that are the location of sacred buildings." The forms that emerge in this way are seen as frozen music, as defined by Hans Kayser. They embody universal harmony.

BioGeometry does the opposite. Where Pythagorean harmonics uses number proportions to achieve tonal qualities, BioGeometry begins with the energy quality of sacred places and searches for the numbers that generate them. These numbers have no mathematical relationship, just the same quality of energy. Here a „qualitative harmony" is created with a „sacred, subtle energetic spirit".

The shape-forming power of sound (word), much celebrated in old creation myths, became accessible in 1785 through the work of Ernst F. Chladni as an immediately visible phenomenon, when he made a glass plate sprinkled with sand resound. Today, referred to as „Chladni sound figures", they still form the starting point for the „visualization" (today with the help of modern technical devices) of various sound propagations, for example on the surface of a musical instrument.

With our normal senses we are not able to perceive the vibrational pattern of a guitar top.

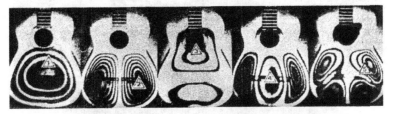

Different modes of vibration on a guitar top (EV Jansson in Acustica 1971).

This insight then formed the basis for 6 different guitar top constructions to date.

2 examples of guitar top constructions

Dr. Karim showed me that, with the techniques used in BioGeometry, it is possible to detect points along the string which, when used to determine its length, cause it to resonate with what is called BG3 energy.

As these partial tones do not lie at the same points along the string as the tones in the different scales used in music, the aim of the research is to achieve this BG3 quality through different applications, in accordance with the principles of the science of Biogeometry, for the complete sound range of the instrument, so that this quality is present in every scale or harmony used.

For example: The integration of a BG3 quality tube with a Bio-Geometry rosette pattern in the frame as an additional centering sound opening, resulted in a significantly increased overtone spectrum while plucking the 6 strings one after the other.

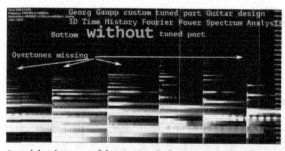

Sound development of the 6 strings before inserting the tube ...

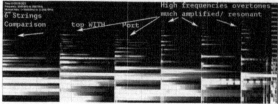

and after inserting the tube with rosette.

This experience then led to various further experiments in guitar construction incorporating tubes and rosettes according to Bio-Geometry principles with interesting results in the sound spectrum.

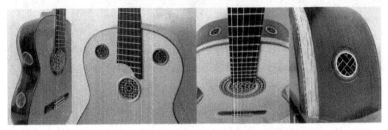

Examples of further experiments

Since 2008, I have been experimenting with BioGeometry in connection with the sound world, and in connection with research in the field of instrument building, with regard to sound quality and music therapy applications. I have meanwhile designed and built about 30 instruments, each different in sound and construction, incorporating different elements of BioGeometry.

Different instruments with BioGeometry application

Sound-dome with two sets of 16 strings at the back

Measurements from sessions in the sound dome revealed amazing improvements in heart rate variability which led to further constructions.

Sound bed and sound tube

Since the effectiveness of a sound takes place on a physical, mental and spiritual level, the science of BioGeometry represents an additional interesting component. Or in other words, the sound world with its overtones, resonances, numerical values, etc. is actually a partial aspect of BioGeometry.

"BioGeometry is actually the science of detecting the centering or balancing energy quality of BG3, studying its harmonizing effect in nature and reproducing it using a system of BioGeometry harmonics to create a design language of shape that achieves harmony in the inner and outer environment." (Karim, 2009)

In this context, it should also be mentioned that the sound quality also depends on the room in which it is heard. In an octagonal Templar church, I once had a special, almost otherworldly sound experience under the dome, which was mainly due to the nature of the room.

Geometry, especially the science of BioGeometry, which also includes the field of geometry, can also be a designation for a special "field" that can be implosive and fractal, or for a science that understands why and how sacred space exists.

With the knowledge that sounds can also be viewed as information carriers, a large new area of research opens up, which already had its place in "Ancient Egypt". By studying, understanding and applying knowledge from the past, we can enrich and expand our current science, maybe even reorient it and find a new approach.

It may be that sound incorporates the highest science of creation. Sounds as singing numbers (as quantitative physically measured frequency in Hz, i.e. number of vibrations per second/periodicity of the sound waves) can make cosmic order audible and visible in the sound images of cymatics.

As a life and form pattern, biological life is also bound to periodicity. The living is never in rigid balance. In its pulsating changes – as in sound forms, nature and in it the human being resembles a self-organizing system, which can be supported by aspects of BioGeometry. This support is also achieved through the construction of sound bodies which include aspects of BioGeometry.

The development of physics over the last 70 years has fundamentally changed our everyday view of the nature of matter. Matter is no longer a frozen dead thing. Corresponding to the organic formative processes, the rhythmically pulsating processes that begin in something that is fluid and moving (e. g. an embryo) and whose design continues to crystallize in the same flowing forms, we find, in a simplified form, a purely mechanical vibrational movement caused by standing waves in cymatics.

Although often similar in manifestation, these must not be equated with an animated being since we can neither know nor say how nature or life creates vibrations. But it seems that solid matter is also based on a similar process, and we are only at the beginning of a deeper understanding of coagulated vibration nodes and lines in an infinite vacuum.

A Resonance or a harmonic relationship with other particles throughout the energy spectrum also involves a qualitative effect registered by living systems.

From the densest matter to the subtlest cosmic rays, everything is atomic and molecular vibration. The whole „substance" of creation makes itself known in all its infinite manifestations as differently vibrating oscillations in an infinite symphony.

In both audible and visible vibrational frequencies, as physical manifestations, there are energy qualities. However, energy qualities are, of course, found throughout the vibrational range – and the key to understanding BioGeometry lies in the effect that they have and in the connection between the qualitative and quantitative aspects of energy.

Both scales are sides of the same coin, and each energy interaction involves both a quantitative and a qualitative effect. (Karim)

Harmonic sound creates harmonic structure. And vice versa, harmonics arise when the form factors work in harmonic order, for example in a musical instrument. In its diversity of archaic patterns, harmony is omnipresent, as a universal ordering principle, from the cosmos to the atomic level.

The human body tends towards order through its self-healing powers, whereas any form of stress creates an increased degree of disorder (pathology as a local area of entropy).

In order to reduce disorder, an impetus is required, a certain ordering energy of a higher order.

"By playing their instruments, musicians bring the molecules of the air around them and the listener into a very specific order, which we call „music‘. When we listen, we transmute the vibrations of the air; first into mechanical movements of the middle ear apparatus, then into the rising and falling waves of the inner ear fluid and finally into neuronal energy flows in the central nervous system. At the end there is the perception: I hear musi" (Kapteina/Zhang 2008)

This still very physical view should be expanded:
Sound can be an expression of a pure heart, it can convey the innermost sound of life, it can raise one up to the throne of the Creator. Its effect corresponds to the mental or spiritual forces which ultimately unfold in a tone.

As the heart – which not only beats but also is a huge vibrational field that can be full of love and mystery – so the tone, with its beginning, sounding and fading away.

One fundamental tone frequency differs from other fundamental tone frequencies, apart from in the respective pitch and amplitude, in the harmony of its respective resonating overtones (resonating intervals such as octaves, fifths, fourths..., generated by the vibration nodes), which give it its own tone color and harmonic structure. In addition to the fundamental tones, the overtones play an outstanding role, the importance of which has been recognized, understood and practiced in religious traditions, in shamanism and in the healing arts of many peoples, and is also attracting attention again today in a wide variety of ways.

When water in a container is sonicated, a measurable (electromagnetic) field forms outside. (TU Buchs)

Masaru Emoto's method was also used to document the differences in water structure, or the ability or inability of the subsequently frozen water to form hexagonal crystals after sonication.

Thus, bearing in mind that the human body consists of about 75% water (brain 90–95%), it can be assumed that the human body's own field is also influenced and structured by external sound influence.

In the search for the special quality of a sound, we find, firstly, diverse components that exert their influence, and, secondly, ways in which the science of BioGeometry can be involved.

When building a musical instrument, the initial factor is the quality of the material; e.g. with regard to stringed instruments with the wood – on which day of the year the tree was felled, how old it was, what kind of high-quality wood it is, from which area, how it was further processed, by machine or by hand, etc. – also the construction and shape geometry, the quality aspects of the strings and bridges, and much more. The nature of the surface in particular (waxed or varnished, natural varnish or artificial varnish, etc.) plays an important role. The sound can seem imprisoned and slowed down, for example, by an artificial varnish. On the other hand, the speed of sound can be accelerated by the surface quality and create a piezoelectric effect.

Primer and varnish can have an influence on the mouldability and response, the carrying capacity, dynamics and sound intensity of the tone. There are many criteria that play a role in creating an excellent sound, from the technical ability, to finally, the condition and the consciousness of the player. These criteria also play a role in building the instrument.

The tonal quality of an instrument also develops over time through the manner in which the instrument is played. The molecules in the material rearrange themselves through the vibrating sound in the instrument. Two visits to a friend who plays Indian music made this particularly tangible. On my first visit, I tried his newly arrived surbahar (Indian plucked string instrument) and found the sound nice but not particularly good. After two years, when I visited him again, the sound of the tones made me feel as if I was sitting in the middle of a fire because the instrument had achieved such an amazing sound intensity through the player and his playing.

In the case of a good instrument, one can also speak of a type or ability of mediumship. Such an instrument implements the smallest nuances at lightning speed. Through this, the player experiences increased inspiration, imagination, and intuition, a uniform experience of the tangible and intangible, of the inner and outer essential forces of the human being, through which a connection with higher things can be experienced, grasping oneself and the forces of this world. The sound becomes like a cleansing firelight. We experience potency and potentiality, intention – not yet visible or audible, but present like the power in the seed.

All these aspects can also be improved through BioGeometry, as the inclusion of BioGeometry also brings us closer to the importance of the center. The image of center is archetypal, evoking the feeling of the whole. Through the center, through centering, we can experience ourselves in our full depth, in a feeling of cosmic and inner unity, as a movement towards conscious evolution, as a picture of a process of balanced self-development, inner and outer, as a process of transformation for the human being.

Just as, by using the principles and techniques of the BioGeometry Design Language, the subtle energy quality of the center can spread and radiate throughout the object or space, so it can in the musical instrument and in the sound.

Since the importance of the center and the centering quality is a main part of the science of BioGeometry, all of these aspects can lead to a deeper understanding through the inclusion of „BioGeometry".

An understanding of periphery and center, requires the inclusion of a spiritual component, such as is found in the science of „Biogeometry". Through this additional element, the complexity of the sound, which on all levels (physical, mental, spiritual) brings certain qualities to resonance, becomes more understandable.

The science of BioGeometry, due to its understanding that sound, as an information carrier, as an archaic pattern, as a universal ordering principle, works everywhere in all areas and on all levels of creation and life, is of great importance.

After fascinating experiences with the latest sound results on guitars that have just been finished (which I compared with the sound of high-quality guitars), my hope is that, through these techniques – which are still in a process of development – of incorporating BioGeometry into the „world of sound", a large field of activity will open up.